FAMILY LAWS IN PAKISTAN

AF895790

FAMILY LAWS IN PAKISTAN

SECOND EDITION

Muhammad Zubair Abbasi
Shahbaz Ahmad Cheema

OXFORD
UNIVERSITY PRESS

OXFORD
UNIVERSITY PRESS

Oxford University Press is a department of the University of Oxford. It furthers the University's objective of excellence in research, scholarship, and education by publishing worldwide. Oxford is a registered trade mark of Oxford University Press in the UK and in certain other countries

Published in Pakistan by
Oxford University Press
No. 38, Sector 15, Korangi Industrial Area,
PO Box 8214, Karachi-74900, Pakistan

© Oxford University Press 2018

The moral rights of the author have been asserted

First Edition published in 2018

Second Edition 2024

All rights reserved. No part of this publication may be reproduced, stored in a retrieval system, or transmitted, in any form or by any means, without the prior permission in writing of Oxford University Press, or as expressly permitted by law, by licence, or under terms agreed with the appropriate reprographics rights organization. Enquiries concerning reproduction outside the scope of the above should be sent to the Rights Department, Oxford University Press, at the address above

You must not circulate this work in any other form
and you must impose this same condition on any acquirer

ISBN 9789-69-734756-8

Typeset in Times New Roman
Printed on 63gsm Offset Paper

Printed by Delta Dot Technologies (Pvt.) Ltd., Karachi.

Contents

PART IV
Personal Laws and Family Court Procedures

Foreword

It is with much pleasure and pride that I write this foreword for *Family Laws in Pakistan* authored by two very promising, competent, and motivated legal scholars—Dr Muhammad Zubair Abbasi and Dr Shahbaz Ahmad Cheema. I have had the privilege of seeing both grow from strength to strength, developing and completing doctoral projects, and publishing thoughtful scholarship. Shahbaz was my doctoral supervisee at Warwick Law School, United Kingdom, where I witnessed remarkable blossoming of his ideas resulting in an excellent doctoral thesis. I had the pleasure of first meeting Zubair at a conference in London when he was writing his DPhil thesis at Oxford University, and came away deeply impressed by his conference paper on *waqf* in colonial India as well as his scholarship on Islamic law. Having followed their work over the years, it therefore came as no surprise when, after years of research, I received the manuscript of *Family Laws in Pakistan* from the authors along with a request to write a foreword for the book.

Family laws are deceptively simple in that while the general and broad principles are fairly straightforward, this very simplicity is lost in the complexity of interactions with other areas of law—i.e. constitutional, criminal, property, and others. Islamic family law has added layers of complexity including intricacies inherent in the various sects and sub-sects of Islam and how this impacts the outcome of a family law case. Family laws are, therefore, best understood and applied through a contextual approach thereby making both the law as well as its application more accessible to law students as well as a wider readership. This is the approach adopted by Dr Abbasi and Dr Cheema in their analysis of law and practice, including case law on various aspects of family laws in Pakistan. I see this as a strength of the book.

For years, students of family laws in Pakistan have read and repeatedly used a handful of books authored in the early part of the twentieth century by highly skilled legal professionals. Whilst these books have been very useful in collating basic principles of Muslim family law as well as landmark decisions and statute laws mainly in colonial times, subsequent editions have mainly added new cases and legal reforms to these classic textbooks. Dr Abbasi and Dr Cheema's book brings forth the latest and an updated account of family laws in Pakistan in a more contemporary and holistic framework of rights and citizenship. Case law is not only cited in a systematic and organized manner at appropriate points to highlight aspects of family law but the authors have also presented their evaluation of the legal reasoning informing the decisions arrived at by courts.

The contextual approach also demands that author/s move beyond doctrinal principles and engage with socio-legal, economic, and political factors impacting law-making and its application. Legislation and case law on family laws in Pakistan reflect complexity as well as the inherent plurality of the Islamic legal traditions. The book is unique in that it makes a conscious effort to analyse and assess case law through the lens of gender and women's rights bringing to the fore some conflicting decisions in this area. It is also the first book on family laws in Pakistan which I have seen covering personal laws of non-Muslim citizens—an area of family law that has led to contested application of family law in multi-religious jurisdictions such as Pakistan, India, and Malaysia among others.

Dr Abbasi and Dr Cheema are experienced academics with significant experience in research and teaching Muslim Personal Law for several years, and this is reflected in the present work. The *Family Laws in Pakistan* is an excellent contribution to family law scholarship for students, lawyers, and judges as well as for the general reader. I am confident that the book will appeal to a broad audience within and outside Pakistan.

Dr Shaheen Sardar Ali
Professor of Law
Warwick Law School
Coventry, United Kingdom
23 December 2017

Preface

Legal and scholarly communities welcomed the publication of the *Family Laws in Pakistan* in 2018. It is primarily due to the positive feedback, comments, and suggestions from academics, judges, lawyers, and practitioners that we started to work on the second edition immediately. During the past four years, superior courts have delivered many important judgments related to marriage, dower, divorce, wills, and inheritance. Simultaneously, national and provincial legislatures have also contributed to amend various statutes related to family laws. The national legislature has added two important provisions in the Muslim Family Laws Ordinance 1961 to confer inheritance right to immoveable property to a childless widow of a Shia husband and to declare that triple *talaq* is ineffective under Shia law (*Jafria* school). The first amendment is a direct result of the judgment of the Lahore High Court in *Khalida Shamim Akhtar v Ghulam Jaffar* PLD 2016 Lah 865 in which the court granted a childless widow of a Shia husband inheritance rights in the immovable property of her deceased husband. The Muslim Family Laws (Amendment) Act 2021 added subsection 2 in section 4 of the MFLO to recognise this right. The new law however did not give a childless widow the right to inheritance in the corpus of the property but limited it to one-fourth share of 'the fixed price or value' of the property. The Muslim Family Laws (Second Amendment) Act 2021 added a proviso in subsection 1 of section 7 of the MFLO to clarify the procedure of *talaq* under the Shia school (*Fiqah-e-Jafria*).

Another noteworthy legislative intervention has been the introduction of a strict regulatory regime for Muslim religious endowments/trusts (*awqaf*) by the central and provincial legislatures. Similar changes have also been brought into the regulatory regime for trusts. Most of these changes apply to public endowments and trusts and therefore are unlikely to impact family endowments and trusts but they are likely to affect mixed public-private endowments and trusts.

In recent judgments, the judges of the Supreme Court have relied upon the trilogy of Constitution, human rights law, and Sharia to develop jurisprudence for the protection of inheritance rights of Muslim women.[1] The roots of such judicial trend can be traced back to Islamic human rights jurisprudence developed in 1990s.[2] The Federal Shariat Court has also contributed to Islamic family law jurisprudence through its recent judgments in which it rejected the petition that challenged the Child Marriage Restraint Act 1929,[3] declared as un-Islamic the practice of giving girls in marriage to aggrieved parties to resolve blood feuds (*vani* and *swara*)[4], and declared as repugnant to the injunctions of Islam the 2015 amendment by the Punjab legislature in the Family Courts Act 1964 because it required wives to partially return dower even in cases where the husband caused breakdown of marriage.[5] In May 2023, the FSC declared certain sections of the Transgender Persons (Protection of Rights) Act 2018 repugnant to the injunctions of Islam.[6] An appeal has been filed before the Shariat Appellate Bench, SC against this judgment. The judgment of the FSC will not take effect until the appeal is decided. We have updated case law and statutes in this second edition of the book.

Muhammad Zubair Abbasi and Shahbaz Ahmad Cheema
August 2023
Oxford

Notes

1. See for instance Atta Mohammad v Mst. Munir Sultan 2021 SCMR 73; Farhan Aslam v Nuzba Shaheen 2021 SCMR 179; and Ghulam Qasim v Razia Begum PLD 2021 SC 812.
2. Ghulam Ali v Ghulam Sarwar Naqvi PLD 1990 SC 1.
3. Farooq Omar Bhoja v Federation of Pakistan PLD 2022 FSC 1.
4. Mst. Sakeena Bibi v Secretary Law Pakistan PLD 2022 FSC 64.
5. Imran Anwar Khan v Government of Punjab PLD 2022 FSC 25.
6. Hammad Hussain v Federation of Pakistan [Shariat Petition No. 5/I of 2020].

Acknowledgement

This book took several years in the making and we incurred numerous debts during this process. We thank our teachers at the International Islamic University, Islamabad (IIUI) for instilling in us a yearning for knowledge. I especially acknowledge the role of Dr Muhammad Munir, Dr Khalid Masud, Dr Abdul Haye Abro, Dr Tahir Mansoori, and Dr Aziz-ur-Rahman. Dr Muhammad Munir has been a source of inspiration for me since my first year as a law student at the IIUI. His writings provide me insights into the intricacies of Islamic family law. My co-author, Dr Cheema, acknowledges the role of his doctoral supervisor, Professor Shaheen Sardar Ali in sharpening his research skills. Asad Ullah Khan, Aleena Khan, Mariam Noor, Ashraf Ali, and Hafiz Kalim Ullah provided excellent research assistance. Orubah Sattar Ahmed, Salman Ijaz, Ayesha Ahmed, Muhammad Faisal Sattar, Mustafa Khan, Nimra Arshad, and Maham Naweed proofread various drafts of the book. We thank them for their contribution. Our students of Muslim Personal Law at the Lahore University of Management Sciences (LUMS), and the University Law College, University of the Punjab, provided inspiration for writing this book. We are grateful for their valuable suggestions. We thank our colleagues, especially Professor Martin Lau, Dr Syed Muhammad Azeem, and Professor Khyzar Hussain for their suggestions and comments in designing the book. Parts of this book were used as teaching material for our lectures at the Punjab Judicial Academy and the Shari'a Academy, IIUI; we are grateful to the participants for their excellent feedback. We especially thank Uzma Akhtar Chughtai (former DG), and Muhammad Amir Munir (Senior Instructor) of the Punjab Judicial Academy; Qaisar Abbas, Mohsin Mumtaz, and Shagufta Shafique of the Research Centre of the Lahore High Court for sharing their valuable practical experiences regarding family disputes.

My mother Salma Munir, wife Ayesha Ahmed, and daughter Aiza Amelle are the muses for my continuing research on family laws. My son Mikail Hani provided his joyful company while I updated the first edition of this book. I also thank my father Muhammad Munir, and brothers Umair, Wajid, and Waleed for their support. I am grateful to my friends Shafqat Mahmood Khan Mastoi, Hasnain Ashraf, Akif Khan, and Dr Hafiz Muhammad Siddique with whom various chapters were discussed. Dr Cheema is grateful to his mother Parveen Akhter, wife Shazia Shahbaz, and children Rida, Taha, and Talal for allowing him space to engage in this research project.

We thank Khalid Mehmood Siddiqui, Muhammad Imran, Shahnawaz Ali, and Iftikhar Ahmed, staff members at LUMS, for their excellent assistance.

A Note on Translation, Transliteration, and Terminology

We rely upon several sources available in Arabic and Urdu. The translations of the verses of the Qur'an are from Abdullah Yusuf Ali unless there are direct quotes from the judgments which refer to other translations of the Qur'an. The translations of passages from *fiqh* books and material in Urdu are ours unless there are direct quotes or indicated otherwise.

We have tried to provide simple transliterations as much as possible but have occasionally used macron and other diacritics to convey accurate pronunciation. We use ['] for *ayn* and ['] for *hamza*. Non-English words, except the ones which frequently occur, e.g. *waqf*, have been translated whenever they are used and a glossary is provided at the end of the book.

We omit Mst short form of *Massamat* (equivalent of Ms), before the names of women in judgments unless their names come second. Thus Mst Shafqat Parveen is written as Shafqat Parveen unless the context requires the use of Mst to correctly identify the parties. We also omit the words 'and others' in the titles of the cases. For instance, *Haji Muhammad Ali and others v Muhammad Akram and others* is written as *Haji Muhammad Ali v Muhammad Akram.*

We understand the contested nature and the variety of meanings ascribed to some of the most frequently used terms in this book, such as '*shari'a*', '*fiqh*', 'Muhammadan law', 'Muslim law', and 'Islamic law'. In the Introduction, we have provided a historical account of the use of these terms over the years. We observe that both their usage and meanings have been subject to change during the past few centuries. Therefore, these words are used in their general sense and we do not assign any particular or fixed meanings to them.

We use the terms 'classical' and 'modern/contemporary' jurists to differentiate between earlier and current day jurists without following any specific periodisation and/or attaching any normative authority to them.

Following section 13 of the General Clauses Act 1897, statutes and case law in Pakistan tend to use masculine gender which is 'taken to include females'. While such usage is convenient, we do not think that it is appropriate to do so any longer. Therefore, we use 's/he' and 'him/her' to denote gender as far as possible. Where this is not possible, we try to use gender neutral words or phrases such as 'person', 'any person', or 'every person'. However, we have not changed the language in direct quotations from cases, textbooks, and other sources.

Introduction

This book provides a concise introduction to family laws in Pakistan. Ostensibly, family law is the simplest and the easiest branch of law as compared with other areas of the law such as tax law, land law, constitutional law or criminal law. However, despite its apparent simplicity, issues arising under family laws sometimes pose challenging questions when they interact with other branches of law such as constitutional law, criminal law, or private international law. Let us explain this through an example: section 5 of the Muslim Family Laws Ordinance 1961 (MFLO) requires that every marriage solemnised under Muslim law must be registered with a *nikah* registrar. One of the most important functions of the registration of marriages is to minimise litigation concerning the legitimacy of children. Substantively, the issue of legitimacy is linked to a child's property rights such as the right to maintenance and inheritance. The right to property is constitutionally guaranteed and the right to maintenance and inheritance of a child depends on his/her legitimacy. Further, it is to be borne in mind that the legitimacy of a child is established under the rules of evidence. Legitimacy is conferred upon children born during wedlock. On the other hand, sex outside marriage is a criminal offence which is established through the application of criminal procedure and evidence law. Such an interplay among family, constitutional, criminal, and evidence law, can give rise to complex factual as well as legal issues ranging from the relevance of evidence to the applicable standards of proof in a particular case. Curiously, the MFLO is silent on the status of marriages solemnised outside Pakistan. The legal issues arising out of such marriages are dealt with under the conflict of laws or private international law, which pose further questions as to the sovereignty of a state.

In the following chapters of this book, we shall come across many examples of this interplay between family law and other branches of law in the context of Pakistan. In this regard, we observe that many important legal principles of family laws have been developed in cases which primarily dealt with issues related to constitutional, criminal, property, evidence, or private international law.

The primary objective of this book is to introduce its readers to the principles and practices of family laws in Pakistan. To this end, the book discusses latest case law and statutes related to every important aspect of family laws in Pakistan. To make this book accessible to a wide range of readers, we refrain from making detailed references to *fiqh* books unless the context requires so to either verify such references in judgments or to clarify legal principles. Likewise, we do not refer to foreign case law or statutes unless the context requires so regarding certain legal principles such as post-divorce maintenance or polygamy. We take into account important academic discourses regarding family laws in the Muslim world in general and Pakistan in particular. These discourses involve debates about gender equality and children's rights. We refer to these discourses in almost every chapter of the book, particularly in the introduction and the conclusion. However, for the sake of brevity and to avoid complexity, we keep such references to a minimum in the rest of the chapters.

While selecting case law, we have not only discussed the latest judgments, but have also included earlier landmark judgments such as *Moonshee Buzloor Ruheem v Shumsoonnissa Begum* (1867) on women's right to no-fault judicial divorce (*khula*) and restitution of conjugal rights; *Abdul Kadir v Salima* (1886) on the nature of marriage under Islamic law; *Balqis Fatima v Najam-ul-Ikram* (1959) on the extension of women's right to no-fault judicial divorce (*khula*); *Syed Ali Nawaz Gardezi v Lt. Col. Muhmmad Yusuf* (1963) on the procedural requirements of notice for divorce; and *Khurshid Bibi v Baboo Muhammad Amin* (1967) on the confirmation of women's unilateral right to no-fault judicial divorce (*khula*).

We recommend that our readers should read the complete judgments to develop a profound understanding of various legal principles of family laws. Our book provides a concise summary of each judgment; this summary, however, is not a substitute to the complete judgment. At the same time, we suggest that our prudent readers should not take the substantial parts of the book as mere summaries of judgments. Besides systematically organising the case law, we evaluate the legal reasoning of the judges and have not refrained from pointing out the misapplication of laws in various judgments. In addition, we also propose legal reform wherever it is required.

In addition to statutes and latest case law, we have also relied upon the books on Muslim family law written by Dr Tanzil-ur-Rahman,

Dr Tahir Mansoori, D. F. Mulla, Asaf Fyzee, Faiz Badruddin Tyabji, Syed Ameer Ali, Ronald Knyvet Wilson, Abdur Rahman, Abdur Rahim, David Pearl and Werner Menski, Keith Hodkinson, Cassandra Balchin, Lynn Welchman, Jamal Nasir, Alamgir Serajuddin, Shaheen Sardar Ali, and M. Mahmood. We have further developed the scholarship of these esteemed scholars since our book complements their work by providing the latest and updated account of family laws in Pakistan. Our book, however, differs from earlier works in several ways. To mention but a few variances: firstly, we include material facts of judgments along with legal principles to enable our readers to appreciate the context in which the law is applied; secondly, we present a systematic account of legal developments by highlighting the principles which are settled, or are in the process of being settled, as well as the ones which need to be reformed in light of new social developments; thirdly, we have added new chapters regarding the personal laws of non-Muslims and the conflict of personal laws. We believe that these two chapters along with a chapter on the procedures of the Family Courts have immense practical value in Pakistan. In these chapters, we have explored such aspects of family laws that have either been completely ignored or were only partially discussed by other authors.

Structurally, the book is divided into four parts. Part I deals with the institution of marriage, its formation, operation, and dissolution by looking into the nature of marriage, dower and dowry, provision of maintenance to family, and divorce. Part II deals with the rights of children by exploring the issues of legitimacy, custody, and guardianship of children. Part III is about the transfer of private property through gifts, wills, *waqf* (Islamic endowment), and inheritance. Part IV discusses the personal laws of non-Muslims, conflict of personal laws, and the procedures of the Family Courts.

The first chapter of the book traces the historical development of Muslim Personal Law (Islamic Family Law) in South Asia through the colonial period and in Pakistan during the post-colonial period. The historical analysis explores various historically contingent definitions of Muslim Personal Law. It not only identifies current academic discourses, but also provides an anchor for the discussion of Islamic family law in the post-colonial context of Pakistan. The conclusion of the book discusses the role of the judiciary in accommodating classical Islamic family law within the framework of constitutional law and international human rights law. In this regard, we highlight not only the positive role of the judiciary regarding the protection and promotion of women and children's rights, but also the instances where the judiciary could have adopted a pro-women and pro-children rights approach but did not do so despite ample choice. Such instances include: the failure to declare the remedy of restitution of conjugal rights as illegal; the recommendation of the Federal Shariat Court to criminalise surrogacy without suggesting mechanisms for the protection of the rights of surrogate mothers and surrogate children; and restrictive judicial interpretation of section 4 of the MFLO that is related to the inheritance rights of orphaned grandchildren.

To make family laws accessible to both advanced learners and beginners, each chapter of the book is divided into three main parts. The first part provides a brief but comprehensive introduction to various aspects of the topic. The introduction is followed by a systematic analysis of relevant case law, which is organised under various headings and sub-headings. The main legal principle established in each case is clearly stated at the outset, followed by the relevant facts of the case leading to the application of the principle along with judicial reasoning. Finally, the conclusion of each chapter highlights the established legal principles regarding the respective topic; underlines the areas where law is still developing and/or is characterised by conflicting judicial authorities; and identifies the principles that require reform in light of changing social needs. At the end of each chapter, lists of further cases, readings, and review questions are also provided to assist the readers in further research.

1

HISTORICAL CONTEXT OF MUSLIM FAMILY LAW IN PAKISTAN

This book is about family law. Many cases are litigated on issues relating to family law and many family disputes lead to further civil and criminal litigation. In a survey conducted under the European Union Punjab Access to Justice Project, family issues were cited as the most common reason for legal disputes.[1] Another survey on litigation in Lahore shows that the number of cases related to family disputes is about 30 per cent. The highest number of disputes (52 per cent) relate to land and property,[2] which also partially fall within the purview of family law because personal property encompasses gifts, wills, family endowments (*awqaf*), and inheritance. Therefore, a firm grasp of family law becomes quite important for law students, lawyers, judges, policymakers, and practitioners to ensure effective dispute resolution.

This chapter provides a brief historical context to the development of Islamic/Muslim family law in Pakistan. It does not provide an exhaustive illustration of the historical developments of legal doctrines of Islamic family law; rather, this chapter highlights only those historical processes which led to the development of Islamic family law in Pakistan.

1.1 Historical Development of Islamic Family Law in Pakistan

Islamic family law as practised in Pakistan today has passed through various transformative phases. To develop an in-depth understanding of the theory and practice of Islamic family law, it is important to trace the course of its development at various historical junctures.

1.1.1 Formative Period of Islamic Law (*Shari'a/Fiqh*). The Qur'an was revealed to Prophet Muhammad (PBUH), gradually over a period of almost twenty-three years. The Prophet (PBUH) transmitted the Qur'an to his companions (may Allah be pleased with them). After the death of the Prophet (PBUH), the companions looked towards the Qur'an and the traditions of the Prophet (PBUH), Sunnah, for guidance. In this way, the Qur'an and Sunnah provided the basic sources of Islamic law (*fiqh*).[3] To derive new legal principles, jurists used the methodology of *ijtihad* (independent reasoning). According to Imam Shafi'i, *qiyas* (analogy) was the only methodological tool to exercise *ijtihad*. However, some jurists used *istihsan* (juristic preference) to derive new legal principles by referring to the underlying spirit of the law (*qiyas khaffi*) over the ostensible analogy (*qiyas jalli*). Later, jurists further developed the list of methodological tools which included: *ijma* (consensus), *maslaha* (public welfare), *maqasid* (purposive approach), *istishab* (presumption of continuity), *sadd al-dhara'a* (pre-emptive means), *darura* (necessity), and *hiyal* (stratagems).

After intense intellectual activity during the formative and classical periods (seventh to tenth centuries CE) of Islamic law and jurisprudence, Muslim jurists felt the need to discipline scholarly developments by adhering to the views of earlier jurists. This led to the emergence of various schools, prominent among them were the four Sunni schools: Maliki, Hanafi, Shafi'i, and Hanbali; the three Shia schools: Ithna Ashariya, Ismailya, and Zaidiya; and one literalist school, Zahriya. After the formation of these schools, subsequent scholarly endeavours were confined within the limits of existing theoretical frameworks and legal literature.[4]

Amongst the Sunni schools, jurists were ranked on a scale that had seven levels. The higher-level jurists, primarily the founders and eponyms of the schools, enjoyed the absolute authority to expound the law based on primary sources, while the lower-level jurists were required to follow the rules established by the higher-level jurists.[5] This did not mean that the lower-level jurists could not provide answers to new legal problems. The answers, however, had to be found within the existing literature by using the established methodology and the theoretical framework of Islamic jurisprudence—*usul al-fiqh*.[6]

In contrast with the Sunni schools, the Shia schools consider the *Imam* to be the final interpreter of the law. They consider the Qur'an and Sunnah as the sources of Islamic law. A Hadith is accepted only if it is narrated by an Imam descended from the Prophet (PBUH). Unlike Sunni jurists, Shia jurists do not accept *qiyas* (analogy); however, they regard human reasoning (*aql*) as a valid source of law. Only the Imam and, in his absence, the *mujtahidin* (jurists) can provide the correct interpretation of the law. In this way, jurists play an important role in the development of legal rules under the Shia schools.[7]

1.1.2 Islamic Law in South Asia. Arab Muslims arrived in India through Sindh in the early eighth century, but they did not settle there permanently. In the twelfth century, Muslims of Central Asia established their rule in modern-day South Asia. Four centuries later, the Mughals laid the foundation of an Indian Empire that lasted until the mid-nineteenth century. In the Mughal Empire, the emperor was the central authority of the political system. His main instrument of order was called *zawabit* (regulations). He was considered directly responsible to God and to no other individual or institution. Being the supreme leader of the faithful, he embodied within his title and person the roles of the chief military commander, the executive head of the state, and the final dispenser of justice. The emperor appointed the chief judge (*qadi al-qudat*). The lower judges, however, were appointed upon the recommendations of the lord chancellor (*sadar al-sudur*). Apart from performing the functions of the administration of justice in civil and criminal matters, a judge could be vested with the executive powers to supervise prisons. He could also be required to advise the emperor and governors on legal issues regarding cases brought before them under their *siyasa* jurisdiction.[8]

The compilation of *al-Fatawa al-Alamgiriyya*, under the patronage of the Mughal Emperor Aurangzeb Alamgir in 1672, was an important contribution to Islamic legal literature.[9] A board of Muslim jurists worked for about eight years to complete this encyclopaedic work.[10] The text of *al-Fatawa al-Alamgiriyya* reflects the tradition of legal pluralism in pre-colonial India. Following the local Indian tradition, it endorsed a status-based construction of society by dividing state-based punishments (*tazir*) into four categories in accordance with the social status of the offender: (i) Nobles, *ulama*, and Sayyids were exempted from humiliation and physical punishments; (ii) Landholders could be subjected to humiliation but not to physical punishment or imprisonment; (iii) Middle class (*awsat*) could be humiliated and imprisoned but not punished physically; (iv) Lower classes (*khasis* and *kamina*) could be humiliated, physically punished, and imprisoned.[11]

1.1.2.1 Transformation of Islamic Law in British India. The advent of the British in India was significant for the development of Islamic law in South Asia. During the colonial period, two paradoxical changes took place: on the one hand, the sphere of Islamic law became restricted to private life, while in other areas such as criminal, commercial, and procedural law, extensive legal codes based on English legal doctrines replaced the traditional Islamic law. On the other hand, even though

Islamic law was restricted to the private sphere, it was nevertheless applied as state law. During the pre-colonial period, although the state played an important role in implementing the law, rulers did not have a prominent role in the process of law-making. As is evident from the example of the compilation of *al-Fatawa al-Alamgiriyya*, Muslim jurists preserved and developed Islamic law through their private efforts. Neither the edicts of a ruler nor the decrees of a *qadi* had any normative legal value.[12] However, the introduction of the modern nation-state in British India established the monopoly of the state on legislation, displacing the traditional status of Muslim jurists as the sole legal authority in Muslim society. Scholars describe this change in the nature of Islamic law during the colonial period as the transformation of *shari'a* from jurists' law to state law.[13]

This transformation, however, was a gradual process, which was affected primarily by four mechanisms: translation, adjudication, legislation, and education.

Firstly, leading Islamic legal textbooks were translated into English to enable British judges to adjudicate legal disputes without the help of local legal experts who assisted British judges during the early days of colonialism. Secondly, once these textbooks were translated, British judges treated them as the 'codes of Islamic law'. Based on these 'codes', they adjudicated legal disputes and produced new legal principles as judicial precedents. Legal commentators incorporated these precedents into their commentary books, which were constantly updated to include the ever-increasing number of judgments of superior courts which laid down new legal principles of Islamic law. In this way, the hierarchical judicial system served as a legal machine, which produced new legal principles while adjudicating legal disputes.

Thirdly, in order to be effective, judicial law-making was to be supplemented with reformative legislation. This was done for several purposes: to lay down procedures, e.g. the Guardians and Wards Act 1890; to implement policy decisions such as fixing the minimum age of marriage under the Restraint of Child Marriage Act 1929; to remove the effect of judicial precedents like the validation of family endowments under the Mussalman Wakf Validating Act 1913; to protect women's right of inheritance under the Muslim Personal Law (Shariat) Application Act 1937; and to extend women's right of divorce under the Dissolution of Muslim Marriages Act 1939.[14]

Finally, the universities cemented this process of transformation by imparting legal education based on judicial precedents as well as legislation. Ultimately, the university-educated lawyers replaced *ulama* as intermediaries between the state and Muslim society. Therefore, it is not surprising that an overwhelmingly large number of Muslim political leaders in British India were lawyers, rather than religiously trained *ulama*.

1.1.2.2 Textbooks on Muhammadan Law. Legal textbooks on Islamic family law provide a perfect illustration of the process which transformed *shari'a/fiqh* during the colonial period. These books also highlight the role of Indian legal scholars, commentators, lawyers, judges, and politicians in the legal transformation that shaped the fundamental features of Islamic family law in South Asia. The details of these textbooks are discussed in the following paragraphs.

After the conquest of Bengal around the mid-eighteenth century, the Nawab-Governor General Warren Hastings promulgated the Regulations of 1772 which provided for the application of Islamic law for the private affairs of Muslims. Initially, the executives of the East India Company (EIC) relied upon indigenous population and local institutional structures for the administration of justice. However, the British gradually started to familiarise themselves with local legal traditions. For this purpose, in 1786, Francis Gladwin translated a small booklet, the *Mirat ul Missayil* from Persian into English. This short 82–page booklet, however, could not be used for administrative or judicial purposes because it lacked sufficient details.[15] Therefore, the EIC commissioned Charles Hamilton to translate a popular Hanafi legal textbook, the *Hidaya*, into English. Like Gladwin's translation, Hamilton did not translate the *Hidaya* directly from its Arabic text. As Hamilton did not know Arabic, a Persian translation of the *Hidaya* was prepared for him, which he subsequently translated into English and published the first edition in 1791. In this process, Hamilton did not act as a mere translator; he also edited the *Hidaya* by purging the text of, what he considered, unnecessary details and omitted the translation of the chapters that he regarded as purely religious obligations dealing with ablution, prayer, fasting, and pilgrimage.[16] In 1870, a second edition of Hamilton's translation of the *Hidaya* was published with a preface by Standish Grove Grady. Grady further excluded some chapters in order to reduce the four volumes into one.[17] The *Hidaya* covered various areas of family law except for inheritance. In order to fill this gap, the famous English orientalist, William Jones, translated a popular textbook on inheritance known as the *Sirajiyya* of Siraj al-Din Sajawandi (fl. c. 600 AH/1203 CE) into English in 1792.[18] It is not without interest that in the following year, the Bengal Regulations 1793 replaced custom with Islamic inheritance law.[19] This shows that colonial projects of translation were intimately connected with their system of governance and control.[20]

Over the next few decades, the *Hidaya* and the *Sirajiyya* remained key texts for judicial and revenue officers for the determination of 'Muhammadan law'. It was more than half a century later that Neil B.E. Baillie translated certain parts of *al-Fatawa al-Alamgiriyya* into English in the form of *The Moohummudan Law of Sale* (1850), *The Land Tax of India* (1853), and *A Digest of Moohummedan Law* (1875). Baillie also partially translated the *Shara'a'a al-Islam*, a popular *Jafari Shia* school text of Al-Muhaqqiq al-Hilli (d. 676 AH/1277 CE), as the *Digest of Moohummudan Law* (1869). These works were used by the courts as the 'civil code' of Muhammadan law. Having gained access to the 'codes' of Islamic law, the British judges could now know Islamic law for themselves without the help of local *ulama*. Thus, these 'codes' gradually substituted the local *ulama* and helped the colonial state rid the local agency of the administration of justice.[21]

In the mid-nineteenth century, the British introduced a hierarchical judicial system that operated under the doctrine of precedent in colonial India.[22] Under this system, the court decisions provided material for another mode of transformation. The Anglo-Indian courts were not simply adjudicating legal disputes; they were also creating legal principles on the basis of their decisions.[23] Later, legal textbooks systematised court decisions for practitioners and judges. William Hay Macnaghten published the first such book, *Principles and Precedents of Moohummudan Law* in 1825.[24] Subsequent legal commentators followed the tradition of Macnaghten.

In the same vein, Shama Churun Sircar published *The Muhammadan Law* in 1873.[25] This book was primarily based on Hamilton's translation of the *Hidaya* and Baillie's translation of *al-Fatawa al-Alamgiriyya*. However, unlike its predecessors, Sircar also incorporated in his treatise the judicial precedents laid down by the Indian High Courts and the highest court of appeal in the British Empire—the Judicial Committee of the Privy Council. A decade later, a prominent Muslim lawyer and politician, Syed Ameer Ali published the *Tagore Law Lectures 1884*.[26] The distinctive feature of this book was its critical evaluation of the translations of Hamilton and Baillie. Syed Ameer Ali pointed out several mistakes committed by the judges while adjudicating legal disputes. In 1892, Ameer Ali published an updated version of his treatise in two volumes in which he relied upon the translations of a wide variety of classical legal textbooks.[27]

In 1895, R.K. Wilson published his influential book, *A Digest of Anglo-Muhammadan Law*.[28] This was the first book that organised Muhammadan law in the form of a legal code. Each chapter of this book contained several numbered sections like an Act of Parliament. Another distinctive feature of this book was the incorporation of statutes along with Hamilton and Baillie's translations, and judicial precedents of the Indian High Courts and the Judicial Committee of the Privy Council.

In the early twentieth century, D.F. Mulla[29] and Abdur Rahman[30] published their influential treatises. Mulla's *Principles of Mahomedan Law* followed the pattern of Wilson's book. However, it was only one-third of its size. Notwithstanding that the book was written primarily for law students, its brevity and clarity made it equally popular amongst the bar and the bench. Even today, Mulla's book is widely used as an authoritative text in South Asian courts. On the other hand, Abdur Rahman's *Institutes of Mussalman Law* was based on Muhammad Qadri Pasha's *Code of Personal Law*. Qadri Pasha was an Egyptian judge who prepared the code with the help of the *ulama* of Al-Azhar University, Cairo. To ground his treatise within the legal tradition developed in British India, Rahman provided references to Hamilton and Baillie's translations, Macnaghten's *Principles*, case law, and Indian statutes. However, despite being an erudite treatise, this work did not attract much scholarly attention and remained confined to the first edition.

In this tradition, Abdur Rahim's *Principles of Muhammadan Jurisprudence* was the first book in English on the science of *fiqh* (*usul al-fiqh*).[31] It was based on a number of classical texts and remained the only textbook on the subject of Islamic jurisprudence in British India. Abdur Rahim wrote this book on the pattern of Salmond's famous treatise, *Jurisprudence*. Afterwards, F.B. Tyabji published the *Principles of Muhammadan Law* in 1913. Its extended editions were subsequently published in 1919 and 1940.[32] He meticulously analysed several legal principles and vehemently argued for the recognition of limited interests under Islamic property law. The introduction of the third edition of the book provides an incisive critique of the methodology of the judges of Anglo-Indian courts. Vesey-Fitzgerald's *Muhammadan Law* was written for the training of colonial officers.[33] In this series of textbooks, Fyzee's *Outlines of Muhammadan Law* was published in 1949. This book was written primarily for law students.[34]

It is interesting to note that the authors of the above-mentioned legal commentaries were not simply academics. Syed Ameer Ali, D.F. Mulla, and Abdur Rahim were practitioners who were later appointed as judges of the Indian High Courts. Ameer Ali and Mulla were subsequently elevated as the judges of the Judicial Committee of the Privy Council. Ameer Ali and Abdur Rahim were also leading Muslim politicians; the latter was a member of the legislative assembly as well. These textbooks were not simply a systematic organisation of judicial decisions; they also analysed, commented upon, and identified the limitations of judicial authorities relied upon by the courts. In this regard, Syed Ameer Ali's treatises provided a critique of judicial decisions, especially in the light of classical *fiqh* books. Wilson and Vesey-Fitzgerald taught law at Cambridge University, and the School of Oriental and African Studies, University of London, respectively. They also trained officers of the Indian Civil Service. Syed Ameer Ali wrote a short students' edition of his book and Abdur Rahim's treatise was a recommended text for the LLB course on Muhammadan law. Mulla's book was also taught at various universities.[35] Mulla, Tyabji, and Fyzee also taught at the Bombay Law College.

1.1.2.3 Political Context of Islamic Family Law in British India. In the early twentieth century, the British yielded to the demands for the representation of local Indians in the legislative institutions and introduced an electorate system in India. The Indian Councils Act 1909 envisaged a separate electorate system. Under this system, Muslims voted for Muslim candidates and Hindus for Hindu candidates. In this way, the separate identity of Muslims became politically significant and distinct from other religious communities of India. This separate identity, however, was to be defined in legal terminology. From a legal perspective, a Muslim was a person who professed Islam and followed Islamic law. However, in many parts of India, Muslims followed customary law which they usually prioritised over Muhammadan law (later called Muslim Personal Law). For instance, under the Punjab Laws Act 1872, all family law matters were to be decided according to custom or Muhammadan law modified by custom. Generally, Punjabi Muslims did not strictly follow Islamic inheritance law, especially in rural areas: female relatives did not get their prescribed share in inheritance in agricultural land, and wives were given only life interests in land in order to keep the land within the ownership of a particular family or clan. Moreover, there were some Muslim communities such as Khojas and Memons, who followed Hindu inheritance law as a customary practice. In this way, personal law and customary law existed side by side, notwithstanding that legally the latter had priority over the former.

The introduction of separate electorate systems for Muslims and Hindus, however, required a clear distinction on the basis of religious identity. For Muslims, this meant greater adherence to their personal law. The enactments of the North-West Frontier Province Muslim Personal Law (Shariat) Application Act 1935 at the provincial level and the Muslim Personal Law (Shariat) Application Act 1937 at the federal level should be seen in this political context. These Acts protected women's rights to property. Similarly, the promulgation of the Dissolution of Muslim Marriages Act 1939 provided Muslim wives with the right to judicial divorce. The objective of this Act was to prevent the apostasy of Muslim wives who renounced their religion to get out of bad marriages. The Act, however, was presented as an emancipatory legislation to promote women's right to divorce. Interestingly, *ulama* played a key role in the promulgation of these Acts to promote the rights of Muslim women in British India.

As we shall see in the next section, family law reform became one of the most important political and legal issues in the nascent state of Pakistan.

1.2 Islamic Family Law in Pakistan

The Muslim Personal Law (Shariat) Application Act 1937 did not apply to agricultural land because, under the Government of India Act 1935, agricultural land was a provincial subject. Thus, only a provincial assembly could legislate on it. Therefore, the Punjab Muslim Personal Law (Shariat) Application Act 1948 was passed to apply the Islamic inheritance law to agricultural land. A similar Act was passed in Sindh in 1950.

The most important legal development in family law in Pakistan was the Report of the Marriage and Family Law Commission 1956 and the subsequent promulgation of the Muslim Family Laws Ordinance 1961 (MFLO). In 1955, the Government of Pakistan established the Commission on Marriage and Family Law to propose reforms in family laws.[36] The commission recommended several measures to protect women's rights by increasing the age of marriage for girls to sixteen years, putting restrictions on polygamy, and requiring the registration of marriage and divorce.[37]

A majority of religious scholars, however, strongly criticised the report of the commission. They branded it as an attempt to Westernise society in the garb of legal reform.[38] The report generated heated debates among traditionalists and modernists; each side presented its arguments to the public in the form of pamphlets, articles, and books.[39] These debates, however, remained inconclusive and the government ultimately decided to shelve the report. A few years later, the powerful government of the military dictator, Ayub Khan, promulgated the MFLO, which was primarily based on the report. Even though the MFLO did not incorporate all the recommendations of the commission, a majority of religious scholars termed it un-Islamic. To this date, the promulgation of the MFLO remains the most important legal development regarding Islamic family law in Pakistan. Despite several attempts to get it repealed, the MFLO continues to be the law of the land.[40]

After the promulgation of the MFLO, the next important legal development in Islamic family law was the Islamisation of laws during the Zia era (1977–1988). The focus of Zia's Islamisation was primarily on Hudood laws, which is probably the reason he did not introduce any specific statute on family law or repeal the MFLO in its entirety. However, in 1978, Zia ul-Haq directed the Council of Islamic Ideology to review the MFLO. The Council sent its recommendations to the Ministry of Law, which in its letter dated 15 January 1980, responded in the following words:

> The Muslim Family Laws Ordinance 1961 is utterly un-Islamic. It is against the holy Qur'an and Sunnah. It has dared to amend the Qur'anic law to the extent of *Irtidad* [apostasy] and its existence is a slur, a blot, a bad blot on the glorious name of Islam and our Islamic country. Such a legislation or even its name need not be protected. Let us clean the blot altogether by its total repeal.[41]

The Ministry of Religious Affairs also agreed to repeal the MFLO. Two male and one female members of the Council, however, proposed that the MFLO should be amended and not repealed.[42] Ultimately, instead of amending the MFLO, the Zia regime repealed its sections 12 and 13 in 1981. Section 12 had increased the age of marriage under the Child Marriage Restraint Act 1929 to sixteen years for females and eighteen for males, and section 13 had declared the second marriage of a husband, without the consent of the first wife, a ground for divorce under the Dissolution of Muslim Marriages Act 1939. At the same time, section

488 of the Code of Criminal Procedure 1898 was also repealed, which provided for the maintenance of wives and children, including illegitimate children.[43]

Interestingly, the most effective tool of Islamisation under the Zia regime was not legislation; rather, the process of Islamisation was effectuated through adjudication. The Federal Shariat Court (FSC) was assigned the task to examine and decide whether any law or provision of law is repugnant to the Injunctions of Islam as laid down in the Qur'an and Sunnah. Since Muslim Personal Law (MPL) is based on the interpretations of the Qur'an and Sunnah by jurists belonging to various schools and there are important differences between Sunni and Shia personal laws, the Zia regime excluded it from the jurisdiction of the FSC. After the death of Zia ul-Haq, however, the Shariat Appellate Bench (SAB) of the Supreme Court extended its jurisdiction by narrowly construing the definition of MPL provided in the Constitution.[44] Under this power, in the *Allah Rakha* case, the FSC scrutinised various sections of the MFLO.[45] The provisions concerning polygamy and regulating the process of *talaq* by requiring a husband to give notice to the wife and the Chairman of the Union Council survived judicial scrutiny. However, the FSC declared the right of representation for orphaned grandchildren in the grandfather's legacy and the fixed period of *iddat* as un-Islamic. The judgment, in this case, has not attained finality because an appeal against it has been pending before the SAB since 2000.

As we shall see in the following chapters of this book, the FSC and SAB have delivered landmark judgments elaborating upon various principles of Islamic criminal law.[46] These judgments have implications for Islamic family law, which continues to be influenced by the process of judicial Islamisation of laws.

1.3 What is Muslim Personal Law?

During the early days of British rule in India, the term Muhammadan, with its varying spellings, was used for Muslims. This term seems analogous to the term Christian. The British used the term Muhammadan since they perceived Muslims as the followers of Muhammad (PBUH). As the followers of Christ were called Christians, it was apt to call the followers of Muhammad as Muhammadans. The same pattern was followed for Islamic law/Muslim law, which was termed as Muhammadan law. After the translation of classical Islamic legal textbooks such as the *Hidaya* and *al-Fatawa al-Alamgiriyya* into English, and the compilation of judicial precedents in various textbooks, the Anglicised expression, Anglo-Muhammadan law, came into vogue.

As is described above, during the colonial period, none of the textbooks used the expression 'Muslim Personal Law' in their titles.[47] Despite his dislike for the term 'Muhammadan Law', Fyzee used it in the title of his book. He explained that the term 'Muhammadan Law' was 'neither accurate nor felicitous'.[48] The use of the term 'Shariat', in the title of the NWFP Muslim Personal Law (Shariat) Application Act 1935, is worth noting. Such use of this term distinguished Muslim Personal Law as being 'Shariat' from Muhammadan law, which was not always in conformity with the Injunctions of the 'Shariat'.

The term 'personal law', in legal parlance, is used in contrast with territorial law. The former is applied on the basis of an individual's personal beliefs, unlike the latter which applies to all citizens irrespective of their religious affiliations. In South Asia, there are various personal laws, e.g. Muslim, Hindu, Christian, and Parsi. Personal law only covers an individual's family life and associated matters. It does not cover other areas of law, e.g. constitutional law or commercial law, though a religion-based argument can be raised, and is often raised, in matters related to constitutional and commercial law.[49]

While defining the jurisdiction of the FSC, Article 203B(c) of the Constitution of the Islamic Republic of Pakistan 1973 excludes Muslim Personal Law (MPL) along with the Constitution and any law relating to the procedure of any court or tribunal. Under this Article, the SAB examined the issue of the definition of MPL in two judgments. In *Federation of Pakistan v Mst Farishta*, the court held:

> [P]hrase "Muslim Personal Law" may have two meanings depending on the context in which it is used. In one generally and commonly understood sense, it may mean, such religious or Divine law of Muslims by which they believe to be governed as a matter of their religious faith. It is a law which a Muslim carries with him wherever he goes, and this is because, according to him, Islam is not merely a religion but Din imparting the sense of obedience to Allah's commandments and embraces a man's life from cradle to the grave. It is a whole way of life, and from that point of view, Islam, as such, is a pure personal law of every Muslim. In the second sense it may mean all such special statutory laws which apply only to the religious community known as Muslims of Pakistan, as distinct from general laws of this country which apply to all classes and types of people in general. In other words, by the term *"Muslim Personal Law" is meant that portion of*

the Civil Law of Pakistan which is exclusively applied or which authorises application of certain specified law to Muslim residents of this country as a special and personal law for them.[50] (Italics added for emphasis.)

In the *Farishta* case, the Shariat Bench of the Peshawar High Court had declared section 4 of the MFLO relating to the inheritance right of orphaned grandchildren repugnant to the Injunctions of Islam. In an appeal against this decision, the SAB overturned this decision on the ground that the MFLO fell within the definition of MPL, and therefore, it was excluded from the jurisdiction of the FSC. The SAB defined MPL as:

> "Muslim Personal Law" in this special context [of the jurisdiction of Shariat Court], therefore, means such codified or legislated law which is being applied to Muslim residents of Pakistan as or with the denomination "Muslim" which governs their persons as such and as distinct from general law of the land which applies to everybody.[51]

In *Dr Mahmood-ur-Rehman Faisal v Government of Pakistan*, the SAB reviewed its decision in the above case, and provided a relatively narrow definition of MPL:

> The expression "Muslim Personal Law" used in Article 203B(c), therefore, in our view means the personal law of each sect of Muslims based on the interpretation of [the] Qur'an and Sunnah by that sect. The expression "Muslim Personal Law" used in Article 203B (c) (supra), therefore, will be limited in its meaning only to that part of [the] personal law of each sect of Muslims which is based on the interpretation of Holy Qur'an and Sunnah of Holy Prophet (peace be upon him) by that sect.[52]

It means that if a law applies to all Muslims irrespective of their sectarian affiliations, it does not fall within the definition of MPL. Therefore, the MFLO does not form part of MPL because various provisions of the MFLO apply to all Muslim citizens of Pakistan irrespective of their sectarian affiliation. The SAB justified this change based on the Explanation added to Article 227(1) of the Constitution, which provides: 'In the application of this clause to the personal law of any Muslim sect, the expression "Qur'an and Sunnah" shall mean the Qur'an and Sunnah as interpreted by that sect'.[53] Justice Saeeduzzaman Siddiqui contended that this explanation provided an 'insight' into the real meaning of the expression 'Muslim Personal Law'. With due respect to the full bench of the SAB, we note that Article 227 is included in Part IX of the Constitution. This part relates to the Council of Islamic Ideology, which is an advisory body. Therefore, the reliance on this article for the interpretation of the definition of MPL included in Part VII of the Constitution, which deals with the judicature, is problematic from the perspective of the rules of interpretation of statutes.

It should also be noted that the definition of MPL in the *Mahmood-ur-Rehman Faisal* case is limited to the cases related to judicial Islamisation of laws falling under Part VII, Chapter 3–A of the Constitution. For the purposes of our book, we define MPL as:

> Muslim Personal Law is the branch of private law of Muslims that applies to family life (marriage, dower, dowry, maintenance, and divorce), and the associated matters such as custody and guardianship of children, and disposal of property *inter vivos* (gift and waqf) or testamentary (will) or through inheritance law.

1.4 Definition of a Muslim

The definition of MPL is incomplete without defining the term 'Muslim'. The colonial Indian courts defined a Muslim as any person who believes in the unity of God and the Prophethood of Muhammad (PBUH). Article 260(1) (a) of the constitution, after the Second Amendment, defines a 'Muslim' as:

> "Muslim" means a person who believes in the unity and oneness of Almighty Allah, in the absolute and unqualified finality of the Prophethood of Muhammad (peace be upon him), the last of the prophets, and does not believe in, or recognise as a prophet or religious reformer, any person who claimed or claims to be a prophet, in any sense of the word or of any description whatsoever, after Muhammad (peace be upon him).

Article 260(1) (b) defines a 'non-Muslim' as:

> "non-Muslim" means a person who is not a Muslim and includes a person belonging to the Christian, Hindu, Sikh, Buddhist or Parsi community, a person of the Quadiani Group or the Lahori Group who call themselves 'Ahmadis' or by any other name or a Bahai, and a person belonging to any of the Scheduled Castes.[54]

After the Second Amendment to the constitution in 1974, the question arose whether MPL applies to Qadianis and Ahmadis. In *Abdur Rahman Mobashir v Syed Amir Ali Shah Bokhari*, Justice Aftab Hussain of the Lahore High Court held that Islamic law cannot be applied to non-Muslims in general; however, since Qadianis/Ahmadis claim to be bound by the Qur'an and Sunnah, therefore, Muslim law will apply to them under the principles of justice, equity, and good conscience.[55] However, in *Farida Malik v Khalida Malik*, Justice Khalil-ur-Rehman Khan of the Supreme Court observed that the members of the Qadiani faith are not governed by Muslim Personal Law;[56] and in *Farah Chaudhry v Shahid Mahmood Malik*, the Lahore High Court held that the MFLO does not apply to Ahmadis.[57] Likewise, in *Amjad Khan Yousafzai v Arshad Khan*, the Sindh High Court held that the Ahmadis cannot make an oral gift which is valid only under Muslim law.[58] Moreover, in *Mubbasher Ahmad v Talat Khurshid*, the Lahore High Court held that the Family Courts Act 1964 applies to Ahmadis, but the Dissolution of Muslim Marriages Act 1939 does not apply to them.[59] In a recent case, the same court held that an Ahmadi wife does not have the right to *khula* because this right is not available to non-Muslim wives.[60] The courts have held that whether a person is an Ahmadi is a question of fact,[61] and the court cannot test or gauge the sincerity of the religious beliefs of a person. It was sufficient for a court to be satisfied that the person professes to belong to a certain faith, without inquiring further into his/her state of mind.[62]

Regarding the issue of the application of a particular school in a family law dispute, the Supreme Court held that as the majority of Muslims in Pakistan follow the Hanafi school, there is a legal presumption that a case falls under the rules of the Hanafi school unless either party proves to the contrary. Similarly, a sizeable population in Pakistan follows the Shia Ithna Ashariyya school and the courts tend to draw a legal presumption that Shia Muslims follow this school unless proven otherwise.[63]

The next question is if the parties to a dispute follow different schools, which rules will apply? The colonial Indian courts developed two general principles to deal with such cases: (i) the rules of the defendant's school will prevail;[64] and (ii) the principles of equity, justice, and good conscience will apply.[65] However, we observe that in various judgments these general principles were not consistently applied. In fact, the courts have developed quite a few exceptions to these principles.[66] For instance, inheritance cases are decided in accordance with the school of the *propositus*, not the school of the parties. Similarly, in custody cases, the courts take into account the personal law of the child but decide the case in accordance with the welfare of the child.[67]

1.5 Current Debates in Islamic Family Law

One of the key debates amongst the scholars of Islamic law generally, and that of Islamic family law in particular, relates to the relationship between classical Islamic law (*shari'a*) and Western values. In this debate, *shari'a* is presumed as traditional, and Western values as modern. The whole debate takes place within this binary where tradition and modernity are pitched against each other.[68] While there are many manifestations of this conflict, we shall focus primarily on the issues of the compatibility of *shari'a* with the modern state and international human rights law.

A number of scholars have argued that *shari'a* is based on a religious belief that is personal and voluntary, while positive state law is impersonal and coercive. It necessarily follows that *shari'a* cannot be applied through the instrument of the state as the normativity of *shari'a* dies when any element of coercion is involved in its enforcement. This argument is based on the premise that *shari'a* does not envisage a politically organised society in the form of a state. The modern state, according to this argument, only developed in Europe due to its peculiar historical circumstances.[69] Critics point out that this argument is not only ahistorical but also Eurocentric. It tends to essentialise *shari'a* and does not view its historical peculiarities, whereas historical records show that *shari'a* developed differently in various parts of the world, without losing its core features.[70]

A majority of modern Western scholars, however, ignore these historical peculiarities and imagine *shari'a* as being incompatible with state law. They depict this as a 'dilemma' or 'paradox' for Muslim states. They point out the removal of the monopoly of the *ulama* as the sole custodians of *shari'a* and the abandonment of 'classical Islamic legal methodology' as the main sources of transformation in the nature of *shari'a* in modern times.[71] They argue that although classical *shari'a* has distinguished itself from state law and has maintained its distinctive features, it has degenerated into a thing of the past—an archaic discipline. They assert that the codification of *shari'a* by the state has resulted in its 'secularisation and democratisation'.[72]

The above assertions appear persuasive in the context of Pakistan where conservative *ulama* have been resisting the reforms of Islamic family law by the state. The reaction of *ulama* against the Family and Marriage Commission Report 1956 and the MFLO is one such example of the tussle between the 'custodians of *shari'a*' and the 'modern legislating state'. This, however, is only one way of looking at the relationship between the *ulama* and the state. The same *ulama* who resist the codification of Islamic family law by the state, vehemently opposes any changes in the codified Islamic criminal law (Hudood laws). This shows that they are not against the codification of Islamic law and its implementation by the state *per se*. In fact, they want more Islamisation of laws and have repeatedly offered their services for this purpose.[73] Historical record suggests that even during the colonial period, not only did *ulama* perform their traditional functions, but they also participated in judicial and legislative processes, albeit with much weaker bargaining power.[74] The *ulama* of India at that time established closer contact with ordinary individuals after they were deprived of state patronage. Consequently, in an effort to increase their influence in society, they organised themselves in institutional forms such as the famous seminaries of Deoband, Nadwat al-Ulama, and Bareli.[75] Moreover, it should also be noted that Muslim jurists never denied the existence of state legislation, judicial decisions, and custom within the Islamic legal system.[76] Rather, they justified the state law under the doctrine of *siyasa shari'a*, and judicial decisions and custom (*'urf*) under the doctrines of continuity (*istishab*), juristic preference (*istihsan*), and welfare (*maslaha*).[77]

An interesting aspect of the attitude of *ulama* towards state legislation and women's rights is manifested in their contrasting responses towards two sets of legislation during the colonial and post-colonial periods. They were the proponents of the Muslim Personal Law (Shariat) Application Act 1937 and the Dissolution of Muslim Marriages Act 1939 during the colonial period and supported these Acts for the protection of women's rights to property and divorce. However, during the post-colonial period, *ulama* opposed every piece of legislation that intended to protect women's rights such as the MFLO, the Protection of Women (Criminal Laws Amendment) Act 2006, and the Punjab Protection of Women against Violence Act 2016. Therefore, it is incorrect to portray *ulama* as essentially conservative, traditionalist, and orthodox. Not only are the *ulama* diverse as a religious class but also their relationship with the state and society, in the context of Pakistan, has been considerably dynamic and historically contingent.

Another important debate in Islamic family law relates to the issue of the compatibility of *shari'a* with international human rights law.[78] In this respect, the Convention on the Elimination of All Forms of Discrimination against Women (CEDAW), and the Convention on Rights of the Children (CRC) are two important international legal instruments. Many Muslim states ratified these conventions, but added their reservations, making the efficacy of these instruments 'subject to the principles of *shari'a*'. One of the main concerns of many Muslim countries has been the issue of gender equality, which complicates the permissibility of polygamy, differential rights of spouses to marriage, maintenance, divorce, custody of children and inequality in the rights of family property and inheritance as regards male and female relatives.

On the basis of these perceived complications, some scholars argue that the compatibility between international covenants on human rights and Islamic law is difficult, if not impossible. According to these scholars, there is only one way out of this conundrum: the subordination of Islamic law to the human rights covenants.[79] Such proposals reflect a lack of sensitivity towards the religious sentiments of Muslims and assume Islamic law as essentialist and ahistorical. Considering these aspects of the debate, other scholars contend that Islamic law can be construed in a manner which would be in consonance with the standard of universal human rights and gender equality.[80] They are of the opinion that the only viable and authentic alternative to the subordination of Islamic law to international human rights law is to develop Islamic interpretations to counter the culturally prevalent and historically embedded constructions of gender inequality in Muslim countries. However, in order to be effective and legitimate in the eyes of Muslims, such interpretations must be based on the traditional sources of Islamic jurisprudence.

In the rest of the chapters of this book, we shall see that the judges of the superior courts of Pakistan have gradually reformed Islamic family law by directly relying upon the primary sources of Islamic law—the Qur'an and Sunnah. For this purpose, the judges are guided by the opinions of classical jurists, but without being constrained by them. They develop new legal principles or reform the existing ones through fresh interpretations of the Qur'an and Sunnah. We call this practice of judges 'judicial *ijtihad*'.[81] A few examples of this practice include the extension in women's right to no-fault divorce (*khula*);[82] the endorsement of a widow's right to the immovable property of her Shia husband;[83] and the affirmation of a mother's right to the custody of her child even when she enters into a second marriage to a person who does not fall within the prohibited degree of marriage with the child.[84] The judges also refer to general principles of Islamic jurisprudence while performing 'judicial *ijtihad*'. A recent example of this practice includes the FSC judgment in which the Court justified setting the minimum age of marriage for children under the Child Marriage Restraint Act 1929 on the basis of the principle of the protection of intellect which is one of the objectives of *shari'a*. The Court observed that setting the minimum age of marriage would generally help girls to get an education and acquisition of education is mandatory for every Muslim irrespective of gender to develop themselves intellectually. Therefore, the law setting the minimum age of marriage is justifiable to promote one of the basic goals of *shari'a*—protection of intellect. The Court further observed that intellectual development and mental maturity are necessary for a healthy marriage which further promotes the goals of *shari'a*.[85]

Notes

1. Public Knowledge, Attitudes and Perceptions of Justice: Report of a Household Survey in Southern Punjab Districts (EU Punjab Access to Justice Project, March 2015), 98. These findings are confirmed by the annual reports of the Lahore High Court. According to Annual Report 2015, 93,000 family cases were pending before the family courts in Punjab. The data shows that the number of pending family cases has increased from 60,000 to 91,000 within a short period of five years. In 2010, the number of pending family cases was 60,000; in 2011 it increased to 70,000; in 2012 to 77,000; in 2013 to 90,000; and in 2014 to 91,000.
2. The survey reveals the following per centage of litigation in various areas of law: 10.5 per cent marital disputes; 7.5 per cent guardianship disputes; 6.5 per cent inheritance disputes; 5 per cent other family disputes (Total: 29.5 per cent); 52.5 per cent land and property; 7.5 per cent transactional/contractual, and 3 per cent rent. O. Siddique, *Pakistan's Experience with Formal Law: An Alien Justice* (Cambridge: Cambridge University Press, 2013), 117.
3. *Fiqh* literally means understanding. It denotes the meanings of human interpretation of *shari'a*, which is found in the revealed sources: the Qur'an and the Sunnah of Prophet Muhammad (PBUH). Whereas *shari'a* is all-encompassing, and covers both beliefs and legal injunctions, *fiqh* is limited to human actions. The founder of the Hanafi school, Imam Abu Hanifa, defined *fiqh* as the knowledge of rights and obligations. Later, jurists drew a distinction between *shari'a* and *fiqh* in terms of the generality and immutability of the former and the specificity and adaptability of the latter. 'Ubayd Allāh ibn Mas'ūd Maḥbūbī, *Tawḍīḥ ma'a al-talwīḥ* (Qazān: al-Maṭba'a al-Impīrāṭūriya, 1884), 11–12, and M. K. Masud, *Shatibi's Philosophy of Islamic Law* (Islamabad: Islamic Research Institute, Islamabad, 1995), 18–20.
4. This phenomenon is described as the theory of the closure of the doors of *ijtihad* which has been criticised by various scholars and researchers. See S.M. Iqbal, *The Reconstruction of Religious Thought in Islam* (Oxford: Oxford University Press, 1934), 139–70; W.B. Hallaq, 'Was the Gate of Ijtihad Closed?', *International Journal of Middle East Studies*, 16 (1) (1984), 3.
5. A. Rahim, *The Principles of Muhammadan Jurisprudence* (London: Luzac & Co. 1911), 182–85.
6. M. Fadel, 'The Social Logic of *Taqlīd* and the Rise of the *Mukhataṣar*', *Islamic Law and Society* (1996) 3 (2), 193.
7. A.A.A. Fyzee, *Outlines of Muhammadan Law,* 5th edn (first published Oxford: Oxford University Press, 1949; New Delhi, 2009), 27–28.
8. M.L. Bhatia, *Administrative History of Medieval India (A Study of Muslim Jurisprudence under Aurangzeb)* (New Delhi: Radha Publication, 1992), 135–63, 84–94. See also M.B. Ahmad, *The*

Administration of Justice in Medieval India (Allahabad: The Aligarh Historical Research Institute, 1941).

9. A.M. Guenther, 'Hanafi Fiqh in Mughal India: The Fatāwá-i 'Ālamgīrī'', in R.M. Eaton (ed.), *India's Islamic Traditions, 711–1750* (New Delhi: Oxford University Press, 2003), 215. Also see M.I. Bhatti, *Barr-i Saghir Pak-o Hind mein 'Ilm-i Fiqh* (Lahore: Institute of Islamic Culture, 1973).
10. J. Schacht, 'On the Title of the *Fatāwā al-'*Ālamgīriyya', in C.E. Bosworth (ed.), *Iran and Islam* (Edinburgh: Edinburgh University Press, 1971); H. Liebesny, 'English Common Law and Islamic Law in the Middle East and South Asia: Religious Influences and Secularization', *Cleveland State Law Review* (1985) 34, 19, 21.
11. Al-Shaykh Niẓām, *Al-Fatāwā al-'Ālamgīriyya,* vol. 3, Maulanā Syed Amīr tr., (Karachi: Dār al-isha'at 2011), 353.
12. This does not mean that rulers and judges did not play any role at all in the development of Islamic law. M. Hoexter, 'Qāḍī, Muftī and Ruler: Their Roles in the Development of Islamic Law', in R. Shaham (ed.), *Law, Custom, and Statute in the Muslim World* (Leiden: Brill, 2006), 67.
13. M.R. Anderson, 'Legal Scholarship and the Politics of Islam in British India,' in R.S. Khare (ed.), *Perspectives on Islamic Law, Justice, and Society* (Oxford: Rowman & Littlefield, 1999), 65–91; S.A. Kugle, 'Framed, Blamed and Renamed: The Recasting of Islamic Jurisprudence in Colonial South Asia', *Modern Asian Studies* (2001) 35, issue 257; E. Giunchi, 'The Reinvention of Sharia under the British Raj: In Search of Authenticity and Certainty', *The Journal of Asian Studies* (2010) 69 (4), 1119.
14. Despite considering the option of codification in the mid-nineteenth century, the colonial state did not codify Islamic family law. R.K. Wilson, 'Should the Personal Laws of the Natives of India be Codified?' *Asiatic Quarterly Review* (1898) 6, 225.
15. In its preface, the translator stated that the book was written in Persian for the use of Emperor Muhammad Shah. He wrote that his translation conveys the general idea of Muslim law about which little was known by the British. He opined that his work might be useful for the public during the period till the translation of the *Hidaya* produced by Captain Hamilton and Mr James Anderson was published. F. Gladwin, *An Epitome of Mohammedan Law* (Translated from the original Persian, Calcutta: William Mackay, 1786).
16. C. Hamilton, *The Hedaya, or Guide; A Commentary on the Mussulman Laws*, 4 vols (London: T. Bensley 1791).
17. Charles Hamilton (trans.), *The Hedaya, Or Guide: A Commentary on the Mussulman Laws*, 2nd edn. (London: W/H. Allen 1870). Second edition, with Preface and Index by Standish Grove Grady,
18. Siraj al-Din Muḥammad Ibn Muhammad Sajawandi, *Al Sirajiyya; or, the Mahommedan Law of Inheritance* (Reprinted from the translation of Sir William Jones, published at Calcutta in 1792, with notes and appendix by Almaric Rumsey W. Amer 1869).
19. Pal argued that Regulations 1793 intended to divide the estates of landlords. R. Pal, *The History of the Law of Primogeniture with Special Reference to India, Ancient and Modern* (Calcutta: University of Calcutta, 1929), 347–65.
20. J.G. Thiessen, 'Orientalism and the East India Company, 1773–1858' (PhD Thesis, The John Hopkins University 1992), 361–62.
21. Hamilton had pointed out that the practical utility of these 'codes' was not simply limited to governance and the administration of justice, it also served the commercial interests of the British Empire by serving as 'a source of desirable knowledge to the merchant and traveller' all over the Muslim world. Hamilton, *The Hedaya*, lxxxvii.
22. Under the principle of precedent or *stare decisis* ('to stand by things decided'), courts adhere to their previous rulings or the rulings of higher courts. The doctrine of precedent was the product of the 19th century, caused by changes in legal theory purported by Bentham and Austin, also changes in the judicial hierarchy and a growing requirement for certainty in the law, ref. J. Evans, 'Change in the Doctrine of Precedent During the Nineteenth Century', in Laurence Goldstein (ed.), *Precedent in Law* (Oxford: Clarendon Press, 1987), 35–72. For the earlier history of the development of the doctrine of precedent, see T.E. Lewis, 'The History of Judicial Precedent,' *Law Quarterly Review* (1930–32) 46, 207–24 & 341–60, also 47 *LQR* 411–27, 48 *LQR* 230–47.

23. B.S. Cohn, 'Anthropological Notes on Disputes and Law in India', *American Anthropologist* (1965) 67, 82, 105.
24. Macnaghten was born in Calcutta and was fluent not only in Persian and Sanskrit but also in Arabic. He had served as a magistrate and registrar of the Sadr Diwani Adalat. K. Prior, 'Macnaghten, Sir William Hay, baronet (1793–1841)', *Oxford Dictionary of National Biography* (OUP, 2004), <http://www.oxforddnb.com/view/article/17705> accessed 14 September 2016.
25. S.C. Sircar, *Tagore Law Lectures—1873: The Muhammadan Law* (Calcutta: Thacker, Spink and Co., 1873).
26. S.A. Ali, *Tagore Law Lectures–1884: The Law relating to Gifts, Trusts, and Testamentary Dispositions among the Mahommedans* (Calcutta: Thacker, Spink & Co., 1885).
27. S.A. Ali, *Mahommedan Law* (Lahore: Law Publishing Company, 1976 [first published in 1892]).
28. R.K. Wilson, *A Digest of Anglo-Muhammadan Law,* 1st edn. (Calcutta: W. Thacker & Co., 1895).
29. Mulla, *Principles of Mahomedan Law* 20th edn (1st edn Calcutta: W. Thacker & Co 1905; Haryana: LexisNexis, 2013).
30. Rahman, *Institutes of Mussalman Law* (Calcutta: Thacker, Spink & Co., 1907).
31. He mentioned seventy-one original authorities as his primary material for this treatise. A. Rahim, *The Principles of Muhammadan Jurisprudence* (London: Luzac & Co, 1911), xi–xiii.
32. F.B. Tyabji, *Principles of Muhammadan Law*, 2nd edn (Calcutta: Butterworth & Co. 1919). There is also F.B. Tyabji, *Muhammadan Law*, 3rd edn (Bombay: N.M. Tripathi 1940).
33. S. Vesey-Fitzgerald, *Muhammadan Law: An Abridgement* (Oxford: Oxford University Press, 1931).
34. Fyzee, *Outlines of Muhammadan Law* (Oxford: Oxford University Press, 1949).
35. A complete syllabus for the first year of LLB degree at Allahabad University is provided in G.C. Kozlowski, 'Muslim Endowments and Society in British India' (PhD Thesis, University of Minnesota, 1980), 209.
36. The formation of this commission was the result of a campaign launched by the All Pakistan Women's Association (APWA), which called for the family law reform following the second marriage of the then Prime Minister Muhammad Ali Bogra. S. Ansari, 'Polygamy, Purdah and Political Representation: Engendering Citizenship in 1950s Pakistan', *Modern Asian Studies* (2009), 43, 1421 and F. Abbott, 'Pakistan's New Marriage Law: A Reflection of Qur'anic Interpretation', *Asian Survey* (1962) 11(1), 26.
37. M.A. Rashid, 'Report of the Commission on Marriage and Family Law,' in Khurshid Ahmad (ed.), *Studies in the Family Law of Islam* (Karachi: Chirag-e-Rah Publications, 1959), 33–97.
38. Khurshid Ahmad (ed.), *Marriage Commission Report X-Rayed: A Study of the Family Law of Islam and a Critical Appraisal of the Modernist Attempts to 'Reform' It* (Karachi: Chiragh-e-Rah Publications, 1959), i–xiii.
39. Q.M. Tahir, *Aali Qawanin* (Lahore: Jang Publishers, 1999), 135–47 and Dr Tanzil-ur-Rahman, *Muslim Family Laws Ordinance: Islamic & Social Survey* (Karachi: Royal Book Company, 1997), 4–7.
40. A bill to repeal the MFLO was introduced in the National Assembly in 1962 but it was rejected by a majority vote. A decade later, in 1972, yet another attempt was made to bring the MFLO in 'accordance with the Qur'an and Sunnah' by setting up a board of *ulama*. K. Mumtaz, 'Political Participation: Women in National Legislatures in Pakistan', in F. Shaheed, S.A. Warraich, C. Balchin and A. Gazdar (eds.), *Shaping Women's Lives: Laws, Practices & Strategies in Pakistan* (Lahore: Shirkat Gah, 1998), 328–38.
41. Council of Islamic Ideology, Report on Muslim Family Laws, 1st–2nd edn (Islamabad: Government of Pakistan, first edn. 1983, second edn. 1993), 32.
42. Ibid., ii–iii, 33.
43. Omitted by s 2 and second schedule, the Federal Laws (Revision and Declaration) Ordinance 1981.
44. *Dr Mahmood-ur-Rahman Faisal v Government of Pakistan* PLD 1994 SC 607.
45. *Allah Rakha v The Federation of Pakistan* PLD 2000 FSC 1.
46. *Shoukat Ali v The State* 2004 YLR 619 (FSC) (*Talaq* is valid despite non-fulfilment of a notice requirement); *Muhammad Aslam v The State* 2012 PCrLJ 11 (FSC) (Consent of marriage obtained through fear is invalid); *Tariq Masih v The State* 2004 PCrLJ 1017 (FSC) (Consent by an adult convert

to Islam is valid for *nikah*); and *Muhammad Shahid Sahil v State* PLD 2010 FSC 215 (A DNA test can be conducted to establish the offence of rape).

47. Tanzil-ur-Rahman used the term Muslim Personal Law for his book, *A Code of Muslim Personal Law* (Karachi: Hamdard Academy, 1978). A decade later, David Pearl titled the second edition of his book, *A Textbook on Muslim Personal Law* (Kent: Croom Helm, 1987). The first edition of his book was called, *A Textbook on Muslim Law* (Kent: Croom Helm, 1979). The third edition of his book, coauthored with W. Menski, is titled, *Muslim Family Law* (New Delhi: Sweet & Maxwell, 1998 and 2015).
48. A.A.A. Fyzee, *The Reform of Muslim Personal Law in India* (Bombay: Nachiketa Publications, 1971), 11.
49. See Y. Sezgin, *Human Rights under State-Enforced Religious Family Laws in Israel, Egypt and India* (Cambridge: Cambridge University Press, 2013).
50. PLD 1981 SC 120, 122.
51. Ibid., 125.
52. PLD 1994 SC 607, 620.
53. Ibid., 617.
54. This sub-Article was inserted under the Constitution (Third Amendment) Order, 1985 (President's Order No. 24 of 1985). It replaced the following sub-Article, which was inserted under the Constitution (Second Amendment) 1974: '(3) A person who does not believe in the absolute and unqualified finality of the Prophethood of MUHAMMAD (Peace be upon him), the last of the Prophets or claims to be a Prophet, in any sense of the word or of any description whatsoever, after MUHAMMAD (Peace be upon him), or recognizes such a claimant as a Prophet or religious reformer, is not a Muslim for the purposes of the Constitution or law'.
55. PLD 1978 Lah 113.
56. 1998 SCMR 816.
57. 2005 YLR 29 [Lah].
58. 2009 CLC 1057 [Kar].
59. 1996 CLC 1963 [Lah].
60. *Basharat Ahmed v Mst Shamim* PLD 2016 Lah 271.
61. *Bashir Ahmed v Muhammad Boota* 1991 CLC 1153.
62. *Mst Bhagari v Khia* 2006 YLR 394.
63. *Ghulam Shabbir v Mst Bakhat Khatoon* 2009 SCMR 644.
64. *Bikani Mia v Shuk Lal* (1892) 20 Cal 116, 179.
65. *Muhammad Raza v Abbas* (1932) 59 IA 236, 245.
66. For details see Fyzee, *Outlines of Muhammadan Law*, 56.
67. S 17, the Guardians and Wards Act 1890.
68. A. Shalakany, 'Islamic Legal Histories', *Berkeley Journal of Middle Eastern & Islamic Law* (2008) 1, 2.
69. W.B. Hallaq, *The Impossible State: Islam, Politics, and Modernity's Moral Predicament* (New York: Columbia University Press, 2013). Hallaq argues that a coercive modern state and ethically oriented *shari'a* cannot co-exist. A different version of this argument is presented by Abdullahi An-Na'im in his several writings. See A.A. An-Na'im, 'Shari'a and Positive Legislation: Is an Islamic State Possible or Viable?', in A. Ghazaleh (ed.), *Intellectual Property Laws of the Arab Countries* (The Hague: Kluwer Law International, 2000) 29–41 and A. A. An-Na'im, *Islam and the Secular State* (Cambridge: Harvard University Press, 2008).
70. M. Fadel, 'A Tragedy of Politics or an Apolitical Tragedy?', *Journal of the American Oriental Society* (2011) 131 (1), 109. Brian Wright, *A Continuity of Sharīʿa: Political Authority and Homicide in the Nineteenth Century* (American University in Cairo Press 2023) 5 and Rachel M. Scott, *Recasting Islamic Law: Religion and the Nation in Egyptian Constitution Making* (Cornell University Press 2021) 5.
71. W.B. Hallaq, 'Juristic Authority vs. State Power: The Legal Crises of Modern Islam', *Journal of Law and Religion* (2003) 19 (2), 243, argues that classical Islamic law operated outside the state authority

and notes that the power of the coercive state has replaced the moral authority of *shari'a* as a means of legitimacy.

72. A. Layish, 'The Transformation of the Sharī'a from Jurists' Law to Statutory Law in the Contemporary Muslim World', *Die Welt des Islams* (2004) 44 (1), 85, 93. R. Peters, 'From Jurists Law to Statute Law or What Happens When the Shari'a is Codified', *Mediterranean Politics* (2002) 7 (3), 82.
73. M.T. Usmani, 'The Islamization of Laws in Pakistan: The Case of Hudud Ordinances', *The Muslim World* (2006) 96, 287, 303. Usmani argues for further legal reforms to make Hudood laws effective instead of scrapping them. K. Pemberton, 'An Islamic Discursive Tradition on Reform as Seen in the Writing of Deoband's Muftī Muḥammad Taqī 'Ušmānī', *The Muslim World* (2009) 99 (3), 452, describes Justice Usmani as a reformer of Islamic law reformers because of his emphasis on strictly following the principles of classical Islamic law.
74. M.Q. Zaman, *The Ulama in Contemporary Islam: Custodians of Change* (Princeton: Princeton University Press, 2002), 15–37.
75. K.A. Nizami, 'Socio-Religious Movements in Indian Islam, 1763–1898', *Islamic Culture* (1970) 44 (2), 131.
76. M.K. Masud, *Shatibi's Philosophy of Islamic Law* (Islamabad: Islamic Research Institute, 1995), 14–15.
77. G. Libson, 'On the Development of Custom as a Source of Law in Islamic Law', *Islamic Law and Society* (1997) 4 (2), 131; F.M.M. Opwis, *Maṣlaḥa and the Purpose of the Law: Islamic Discourse on Legal Change from the 4th/10th to 8th/14th Century* (Leiden: Brill, 2010).
78. E. Afsah, 'Contested Universalities of International Law: Islam's Struggle with Modernity', *Journal of the History of International Law* (2008) 10, 259.
79. A.E. Mayer, *Islam and Human Rights: Tradition and Politics* (Oxford: Westview Press, 1991).
80. S.S. Ali, *Gender and Human Rights in Islam and International Law: Equal before Allah, Unequal before Man* (London: Kluwer Law International, 2000); M.A. Baderin, *International Human Rights and Islamic Law* (Oxford: Oxford University Press, 2003) and N.A. Shah, *Women, the Koran and International Human Rights Law: The Experience of Pakistan* (Leiden: Martinus Nijhoff Publishers, 2006).
81. For details see M.Z. Abbasi, 'Judicial *Ijtihād* as a Tool for Legal Reform: Extending Women's Right to Divorce under Islamic Law in Pakistan', *Islamic Law and Society* (2017) 24, 384.
82. *Balqis Fatima v Najam-ul-Ikram* PLD 1959 Lah 566.
83. *Khalida Shamim Akhtar v Ghulam Jaffar* PLD 2016 Lah 865.
84. *Amar Ilahi v Rashida Akhtar* PLD 1955 Lah 412.
85. *Farooq Omar Bhoja v Federation of Pakistan* PLD 2022 FSC 1.

Part I
MARRIAGE

Formation, Operation, and Dissolution

2

MARRIAGE

2.1 Introduction

Under Islamic law, marriage (*nikah*) is a contract, entered into between a man and a woman with their free consent. The Qur'anic verse 4:21 describes marriage as a solemn covenant, '*mithaq ghaliz*'.[1] This means that, unlike a purely civil contract, a marriage contract has a certain religious aspect to it. The default terms of a marriage contract can be altered by the parties to suit their individual circumstances. It is a recommended act (*sunnah/mandub*), which may become obligatory (*fard*) or prohibitory (*haram*) under certain circumstances. For instance, marriage is obligatory for men who have sufficient means to pay dower and maintain their families, and they are certain that they will commit extra-marital sexual offences to fulfil their biological desires if they remain unmarried. In this regard, classical Muslim jurists presume marriage to be a shield against the commission of sexual offences. Similarly, marriage is prohibited for persons who do not have sufficient means to maintain their wives and children, and/or who are suffering from serious sexually transmitted diseases. This suggests that marriage in Islam is not simply a matter of strict religious injunctions, but a sophisticated combination of *ibadat* (worship) and *muamalat* (worldly affairs).

2.2 Requirements of a Valid Marriage

A valid marriage must fulfil all the legal requirements of a contract. The contract must be: (i) a result of an offer and acceptance at one meeting; (ii) entered into with the free consent of the parties, or of their guardian in case of minors,[2] who have the option to validate or repudiate their marriage contracts upon attaining the age of puberty (this is known as *khiyar al-bulugh* or the 'option of puberty'[3]); (iii) for an indefinite period of time (with the exception of *muta* marriages under Shia law)[4]; and (iv) the parties must not fall within the prohibited degree of marriage based on blood relations, affinity, and fosterage.

2.3 Prohibited Degree of Marriage

The prohibited degree of marriage is related to the nature of the relationship between the parties. If the parties fall within the following range of relationships, the marriage will be invalid. Blood relations include:

i. mother or grand-mother, how high so ever;
ii. daughter or grand-daughter, how low so ever;
iii. sister (full, uterine, and consanguine);
iv. niece or grand-niece, how low so ever; and
v. aunt or grand-aunt (paternal and maternal), how high so ever."

Affinity to the relations of:

i. wife (wife's mother or grand-mother, daughter or grand-daughter);
ii. father (his wife and grand-father's wife, how high so ever); and
iii. son (his wife or the wife of his son's son or the wife of his daughter's son, how low so ever)."

As regards fosterage, generally, such relations are to be treated the same way as real relations, with the exception of certain foster relations such as sister's foster-mother, foster-sister's mother, foster-son's sister, or foster-brother's sister.[5]

2.4 Temporary Prohibitions

Under certain circumstances, marriage is prohibited as long as a legal impediment exists. When the legal impediment is removed, it becomes lawful to enter into a marriage. These circumstances include the following:

i. an unlawful conjunction: a man is not allowed to have two wives, at the same time, who are so related to each other that if either of them had been a male, they could not have lawfully intermarried, e.g. two sisters, or aunt and niece;
ii. a man cannot enter into a marriage with a married woman until she is divorced or her husband dies and she completes her *iddat* period;

iii. a marriage contract of a Muslim man with a woman who is not a *kitabiya* (Jewish or Christian) is prohibited until she embraces Islam, Judaism, or Christianity. A Muslim woman, on the other hand, cannot enter into a valid marriage with a non-Muslim whether he be a *kitabi* or not;[6]
iv. a fifth marriage by a Muslim husband; as a Muslim, he is allowed to marry a maximum of four wives at a time;
v. a person who enters the precincts of Kaaba and puts on a pilgrimage dress cannot enter into a marriage contract. Hanafi jurists allow such a person to contract a marriage, but disallow its consummation; and
vi. a woman who is divorced thrice cannot enter into a valid marriage with her former husband without an intervening marriage (*halala*).

2.5 Legal Consequences of Marriage

A marriage contract can be valid (*sahih*), void (*batil*), or irregular (*fasid*). A valid (*sahih*) marriage establishes a legal relationship between the spouses and gives rise to mutual rights and obligations. It also confers legitimacy on the children born during the marriage, and obligates the husband to pay dower and provide maintenance to the wife and children (if any). Validly married spouses inherit from each other and from their children. Legitimate children also inherit from their validly married parents. A valid marriage also establishes the prohibition of affinity based on marriage (*hurmat e masaharat*) between each spouse and certain relatives of each other.

A void (*batil*) marriage is unlawful in itself, and its prohibition is absolute and perpetual. For instance, a marriage with a person falling within the prohibited degree of marriage is unlawful absolutely and perpetually. Such a marriage does not create any rights and obligations between the parties. Moreover, the offspring of a void marriage are regarded as illegitimate. Such a marriage cannot be legalised through any process.

There is a third category between a valid marriage and a void marriage, called an irregular (*fasid*) marriage. Such a marriage is not unlawful in itself, rather external factors make it unlawful for a temporary period. Therefore, it is not essentially unlawful but can become so if certain requirements are not fulfilled, e.g. the absence of witnesses to the marriage. Such a marriage does not have legal effects before consummation. However, if an irregular marriage is consummated, it has the following consequences:

i. the wife is entitled to dower, specified or proper whichever is lower;
ii. she is bound to observe *iddat*[7] upon the termination of the marriage;
iii. legitimacy is conferred upon the offspring; and
iv. mutual rights to inheritance between the spouses do not arise.

The legal impediments for an irregular marriage are not absolute or permanent; they can be removed to make a marriage valid. For instance, a marriage conducted without witnesses is irregular. However, the parties can enter into a fresh marriage in the presence of witnesses, making it a valid marriage.

2.6 Stipulations in Marriage Contracts

The parties may set certain conditions in their marriage contracts. Women may use stipulations in marriage contracts to protect their rights. For instance, a marriage contract may contain a condition that if the husband enters into a second marriage, the first wife will get a right to opt for divorce or get financial compensation. There are, however, certain limitations upon stipulations. For example, stipulations that contravene the basic purpose of marriage are void. Thus, the condition that the groom will divorce the wife after marriage so that she may remarry her previous husband who triply divorced her, the so-called *halala* marriage, is void. Similarly, default rules of Islamic family law cannot be altered through stipulations e.g., wife's right to dower and maintenance. Amongst the Sunni schools, Hanbali school is the most flexible by allowing a wide scope for stipulations to benefit women. Hanbali jurists regard as valid the stipulation that the husband shall not enter into a second marriage unlike jurists belonging to the other three Sunni schools, who regard such stipulation as void.[8]

2.7 Registration and Witnessing of Marriage Contracts

Writing or registration is not a mandatory requirement for the validity of a marriage contract under classical Islamic law (*fiqh*). Therefore, even an oral and unregistered marriage can be regarded as valid under *fiqh*. However, written and registered marriages are easier to prove in a situation where the existence of marriages are disputed either during the lifetime of the spouses or after their death. Such proof becomes crucial where rights in inheritance need to be established. Therefore, the evidentiary significance of registration cannot be disregarded. Section 5 of the MFLO requires registration of all marriages, whether solemnised by an official *nikah* registrar or anyone else. One *nikah* registrar is licensed in each ward by the union council to supply the standard form of a *nikahnama*. It should be noted that an unwritten and/or unregistered marriage is still valid, though the persons who violate the requirement of registration are liable to punishment under section 5 of the MFLO. The punishment includes simple imprisonment for up to three months or a fine of up to Rs 1000, or both. In its Report No. 74 of 2005, the Law and Justice Commission of Pakistan recommended that the fine should be increased to Rs 10,000 in order to make the deterrent more effective.

A marriage contract should be witnessed by two persons (two males, or one male and two females), who are sane, adult Muslims. According to the majority of Muslim jurists, the presence of witnesses is an essential requirement for a valid marriage. However, Imam Malik does not consider the presence of witnesses essential at the time of marriage for its validity as long as the marriage is duly publicised, e.g. by beating of drums. Similarly, according to Shia jurists, the presence of witnesses is not a mandatory requirement for the validity of a marriage contract.

According to the majority of Sunni jurists, a marriage conducted in the absence of witnesses is irregular (*fasid*). Consequently, if the irregularity in a marriage is revealed, the couple should separate themselves or a court shall order them to separate. In order to validate their relationship, the couple may conduct a fresh marriage contract in the presence of witnesses.

2.8 Presumption of a Valid Marriage

In the absence of any evidence to prove a marriage, a presumption of a valid marriage arises as a result of prolonged and continuous cohabitation as husband and wife. This presumption also arises if a man acknowledges a woman as his wife or if he acknowledges the paternity of a child born to a woman.[9]

2.9 Outline of Case Law

2.9.1 Nature of Marriage under Islamic Law. The cases in this section elaborate on the nature of marriage under Islamic law. In Islam, marriage is considered a civil contract, and not a sacrament or a religious covenant.

Payment of the dower is an essential effect of a valid marriage contract. In *Abdul Kadir v Salima*,[10] Justice Syed Mahmood construed dower as a consideration. Like any contract, parties to a marriage contract can agree on certain terms and conditions that restrict the legal rights of either spouse, provided they are not against the law and public policy. Since marriage has been conceptualised as a civil contract, a logical corollary would be that damages can be sought in case of its unwarranted breach. In *Shahida Parveen v Samiullah*,[11] the Lahore High Court held that under Islamic law, a marriage is not similar to an ordinary contract; it is a special type of contract, meaning thereby that the general contract law for breach of contract does not apply to a marriage contract.

Abdul Kadir v Salima (1886) ILR 8 All 149

Marriage in Islam is a civil contract and not a sacrament.

This is a seminal case on the nature of marriage in Islam. The plaintiff filed a suit for restitution of conjugal rights[12] against his wife, who argued that her husband could not claim this right since he did not pay her dower. The plaintiff, in response, deposited the full amount of the dower in the court. The wife was an adult before her marriage and cohabited with the husband for three months after their marriage. She subsequently had gone to visit her parents' home and refused to return to live with her husband. Therefore, the husband filed a suit for restitution of conjugal rights to force her to live with him as his wife. There was no evidence that she had demanded the payment of her dower or refused cohabitation for non-payment of the dower before her husband filed the suit. She also alleged that her husband had orally divorced her and treated her with cruelty prior to the divorce. However, she could not substantiate these allegations through cogent evidence. In light of these circumstances, the trial court decreed the husband's suit for restitution of conjugal rights.

On appeal, the Appellate Court reversed the decision of the trial court on the ground that since the husband had not paid the dower at the time of filing the suit, his demand for restitution of conjugal rights was liable to be dismissed. Consequently, the husband filed an appeal before the Allahabad High Court. In the High Court, the case was referred to the full bench due to divergent juristic opinions on this point of law. Justice Syed Mahmood, son of Sir Syed Ahmed Khan—the leading Muslim reformer and the founder of the Aligarh University—authored the judgment. Justice Mahmood elaborated on the nature and effect of marriage in Islam along with the mutual rights and obligations of spouses under Islamic law. He observed that marriage in Islam is a civil contract, not a sacrament, even though it is generally solemnised with the recitation of the Qur'an. Like a civil contract, it becomes complete upon the acceptance of an offer made by a party or their guardians before competent witnesses. The legal effect of this contract is that it legalises the relationship between a man and a woman, and creates mutual rights and obligations, such as provision of dower, maintenance of wife, legitimacy of children, and mutual rights of inheritance. He assessed the nature of the dower under Islamic law and the effect of its non-payment at the time of marriage. Consequently, he defined a dower as 'a sum of money or other property promised by the husband to be paid or delivered to the wife in consideration of marriage'.[13] He came to the conclusion that the dower was 'consideration' for a marriage contract, which was deferrable until the dissolution of the marriage or the death of either spouse. Highlighting the significance of the dower, he stated that even where no dower is expressly fixed or mentioned at the time of marriage, the law confers the right of dower upon the wife as a necessary consequence of marriage.

Under the Hanafi school, a wife can deny herself to her husband until she receives the dower. The primary legal issue, in this case, was: whether a wife, who had willingly consummated her marriage without demanding the payment of a dower, could later refuse to maintain conjugal relations with her husband on the ground of non-payment of the dower. After referring to a plethora of case law and classical *fiqh* texts, Justice Mahmood decided the issue against the wife. He argued that a husband's right to cohabitation and a wife's right to dower accrue simultaneously as a result of a marriage contract. He elaborated this point through an analogy to a seller's right to a lien on the sold goods as long as they remain in his possession and the price remains unpaid.[14] He held that the wife's right to deny her body to the husband is similar to a seller's right to lien. Just as a right to lien is extinguished upon the delivery of the goods to the vendee, a wife cannot deny a husband's right to conjugal relations on the ground of non-payment of dower if she had willingly consummated her marriage. She could, however, sue him for its payment.

We observe that Justice Mahmood's analogy of a wife's right and control over her body with a seller's right to lien upon a commodity is misplaced. The conjugal rights are not comparable to the rights over a commodity which once surrendered cannot be retrieved. In contrast, a husband's right to cohabit with his wife accrues over a period of time during the subsistence of marriage. In accordance with the Qur'anic verse 4:34, husbands are allowed to refuse cohabitation with their wives to discipline them, likewise, wives should also have a right to refuse cohabitation with their husbands to enforce their rights such as the payment of prompt dower.

Shahida Parveen v Samiullah PLJ 2006 Lah 1215

Damages are not available for the breach of a marriage contract because general contract law does not apply to a marriage contract.

This case discusses the issue of remedies for breach of a marriage contract. According to the facts of the case, the respondent's wife departed from the house of her husband immediately after marriage without consummating her marriage on the pretext that her father was ill. She subsequently filed a suit for the dissolution of the marriage, alleging that her husband was a professional dancer. The Family Court passed a decree for the dissolution of marriage based on *khula*.

The husband filed a suit for damages against the wife and her father. He also claimed recovery of the dower and other expenses incurred by him on the marriage ceremony. He argued that in the suit for dissolution of marriage, the respondent levelled false, frivolous, and malicious allegations against him, which were defamatory in nature. He sought damages of Rs 2,400,000 for defamation, and further damages arising out of the expenses of the wedding. The trial court decided the suit in his favour and awarded him Rs 1,000,000 in total as damages (Rs 800,000 for defamation, and Rs 200,000 on other accounts). Both parties appealed before the Lahore High Court.

Mr Justice Mian Saqib Nisar, as he then was, observed that the respondent's allegations against her ex-husband being a professional dancer could not be proved. He found that these allegations were indeed defamatory in nature. However, Justice Nisar held that damages to the amount of Rs 800,000 for defamation/libel were punitive in nature and reduced the amount to Rs 100,000. Regarding damages for the breach of a marriage contract, Justice Nisar held that although marriage in Islam is a civil contract, it could not be equated with ordinary contracts of sale/purchase, property transactions, or personal service contracts. Therefore, a suit for breach of a marriage contract does not attract the remedies that are available for breach of contracts under sections 73 and 74 of the Contract Act 1872 or the general law.

Muhammad Masood Abbasi v Mamona Abbasi 2004 YLR 482 (Lah)

Restrictions on the husband's right to divorce in a marriage contract are valid.

This case deals with the object and scope of the restrictions on a husband's right to divorce. The wife filed a suit for the recovery of Rs 100,000 against her former husband for unjustifiably divorcing her. The parties were married in April 1994. They lived together till September 1995, when the petitioner's husband expelled the respondent's wife from his house. The husband subsequently divorced her without any justification. The *nikahnama* of the parties included a stipulation that in case the husband divorced his wife without any justification or contracted another marriage, he would be liable to pay a sum of Rs 100,000. The trial court dismissed the suit. However, the Appellate Court set aside the judgment of the trial court and decreed the suit in favour of the wife. The husband challenged this decision before the High Court.

The counsel for the petitioner contended that a restriction on a husband's right to divorce his wife is against the injunctions of Islam and public policy. Justice Farrukh Latif rejected this argument and held:

> To preserve the marriage contract and to safeguard the interest of the wife against its unjustified termination by the husband, if any stipulation is made in the *Nikahnama* whereby the husband agrees to pay some damages in the event of divorcing the wife without any just cause, such stipulation is neither against injunction[s] of Islam nor against public policy. It is true that Islam allows husband to divorce his wife without assigning any cause but it is equally true that Islam also approves preservation and protection of marriage and does not approve unjustified exercise of this right by the husband which certainly leads to innumerable social problems for the divorcee and the children which consequently has an adverse effect on the society as well. By imposition of such condition, the right of husband is neither taken away nor is restricted in the sense that he can still divorce the wife in spite of the condition but in case he divorces her without any reasonable cause or justification he would be liable to pay the agreed amount as damages so that the destitute divorcee and the children may make some arrangement for their food and shelter for the time being.[15]

Therefore, the court dismissed the petition *in limine*, upholding the condition restricting the husband's right to divorce.

Muhammad Zaman v Mst Irshad Begum PLD 1967 Lah 1104

An agreement to provide maintenance to a wife even when she is not living with her husband is valid and is not against public policy.

According to the facts in this case, the plaintiff, Muhammad Zaman, got married to Irshad Begum. A daughter was born during the marriage. In 1951, the plaintiff executed an agreement with his wife to the effect that if he contracted a second marriage she would be entitled to maintenance in a separate house or in her parental house if she so wished. In 1960, the husband filed a suit for the restitution of conjugal rights against the wife. The wife pleaded that the husband had not paid her prompt dower and maltreated her. She contended that the suit for the restitution of conjugal rights was a mere counterblast to her application under section 488 of the Criminal Procedure Code for the provision of maintenance for herself and her daughter.[16]

The entire case rested on the effect of the agreement executed by the plaintiff stipulating that if he took a second wife, Irshad Begum would be entitled to live away from him. The trial court noted that, by executing the agreement, the plaintiff had unconditionally agreed not to take a second wife, and if he did so, Irshad Begum would be allowed to live separately. On this ground, the plaintiff's suit for the restitution of conjugal rights was dismissed. On appeal, the District Judge upheld the decision of the trial court. Aggrieved by these decisions, the husband filed a second appeal before the High Court.

The counsel for the appellant contended that the courts below erred by relying upon the agreement. It was a void agreement because it contained a stipulation in restraint of marriage and provided a condition for the husband and wife to live separately from each other. The counsel submitted that this agreement was opposed to public policy within the meaning of section 23 of the Contract Act 1872 and, therefore, should not be enforced. In support of his arguments, he relied upon the two judgments of the Bombay and Lahore High Courts: *Bai Fatima v Ali Muhammad Aiyeb*[17] and *Bibi Fatima v Nur Muhammad*.[18] In these judgments, the courts declared such agreements, which provided and encouraged future separation between spouses against public policy.

However, in *Manzoor v Azizul*,[19] the Chief Court Oudh held otherwise. In this case, the two wives of the plaintiff could not get along well. Therefore, the husband executed an agreement to provide maintenance to one of the wives in a separate house. In a suit by the wife for maintenance, the husband contended that he was not liable to maintain her under the agreement as she was not living with him. The trial court decreed the wife's suit, and the Appellate Court upheld it. In the second appeal before the Chief Court, the husband argued that the agreement was without consideration and opposed the public policy. The court observed:

> If a Muhammadan marries a second wife and finds that his first wife cannot pull on well with his second wife and he does not and cannot provide a separate apartment or habitation for her exclusive use, and for the sake of preservation of the family peace executes an agreement in her favour giving her maintenance, even if she does not reside in the same house with him and his second wife, that agreement is not in our opinion against public policy. This arrangement does not necessarily result in [a] separation between husband and wife.[20]

After a detailed examination of the case law, Justice Muhammad Fazle Ghani rejected the proposition that the agreement was against public policy either under Muslim law or within the meaning of section 23 of the Contract Act 1872:

> A marriage between [a] Muslim male and female is purely of a nature of civil contract and the wife is entitled to protect herself at the hands of her husband in case of their future differences. In the present case[,] the agreement is to the effect that the wife is entitled to receive alimony in the house of her parents or anywhere else where she chooses to reside in case the husband takes a second wife and there is nothing in such an agreement which may be considered to offend against the term "public policy" which is very broad and it is not safe to rely upon it in such cases as a ground for [a] legal decision.[21]

The appellant's counsel raised an alternative contention that in case the agreement was found valid, the wife, at the most, could enforce her right to maintenance in a separate house. But the existence of such an agreement, or failure of the husband to fulfil the obligations under the agreement, could not serve as a defence to the plaintiff's suit for restitution of conjugal rights against his wife. The court rejected this contention and held that although it is the wife's duty to follow her husband wherever he wishes her to go, such an obligation of a wife is not absolute. The law recognises circumstances in which the wife has a right to refuse to live with her husband. Under Muslim law, the bad conduct or gross neglect of the husband is a good defence to a suit for the restitution of conjugal rights. Furthermore, a husband can file a suit for the restitution of conjugal rights in a court, but it is the discretion of the court to dismiss or decree such a suit considering the safety of the wife. The court upheld the agreement and dismissed the appeal.

2.9.2 Validity of Marriage. The free and voluntary consent of the parties is the most significant criterion for determining the validity of a marriage. In a society like Pakistan especially in rural areas, the elders of the family have the final say in the marriage, which oftentimes disregards the will of the parties. The superior courts have clearly laid down the principle that the consent of the parties is an essential requirement for a valid contract. In *Issa Khan v Mst Razma*,[22] the Supreme Court held that an agreement of engagement affected by the elders without the consent of the parties is not binding. Similarly, in *Hafiz Abdul Waheed v Asma Jehangir*,[23] the court thwarted the notion that a guardian's consent is necessary for the marriage of an adult female. It was held that a *wali*'s lack of consent does not invalidate a marriage contracted by a *sui juris* Muslim female.

2.9.2.1 Consent of the Parties for the Validity of Marriage

Issa Khan v Mst Razma 1991 SCMR 2454

An agreement of engagement between the elders without the consent of the parties is not binding.

This case deals with the scope and effect of a betrothal agreement between elders to unite their children in wedlock in future. The respondent Mst Razma filed a suit to contest the petitioner's (Issa Khan) claim that he had been betrothed to her for marriage. The trial court dismissed the suit, but it was decreed in her favour by the Appellate Court. The petitioner filed a civil revision against the decision of the Appellate Court, which was also dismissed. Ultimately, he sought leave to appeal against the dismissal before the Supreme Court. The petitioner argued that the respondent had been betrothed to him, and her father was bound by the agreement to arrange their marriage. He further claimed that the betrothal had matured into a marriage, and thus sought restitution of conjugal rights. The judge of the High Court while dismissing the petition observed:

> It is well-settled that mere betrothal (*mangani*) does not constitute any valid contract. This is generally [a] customary arrangement arrived at between

> relations of parties with a view to entering into [a] contract of marriage. It being pre-nuptial negotiations does not create any civil right[s].[24]

The Supreme Court, while refusing the leave to appeal, noted that in most betrothal arrangements in our society, the parents or other elders decide to bind the two persons in wedlock of marriage in future. Regarding the validity of such an arrangement, the court held:

> To bind a girl with such an agreement in the nature of betrothal in such a manner that she should be compelled to give her consent at the time of marriage or for that matter a decree for conjugal rights or for a direction for marriage be passed against a female in the above circumstances is unimaginable. The whole fabric of Islamic Law and jurisprudence on the subject is against such a notion. The lady remains free to give or to withhold consent for marriage till the moment when [the] marriage contract takes place.[25]

Muhammad Aslam v The State 2012 PCrLJ 11 (FSC)

A consent of marriage obtained through fear is invalid.

The complainant, Ayesha Bibi conducted *sharai nikah* of her daughter, Parveen Akhtar with Muhammad Zaheer. *Rukhsati* was due to take place at a later stage. The complainant alleged that the accused, Muhammad Tanveer developed illicit relations with her daughter and abducted her in connivance with Muhammad Aslam and others. The alleged abductee, Parveen Akhtar, was summoned before the *ilaqa* magistrate and her statement was recorded. She stated that both the accused, Muhammad Aslam and Muhammad Tanveer kept committing *zina* (rape) upon her and they obtained her thumb impressions on a blank paper. The trial court convicted the accused under sections 10(3) and 11 of the Offense of Zina (Enforcement of Hudood) Ordinance 1979.

After going through the facts of the case, the Appellate Court observed that the appellant in his statement under section 342 of the Criminal Procedure Code claimed that he had performed *nikah* with the abductee with her own free will. According to one of the prosecution witnesses, the age of the abductee was 16 years at the time and the alleged *nikah* had taken place one and a half years earlier. None of the abductee's parents or relations was informed of this alleged *nikah*. According to the Child Marriage Restraint Act 1929, Parveen Akhtar had not attained the legal age (16 years) required to enter into a valid marriage contract. Considering her age and the fact that the appellant was a 44 years old man, it seemed unlikely that Parveen Akhtar would freely consent to marry him. These facts and circumstances led the court to conclude that the commission of sexual intercourse with the abductee fell within the ambit of *zina-bil-jabr*.

The court held that in order to analyse the quality, value, and features of free consent, the following factors need to be considered: the ability to exercise free choice; capacity (legal capacity: not only sane but mature mind, i.e. not only puberty or majority but the age of responsive and conscious consent); capability to use the capacity; depending upon capacity, impediments to or assistance available for the application of mind, for example, availability of assistance of a *wali* and/or a *wakil*; extent of free availability of options to choose from; and an environment of freedom.

In the circumstances of the case, the court held that if the alleged consent of the abductee was obtained through fear, then it was not a free consent. Bearing in mind the age difference, the court held that Parveen Akhtar was too young and impressionable and needed the opportunity to seek assistance from her parents or a *wakil*, which evidently, she did not have. The *nikah* was, therefore, performed under duress and any sexual offence committed against the abductee would be forceful and qualified as being *zina-bil-jabr*. In light of these reasons, the court upheld the conviction of the appellant for the offence of kidnapping and *zina-bil-jabr*.

Rabia Khizer v Station House Officer PLD 2009 Lah 223

A marriage contract by a minor female is valid if she has reached puberty.

In this case, petitioner no. 1, Rabia Khizer, claimed that she married petitioner no. 2, Inam Ullah, of her own free will. Dissatisfied with the marriage, Rabia's father registered an FIR alleging abduction of his daughter by petitioner no. 2 and other accused. Petitioner no. 1 sought quashing of the FIR through the present writ petition. She vehemently denied the allegation of her abduction and maintained that she married petitioner no. 2 of her free will. The counsel for the respondents relied upon the School Leaving Certificate of petitioner no. 1 on which her year of birth was 1997, which meant that she was only 12 years old. The respondents argued that she had not yet attained the age of majority under the Child Marriage Restraint Act 1929. The medical examination, however, showed her to be of 18/19 years of age, which meant that she had attained the age of majority. The court held:

> Even if the contention of the learned counsel for the respondents regarding the age of petitioner No.1 Mst Rabia Khizer is not disputed, the marriage contracted by the petitioners would not be invalid or void … the female though not having the age of majority had attained puberty could not be compelled to sever her Nikah/marriage entered by her own free-will.[26]

Even if there was doubt as to petitioner no. 1's attaining the age of majority, there was none as to her attaining the age of puberty. Based on the medical report, the court treated her marriage as valid and quashed the FIR.

Mumtaz Bibi v Qasim and Others Writ Petition No. 4227 of 2021 IHC

A marriage contract by a minor is unlawful and *void ab initio.*

In this case, the Islamabad High Court dealt with two important legal questions: (i) whether a minor can contract a valid marriage? (ii) whether a minor has legal capacity to enter into a contract before attaining the age of majority under the Contract Act 1872?

The brief facts of the case are that the petitioner, Mst. Mumtaz Bibi, filed a constitutional petition for the recovery of her abducted daughter. The police produced the minor before the court. The minor stated that she married respondent no. 1 and was unwilling to go with her mother, the petitioner. While determining the question for validity of marriage by a minor, Justice Babar Sattar of the Islamabad High Court held that the marriage contract of children under the age of 18 is unlawful and *void ab initio*. In doing so, Justice Sattar did not follow the earlier judgment of the Supreme Court in *Mst. Bakhshi v Bashir Ahmad.*[27] In this case, the Supreme Court had observed that while the person violating the provisions of the Child Marriage Restraint Act 1929 would be penalised under the Act, the marriage of a minor who has attained the age of puberty itself would not become invalid. Justice Sattar justified departing from the Supreme Court judgment on the basis of the United Nations Convention on the Rights of the Child 1989 (UNCRC). He argued that Pakistan ratified the UNCRC in 1989, after the Supreme Court judgment, and the UNCRC required restraints on child marriages.

Justice Sattar further supported his argument on the basis that sexual intercourse with a child under the age of 16 falls under the definition of 'statutory rape' under sections 375 and 376 of the Pakistan Penal Code 1860 as amended in 2006. He argued that if an act is a criminal offence, it is not logical to regard as valid the marriage of a minor girl who has attained puberty. He argued that even if a child were to give consent to engage in sexual intercourse, the action of the accused would still constitute rape under section 375 of the PPC and would be punishable with death or maximum imprisonment of 25 years under section 376 of the PPC. Moreover, sections 377A and 377B were added to the PPC through an amendment in 2016. Under these sections, any persuasion, inducement, or enticement for the sexual activity of a child below the age of 18 is a crime punishable with imprisonment for up to 25 years. On the bases of these legal provisions, Justice Sattar argued that any contract of marriage where one of the contracting parties is below the age of 18 would be a contract which is executed for an unlawful purpose (child rape and sexual abuse). Therefore, such a contract would be void *ab initio* under section 23 of the Contract Act 1872.

On the bases of the above reasoning, the Islamabad High Court approved the petition and handed over the custody of the minor to the petitioner, her mother.

The judgment, in this case, is relevant for several reasons. First, it relies upon the international human rights convention, the UNCRC along with the subsequent relevant legislation to deviate from the judgment of the Supreme Court. Second, it gives precedence to codified law over uncodified principles of Muslim Family Law. In doing so, it differs from the conciliatory approach of the Supreme Court which had construed the provisions of the Child Marriage Restraint Act 1929 in a way that it does not conflict with the principles of Muslim family law.[28] It is important to note that in its recent judgment, the Federal Shariat Court in *Farooq Omar Bhoja v Federation of Pakistan* dismissed a challenge to sections 4, 5, and 6 of the Child Marriage Restraint Act 1929 on the basis of the injunctions of Islam.[29] The FSC held that although there is disagreement among Muslim jurists about the validity of the marriage of a minor, it is not un-Islamic for the state to determine the age of marriage for entering into a marriage contract. The judges of the FSC argued that if a permissible act (*mubah*) appears harmful to society, the state has the authority to prohibit it. The FSC referred to the action of Hazrat Umar (RA) of prohibiting marriage with Jewish and Christian (*ahl al-kitab*) women in the larger interest of the Muslim community even if the marriage was permissible in Islam. The FSC further relied upon the principle of blocking of means (*sadd al-dharia*), which authorises the state to take pre-emptive measures to curtail and curb any harmful act.

2.9.2.2 Consent of the *Wali*

Hafiz Abdul Waheed v Asma Jehangir PLD 2004 SC 219

Consent of a guardian is not required for the marriage of an adult Muslim female.

This case disposed of two appeals which involved a common question of law: whether the consent of a *wali* is essential for the validity of the marriage of a *sui juris* Muslim female. The first appellant, Saima Waheed, contracted a marriage of her own free will, despite her father's disapproval. She fled her father's house and took refuge in the institution 'Dastak', run and managed by Asma Jehangir—a lawyer and human rights activist. In the second appeal, the appellant Muhammad Iqbal married Shabina Zafar, a *sui juris* Muslim female. Shabina's father lodged an FIR under section 10(2) of the Offense of Zina (Enforcement of Hudood) Ordinance 1979 on the grounds that the appellant seduced his daughter and developed illicit relations with her. Shabina, on the other hand, maintained that she had entered into a valid marriage of her own free will.

The first appeal was a high-profile case, commonly known as the *Saima Waheed* case. Saima's father was allegedly forcing her to marry a much older man. Therefore, she eloped with the tutor of her younger brothers. The full bench of the Lahore High Court, by a ratio of two to one, held that her marriage without the consent of her *wali* was valid. Her father appealed before the Supreme Court.

The Supreme Court observed that there were several judicial authorities of the Federal Shariat Court,[30] which held that a *sui juris* Muslim girl can contract a marriage of her own accord, without the consent of her *wali* or other relations. In *Mauj Ali v Safdar Hussain Shah*,[31] the Supreme Court held that a Muslim girl, who has attained the age of puberty is competent to marry of her own free will and, therefore, her custody was declined to her father. The Supreme Court held that the judges of the Lahore High Court were bound to follow these authorities and it was improper for them to question the validity of the marriage in a writ of *habeas corpus* because only the Family Court could decide this issue:

> In the facts and circumstances of the case particularly in view of the stance of the alleged *detenue* that she was voluntarily putting up at 'Dastak', the High Court clearly transgressed its jurisdiction and by formulating the question of validity of marriage and then answering the same, assumed to itself the exclusive jurisdiction of the Family Court in such matter. The point need not be labored further and may be concluded by observing

> that it was inappropriate and undesirable, if not illegal for the High Court to have determined the fate of the couple by adjudicating the validity of marriage on the touchstone of Injunctions of Islam in proceedings under section 491, Cr.P.C.[32]

Finally, the court held that according to the judgments of the Federal Shariat Court, the consent of a *wali* is not required and a *sui juris* Muslim female can enter into a valid marriage of her own free-will. The court emphasised that these judgments of the Federal Shariat Court are binding on the High Courts and all other subordinate courts.

2.9.2.3 With Whom is Marriage Valid?

Sani Gul v Civil Judge-III, Swat 2000 CLC 1228 (Pesh)

Marriage between fostering siblings is invalid.

In this case, the marriage of the petitioner, Sani Gul was solemnised with the respondent, Mst Nazakat. *Rukhsati* was agreed to be performed upon the wife (respondent) attaining the age of majority. She was only 13 years old at the time of the marriage. However, before *rukhsati* could take place the wife filed a suit for the dissolution of her marriage on the basis that her mother had suckled the petitioner when he was an infant. Therefore, her marriage with the petitioner was prohibited on the ground of fosterage. She only came to know about this after the marriage. The trial court decreed her suit and dissolved her marriage. The petitioner challenged this decision before the High Court. The counsel for the petitioner raised the objection to the validity of the evidence of the respondent's mother. The court held:

> In Shariah the evidence of the woman, who has nurtured both the spouses is valid and enough to prove the relationship by reason of fosterage. There are many instances available where Prophet Muhammad (PBUH) accepted the evidence of [a] foster mother. It is obvious that the consequences otherwise would have been detrimental, since offsprings of such a void vow/marriage will be illegitimate.[33]

The court held that it is an undisputed fact that *nikah* between a foster brother and a sister is prohibited in Islam. In light of these findings, the court dismissed the petition.

Farzand Ali v Raja Muhammad Ibrahim PLD 1996 FSC 29

Marriage with a wife's stepmother is valid.

This case discusses the scope and effect of a marriage within the prohibited degree with respect to unlawful conjunction and affinity to the relatives of one's wife. Petitioner no. 1, Farzand Ali, married petitioner no. 2, Ferozi, his first wife's stepmother (the widow of his first wife's father) while the first marriage still existed. Raja Ibrahim filed a complaint against the petitioner under section 10(2) of the Offense of Zina (Enforcement of Hudood) Ordinance 1979. The complainant alleged that petitioner no. 1 could not marry petitioner no. 2, the stepmother of his first wife as the unlawful conjunction of a mother and her daughter at the same time in marriage is prohibited under Islamic law. This argument of the complainant was acceded to by the Sessions Court and the private complaint was processed. The petitioners brought the matter before the Federal Shariat Court for setting aside the complaint against them.

The issue before the court was whether a man can simultaneously keep a stepmother and her stepdaughter in a marital relationship. In this context, Islamic law laid down two kinds of prohibitions: one relating to affinity, and the other about unlawful conjunction. As far as the prohibition of affinity was concerned, the court held that this prohibition applied to the mother of one's wife. Since petitioner no. 2 was not the real mother of the first wife of petitioner no. 1, therefore, this prohibition had no bearing on this case.

It is important to note that the legal prohibition based on affinity to the relatives of a wife, called *hurmat e masaharat*, is of two kinds: first, marrying the daughter of one's wife (stepdaughter); and second, marrying the mother of one's wife (mother-in-law). In the first case, there is a condition that the marriage should have been consummated with the wife and if the marriage is not consummated then the marriage with the daughter of one's wife is lawful. In the second case, the mere occurrence of *nikah* with the wife renders the mother of the wife unlawful for marriage and there is no condition of the consummation of marriage with the wife.

As far as the issue of unlawful conjunction was concerned, the court observed that 'a man is prohibited to have at the same time two wives who are *inter se* sisters, aunt, and niece or are so related to each other that if either of them had been a male they cannot have lawfully intermarried'.[34]

In the instant case, if the stepdaughter had been a male, she could not have lawfully married the wife of her father because the Qur'anic verse

(4:22) does not allow a son to marry the woman who had been the wife of his father. However, if the stepmother had been a male, she would not have been prohibited from marrying her stepdaughter, as there is nothing on record to show that they are related to each other by consanguinity, affinity, or fosterage. Therefore, a majority of Muslim jurists hold the opinion that combining a daughter and her stepmother in marriage at the same time is lawful.

Considering the marriage between petitioner no. 1 and petitioner no. 2 from the perspectives of affinity and unlawful conjunction, the court concluded that their marriage was lawful and valid despite the fact that petitioner no. 1 was also in a subsisting marital relationship with petitioner no. 2's stepdaughter.

2.9.2.4 When is a Marriage Valid?

Allah Dad v Mukhtar 1992 SCMR 1273 (Shariat Appellate Bench)

A marriage contracted during *iddat* period is void.

The petitioner sought leave to appeal against the acquittal of Mukhtar (respondent no. 1) and Rashida Akhtar (respondent no. 2) by the trial and Appellate Courts. The petitioner filed a private complaint against the respondents under sections 10 and 16 of the Offense of Zina (Enforcement of Hudood) Ordinance 1979. He alleged that respondent no. 2 was his legally wedded wife, who under the influence of respondent no. 1 had left his house. The petitioner alleged that both the respondents were committing adultery. The trial and the Appellate Courts acquitted the respondents based on the evidence which suggested that the complainant had divorced respondent no. 2, after which she contracted a valid marriage with respondent no. 1. Hence, no question of *zina* arose in these circumstances.

Before the Supreme Court, the counsel for the petitioner argued that the alleged divorce deed was illegal and invalid, as notice of *talaq* had not been given to the chairman union council as required under section 7 of the MFLO. Even if it could be proved that the complainant had in fact divorced respondent no. 2, the divorce could not be held as legally effective because mandatory provisions of section 7 had not been complied with. Hence, the alleged *nikah* between the respondents without valid *talaq* was invalid. Justice Taqi Usmani found this argument misplaced and observed:

> The words 'validly married' occurring in the definition of 'Zina' in section 4 of the Ordinance [Zina Ordinance] have not been defined in the Ordinance. The definition, therefore, will be sought from the Injunctions of Islam because the Ordinance intends to bring the existing law relating to zina in conformity with them … if there is a clash between an existing law and Injunctions of Islam with regard to the validity of a marriage, the Injunctions of Islam shall prevail for the purpose of this Ordinance. Thus, if a marriage is valid in Shariah, it shall be held valid for the purpose of this Ordinance even though it is not recognised as valid in any other law for the time being in force.[35]

The counsel for the petitioner contended that even if the complainant validly divorced respondent no. 2, the *nikah* between the respondents could still not be valid before the expiry of 90 days from the date of *talaq*. Justice Usmani observed that a marriage performed during *iddat* period is not merely irregular; it is void (*batil*).[36] He noted that the period of *iddat* as laid down in the Qur'an is three menstrual cycles, which does not necessarily extend to 90 days, and it could be a minimum of 39 days. The *nikah* between the respondents was performed after 79 days of *talaq*. Therefore, the said period was sufficient for the completion of the *iddat* period as prescribed in the Qur'an. In light of the foregoing reasons, the court dismissed the petition.[37]

Muhammad Aslam v Ghulam Muhammad Tasleem PLD 1971 Lah 139

Second marriage in contravention of the MFLO is valid.

In this case, the petitioner filed an application under section 491 of the Code of Criminal Procedure 1898 to recover the detenue from the custody of her father. The petitioner who was not related to the alleged detenue, claimed to be a family friend. He alleged that he happened to visit the house of the respondent accompanied by his wife and daughters and was surprised to learn that the respondent was detaining his daughter in a locked room. This was in view of the fact that she did not agree to marry a person of the respondent's choice, who happened to be a man much older than the detenue.

During the proceedings of the case it was revealed that the detenue wanted to marry another man who was already married. The father of the detenue raised two objections against her marriage to the person of her choice. First, she was less than 18 years old; and second, the person she wanted to marry was already married and polygamy was prohibited under the MFLO, except with the prior written permission of the arbitration council. The court dismissed both these objections. First, it held that every Muslim of sound mind who has attained the age of majority can enter into a marriage contract. Second, it held that according to the principle laid down in *Syed Ali Nawaz Gardezi v Lt. Col. Muhammad Yusuf*,[38] the second marriage contracted during the subsistence of the first marriage without the permission of arbitration council in contravention of section 6 of the MFLO attracts penal action, but it is not invalid in itself.[39]

2.9.2.5 Inter-marriages between Muslim Sects

Aziz Bano v Muhammad Ibrahim Husain 89 Ind Cas 690

Marriage between a Shia woman and a Sunni man is not void. A Shia girl has a right to repudiate her marriage with a Sunni man upon attaining the age of puberty.

In this case, the court discussed two important legal questions: (1) whether, under Shia law, a marriage performed between a Shia woman and a Sunni man is void; and (2) whether a minor has a right to repudiate her marriage upon attaining puberty when the marriage was contracted with her guardian's consent?

Brief facts of the case are such that Muhammad Ibrahim, a Sunni Muslim, filed a suit for restitution of conjugal rights against, *inter alia*, defendant no. 1, Aziz Bano who is a Shia Muslim. The plaintiff claimed that he was married to defendant no. 1 on 25 September 1918 with the consent of her father acting as her guardian. The marriage was performed in exchange for a deferred dower amounting to Rs 500 plus 2 dinars. However, after the marriage, the defendant's father and other concerned relatives refused to send her to the plaintiff.

In these circumstances, the plaintiff filed a suit for restitution of conjugal rights, which was decreed by the trial court. In doing so, the trial court dismissed defendant no. 1's contention that the marriage was *void ab initio* because (i) her father, the guardian, never consented to it; (ii) under Shia law, no marriage can be valid between a Sunni and a Shia; and (iii) she had repudiated the marriage upon attaining the age of puberty. The trial court held that the parties were duly married under the supervision of the woman's father acting as her guardian and she could not repudiate such marriage on her own; moreover, the marriage suffered no illegality because of the difference in parties' religion and, therefore, was valid in the eyes of law. Aggrieved by this decision, the defendants approached the lower Appellate Court which dismissed the appeal. Ultimately, the defendants challenged the decrees before the Allahabad High Court.

While determining the question as to which law should govern the dispute, the High Court observed that 'it is a well-settled rule that the law to be observed in the trial of suits shall … in the absence of any specific law and usage, be justice, equity and good conscience'.[40] The court further noted that in the present case:

> The plaintiff desires to force an alleged marriage on the contesting defendant. The defendant is, therefore, entitled to say that, under the law by which she herself is governed, such a marriage was void or voidable. It would be grossly unjust to decree the claim on the strength of the personal law governing the plaintiff.[41]

Therefore, there can be no doubt that 'justice, equity and good conscience require that the question of the validity of the alleged marriage must be determined according to the personal law of the defendant, that is, the Shia Law'.[42]

The court subsequently considered the issue of the validity of inter-sect marriages in Shia law. After perusing a number of authoritative textbooks such as Baillie's *Digest of Muhammad Law*, Ameer Ali's *Muhammadan Law*, and Tyabji's *Principles of Muhammadan Law* and some legal precedents, the court noted that the prevalent legal position in India was that such marriages were not absolutely illegal. It was noted that under Shia law, one of the most significant conditions for the validity of the marriage was equality as to religion; the term equality meant that the parties should be Muslims in the general sense of the word. Therefore, the court noted that the difference in sectarian affiliation of the parties had no bearing on the validity of a marriage contract. Putting the burden of proof on the appellants, the court observed that the appellants were to persuade the court against all these authorities.

In this regard, the counsel for appellants asserted that the legal position proclaiming the validity of the marriage between a Shia and a Sunni was based solely on one classical text, *Sharaya-ul-Islam*, whose credibility was disputed among classical jurists. He maintained that there were other, more credible legal authorities such as *Shara Luma* and *Jawahir-ul-Kalam*, which expounded the opposite opinion that such a marriage is absolutely illegal. Relying on these authorities, he asserted that according to the true interpretation of Shia law, the marriage of a Shia girl with a

Sunni husband is absolutely void, although the marriage of a Shia man with a Sunni girl will not be so.

He further maintained that these authorities proclaimed that the condition of equality between spouses entailed not only equality as to Islam but also equality as to their *iman*; whereby the term *iman* referred to the sectarian affiliation of the parties. Thus, in order for a marriage to be valid, the sectarian affiliation of the parties, i.e. their *iman*, needed to be equal. If the parties belonged to different sects, the marriage would automatically be void under Shia law. The court dismissed this contention, holding thereby that in the times of the Prophet (PBUH) the Muslim community was not divided into sects and, therefore, the term *iman* was not considered to mean any particular sect. The special meaning of *iman* as referring to only Shia Muslims was of later origin and could not be read into the traditions of the Prophet (PBUH) which prescribed the condition of equality for the validity of marriage. Addressing the counsel's contention as to the credibility of the *Sharaya-ul-Islam*, the court observed:

> Sharaya-ul Islam is undoubtedly the most universally known authority on Shiah Law so far at least as India is concerned. The view of Al. Muhakkiq, its author, is undoubtedly that such a marriage is not illegal … [Considering the prevalent practice if inter-sect marriages in India], it is … a fair inference to draw that the view of the author of Sharaya-ul-Islam has been accepted so far as India is concerned and that the contrary view that such a marriage is illegal has not been accepted here … His is a liberal view which considers that persons belonging to sects other than Shiahs are within the pale of Islam and there is equality between them so far as marriage is concerned.[43]

Subsequently, the court considered the credibility of competing legal authorities as provided by the counsel for appellants. It was observed that even though these authorities did not declare an inter-sect marriage absolutely illegal; it was at most regarded as *makruh* (disapproved). The court further noted that even apart from these considerations, it was a well-established principle that in cases of divergent opinions, the court would choose the view which was 'most conformable to equity and the requirements of the times'.[44] Considering that accepting the view that inter-sect marriages are void 'would render illegitimate not only the children of a Shia wife, married to a Sunni husband but also of all Imamia women married to *ghair* Imamia Shias', the court held that 'in this case, there can be no doubt that the view that the marriage is not illegal is "most conformable to equity and the requirements of the times".'[45]

As regards the issue of repudiation, the court relied upon the opinions of Ameer Ali and Tyabji to hold that 'in certain special cases there is an option left to the minor boy or girl even though the marriage has been performed by the father or grandfather'.[46] According to these texts, a Shia girl can repudiate her marriage upon attaining the age of puberty provided that the marriage was to her 'manifest disadvantage'.[47] It was noted that an inter-sect marriage, though not void, had been considered *makruh* (disapproved) by almost all leading authorities on Shia law. Therefore, it would be against justice, equity, and good conscience to force a woman into sustaining a marriage which might be hateful to her religious sentiments. The court noted:

> It seems to me that if a minor Shiah girl has been given away in marriage by her father while of nonage, when it was impossible for her to have any voice in the matter, and on attaining puberty she considers the marriage to be repugnant to her religious sentiments and grossly disadvantageous to herself, it would be contrary to all rules of equity or justice to force such marriage on her and thereby compel her to live with a person who is abhorrent to her. When her religion says that such a marriage is abhorrent she must be allowed the option to repudiate it if any option can ever exist.[48]

However, the court also mentioned a caveat; it was observed that had the marriage been consummated, the marriage would have become irrevocable, and the woman would have lost her right to repudiate the union. The fact that she repudiated the marriage before consummation enabled her to avoid the marriage.

In light of these reasons, the court held the following and dismissed the appeal accordingly:

> [Although], the marriage of a Shiah woman with a Sunni husband, if entered into when the parties are of age or if performed by her guardian and ratified by her on attaining puberty, is valid and legal and her offspring are legitimate … [However], such a marriage, if performed by her guardian, no matter whether he is the father or the grandfather, is capable of being repudiated by her attaining puberty because it may affect her religious sentiment and may therefore be said to be to her manifest disadvantage. This is a liberal view to take and is obviously in accordance with justice, equity and good conscience as well as the requirements of the times.[49]

2.9.3 Proof of Marriage. A simple statement of spouses is sufficient evidence to prove the validity of a marriage. In this regard, the courts have frequently held that the testimony of witnesses and/or the registration of the *nikahnama* as required under the MFLO are generally not essential to the validity of a marriage contract. In certain cases, where the validity of a marriage was disputed, the courts have invoked the presumption of continuous and prolonged cohabitation as a ground for determining the validity of the marriage contract. This presumption, however, was not extended to the cases of women who were known to be prostitutes. In *Abdul Majid Khan v Anwar Begum*,[50] the Supreme Court of Pakistan referred to the constitutional rights of citizens to marriage and family to apply this presumption in cases of prostitutes.

Azra Bibi v S.H.O, Police Station, Thingi, District Vehari 2005 YLR 1859 (Lah)

A simple statement of spouses is sufficient to prove the validity of a marriage.

Through a writ petition, the petitioner, Azra Bibi, sought quashing of an FIR that was registered under section 16 of the Offense of Zina (Enforcement of Hudood) Ordinance 1979 by her brother, Muhammad Azeem. Azra's brother accused her of having illicit relations with the accused, Muhammad Akram. The brother claimed that she was already married and produced a *nikahnama* to this effect. He further alleged that the accused demanded the hand of Azra Bibi and upon being refused he, along with others, abducted her.

The counsel for Azra Bibi argued that she was not already married and that she contracted marriage with Muhammad Akram with her own consent. Therefore, she did not commit any offence. Azra Bibi's alleged previous *nikahnama* with Ghulam Fareed had various discrepancies and was therefore declared forged. The court relied upon the established principle that if the spouses claim themselves to be the husband and wife, other formalities can be ignored, and their statement is sufficient to prove the validity of their marriage. The court, therefore, accepted the writ petition and quashed the FIR.

Humaira Mehmood v The State PLD 1999 Lah 494

A presumption of truth is attached to a *nikahnama* acknowledged by the spouses.

The petitioner, Humaira, contracted marriage with Mehmood with her own free will, but against her father's wishes. The respondent, Moazzam

Ghayas Khokar registered an FIR under section 16 of the Offense of Zina (Enforcement of Hudood) Ordinance 1979, alleging that the petitioner was his wife and Mehmood along with others abducted her. Humaira denied these allegations and maintained that she had validly married Mehmood with her own consent. Furthermore, she maintained that the alleged *nikahnama* was forged and deliberately ante-dated to her genuine *nikah* with Mehmood. The petitioner claimed that her thumb impressions on the alleged *nikahnama* were obtained through force and without her consent. The court observed:

> It is a settled proposition of law that in Islam a *sui juris* woman can contract Nikah of her own free will and a Nikah performed under coercion is no Nikah in law. Instances are not lacking from Hadith and the Islamic history that the consent of *sui juris* woman was held to be *sine qua non* for a valid marriage in absence of which marriage was declared void … the term 'consent' means a conscious expression of one's desire without any external intimidation or coercion … in situations where consent to a marriage is in dispute and a challenge is thrown to a Nikahanama which is being owned by a man and a woman who claim to be a husband and a wife then a presumption of truth attaches to the Nikahnama which is being acknowledged by both the spouses and not the intervener.[51]

The court observed that a presumption of truth was attached to the *nikah* between the petitioner and Mehmood as it had been acknowledged by both spouses. Consequently, the court quashed the FIR.

Farzana Siddique v The State through Advocate General Azad Jammu and Kashmir 2014 CrLJ 897

The statement of a woman plays a vital role in deciding the validity of her marriage.

In this case, the petitioner, Farzana Siddique, sought quashing of an FIR registered against her husband, herself, and others under the Offense of Zina (Enforcement of Hudood) Ordinance 1979. The petitioner contended that contrary to the abduction charges in the FIR, she wilfully contracted marriage with Muhammad Mushtaq Awan. The main element of the case was to prove the validity of the *nikah* between the petitioner and Muhammad Mushtaq Awan. The court observed:

> Where there are two claimants of Nikah of a woman the statement of that woman was of vital importance to decide the controversy between the

> parties. Moreover, according to the injunctions of Islam, the consent of [an] adult, sane couple, was sufficient for "Nikah".[52]

The court concluded that the petitioner was validly married because she recorded her statement before the civil judge/judicial magistrate that she was not abducted by anyone and wilfully solemnised *nikah* with Muhammad Mushtaq Awan. Therefore, no offence was committed by them.

Rasool Bibi v Waryam 1992 SCMR 1520

Testimony of all witnesses to a *Nikahnama* is not required to prove its validity.

This case demonstrates how a *nikah* can be proved in a court of law. The appellant, Rasool Bibi claimed to be Barkat's widow who died in 1972. She claimed her entitlement in the estate of her late husband. She filed a suit for declaration in this regard. Both the lower courts dismissed her suit. The High Court also dismissed her civil revision petition. Therefore, she approached the Supreme Court. The court had to answer the key question: whether or not the appellant was the deceased's widow. The appellant produced her *nikahnama* to show that she was the legally wedded wife of Barkat. The Supreme Court observed that the courts below wrongly assumed that all the persons mentioned in the *nikahnama* were to be examined in the court as if the formality of the *nikah* had to be repeated:

> This is now well-settled that for establishing the Nikah, the Registrar or for that matter all the witnesses need not appear. One or more of them and/or other witnesses can prove the Nikah.[53]

The Supreme Court declared that the appellant was the legally wedded wife of Barkat and was entitled to one-fourth of the share of the property left by her husband.

2.9.3.1 Registration of Marriage

Mirza Allah Ditta alias Mirza Javed Akhtar v Amina Bibi 2004 YLR 239 (Lah)

Registration of a *nikah* is not mandatory for its validity.

This case discusses the standard of proof for a marriage (*nikah*). Wali Muhammad was the owner of a house and a shop. The claim of the respondent, Amina Bibi, the wife of Wali Muhammad, was that her husband gave her the house and shop at the time of marriage in lieu of a dower. The contention of the petitioner, Allah Ditta was that he had purchased the shop and house from Wali Muhammad through a sale deed. The petitioner filed a suit for possession of the property. The respondent contended that the sale deed was fraudulent and hence it was ineffective upon her rights with respect to the property. She also sought a permanent injunction restraining the petitioner from interfering with her possession of the suit property. Both the suits were consolidated and decreed in favour of the petitioner.

On appeal before the High Court, the counsel for the petitioner argued that the respondent's *nikah* with Wali Muhammad was not registered in accordance with section 5 of the MFLO. The counsel for the respondent contended that *nikah* could not be rendered void simply on this ground. The court observed that the first and foremost issue that needed to be resolved between the parties related to the effect of non-registration of marriage. Amina Bibi and Wali Muhammad stated on oath that their *nikah* was performed on 4 July 1976. They also produced witnesses to support their versions. The court held that the registration of *nikah* was in accordance with section 5 of the MFLO, and even otherwise such registration was not mandatory for the validity of the marriage. The court observed that although the presence of two witnesses is mandatory for the validity of the *nikah*; a presumption of truth is attached to the *nikah*, which is acknowledged by the spouses and there is no need to produce two witnesses.

2.9.3.2 Presumption of Marriage Based on a Continued and Prolonged Cohabitation

Loung v Allah Ditto 2002 CLC 1307 (Kar)

The presumption of a marriage can be raised where there is a prolonged and continuous cohabitation as husband and wife.

In this case, the plaintiffs filed a suit for declaration and permanent injunction against the defendants relating to the estate of Ditto, who died leaving several children from two wives. The defendants contended that plaintiff no. 2 was not a legally wedded wife of the deceased as there was no valid proof of her marriage and, therefore, the plaintiffs were not his legitimate heirs. The trial court dismissed the petition, and the Appellate

Court upheld that decision. Therefore, the plaintiff brought the case before the High Court.

While appraising the evidence, the High Court pointed out towards certain common practices in the rural areas of Sindh relating to marriage. Oftentimes, the parents take consideration for the marriage of their daughters in cash or in kind, or the hand of another female is taken in exchange. It was argued on behalf of plaintiff no. 2 that she was married to Ditto in exchange for his daughter being married to her brother. The defendants, however, argued that the brother of plaintiff no. 2 in fact abducted Ditto's daughter. However, they did not provide any evidence to prove such abduction. Plaintiff no. 2 had lived with her husband as his wife and had given birth to two children. In the circumstances of the case, the court held that in the absence of any contradictory evidence, the presumption of a valid marriage arises where there is a prolonged and continuous cohabitation as husband and wife. Therefore, the court allowed the petition.

Abdul Majid Khan v Anwar Begum PLD 1989 SC 362

The presumption of a valid marriage as a result of a prolonged and continuous cohabitation as husband and wife arises even in cases of prostitutes.

In this case, the son and first wife of Amir Abdullah Khan challenged the validity of a gift by him to his second wife. The lower courts dismissed their petition by holding that the respondent was a duly wedded wife of Amir Abdullah Khan, who validly made a gift in her favour. The petitioner contended that the respondent was a dancing girl whose marriage with Amir Abdullah Khan was not established and thus, a gift could not be given to a concubine or a prostitute.

Justice Afzal Zullah rejected these arguments and laid down the principle that a presumption of a valid marriage is based on a prolonged and continuous cohabitation as husband and wife and as such, is admissible even in cases of prostitutes. In doing so, Justice Zullah overruled the prior case law which did not allow for this presumption in cases of prostitutes. He observed that all prostitutes do not adopt or continue to practice this profession of their own volition; rather, a large number of them are compelled to do so on account of social conditions, mishaps in their childhood due to broken families, and cruelty of criminals. Therefore, the court held that it would be unjust to assume that a prostitute could not abandon her profession and live a respectable married life. The court endorsed this view by referring to Articles 35, 25, and 14 of the Constitution of Pakistan 1973. Article 35 provides protection to the marriage and family; Article 25 ensures the fundamental right of equality of citizens and prohibits discrimination based on sex, and Article 14 guarantees the dignity of man.

2.9.3.3 Marriage of Transgender Persons

Ghulam Mustafa v Judge Family Court 2021 CLC 204

The right of privacy is protected under Islamic law, human rights law, and constitutional law. The Family Court can only order for the medical examination of the person for the determination of their sex if it is absolutely necessary. The Transgender Persons (Protection of Rights) Act 2018 recognises the right to self-perceived gender identity.

In this judgment, the Lahore High Court deals with two important questions. First, whether the Family Court has the authority to ask a person to take a medical examination for the determination of their sex, and second, whether a transgender person can enter into a valid marriage contract under Islamic law.

According to the facts of the case, the wife initiated a case against her husband arguing that he had expelled her from his house and sought recovery of dower, maintenance allowance, and dowry articles. The husband alleged that his wife was 'defective' and lacked 'feminine characteristics' and was not fit for marriage. The counsel of the husband contended that the wife and her family had defrauded him, and she was not entitled to maintenance rights. The Family Court dismissed the application of the husband for the medical examination of the wife on the ground that the wife had a right to privacy under articles 9 and 14 (1) of the Constitution.

The husband challenged the judgment of the Family Court before the Lahore High Court. The Court framed two issues: (i) whether the wife had a fundamental right to privacy; and (ii) whether the Family Court is authorised to direct a party to undergo a medical examination.

After consulting various sources on privacy, Justice Tariq Saleem Sheikh held that privacy is a fundamental right. It is supported by the Qur'an and Hadith, and international human rights law recognises privacy as a fundamental right. While defining the scope of privacy, Justice Sheikh observed that the right to privacy includes sexual identity and gender information. Islam prohibits prying into the lives of others and preserves the sanctity of home in verses 27–28 of Surah al-Noor. In addition, there are several Hadiths that support this view. The right to privacy can only be infringed by the public authority in case of national security and that too in limited circumstances. The right to privacy is a fundamental right; however, it is not an absolute right. Therefore, the court can order the medical examination for the determination of sex in specific circumstances where it is absolutely necessary and there is sufficient evidence available to the court to make such an order. If the concerned person refuses to undergo a medical examination, they cannot be compelled but the court may draw 'appropriate inference' from such refusal from the facts and circumstances of the case.

On the issue of the marriage of transgenders, Justice Sheikh elaborated that Islamic law recognises four types of gender: male, female, *khunsa* (intersex or hermaphrodite) and *mukhannath* (effeminate male). The category of *khunsa* is further divided into *wadhih* (discernible) who can be identified as male or female based on dominant attributes and *mushkil* (problematic/intractable) who cannot be identified as either male or female. Justice Sheikh then referred to the Transgender Persons (Protection of Rights) Act 2018 which recognises an individual's right to self-perceived gender identity. Justice Sheikh observed that according to some scholars, *khunsa wadhih* can contract marriage with the opposite sex whereas *khunsa mushkil* is prohibited from marriage.

In the instant case, the marriage between the parties had lasted for more than eight months and the husband did not divorce the wife despite claiming that she lacked 'feminine characteristics'. Justice Sheikh held that the Family Court should ask the husband to produce evidence about the gender of his wife. The court will allow the medical examination only if there is material evidence to prove the husband's assertion and the facts of the case require that a medical examination is absolutely necessary.

2.10 Conclusion

Marriage under Islamic law is a contract. The parties are autonomous to agree upon the terms and conditions of the contract and the courts tend to uphold such terms as long as they are not against the law and public policy. It must be noted that although marriage under Islamic law is a contract, the parties cannot claim damages and remedies for its breach under the Contract Act 1872. In this respect, a marriage contract is distinguished from an ordinary contract and is regulated under the principles of Islamic law.

Being similar to a civil contract, a valid marriage must fulfil all the legal requirements of a contract. In this regard, the free and voluntary consent of the parties is an essential requirement. A marriage contract concluded with force, threat, or undue influence is invalid. The consent of parties, even without the approval of a guardian/*wali*, is adequate for the validity of a marriage contract. However, the consent of guardians is required for the marriages of minors.

A marriage contract does not need to be formally written and/or registered. In several cases, the courts have held informal and verbal marriages to be valid. In this regard, the statements of the spouses have a decisive role to play. The courts have established that a third person cannot challenge the validity of a *nikahnama* if the spouses claim it to be valid. The courts have upheld marriages where a man and woman lived together as husband and wife for a prolonged and continuous period without there being any formal proof of *nikah*. There was an exception to this rule in cases of women of ill repute or prostitutes. However, the Supreme Court overruled this exception in light of the principles of Islamic law and human rights.

Section 5 of the MFLO requires the registration of marriages, and its rationale is to reduce litigation relating to the proof of marriage and transfer of personal property through gifts, wills, and inheritance. The records of the registered marriages are kept at the union council. Failure to comply with the requirement of this section leads to the imposition of a penalty but does not render unregistered marriages invalid.

Questions

1. What is the nature of a marriage contract under Islamic law? How is it different from other types of contracts?
2. Are pre-nuptial agreements valid under Islamic law? If yes, to what extent?
3. Can a minor female, who has not attained the age of puberty, enter into a valid marriage contract without the consent of her parents?
4. How is a marriage contract proved in a court?
5. Why is a continued and prolonged cohabitation as husband and wife presumed to be a valid marriage? What is the legal or moral justification for this presumption?

Further Reading

Books/Articles

Ali, Kecia, 'Marriage in Classical Islamic Jurisprudence: A Survey of Doctrines', in Asifa Quraishi and Frank Vogel, *The Islamic Marriage Contract* (Cambridge: Harvard University Press, 2008), 11–45.

Fyzee, A.A.A., *Outlines of Muhammadan Law*, 5th edn (New Delhi: Oxford University Press, 2008), 69–104.

Mansoori, M.T., *Family Law in Islam* (Islamabad: Shari'ah Academy, 2012), 1–70, 83–95.

Meron, Y., 'The Moslem Marriage between Status and Contract', *Studia Islamica* (2001) 92, 197.

Cases

Aftab Ahmad v Judge Family Court 2009 MLD 962 (Lah) (Non-registration of marriage does not invalidate it.)

Bakht-e-Rawida v Ghulam Habib PLD 1992 Kar 46 (Family Courts have acted illegally and not in accordance with the law when the basic document of marriage, the nikahnama, is ignored or when they have not given full effect to the terms contained therein.)

Dr A.L.M. Abdullah v Rokeya Khatoon PLD 1969 Dacca 47 (The solemnisation of marriage, if validly effected, might not be affected by non-registration under the MFLO. But the non-registration of the marriage causes a doubt on the solemnisation of the marriage itself.)

Farooq Omar Bhoja v Federation of Pakistan PLD 2022 FSC 1 (Sections 4, 5, and 6 of the Child Marriage Restraint Act 1929 are not against the injunctions of Islam.)

Gul Khatoon v Haji Muhammad Aslam 2015 PCrLJ 193 (Quetta) (Wali's lack of consent does not invalidate a marriage contracted by a sui juris Muslim female.)

Hajra Khatoon v SHO, Police Station Fateh Jang, Attock PLD 2005 Lah 316 (Marriage contracted by a woman not having attained the age of majority as defined in law, but having attained puberty as defined in the Offence of Zina (Enforcement of Hudood) Ordinance 1979, is valid and not void.)

Iqra Javed alias Saba v Station House Officer PLD 2013 Lah 538 (The validity of a nikahnama cannot be challenged if the spouses admit it as valid.)

Jan Muhammad v Salamat Bibi 2002 SCMR 1408 (Testimony of witnesses is not required to prove the validity of a nikahnama.)

Muhammad Akram v Farman Bi PLD 1989 Lah 200 (Where the factum of marriage is in serious doubt, non-registration of marriage might cause some doubt on its existence and solemnisation.)

Shaukat Hussain v Civil Judge, Multan 2006 YLR 349 (Lah) (Registration of a nikah is not mandatory for its validity.)

Notes

1. 'And how could ye take it when ye have gone in unto each other, and they have Taken from you a solemn covenant?'
2. The Child Marriages Restraint Act 1929 puts restrictions on the marriage of a male if he is less than 18 years of age and female if she is less than 16 years of age. The minimum age of marriage for both males and females is 18 years under the Sindh Child Marriages Restraint Act 2013.
3. According to s 2 (iv) of the Dissolution of Muslim Marriages Act 1939, option of puberty can be exercised by a minor female who has been given in the marriage by her father or other guardian before she attained the age of sixteen years, the minor can repudiate the marriage upon attaining the age of eighteen years, provided the marriage has not been consummated. For males, the right to exercise option of puberty continues until the marriage is ratified either expressly or by implication, for instance by payment of dower or cohabitation.
4. For the validity of a *muta* marriage, the period of cohabitation should be fixed and the dower should be specified. The children from such marriage are legitimate and can inherit from both parents, though the mutual right of inheritance between spouses does not arise. For details see D.F. Mulla, *Principles of Mahomedan Law*, 20th edn (Haryana: LexisNexis, 2013), 344–46.
5. Mulla, *Principles of Mahomedan Law*, 339. See also: S.S. Shah, 'Fosterage as a Ground of Marital Prohibition in Islam and the Status of Human Milk Banks', *Arab Law Quarterly* (1994) 9 (1), 3, 7. Shah argues that fosterage prohibition should also apply in cases of human milk banks.
6. The Special Marriage Act of 1872 regulates the marriages between persons who do not profess the following religions Christianity, Judaism, Hinduism, Zoroastrianism, Buddhism, Sikhism, or Jainism. Persons who profess Hinduism, Buddhism, Sikhism, or Jainism religion may also register their marriages under this Act. Christians, Jews, and Muslims cannot register their marriages under this Act. The marriages under this Act are monogamous and the divorce is regulated under the Divorce Act 1869. In India, the Special Marriage Act 1954 governs secular marriages. The Indian Succession Act 1925 applies to the estates of the parties married under this Act.
7. '*Iddat*' translated as 'prescribed waiting period' is the practice whereby a woman, whose marriage is dissolved by divorce or death, remains in seclusion and does not marry for a specific period of time. (i) When the marriage is dissolved by divorce, the *iddat* period is three courses of menstruation. If she does not menstruate, the period is three lunar months; and if she is pregnant, the *iddat* period ends upon delivery. (ii) When the marriage is dissolved by death, the *iddat* period is four months and ten days. If the woman is pregnant at the time of the death of her husband, the *iddat* period is four months and ten days or until the delivery, whichever period is longer. For details, see M.T. Mansoori, *Family Law in Islam* (Islamabad: Shari'a Academy, 2012), 181–7.
8. Kecia Ali, 'Marriage in Classical Islamic Jurisprudence: A Survey of Doctrines', in Asifa Quraishi and Frank Vogel, *The Islamic Marriage Contract* (Cambridge: Harvard University Press, 2008), 11–45.
9. For details on the Islamic legal principle of acknowledgement, see Chapter 6.
10. (1886) ILR 8 All 149.
11. PLJ 2006 Lah 1215.
12. One of the obligations arising out of the marriage contract is that spouses are entitled to the company of each other. Therefore, spouses can sue each other for the restitution of conjugal rights when one of them refuses to live with the other without any lawful excuse. Normally, husbands exercise this right against their wives because if a wife exercises this right, the husband is likely to divorce her. This right, however, is not absolute. The courts take into account the circumstances of each case.
13. (1886) ILR 8 All 149, 157.
14. The right to lien is provided under s 95 of the Contract Act 1872.
15. 2004 YLR 482, 485.
16. This section was repealed in 1981 under Zia ul-Haq's programme of the Islamisation of laws in Pakistan. S 2 and second schedule, Federal Laws (Revision and Declaration) Ordinance 1981 (XXVII of 1981).
17. ILR 37 Bom 280.
18. (1921) 60 IC 88 (Lah).

19. AIR 1928 Oudh 303.
20. Ibid., 304.
21. PLD 1967 Lah 1104, 1109.
22. 1991 SCMR 2454.
23. PLD 2004 SC 219.
24. 1991 SCMR 2454, 2456.
25. Ibid.
26. PLD 2009 Lah 223, 227.
27. PLD 1970 SC 323.
28. It must be noted that in *Mst. Bakhshi v Bashir Ahmad* PLD 1970 SC 323, the Supreme Court did not analyse the issue in detail. Rather, Justice M.R. Khan briefly held that the Child Marriage Restraint Act 1929 'does not permit the marriage of a girl below the age of 16 years, but if a girl below the age of 16 years marries in violation of that law, the marriage itself does not become invalid on that score, although an adult husband contracting the marriage or the persons who have solemnized the marriage may be held criminally liable.'
29. PLD 2022 FSC 1.
30. *Muhammad Imtiaz v The State* PLD 1981 FSC 308; and *Muhammad Yaqoob v The State* 1985 PCrLJ 1064.
31. 1970 SCMR 437.
32. PLD 2004 SC 219, 235.
33. 2000 CLC 1228, 1230.
34. PLD 1996 FSC 29, 32.
35. 1992 SCMR 1273, 1280.
36. Dr Tanzil-ur-Rahman supports this view. He, however, provides an exception where such a marriage is conducted unknowingly, then it will be regarded as irregular. Dr Tanzil-ur-Rahman, *A Code of Muslim Personal Law,* 1 of 2 vols (Karachi: Hamdard Academy, 1978), 153–57. According to Mulla and Fyzee, a marriage conducted during the *iddat* period is irregular. Mulla, *Principles of Mahomedan Law*, 334; A.A.A. Fyzee, *Outlines of Muhammadan Law*, 5th edn (New Delhi: Oxford University Press, 2008), 82.
37. For a contrary view, see *Muhammad Sher v ASJ District Khushab* 2016 CLC 717 (Lah). In this case, the court relied upon Mulla and observed that the marriage conducted during the *iddat* period is irregular and not void. Interestingly, in this case, Justice Hafiz Shahid Nadeem Kahloon relied on the judgment in the *Allah Dad* case regarding the minimum number of days. He, however, did not note that in this judgment the SC regarded a marriage during the *iddat* period as void rather than irregular.
38. PLD 1963 SC 51.
39. In a few reported cases, the courts punished the husbands who entered into a second marriage in contravention of the provisions of the MFLO. See *Raja Muhammad Azram v Mst Jamila Banaras* 2011 YLR 1595; *Salma v Zamir Ahmad Hussain* 2004 PCrLJ 278.
40. 89 Ind Cas 690, [5].
41. Ibid.
42. Ibid.
43. Ibid., 46.
44. Ibid., 51.
45. Ibid., 52.
46. Ibid., 57.
47. Ibid., 79.
48. Ibid., 58.
49. Ibid., 59. To avoid repetition, we have summarised the judgement of one judge only. Another judge wrote a concurring judgment in this case.
50. PLD 1989 SC 362.
51. PLD 1999 Lah 494, 501.
52. 2014 PCrLJ 897, 899.
53. 1992 SCMR 1520, 1523.

3

DOWER AND DOWRY

3.1 Dower

3.1.1 Introduction. Dower (*mahr*) is a gift that a husband gives to his wife at the time of marriage. It is a token of respect for the wife that a husband is obliged to pay her and is not a 'consideration' of the marriage contract. Unlike consideration under English contract law, the dower is not an element of a valid marriage contract under Islamic law; rather, it is an effect of a valid marriage. The payment of the dower is a default rule, and the parties cannot enter into the contract without it, though a wife may waive it. Dower is a right of the wife and hence, should be paid to her, rather than to her father or any other family member. A wife can insist on the payment of her dower and refuse restitution of conjugal rights for non-payment of the dower.

The obligation of the payment of the dower does not necessarily arise at the time of entering the marriage contract. The whole dower becomes payable upon one of the following three incidents: after valid retirement (*khalwa sahiha*),[1] the consummation of marriage, and death of either spouse even when valid retirement or consummation did not take place. Only half of the specified dower is payable if the marriage is dissolved before valid retirement or consummation. If the dower was not specified and the marriage is dissolved, the wife will get a parting or consolatory gift. The wife will get no dower if she is solely responsible for the dissolution of the marriage. For instance, if she exercises her option of puberty (*khiyar al-bulugh*)[2] or right to no-fault divorce (*khula*).

3.1.2 Classification of Dower. The amount of dower can either be specified at the time of marriage or left unspecified. Where the amount of dower is fixed by the parties, it is called a specified dower (*mahr musammat*). In cases where the dower amount is not specified, the wife is entitled to receive the proper dower (*mahr mithal*). The specified dower is divided into several sub-categories: (i) prompt dower (*mu'ajjal*) payable at the time of marriage, and (ii) deferred dower (*mu'wajjal*) payable after a specified time or upon the dissolution of marriage by divorce or death.

The payment of dower can also be partially prompt and partially deferred. When the mode of payment of the dower is not specified, the default rule is that the whole of it is deemed to be prompt. This rule is incorporated in section 10 of the MFLO which provides that when no details about the mode of payment of dower are specified in the *nikahnama*, the entire amount of dower is presumed to be payable on demand. Section 6(5)(a) of the MFLO provides that if a man contracts another marriage without the permission of the arbitration council, he shall immediately pay the entire amount of dower, whether prompt or deferred to the existing wife or wives.

If a time period is fixed for the payment of a deferred dower, e.g. one year, then it is payable at that time. However, if no time period is fixed for the payment of the deferred dower, can a wife demand it anytime? Classical jurists have differed on this point and some of them have held that in such a case, the deferred dower is payable upon the dissolution of marriage by divorce or death of one of the spouses. This strict rule has progressively become the default rule in South Asia though it is not based on sound legal argument and has thus been challenged by many scholars. In fact, it has led to the development of a third category of dower, i.e. the dower 'payable on demand' ('*inda al-talab*) of a wife.[3] It is also called *mu'akhar* or *ghair mu'ajjal*. It appears to be a sub-category of deferred dower and is commonly used in Pakistan.

This classification shows the changing practices in the payment of dower in society. Lawmakers are well aware of these developments. Therefore, the standard *nikahnama*, provided by the Rules under the MFLO, was amended and the term '*mu'wajjal*' was replaced by the term '*ghair mu'ajjal*'. This means that if the dower is deferred and no time period is specified, it will be payable upon demand of the wife.[4]

3.1.3 Quantum of Dower. Sunni and Shia jurists agree that there is no higher limit to a dower, but they disagree as to the minimum amount permissible as a valid dower. According to the Hanafi school, the minimum amount of dower is ten dirhams or its equivalent (which is only a few rupees). There is no higher limit for dower. It is not necessary for a dower to have a monetary value. The Prophet (PBUH) allowed a man to marry a woman on the condition that he would teach her the Qur'an. The dower is to be specified at the time of marriage; however, if it is not specified, it has to be fixed by considering the social status of the wife's family and her personal qualities such as age, beauty, education, and virtuousness. A court may determine the amount of unspecified dower (*mahr al-mithal*, literally 'dower of the like' and also known as proper dower) after taking into account the dower of other women belonging to the wife's family such as her sisters and paternal aunts.

The amount of dower may differ based on the social and financial status of families, and customary practices. In some parts of Pakistan, there is a custom of the payment of '*Shara'i mahr*' which is Rs 32.50.[5] The minimum dower was supposed to be the dower of the Prophet's (PBUH) daughter Fatima (RA). A husband may increase the amount of dower subsequent to the marriage and a wife may remit the dower with her free consent. However, a wife's remission of dower to gain the favour of her husband or due to mental stress is not deemed as remission with free consent.[6]

3.1.4 Functions of Dower. The outstanding amount of dower functions as a check on a husband's impulsive exercise of his right of unilateral divorce (*talaq*) as he has to pay such amount immediately upon divorce, and hence, is likely to think twice before terminating the marriage. The deferred dower also protects the interests of childless widows in the estate of their husbands. Under Islamic inheritance law, a childless widow is entitled to only one-fourth of the property, the remaining of which is divided amongst other legal heirs of the deceased such as his siblings or parents (if alive). The unpaid dower is given preference over bequests and inheritance and is regarded as a debt over the estate of the husband. A widow, who is in lawful possession of her deceased husband's estate, is entitled to retain such possession until the amount of her deferred dower is paid. If she is wrongfully deprived of her possession, she can sue for its recovery. She, however, cannot alienate such property through sale, mortgage, gift, or otherwise.

3.2 Dowry

Dowry (*jahez*) comprises gifts given to a bride by her parents at the time of marriage. It commonly includes moveable property in the form of cash, jewellery, clothes, and household items such as furniture, kitchen utensils, and electronic appliances (TV, air conditioner, fridge, fan, etc.). It is a customary practice in some parts of Pakistan that daughters are denied their due share in inheritance in the family property and dowry is treated as their share in lieu of their right to inheritance. This customary practice is not based on Islamic law and the courts in Pakistan have condemned it unambiguously.[7]

Dowry is usually considered as a symbol of the wealth and prestige of the bride's family. This often puts huge pressure on girls' parents who are forced to save for their daughters' dowries in the hopes of securing good matches. The legislature in Pakistan introduced the Dowry and Bridal Gifts (Restrictions) Act 1976 to curb this fault in society. This Act limits the amount of dowry to Rs 5,000. However, this amount has not been increased since its enactment to incorporate the devaluation of the currency. This makes the set limit very low in the present times. Section 9 of the Act makes any contravention of the provisions of the Act punishable with imprisonment up to six months or a fine, which shall not be less than the amount proved to have been spent in excess of the maximum limits laid down in this Act, or with both. The federal government can forfeit excessive dowry, bridal gifts, and presents to utilise the same for the marriage of poor girls. A complaint under this act can only be filed with the deputy commissioner and only Family Courts are authorised to try offences under the Act. Hence, it is not surprising that the Act remains a dead letter and has failed to serve its purpose. Trends in the reported case law exhibit that husbands try to use this Act to defend themselves against the suits filed by their wives for recovery of dowries. The courts, however, have rejected this defence.[8] The case law further shows that divorced women use the list of dowry items that are required to be furnished to the *nikah* registrar under section 8 of the Act as evidence for the recovery of dowry.[9]

3.3 Outline of Case Law

3.3.1 Nature of Dower. The courts have adopted a flexible approach towards the determination and payment of dower with an aim to ensure smooth enforcement of women's right to dower. They have clarified that life interest in the property is a valid subject matter of dower. It has also been settled that deferred dower without specification of its mode of payment in the *nikahnama* becomes payable on demand by the wife and is not to be postponed until the dissolution of the marriage.

3.3.1.1 Specified Dower Without Consummation of Marriage

Muhammad Akbar v Shazia Bibi PLD 2014 SC 693

In case of consummation of marriage, full dower is payable, and in the absence of consummation, half dower is to be paid.

It is a settled principle among Muslim jurists that once a marriage is consummated, the entire amount of specified dower becomes payable by the husband to his wife; and if consummation does not take place, the wife's entitlement to dower is reduced to half of the specified dower. In this case, all three courts (the Family Court, the First Appellate Court, and the High Court) failed to consider this principle. The Supreme Court took notice of this lapse and applied the correct principle.

The marriage of Muhammad Akbar and Shazia Bibi was solemnised on 13 February 2004, and 99 kanals of land was mutated in favour of the wife on 31 January 2004 as dower. However, *rukhsati* did not take place. After about two years of the marriage, the husband filed a suit for declaration that the land allegedly transferred as dower belonged to him and was fraudulently mutated in favour of the respondent (wife). The respondent contended that the land was given to her in lieu of dower. The court of first instance decreed the husband's suit. Thereafter, the respondent appealed to the first Appellate Court, which was accepted.

The Lahore High Court dismissed the husband's appeal while upholding the decision of the first Appellate Court.

Before the Supreme Court, the appellant-husband disputed the respondent's entitlement to the entire piece of land on the ground of non-consummation of marriage. The court, while referring to the Qur'anic verse 2:237, concluded that the respondent was only entitled to half of the settled dower as the marriage had not been consummated. Hence, the court ordered the division of the disputed land between the appellant and the respondent in equal shares and held that any controversy as to the distribution should be referred to and settled by the executing court.

3.3.1.2 Lifetime Interest as Dower

Ajab Gul v Rahim Gul 1991 SCMR 2500

A lifetime interest in immovable property is a valid subject of dower.

A lifetime interest in property provides the holder with the right to enjoy the usufruct of the property during his/her life. For instance, a husband may give his wife the right to occupy a house during her lifetime. She can live in the house until her death but cannot sell it. After her death, the house will be transferred to the legal heirs of the husband. This case discusses the question of the possibility of fixing lifetime interests as dower under Islamic law. The Supreme Court, after analysing a number of legal authorities concluded that lifetime interests are the valid subject of dower. After considering the facts of the case, the court, however, held that in the present case, lifetime interest was not fixed as a dower.

According to the brief facts of the case, Mst Shamala was married to Waheed Gul. The latter's father, Habibullah gave her one house and two shops as dower through a registered deed executed on 21 October 1936 and registered on 26 February 1937. According to the agreement, she would be entitled to enjoy the property only in her life and would not have any right to dispose of it in any manner whatsoever. Upon her death, the property would revert to the legal heirs of Habibullah. However, Mst Shamala did not adhere to the terms of the agreement and transferred the property. Consequently, Habibullah's legal heirs filed a suit for declaration to the effect that they were the legal heirs of the disputed property and Mst Shamala had no right to alienate it. They claimed that Habibullah's transaction in her favour was only an *areet*, not a transfer of absolute proprietary rights. The trial court decreed their suit holding thereby that Mst Shamala had no right to dispose of the suit property and therefore any alienation made by her was of no legal effect.

When the matter was brought before the Peshawar High Court, the impugned decision of the trial court was reversed. The court observed that the agreement was in nature of a dower deed and was not a simple *areet*. Hence, Mst Shamala had a full ownership right of the property and any condition restraining her proprietary rights would not have any legal consequences.

On appeal before the Supreme Court, the legal heirs of Habibullah reiterated their claim that the agreement was only for the enjoyment of the usufruct of the property and not for the exercise of ownership rights. On the other hand, the counsel for Mst Shamala argued that the property was permanently transferred to her as dower. Despite confirming the validity of lifetime interest as dower under Islamic law, the court concluded:

> [T]he very document fixing the dower unmistakably shows that the demand of the prospective wife was for the transfer of the house and the shops in lieu of [the] dower. It was not life interest in them or Areet that she was asking for. The donor was ostensibly complying with her demand. In complying with it, he could not stop short of it, deviate from it or modify it, without her express

> consent. There is nothing to show her express consent in it. In its absence, she takes the property as per her demand as a condition of marriage.[10]

The court held that the wife was the exclusive owner of the property, and the condition attached to it did not adversely affect her proprietary rights. Consequently, the court dismissed the appeal filed by the legal heirs of Habibullah.

3.3.1.3 Deferred Dower

Saadia Usman v Muhammad Usman Iqbal Jadoon 2009 SCMR 1458

A wife cannot demand deferred dower during the subsistence of marriage; instead, it is to be paid upon dissolution of marriage or death of either spouse.

This case concerns the question that whether a deferred dower (*mahr mu'wajjal*) could be converted into a prompt dower (*mahr mu'ajjal*) when a wife demands it. Saadia Usman (appellant) was married to Muhammad Usman Iqbal Jadoon (respondent). An amount of Rs 1,000,000 was settled as her dower. Half of the dower was prompt and was given to the appellant in the form of gold ornaments at the time of the marriage. The other half was deferred. The dispute between the parties arose when the respondent moved abroad and left the appellant and her daughter in Pakistan. He did not provide maintenance to the appellant and her daughter. Consequently, the appellant filed a suit for recovery of dower of the remaining amount of Rs 500,000 along with maintenance allowance for herself and her daughter. In return, the respondent filed a suit for restitution of conjugal rights. The Family Court jointly decided both suits and decreed the appellant's suit for recovery of Rs 500,000 as dower and also fixed a small amount as maintenance. Both parties being aggrieved by the decision, appealed to the First Appellate Court. The first Appellate Court did not deal with the issue of the recovery of dower but increased the amount of maintenance. Both parties were dissatisfied with this decision and consequently filed separate writ petitions before the Islamabad High Court.

The Islamabad High Court decided that the unpaid amount of dower was in nature of deferred dower, and it could not be ordered to be paid during the subsistence of marriage unless it was agreed between the parties. As there was nothing on record to establish the condition of its early payment the court deferred the payment of unpaid dower until the dissolution of marriage either by divorce or upon the death of either spouse.

The appellant took the matter before the Supreme Court. The appellant's counsel argued that, by making payment of deferred dower dependent upon the eventuality of either death or divorce, the High Court failed to appreciate the significance of dower in an Islamic marriage contract. He asserted that it was obligatory upon the husband to pay dower to his wife without any hesitation. On the other hand, the respondent's counsel argued that the decision of the High Court did not warrant any interference as it was based on the correct interpretation of the law.

After hearing the arguments and perusing the record, Chief Justice Iftikhar Muhammad Chaudhry analysed the relevant verses of the Qur'an, the exegeses of renowned scholars, and the case law. He observed:

> The Qur'anic word 'Nihla' signifies the giving something willingly, of one's own accord, without expecting a return for it. Thus, [the] dower is a gift given by the bridegroom to the bride. However, the Holy Qur'an is silent on the two types of dower[s], i.e. prompt and deferred.[11]

Justice Chaudhry referred to the views of the Hanafi jurists who held that the deferred dower is payable either upon death or divorce. He observed that Maulana Maududi, whom he described as 'a renowned jurist of Pakistan of the modern times'[12] dissented from the opinions of classical jurists and held that deferred dower is payable on demand. Justice Chaudhry was not persuaded by the views of Maulana Maududi and held:

> [W]here a part of [the] dower is described as Mu'wajjal, i.e. deferred, but no time limit is fixed for its payment, according to some jurists, the condition is valid[,] and the time of deferred payment is either death or divorce. And this is considered to be the correct exposition of law.[13]

Consequently, the court upheld the decision of the High Court that a deferred dower is payable upon the eventuality of dissolution of marriage either by the death of one of the spouses or their divorce.

We observe that it is unfortunate that Justice Chaudhry and two other judges on the Bench (Mian Shakirullah Jan and Raja Fayyaz Ahmad JJ) did not appreciate the views of Maulana Maududi expressed in his famous book *Huqooq e Zaujain* to extend women's right to deferred dower by making it payable on demand.[14] This could have provided an effective remedy against husbands who fail to fulfil their marital obligations. Ameer Ali, whose commentary on *Mahommedan Law* was referred to in this judgment, alluded to this function of the deferred dower among Indian

Muslims. He observed that deferred dower is intentionally allowed to remain unpaid with the 'object of compelling the husband to fulfil the terms of the marriage-contract in their entirety'.[15] Justice Chaudhry relied upon Abdur Rehman Al-Jaziri's *Kitab al-Fiqh ala al-Madhahib al-Arba* to support his view. Al-Jaziri mentions that 'according to some jurists'[16] the time of deferred payment is either death or divorce. The phrase, 'according to some jurists' suggests that Al-Jaziri's view was not based on the opinion of a majority of Muslim jurists. In order to safeguard the wife's right to dower, the Supreme Court could have adopted a different view but, ultimately, was unwilling to do so.

The Lahore High Court, however, adopted a different approach to the issue of the payment of deferred dower. The court not only examined the jurisprudential debates but also explored the functions of deferred dower within Pakistani society. This judgment is discussed below.

Muhammad Sajjad v Additional District and Session Judge PLD 2015 Lah 405

Deferred dower without specification of period or stipulation shall be payable at any time upon demand.

In this case, Justice Sohail Iqbal Bhatti of the Lahore High Court discussed the significance of various categories of dower and clarified some general perceptions in regard to it. This was an ordinary family law case where a wife had filed for recovery of maintenance, dower, and dowry after separation but during the subsistence of marriage. The Family Court decreed the suit, and the Appellate Court upheld the decree. This prompted the petitioner (husband) to file a writ petition before the Lahore High Court. He assailed the decree on the ground that during the subsistence of his marriage, he could not be required to pay the dower as it was specified to be deferred. The court did not find his argument convincing as it was never raised before the trial court, and he failed to establish it through evidence.

The court while dismissing the petition discussed the significance of various categories of prompt and deferred dower. Relevant portions of the judgment are reproduced below:

> In general terms, dower is defined as "Muajjal" and "Muwajjal" which is called prompt and deferred respectively. The prompt dower is payable immediately on demand whereas [the] deferred dower is payable at a specified time and on consummation of marriage, the dower is [the] right of the wife, whether prompt or deferred and there is no difference of opinion

> between Islamic jurists regarding payment of prompt dower at the time of marriage or when it is demanded by the wife. However, various schools of thoughts have divergent opinion[s] about the payment of deferred dower. According to "Hanfi Fiqah" to which the most of the society belong in our Country, if the deferment or postponement is not specified and is generally described as deferred, this dower will be considered prompt and shall be payable accordingly.[17]

By referring to various books of the Hanafi school, the court observed:

> This Court would refer to *Kitab-al-Fiq Ala-Madhahib-Al-Arbaha* [*sic*] by Abdul Rehman Al-Jazairi, Volume 4, Page 153, Chapter of Nikah, Published at Darul Fiq, and *Bidaie-As-Sanaie Fi Tarteeb Ash-Sharai* by Allama Abu Bakar Alla-ud-Din Al-Qasmi Al-Hanfi, Volume 2, Page 288, to hold that the view that deferred dower is not payable unless the marriage is dissolved is not supported by any recognized principle based on some authority whereas[,] on the other hand, the deferred dower shall always be treated as prompt if no specified period for the payment of dower is fixed. This view is in conformity to the command of [the] Holy Quran, therefore, in terms of section 6(5)(a) of the Muslim Family Laws Ordinance, 1961 the immediate payment of [the] entire amount of dower, whether prompt or deferred is obligatory in such cases.
>
> The only difference [between] Mu'wajjal and Mu'ajjal[,] i.e. prompt and deferred is that deferred dower is not payable till the arrival of [the] stipulated period whereas prompt dower is payable immediately on demand and if for the payment of deferred dower[,] no stipulated time is fixed, it would be treated as prompt i.e. payable on demand. This leads this Court to the conclusion that deferred dower without specification of period or stipulation, shall be payable at any time upon demand.[18]

The court further observed:

> [T]he classification of dower as prompt and deferred has no legal sanction behind it, except the general practice in Muslim society for the convenience of the parties. The concept and wisdom in [the] classification of dower as prompt and deferred depends upon the relationship of party and protection of [the] right[s] of women in un-foreseen circumstances without taking away her right of demand of payment of dower till the marriage is not dissolved. The postponement of the payment of dower for an indefinite period would not mean that the same cannot be claimed before the dissolution of marriage and if it is considered as such, it would

> negate the concept of dower in Islam as well as defeat the Muslim Family Laws Ordinance, 1961. The deferred dower is [a] source of guarantee for a woman against ill-treatment, non-maintenance, desertion or any other abnormality in the family life. Thus, the payment of deferred dower is deemed to be postponed till either the specified time and if no time is specified, till the wife demands it.[19]

During the course of his analysis, Justice Bhatti did not refer to the Supreme Court judgment in the *Saadia Usman* case[20] for distinguishing his expositions from it. This lapse has been rectified by the Shariat Court of Azad Jammu & Kashmir in its judgment, which is discussed below.

Tahir Hanif v Saira Kosar 2016 YLR 440

Mahr ghair mu'ajjal becomes prompt on demand of wife after consummation of marriage.

In this judgment of Shariat Court (AJ&K), Justice Sardar Abdul Hameed Khan analysed the classification of dower and its implications. The wife filed two suits for maintenance and recovery of the deferred dower. The trial court decreed both suits. In the appeal, the counsel for the husband argued that the whole amount of dower is deferred which is payable upon dissolution of marriage either by the death of the husband or because of divorce. He relied upon the judgment of the Supreme Court in *Saadia Usman* case.[21] Justice Khan examined the Supreme Court judgment by referring to an earlier judgment of Justice Muhammad Nawaz Abbasi of the Lahore High Court in *Dr Subira Sultana v Maqsood Sulari*.[22] In the latter judgment, Justice Abbasi held that if the time for the payment of the deferred dower is not specified it will be payable on demand of the wife.

Justice Khan distinguished the principle laid down in the *Sadia Usman* case by referring to the fact that the legislature amended the standard *nikahnama* which contains the expression '*ghair mua'jjal*'. He contended that the legislature replaced the expression '*mu'wajjal*' (deferred) with '*ghair mua'jjal*' to remove ambiguity:

> It is useful to add that the legislature is wiser than anybody else, hence in this view of the matter it is [a] correct exposition of the term that Mehr "Ghair-e-Mu-ajjal" means deferred dower which becomes "prompt on demand of the wife at any time after consummation of marriage, and the husband is bound to pay the balance amount of the dower to the wife immediately". It may also be stated that [the] term/word "Mu Wajjal"/

> Deferred has been omitted with the use of proper wisdom of law makers to remove the ambiguity of [Mehr Muwajjal] deferred dower is payable only on the eve of [the] dissolution of marriage by Talaq or death, if there being no condition is specifically stipulated in the instruments of Nikkah.[23]

Justice Khan further observed that the classification of dower into the prompt and deferred is based on the practice in society; it is incorporated for the convenience of the parties and does not have any legal sanction behind it. He emphasised that the payment of the dower is an obligation of a husband and if the dower is deferred it does not mean that it has been waived or is postponed until the dissolution of the marriage.

3.3.1.4 Change in the Fixed Amount of Dower

Naziran Begum v Khurshid Begum 1999 SCMR 1171

A husband can increase the amount of dower fixed at the time of marriage.

This case deals with a husband's right to enhance the amount of settled dower. The facts of the case date back to the 1950s and 1960s and the parties mentioned in the title of the case are the legal heirs of the original parties who died long ago. The relevant facts of the case are such that Mumtaz Begum was married to Bashir Ali Shah who died issueless during the subsistence of the marriage leaving behind two other legal heirs (a brother and a sister) in addition to his widow. The deceased owned a reasonable extent of landed property that became a subject of disagreement among all three legal heirs. The disputed properties were transferred in the name of all three legal heirs by the revenue authorities in proportion to their respective shares under Islamic inheritance law.

Legal heirs, not satisfied with the said mutation, brought the matter before the Civil Court. The widow argued that she had an exclusive right to the entire disputed property on the basis of an agreement executed by the deceased a few days before his death in her favour that thereby suppressed a previously written dower deed dated 13 March 1957. The brother and the sister of the deceased challenged the widow's entitlement to the deceased's property. The Civil Court decreed the suit in favour of the widow based on the evidence that she adduced. However, the Appellate Court reversed the decision. Thereafter, the case reached the High Court which restored the decision of the Civil Court. Resultantly, the parties agitated the matter before the Supreme Court.

It was argued on behalf of the appellant that since the claim of dower by Mumtaz Begum stood finally settled by a document dated 13 March 1957, there was no occasion for the deceased to execute another agreement a few days before his death agreeing to once again pay the dower debt that was discharged long ago. On the other hand, it was contended on behalf of the legal heirs of the widow (respondent) that a Muslim man has an unfettered right under Islamic law to transfer or agree to transfer any amount in lieu of dower. Therefore, the agreement was a valid transaction under Islamic law and was known as *hiba-bil-ewaz*.[24] The counsel of the appellant argued that even if it was conceded that the agreement in question was *hiba-bil-ewaz*, it cannot be given effect because it was incomplete due to the non-delivery of possession to Mumtaz Begum. This argument from the appellant's side was countered on the ground that although the delivery of possession was an essential condition for the fulfilment of simple *hiba*, it was not a requisite for the completion of a transaction in the case of *hiba-bil-ewaz*.

The Supreme Court had to settle two issues: the first issue related to a husband's unfettered right under Islamic law to increase the amount of dower even to the extent of disposing of his entire property. The second issue was concerned with the nature of the agreement presented by the widow. The court affirmed the husband's right to increase dower and as to the second issue, it concluded that the decision of the High Court regarding the treatment of the agreement as *hiba-bil-ewaz* did not warrant any interference as it was based on sound principles of law and accurate appreciation of evidence on record. The court reproduced the agreement and while going through its various clauses observed that the mere fact of postponement of the transfer of title of the properties until the death of the husband was not of such a consequence as to affect its validity. Consequently, the widow's entitlement to an enhanced amount of dower, which in fact disinherited the rest of the legal heirs through the mode of *hiba-bil-ewaz*, was upheld.

Malik Amir Akbar v Mian Murid Hussain, ADJ, Lahore 2008 SCMR 505

A wife may settle on a lower amount of dower if the husband is unable to pay.

This case deals with the issue of reduction in the amount of dower. The question before the court was whether it is lawful for a wife to agree on a reduced amount of dower once the court has affirmed her claim. The Supreme Court answered this question in the affirmative.

The marriage of Malik Amir Akbar (appellant) was solemnised with Shahzadi Umarzadi Amir (respondent no. 3). Two children were born from wedlock. After some time, the relations between the parties became strained and they approached the Family Court for various reliefs such as custody of children, payment of maintenance and recovery of dower. The Family Court passed a decree in favour of respondent no. 3 and awarded her Rs 600,000 as the amount of dower. The first Appellate Court and the High Court upheld the decree.

The appellant challenged the decree before the Supreme Court. The appellant's counsel argued that due to his client's financial incapacity, he was unable to meet the liability imposed by the decree of the Family Court. The counsel requested the court to look into the matter sympathetically. However, the fixation of the dower amount and the husband's basic liability to its payment was not questioned in the court. Considering the financial incapacity of the appellant, respondent no. 3 gracefully agreed to reduce the decreed amount of dower from Rs 600,000 to Rs 450,000 on the condition that the latter amount is paid within two months in the executing court. The court accepted the reduction in the amount of dower by the wife and held that if the payment was not made within the stipulated time, the appellant would be required to pay the original amount of dower, i.e. Rs 600,000.

Muhammad Sanaullah v Shamin Naz Kausar 1995 SCMR 1208

Where immovable property is provided as a dower, the property itself has to be transferred to the wife and it is not sufficient that its price is paid.

This case addresses the issue that whether a court can, on its own, modify the nature of liability of the dower disregarding the contents of the *nikahnama* and the wife's consent. Briefly, the facts of the case are that Muhammad Sanaullah (appellant) was married to Shamin Naz Kausar (respondent) on 6 October 1977 and their marriage remained intact till 1989. The dower agreed between the parties comprised half a portion of the house and 6 kanals of agricultural land in addition to some gold ornaments. Both the immovable properties were mentioned in the *nikahnama* in a detailed and precise manner as required. There was no alternative arrangement described in the *nikahnama* in case the properties were not transferred to the respondent.

After the dissolution of the marriage, the respondent filed a suit for the recovery of her specified dower. The trial court awarded her decree but not according to the terms described in the *nikahnama*, but rather in the form of cash of Rs 10,000. Both parties were dissatisfied with the decision of the trial court and approached the first Appellate Court, which did not interfere with the impugned judgment. Hence, the parties agitated before the High Court in its constitutional jurisdiction. The High Court observed that the lower courts had misapplied the law on the subject by granting a decree worth Rs 10,000 instead of the properties listed in the *nikahnama*. The judge substituted the nature of liability from the cash amount to that specifically mentioned in the *nikahnam*a, i.e. the half portion of the house and 6 kanals of agricultural land.

The appellant sought leave to appeal before the Supreme Court against the decision of the High Court. The court refused the appeal on the grounds that the *nikahnama* clearly stated that the husband had agreed to pay the dower in terms of half portion of the house and the specified piece of land. There was no condition in the *nikahnama* that suggested that the husband would pay the specified amount instead. Therefore, the High Court was justified in awarding the decree for the properties listed in the *nikahnama*.

3.3.1.5 Principle of *As-sum'at*

Nasir Ahmad Khan v Ismat Jehan Begum PLD 1969 SC 194

Under the Islamic legal principle of *As-sum'at*, a higher amount of dower can be declared in public while actually paying a lower amount in private.

This case deals with a principle of Islamic law termed *as-sum'at*. According to this principle, one may fix two different amounts of dower in a marriage: one announced in public and the other settled in private. The former is usually higher than the privately settled amount without any intention to pay it. The principle allows this arrangement to enhance the prestige of the family of the bridegroom without obliging the husband to pay the inflated amount of dower. While delivering its judgment, the Supreme Court reproduced passages from Ameer Ali's *Mahommedan Law*, and the *Fatawa-i-Alamgiri* to illustrate the recognition of this principle under Islamic law. However, it was made clear that the present case did not fall within the ambit of this principle due to its peculiar circumstances.

Nasir Ahmad Khan (appellant) was married to Ismat Jehan Begum (respondent) and on the eve of the marriage, a dower deed was executed describing 70 *jaribs* of land as dower. After the separation of the spouses, the respondent filed a suit for the recovery of her fixed dower. The appellant contested the suit on two grounds: first, that the dower deed was a fictitious transaction and was never intended to be acted upon; and second, the deed was executed under undue influence. The trial court rejected these contentions and declared that the respondent was entitled to a fixed amount of dower. The first Appellate Court confirmed the trial court decision. Ultimately, the appellant brought the matter before the superior judiciary. The appellant invoked the principle of *as-sum'at* in his favour by arguing that Islamic law allowed the fixation of a higher amount of dower in public for the glorification of families while settling a lower amount for payment. The respondent's counsel relied upon sections 90 and 91 of the Evidence Act 1872 (presently Articles 102 and 103 of the Qanun-e-Shahadat Order 1984) to argue that once a transaction was rendered into a written document, no oral evidence contradicting or modifying the same would be admissible. This rule is based on a common law principle called the parol evidence rule, where extrinsic evidence is not accepted once a transaction is reduced into writing.

The Supreme Court, after hearing both the parties and going through the relevant evidence concluded that there was no cavil as to the recognition of the principle of *as-sum'at* in Islamic law but the facts of the present case did not attract its application. The court observed:

> [T]hat in the written statement filed by the appellant there was no averment of privately fixed dower which is essential for [the] application of the principle of As-Sum'at. The evidence led in support of the alleged fictitious nature of the dower was also found to be contradictory and rejected concurrently by the courts below … [From] this state of pleadings and the evidence led by the appellant, the learned Judges in concurrence with the trial court concluded that the transfer of the suit land in favour of the respondent was not a fictitious transaction, that it was intended to be acted upon.[25]

The court further noted that the establishment of *as-sum'at* in clear terms would have averted the application of sections 90 and 91 of the Evidence Act 1872, but the appellant failed to do so. Thus, the said provisions rendered the oral evidence presented by the respondent about the fictitious nature of the dower inadmissible.

3.3.2 Recovery of Dower. The case law suggests that while adjudicating upon the issue of recovery of dower after the dissolution of marriage, the judges are conscious of the disparate gender relations in our society. This is evident from the fact that the burden of proof to establish the payment of the dower is placed upon the husband. The dower is to be recovered even if the property was not properly described at the time of marriage. Furthermore, the courts do not strictly construe the period of limitation for execution of the decree for the recovery of prompt dower provided under the Limitation Act 1908. Treading the same path, the courts have also held that the relinquishment of the dower will be invalid if the wife was acting under coercion or undue influence, and not as a free agent.

Rab Nawaz Ahmed v Hasina Iqbal 2011 SCMR 972

The burden of proof is upon the husband to establish the payment of the dower.

In this case, the Supreme Court laid down the principle that a husband's plea of discharging his liability of the payment of dower should be established through relevant and cogent evidence.

The marriage between Rab Nawaz Ahmed (appellant) and Hasina Iqbal (respondent) was solemnised, and the amount of dower was agreed to be Rs 500,000. After some time, the respondent filed a suit for the recovery of the dower amount in the Family Court, which was decreed in her favour. The first Appellate Court reversed the decision of the Family Court on the plea of the appellant that he had transferred half of his house to the respondent in lieu of a dower. The court held that when a valuable property/consideration had already been transferred to the respondent in lieu of dower, the appellant could not be asked to pay the same again. It is important to note that the appellant did not produce the original transfer deed in court.

The respondent filed a writ petition before the Peshawar High Court where the decision of the first Appellate Court was set aside. The respondent's right to the amount of dower was restored as the appellant had not discharged his burden of presenting proof that he had fulfilled his responsibility of payment of the dower.

The husband filed a petition for leave to appeal before the Supreme Court. During the course of his argument, the appellant contended that he could not produce the original deed of transfer of property because it was lying with his previously engaged attorney. The court disapproved of this contention and held that the burden of proof was on the appellant to substantiate his case by producing relevant evidence. The court concluded that the appellant failed to establish that half share of the house had actually been transferred by him in favour of the respondent. Resultantly, the leave petition was refused and the respondent's right to dower was affirmed.

Shah Bano Begum v Iftikhar Muhammad Khan PLD 1956 Kar 363

Relinquishment of dower by a wife is not binding upon her if she is not acting as a free agent.

This case deals with the issue of recovery of a dower by a wife when a husband alleges its relinquishment. The plaintiff, Shah Bano Begum filed a suit for recovery of her dower amounting to Rs 50,000 from the defendant Iftikhar Muhammad Khan. The parties were married in 1944, and the amount of dower was fixed at Rs 50,000. According to the plaintiff, the dower was prompt. The defendant married another woman and left for the UK along with his second wife. The plaintiff demanded her dower by means of serving a notice upon the defendant, but he refused to pay. He asserted that the plaintiff had relinquished the entire dower amount. It appeared that in 1951, the plaintiff had filed another suit for dissolution of marriage, which was decreed on the grounds of gross cruelty for keeping relations with other women, neglecting the plaintiff and their minor children, and ultimately marrying another woman. The defendant did not file an appeal against the decree for dissolution of marriage and the parties were no longer in a matrimonial relationship. It should be noted that this case was decided in 1956. Now there is no right of appeal against a decree of dissolution of marriage under section 14 (2) (a) of the Family Courts Act 1964.

The court noted that the burden of proving the alleged relinquishment was upon the defendant. The defendant produced two letters allegedly written by the plaintiff. One of them was found to be the most relevant in the circumstances of the case. The court noted that the circumstances under which the letter was written were clear from its language, which read as: 'we pledge to live a [*sic*] loving and devoted husband and wife hereafter and I forego the *meher*'.[26] The court noted the context in which the letter was written that the husband wanted to enter into a second marriage and the plaintiff, as the first wife, tried to appease him by foregoing her dower. Considering the language of the letter and the attending circumstances, the court concluded that the relinquishment was not with the plaintiff's free consent. Though the alleged relinquishment was not extorted by physical force, it was definitely obtained through undue influence that a woman in the position of the plaintiff could hardly resist.

The court held that the plaintiff was not acting as a free agent, and it was not justified to hold that a woman who remitted the dower in such circumstances should be bound by it. Hence, the plaintiff's letter did not amount to a deliberate and intentional relinquishment. Therefore, she was entitled to recover her dower amounting to Rs 50,000.

Dr Asma Ali v Masood Sajjad PLD 2011 SC 221

Dower is to be recovered even if the property is not properly described in the *nikahnama*.

In this case, the Supreme Court dealt with the issue of the effect of a non-description or inaccurate description of the property in the *nikahnama* on a wife's right to dower. The bench included three judges, Mian Shakir Ullah Jan, Tariq Parvez Khan, and Nasir ul Mulk. The first two judges favoured the wife's right to recover the dower in circumstances where the property was not properly identified. Justice Nasir ul Mulk, however, objected to the majority decision based on the practical difficulty in the execution of a decree regarding the property that was not properly identified.

Dr Asma Ali (appellant) was married to Masood Sajjad (respondent no. 1) on 17 July 1992 vide a registered *nikahnama*. According to the entries in the *nikahnama*, respondent no.1 was bound to pay prompt dower to the appellant. The father of respondent no. 1, Dr Sajjad Ahmad (respondent no. 2), served as a surety through *iqrarnama* to this arrangement in case respondent no. 1 failed to discharge his liability. The appellant brought a suit for the recovery of dower, which according to her claim comprised Rs 200,000 in cash, 60 *tolas* of gold, a two-kanal house situated in village Mirza, tehsil and district Attock, or its market value stipulated in the *nikahnama* as Rs 3,000,000, and 100 kanals of agricultural land located at village Chassian, tehsil and district Attock, or its market value of Rs 5,000,000. In the *nikahnama,* the agricultural property was neither described in detail nor was its market value determined. Therefore, the issue was whether the 100 kanal agricultural property was sufficiently described for the enforcement of the appellant's right to dower.

In the Family Court, respondent no. 1 stated that the ornaments of gold and cash amount of Rs 200,000 had already been given to the appellant and these were the only items mentioned and they were fixed as prompt dower, whereas the other entries pertaining to the house and agricultural land were fictitious. He further argued that the alleged *iqrarnama* did not exist as no such instrument had ever been signed by his father. The Family Court partially decreed the petition by ordering the recovery of Rs 200,000 and did not pass any order for the house and the agricultural land measuring 100 kanals.

Both parties approached the first Appellate Court, which confirmed the decision of the Family Court. Thereafter, the appellant approached the Peshawar High Court in its constitutional jurisdiction but failed to get any relief. The appellant then brought her case before the Supreme Court.

The court went through the evidence recorded in the case file and found that the testimonies of the two important witnesses who appeared on behalf of the appellant were not accorded the level of credence they deserved. One of these witnesses was the person who recited the *khutbah* of the *nikah* and the other was the one who had recorded entries into the *nikah* register. Both of them confirmed that the entries of the two-kanal house and agricultural land measuring 100 kanals were genuine. One of them disclosed that respondent no. 1 had married another woman without the permission of the appellant. On the other hand, the respondent's counsel argued that as there was no description of agricultural land specified in terms of its *khasra* numbers nor was the house earmarked with respect to its boundaries, the three courts below had correctly concluded the controversy about the vague and disputed entries by not decreeing the house as well as the agricultural land in favour of the appellant.

After hearing the arguments of both sides and perusing the evidence, the majority of the judges of the Supreme Court concluded that the appellant was entitled to the house in the form of an amount of Rs 700,000, a price mentioned in the *nikahnama* along with compound interest since the time of marriage, and also, she was entitled to receive the agricultural land of 100 kanals. However, there were still other issues to be addressed such as: which tract of agricultural land was it, where was it located, and how could its market value be determined if no description of the property was mentioned in the *nikahnama* apart from the name of village, tehsil, and district.

Justice Tariq Parvez Khan responded to this issue:

> In respect of 100 kanals of agricultural land, since no description of the land was given in the Nikkah Nama in terms of its khasra numbers or identifying data, a decree is given in favour of [the] appellant-wife as prayed for in her plaint. In view of [the] absence of particulars of 100 Kanals land, the Trial Court shall appoint [a] commission by directing a member of [the] Revenue hierarchy to determine the average price of per Kanal agricultural land in village Chassian, Tehsil and District Attock and after such determination the appellant will be entitled to receive the 100 Kanals or its market value so determined.[27]

Justice Mian Shakir Ullah Jan, while supporting the contentions of Justice Tariq Parvez Khan, expressed his views as follows:

> That once we decide that if the property/house [is] mentioned in the Nikahnama on account of lack of sufficient description leading to its identification then its price, if mentioned in the Nikahnama, can be awarded then in the same way the value of the other property (agricultural), the price of which has not been mentioned in the Nikahnama, can also be granted if the evolvement of a mechanism for determination of value is possible, which is not in conflict with any provision of law rather in consonance with the established principles for determining the value of [the] property, then the same be resorted to.[28]

The minority view of Justice Nasir ul Mulk was based on the Family Courts Act 1964 and certain provisions of the Civil Procedure Code 1908, particularly relating to the execution of a decree for the recovery of immovable property. He concluded:

> [F]or the present purpose, one may refer to Rule 19 of Order XXII of the Civil Procedure Code, mandating that a decree for recovery of immovable property shall contain its description sufficient for its identification. This would only be possible if the property is sufficiently described in the plaint or in the evidence. The identification of the immovable property is necessary for the execution of the decree by the Executing Court as it cannot go beyond the terms of the decree. Undisputedly, the 100 kanals of agricultural land claimed by the appellant as part of her dower, are not identified. Describing property in terms of its area in a particular village, without giving its exact location, would not be sufficient description for the grant of decree for its recovery. A decree granted in such ambiguous terms would be incapable of execution. It was on these premises that all three Courts have consistently held that on account of the lack of proper description of the 100 kanals of agricultural land, no decree could be granted to the plaintiff for its recovery. Even a money decree in the alternative cannot be awarded in the absence of the identity of the property as there would exist no basis for evaluation.[29]

An important aspect of this case is that all three judges granted the wife compound interest on the amount of her dower that remained unpaid. Justice Nasir ul Mulk held:

> To compensate the appellant for the inflation in the currency and the increase in the value of [the] real property, I agree that interest be granted on the decree for recovery of Rs. 700,000 from the date of the Nikahnama, namely, 17th July, 1992.[30]

The granting of compoundable interest on a deferred dower has far-reaching implications for women's financial rights since such a dower is paid many years after the marriage.

Fawad Ishaq v Mehreen Mansoor PLD 2020 SC 269

A wife/mother-in-law who did not sign the *nikahnama* nor committed to discharge the responsibility of dower at any stage, could not be obliged to pay when such responsibility was incurred by her husband/father-in-law.

An intriguing situation arose in a dower-related controversy in this case. At the time of marriage of Ms Mehreen Mansoor (the respondent), she was promised in writing in the *nikahnama* that she would be given as dower a constructed house on a plot. This responsibility was taken by her father-in-law, but the plot was owned by the mother-in-law.

The respondent initiated the judicial proceedings for the acquisition of the constructed house on the plot as a dower in league with her husband. It was assumed by the respondent that her father-in-law's commitment would be discharged from the plot/house owned by her mother-in-law. It is interesting to note that the respondent only made her parents-in-law a necessary party and she did not think it appropriate to make her husband a party who was primarily obliged for the payment of her outstanding dower. During the course of the litigation, the mother-in-law passed away and her children stepped into her shoes.

The Peshawar High Court decided in the favour of the respondent on three grounds: firstly, the wives of other sons had also been granted plots measuring two kanals, secondly, the mother-in-law did not question the *nikahnama* and the responsibility of the dower mentioned therein, and thirdly, the father-in-law was a guarantor of her property. The Supreme Court did not agree with any of the grounds relied upon by the High Court and set aside its judgment.

The Supreme Court highlighted the distinctive feature of Islamic law that favoured women's property rights. Specifically, the Court criticized the English doctrine of coverture and its French counterpart *feme covert* that led to the merger of the wife's persona into her husband after marriage in which the former could not exercise her property rights without the consent of her husband. The Court speaking through Justice Faez Isa distinguished how Islam emphasised upon women's individuality in the context of her right to property. She alone is the owner and master of her property, and no one could transfer her property unless she has explicitly given consent with free will.

In the context of the facts of this case, Justice Isa raised three points. Firstly, each and every contract of marriage is a different transaction from other marriage contracts and it should be evaluated on its facts and circumstances. Secondly, the mother-in-law was not a signatory to the marriage contract of the respondent nor agreed at any later stage to part with her property in favour of the respondent. And thirdly, keeping in view the individuality emphasised in Islamic law, a husband cannot be treated as a guarantor of his wife's property particularly when she had not permitted him to assume that position.

3.3.3 Limitation Period for the Recovery of Dower

Syed Muhammad v Mst Zeenat PLD 2001 SC 128

A specific period of limitation for the execution of the decree for the recovery of prompt dower cannot be fixed.

This case discusses the limitation period for the recovery of dower. Briefly, the facts of the case are that the petitioner and respondent no. 1 were married. Respondent no. 1 obtained a decree for recovery of her prompt dower against the petitioner on 24 October 1979. However, she filed a suit for the execution of the decree on 10 November 1996. The petitioner raised the objection against the execution on the grounds of limitation. The executing court, on 27 February 1997, overruled the petitioner's objection. The petitioner filed an appeal against the order before the additional district judge, who accepted the appeal, and dismissed the execution application of respondent no. 1. The respondent no. 1 filed a constitutional petition before the High Court, which was allowed. Consequently, the present petition for leave to appeal was filed before the Supreme Court.

The counsel for the petitioner contended that the execution application filed by respondent no. 1 on 10 November 1996 was time-barred, and hence the additional district judge rightly set aside the order of the executing court. Justice Iftikhar Muhammad Chaudhry noted that as per Article 103 of the Limitation Act 1908, all suits for recovery of prompt dower can be instituted within three years from its demand whereas the time prescribed for the suit of deferred dower is three years under Article 104 of the Act. In the instant case, as the marriage still existed between the parties, therefore the decree of the Family Court for recovery of dower in favour of the respondent would be deemed to be in respect of her prompt dower. The question left to be determined was the period of limitation for filing of execution application for the satisfaction of the prompt dower.

The court placed reliance upon Article 181 of the Limitation Act 1908, which provides a period of three years from the time the right to sue accrues. The court held:

> … because the prompt dower is to be recovered during the subsistence of marriage, therefore, no specific period of limitation for implementation of [the] decree of such nature can be fixed due to subsistence of marriage. The judgment-debtor i.e., the husband acknowledges the right of his wife[,] and he is deemed to remain under a legal obligation to satisfy the decree whenever the decree-holder/wife has moved the legal forum for [the] satisfaction of her right. This proposition can be considered from another angle i.e., that as [the] tie of marriage exists between parties, therefore, the decree-holder/wife out of [the] number of consideration[s] may have postponed the implementation of the decree including the consideration that let relations between the spouses remain cordial or the husband is looking after her as well as other family members or the husband on account of his poor financial position is not in a position to implement the decree but such postponement for any consideration during [the] subsistence of marriage would not deprive the decree-holder/wife from [the] execution of the decree being barred by time.[31]

For the foregoing reasons, the petition was dismissed, and leave was refused to the husband. Consequently, the wife's right to get her decree executed even after fifteen years of its pronouncement, was held to be within the limitation period.

3.3.4 Recovery of Dowry. Section 5 of the Dowry and Bridal Gifts (Restriction) Act 1976 provides that the ownership of dowry articles vests absolutely in the bride. In Pakistan, women usually file suits for the recovery of their dowry articles upon the dissolution of marriage. Such suits are often defended on the ground that since the amount of dowry item exceeds the specified limit provided under section 3 of the Dowry and Bridal Gifts (Restriction) Act 1976, the court should not order their recovery. To counter this, the judiciary has held that a husband cannot rely upon the provisions of the Act to deny recovery of dowry to a wife.

Muhammad Tazeel v Mst Khair-un-Nisa 1995 SCMR 885

A husband cannot rely upon the Dowry and Bridal Gifts (Restriction) Act 1976 to deny recovery of dowry to a wife.

This case addresses the issue of the effect of contravention of the Dowry and Bridal Gifts (Restriction) Act 1976 on the recovery of dowry items by a wife. Briefly, the facts of the case are that the petitioner married the respondent on 16 May 1976. The marriage broke down, and the respondent's suit for dissolution of marriage was decreed. The respondent subsequently filed a suit for recovery of her dowry articles or alternatively that she be paid their price amounting to Rs 24,000. The suit was decreed in favour of the respondent. The petitioner filed an appeal before the District Court, which was dismissed. He then filed a revision petition in the High Court, which was also dismissed. He then sought leave to appeal before the Supreme Court.

In support of contentions raised by the petitioner, his counsel relied upon two main provisions of the Act, sections 3 and 8. Section 3 puts a ceiling of five thousand rupees on the value of dowry and bridal gifts given to the bride at the time of marriage. It also prohibits the giving of gifts to the bride before or after six months of *nikah*, and if *rukhsati* takes place sometime after the *nikah* then six months after the *rukhsati*. Section 8 requires the list of dowry items to be furnished to the *nikah* registrar. The petitioner's counsel contended that the violation of the two sections is an offence under section 9 of the Act. Therefore, the respondent by claiming that she had received dowry articles of the value of Rs 24,000 had been guilty of the offence under section 9, and hence the court cannot assist her in the recovery of her dowry articles. Furthermore, the list of dowry articles produced by the respondent was not provided to the *nikah* registrar as required under section 8 of the Act, therefore it was inadmissible as evidence.

The court observed that the aforementioned contentions were not raised before the courts below and had only been advanced at this forum to deprive the respondent of her property. The court further noted that it was true that violation of the provisions of sections 3 and 8 constitute offences under section 9, but this section provides that the cognizance of such offences cannot be taken by courts except on a complaint made by or under the authority of the deputy commissioner within nine months from the date of *nikah* or *rukhsati*, whichever is later. In the instant case, the deputy commissioner did not lodge any complaint within the prescribed period. Furthermore, at the time of the *rukhsati* when the dowry articles were taken to the petitioner's house, he did not raise any objection as to their value being in excess of the ceiling provided under section 3 of the Act. Therefore, he could not deprive the respondent of her property by making the violation of the Act as a ground. As far as the list of dowry items was concerned, it was not inadmissible evidence merely because it was not furnished to the *nikah* registrar. Therefore, the leave to appeal was refused.

Muhammad Arshad v Additional District Judge 2015 CLC 463 (Lah)

Limiting the maximum amount of dowry articles and bridal gifts as enacted by the Dowry and Bridal Gifts (Restriction) Act 1976 is against the injunctions of Islam.

In this case, respondent no. 3 filed a suit for recovery of maintenance allowance and dowry articles. The trial court decreed the suit and directed the petitioner to return the dowry articles as per the list annexed with the plaint or pay its price, i.e. Rs 579,500. The petitioner filed an appeal before the additional district judge. The judge partially allowed the appeal while modifying the impugned judgment to the extent that respondent no. 3 was entitled to either recover dowry articles or be paid their price amounting to Rs 331,000. Hence, the present writ petition was filed.

The counsels for the parties advanced their arguments and produced evidence in support of their contentions. The court, after hearing the arguments and perusing the record, noted that despite the bar mentioned in the Act, if parents had given dowry valued at more than Rs 5,000, then it will remain the property of the bride and the husband cannot usurp the same on the ground that it has been given in violation of section 3(1) of the Act. Section 5 of the Act clearly states that dowry items shall remain the property of the bride. Even otherwise, the husband cannot refuse to return the dowry articles on the ground of the violation of section 3 of the Act when the husband had failed to adopt the procedure of complaint specified in section 8(A) of the Act. While dismissing the petition, the court passed some important remarks on the purpose of the Act and its validity in light of Islamic injunctions, which are reproduced as follows:

> Act XLIII of 1976 was enacted for the benefit of the women to be married and their parents so that they may not remain unmarried for lack of dowry of heavy value. It was not enacted to deprive the wives of the ownership of their dowry and Wari. As a matter of fact, the said Act is a paper law and has seldom been acted upon. The said law has been used only against the women and wives and efforts have been made by the husband to deprive the wives of their such property on the basis of the said law. In other words, the said law instead of being beneficial to women and wives is detrimental to their rights and interests. It may be added that there is no Islamic sanction behind the said law. In a way, the said law offends [*sic*] against the Injunctions of Islam as set out in the Holy Qur'an and Sunnah. In Aya No. 20 of Sur-Al-Nisa of the Holy Quran, it has been ordained

> that in case a husband marries another woman he should not take back any of the property given to her. In Aya No. 21 thereof it has been further ordained that a husband cannot take back the same after the marriage has been consummated. The said Ayas have been interpreted by all translators and Mufasareen to mean and include the property of any value, however, great it may be. Some of them have given it the meaning of treasure. This means that there is no limit on the value of bridal gifts which may be given to her by her parents or by the husband or his parents.[32]

3.4 Conclusion

Dower is a mark of respect for a wife, and it also serves as a check on a husband's unfettered right to divorce his wife. Dower is an essential consequence of a valid marriage. The Pakistani courts have adopted a protective approach towards women's right to recover dower, especially after the dissolution of marriage. The case law exhibits the cautious approach of the courts in deciding cases of alleged relinquishment of dower by a wife. Such relinquishment is not considered valid unless done by the wife with her free consent and not in order to win her husband's favour or after being subjected to any kind of undue influence. An important principle consistently followed by the courts is that the dower is an obligation on a husband and the burden of proof lies on him to prove that the dower has been paid. These measures ensure that a wife is not deprived of her right to dower without any lawful reason.

Furthermore, lifetime interest in an immovable property is deemed a valid subject of dower. The courts have acknowledged the Islamic legal principle of *as-sum'at*. This principle permits one to fix two different amounts of dower: one in public and the other in private. The former is higher than the privately settled amount and there is no intention to pay the former. The courts interpret this principle strictly in order to protect the financial interests of wives. In some cases, the husbands have attempted to escape liability to pay the dower in the case of immovable property on the ground that the property which is the subject of the dower is not properly described in the *nikahnama*. The Supreme Court has held that the dower is to be recovered even in such circumstances where the property is not adequately described.

It is unfortunate that the Supreme Court did not adopt a pro-women's rights position on the issue of the payment of deferred dower. In the *Saadia Usman* case, Chief Justice Iftikhar Muhammad Chaudhry chose to follow the restricted view that deferred dower is only payable on dissolution of marriage by divorce or death, despite referring to the contrary opinion which regarded the deferred dower to be payable on demand.[33] Justice Chaudhry could have opted to follow the latter view to protect the financial interests of wives who should not be forced to either file for divorce or wait for the death of their husbands to get their deferred dower. In *Muhammad Sajjad* case, the Lahore High Court adopted a purposive approach to this issue and held that deferred dower without specification of period or stipulation shall be payable at any time upon demand.[34] The Shariat Court (AJ&K) clarified that the term '*ghair mu'ajjal*' (deferred dower) in the amended standard *nikahnama* should be interpreted to mean 'payable at the demand of a wife'.[35] We hope the Supreme Court will endorse the principle laid down in the judgments of the Lahore High Court and the Shariat Court (AJ&K) as and when the issue appears before it.

Parents giving dowry to the bride at the time of marriage is a customary practice in many parts of Pakistan. Although the Dowry and Bridal Gifts (Restriction) Act 1976 was enacted to curb the practice of huge dowries and to protect the poor, husbands have attempted to usurp the dowry articles of their wives by using this Act. The courts, however, have thwarted the attempts of husbands to use the Act for their benefit by laying down the principle that the limitation upon the value of dowry under this Act is only restrictive and not prohibitive in nature; such property remains with the wife irrespective of its value.

Overall, the trend in the case law on dower and dowry shows a dynamic approach of the Pakistani judiciary towards securing women's financial rights.

Questions

1. What is dower? Describe its types and functions.
2. Critically analyse the role of the judiciary in Pakistan in protecting the financial rights of women while applying the Islamic legal principles on dower.
3. The Dowry and Bridal Gifts (Restrictions) Act 1976 was promulgated to curb the menace of excessive dowries which adversely affect poor women and their parents. Critically evaluate the extent to which this Act achieved its objectives.

Further Reading

Books/Articles

Mansoori, M.T., *Family Law in Islam* (Islamabad: Shari'ah Academy, 2012), 71–82.
Azahari, R. and H.M. Ali, 'Mahr as a Form of Economic Security: A Preliminary Study', *Arab Law Quarterly* (2015) 29(3), 296.

Cases

Ashiq Ali v Mst Zamir Fatima PLD 2004 SC 10 (Once a property has been gifted by the husband to his wife in lieu of dower, he cannot subsequently exercise his proprietary rights over the same.)

Ayesha Shaheen v Khalid Mahmood 2013 SCMR 1049 (A wife is entitled to the gold ornaments or their current market value at the time of the execution of the decree.)

Aziz-ur-Rehman v Mst Bibi Jameela 2020 CLC 380 (Quetta) (In the recovery of dowry articles, the solitary statement by the wife is enough to prove them.)

Azra Bibi v Lateef 2020 YLR 282 (Lah) (When no list of dowry articles is available, the financial status of parents is determining factor in the recovery of dowry articles.)

Dr Muhammad Ali Chohan v Fakhur-un-Nisa 2009 CLC 255 (Pesh) (When dowry articles are not objected to at the time of *rukhsati* of the wife, no objection can be raised subsequently on the ground of violation of the Dowry and Bridal Gifts (Restriction) Act 1976.)

Ghania Hassan v Shahid Hussain Shahid 2016 SCMR 2170 (The property mentioned in the *nikahnama* as dower belongs to the wife, and it cannot be subjected to attachment or sale in an execution proceeding against the husband.)

Ghulam Sabir v Chairman Union Council, Ward No. 27, Samanabad Lahore PLD 1981 Lah 232 (Decisions in matters regarding dower do not lie within the jurisdiction of the union council.)

Gul Akbar v Jameela Afridi PLD 2016 Pesh 109 (Though the payment of dower is primarily a responsibility of the husband, some other person can also bind himself to accept such responsibility by becoming a surety to the marriage contract.)

M. Ishaque v Rukhsana Begum PLD 1988 Kar 625 (Prompt dower is payable on demand and in full. It may also be demanded before the *rukhsati*/consummation of the marriage.)

Nabeela Shaheen v Zia Wazir Bhatti PLD 2015 Lah 88 (Presumption of truth is attached to the entries made in the *nikahnama* including those pertaining to dower. And the one who disputes any entry has to bring cogent and convincing evidence to rebut the same.)

Saif-ur-Rehman v ADJ Toba Tek Singh 2018 SCMR 1885 (The Court held that under section 14(2)(b) of the Family Courts Act 1964, the wife could appeal against the decision given upon dower money, but the husband did not have the right to appeal because the law put a restriction on the right of appeal of a husband and not that of a wife who is protected from lengthy and expensive litigation.)

Samreen Bibi v Judge Family Court PLD 2015 Lah 504 (There is no general formula available under which wear and tear of dowry articles can be exactly determined. Wear and tear of dowry articles depend upon multiple factors, like nature and quality of dowry articles, their use by the woman, relationship level between the spouses during the marriage, retaliatory attitude after separation, the period during which dowry articles remained under use of the lady and period after which the claim of dowry articles was made, etc. Different items have different rates of depreciation. Tentative assessment should not be presumptive, but it should be based on subjective analysis of dowry articles on physical verification which could be done in various ways.)

Notes

1. *Khalwa sahiha* is translated as valid retirement. Technically, it means getting the husband and wife together at a place where there is no legal, moral, or physical impediment to their having sexual intercourse.
2. An option of puberty is a right of a Muslim minor who is married during minority by a guardian, to repudiate the marriage upon attaining majority/puberty.
3. Some authors treat prompt dower and dower payable on demand as a single category having mixed characteristics of both. According to them, the prompt dower is either payable at the time of marriage or when the wife demands it. Mulla, *Principles of Mahomedan Law*, 374–76; and Dr Tanzil-ur-Rahman 53, *A Code of Muslim Personal Law*, 221.
4. 2016 YLR 440, 451–52.
5. J.H. Korson, and M.A. Sabzwari, 'Age and Social State at Marriage, Karachi, Pakistan 1961–64 and 1980: A Comparative Study', *Journal of Comparative Family Studies* (1984) 15(2), 257, 272.
6. *Shah Bano Begum v Iftikhar Muhammad Khan* PLD 1956 Kar 363.
7. PLD 1990 SC 1.
8. 1995 SCMR 885; 2015 CLC 463 (Lah); 2014 MLD 1400 (Kar); 2009 CLC 255 (Pesh). In *Muhammad Imran Ahmad v Hina Faheem* 2014 MLD 1400, the Sindh High Court held that the limitation to the value of dowry articles under the Act is only restrictive and not prohibitive in nature. It means that the ownership of the dowry items remains with the wife irrespective of its monetary value.
9. PLD 2013 Isb 11; 1988 CLC 1888 (Kar).
10. 1991 SCMR 2500, 2503.
11. 2009 SCMR 1458, 1467.
12. Ibid., 1470 f.n. 3.
13. Ibid., 1470.
14. Justice B.Z. Kaikaus specifically relied upon the *Huqooq e Zaujain* to extend women's right to no-fault divorce '*khula*' by removing the requirement of the consent of the husband for its validity. *Balqis Fatima v Najam-ul-Ikram* PLD 1959 Lah 566.
15. A. Ali, *Mahomedan Law* (Lahore: Imran Law Book House, 2012), 1383.
16. 2009 SCMR 1458, 1470.
17. PLD 2015 Lah 405, 410.
18. Ibid., 411.
19. Ibid., 412.
20. 2009 SCMR 1458.
21. Ibid.
22. 2000 CLC 1384.
23. 2016 YLR 440, 451.
24. As opposed to a simple gift, it is a gift for consideration. It possesses the elements of a contract of sale. The two conditions that must be fulfilled to make such a gift valid are: *bona fide* intention on the part of the donor to transfer the ownership of the subject of the gift, and payment of consideration on the part of done.
25. PLD 1969 SC 194, 196.
26. PLD 1956 Kar 363, 369.
27. PLD 2011 SC 221, 229.
28. Ibid., 231.
29. Ibid., 234.
30. Ibid.
31. PLD 2001 SC 128, 131.
32. 2015 CLC 463, 467
33. 2009 SCMR 1458
34. PLD 2015 Lah 405.
35. 2016 YLR 440.

4

MAINTENANCE OF WIVES AND CHILDREN

4.1 Introduction

Maintenance includes food, clothing, lodging, and other necessary expenses for the mental and physical well-being of a person. A husband is liable to provide maintenance to his wife during the marriage and after divorce during the *iddat* period. This principle is drawn from the Qur'anic verse 4:34, which provides that men are protectors and maintainers of women, i.e. '*al-qawamun*'. A father is obligated to maintain his children: sons until they attain the age of majority and daughters till their marriage, irrespective of the fact that they live away from the father with the divorced mother or even if the mother earns a livelihood. The father is also required to maintain his divorced or widowed daughter(s). If a father is unable to provide maintenance, then the paternal grandfather is liable to provide maintenance to his grandchildren. There is also a corresponding duty upon children to maintain their poor and old parents and grandparents, once they grow up and start earning their livelihood.[1]

Under section 2(ii) of the Dissolution of Muslim Marriages Act 1939, if a husband fails or neglects to provide maintenance for a period of two years to his wife, she is entitled to ask for judicial dissolution of her marriage. A wife can seek an order from the arbitration council for maintenance under section 9 of the Muslim Family Laws Ordinance 1961 (MFLO) in case the husband fails to maintain her adequately, or where there is more than one wife, he fails to maintain them equitably. A wife can also file a suit for maintenance before the Family Court under section 7 of the Family Courts Act 1964. Under section 17A of the Act, the court may fix an interim maintenance and if the husband does not pay it, he could be deprived of his defence and the case against him decreed on the basis of the plaint and other supporting documents. This provision also empowers the courts to grant a higher amount of maintenance than what has been prayed for keeping in view the lapse of time in pursuing the judicial proceedings and other relevant circumstances, such as inflation. Furthermore, if the court does not mention the annual increase in the amount of maintenance granted, then it would automatically increase at the rate of 10 per cent.

The quantum of maintenance is to be determined by taking into account the needs of the beneficiaries and the income of the father or maintenance provider (e.g. the grandfather). All children are to be treated equitably for the purposes of the provision of maintenance. Therefore, the capacity of the maintainer and the adequacy of the maintenance are essentially, questions of fact to be determined by the courts by considering all relevant circumstances of a particular case.

However, the wife's right to maintenance is not absolute; it may be denied in some circumstances. It can be suspended in the presence of a decree for restitution of conjugal rights against her. A wife may not be entitled to maintenance if she refuses to reunite with her husband without any reasonable cause. The right to maintenance also extinguishes with the termination of a marriage contract. In case of *talaq*, the husband is liable to pay maintenance to the divorced wife only during the *iddat* period. To avoid the payment of maintenance to his wife, a husband may divorce her even though she has got a court decree for the payment of maintenance. This is because a husband has a unilateral right to no-fault divorce under Islamic law.

In case a wife is divorced because of no fault on her behalf, she is entitled to the payment of a 'parting gift' or 'consolatory gift' called *mata'a*, in addition to the payment of her deferred dower and maintenance during the *iddat* period. *Mata'a* is different from maintenance after divorce and is paid by a husband to his wife as a compassionate gift to lessen her difficulties caused by the divorce. The concept of *mata'a* has been clearly referred to in several verses of the Qur'an (2:235, 2:240–41, and 33:49). In case of dissolution of an unconsummated marriage contracted without specific dower (*mahr musamma*), only *mata'a* is payable and the woman is not entitled to claim dower or maintenance. In many Muslim countries like Algeria, Egypt, Jordan, Libya, Morocco, Syria, and Tunisia, *mata'a* is paid to a divorced wife in addition to dower and maintenance. If after the consummation of marriage, a husband pronounces *talaq* against the wishes of his wife and without any fault on her part, the husband is liable to pay *mata'a* according to his financial capacity in addition to the payment of maintenance during the *iddat* period. The courts have to determine the quantum of *mata'a* by taking into account the financial status of a husband, the duration of the marriage, and the circumstances of the divorce.[2]

In its 2009 Report, the Law and Justice Commission of Pakistan proposed that a new section must be added to the MFLO to provide for *mata'a* at the time of divorce by a husband. In its section 2(bb), the proposed amendment Bill defined *mata'a* as 'a fair provision in kindness by the husband according to his means and includes anything in cash or kind either movable or immovable.'[3] This proposal has not yet been incorporated into the MFLO.

4.2 Outline of Case Law

4.2.1 Maintenance of Wife. A thorough analysis of the case law suggests it is now a settled principle of law that maintenance is not a gift but a right of the wife. She is to be provided with proper maintenance during the marriage and after divorce during the *iddat* period even when the divorce is initiated by the wife on the basis of *khula*. It is the duty of the husband to provide maintenance, even if the wife does not reside with him for a valid reason. The burden of proof is not as stringent in maintenance suits as it is in other financial disputes. The courts have absolved the wife of the burden to provide documentary evidence of the husband's income. Additionally, the courts consider all relevant circumstances including the needs of claimants and the resources of defendants in order to fix the amount of maintenance.

4.2.1.1 Maintenance—a Right of a Wife

Shazia v Muhammad Nasir 2014 YLR 1563 (Pesh)

Maintenance is not a gift but a right of a wife.

This case sheds light on the scope of a wife's right to be maintained by her husband. The petitioner, Shazia and her minor son, Suleman, filed a suit against the respondent, Nasir. She claimed the recovery of gold ornaments given as dower, maintenance allowance at the rate of Rs 4,000 per month for herself for the last twenty-seven months and onwards, maintenance allowance at the rate of Rs 2,000 per month for the minor for the last twenty-four months and onwards, and Rs 30,000 as medical expenses. We shall only discuss the issue regarding maintenance allowance here.

The petitioner argued that the respondent, Nasir, used to maltreat her and beat her whenever she demanded her dower. After being driven out of the house by the respondent, she resided with her parents. Later, the minor, Suleman, was born. The respondent also contracted a second marriage without the permission of the petitioner. The respondent, through his written statement, asked for restitution of conjugal rights. The trial court decreed the suit of the petitioner for maintenance at the rate of Rs 2,000 per month for the period she prayed for, and the minor, Suleman, was awarded maintenance at the rate of Rs 1,500 per month for the period the petitioner prayed for until his majority with 10 per cent annual increase. At the same time, the court granted a decree for the restitution of conjugal rights in favour of the respondent subject to the payment of dower and past maintenance. Both parties filed separate appeals before the first Appellate Court that were dismissed. Hence, the petitioner brought her case before the High Court.

The court noted that the respondent could not prove that the petitioner voluntarily left his house. On the other hand, the petitioner successfully proved that the respondent did not pay her dower and hence she was justified in living away from her husband. The petitioner also showed that the matrimonial tie between the parties still existed. Therefore, the petitioner being the wife of the respondent was entitled to be maintained by him. The court held that maintenance is neither a gift nor a benefit but an undeniable legal obligation of a husband. As far as the maintenance allowance for the minor, Suleman, was concerned, the court observed that he was the son of the respondent, and the father was bound to maintain him until the age of puberty. The court further held that the mere fact that the son was in the custody of his mother was not a valid ground for the father to withhold maintenance.

Ghazala Sadia v Muhammad Sajjad 2012 YLR 2841 (Lah)

Khula-based divorce does not deprive a wife of her right to be maintained during *iddat* period.

This case deals with the right of maintenance of a wife who exercised her right to no-fault divorce, *khula*. The Family Court dissolved the marriage between the petitioner and respondent no. 1 on the basis of *khula* in lieu of dower. In addition, the Family Court held that the petitioner was entitled to dowry and maintenance of Rs 1,415 per month from the date of *nikah* till the end of *iddat* period. Both parties preferred appeals against the decision. The Appellate Court slightly modified the decree of the Family

Court with regard to dowry articles and held that the petitioner was not entitled to any maintenance. The petitioner challenged the Appellate Court decision before the High Court.

The Appellate Court had set aside the order of the Family Court for maintenance to the petitioner on the basis that the petitioner was not entitled to the benefit of maintenance because she dissolved the marriage of her own volition. The High Court held that a Muslim wife is entitled to be maintained by her husband as of right. Respondent no. 1 attained the status of a wife after entering into a marriage with the respondent, and therefore, she was entitled to be maintained by her husband. The court placed reliance upon the *Muhammadan Law* by D.F. Mulla to establish that a divorce affected by *khula* or *mubarat* operates as a release by the wife of her dower, but it does not affect the liability of the husband to maintain the wife during her *iddat* period. Therefore, the High Court restored the decree of the Family Court which awarded maintenance to the petitioner until the end of her *iddat* period.

Syed Abu Talib Shah v Bibi Rukhsar Zahra 2012 CLC 1272 (Pesh)

A wife residing away from her husband with a lawful excuse is entitled to maintenance.

This case deals with the issue of maintenance of a wife (respondent no. 1) who was not residing with her husband (the petitioner). Respondent no. 1 filed three suits against the petitioner and one of them was the suit for recovery of maintenance. All three suits were decreed in her favour, and she was awarded maintenance at the rate of Rs 2,000 by the court of first instance. The decision was also upheld by the first Appellate Court. The petitioner challenged the concurrent findings of the two courts before the High Court. Only the relevant portions of the judgment are discussed here.

The counsel for the petitioner argued that respondent no. 1 herself left the house of the petitioner, and therefore, she was not entitled to maintenance. The court rejected this argument and held:

> It is well-established law that it is incumbent upon the husband to maintain his wife and he is not absolved of his liability to maintain her even though she be [*sic*] not residing with him provided she has a lawful excuse or a legal right to refuse to live with her husband on account of non-payment of prompt dower.[4]

In the instant case, it was on record that the petitioner had not paid the respondent wife her dower, hence she was held to be justified in living away from him. The writ petition was dismissed, and the decision of the lower courts was maintained.

Kashif Akram v Mst Naila 2011 MLD 571 (Kar)

A wife who deserted her husband without any lawful reason is not entitled to past maintenance.

This case deals with the issue of the right of maintenance of a wife who deserts her husband without any lawful excuse. The petitioner was married to respondent no. 1 (the wife). A child, Muhammad Uzair (respondent no. 2), was born during the marriage. After some time, relations between the spouses became strained, and the husband divorced the wife through a divorce deed dated 26 May 2004. In her civil suit, the respondent wife contended that the petitioner husband left her and their child (respondent no. 2) at her parents' house in 2002 and never returned to take them back. She asserted that the petitioner also failed to maintain them since that occurrence. She admitted receiving a pay order dated 2 March 2003 of Rs 12,000 from the petitioner and getting Rs 2,000 from him after each alternate month as a maintenance amount for the minor. However, she contended that maintenance payment was discontinued after April 2004. She alleged that the petitioner was an architect who drew a handsome salary. He owned a double-story bungalow and received a monthly rent of Rs 40,000 apart from his salary. The petitioner contested all these allegations in his written statement. He maintained that respondent no. 1 voluntarily left him and took their son (respondent no. 2) with her after leaving a note to that effect. He maintained that in spite of the best efforts of the elders of the family, respondent no. 1 and her family did not reconcile with him, and this led to their divorce.

The court of first instance examined the evidence presented by both parties and decreed the suit of the respondents, but maintenance was awarded at a much lower rate than claimed. Respondent no. 1 was awarded maintenance at the rate of Rs 3,000 from April 2002 till the end of her *iddat*, while respondent no. 2 was awarded Rs 6,000 per month from the date of filing of the suit till his puberty with an increment of 20 per cent per annum. Both parties appealed, but their appeals were dismissed. Therefore, the petitioner filed a writ petition before the High Court.

The counsel for the petitioner contended that respondent no. 1 voluntarily left the petitioner and never let him meet his minor son. He claimed that respondent no. 1 failed to discharge her marital obligations and hence was not entitled to any maintenance. He also argued that both the courts below had failed to ascertain the financial position of the petitioner whose salary certificate was submitted and was not disputed. Respondent no. 1 was entitled to maintenance for *iddat* period only with effect from the pronouncement of *talaq*. In addition, the amount of maintenance to the minor should be awarded while keeping in view the financial capacity of the petitioner. It was maintained that the petitioner earned only Rs 11,750 per month and the alleged rental income in respect of the house mentioned by the respondents did not accrue to the petitioner, as the house had been sold in 2003. The petitioner's father who owned the house had received the amount from the sale proceeds. Furthermore, the counsel argued that a 20 per cent annual increase in the maintenance of the minor was exorbitant. The counsel for the respondents rebutted these arguments by asserting that the petitioner was the only son of his parents, lived in the Defence Housing Society and was an architect by profession. Hence, it was not difficult for him to pay the amount of maintenance as decreed by the lower courts.

The High Court noted that there was no cavil in the proposition that it is the duty of the husband to maintain his wife according to his financial status, but if the wife leaves the house of the husband of her own accord without any lawful excuse, then her claim of maintenance is vitiated unless otherwise agreed upon between the parties. The social and financial status of the father is an important factor in determining the quantum of maintenance payable by him. In the instant case, the lower courts did not consider the financial status of the father while fixing the amount of maintenance. The court placed reliance upon various judicial authorities that lay down the principle that past maintenance can only be claimed by a wife who is willing to perform conjugal rights and discharge her marital obligations and has been deserted by her husband without any lawful excuse. In this case, there was a handwritten note on record, which was allegedly written by respondent no. 1 expressing her decision to desert the petitioner without giving any excuse. The execution of the document was not denied by respondent no. 1. Furthermore, she could not produce any evidence to prove that the petitioner had defaulted in maintaining her without any lawful excuse. Hence, the fact of voluntary desertion of respondent no. 1 without any lawful reason was sufficiently proved. In addition, the court noted that 20 per cent annual increase in the maintenance of respondent no. 2 was not based on any evidence and the lower courts had not given any reason justifying this increase. Hence, in light of these findings, the court reduced the annual increase in the maintenance of respondent no. 2 to 5 per cent. At the same time, the period of maintenance granted to respondent no. 1 was reduced to the period of *iddat* only.

Ghulam Shabbir v Mst. Abbas Bibi 2022 CLC 963 (Lah)

A husband can agree to arrange for maintenance or extend the financial advantage to the wife even after divorce and such condition is not contrary to injunctions of Islam.

According to the facts of this case, the parties agreed at the time of marriage that in case of an unreasonable divorce, the wife would be provided with gold ornaments/finances. This condition was mentioned in Clause 19 of the *nikahnama* which contained the question 'whether the husband's right of divorce is in any way curtailed?' Unfortunately, the husband divorced his wife, and she claimed the gold ornaments/finances. The Family Court and the first appellate court decided in favour of the wife. The husband brought the dispute before the Lahore High Court in written jurisdiction and raised two major objections. First, the requirement of payment in the form of ornaments/finances amounts to a restriction on a husband's right of divorce provided under Islamic law. Second, such payments are akin to the maintenance after the lapse of the period of *iddat* which is not allowed under Islamic law. Justice Asim Hafeez of the Lahore High Court rejected both objections and held that since marriage is a civil contract, spouses are free to introduce terms and conditions for the protection of their rights and interests. Regarding the facts of the case, Justice Hafeez observed that this provision of ornaments/finances in case of unreasonable divorce is in nature of spousal support and Islamic law is not against the provision of such alimony aimed for the dignified and comfortable life of an ex-spouse after the divorce. Such a provision does not in any way prevent the husband to exercise his option of divorce rather it merely obliges him to give the agreed benefits to his wife upon divorce. Furthermore, this provision of ornaments/finances is not in nature of continued maintenance after the period of *iddat* rather it represents a sense of responsibility and affection on the part of the ex-husband for the future financial security of his ex-wife. Consequently, the Court found the petition devoid of any merit and dismissed it.

4.2.1.2 Requirement of Evidence for Proving Income of Husbands for Maintenance

Abdul Jabbar v Additional District Judge 2009 CLC 364 (Lah)

Maintenance is to be fixed by taking into account the needs of claimants and the resources of defendants.

In this judgment, the court laid down the legal principle regarding the factors that are to be considered while determining the quantum of maintenance. Respondent no. 3, Sarwari Bano, was married to the petitioner, Abdul Jabbar. Respondent no. 4, Talha, was born during the wedlock. Later, the relationship between the spouses became strained and ended in the dissolution of the marriage. Respondent no. 3 filed a suit for maintenance for herself and her son and for the recovery of her dower. Only the suit for maintenance is discussed here. The Family Court granted maintenance allowance to respondent no. 3 and 4 at the rate of Rs 1,000 per month. The petitioner challenged the quantum of maintenance through a writ petition.

The High Court observed that the quantum of maintenance has to be fixed keeping in account the requirements of the claimant and the resources of the father. In the instant case, the petitioner's resources were not too meagre to meet the requirements of maintenance of Rs 1,000 per month each. In fact, keeping in view the living expenses of the mother and the child, Rs 1,000 per month to each was less than the bare minimum to meet their requirements. The court observed that the present decree of maintenance by the Family Court was not appealable under section 14(2)(c) of the Family Courts Act 1964 which provides that a decree of maintenance of Rs 5,000 is not appealable. Therefore, when the decree is not appealable, then the discretionary relief of writ jurisdiction could not be availed unless an impugned order is perverse or against proved facts. In light of these observations, the court dismissed the petition with costs.

Tariq Mehmood v Farah Shaheen 2010 YLR 349 (Lah)

Judges should not take the words of husbands for granted in respect of their income, and must not require documentary proof from wives.

In this case, the court laid down guidelines to be followed for determining the amount of maintenance allowance. Respondent no. 1 (wife) was married to the petitioner. Respondent no. 2 was born during wedlock. Soon after the marriage, the wife found out that her husband had previously been married twice and had divorced both of the other wives. She alleged that the petitioner was involved in some nefarious activities and wanted her to indulge in them. Upon her refusal, he drove her out of his house. She gave birth to respondent no. 2 at her parents' house.

Respondent no. 1 filed a suit for recovery of gold ornaments, personal belongings, and maintenance for herself and respondent no. 2 at the rate of Rs 2,000 per month from January 2005 and prayed for the dissolution of her marriage. She claimed delivery expenses and averred that the petitioner's monthly income was Rs 50,000. The petitioner contested the suit and argued that he was a poor labourer and was ready to pay Rs 200 per month for respondent no. 2 only. The Family Court dissolved the marriage between the parties and held that respondent no. 1 was not entitled to any maintenance allowance as she was living apart from the petitioner despite the decree of restitution of conjugal rights in his favour. The Family Court granted her maintenance at the rate of Rs 1,000 during the *iddat* period along with maintenance for respondent no. 2. The husband filed a writ petition before the High Court.

Justice Jamila Jahanoor Aslam observed that courts should adopt a more dynamic approach when it comes to the grant of maintenance allowance. It has been repeatedly proved that women are either thrown out of their marital abode by their husbands or are compelled by circumstances to leave the same. Husbands then do not maintain their wives and minors residing away from them, which gives rise to suits for recovery of maintenance. The husbands counter such suits by filing suits for restitution of conjugal rights just to prove their *bona fides* and to counteract the wives' right to maintenance. When wives fail to abide by the decrees of restitution of conjugal rights passed in favour of their husbands, they are declared '*nashizas*' (disobedient) by the courts without taking into consideration the motives of their husbands. Had the husbands really come to courts with *bona fide* intentions when they file suits for restitution of conjugal rights, they could have shown their goodwill by maintaining their estranged wives.

On the issue of determining the rate of maintenance, the court noted that hardly any wife collects evidence against her husband when they are living together, therefore, the expectation of courts from a wife to come up with documentary evidence against her husband is misplaced. The courts must use their own discretion in order to ascertain the income of the husband rather than taking his word for granted when he claims to be destitute. The court upheld the quantum and duration of maintenance granted to the respondents and dismissed the petition.

4.2.2 Maintenance of Children. The following cases show that the maintenance of children is an inescapable duty of the father even if the mother earns a living. The courts have held that the father is bound to provide maintenance not only to his unmarried adult daughters but also to his widowed and divorced daughters even if they live separately with their mother. If a father fails to do so, the court might hold the grandfather liable for the maintenance of his grandchildren. In *Humayun Hassan v Arsalan Humayun,*[5] the Supreme Court extended the scope of 'maintenance', holding thereby that a father might be required to maintain his son until he acquires the education necessary to earn a decent livelihood. The Lahore High Court relied upon the doctrine of constructive guardianship to make the adopting father liable for the maintenance of the adopted children after divorce.[6]

4.2.2.1 Obligation of a Father to Maintain his Child

Khalid Bashir v Shamas-un-Nisa 2015 MLD 11 (Lah)

A child is to be maintained by the father even though the mother earns a livelihood.

This case discusses a father's obligation to maintain his children and whether or not he is absolved of this responsibility if the mother earns a livelihood. The wife (respondent no. 1) had filed two suits against the husband (the petitioner): one for the recovery of dowry articles and the other for the recovery of the maintenance allowance for herself as well as for their child (respondent no. 2). Only the latter suit is discussed here. The trial court disposed of the suits through a consolidated judgment. The suit of respondent no. 1 for maintenance was dismissed except for *iddat* period at the rate of Rs 8,000 per month, while the maintenance allowance for respondent no. 2 was fixed at the rate of Rs 8,000 per month with an annual increase of 30 per cent. The petitioner filed an appeal against the decision, which was accepted to the extent of dowry articles whereby the respondent's prayer was declined. Both parties filed constitutional petitions before the High Court.

The counsel for the petitioner argued that the lower courts erred in law while awarding maintenance allowance to the minor at such an exorbitant rate that was beyond the capacity of the petitioner to pay. He argued that as the mother was earning, the petitioner should not be made to bear the maintenance cost of respondent no. 2. Furthermore, the counsel challenged the order of the lower court for the annual increase of the maintenance allowance of respondent no. 2 at the rate of 30 per cent because there is no provision for such enhancement in the Family Courts Act 1964.

The High Court held that a father cannot be absolved of his responsibility to maintain his children merely because the mother earns money. In the present case, the mother was working as a homoeopathic doctor and the court did not consider this fact sufficient to relieve the father from his responsibility. The court discussed the quantum of maintenance of respondent no. 2 and held:

> The intent and purport of [awarding] maintenance allowance to a minor child is to enable her/him to continue living at least, in the same state of affairs as the child was used to prior to separation/divorce amongst the parents. It would be quite unjust and against the norms of propriety if due to separation amongst the parents the child has to relegate to a lower level of living standard or he/she is declined [sic] the level or standard of education which was being achieved by him/her prior to such unfortunate happening i.e. separation of parents.[7]

After determining the source of income of the petitioner, the court concluded that the maintenance allowance fixed at the rate of Rs 8,000 was neither exorbitant nor harsh. However, the court found that the enhancement of the allowance at the rate of 30 per cent annually was unjustified and hence reduced it to 15 per cent.

Mariam Bibi through Abida Parveen v Naseer Ahmad PLD 2015 Lah 336

An adopted child is to be maintained by the adopting father as a constructive guardian.

This is an important case that deals with the right of an adopted child to be maintained by the adopting father. The Family Court decreed the minor's/ petitioner's suit for recovery of maintenance against the adopting father (the respondent), and she was declared entitled to maintenance at the rate of Rs 800 per month with a 5 per cent prospective annual increase from the date of the institution of the suit till her marriage. The court held that although the petitioner was not the real daughter of the respondent, he was still bound by his adoption agreement to maintain her. On appeal, the Additional District Judge dismissed the petitioner's suit primarily on the ground that the petitioner was not the real daughter of the respondent, and Islam does not recognise the concept of adoption. Hence, the petitioner filed this petition before the High Court.

The counsel for the petitioner contended that the respondent had given a solemn pledge that he would maintain and bring up the petitioner as his daughter and could not discontinue his commitment. No one appeared on behalf of the respondent. Justice Shezada Mazhar, after hearing the arguments and perusing the record, held that it is an admitted fact of the case that the petitioner was adopted by the respondent and his wife at a very tender age, and was presented as such before the public at large. Justice Mazhar discussed the Islamic concept of adoption by narrating the incident of Zayd bin Haritha's adoption by the Prophet Muhammad (PBUH). From this incident, he deduced the following principles: adoption is allowed in Islam, however, changing the family name of the adopted child is not allowed. If the child was two years old or less and was also breastfed directly by the adoptive mother for at least a day and night (or fifteen times consequently), then the child will become *mahram* to the new family. But if not breastfed as mentioned, the child will remain *non-mahram* to the new family. In view of these principles, the petitioner cannot have any claim of maintenance against the respondent. Furthermore, there is nothing on record to show that the petitioner is the *rizai* (foster) daughter of the respondent under which the petitioner may have a claim of maintenance against the respondent.

Justice Mazhar, however, noted that there is another aspect to the issue that entitles the petitioner to claim maintenance allowance from the respondent. Islam categorically ordains to help the poor and needy, especially orphans. If there is no one to take care of orphans and the needy, then this becomes the responsibility of the state. If the adopting parents take it upon themselves before the public at large to take care of adopted minors, then they assume the role and status of constructive guardians of the minor. This constructive guardianship creates a fiduciary obligation/relation between the adopting parents and the adopted child. The doctrine of constructive guardianship has long been a part of the law of guardianship. In view of the facts of the instant case, it is clear that the respondent adopted the petitioner and presented her as a daughter to the public at large. These acts of the respondent have created a relationship of trust and constructive guardianship between the petitioner and the respondent. This relationship also entails fiduciary duties to be performed by the respondent that inevitably include the maintenance of the minor. In view of this discussion, this petition was accepted, and the impugned judgment of the Appellate Court was set aside.

Shayan through Mst Shamim v Nisar Ahmad 2010 MLD 695 (Lah)

A mother cannot waive the maintenance right of a child by entering into an agreement with the father.

This case discusses the validity of a waiver by a mother of the minor's right to claim maintenance from his father. The petitioner being the daughter of respondent no. 1, filed a suit for recovery of maintenance against him. She alleged that she was born in wedlock between Shamim and Nisar Ahmad in 1994 at the house of Shamim's parents. Respondent no. 1 had never seen her and failed to maintain her. Additionally, respondent no. 1 had obtained the signatures of the petitioner's mother on various papers on different pretexts and had been blackmailing her. She claimed maintenance from 30 April 1999 at the rate of Rs 6,000 per month. Respondent no. 1 contested the suit alleging that he had divorced the mother of the petitioner in 1994 before a *panchayat.* It was resolved therein that respondent no. 1 would pay Rs 175,000 to the mother of the petitioner, and she would not claim any further maintenance for the petitioner. A divorce deed, agreement deed, and receipts were also executed which bore the signatures of the petitioner's mother and her maternal grandparents. Furthermore, it was agreed that respondent no. 1 would not ask for the custody of the child. The trial court decreed the suit in favour of the petitioner and awarded her maintenance at the rate of Rs 3,000 per month from the date of the institution of the suit.

Respondent no. 1 filed an appeal against the trial court decision, and the Additional District Judge reduced the rate of maintenance to Rs 2,000 per month and found the petitioner entitled to past maintenance with effect from 30 April 1999. Being aggrieved by the judgment, respondent no. 1 filed a writ petition before the High Court whereby the case was remanded to the trial court to decide the controversy as to whether, by receiving Rs 175,000 in a lump sum from respondent no. 1, the mother of the petitioner had waived the petitioner's right to claim future maintenance from her father.

The trial court decreed the suit of the petitioner and declared her entitled to receive maintenance allowance at the rate of Rs 2,000 per month with effect from 3 April 1999 to 30 April 2005, and for the future, from the date of the institution of the suit until her marriage. Both parties felt aggrieved by the decision and preferred appeals. The petitioner's appeal was dismissed and respondent no. 1's appeal was partly allowed to the extent that the petitioner's claim for past maintenance was set aside. Hence, the present constitutional petition.

The controversy to be decided was whether the mother of the petitioner waived the petitioner's right to claim future maintenance from her father by allegedly receiving a lump sum of Rs 175,000 from respondent no. 1 and agreeing not to claim any further maintenance for the petitioner. The court held:

> Any agreement by the minor would be void unless Court expressly appoints a guardian or a next friend keeping in view the interest of the minor for the execution of such an agreement, as such, the agreement deed (Exh.D-1) and receipt (Exh.D-2) are not binding on the petitioner. Even otherwise, it is the inalienable right of the petitioner to be maintained by her father. Viewed from any angle, the petitioner is entitled to receive maintenance from her father till her marriage.[8]

The court held that the petitioner was entitled to receive past maintenance as claimed by her because the father is bound to maintain his daughter's rights from the time of her birth until her marriage.

Gakhar Hussain v Surrayya Begum PLD 2013 Lah 464

A father is required to maintain his unmarried daughter even when she is earning her living.

This case discusses the extent and nature of a father's duty to maintain his daughter. In doing so, the court also explains the definition of maintenance. The petitioner married respondent no. 1 in 1981. A daughter (respondent no. 2) was born in wedlock. The petitioner expelled the respondents from his house in 1987 and contracted his third marriage. Respondent no. 1 claimed maintenance and educational expenses of respondent no. 2. The petitioner contested this claim on various grounds including that respondent no. 2 is disobedient because she refused to marry his nephew as suggested by him. The two courts below ruled in favour of the respondents. Therefore, the petitioner filed a writ petition before the High Court.

The counsel for the petitioner maintained that respondent no. 2 is an educated woman who is earning money as a schoolteacher, whereas the petitioner is an old and ailing man, hence the granting of past maintenance for six years to the respondents is harsh and illegal. He argued that it is rather the responsibility of the children, who are earning their livelihood, to support their sick and elderly parents. On the other hand, the counsel for the respondents argued that the petitioner married three women and he was maintaining the children from other wives, while respondent no. 2 was being discriminated against in this regard. Since the petitioner divorced the mother of respondent no. 2, he never bothered to inquire about the well-being of his daughter (respondent no. 2).

The court noted the definition of maintenance as provided in section 369 of Chapter XIX of the *Muhammadan Law* by D.F. Mulla. 'Maintenance' includes food, raiment, and lodging. Under section 370, Mulla noted that a father is bound to maintain his daughter until she is married, and the father is not bound to maintain a child who is capable of maintaining himself/herself out of his/her own property. The court differed with Mulla's views and held that the definition of maintenance is to be liberally construed, which means it includes the process of maintaining or being maintained and the provision of the means to support life. In this context, the Court alluded to the Lahore High Court judgment in *Mian Muhammad Sabir v Uzma Parveen* wherein a father was held to be bound to maintain his divorced daughter despite the fact that she was living with her mother.[9]

In the present case, the father was providing maintenance to his other children. The court observed that the contention of the petitioner that respondent no. 2 is disobedient did not have any force because the petitioner, as a father, never showed any love and affection towards his daughter rather he had deserted her. Therefore, he could not expect her to show love towards him. Moreover, under Islamic law, there is no such thing as abandonment (*aaq*) of the disgruntled son or daughter, depriving him or her of his/her share in inheritance. For the foregoing reasons, the petition was dismissed.

4.2.2.2 Father has to Maintain his Unmarried and Divorced Daughters

Ch. Muhammad Bashir v Ansarun Nisa 2012 MLD 1394 (Lah

A father is to maintain unmarried adult daughters.

This case sheds light on the issue of whether the mere age of majority can be a ground to disentitle a daughter to claim maintenance from her father. The respondents filed two separate suits for recovery of maintenance against the petitioner. Respondent no. 1, Ansar-un-Nisa, filed the first petition for herself and for her three minor children. Respondents no. 2 and 3 (Bushra Bashir and Aleena Bashir), adult daughters of the petitioner, filed the second suit. According to the facts stated in the plaint, respondent no. 1 got married to the petitioner and five children were born in wedlock. At the time of the filing of the first suit, respondents were residing with their father (the petitioner) in Dubai. However, the petitioner subsequently sent them back to Pakistan and contracted a second marriage. The respondents contended that the petitioner was a man of means and could easily pay the maintenance claimed by them. On the contrary, the petitioner claimed that his maximum monthly income was Rs 50,000 only. The Family Court granted maintenance to the petitioner's children only and that too at a reduced rate than the one claimed by the respondents. The respondents filed appeals against the judgment. Only respondent no. 1's appeal was accepted to the extent of granting her the maintenance allowance. The appeals of other respondents for enhancing the amount of maintenance were dismissed. The petitioner filed a writ petition against this decision.

The counsel for the petitioner argued that both respondents no. 2 and 3 were major and were disobedient daughters, and hence they were not entitled to any maintenance. Moreover, the lower courts did not fix the quantum of maintenance while keeping in consideration the financial status of the petitioner. On the contrary, the counsel for the respondents argued that the source of income and financial status of the petitioner was proved through evidence. In addition to that, respondents no. 2 and 3 were unmarried and still studying, hence under Muslim law the petitioner was bound to maintain them, especially when there was nothing on record to prove that they were disobedient daughters. The court held:

> Mere age of majority itself is not sufficient to declare unmarried daughters disentitled to maintenance allowance if otherwise it is not proved with cogent and sufficient evidence that daughters were living apart from the father against his wishes and were not ready to obey his lawful and reasonable demands.[10]

The mere fact that respondents no. 2 and 3 refused to get married in the petitioner's family does not make them disobedient. However, had the offer been proper and according to the wishes of respondents no. 2 and 3 one could have inferred otherwise. The circumstances of the case and the attitude of the petitioner showed that respondents no. 2 and 3 must have rejected the marriage proposals for some cogent reasons. In light of the foregoing reasons, the court dismissed the petition.

Muhammad Ali v Judge Family Court, Depalpur 2010 YLR 520 (Lah)

An unmarried daughter who refused to marry according to the wishes of her father is entitled to be maintained by him.

This case discusses whether a daughter after attaining the age of majority is entitled to maintenance from her father. This writ petition was filed against two impugned judgments whereby respondent no. 3's suit for recovery of maintenance against the petitioner was decreed. The matter agitated before the High Court pertains to the quantum and period of maintenance allowed in favour of respondent no. 3 who is the petitioner's daughter. The petitioner challenged the decree on the basis that the maintenance allowance awarded in favour of respondent no. 3 was excessive and the period for which it was allowed was too long.

The counsel for the petitioner contended that the petitioner had been paying maintenance to respondent no. 3 till she attained majority and afterwards, since she was then a major, she was not entitled to any maintenance. Furthermore, respondent no. 3 failed to accept a marriage proposal suggested by the petitioner thus disentitling herself from claiming any maintenance from him. The court held that the father is bound to maintain his daughter till her marriage. The mere fact that the daughter attained majority does not disentitle her from claiming maintenance from her father. The court rejected the argument that respondent no. 3 should be denied maintenance just because she refused to accept the marriage proposal suggested by the petitioner. The court noted that since the petitioner neglected her for so many years he could not interfere in her life and impose his will upon her. Furthermore, the court held that a girl could not be compelled into a marriage against her will under Islamic law. Therefore, the writ petition was found devoid of merits and was dismissed *in limine.*

Mian Muhammad Sabir v Uzma Parveen PLD 2012 Lah 154

A divorced daughter even when living with her divorced mother and not the father is entitled to be maintained by the father.

This case deals with the issue of whether a divorced daughter who lives apart from her father, is entitled to maintenance from him. The respondent, who was the daughter of the petitioner, filed a suit against him for the recovery of maintenance allowance at the rate of Rs 10,000 per month along with past maintenance for five years. According to the plaint, the respondent was 27 years old and lived with her mother who had been divorced by the petitioner when the respondent was only a year old. The respondent further averred that she herself was a divorcee with no means of sustenance of her own and was entitled to be maintained by the petitioner who worked in a bank and drew a monthly salary of Rs 50,000. The Family Court decreed the suit of the respondent and fixed her maintenance allowance to be Rs 2,000 per month from the date of the institution of the suit till her marriage with a 10 per cent annual increase. Both parties filed appeals against the decree. The petitioner's appeal was dismissed while the respondent's appeal was allowed to the extent that her monthly allowance was increased to Rs 5,000 per month. The present petition challenged the legality of the judgments whereby maintenance was awarded to the divorced daughter.

The counsel for the petitioner argued that the petitioner extended full financial support to the respondent until her marriage when her right to maintenance came to an end. The same does not stand revived upon the dissolution of her marriage. The court observed that it is a settled law that a father is bound to maintain his daughter regardless of her age until she is married:

> The rationale for providing maintenance to a Muslim female until her marriage is understandable as in most cases she would need the financial support of her father for having no means of her own. The responsibility of the father continues till his daughter's marriage when it is passed on to her husband, who is under legal obligation to maintain his wife. However, the obligation of the husband to maintain his wife lasts as long as the marriage is intact with the consequences that upon the dissolution of the marriage, the husband is no longer liable and has no obligation to maintain his erstwhile spouse. Upon losing her marital status, a female reverts to her status of a single lady who needs financial support in the same manner as she needed it before she was married. Her right to receive maintenance should not be defeated by her marriage no longer in existence. The rationale for providing maintenance to an unmarried lady is equally applicable to a divorced lady as in either case the single lady has no independent source of income. As such, there is no reason to treat a divorced lady differently and deny her the maintenance [when] she is in need of it.[11]

In the instant case, it was on record that the petitioner's divorced daughter had no source of income of her own and was dependent upon her mother who could hardly provide her any maintenance. On the contrary, the petitioner earned a monthly income of at least Rs 30,000. In view of these circumstances, and the blood tie between the respondent and the petitioner, some burden was to be placed on the petitioner's shoulders to take care of his divorced daughter. The court further noted that the respondent could not be denied maintenance owing to the fact that she chose to reside with her mother and not the petitioner. Therefore, the petition was dismissed.

4.2.2.3 Father Might be Required to Maintain his Adult Son

Humayun Hassan v Arsalan Humayun PLD 2013 SC 557

A male adult child may be maintained by a father under exceptional circumstances.

This case discusses two issues: (a) whether a son, who has attained the age of majority, is entitled to be maintained by his father; and (b) whether the executing court has jurisdiction to compel the father to pay the maintenance to his adult son on the basis of the decree which was delivered in his minority. The respondent, Arsalan, being the minor son of the appellant, filed a suit for maintenance against his father. The suit was decreed in his favour. While the execution petition filed by the respondent was pending, the appellant on 14 September 2011 moved an application before the executing court maintaining that the decree-holder attained the age of majority on 1 March 2011, and therefore, the appellant is no more under the obligation to pay maintenance. Furthermore, the executing court ceased to have any jurisdiction in the matter, hence the execution petition be dismissed. The executing court dismissed the application and held that the father could not be absolved of his responsibilities to maintain his minor son. Furthermore, the court held that it is in the interest of justice that the father should maintain his son until he completes his education and starts working. The father challenged this decision before the High Court in a writ petition that was dismissed. Therefore, an appeal was filed before the Supreme Court.

The counsel for the appellant relied upon various judicial authorities establishing that a father is not bound to maintain his male child after he attains the age of majority. Moreover, the father is not bound to bear the study expenses of his major son. Furthermore, the counsel contended that the respondent was 19 years of age and was studying in Australia. His mother, who was divorced by the appellant had sent him there without the consent of the appellant. Additionally, the respondent kept no contact with the appellant; therefore, the appellant is not bound to maintain an estranged son. The counsel argued that after the son has attained the age of majority the decree against the appellant lapsed and the executing court divested of its jurisdiction to execute the decree. On the contrary, the counsel for the respondent contended that the respondent was still studying and was not able to maintain himself, hence the appellant was under a duty to maintain his son until he completes his education and becomes capable of earning his livelihood.

The court referred to the definition of maintenance as given in D.F. Mulla's *Muhammadan Law*. According to Mulla, maintenance includes food, clothing, and lodging. The court noted that this definition is neither conclusive nor exhaustive. It should be given a wider meaning for the purposes of meeting the present-day needs in respect of social, physical, and mental growth, upbringing, and well-being of the minor while keeping in mind the status of the family, the norms of the society, and his/her educational requirements, but obviously corresponding to the means and the capacity of the father to pay. The court observed that, generally, the father is only bound to maintain his son until he attains puberty unless the son is disabled by some infirmity or disease. However, the court noted that the scope of this exemption has now been extended to include those children who have not yet completed their basic education and are unable to earn their livelihood. The court also relied upon the dictum in *Alaf Din v Parveen Akhtar*,[12] whereby the Supreme Court held:

> Normally a child, after attaining majority, would be physically in a position to maintain itself, for, it would then be capable of earning some kind of a livelihood. But this again is a question which will depend upon the status and circumstances of each individual family … an infirm or decrepit or deformed son or daughter may be entitled to claim maintenance even up to a very advanced age, while an able-bodied son or daughter may be deprived of the right if he/she has already found suitable gainful employment and is in a position to maintain himself or herself. Again in interpreting the word 'maintenance' some reasonable standard must be adopted. Whilst it is not confined merely to food, clothing and lodging, it cannot, by any stretch of imagination, be extended to incorporate within it education at higher levels *ad finitum*. What is necessary to decide in this connection is to find out as to what amount of education has to be attained by the child concerned, having regard to the status and other circumstances of his family, to enable it to earn a complete livelihood by honest and decent means.[13]

The court noted that the obligation of the father to maintain his son, who has not yet achieved his basic education enabling him to earn his livelihood, might be considered by a court in an independent suit considering all relevant factors. This situation falls within the exception to the general rule laid down by Mulla and various factors need to be kept in mind in this regard. Thereafter, the court enlisted the following factors: age (of adult son); whether he has his own resources to sustain his studies; the nature and stage of his studies; his academic results; his fervour and zeal for education and the extent of education which is essential to enable him to earn a livelihood. The court held that this shall not include higher studies and education abroad, especially where the (adult) son has gone aboard for such education either on his own, without there being any promise by the father, or at the behest of someone else who had assured to support him. Moreover, it must be considered if the son shows respect towards his father and is not a disobedient or estranged son. A father's capacity to pay is another important factor to be duly considered.

The court also observed that once the respondent attained majority, the decree of maintenance passed in his favour during his minority becomes non-executable and the executing court is divested of jurisdiction to enforce such decree or to extend its life. Therefore, the appeal was allowed and the entitlement of the respondent to be maintained for his higher education after attaining majority was left to be decided through an independent suit.

Saifuddin v Mubarak Sawal 2009 YLR 1226 (Karachi)

An adult student is not entitled to be maintained by his father with a meagre income.

This case deals with the issue of whether a father is bound to maintain his son who has attained majority. A suit was filed against the petitioner by his ex-wife for recovery of her own maintenance and that of her son. The Family Court decreed the suit. Two appeals were preferred against the judgment whereby the Appellate Court upheld the judgment of the Family Court with a slight modification. The maintenance for the ex-wife was granted for the same period and at the same rate as fixed by the Family Court. However, the maintenance allowance for the petitioner's son who was a student of MBBS was increased by the Appellate Court from Rs 2,000 per month to Rs 8,000 per month. The father filed a writ petition before the High Court against the decision of the Appellate Court.

The High Court had to ascertain whether the petitioner was in a position to maintain his son who attained the age of majority and was in the fourth year of MBBS. The court noted:

> It is a settled principle that a father is bound to pay the children/son only up to the age of attaining the majority and that after the son attains such age of the majority, the son would not be entitled to receive the maintenance allowance from the father, except in the exceptional circumstances, [the] burden of which lies upon the son to prove that the circumstances around him are such that though he has attained the age of majority, even then the father would be liable to continue to pay to him towards maintenance, as otherwise the future of the son would be at stake, and as and when such extraordinary circumstances as proved by the son [*sic*], the Court may in its discretion direct the father to go on paying the maintenance allowance to the son, even he may have attained the age of majority.[14]

In the instant case, the petitioner presented evidence showing that the profits earned by him on his savings, amounted to Rs 37,500 per month. He further pleaded that the said amount was spent on his own medical treatment and the treatment of his ailing wife. He did not have any other source of income; hence, he could not pay for the maintenance of his adult son. The respondents could not produce any such evidence strengthening their case except the evidence relating to the petitioner's income arising out of his savings that was produced by the petitioner himself. The adult son could not show that the petitioner had any extra income enabling him to continue paying towards his maintenance. Therefore, he was held to be not entitled to any maintenance. The constitutional petition was allowed, and the impugned judgments were set aside to the extent of awarding a maintenance allowance to the adult son.

Sultan Ahmad v Judge Family Court PLD 2012 Lah 148

A grandfather is liable to maintain the grandchildren if the father fails to do so.

This judgment lays down the principle about the responsibility of a grandfather for the maintenance of his needy minor grandchildren in case the judgment debtor father fails to do so. Brief facts of the case are such that respondents no. 2 to 5 filed a suit for maintenance allowance, which was decreed by the Family Court. The decree-holders filed an execution petition whereby the judgment debtor father was arrested for his failure to satisfy the decree. He was freed after one year. For the realisation of the maintenance expenses, the executing court attached a house that belonged to the grandfather of the minors and ordered its auction. The order of the attachment was assailed through the present petition by the petitioner grandfather. Along with other arguments, the counsel for the petitioner submitted that the petitioner was not a party to the suit, and hence, the house could not be auctioned. Moreover, the counsel claimed that the judgment debtor was a physically and mentally fit person; hence, the decree could be executed only against him and not against any other person.

The court noted that the petitioner is the grandfather of the minors/decree-holders, while the father is the judgment debtor who is hiding himself to avoid satisfying the decree. In such circumstances, the minors cannot be left unattended. The court relied upon a judicial authority establishing the following principle:

> It is from the … provisions of the Islamic Law on the question of the obligations and rights of the opulent and needy relations in Muslim society that as [a] corollary it has been unquestionably accepted that a grandfather in easy circumstances is bound to maintain and support his needy grandchildren.[15]

In light of the above-stated principle and circumstances of the instant case, the court held that the petitioner being the grandfather of respondents no. 3 to 5, is bound to maintain them in the absence of their father. The petition was dismissed accordingly.

4.2.3 Quantum of Maintenance Allowance. The case law with regard to the quantum of maintenance shows that, in order to determine the amount to be paid by the husband/father, the courts take into account all the relevant circumstances—the needs of the claimants as well as the status and income of the defendant.

Tauqeer Ahmad Qureshi v Additional District Judge, Lahore PLD 2009 SC 760

The Quantum of maintenance is to be determined by taking into account the status and income of the father.

This case emphasises that the Family Court is required to adopt a holistic approach while fixing the quantum of maintenance. Respondents no. 2 and 3 were the daughters of the appellant. They filed a suit against the appellant in 2002 for the recovery of maintenance allowance. The Family Court decreed the suit in 2003 and ordered the appellant to pay Rs 3,000 per month to each minor, with a 20 per cent yearly increase with effect from 4 March 2002. Both parties filed appeals, which were dismissed by the Appellate Court in 2004. The High Court dismissed the writ petition of the father against the Appellate Court decision.

In 2005, the respondents/minors filed an execution petition. The appellant filed an application in the executing court requesting the payment of arrears of maintenance allowance in easy instalments. The executing court allowed the appellant to pay the arrears in instalments of Rs 12,000 per month. This order of the executing court was again assailed by the respondents/minors through a revision petition. In light of this petition, the appellant was directed to pay the arrears in monthly instalments of Rs 50,000. The petitioner challenged the order through a writ petition. The court rejected the argument of the appellant's counsel that a 20 per cent yearly increase in the maintenance allowance awarded to the respondents by the Family Court was without jurisdiction. The court, however, granted him partial relief by directing the appellant to pay the maintenance allowance at the rate as decreed by the Family Court from 1 April 2008, and to deposit a sum of Rs 15,000 per month to be adjusted against maintenance arrears. Thereafter, the appellant filed a civil petition before the Supreme Court in which leave to appeal was granted.

The counsel for the appellant argued that the appellant has been paying the maintenance allowance at the rate of Rs 3,000 per month from 4 March 2002 as decreed by the Family Court. The appellant urged that the second part of the decree passed by the Family Court whereby a 20 per cent yearly increase in maintenance amount was ordered could not be executed. He argued that it was not asked for in the plaint and it was neither fair nor reasonable. The total maintenance allowance payable by the appellant along with a 20 per cent annual increase at the end would amount to Rs 68,800,000. The appellant further submitted that the Family Court ordered the increase while keeping in account the rising rate of inflation, but it was mere speculation because the situation might reverse in future, and in any case, the respondents/minors could always resort to the Family Court for enhancement in the rate of maintenance allowance. The appellant submitted that he was suffering from schizophrenia and was employed in a temporary job from which he only earned Rs 20,000 per month. On the contrary, the counsel for the respondents argued that the appellant had not challenged the annual increase in the maintenance allowance before the Appellate Court or the High Court, hence the decree attained finality and was a past and closed transaction. He further submitted that the appellant's monthly salary was Rs 50,000. After hearing the arguments, the court held:

> The minors are entitled to be maintained by the father in the manner befitting the status and financial condition of the father and for this reason the Family Court is under obligation while granting the maintenance allowance, to keep in mind the financial condition and status of the father. It has to make an inquiry in this regard. It cannot act arbitrarily and whimsically. Furthermore, at the same time, unjust enrichment of the minors cannot be permitted at the cost [of] the father.[16]

In the instant case, there was nothing on record to show that the appellant/father was a rich man who could afford to pay a total of Rs 68,800,000 towards the maintenance of the minors. Moreover, the Family Court had no basis before it for granting the yearly increase of 20 per cent in the maintenance allowance awarded to the respondents. A father's obligation to maintain his minor children is only to the extent of his financial status. For the foregoing reasons, the court reduced the annual increase in the maintenance allowance of the respondents/minors from 20 to 5 per cent.

4.2.4 Procedure. The following cases suggest that in order to safeguard the rights of wife and children, the courts have softened the rigidity of various formal legal procedures related to the issue of maintenance. In *Muhammad Ali v Judge Family Court, Depalpur*,[17] the court held that the principle of *res judicata* does not apply in maintenance cases. Similarly, in another case the court declared that interim maintenance can be awarded to ameliorate the financial problems of the claimants and the same cannot be challenged in a writ petition.[18]

Muhammad Ali v Judge Family Court, Depalpur 2010 YLR 520 (Lah)

The principle of *res judicata* does not apply in maintenance cases.

This case has already been discussed above; but, in this section, we shall focus on the principle of *res judicata* in cases of recovery of maintenance for progeny. The writ petition was filed against two impugned judgments dated 20 March 2008 and 17 June 2009. The first suit was dismissed on technical grounds, while the second suit for recovery of maintenance by respondent no. 3 (daughter) against the petitioner father was decreed. The petitioner brought the matter before the High Court agitating against the quantum and period of maintenance allowed in favour of respondent no. 3 on numerous grounds *inter alia* the principle of *res judicata*.

The counsel for the petitioner argued that respondent no. 3's first suit for recovery of maintenance was dismissed on merit; hence, the principle of *res judicata* was applicable against the initiation of the second suit. Justice Jamila Jahanoor Aslam noted that the first suit was not dismissed on merit rather it was dismissed on the basis of a technicality namely that respondent no. 3 being a major, who should have filed the suit herself, filed her suit through her mother as her next friend. This technicality could have been fixed by directing respondent no. 3 to file an amended plaint in her name. Hence, it was not dismissed on merit. It was noted that the principle of *res judicata* does not have much relevance in matters pertaining to recovery of maintenance as new circumstances may require the courts to determine the nature of liability and the amount of maintenance afresh. So far as the merit of the petition was concerned, the court held that the petitioner was legally bound to maintain her adult daughter (respondent no. 3) till she married. The petition was dismissed accordingly.

Zulfiqar Ali v Shazia Bibi 2009 SCMR 1037

Pending the suit before the Family Court, a parallel proceeding for the recovery of maintenance could not be initiated before the arbitration council.

This case discusses the scope of the authority of the arbitration council to grant maintenance to a wife and a minor. The respondent, Shazia Bibi was married to the petitioner Zulfiqar Ali on 3 April 1999. They were blessed with two sons and one daughter. While the respondent's suit for recovery of maintenance for herself and her children was pending before the Family Court, the petitioner divorced her on 15 March 2007. During the pendency of the suit the respondent also filed a suit for maintenance before respondent no. 2, *nazim*, union council as chairman arbitration council on 16 November 2006. Respondent no. 2 issued a certificate in favour of the respondent, granting her maintenance at the rate of Rs 5,000 per month from the date of the marriage onwards. The petitioner challenged this order through a revision petition, but it was dismissed. The petitioner then filed a writ petition that was also dismissed. Therefore, he filed an appeal before the Supreme Court.

The counsel for the petitioner argued that during the pendency of the suit before the Family Court, the respondent agitated the same cause for the same relief before the arbitration council. Hence, the chairman arbitration council could not commence any proceedings in this regard as the Family Court, where the suit was initially filed, had the exclusive jurisdiction to adjudicate upon the matter at hand. Therefore, the issuance of a certificate awarding maintenance allowance at the rate of Rs 5,000 per month for an indefinite period was unlawful, as the marriage bond between the spouses had already broken down upon the pronouncement of divorce on 15 March 2007. The respondent was not entitled to past maintenance as there was nothing on record to show that the petitioner had not maintained her when she was residing with him. The petitioner's counsel also challenged the validity of the constitution of the arbitration council.

The court, after hearing the arguments, noted that it is true that the arbitration council has the authority to award maintenance under section 9(2) of the MFLO, but it is not fair that parallel proceedings for the same cause and relief should be allowed to the respondent, as it may result in contradictory decisions. The suit filed by the respondent for recovery of maintenance for herself and the minor was prior in time to the application filed by her before the arbitration council, hence she could not be allowed to proceed with the latter application, as she had already resorted to the exclusive jurisdiction of the Family Court. The maintenance granted by the chairman was awarded without taking into account the fact that the petitioner divorced the respondent. Furthermore, maintenance could not be awarded to the divorced wife from the date of her marriage onward without specifying the point of termination. Even the grant of maintenance from 1 May 1999 was illegal because there was no proof that the petitioner was not maintaining the respondent. The grant of maintenance for a period of more than three years was illegal, as the arbitration council had no power to grant maintenance against the law of limitation. Furthermore, the arbitration council was not validly constituted as no representative had been appointed from the petitioner's side. There was nothing on record to show that the petitioner had been issued a notice to nominate his representative and he had failed to do the same. Hence, the order of the Lahore High Court upholding the certificate of maintenance issued by the arbitration council was set aside.

Abrar Hussain v Mehwish Rana PLD 2012 Lah 420

The objective of awarding interim maintenance is to ameliorate the financial problems of minors, and it cannot be challenged in a writ petition raising new issues of facts which require the recording of evidence.

This case elaborates on the object and scope of interim maintenance. In this case, respondent no. 1 got married to the petitioner in 1996. Respondents no. 2 and 3 were born in wedlock. In 2007, the relationship between the spouses became strained. Consequently, the petitioner expelled the respondents from his house and did not pay any maintenance allowance.

In 2010, the respondents filed a suit for the recovery of dowry articles and maintenance. They also filed an application for the recovery of interim maintenance. During the pendency of the case, the petitioner divorced respondent no. 1. The Family Court fixed the interim maintenance allowance at the rate of Rs 10,000 per month per head. The petitioner, being aggrieved by the decision, challenged it before the High Court.

The counsel for the petitioner contended that the quantum of interim maintenance as fixed by the Family Court was exorbitant and beyond the means of the petitioner, as the petitioner resigned from his job in 2010 and was unemployed at the time of the petition. He argued that the Family Court is required to fix the interim maintenance according to the financial status of the parties. On the other hand, the counsel for the respondents argued that the petitioner was a retired Major from Pakistan Army, and his monthly pension was more than Rs 30,000. Apart from his pension, he worked at a multinational company and drew a very handsome salary. He also owned various commercial and residential properties from which he received a rent of more than Rs 300,000 per month. Moreover, respondents no. 2 and 3 had been admitted to the Beaconhouse School System by the petitioner himself where the monthly fee was more than Rs 12,000 per month. The maintenance as fixed was already too meagre to meet the expenses of the minor respondents.

After hearing the arguments and perusing the record, the court noted that the Family Court is empowered to grant interim maintenance during the pendency of the proceedings to ameliorate the financial constraints faced by the minors. The court observed that while fixing the quantum of interim maintenance, a judge must look broadly into the social status of the parties; the amount the defendant earned; his capacity to pay and the requirements of the minors. Since such an order is interim in nature and is not appealable, the court must be very careful in fixing such maintenance to avoid any possibility of injustice. Furthermore, the court evaluated the written statement filed by the petitioner to determine his earnings and capacity to pay. The contents of the written statement proved that the petitioner was a rich man. Hence, the quantum of the interim maintenance fixed in the impugned order was not exorbitant. The court noted that the petitioner raised disputed questions of facts regarding his resignation from the job, source of income, and social status. However, it is not possible to determine the truth of these claims without recording evidence. Such exercise cannot be undertaken by the court in its constitutional jurisdiction, especially when the finding is interim in nature, thus the petition was dismissed.

The High Court delved into the question of exercising the jurisdiction under Article 199 of the Constitution against an interim order particularly when the relevant statute has specifically ousted an appeal against such orders. The court observed that this exceptional jurisdiction could only be resorted to when the impugned interim order is *void ab initio* and without jurisdiction. However, in those cases where the courts are competent to pass such orders and they have issued them after giving a proper opportunity of hearing to the parties, like the present petition, the petitions are not maintainable under the law.

Farkhanda Mumtaz v Muhammad Sharif PLD 2006 Pesh 96

The period of limitation for a suit for recovery of past maintenance is six years.

In this case, the court held that a wife could seek past maintenance from her husband for a maximum period of six years. The petitioner, Farkhanda Mumtaz, filed a suit against her husband (respondent) for recovery of dowry articles and maintenance and the respondent filed a suit for restitution of conjugal rights. The discussion will focus on the suit for maintenance. The facts of the case according to the petitioner's claim are that after the parties' marriage in 1968, the respondent left for Dubai. The respondent neglected the petitioner and failed to provide her with any maintenance since 1996. The trial court dismissed the petitioner's suit and decreed the respondent's suit for restitution of conjugal rights. This is one of the rare cases in which the court decreed a suit for restitution of conjugal rights. The petitioner filed an appeal before the District Judge. The District Judge passed a decree for the recovery of maintenance at Rs 3,000 from January 2002 for the future without passing any order as to past maintenance. Both the parties filed writ petitions before the High Court.

The counsel for the petitioner argued that she was entitled to receive maintenance for a period of six years preceding the institution of the suit. On the other hand, the counsel for the respondent claimed that since the petitioner left her husband's house of her own free will, she is not entitled to any maintenance allowance and hence the decree passed by the District Judge should be struck down.

The court observed that the petitioner successfully established that the respondent failed to maintain her and in circumstances when the respondent was residing in Dubai with his second wife, it was immaterial whether the petitioner left the house at her own volition, or the respondent expelled her. It was the responsibility of the respondent to maintain his wife. Regarding past maintenance, the court concluded that 'the law is well settled that suits for past maintenance are governed by article 120 of the Limitation Act, 1908 that prescribe a period of 6 years from the date of accrual of cause of action.'[19]

Considering the factual position and the legal entitlement of the petitioner, the court decreed her suit for maintenance at the rate of Rs 3,000 per month for a period of six years preceding the institution of suit and onwards.

4.3 Conclusion

Entitlement to maintenance is one of the important aspects of family law. There is a plethora of case law on this subject which highlights the progressive approach of Pakistani courts to protect the financial interests of wives and children. An analysis of the case law discussed in this chapter reflects that important principles pertaining to the right of maintenance of wives and children have already been settled. With regard to a wife's entitlement to maintenance, it has been held that maintenance is neither a gift nor a benefit but an undeniable legal obligation of a husband towards his wife. The trends in case law reveal that the judges take a favourable approach towards a wife's right to maintenance. The courts have established that the right to maintenance during *iddat* period is not forfeited when a wife dissolves her marriage on the basis of *khula*. It is also well-established that the mere fact that a wife is residing away from her husband does not absolve the latter of his responsibility to provide maintenance to the former provided she has a lawful excuse to do so. However, the courts do not blindly favour the wife in every case, rather they tend to take a more balanced approach by relieving the husband of his liability to pay maintenance in circumstances that warrant such exemption. In cases where the wife resides away from the husband without any reasonable cause, the wife is denied past maintenance as it can only be claimed by a wife who is willing to perform her marital obligations.

The courts have established that a father is to maintain the children born during the marriage: sons until they attain the age of majority and daughters until they are married, irrespective of the fact that they live away from the father with the divorced mother or whether their mother earns a livelihood. Moreover, the courts have been considerate in regard to the financial difficulties faced by divorced or widowed daughters and have assigned the responsibility of their maintenance to their fathers. The judiciary has also been progressive and thoughtful in its approach towards grant of maintenance to adopted children by resorting to the doctrine of constructive guardianship and making the adopting father responsible for their maintenance. The development of this principle through an ingenious application of the principles of equity is a laudable act.

Furthermore, the courts have extended the definition of maintenance to include the social, physical, and mental growth, upbringing, and well-being of the minor, while keeping in mind the status of the family, the norms of the society, and his/her educational requirements, but obviously corresponding to the means and the capacity of the father to pay. It means that a father might be required to maintain his adult son until the completion of his education under exceptional circumstances. Again, the courts have adopted a very reasonable approach in giving extended meaning and scope to the word 'maintenance' which includes the education necessary to enable him/her to earn a decent livelihood. If a father is unable to provide maintenance, then the grandfather is liable to provide maintenance to his grandchildren. This shows that the courts have gone to the maximum extent possible in ensuring that the children are well taken care of by their fathers or grandfathers and are not left at the mercy of anyone else.

As regards the quantum of maintenance, the courts have established that it is to be fixed while keeping in account the requirements of the claimant and the resources of the father. However, the courts have relieved the wives of the responsibility of proving their husbands' real income by documentary evidence in the courts as it is impracticable to expect wives to collect evidence against their husbands when they are living together in a friendly and peaceful atmosphere. The courts have adopted a dynamic approach in this regard by fixing maintenance after evaluating the entire evidence and circumstances, and not taking husbands for their words. Furthermore, the case law suggests that courts are now more sceptical of the suits filed by husbands for restitution of conjugal rights as most of the time, they are not filed *bona fide* and are merely resorted to as a calculated attempt to counter the suits for maintenance filed by the wives.

The way the jurisprudence is unfolding, in respect of maintenance cases, suggests that the courts are likely to adopt a more progressive and dynamic approach in future by granting wives and children extensive maintenance rights, but at the same time, balancing them against the earning capacities of their husbands and fathers.

Questions

1. What is maintenance and how does a court determine the quantum of maintenance?
2. Who has the right to maintenance and why? Why should old fathers maintain divorced adult daughters, especially when they are earning their living?
3. Do adopted children have a right to be maintained by the adopting father despite the fact that under Islamic law adoption does not establish the relationship of parentage? Should this right be extended to illegitimate children against the biological father?
4. Is a beneficiary of a right to maintenance (child or wife) required to obey the person who provides maintenance (father or husband)?

Further Reading

BOOKS

Mulla, *Principles of Mahomedan Law* (Haryana: LexisNexis, 2013), 351–57, 454–58.
Tanzil-ur-Rahman, Dr, *A Code of Muslim Personal Law*, vol. 1 (Karachi: Hamdard Academy 1978), 257–88.

CASES

Ali Adnan Dar v Judge Family Court PLD 2016 Lah 73 (The Family Court has the power to pass interim maintenance order at any stage of the suit. Such an order is normally passed after the filing of a written statement by the defendant.)

Ali Haider v Syed Muhammad Asghar Shah 2015 YLR 511 (A father is bound to maintain his children till they attain the age of majority in the case of a son and, till her marriage, in the case of a daughter. The law does not debar children to claim maintenance allowance from their father even after attaining the age of majority. However, if children after becoming major have their independent sources of income, then the father is not bound to maintain them.)

Hassan Ahmad Kanwar v Adnan Hassan 2020 CLC 1701 (Lah) (When the legal heirs are enjoying the property of the deceased grandfather, they are bound to maintain the grandson through maintenance allowance and also give a due share in the property.)

Lt. Col. Nasir Malik v Additional District Judge, Lahore 2016 SCMR 1821 (An application can be filed in the Family Court for enhancement of maintenance after the court has awarded it and there is no need to file a fresh suit.)

Muhammad Najeeb v Talat Shahnaz 1989 SCMR 119 (When an application is filed by an ex-wife for maintenance for the period when the wedlock was intact and also for the *iddat* period, she would be covered by the word 'wife' as contained in section 9 of the MFLO.)

Muhammad Nawaz v Khurshid Begum PLD 1972 SC 302 (The arbitration council is competent to award past maintenance subject to the question of limitation.)

Muhammad Nawazish Ali v Family Judge 2021 CLC 1841 (Lah) (Where a father could not be traced or is living abroad, the grandfather is required to pay for the maintenance of grandchildren.)

Sardar Muhammad v Mst Nasima Bibi PLD 1966 Lahore 703 (The mere fact that a neglected wife has been hesitant in promptly coming to the Court or has been pursuing alternative remedies out of Court cannot in all fairness be construed as to deprive her of the right of maintenance from the day when the cause of action accrued to her.)

Syeda Adrish v Syed Anwar-ul-Haq PLD 2011 Lah 569 (An unwilling wife without a lawful excuse could not recover past maintenance.)

Notes

1. Under Islamic law, persons are bound to maintain their poor relatives within the prohibited degrees in proportion to their share which they would inherit from them after their death.
2. Terms such as '*mut'a*' and '*ta'wid*' are also used for *mata'a*. L. Welchman, *Women and Muslim Family Laws in Arab States* (Amsterdam: Amsterdam University Press 2007), 185–90.
3. Report 103 on Post-Divorce Mata'a for Wife, available at <http://ljcp.gov.pk/lfr/103/> (accessed 25 July 2016).
4. 2012 CLC 1272, 1273.
5. PLD 2013 SC 557.
6. PLD 2015 Lah 336.
7. 2015 MLD 11, 16.
8. 2010 MLD 695, 698.
9. PLD 2012 Lah 154.
10. 2012 MLD 1394, 1399.
11. .PLD 2012 Lah 154, 158.
12. PLD 1970 SC 75.
13. Ibid.
14. 2009 YLR 1226, 1229.
15. PLD 1976 Lah 930 as quoted in PLD 2012 Lah 148, 149.
16. PLD 2009 SC 760, 766.
17. 2010 YLR 520 (Lah).
18. PLD 2012 Lah 420.
19. PLD 2006 Pesh 96, 98.

5

DISSOLUTION OF MARRIAGE

5.1 Introduction

A spouse may dissolve the marriage either without assigning a cause (no-fault-based) or after assigning a cause (fault-based) pertaining to the conduct of the other spouse. A husband can pronounce a *talaq* without assigning any reason. Likewise, a wife can ask for *khula*. The distinction between the two lies in the procedure. In case the husband does not agree to dissolve the marriage, the wife needs to approach a court. While a husband does not need the wife's consent for *talaq* and is entitled to dissolve the marriage without judicial intervention; the wife needs to justify her decision in a court by declaring that her marriage has irretrievably broken down and it is not possible for her to live with her husband 'within the limits prescribed by Allah'.[1]

A marriage can also be dissolved with the mutual consent of spouses. This type of dissolution of marriage is called *mubarat*. Spouses may agree on the dissolution of their marriage without the intervention of the court. Under certain circumstances, either spouse may go to court for dissolution of marriage. Since a husband's right to divorce is absolute, it is usually the wife who goes to the court for dissolution of her marriage. This type of dissolution is called *faskh*, and it can only be availed under specific circumstances. Section 2 of the Dissolution of Muslim Marriages Act 1939 (DMMA) provides the following grounds for the dissolution of marriage:

1. The disappearance of the husband for four years.
2. Husband's failure to provide maintenance for two years.
3. Husband's final sentence to imprisonment for seven or more years.
4. Husband's failure to perform his marital obligations for three years.

5. Husband's impotence at the time of marriage and its continuity.
6. Husband's insanity for two years or suffering from leprosy or virulent venereal disease.
7. Wife given in marriage by her father or another guardian before she attained the age of 16 years, repudiates the marriage before attaining the age of 18 years, provided that the marriage has not been consummated.
8. *Li'an*: where the husband has accused his wife of *zina* and the wife does not accept the accusations as true.
9. Cruel treatment of the wife by the husband (includes mental cruelty, association with women of ill-repute or leading an infamous life, forcing a wife to live an immoral life, interference with wife's property, obstruction in her observance of religious profession or practice, and failure to treat wives equitably, in case of polygamy).
10. Any other ground recognised as valid under Muslim law.

Under the Muslim Family Laws Ordinance 1961 (MFLO), a husband's taking of an additional wife without the consent of the first wife as required under the Ordinance was incorporated as an additional ground for the dissolution of marriage.[2] However, this ground was removed in 1981 under Zia ul-Haq's Islamisation of laws.[3]

A decree of dissolution of marriage passed on the basis of the disappearance of a husband for four years shall take effect after six months, and if the husband appears either in person or through an authorised agent within that period and satisfies the court that he is prepared to perform his conjugal duties, the court shall set aside the said decree.[4]

Before passing a decree on grounds of the impotency of the husband, the law provides a husband with a chance to prove otherwise. Therefore, the court shall on application of the husband, make an order requiring the husband to satisfy the court within a period of one year that he has ceased to be impotent, and if the husband so satisfies the court, no decree shall be passed on this ground.[5]

A marriage terminates automatically with the death or apostasy of either spouse.[6] A widow has to observe *iddat* for a period of four months and ten days, and if she is pregnant at the time of the death of her husband or if during the *iddat* period, it appears that she is pregnant, then until the delivery.

In the following paragraphs, further details on various types of dissolution of marriage are provided.

5.2 *Talaq*

The word *talaq* literally means 'freedom from bondage'. As mentioned earlier, it is the absolute right of the husband to pronounce *talaq*. He may exercise this right in one of the following ways:

1. *Ahsan*: A single pronouncement of *talaq* made during a period between menstruations (*tuhr*), followed by abstinence from sexual intercourse during the *iddat* period. This is the ideal form of *talaq* under Islamic law.
2. *Hasan:* Three successive pronouncements of *talaq* during three successive periods between menstruations (*tuhr*), with no sexual intercourse during the *tuhr*. It is a lesser approved form of *talaq* than *ahsan*.
3. *Bidat*: Three pronouncements of *talaq* on a single occasion at any time (during menstruation or non-menstruation period). It is also commonly referred to as a triple *talaq*. It is disapproved (*makruh*) but is still valid according to a majority of Muslim jurists. Such a *talaq* becomes effective immediately and is irrevocable.

Ahsan and *Hasan* are also called *talaq as-sunna*.

With regard to its legal effects, *talaq* is divided into *Raja'i* and *Ba'in*. *Raja'i* (revocable) may be a single or double pronouncement of *talaq*. A husband may revoke it during the *iddat* period. The revocation may be by words or deeds. *Ba'in* (irrevocable) is further divided into *Bainunah sughra* (irrevocable divorce of minor degree) and *Bainunah kubra* (irrevocable divorce of major degree).

Bainunah sughra talaq becomes irrevocable when a husband pronounces it once or twice and does not revoke it during the *iddat* period. *Talaq* also becomes irrevocable if it happens before the consummation of marriage or through *khula* or *faskh* (judicial decree). In these circumstances, the couple can remarry by entering into a new marriage contract.

A *talaq* becomes irrevocable to a major degree when a husband pronounces it thrice either simultaneously or in three successive periods. It becomes effective immediately in the first situation, while in the second, it becomes irrevocable on the third pronouncement. After this *talaq*, the divorcee cannot remarry her ex-husband without an intervening marriage (*halala*).

5.2.1 *Tafwid al-Talaq*. A husband may delegate his right of *talaq* to his wife or to a third person, either conditionally or absolutely. Such delegation may be made at the time of marriage or after it. Once the right of *talaq* is delegated to the wife, the husband cannot withdraw it unless it has been agreed otherwise, though he still retains the right to *talaq*. An example of a conditional delegation of the right of *talaq* is that the wife shall have this right if the husband enters into a second marriage without the consent of the first wife, or if he fails to provide her maintenance for a specified period.

5.2.2 *Khula*. Divorce at the instance of the wife, where she agrees to relinquish her dower in exchange, is called a *khula*.[7] This is a wife's right to end the marriage, comparable to a man's right of *talaq*. It operates as a single irrevocable divorce (*talaq e ba'in*), and the wife can remarry her ex-husband without an intervening marriage (*halala*).

5.2.3 *Mubarat* (dissolution through mutual consent). This is the dissolution of marriage with the consent of both the husband and the wife. It may be conditional or unconditional, and the wife may or may not surrender the dower, or any other right, to the husband in exchange. Like *khula*, it takes effect as a single irrevocable divorce and the couple may remarry without an intervening marriage (*halala*).

In addition to the above, Muslim jurists also recognise the following circumstances that may cause the dissolution of marriage.

5.2.4 Li'an (Imprecation). The term literally means 'mutual cursing'. If a husband accuses his wife of adultery, the wife denies it, and there is no evidence to substantiate this claim, a judge asks them to provide testimony on oath. The husband will say four times, 'I swear by Allah that I am surely truthful in my accusation of adultery against my wife', and the fifth time he will say, 'Allah's curse be upon me if I am a liar in my accusation of adultery against my wife'. After the husband's oath, the wife will say four times, 'I swear by Allah that my husband is surely a liar in his accusation of adultery against me', and the fifth time she will say, 'Allah's wrath be upon me if he is truthful in his accusation of adultery against me'. Once this process is complete, the judge dissolves their marriage.

5.2.5 *Ila* (Vow of continence). In *ila*, the husband vows to abstain from sexual intercourse with the wife for a time period of four months or more.

The husband may revoke his vow and resume conjugal relations. If he does not do so, according to the Hanafi school, the marriage is dissolved without the order of the court after the expiry of four months.

5.2.6 *Zihar* (Injurious assimilation). *Zihar* is derived from *zahr* which means 'the back'. In *zihar*, the husband swears or solemnly states that, to him, his wife is like 'the back of his mother'. This is tantamount to saying that 'for me to have sexual relations with you would be like having sex with my mother'. During the pre-Islamic period, this statement of a husband kept the wife in limbo as to her status as a wife because she was not treated as a wife despite the fact that she was in a marital relationship. Husbands adopted this mode to intimidate their wives by keeping them uncertain about their marital status. However, Islam reformed this rule by requiring husbands either to revoke the vow after expiation or terminate the marriage. Under Islamic law, the husband can revoke this vow after (i) the manumission of a slave; (ii) fasting for two months; or (iii) feeding sixty poor persons. The wife has a right to go to court asking either for divorce or for restitution of conjugal rights upon expiation. The court can oblige the husband to expiate or repudiate his wife.

5.2.7 *Kafa'a*. *Kafa'a* literally means equality. One of the desirable conditions of a valid marriage is that the husband should be equal to the wife with respect to religion, family, profession, freedom, character, piety, and wealth. If the husband is not equal to the wife, the marriage could be dissolved by a judge at the instance of the wife, irrespective of whether she herself contracted the marriage or her guardian. As, traditionally, the wife takes the social status of her husband after marriage; therefore, this right is only available to the wife and there is no requirement that the wife should be equal to the husband in these respects.

5.2.8 Notice of *Talaq*. Under classical Islamic law, a marriage can be dissolved orally and there is no need for writing or registration. However, the significance of documentary evidence cannot be disregarded as an oral divorce can only be proved by the testimony of witnesses. Therefore, the absence of documentary evidence poses many problems in proving whether a marriage was validly dissolved. Such proof has crucial implications in criminal cases regarding sexual offences, and civil litigation relating to legitimacy and inheritance. To this end, section 7 of the MFLO requires a husband to give a written notice of *talaq* to the

Chairman of a Union Council and provide a copy to the wife. This section also applies to a wife if she exercises her right to delegated divorce, or dissolves the marriage based on *khula*. The Law & Justice Commission in its Report No. 74 of 2005 recommended that the notice should be given within seven days of the pronouncement of *talaq*; and where a husband fails to give such notice, the wife may give such notice to the Chairman. This recommendation, however, has not been incorporated into the MFLO.

In December 2021, the national legislature amended section 7 of the MFLO through the Muslim Family Laws (Second Amendment) Act 2021 to clarify that for *talaq* to become effective under *Fiqah-e-Jafria*, the husband must pronounce voluntarily and with his free will Arabic words (*seegha*) in the physical presence of two witnesses. It further provides that the pronouncement of *talaq* shall not be effective if it is done 'jokingly or under anger, intoxication, insanity, duress or coercion of any kind and from any corner.'

5.3 Outline of Case Law

5.3.1 Dissolution of Marriage under the DMMA. The DMMA provides various grounds to a wife for getting a decree of dissolution of marriage. In case law, the cruelty of a husband and his failure to provide maintenance to the wife are the two most referred grounds for dissolution of marriage. The reported judgments dealing with cruelty suggest that the courts tend to interpret this provision broadly. For instance, the courts have treated the husband's homosexuality and his habitual disagreements with the wife within the ambit of this provision.

Malik Tanveer Khan v Amber Liaqat 2009 CLC 1210 (Pesh)

The homosexuality of a husband is sufficient grounds for the dissolution of marriage on the basis of cruelty.

In this case, the marriage between the parties took place in 2006. The petitioner, the husband, was serving in the Pakistan Army as a lieutenant. After the marriage, he took his wife to Quetta to reside with him as he was posted there. After a short time, relations between the parties became strained. The respondent, the wife, came back to her parent's home in Abbottabad. She filed a suit for dissolution of marriage, recovery of dower and dowry articles, and maintenance allowance. In her petition, she stated that during her stay with the petitioner in Quetta, she learnt that he was a homosexual—a fact that was publicly known. Therefore, army officials conducted an inquiry against him, and consequently, his service was terminated. She asked the petitioner to mend his ways, but he did not care. The petitioner, on the other hand, asserted that the respondent was a crude, disobedient, and irresponsible woman. She often received phone calls from unknown people, and despite the petitioner's warning, she failed to mend her ways. The trial court decreed in favour of the wife and dismissed the husband's suit for restitution of conjugal rights.

Aggrieved by the decision of the trial court, the petitioner filed a writ petition before the High Court. Keeping in view the allegations levelled by the respondent against the petitioner, the court looked into the concept of marriage in Islam. It observed that one of the primary ends of marriage is the happy companionship of spouses. The court noted that there could be no happiness in marriage if the wife feels that her life had become miserable owing to the immoral and infamous lifestyle of her husband. The court observed that it was clear from the facts and circumstances of the case that there was hatred between the spouses. The court accepted the wife's allegation of cruelty, holding that cruelty does not need to be physical in all circumstances and mental torture may also qualify as cruelty in appropriate cases. The habits and conduct of the petitioner constituted 'a mental cruelty in the worst'[8] as he was a known homosexual. In view of the circumstances of the case, the court dismissed the petition as meritless.

Rukhsana Younas v Aziz-ur-Rehman 2014 CLC 1751 (Pesh)

Dissolution of marriage for non-payment of maintenance.

In this case, the plaintiff was the third wife of the defendant, who had not disclosed his earlier marriages to her. The marriage was solemnised in 2003. The husband and the in-laws maltreated the wife. In 2007, she was forced to leave her husband's house. She filed a suit for dissolution of marriage, and recovery of maintenance allowance, dowry articles, dower, and gold ornaments. The Family Court accepted her petition regarding the recovery of maintenance, dowry, and dower, but dismissed the suit for dissolution of marriage. At the same time, the husband's suit for restitution of conjugal rights was decreed. Both parties felt aggrieved and filed appeals. The Appellate Court upheld the decision of the Family Court. Thereafter, the case was brought before the High Court.

The court framed two basic issues: (i) whether the petitioner was entitled to the dissolution of marriage along with the recovery of dower and maintenance, or was she entitled to *khula* with no right to dower; and (ii) whether the petitioner was self-deserted and was not entitled to any relief, and the husband was entitled to the decree of restitution of conjugal rights as he had fulfilled all his legal obligations.

The court observed that the husband did not even bother to appear before the Family Court so that efforts for reconciliation could be made, and despite attaining the decree for restitution of conjugal rights, he did not make any attempt for its execution. This was substantial evidence of his indifference towards his wife. He had not maintained her for a period of about seven years and had also failed to provide any maintenance despite the court orders. Therefore, the court dissolved the marriage for the non-payment of maintenance under section 2(ii) of the DMMA. The court also accepted the wife's arguments on the ground of cruelty under the DMMA and absolved her from paying anything for the dissolution of the marriage.

Muhammad Zafar v Kamal Fatima PLD 1981 Lah 732

Habitual disagreements with the wife just to make her life miserable is cruelty.

In this case, the wife was a schoolteacher who filed a suit for dissolution of marriage on the basis of habitual cruelty of her husband, desertion, non-payment of maintenance for two years, non-performance of marital obligations, and misappropriation of dowry. The Family Court passed a decree for the dissolution of marriage. The petitioner challenged this decree before the High Court.

The counsel for the petitioner argued that the two pleas of the wife of desertion and habitual cruelty were mutually destructive since the husband could not treat her with cruelty while he had already deserted her. The court rejected this argument and observed that the respondent's evidence showed that the petitioner thrashed her outside the school where she was employed as a teacher. The petitioner's counsel further argued that differences of opinion between the spouses could not be regarded as cruelty by any stretch of the imagination. The court did not accept this argument and held that if a husband makes it a habit to disagree with his wife on each and every matter, 'without any rhyme or reason, and his conduct on this behalf is motivated by a desire to make her life miserable it would certainly amount to cruelty on his part.'[9]

5.3.2 *Tafwid al-Talaq*. The Muslim Family Laws Ordinance 1961 provides that the husband can delegate his right to divorce to the wife, exercisable by her or by a third party. The Federal Shariat Court held that the husband could delegate this right either absolutely or conditionally, for a particular period or permanently.[10] However, the Islamabad High Court held that this right should be strictly construed in order to avoid any unwarranted presumptions.[11]

Khawar Iqbal v Federation of Pakistan 2013 MLD 1711 (FSC)

Delegated divorce is recognised under Islamic law.

In this case, the petitioner challenged the legality of section 8 of the MFLO, which authorises a wife to exercise her delegated right of divorce, which is provided in Column No. 18 with the standard *nikahnama*. The petitioner had delegated the right to divorce to his wife, who later exercised it. The petitioner challenged the legality of his wife's action in a writ petition before the High Court, which dismissed his petition. His appeal before the Supreme Court also failed. Therefore, as a last resort, he filed a petition before the Federal Shariat Court (FSC) challenging the right of delegation of divorce on the basis of its repugnance to the injunctions of Islam as provided in the Qur'an and Sunnah.

The FSC described the function of *talaq al-tafwid* as a check on a husband who may be cruel to his wife; negligent in maintaining his children; deserts his wife for a prolonged period and still refuses to divorce her at any cost or does not agree to her right of *khula*. The court accepted that even though the power to divorce belongs to a husband, he can delegate this right to his wife or to a third person, either absolutely or conditionally or for a particular period or permanently. This position is agreed upon by jurists belonging to all four Sunni schools of thought. The jurists of Shia Jafaria school, however, do not allow such delegation.

In addition to identifying that there was no objection to the validity of delegated divorce from the Islamic perspective, the court pointed out that it did not have jurisdiction under the relevant constitutional provision to decide the dispute. The court referred to the definition of 'Muslim Personal Law' provided in *Dr Mahmood-ur-Rehman Faisal v Govt of Pakistan*,[12] as 'the personal law of each sect of Muslims based on the interpretation of the Qur'an and Sunnah by that sect'.[13] The court held that section 8 of the MFLO fell under the definition of Muslim Personal Law, which could not be challenged before the FSC.[14] Therefore, the petition was dismissed *in limine*.

Ali Abbas Khan v Palwasha Khan 2010 YLR 1632 [Islamabad]

Delegation of divorce should be made clear, and it cannot be assumed from ambiguous words.

In this case, the petitioner filed a writ petition before the High Court challenging the effectiveness of a divorce certificate issued by the chairman of the union council. The petitioner had married the woman in 2006. After some time, the spouses developed differences, and the wife sent her husband a divorce deed in 2008 on the basis of her right of divorce allegedly delegated to her by the husband in Column No. 18 of the standard *nikahnama*. She also sent a copy of the divorce deed to the Chairman Union Council. The Chairman issued an effectiveness of divorce certificate by accepting the notice of divorce by the wife. The husband had earlier disputed her claim that he delegated her the right to divorce and filed a suit for declaration and permanent injunction in the Civil Court, which was rejected. His appeal against this decision was also rejected. Thereafter, the husband filed a writ petition before the High Court.

Justice Syed Intikhab Hussain Shah strictly construed the words written by the parties in Column No. 18 of the standard *nikahnama*. He noted that Column No. 18 of the *nikahnama* deals with the issue of the delegation of the right of divorce to the wife. The parties had added the words '*sharai haqooq hasil hay*' (the rights granted by *shariah* are available) in this column of their *nikahnama*. The court held that these words did not delegate the right to divorce to the wife, as under *sharia* a wife is not originally entitled to exercise the right to divorce. Such right could only be delegated to her in an explicit manner and nothing short of this would amount to a delegation of divorce. Furthermore, the court held, 'if such type of words are allowed to be considered as a right of *talaq-e-tafweez* it would mean that whatever is incorporated against Column No. 18 would be presumed as a right of *talaq-e-tafweez*'.[15]

5.3.3 *Mubarat*

Sana Shehzad v Secretary Union Council PLD 2014 Lah 632

A husband cannot retract mutually agreed dissolution of marriage.

In this case, the parties were married in 2010. Two years later, their relationship became strained and the husband in the presence of witnesses pronounced *talaq* with mutual consent. He also reduced it to writing and filed an application with the union council stating that he had divorced his wife. The wife requested the secretary of the union council to issue a certificate of the effectiveness of divorce, which was refused on the ground that the husband had withdrawn the divorce before the expiry of ninety days. The wife filed a writ petition before the High Court.

The issue before the court was: whether a husband could withdraw a *talaq*, which is in the form of *mubarat*, during the *iddat* period (90 days). The court held that where divorce is affected with the consent of both parties and confirmed in writing, the requirement of sending a notice to the chairman under section 7 of the MFLO is a mere formality. In reaching this conclusion the court relied upon the principle laid down in *Kaneez Fatima v Wali Muhammad* (discussed below).[16] Furthermore, it was held that if a divorce was pronounced with mutual consent on the basis of *mubarat*, the husband could not retract or withdraw the divorce and the Chairman of the Union Council did not have any authority to adjudicate upon the validity/effectiveness of such divorce.

5.3.4 Evidence Required under the DMMA

Fida Hussain v Naseem Akhtar PLD 1977 Lah 328

Evidence of close relatives of a wife is admissible.

A suit for dissolution of marriage was decreed in favour of the wife on the ground that the husband treated her with habitual cruelty based on the evidence presented by her father and brother. The court took into consideration several scars on the wrists of the wife as proof of beating. The counsel of the husband argued that the statements of the woman's father and her brother were inadmissible in light of the principles of Islamic law of evidence. He contended that section 17 of the Family Courts Act 1964 specifically provides against the applicability of the Evidence Act 1872 (now Qanun-e-Shahadat Order 1984) and, as the matter of dissolution of marriage related to the personal law of the parties, the Family Court should have applied Islamic principles of evidence. If these principles were applied, the evidence of the father and brother of the wife should have been excluded. In that case, the solitary evidence of the respondent could not provide the basis for the decree of the dissolution of the marriage. At least two witnesses were required to support her claim.

He relied upon the *Hidaya* and traditions of the Prophet (PBUH) in support of his arguments.

Justice Aftab Hussain quoted the verses of the Qur'an and various traditions of the Prophet (PBUH) regarding the admissibility of evidence. He observed that the Prophet (PBUH) did not lay down any fixed or rigid rules of evidence, rather he administered justice keeping in view the circumstances of each case. Justice Hussain rejected the argument that at least two male witnesses or one male and two female witnesses are required to prove a matter under Islamic law. He held that the evidence of the father and the brother is admissible, though in some cases it cannot be relied upon. He emphasised the need for *ijtihad* and contended that although the Hanafi school does not accept the evidence of close relatives, the other three Sunni schools do. Therefore, the courts are not bound to follow the Hanafi school on this point.

Justice Hussain held that, in the present case, the evidence of three witnesses was corroborated by the various scars on the wrist of the respondent. In light of these reasons, he dismissed the petition.

5.3.5 *Khula* without the Consent of a Husband and Restitution of Conjugal Rights. The most important judicial development in Islamic divorce law in Pakistan has been the relinquishment of the requirement of the consent of the husband for *khula*. Previously, the legal position was that the consent of the husband was a necessary precondition for the dissolution of marriage through *khula*. However, in *Balqis Fatima v Najam-ul-Ikram*,[17] the Lahore High Court overruled *Moonshee Buzloor Ruheem v Shumsoonnissa Begum*.[18] The court held that a judge could grant a decree of *khula* if he is satisfied that the parties can no longer live within the limits prescribed by Allah. However, upon such dissolution, the judge may ask the wife to return the dower or some other benefits that she had received during the subsistence of the marriage. Recently, the courts have shown a progressive tendency to consider the life spent by the wife with the husband as having an economic value that is to be taken into account while deciding the issue of the return of the dower in *khula* cases.

Moonshee Buzloor Ruheem v Shumsoonnissa Begum (Calcutta) [1867] 11 MIA, 551; UKPC 22

The consent of a husband is required for *khula*.

This is a leading case on the issue of restitution of conjugal rights by a husband and the wife's right of *khula*. Shumsoonnissa, a wealthy widow with five children, married Moonshee Buzloor Ruheem (appellant) in 1847. Her wealth appeared to have become a bone of contention between her and the appellant. After leaving her husband's house because of his maltreatment, she filed a suit for the recovery of her property from him. The husband, in return, filed a suit for the restitution of conjugal rights, which was dismissed by the trial court and the Calcutta High Court. The suit for the recovery of the property was decided by the trial court and the Calcutta High Court in favour of the wife. Hence, an appeal was brought before the Judicial Committee of the Privy Council—the highest court of appeal in the British Empire. We shall focus only on the issue of restitution of conjugal rights.

After observing the contractual nature of the marriage under Islamic law and the difficulty of the specific enforcement of such a contract by a Christian court, the judges of the Privy Council held that 'in the event of disobedience the wife was to be given bodily into her husband's hands'.[19] Furthermore, it was held:

> Upon authority, then, as well as principle, their Lordships have no doubt that a Mussulman husband may institute a suit in the Civil Courts of India, for a declaration of his right to the possession of his wife, and for a sentence that she return to cohabitation; and that suit be determined according to the principle of Mohamedan law.[20]

On the issue of *khula*, the Privy Council held that the matrimonial law of Muslims favours men, as is the case in every ancient civilisation. Therefore, a Muslim husband can dissolve the marriage at his will, but a Muslim wife 'cannot separate herself from him except under the arrangement called Khoola [*sic*], which is made upon terms to which both are assenting parties and operates in law as the divorce of the wife by the husband'.[21]

This case set the leading judicial precedent on the issues of a husband's right to restitution of conjugal rights and the requirement of the consent of the husband for a wife's right to no-fault divorce—*khula*. This principle held its ground for a hundred years until the Pakistani superior courts overruled it.

Balqis Fatima v Najam-ul-Ikram Qureshi PLD 1959 Lah 566

A wife is entitled to *khula* and this right is not dependent upon the consent of a husband.

This case provides the leading authority on the issue of the requirement of a husband's consent for *khula*. It establishes that the consent of a husband is not required for *khula*. Balqis Fatima married Najam ul-Ikram in 1949. Only *nikah* was performed and *rukhsati* was to take place later. However, disputes arose between the parties before the *rukhsati*, and the wife never began conjugal relations with her husband. In 1952 the wife filed a suit for dissolution of marriage on two grounds: non-maintenance for more than two years and the husband's association with women of ill repute. As it often happens in such cases, the husband in return filed a suit for restitution of conjugal rights.

Both suits were consolidated, and the trial court dissolved the marriage, observing that the husband had failed to maintain her for more than two years. The husband's suit for the restitution of conjugal rights was dismissed. On the appeal of the husband, the first Appellate Court reversed the trial court decision on the dissolution of marriage by holding that since *rukhsati* did not take place the wife had no right to maintenance. The husband's suit for the restitution of conjugal rights was also dismissed on the ground that the relations between the parties had become sour and in such circumstances the wife could not be forced to live with her husband.

The wife filed an appeal before the Lahore High Court. The wife argued that *khula* is a right of a wife, which could be availed through a court of law. The full bench dealt with the single question as to whether under Muslim law the wife is entitled to *khula* as a right. All three judges answered this question in the affirmative. Justice Badi-uz-Zaman Kaikaus held that in the Qur'anic verse 2:229 the words 'if you fear' refer to '*ulil amr*', which means the State or the Judge is entitled to pass an order for dissolution of marriage without the consent of a husband to divorce the wife. He supported this interpretation of the Qur'anic verse by referring to the instances of the two wives of Sabit bin Qais, Jamila, and Habiba, whom the Prophet (PBUH) granted *khula*. Justice Kaikaus relied upon the treatise of Maulana Maududi, *Huqooq uz Zaujain*, in support of his argument.

In support of a wife's no-fault-based right to the dissolution of marriage, Justice Kaikaus asked, 'if such power be granted to the husband, why should there be a great disparity between the rights of the wife and the husband?'[22] He contended:

> But it does not seem reasonable that while to one of the two contracting parties has been granted a plenary power to put an end to the contract, there should be no power given to the other party and the wife must in order to get a release [to] prove some such misconduct on the part of the husband as will disentitle him to the continuance of the marriage. The wife ought, in reason, to have a right similar to that of the husband subject only to the order of the Court.[23]

The court observed that Islamic law permits the dissolution of marriage if the spouses cannot live together in harmony. On the issue of restitution of dower, the court held:

> If the dissolution is due to some default on the part of the husband, there is no need of any restitution. If the husband is not in any way at fault, there has to be restoration of property received by the wife and ordinarily it will be of the whole of the property but the judge may take into consideration reciprocal benefits received by the husband and continuous living together also may be a benefit received.[24]

The Supreme Court confirmed the principle laid down in this judgment in the following decision.

Khurshid Bibi v Baboo Muhammad Amin PLD 1967 SC 97

The consent of a husband is not required for *khula*.

In this case, Khurshid Bibi filed a suit for dissolution of marriage when her husband entered into a second marriage. Her husband, in return, filed a suit for restitution of conjugal rights. The trial court dismissed her suit and decreed in favour of the husband. The wife subsequently brought another suit before a Civil Court in another city, alleging that her husband had already divorced her orally and praying that even if the court finds otherwise, she should be granted relief on the basis of *khula* since her relationship could not be reconciled. The husband, in his written statement, refused to divorce her despite her willingness to return her dower. The trial judge accepted her suit and decreed the dissolution of the marriage on the basis of *khula*. The decision was, however, overturned in the appeal.

The High Court judge referred to the judgment in *Balqis Fatima v Najam-ul-Ikram Qureshi*,[25] and distinguished the instant case. He observed the fact that the sister of the husband was married to the brother of the plaintiff-appellant and contended that this fact could have restrained the husband from being cruel towards Khurshid Bibi because of the fear of reprisal.

On appeal, the Supreme Court framed the issue as 'whether the wife is entitled, as of right, to claim *khula*, despite the unwillingness of the husband to release her from the matrimonial tie, if she satisfies the court that there is no possibility of their living together, consistently with their conjugal duties and obligations'.[26] The full bench of five judges unanimously answered in the affirmative. Justice S.A. Rehman examined the contractual nature of marriage in Islam and observed that spouses are placed on equal footing with respect to their rights and obligations. He equated a husband's right to *talaq* with a wife's right to *khula*. He subsequently elaborated on the conflicting opinions of Muslim jurists on this issue. As to the difference of opinion regarding the requirement of the interference of the state or *Qazi* for *khula*, he held:

> This difference arises owing to the fact that two situations are contemplated by the writers. One is where *khula* takes place as a result of the mutual consent of the spouses, which is technically called *mubarat*. In such a case it appears that no reference to the Qazi is necessary. But where the husband disputes the right of the wife to obtain separation by *khula*, it is obvious that, some third party has to decide the matter and, consequently, the dispute will have to be adjudicated upon by the Qazi, with or without the assistance of the Hakams. Any other interpretation of the Qur'anic verse regarding *khula* would deprive it of all efficacy as a charter granted to the wife.[27]

On the issue of the requirement of the consent of the husband for *khula*, the court observed, 'it is significant that according to the Qur'an, she can "ransom herself" or "get her release" and it is plain that these words connote an independent right in her'.[28]

Saleem Ahmad v Government of Pakistan PLD 2014 FSC 43

If a wife is unhappy and reconciliation fails, she is entitled to *khula*.

This case shows that the development in judicial precedents on the issue of the requirement of a husband's consent for *khula* is in conformity with the injunctions of Islam. Traditional scholars belonging to the Hanafi/Deobandi school of thought regard the removal of the requirement of the consent of a husband for *khula* as un-Islamic. They argue that according to the Qur'anic verse (2:237), only a husband has the right to divorce. Regarding the traditions about the two wives of the companion of the Prophet (PBUH) Sabit bin Qais, they argue that the Prophet (PBUH) only advised him and did not act as a judge or head of the state in these instances.[29] The judgment, in this case, rebutted these arguments and provided the Qur'anic justification for a wife's unilateral right to *khula*.

In six *shariat* petitions, section 10(4) of the Family Courts Act 1964 was challenged on the ground that it is repugnant to the Injunctions of Islam as laid down in the Qur'an and Sunnah. The petitioners specifically challenged the following proviso, which was added to this section under the Family Courts (Amendment) Ordinance 2002:

> Provided that notwithstanding any decision or judgment of any Court or tribunal, the Family Court in a suit for dissolution of marriage, if reconciliation fails, shall pass decree for dissolution of marriage forthwith and shall also restore to the husband the Haq Mehr received by the wife in consideration of marriage at the time of marriage.

In effect, this proviso codified the principle developed in the *Balqis Fatima* and *Khurshid Bibi* cases.

Justice Dr Fida Muhammada Khan first elaborated the objectives of marriage in Islam as procreation of children; the preservation and perpetuation of the human race; protection of morals through legally justified satisfaction of natural biological urges; and the establishment of sound emotional, spiritual, happy, lovely, and peaceful life-long companionship. He subsequently observed the contractual nature of marriage in Islam as distinguished from a sacrament. Following this, Justice Khan framed the issue as 'whether dissolution of marriage when asked at the instance of wife can be decreed by a Qazi himself or even then also, it would be subject to the approval of her husband'.[30]

In this respect, Justice Khan put the following question before the scholars and advocates who appeared before the court:

> But a question arises if the husband does not agree to this arrangement and refuses to release her from his marital tie by not accepting any compensation even and also declines to divorce her, what should be the course of action for the wife? What would she do if reconciliation fails and the husband proves adamant to dissolve the marriage? Will it be justified to leave the wife who cannot live happily or perform her marital obligations grope in the darkness? Should she be pushed back to her husband to remain

> tongue tied, tight lipped, depressed, dejected, having a miserable survival throughout her whole life? Should she be kept, at the mercy of her in laws, vulnerable to indecent immoral life? Can anyone call this sort of situation morally justified on any standard? Will this position assigned to her not defeat the very object of marital peace and tranquillity? Who will be considered responsible if she cannot bear the Mental agony in state of affair and put an end to her life by setting herself on fire or adopt any other method for committing suicide, which is our normal observation off and on, in different parts of the country? Who will stop or what will prevent her to administer poison to her husband if she finds herself entangled in a "holy dead lock"?[31]

However, none of the scholars and advocates provided a satisfactory answer to the above questions. Therefore, Justice Khan held:

> Obviously, Islam does not intend to force a wife [to] live a miserable life, in a hateful unhappy union, forever. If she is unhappy and reconciliation fails, she should be entitled to get relief whatsoever. This is what justice demands. This is referred to in the Verse: "Women shall have rights similar to the right against them, according to what is equitable" (2:228).[32]

5.3.5.1 Return of Dower on *Khula*

Muhammad Arif v Saima Noreen 2015 SCMR 804

The court may dissolve a marriage on the basis of *khula* irrespective of the fact that the wife did not pray for it.

In this case, the parties were married in 2010. The marriage, however, did not work out and the wife filed a suit for dissolution of marriage on grounds of cruelty provided under the DMMA. Unlike the usual practice, she did not seek *khula* as an alternative. Instead, she requested that her dowry articles be returned along with her dower. The Family Court decreed in her favour and the next two Appellate Courts upheld the decree. Thereafter, the case was brought before the Supreme Court.

An important aspect of the case was that even though the alleged fact of cruelty was not legally proved before the Family Court, it dissolved the marriage on the basis that the relationship between the parties had become so strained that their reunion was not possible (irretrievable breakdown of the marriage). This was a dissolution based on *khula* where the wife was required to forego her dower. The Family Court, however, did not order the restitution of dower, and instead, the husband was ordered to transfer it to the wife, which was a house as mentioned in the *nikahnama*. The Supreme Court noticed this anomaly and ordered that the wife should return the dower to the husband. The decree for the dissolution of marriage on the basis of *khula*, however, was upheld, despite the fact that it was not prayed for in the suit originally filed by the wife.

Syed Haroon Sultan Bokhari v Syeda Mubarak Fatima 2014 CLC 1270 (Lah)

Dower should not be returned if a husband causes the dissolution of the marriage.

In this case, the spouses were married in 2010. After a few months of marriage, however, the wife filed a suit for dissolution of marriage on the basis of *khula*, claiming that her husband tortured her and due to severe beating while she was pregnant, she suffered a miscarriage. She asserted that she could not live with her husband within the limits prescribed by Allah. The husband agreed to divorce her upon her relinquishment of Rs 100,000 and the property was given to her as a dower. The wife agreed to return Rs 100,000 but not the property. The Family Court dissolved the marriage on the basis of *khula* subject to relinquishment of her dower amount of Rs 100,000 or a portion of the property equal to Rs 100,000. The husband filed a writ petition before the High Court against this decision.

The husband argued that the wife was required to return not only the dower but all the gifts that she had received from him as consideration for *khula*. The wife responded that she was only required to return the dower under section 10(4) of the Family Courts Act 1964. The court observed that the wife had made allegations of physical and mental torture and had sought the dissolution of the marriage on the basis of cruelty. Despite asserting severe hatred against the husband she never sought the dissolution of marriage on the basis of *khula*. The arrangement of *khula* was only reached after the intervention of the elders when a settlement agreement was executed between the parties. Therefore, the court held that a wife has to forgo her dower and benefits derived from the husband when *khula* is claimed without any fault of the husband. However, if the wife developed hatred or aversion towards the husband as a result of his conduct, which could be in the shape of mental or physical torture or non-payment of maintenance etc., then the return of the dower amount is not essential for *khula*. The court also observed that a bridal gift can by no stretch of the imagination be regarded as part of the dower that needs to be returned by the wife in case of the dissolution of marriage on the basis of *khula*. Therefore, the court dismissed the writ petition.

Abdul Rashid v Shahida Parveen 2013 YLR 2616 (Pesh)

A life spent by a wife with her husband could be considered as factor for *khula.*

In this case, the wife's claim for *khula* originated as a result of the husband's petition for restitution of conjugal rights. The Family Court decreed in favour of the husband after rejecting the counterclaim of the wife. She filed an appeal, and the Appellate Court dissolved her marriage on the basis of cruelty. In a writ petition against the decision of the Appellate Court, the High Court converted the decree to the dissolution of marriage on the basis of *khula* instead of cruelty. The husband filed for the execution of the petition to recover the dower as this issue was left undecided by the High Court. The trial court dismissed the husband's execution petition, and he filed a writ before the High Court. After referring to verses 2:228–30, 4:19–20, and 20–21 of the Qur'an, and several judicial authorities, Justice Mrs Irshad Qaisar observed that the wife lived with the petitioner for sixteen years and performed her marital obligations during this time. She spent the precious and prime time of her young age with him. It was in fact the petitioner who created such circumstances that compelled her to come to the court for the dissolution of marriage. Therefore, in such a situation, the life spent by the wife with the husband can be taken as consideration for *khula*, and the dower was not to be returned.

Imran Anwar Khan v Government of Punjab [Shariat Petition No.4–I of 2016]

The law requiring the partial return of dower upon *khula* under section 10 (5) & (6) of the Family Courts Act 1964 is repugnant to the injunctions of Islam.

In this judgment, the Federal Shariat Court examined the amendments in the law which required partial return of dower in cases of *khula*. The petitioners challenged the amendment (subsections 5 and 6) in section 10 of the Family Courts Act 1964 under the Punjab Muslim Family Laws (Amendment) Act 2015. Under the amended law, the court may direct a wife to return up to 50 per cent of her deferred dower or up to 25 per cent of her admitted prompt dower to the husband in case of dissolution of marriage through *khula*. The Family Court is also authorised to direct the husband to pay whole or part of the outstanding deferred dower to the decree for dissolution of marriage.

Before framing the legal issues, Chief Justice Muhammad Noor Meskanzai highlighted the sanctity of marriage in Islam by stating that although under Islamic law marriage is a civil contract, the Qur'an describes it as a 'firm covenant'. Therefore, in the Qur'an and Sunnah divorce (*talaq*) is described as a permissible yet reprehensible (*makruh*) act.

In his judgment, Justice Meskanzai framed three legal issues: (i) whether the Qur'an prescribes any quantum of dower to be returned to the husband upon dissolution of marriage through *khula*, (ii) if the answer to the first issue is no, whether Sunnah prescribes any such quantum, and (iii) whether the said amendments are against the Qur'an and Sunnah?

Justice M. Noor Meskanzai observed that if a husband wishes to divorce (*talaq*) his wife, he is not authorised to take back what he gave her as a dower and gift. The Qur'anic verses 4:20 and 4:21 specifically prohibit husbands from taking back what they have already given to their wives during wedlock while divorcing them. Therefore, if a husband divorces his wife of his own volition and without any fault on the part of his wife, he is not entitled to claim the dower or gifts given to her. However, if a wife exercises her right to the dissolution of marriage through *khula*, she may have to pay some compensation, but the Qur'anic verses do not specify the amount of such compensation.

The Qur'an does not even refer to the dower as compensation for *khula* in verse 2:229 which confers the right of dissolution of marriage based on *khula*. The rule that a wife must return the dower when she exercises her right to *khula* is derived from the tradition of the Prophet Muhammad (PBUH). According to tradition, the wife of one of the Prophet's (PBUH) companions, Thabit bin Qais (RA), told the Prophet (PBUH) that she disliked her husband and wanted to dissolve her marriage. The Prophet (PBUH) asked her to return the garden that she received as a dower and dissolved her marriage. Another wife of the same companion also approached the Prophet (PBUH) to dissolve her marriage and was asked to return the properties that she received from him in return for *khula*. From these traditions, Justice Meskanzai drew the legal rule that a wife is required to return full dower when she exercises her right to *khula* based on her disliking of her husband and without any fault in his conduct. Therefore, he held that the impugned amended law contradicted these traditions and hence declared it invalid.

Justice Meskanzai also found the impugned amended law as violative of women's rights because it requires wives to partially return their dower even in cases where the husband caused the breakdown of the marriage. He observed that the impugned amended law fails to achieve its intended objective of the protection of women's financial rights upon dissolution of marriage rather it is likely to increase breakdown of marriages by offering financial gains. By doing so, the impugned amended law posed a danger to the institution of marriage and rights of mothers and children as protected under article 35 of the Constitution. Therefore, not only the impugned amended law was repugnant to the injunctions of Islam, but it was also violative of the fundamental rights enshrined in the Constitution. The Court declared that subsections (5) and (6) of the Family Courts Act 1964 would be invalid and ineffective from 1 May 2022.

5.3.5.2 Intervening Marriage (*Halala*) after *Khula*

Danish v Fozia Danish PLD 2013 Sindh 209

Khula amounts to a single irrevocable pronouncement of divorce and a wife can remarry her former husband without an intervening marriage, *halala*.

This case shows the application of the Islamic legal principle that *khula* amounts to a single pronouncement of *talaq* and a divorced wife can remarry her former husband without an intervening marriage with a third person (*halala*).

The wife filed a suit for the dissolution of the marriage. The Family Court decreed the suit *ex parte* and dissolved the marriage on the basis of *khula* on 7 November 2009. After about three years, in 2012, the husband approached the High Court for a declaration that his marriage with the respondent wife subsisted and that the *ex parte* judgment of the Family Court should be set aside. He submitted that both spouses resolved their differences and decided to reunite for the betterment of their two minor children. A notice was served to the wife who in her affidavit expressed her willingness to reunite with the petitioner as his wife after the performance of a fresh *nikah* with him. The wife stated on oath that she wanted to reunite with the petitioner out of her own free accord for the welfare of their children. She further averred that the earlier suit for dissolution of marriage was filed because of a misunderstanding between the spouses and at the instigation of her brother and father.

The petitioner's counsel contended that no occasion was provided to the spouses for reconciliation and settling their differences. The counsel relied upon case law that established that the pronouncement of *khula* by the court amounts to a single divorce. In such a case, the parties are free to reunite with each other as husband and wife without an intervening marriage (*halala*) on the solemnisation of a fresh *nikah* between them.

After hearing the arguments of the counsel and perusing the record, the court noted that *Fazli-e-Subhan v Mst Sabereen*[33] (relying upon Maulana Ashraf Ali Thanwi's *Bahishti Zaiwar* and a *fatwa* of Mufti Saifullah

Haqani of Jamia Dar ul Uloom, Akora Khattak) and *Muhammad Ayub Khan v Mst Shehla Rasheed*[34] (relying upon Dr Tanzeel-ur-Rahman's *Majmua-e-Qawaneen-e-Islam*) lend full support to the arguments and averments of the petitioner's counsel. The court further relied upon the *Hidaya* (as translated by Charles Hamilton), which provides:

> In a case of irrevocable divorce, i.e. before three divorces, the husband is at liberty to marry his wife again, either during her 'Idat' or after its completion, as the legality of the subject still continues, such legality depends upon a third divorce; and accordingly until a third divorce takes place, the legality of the subject continues.[35]

The court also noted that sub-section (6) of section 7 of the MFLO states that 'Nothing shall debar a wife whose marriage has been terminated by 'Talaq' effective under this section from re-marrying the same husband, without an intervening marriage with a third person, unless such termination is for the third time so effective'.

In view of the case law, *fatawa* of jurists, and relevant provisions of the applicable statute, the prayer of the petitioner was allowed for a reunion with the wife after the solemnisation of a fresh *nikah* between the two.

5.3.6 Triple *Talaq*. The law with respect to the validity of triple *talaq* is not settled and we find various contradictory judgments on this subject. Other considerations such as a wife's property rights, and husband's financial responsibilities make this issue even more complicated. A close analysis of the case law suggests that the courts tend to accept its validity when it serves to protect women's right, while declare it invalid when it is used as a tool to deprive women of their rights.

Sardar Iqbal v Tahira Parveen 2010 YLR 582 (Lah)

A husband cannot retract triple *talaq*, which has become effective.

This is a typical family law case in which a wife sued for the recovery of her dower, dowry items, and claimed maintenance for herself and her child. Following the standard practice, the husband in return filed a suit for restitution of conjugal rights claiming that his marriage still existed as he did not validly divorce his wife.

The couple in this case was married in 2003. However, four years later, the husband expelled the wife from his house and divorced her vide a divorce deed. He also sent a notice of divorce to the Chairman of the Arbitration Council. Two daughters were born during the marriage. One died when she was only twenty days old and the other was living with his wife. The wife filed a claim for the recovery of her dower of 10 *tolas* of gold as mentioned in Column 17 of the *Nikahnama*, dowry items, and her maintenance during the *iddat* period as well as past and future maintenance of her minor daughter. The husband denied all her averments in his written statement and also filed a suit for restitution of conjugal rights. Both suits were consolidated.

The counsel for the husband argued that the divorce was pronounced thrice by mistake and referred to a *fatwa* at the back of the affidavit filed by the husband stating the same. Such *fatwa*s are normally availed from *ulama* belonging to the Ahle Hadith school who regard the pronouncement of triple *talaq* as equal to one *talaq* and hence revocable.

The trial court decreed in favour of the wife and dismissed the husband's suit for restitution of conjugal rights. The Appellate Court upheld this decision. Therefore, the husband filed a writ petition before the High Court.

The petitioner reiterated that his pronouncement of triple *talaq* was a mistake and that he revoked his notice of *talaq* to the Chairman of the Arbitration Council. Justice Ms Jamila Jahanoor Aslam did not find this argument convincing and observed:

> The main points herein are that the intention of divorce was conveyed unambiguously and thereafter to date there has been no co-habitation. The petitioner as well as respondent No.1 admit this fact. I would also like to point out that in the fatwa on the back of the affidavit it is stated that he has to co-habit during the Iddat period for the Talaq to be considered ineffective. Although the notice of revocation was within the Iddat period[,] the fact that the parties did not retire (Khilwat-us-Sahih), has made the divorce effective. It is mandatory that after revocation of divorce there is co-habitation, in the absence of which and after a ninety days period after pronouncement of divorce be it bayn, Ahsan or Hassan the divorce will become effective.[36]

The honourable judge relied upon the *Tafseer-e-Qur'an* by Mufti Muhammad Taqi Usmani in reaching the conclusion that if a husband pronounces *talaq* thrice, then he cannot revoke it:

> By divorcing respondent No. 1 three times in one go the petitioner has forfeited his right to claim her as his lawfully wedded wife. Any affidavit claiming that the three times pronouncement was a mistake is a bit late in the day for rectifying his mistake and that too only for his own convenience.[37]

Sardar v Malik Khan 2003 YLR 2623 (Lah)

Triple *talaq* is invalid.

The dispute, in this case, pertains to the inheritance of the issueless deceased Sultan Ahmad's estate. The petitioners were the legal heirs of the deceased, while the respondents were the legal heirs of Mst Dhami, the widow of Sultan Ahmad. According to the facts of the case, the deceased gave a notice of divorce to Mst Dhami three days before his death. Mst Dhami filed a suit claiming her share in the estate of the deceased with the averment that the said divorce notice was a forged and fictitious document prepared by the petitioners to deprive her of her legal share as the wife of the deceased. She contended that not only was the deceased in a senseless state of mind at the time of the divorce notice, but also that she was never informed of it. The suit of Mst Dhami was decreed, and she was declared to be entitled to one-fourth of the estate of the deceased. The petitioners filed an appeal against this decision, which was dismissed. Therefore, a revision petition was filed before the High Court.

The counsel for the petitioners contended that a written divorce becomes instantly operative. Therefore, Mst Dhami stood divorced and was thus not entitled to inherit the estate of the deceased. On the other hand, the counsel for the respondents maintained that according to the Qur'anic injunctions, even a triple divorce pronounced in one sitting operates as a single divorce, which could be revoked by the husband during the *iddat* period. Thus, Mst Dhami continued to remain the widow of Sultan Ahmad. Considering the significant issues at hand and the difference of opinion among various Sunni schools regarding the scope and nature of triple *talalq*, the Court recorded its own views by making direct recourse to the relevant Qur'anic verses and commentary thereupon. The court held:

> The difference of opinion on [the] validity of instant divorce through triple Talaq and ensuing escalating vice evoked "legislative compassion" which expressed itself in the form of S.7(3) of [the] Muslim Family Laws

> Ordinance, 1961, providing for revocation of Talaq within a period of ninety days … The said provision is not in conflict with the Injunctions of the Holy Qur'an. The contrary view is only a blurred conception of the commandments of the Almighty Allah and it is so due to the reason that moral principles originally adopted and [the] system found thereon by the passage of time became so rigid that it lost all flexibility.[38]

Justice Syed Jamshed Ali observed that the original text of the Holy Qur'an on the subject and the sayings and doings of the Prophet (PBUH) are refreshingly 'modern and rational'[39] and lamented the inflexible approach of jurists belonging to various schools, who do not believe in 'rationalizing and modernizing the system (within the limits set out by Almighty Allah)'.[40]

After considering the relevant verses of Sura al-Baqara, Sura al-Talaq, and Sura al-Nisa, and commentaries thereupon, the court reached the conclusion that a divorce in the proper form as laid down in the Qur'an becomes final and absolute only after the observance of *iddat*. In this way, enough time is given to the husband to deliberate over his decision and to retrieve it, if he so decides. The main objective of this rule is to give parties the opportunity for reconciliation. In light of this discussion, the court held that the *talaq* pronounced by the deceased Sultan Ahmad, followed by a written notice, had not become final in accordance with the Qur'anic injunctions. Hence, Mst Dhami continued to remain the widow of Sultan Ahmad, and was thus entitled to inherit his estate.

5.3.7 Notice of *Talaq* under the MFLO. Under section 7 of the MFLO, a husband is required to give a notice of *talaq* to the Chairman, Union Council, and also provide a copy of the notice to the wife. This section, however, does not clarify the effects of the failure of a husband to provide such notice. In the famous *Gardezi* case, the Supreme Court held that if a husband fails to give a notice, he is deemed to have revoked his pronouncement of *talaq*.[41] This principle caused many legal complications, especially after the promulgation of the Offense of Zina (Enforcement of Hudood) Ordinance 1979. In the *Shoukat Ali* case, which involved the offence of *zina*, the Federal Shariat Court ruled that the *talaq* was effective even if the husband failed to serve a notice under the MFLO.[42] However, in *Kaneez Fatima v Wali Muhammad*,[43] the Supreme Court held that the notice requirement under the MFLO should be taken into account on a case-by-case basis in accordance with the circumstances of each case.

Syed Ali Nawaz Gardezi v Lt. Col. Muhammad Yusuf PLD 1963 SC 51

Talaq was deemed to have been revoked in the absence of a notice under the MFLO.

This is a leading case on the proposition that if a husband does not give a notice of *talaq* to the Chairman of the Union Council under the MFLO, he is deemed to have revoked his pronouncement. The complainant, Ali Nawaz Gardezi, filed a criminal case against the respondent for adultery and enticing a married woman. The respondent was a serving Lieutenant Colonel in the army. The High Court, acting as a trial court, convicted the respondent. However, on appeal, the Appellate Bench of the High Court set aside the conviction. The judgment provides the minute details of the case. We are, however, primarily interested in the facts that are relevant to our proposition.

In 1951, the complainant married a German girl, Christia Renate Sonntag, in England. She was a Christian and did not convert to Islam. Three children were born during the marriage. The respondent was a family friend with whom Renate developed a personal relationship. She corresponded with him, and they also talked over the telephone. In August 1961, the complainant husband intercepted a letter addressed to his wife by the respondent. The letter provided evidence that the respondent planned to marry Renate. The complainant husband discussed the contents of the letter with his wife but did not take any further action. A few months later, Renate went to Quetta to meet the respondent in her husband's absence from Lahore. Upon learning this, the complainant asked her to return and when she reached home, he reprimanded her and gave her a beating. In December 1961, Renate asked her husband to divorce her by signing a divorce deed, which he refused to do. However, a signed divorce document was presented to the court on behalf of the respondent. The respondent claimed that Renate was divorced by her husband before he entered into a marriage with her.

The trial Judge held that the requirement of giving a notice to the Chairman under section 7 of the MFLO was not fulfilled. Therefore, the *talaq* was not effective. The Supreme Court agreed and held:

> [I]t seems to us that the Legislature had attempted to incorporate the Islamic Law provisions with regard to the two forms of "Talaq-us-Sunnat", viz., "Talaq Ahsan" and "Talaq Hasan", as far as may be, in this section …

> The section clearly contemplates a machinery of conciliation whereby a husband wishing to divorce his wife unilaterally, may be enabled to think better of it, if the mediation of others can resolve the differences between the spouses. The talaq pronounced is to be ineffective for a period of 90 days from the date of which notice under subsection (1) of this section is delivered to the Chairman and this period is to be utilised for the attempt at reconciliation…[44]

While rebutting the argument that the above construction of section 7 of the MFLO is tantamount to allowing a husband to benefit from his own wrong, Justice S.A. Rehman observed that the objective of section 7 is to prevent hasty dissolution of marriages by *talaq*. Therefore, if the husband abstains from giving a notice to the Chairman, 'he should perhaps be deemed' to have revoked the pronouncement of *talaq* and that would be to 'the advantage of the wife'.[45]

In the end, the court found the respondent guilty of enticing and taking away Christa Renate when she was still a lawfully wedded wife of the complainant and convicted him under section 498 of the Pakistan Penal Code.

Kaneez Fatima v Wali Muhammad PLD 1993 SC 901

Requirement of the notice to be taken into account on a case-by-case basis.

In this case, the Full Bench of five judges of the Supreme Court held that a husband's failure to give notice to the Chairman, Union Council under section 7 of the MFLO did not constitute the revocation of *talaq*. The parties were married in 1975, and by 1977 their relationship became strained. During the Martial Law period, the wife filed a petition before the Martial Law Authorities for the recovery of maintenance and dower. The parties entered into a written agreement before the Martial Law Authorities to the effect that the divorce was effective between the parties since 1 November 1977. As a result of this negotiation, the wife received Rs 10,000 and 5 *tolas* of gold. However, in April 1978, the wife filed a suit for recovery of the remaining amount of dower and maintenance in the Family Court. She argued that the compromise was made due to the coercion of the Martial Law Authorities. She supported her argument by stating that no notice of *talaq* in pursuance of the compromise agreement was given to the Chairman under section 7 of the MFLO, and therefore, the marriage between the parties continued to subsist. The trial court decreed in her favour. The Appellate Court reversed the decision of the trial court. The High Court upheld the decision of the Appellate Court after observing that by entering into a compromise agreement, the parties had contracted out of the provisions of section 7 of the MFLO and thus finalised the divorce without having recourse to arbitration proceedings before the Chairman, Union Council. Thereafter, an appeal was filed before the Supreme Court.

Justice Saleem Akhtar reviewed the conflicting judicial authorities on the interpretation of section 7 of the MFLO and observed that the decision in the *Syed Ali Nawaz Gardezi* case could be interpreted to lay down the principle that 'failure to send notice of Talaq to the Chairman of the Union Council does not by itself lead to the conclusion that Talaq has been revoked. It may only be ineffective but not revoked'.[46] Justice Akhtar subsequently recommended a purposive interpretation of the section by 'taking into consideration the facts and circumstances of each case'.[47] He held:

> However, keeping in view the facts of each case the applicability and interpretation of section 7 has to be construed in that light. In a case where with the consent of both the parties divorce is effected and confirmed in writing under their undisputed signatures section 7 should not be strictly construed particularly in cases where [the] penal provision of section 7(2) is to be enforced because in such cases the parties do not wilfully commit breach and bona fide believe that they had been divorced with the consent of each other and sending of notice to the Chairman, Union Council, is merely a formality. The notice can be sent at any time thereafter to comply with the provisions of section 7.[48]

Shoukat Ali v The State 2004 YLR 619 (FSC)

Talaq is valid despite non-fulfilment of a notice requirement.

This is an important case decided by the Federal Shariat Court. In this case, the Court attempted to answer various queries revolving around the requirement of a notice of *talaq*, which is to be provided by the husband to the Chairman, Union Council under section 7 of the MFLO. The brief facts of the case are that Shoukat Ali and Naseem were convicted under section 10(2) of the Offense of Zina (Enforcement of Hudood) Ordinance 1979, along with sections 468 and 471 of the Pakistan Penal Code. Both parties preferred criminal appeals, which were heard on merits.

The proceedings against the parties were initiated at the instance of Zulfiqar Ali (the Complainant) who recorded an FIR against the parties involved. As per his statement, Naseem was married to Naseer Ahmad for about 10–11 years when the alleged offence took place. Naseem developed illicit relations with Shoukat Ali, who resided in her neighbourhood. The Complainant, being the brother of Naseem, warned Shoukat Ali not to visit her house when he came to know about their relationship. On 25 January 2002, the Complainant was visiting his sister's house, and after dinner, he went to sleep with his brother-in-law, Naseer Ahmad, and other family members. In the morning, Naseem was missing. After making certain inquiries, they were informed that Naseem was seen with Shoukat Ali in a car headed towards Kallur Kot. After the registration of the case against the two, an investigation began. During the investigation, both the appellants produced a divorce deed and a *Nikahnama*. They contended that Naseer Ahmad divorced Naseem on 2 October 2001, and hence the appellants contracted marriage on 18 January 2002. The investigation officer stated that he found the divorce deed to be forged and the *Nikahnama* remained unverified. Hence, the appellants were sent to face trial.

The material question around which the entire case revolved rested upon the genuineness of the divorce deed. If the divorce deed was genuine then the subsequent marriage of the appellants was valid and no question of *zina* arose. The prosecution failed to discharge its onus of proof in disproving the genuineness of the divorce deed. It failed to produce any cogent oral or documentary evidence questioning the validity of the divorce deed. However, the prosecution raised the objection that the divorce was not pronounced in accordance with the requirements of section 7(1) of the MFLO. The court found this argument to be misconceived and noted that although a procedure has been laid down for the pronouncement of *talaq*, failure to strictly follow the procedure does not invalidate *talaq*. The court held:

> The necessary requirement or ingredient of Talaq was a conscious and wilful pronouncement of Talaq with intention to release wife from marriage bond. The failure to follow said procedure could entail or be followed by punishment prescribed under succeeding subsections but the validity of Talaq or the separation of spouses from the marriage bond would not be affected.[49]

The *nikahnama* of the appellants was also found to be valid. Therefore, the convictions of appellants were set aside.

5.3.8 Proof of *Talaq*

Farah Naz v Judge Family Court, Sahiwal PLD 2006 SC 457

Giving notice is mandatory for the effectiveness of the dissolution of a marriage.

Farah Naz married Inam Qadir in 1996. After one month, the respondent husband left for Paris leaving his wife behind at her parental home in Sahiwal. He entered into a second marriage in Paris and failed to provide any maintenance to his first wife, who in 2002 filed a suit for recovery of maintenance at the rate of Rs 10,000 per month. The respondent (husband) filed a written statement from Paris asserting that since the petitioner wife was insane and of imbalanced mind, he had pronounced *talaq* in 1997 in the presence of witnesses; therefore, she was not entitled to maintenance. After becoming aware of the so-called divorce, the wife filed a suit for the recovery of the amount of dowry articles. The respondent also resisted this suit. The trial court dismissed the suit for maintenance on the grounds that the petitioner had already been divorced and was not entitled to maintenance. The second suit for the recovery of dowry was decreed to the extent of Rs 400,000.

Upon re-evaluation of the evidence, the Appellate Court held that the wife was entitled to maintenance for one and a half years, at the rate of Rs 8,000 per month. In the suit for the recovery of dowry, the amount was increased from Rs 400,000 to Rs 955,038. The husband filed a writ petition before the High Court, which upheld the decision of the trial court by denying the provision of maintenance as the wife stood divorced. The court also decreased the recovery amount to Rs 400,000.

On this, the petitioner, Farah Naz, filed an appeal before the Supreme Court. Justice Rana Bhagwandas observed that the trial court, the Appellate Court, and the High Court misconstrued the law by accepting the averments of the respondent without any evidence and without subjecting him to cross-examination. He held that under the MFLO, the husband was bound to send a notice of *talaq* by a registered post both to the wife and to the Chairman, Arbitration Council. Since the husband did not send such a notice either to the wife or the Chairman, his oral assertion that he had divorced his wife was invalid. The court held:

> [W]e find that the appellant having been lawfully wedded to the respondent in the absence of any proof of dissolution of marital tie, it was his legal, moral as well as social duty under the Islamic principles to provide adequate maintenance for her respectable living as in law he could not neglect to

> maintain her during the subsistence of the marriage tie. His bald statement that he had announced Talaq to her on 13–12-1997 cannot be accepted at all as he utterly failed to substantiate it. In law, he was required to send notice to the Arbitration Council under the Muslim Family Laws Ordinance 1961 and also to send a copy of notice to the appellant by registered post. No such proceedings having been ever conducted, oral allegation of Talaq would neither be effective nor valid and binding on the appellant, who would, in all fairness, be legally entitled to past maintenance as claimed by her.[50]

Therefore, the Court decreed maintenance in the sum of Rs 10,000 per month, and also decreed the recovery of the amount of dowry of Rs 955,038.

Manzoor Ahmad v Nargis Mirza PLD 2004 SC 132

Talaq is invalid without the notice.

The parties, in this case, were married in 1997. As the wife could not bear any children, her husband expelled her from his house. The wife filed a suit claiming maintenance from the husband, who was a British citizen and a London-based businessman. The husband defended the suit by arguing that he had divorced the wife in 1998 in the presence of a witness. The court rejected this plea since the husband failed to notify both the Chairman of the Union Council and the wife as required under section 7 of the MFLO.

It must be noted that the issue in the above two cases is related to the recovery of maintenance. The Supreme Court refused to allow the husbands to benefit from their own wrongs by denying payment of maintenance to their wives on the basis that they had already divorced them. Therefore, the court required compliance with the requirement of giving notice to the Chairman of the Union Council under the MFLO.

5.3.9 *Talaq* and Right to Inheritance

Chuhar v Ghulam Fatima PLD 1984 Lah 234

The MFLO is for the benefit of women and must be interpreted to promote their rights.

The husband of Ghulam Fatima divorced her orally and did not send the notice of *talaq* to the Chairman of the Union Council as required under section 7 of the MFLO. After the divorce, Ghulam Fatima married

Muhammad Ramzan and had a son during the wedlock. After Ramzan's death, Chuhar, Rizwan's cousin, filed a suit claiming the deceased's estate as his sole heir. He alleged that the marriage of Ghulam Fatima and his cousin was invalid as her former husband had not fulfilled the requirements of section 7 of the MFLO that effectuates *talaq*. The trial court accepted Chuhar's claim but the appellate court reversed the judgment of the trial court. Therefore, the case was brought before the Lahore High Court.

Justice Munir Khan examined the facts of the case and held that the MFLO was meant for the benefit of women and should not be interpreted in a manner which might ruin their lives by denying them their inheritance rights. In the circumstances of the case, Justice Khan observed that the *talaq* was not rendered ineffective due to not giving of notice under section 7 of the MFLO. Therefore, the second marriage of Ghulam Fatima was valid and she along with her son was entitled to inheritance in the estate of her deceased husband.

5.4 Conclusion

An analysis of case law shows that the courts have been developing new legal rules on the dissolution of marriage. The judges have liberally construed Islamic family law along with the provisions of the DMMA and the MFLO to protect the interests of women. They have progressively removed the requirement of the consent of a husband for *khula*. Furthermore, they have started to refuse the return of dower to a husband if he caused the dissolution of marriage. In recent cases, the courts held that a wife's life spent with the husband has economic value and the period of wedlock should be taken into account while deciding the issue of the return of dower in *khula* cases. Trends in case law show that future case law will further clarify the issue of the economic value of a wife's life spent with her husband while performing household chores. This will further reduce the economic burden of dissolution of marriage for wives. The judges have also extended the definition of cruelty under the DMMA and made the evidence produced by the close relatives of the wife admissible though they may be regarded as interested witnesses in other civil matters.

The analysis of relevant case law shows that the law is not yet settled on the issues of the validity of triple *talaq* and the legal effect of a husband's failure to serve a notice of *talaq* under the MFLO. It appears that in various contradictory judgments the judges try to protect the rights of women by interpreting the law in one way or the other. They accept the validity of triple *talaq* when it serves to protect women's right. They, however, question its validity when triple *talaq* is misused to deprive a wife of her right to maintenance and inheritance. Trends in case law are similar with respect to the requirement of a husband's serving of a notice of *talaq* under the MFLO. In a case regarding sexual offence of *zina* the FSC held that *talaq* is valid even when the husband failed to serve a notice of *talaq* under the MFLO. The Supreme Court held that the notice requirement has to be taken into account on a case-by-case basis. It shows that jurisprudence is still developing on this issue and further developments are expected in the near future.

Questions

1. What are the types of dissolution of marriage under Islamic family law in Pakistan?
2. Should the consent of a husband be required for *khula*? Why or why not?
3. Why is a wife required to surrender her dower to avail *khula*? Can a court dissolve the marriage on the basis of *khula* without the restitution of the dower to a husband?
4. Does triple *talaq* become effective immediately after its pronouncement under the legal system of Pakistan?
5. Is *talaq* by a husband effective if he fails to give notice to the Chairman of the Union Council?

Further Reading

Books/Articles

Abbasi, M.Z., 'Judicial *Ijtihād* as a Tool for Legal Reform: Extending Women's Right to Divorce under Islamic Law in Pakistan', *Islamic Law and Society* (2017) 24, 384.

Carroll, Lucy, 'Qur'an 2:229: A Charter Granted to the Wife—Judicial Khul in Pakistan', *Islamic Law and Society* 3.1 (1996), 91–126.

Munir, M., 'Stipulations in a Muslim Marriage Contract with Special Reference to Talaq Al-Tafwid Provisions in Pakistan', *Yearbook of Islamic and Middle Eastern Law* (2005–2006) 12, 235.

Yefet, K.C., 'The Constitution and Female-Initiated Divorce in Pakistan: Western Liberalism in Islamic Garb', *Harvard Journal of Law & Gender* (2011) 34, 553.

Cases

Allah Banda v Khurshid Bibi 1990 CLC 1683 (Lah) (Triple *talaq* pronounced in one sitting becomes effective immediately and is irrevocable, per Justice Mian Nazir Akhtar.)

Ambreen Shah v Chairman, Union (Arbitration) Council 2002 MLD 778 (Triple *talaq* is irrevocable, per Justice Nasira Iqbal.)

Chuhar v Mst Ghulam Fatima PLD 1984 Lah 234 (Failure to give notice of *talaq* under the MFLO gives rise to a rebuttable presumption about its revocation. In this case, this presumption was rebutted as the husband did not revoke the *talaq* expressly or impliedly.)

Dr Fakhr-ud-Din v Kausar Takreem PLD 2009 Pesh 92 (Disobedience of a wife, her role in straining the relations, the second marriage of a husband, and possible destitution of a wife after the divorce are determining factors for fixing the amount of what a wife has to return to a husband upon *khula*). This principle is endorsed in *Saima Gul v Haider Zaman*.[51]

M. Saqlain Zaheer v Zaibun Nisa Zaheer 1988 MLD 427 (While ordering restitution of benefits received by the wife, the court has to take into consideration reciprocal benefits received by the husband. Continuous living together, the performance of marital obligations by the wife, housekeeping, and cooking for the husband, bearing him children and assisting in bringing up children, could also be considered as benefits received by the husband.)

Ms Sadaf Munir Khan v Chairman Reconciliation Committee PLD 2019 Lah 285 (The divorce certificate issued by the Chairman Reconciliation Committee in Pakistan is of no legal effect because *talaq* was given when parties were residing abroad.)

Mst. Asma Bibi v Chairman Reconciliation Committee PLD 2020 Lah 679 (When *talaq* is pronounced abroad, the functions of the Chairman union council are performed by the officers of Pakistan mission abroad.)

Mst. Tuharat Firdous v Imtiaz Khan 2019 CLC 1562 (Pesh) (Where a wife is required to return the dower because of dissolution of marriage through *khula*, she is allowed to keep part of the dower under the principle of reciprocal benefits.)

Muhammad Bashir Ali Siddiqui v Mst. Sarwar Jahan Begum 2008 SCMR 186 (*Nikahnama* had a provision that if the wife obtained *khula* she would be liable to pay Rs 2,50,000 and if the husband divorced her, he would pay her a similar amount. When the wife obtained *khula*, the husband sought to enforce this provision. The court rejected the husband's claim.)

Muhammad Kaleem Asif v ADJ PLD 2009 Lah 484 (If a wife's suit for dissolution of marriage on the basis of *khula* is decreed without determination of *badl-e-khula* considering the cruel and inhumane behaviour of her husband, the wife may afterwards initiate a separate judicial proceeding for the recovery of unpaid dower.)

Muhammad Riaz v Robina Bibi 2000 MLD 1886 (Decree of a Family Court is not necessary to invalidate marriage which has been dissolved by a wife in the exercise of her option of puberty.)

Nasir v Rubina 2012 MLD 1576 (Pesh) (The period of wedlock, the birth of the children, and the second marriage of the husband could preclude the return of the dower to the husband.)

Shahzada Begum v Sh. Abdul Hamid PLD 1950 Lah 504 (Under the doctrine of *kafa'at* (equality), the guardian or other relatives of an adult Muslim girl may have the right to object to an ill-assorted union on the ground that it brings the family into disrepute. However, where the wife was an educated woman of mature age who entered into marriage with her husband who was only 15 years or less senior to her, this doctrine could not be invoked to cancel the marriage.)

Shamas Ali v Additional District Judge, Sambrial PLD 2012 Lah 183 (Dower should not be returned if the husband caused the dissolution of marriage.)

Shamshad Begum v Abdul Haque PLD 1977 Kar 855 (When the marriage was dissolved on the basis of *khula* due to the fault of the husband, it is not lawful for him to get the dower back from the wife. Justice Z.A. Channa relied upon the *Radd al-Muhtar* which quoted the Qur'an 4:20 as an authority: 'But if ye decide to take one wife in place of another, even if ye had given the latter a whole treasure for dower, Take not the least bit of it back: Would ye take it by slander and manifest wrong?'). This principle is endorsed in *Aurangzeb v Mst Gulnaz*[52] and *Abdul Aleem Khan v Tabinda Naseer Qazi*.[53]

Sughran Mai v The State PLD 1980 Lah 386 (*Kafa'at* is not a legal rule, it is only a customary rule.)

Notes

1. The phrase 'within the limits prescribed by Allah' is based on the Qur'an 2:229: 'Divorce is only permissible twice: after that, the husbands should either retain wives on equitable terms or let them go with kindness. It is not lawful for you, [men], to take back any of your gifts [from your wives], except when both parties fear that they would be unable to keep the *limits ordained by Allah*. If ye [judges] do indeed fear that they would be unable to keep the limits ordained by Allah, there is no blame on either of them if she gives something for her freedom. These are the limits ordained by Allah; so do not transgress them. If any do transgress the limits ordained by Allah, such persons wrong [themselves as well as others].'
2. S 2(ii-a) was inserted under s 13 of the MFLO 1961.
3. S 13 of the MFLO was omitted under s 3 and Sch II of the Federal Laws (Revision and Declaration) Ordinance 1981 (XXVII of 1981). The Peshawar High Court noted this amendment in the law and refused to accept a husband's second marriage as a valid ground for the dissolution of marriage in *Syed Rashid Ali Shah v Haleema Bibi* PLD 2014 (Pesh) 226. The Lahore High Court, however, appears to be unaware of this change in law and regarded a husband's second marriage as a valid ground for the dissolution of marriage in *Sajjad Hussain v Judge Family Court, Mailsi* 2015 CLC 1347.
4. Proviso (b), s 2, Dissolution of Muslim Marriages Act 1939.
5. Proviso (c), ibid.
6. Jurists hold different views regarding the effect of apostasy on the marriage of a Muslim wife. For details see Dr Tanzil-ur-Rahman, *A Code of Muslim Personal Law*, 653–661.
7. Under Section 8 of the Punjab Family Courts (Amendment) Act 2015, in case of dissolution of marriage through *khula*, the Court may direct the wife to surrender up to 50 per cent of her deferred dower or up to 25 per cent of her admitted prompt dower to the husband and the Court shall direct the husband to pay whole or part of the outstanding deferred dower to the wife. This amendment has been challenged before the Federal Shariat Court for its being against the Injunctions of Islam in *Imran Anwar Khan v Government of the Punjab*, Petition No. 4/I/2016. The FSC has not yet decided on this case.
8. 2009 CLC 1210, 1217.
9. PLD 1981 Lah 732, 733.
10. 2013 MLD 1711 (FSC).
11. 2010 YLR 1632 (Islamabad).
12. PLD 1994 SC 607.
13. Ibid., 621.
14. Under Art 203B(c) of the Constitution of the Islamic Republic of Pakistan 1973, the FSC does not have the jurisdiction to declare the Constitution, Muslim Personal law, and any law relating to the procedure of any court or tribunal as repugnant to the injunctions of Islam.
15. 2010 YLR 1632, 1636.
16. PLD 1993 SC 901.
17. PLD 1959 Lah 566.

18. (1867) 11 M.I.A. 551.
19. Ibid., 609.
20. Ibid., 610.
21. Ibid.
22. PLD 1959 Lah 566, 581.
23. Ibid., 582.
24. Ibid.
25. PLD 1959 Lah 566.
26. PLD 1967 SC 97, 111.
27. Ibid., 117.
28. Ibid., 118.
29. M.T. Usmani, *Islām Mein Khul' ki Ḥaqīqat* (Karachi: Maiman Islamic Publishers, n.d.: 18, first published in *Fiqhī Maqālāt* in Urdu (Karachi: Maiman Publishers 1996), 137, 194.
30. PLD 2014 FSC 43, 54.
31. Ibid., 58.
32. Ibid., 59.
33. PLD 2003 Pesh 169.
34. PLD 2010 Kar 131.
35. PLD 2013 Sindh 209, 213.
36. 2010 YLR 582, 586.
37. Ibid.
38. 2003 YLR 2623, 8.
39. Ibid., 12.
40. Ibid., 14.
41. PLD 1963 SC 51.
42. 2004 YLR 619.
43. PLD 1993 SC 901.
44. PLD 1963 SC 51, 74.
45. Ibid., 75.
46. PLD 1993 SC 901, 916.
47. Ibid.
48. Ibid., 917.
49. 2004 YLR 619, 625.
50. PLD 2006 SC 457, 463.
51. PLD 2015 Pesh 14.
52. PLD 2006 Kar 563.
53. PLD 2011 Kar 196.

Part II
CHILDREN'S RIGHTS

Chapter 6

PARENTAGE AND LEGITIMACY

Chapter 7

GUARDIANSHIP, CUSTODY, AND WELFARE OF MINORS

6

PARENTAGE AND LEGITIMACY

6.1 Introduction

Parentage is the legal relationship of the parents with their children born during wedlock. Paternity refers to the legal relation that exists between a father and his child and maternity refers to the legal relation between a mother and her child. This legal relationship gives rise to mutual rights and obligations between the parties such as custody, guardianship, maintenance, and inheritance. Islamic law recognises two distinct modes of establishing parentage: by birth during a valid marriage of the spouses, and by acknowledgement of paternity of the child by a man. It should be noted that adoption is not a valid mode of filiation under Islamic law.

6.2 Period of Gestation

It is presumed under Islamic law that a child born after six lunar months of marriage is legitimate unless the father disclaims the legitimacy within forty days of the birth or within a reasonable time upon attaining knowledge of the birth. A child born before six lunar months of the marriage is presumed to be illegitimate except where the father acknowledges him/her, and the circumstances allow such acknowledgement to be valid under Islamic law. There is no difference in juristic opinion about the minimum period of gestation, i.e. six months. There is, however, a difference of opinions amongst various schools regarding the maximum period of gestation: under the Shia school, a child born within ten lunar months of the termination of marriage is legitimate; under the Hanafi school, this period is two lunar years; while, under the Shafi'i and Maliki schools, it is four lunar years. Once the paternity of a child is established, legitimacy is also established.

The classical Islamic law on legitimacy has been incorporated under Article 128 of the Qanun-e-Shahadat Order 1984 following the Hanafi school. This Article states that where a child is born during the continuance of a valid marriage between his mother and any man and not earlier than the expiration of six lunar months from the date of the marriage, or within two years after its dissolution, while the mother remains unmarried, it shall be the conclusive proof that he is the legitimate child of that man. This principle is subject to two conditions: the father has not disowned the child, and the child is not born after the expiration of six lunar months from the date on which the mother accepts that her period of *iddat* had come to an end.

6.3 Principle of Acknowledgment

A man can acknowledge (*iqrar*) paternity of a child even when there is no evidence of his marriage with the mother of the child or the fact of their marriage is shrouded in mystery provided the following conditions are fulfilled:

1. The age difference between the parties (i.e. the acknowledger and the child) must be in consonance with the presumption of paternity.
2. Marriage must be possible between the father/acknowledger and the mother of the child.
3. The parentage of the child acknowledged must be in doubt. A child who is established to be illegitimate cannot be extended paternity by acknowledgement.
4. The child gives his/her consent for the acknowledgement.

An acknowledgement may be expressed or implied by conduct. It may be presumed from the fact that one person has habitually and openly treated another as his child. Such an acknowledgement serves as sufficient proof of legitimacy. A valid acknowledgement establishes legal rights between spouses and children. Consequently, they inherit from each other. Once an acknowledgement is established, it cannot be revoked.

6.4 Rights of an Illegitimate Child

Under Islamic law, a child born out of wedlock is considered *filius nullius* (a child of nobody). There are two possible scenarios for a child born out of wedlock. In the first instance, the woman was married and had committed adultery. In the second instance, an unmarried woman had sexual intercourse with a man. A child born as a consequence of unlawful sexual intercourse is considered illegitimate and owes no lineage to the biological father under both the Sunni and Shia schools.

Under Sunni law, any child born to a woman during the subsistence of her marriage is attributed to the husband and not to anyone else, even if the husband is certain that the child is not related to him. If the husband exercises the option to disown the child through the process of *li'an* (mutual imprecation), the child is attributed solely to the mother. In case of an unmarried mother, the majority of jurists hold the view that the child is to be attributed to the mother only and not to the adulterer father, even though the identity of the adulterer father can be established.

No legal rights of maintenance or inheritance can be established between the illegitimate child, the biological father, or other paternal relatives. Sunni law recognises a mutual right of inheritance between the mother and the child's maternal relatives with the illegitimate child. Shia law, however, does not attribute the illegitimate child to either of the parents. Hence, Shia law does not recognise the rights to maintenance and inheritance of an illegitimate child. Such a child is not entitled to inheritance at all, not even from his/her mother and maternal relatives. Likewise, neither the mother nor any of the maternal relatives of such a child inherit from him/her.

6.5 Outline of Case Law

6.5.1 Legitimacy. The legitimacy of children is essential for their welfare, which is based on their rights to maintenance, guardianship, and inheritance. The case law suggests that the courts tend to attach a strong presumption in favour of the paternity of a child born during wedlock.

Hamida Begum v Murad Begum PLD 1975 SC 624

Islamic law is the substantive law for the determination of paternity.

This case is the leading judicial authority on the subject of legitimacy under Islamic law. It was decided by a full bench of the Supreme Court. It was decided at a time when Article 128 of the Qanun-e-Shahadat Order 1984 had not replaced section 112 of the Evidence Act 1872. Section 112 of the Evidence Act 1872 stated that any person born during the continuance of a valid marriage between his/her parents or within 280 days after its dissolution, the mother remaining unmarried, shall be the legitimate child of that man unless it can be shown that the parties to the marriage had no access to each other at any time when the child could have been begotten. Article 128 of the Qanun-e-Shahadat Order 1984, however, differs in its scope from its predecessor section. The Article states that the fact that any child was born no earlier than the expiration of six lunar months from the date of the marriage or within two years after its dissolution, the mother remaining unmarried, shall be conclusive proof that he is the legitimate child of that man.

The issue, in this case, was whether the provisions of the Evidence Act 1872 would have precedence over the principles of Islamic law (later incorporated in the Qanun-e-Shahadat Order 1984). The Supreme Court held that the principles of legitimacy laid down by Islamic law were a part of the substantive law of Pakistan, and therefore, the same would determine the issue of legitimacy irrespective of their conflict with section 112 of the Evidence Act 1872.

The facts of the case are as follows: Sh. Mehar Din established a *waqf-alal-aulad* through two deeds executed in 1944 and 1945. His third and last wife, Murad Begum, was appointed as the *mutawalli* of the *waqf*. The list of beneficiaries included two daughters of Murad Begum, who were also, along with Murad Begum, the respondents in the case. Hamida Begum, the petitioner, who claimed to be a daughter of Sh. Mehar Din from his previous marriage, was deprived of her share in inheritance and any benefits under the *waqf*. Sh. Mehar Din was about 80 years old when he executed the *waqf*. At the time of the petitioner's birth, he was in his late fifties.

In 1950 after the death of Sh. Mehar Din, the petitioner filed a suit for a declaration that the *waqf-alal-aulad* was invalid. She claimed that it was executed under undue influence and fraud for the sole purpose of depriving her of her share in the inheritance. The respondents contended that the *waqf* was validly executed and the petitioner was not a legitimate daughter of the deceased. The trial court dismissed the suit holding that the petitioner was not a legitimate daughter of the deceased and that the *waqf* had been established in conformity with the law.

The petitioner filed an appeal before the first Appellate Court, which was accepted. The court declared her to be the legitimate daughter of the deceased and held the *waqf* to be null and void on the grounds of undue influence and fraud. Thereafter, the respondents appealed to the High Court. The Court accepted the appeal with regard to the legality of the *waqf* but did not address the issue of the legitimacy of the petitioner.

Therefore, both the parties appealed before the Supreme Court. The Supreme Court summarised the rules of legitimacy as follows:

> Under the Muhammadan Law, as in all civilised systems of the world, the child follows the bed (*firash*), that is, the paternity of a child born in wedlock is presumed to be in the husband of the mother without any acknowledgement and affirmation of parentage on his part and such child follows the status of the father. According to the Sunni schools the presumption of legitimacy is so strong that in cases where a child is born after six months from the date of marriage and within two years after [the] dissolution of the marital contract, either by death of the husband or by divorce, a simple denial of paternity on the part of the husband would not take away the status of legitimacy from the child… The shortest period of gestation, according to all the schools, is six [lunar] months. If, therefore, a child is born within six lunar months of the marriage, no affiliation would take place unless the man acknowledges it to be his own issue. In other words, it is the right of the man to legitimate a child born within this time by acknowledging expressly or impliedly that the conception took place in wedlock… If the husband wishes to repudiate a child so born (after six months and before two years of dissolution), he can only do so by [the] procedure of *laan* [*li'an*] that is to say if he swears before the Qadi that the child is illegitimate and fruit of adultery, in which case the Court pass a decree not only dissolving the marriage but declaring the child to be illegitimate.[1]

The court further reflected on the principle of acknowledgement:

> Legitimacy is a status which results from certain facts, whereas legitimation is a proceeding which creates a status which did not exist before. This proceeding becomes necessary where either the existence of a valid marriage cannot be expressly proved or where the child is born within six months of the marriage. In such cases, acknowledgment of legitimacy in favour of the child either by express, or by necessary implication from the course of treatment by the man of the mother and the child, or from the evidence of repute and notoriety, amongst the members of the family, community and respectable members of [the] locality. Such an acknowledgement raises a presumption of [a] valid marriage and legitimate birth.[2]

Reverting to the facts of the case, the court thoroughly analysed the evidence. Both parties had confirmed the marriage between Sh. Mehar Din and the petitioner's mother. They, however, disputed the fact of the petitioner's birth within less than six months from the date of marriage. The

> petitioner stated that she was born after about ten months of the marriage as her father had informed her by referring to a copy of a document in which he made that entry. That being said, the copy of the document was not produced before any court. However, a *nikahnama* was brought on record which confirmed the daughter's claim. The fact that her marriage was solemnised in the house of Sh. Mehar Din and his name appeared as her father in the *nikahnama* supported her claim that she was his legitimate daughter. The petitioner also produced some letters written to her by the deceased which sufficiently demonstrated an affectionate relationship between the father and the daughter.

On the other hand, the respondents relied upon a birth certificate that showed that the petitioner was born within six months of the marriage. The court examined the register of birth on which the birth certificate was issued. It observed that even though the birth register attracted a presumption of genuineness, the manner in which it had been managed over the years made its authenticity questionable. Some other supporting documents were also produced by the respondents, including a will of Sh. Mehar Din, a *muafi-nama* (a document of apology) purportedly written by the mother of the petitioner and an explanatory memorandum attached to the two *waqf* deeds. The court found these documents fabricated in order to oust the petitioner from her due share and hence refused to place reliance on them. A few witnesses appeared to support the version of the respondents, but the court opined that most of them were biased; therefore, their testimonies were not trustworthy. The court observed that respondent no. 1 should have been penalised for attempting to exclude the petitioner from her legitimate share by way of forging a number of documents. As she had passed away by the time the decision was rendered, the court deemed it inappropriate to impose a punishment for her misdeeds on her daughters (the other respondents).

In addition to declaring the petitioner as a legitimate daughter of Sh. Mehar Din, the court held that the *waqf* deeds were executed by an old man under the undue influence of his younger wife—respondent no. 1, Murad Begum. Consequently, the court accepted the appeal of the petitioner and directed that she should be awarded her legitimate share in the property of her late father.

During the course of arguments, the respondents' counsel, upon realising that the court would accept the appeal of the petitioner, submitted that the case should be remanded to the trial court for a fresh decision based on the correct interpretation of law and evaluation of evidence. The court did not accede to his submission and observed that the petitioner had already spent about two and a half decades of her prime period of life establishing her legitimacy and remanding the case would expose her to the same agony again.

Muhammad Arshad v Sughran Bibi PLD 2008 Lah 302

Paternity of a child born in lawful wedlock carries the presumption of truth and it cannot be rebutted by a simple denial.

The petitioner, Muhammad Arshad, was married to respondent no. 1, Sughran Bibi. After one month of the marriage, she left for Saudi Arabia without his consent. After her return to Pakistan, she lived with him only for a few days and ultimately left his house. According to him, at that time she did not appear to be pregnant, nor did she inform him of her pregnancy. She gave birth to respondent no. 2 during the separation of the spouses.

Eight months after the birth of respondent no. 2, respondent no. 1 filed a suit for the dissolution of marriage and recovery of maintenance. It was at this point that the petitioner denied paternity of respondent no. 2 in his written statement. He further requested a DNA test for ascertaining the child's paternity. After the Family Court refused this request, he impugned that order under the writ jurisdiction of the High Court.

The court referred to the well-established presumption of the Islamic law that a 'child follows the bed' and concluded that the denial of legitimacy could not be claimed in a casual manner. The court noted:

> The plea as raised by the petitioner with reference to [the] legitimacy of the child entails far-reaching impact, therefore, determination of this crucial and vital issue should not be taken in a cavalier manner. The accusation by a husband or his act of disowning the child born out of the wedlock is to be substantiated through tangible proof and credible evidence. Paternity of a child born out of the lawful wedlock invariably carried [the] presumption of truth in its favor and mere simple denial can never take away the status of legitimacy, in as much as, according to Muhammadan Law "child follows the bed". Every presumption is made in favor of [the] legitimacy of the child, is presumed to be an issue of his parents without acknowledgement or affirmation of the parentage on the part of [the] father, the child follows bed (*Firash*).[3]

The court also observed that according to sections 146 to 149 of the *Majmooa-e-Qawaneen-e-Islam* by Dr Tanzeel-ur-Rahman, evidence of a woman is sufficient to prove the parentage of a child. To elaborate on its view, the court relied upon *Hamida Begum v Murad Begum*[4] in which the Supreme Court held:

> [A]ccording to Hanafi School of thought, a child born in wedlock is of his parents even if the husband has no access to the wife. In any case, it is obligatory upon the husband who repudiates the child so born can only resort [to] the procedure of Liyan, by swearing before Qazi that child is illegitimate and result of adultery, and in that eventuality, the Court will pass a two-fold decree by dissolving the marriage and declaring the child as illegitimate. Such type of husband has to disown the child immediately upon birth of child or on having the knowledge thereof, and very strong and unimpeachable evidence is required to substantiate the factum of illegitimacy…[5]

The court stated that there was no evidence on record affirming that the minor son Ahmed was born after divorce, nor did any evidence exist to the effect that respondent no. 1 had been living in adultery. Clearly, the petitioner disowned the child solely to avoid the liability of maintenance. No evidence existed on record to substantiate the frivolous and scandalous version of the petitioner's accusation that the minor child was illegitimate; and admittedly he did not resort to a court of competent jurisdiction for *li'an*, hence the minor child was deemed to be legitimate.

The court observed that the paternity of a child could only be repudiated by resorting to *li'an*, i.e. swearing before a qazi that the child was illegitimate and the outcome of adultery, and thereafter the court would dissolve the marriage. However, the court warned that a husband could not avail this procedure at will. He should initiate this procedure immediately after the birth of a child or after having knowledge of the birth and any unwarranted delay would deprive him of this option. Since the petitioner did not take recourse to the court of competent jurisdiction for *li'an*, the court held that respondent no. 2 was a legitimate child and was entitled to be maintained by the petitioner. Consequently, the petition was dismissed *in limine*.

Muhammad Nazir v Ali Muhammad 2003 SCMR 1183

Law is inclined towards the presumption of paternity rather than illegitimacy.

In this case, the petitioner filed a suit for the declaration that the deceased, Ghulam Haider, had divorced Amina Bibi, his wife, and that Sumaira Begum was not their legitimate daughter. Therefore, she was not entitled to inherit from the estate of the deceased. The petitioner, the sister of the deceased also filed a separate suit claiming the entire estate of the deceased as his sole surviving heir. Both these suits were dismissed by the trial court. The petitioner filed an appeal which was also rejected. The petitioner's civil revision before the High Court against the concurrent findings of lower courts met with the same fate; hence, the present application for leave to appeal was filed before the Supreme Court.

The counsel for the appellants argued that both the first Appellate Court and the High Court simply agreed with the trial court's findings of the facts and did not fully appreciate the arguments advanced before them by the petitioners' counsel. The Supreme Court observed that the record showed that the judgments of the first Appellate Court and the High Court were well-reasoned and were based on oral and documentary evidence. The courts below concurrently found that the deceased Ghulam Haider did not divorce Amina Bibi and that Sumaira Begum was born from their wedlock during the subsistence of their marriage. Therefore, there was no reason to disentitle her from the estate of the deceased. The court held that 'it is well-settled that law leans in favour of presumption of paternity rather than illegitimacy, unless proved otherwise by strong evidence'.[6] Hence, the petition was dismissed.

Abdul Rashid v Safia Bibi PLD 1986 FSC 10

A child born during wedlock has the parentage of the husband. There is no need for an acknowledgement or an affirmation.

In this case, Safia Bibi had filed a suit against her ex-husband, Abdul Rashid, the appellant, under section 3 of the Offence of Qazf (Enforcement of Hadd) Ordinance 1979. She sued the appellant for damaging her reputation by falsely and publicly accusing her of committing *zina* and disowning their daughter. She revealed to the court that when she was going to her parents' house for delivery, her husband warned her that he would only receive her back if she gave birth to a boy. She also filed a civil suit for the recovery of dowry articles and maintenance for her child. In his written statement, the husband contended that he had rightly accused his wife of adultery and that he was not bound to pay maintenance costs since the child did not belong to him. The trial court ruled in favour of the wife and held that the husband was guilty under the Qazf Ordinance 1979. The husband filed an appeal before the Federal Shariat Court.

While examining the facts of the case, the court highlighted the point that the parties were married on 4 July 1980 and the child was born on 30 May 1981. The court observed that there is a presumption that a child born during wedlock is legitimate and is to be attributed to the husband. However, the appellant argued that the date of *nikah* and the date of *rukhsati* were four months apart, therefore, the wife was already pregnant at the time of the *rukhsati*. The court found this argument false on the basis of direct and circumstantial evidence. Furthermore, the court inquired from the appellant about the reasons for the delay in *rukhsati*, since in current Pakistani society there is usually a reason for a delayed *rukhsati*, such as financial problems, or one party not yet having reached the age of majority. The appellant could not provide a cogent reason.

The husband also took a plea of impotency and contended that he had been having sexual problems, which prevented him from having sexual relations with his wife. Therefore the child was illegitimate. The court informed the appellant that the onus of proving a medical problem through medical evidence was upon him. The appellant, however, could not provide any such evidence. The court also observed that if the husband was suffering from impotency, then he would have known about his wife's illegitimate child during the period of pregnancy, but he had remained silent until the birth of the child.

The court found the statements of both the wife and her father reliable insofar as the appellant had threatened his wife that he would not take her back unless she gave birth to a boy. The court upheld the decision of the trial court which had found the husband guilty under section 3 of the Offence of Qazf (Enforcement of Hadd) Ordinance 1979 as he knowingly damaged the wife's reputation with the purpose of disowning the child.

Sharafat Ali Ashraf v Additional District Judge, Bahawalpur 2008 SCMR 1707

The legitimacy of a child cannot be questioned merely because of the claims of the father which have not been substantiated by any evidence.

The petitioner, Sharafat Ali Ashraf married Mst Fazal Elahi alias Saira (respondent no. 3) on 18 December 2004. The amount of dower was settled at Rs 1,500,000 or a residential house along with gold ornaments weighing 25 *tolas*. Sometime later, the petitioner contracted another marriage which led to a strained relationship with the first wife. In December 2005 the petitioner expelled respondent no. 3 from his house.

After the separation of the spouses, respondent no. 3 initiated a suit for maintenance and recovery of dower, whereas the petitioner filed a suit for jactitation of marriage—challenging the validity of his marriage with respondent no. 3. A daughter was born to respondent no. 3 in November 2006 during the pendency of the suits in the trial court and she was added as a party (respondent no. 4) to the proceedings. The trial court decreed the suit for maintenance of respondent no. 3 and respondent no. 4. The claim for recovery of dower was also decided in favour of respondent no. 3. The petitioner's suit for the jactitation of marriage was dismissed. Thereafter, the appeals of the petitioner before the first Appellate Court and the High Court were dismissed.

The petitioner brought his case before the Supreme Court. He argued that the lower courts misread and misinterpreted the evidence and by not allowing DNA tests, the courts materially jeopardised his interests. Therefore, the decisions rendered by them should be set aside.

The court while analysing the facts of the case found that there was convincing and substantial evidence for the lawful marriage between the parties and the lower courts had rightly relied upon that. The petitioner had negated the legitimacy of the child without substantiating his claim. Furthermore, he was unable to prove that respondent no. 4 was born after the dissolution of their marriage, or that respondent no. 3 had committed adultery. Since respondent no. 4 was born after six lunar months of the marriage and two years of the dissolution of marriage her legitimacy and consequent paternity could not be disputed. The court further noted that respondent no. 3 had agreed to have the DNA test conducted but the petitioner did not opt for the test. The court observed that the case of the petitioner was motivated to avoid his liability to provide maintenance to respondent no. 4. In light of these reasons, the court dismissed the petition.

Manzoor Hussain v Zahoor Ahmed 1992 SCMR 1191

A child born to a prostitute who validly married a man is legitimate.

The petitioner in this case was denied his share of inheritance in the estate of his father, Muhammad Khan. According to the petitioner, his mother Mst Kalo was married to Muhammad Khan, and he was born in 1928 during wedlock. His father died in 1972 and thereafter he was precluded from inheriting his share on the ground that he was an illegitimate child born to a mother who belonged to a family of prostitutes.

The petitioner initiated a suit for declaration of his status, but the lower courts and the High Court rejected his suit. The courts were convinced by the fact that his mother hailed from a family of prostitutes and there was evidence that his mother and maternal grandmother had engaged in the disreputable profession of prostitution.

Ultimately, the petitioner brought his case before the Supreme Court. Justice Muhammad Afzal Zullah analysed the evidence and found that some important pieces of evidence supported the legitimacy of the petitioner. Muhammad Khan had been mentioned as the father of the petitioner throughout his educational career and thereafter. The petitioner was a teacher, but the lower courts did not accord due importance to his evidence. During his lifetime, Muhammad Khan took care of the petitioner and his mother and in the revenue records the mother of the petitioner was shown to be the wife of Muhammad Khan.

After going through the records, Justice Zullah observed that the lower courts erred as to two Islamic law rules. Firstly, there is no restriction on a woman who has been a prostitute to go through the process of *tauba* (repentance) and lead a normal married life. Allah in His wisdom may accept *tauba* (repentance) at any time. Secondly, the courts should be inclined towards legitimisation rather than stigmatisation of the petitioner. The courts should have construed the law while considering the presumption of legitimacy in the absence of strong evidence to the contrary. Justice Zullah referred to his judgment in *Abdul Majid Khan v Mst Anwar Begum*[7] and observed that the High Court had not appreciated the presumption of a valid marriage under Islamic law of evidence. The judgments of the Privy Council had created an exception to this general presumption in the marriage of prostitutes. However, in the *Abdul Majid* case, Justice Zullah removed that exception.

Viewing the case from this perspective, the Supreme Court held that the petitioner was a legitimate son of Muhammad Khan from the marriage of the latter with Mst Kalo. Hence, he was entitled to his share from the estate of his father, Muhammad Khan.

6.5.2 Paternity and DNA Profiling. The following case law suggests that the courts have been hesitant to resort to DNA profiling as proof of legitimacy. The courts have held that a father cannot deny the paternity of a child after forty days of the birth and in view of this point of law, a DNA test cannot be ordered as a routine to determine the legitimacy of children. Even if a court allows such a test, it cannot be conducted without the consent of the concerned person. In *Khizer Hayat v Additional District*

Judge, Kabirwala,[8] the court held that such a test could not be ordered when the factum of birth is proved, given the possibility of human error in its administration. However, in criminal cases, the courts have held that a DNA test can be conducted to establish the offence of rape.

Ghazala Tehsin Zohra v Mehr Ghulam Dastagir Khan PLD 2015 SC 327

A father cannot question the paternity of a child after forty days of the birth by asking for a DNA test of the child.

This is an important case regarding the question of conducting a DNA test where a father denies the paternity of a child. The Supreme Court categorically discouraged the conducting of the test in a routine manner. It observed that the interest of the society as a whole should be given preference over the interest of an individual for the test.

The respondent, in this case, was married to the appellant on 9 August 1997. They had been living an amicable married life until 26 March 2001 when the appellant's parents took her back to their home. During the subsistence of the marriage, on 21 March 2000 and on 9 February 2001 a daughter and a son were born to the wife respectively. The immediate cause of discord between the spouses was that the respondent got transferred to his name some land which he had earlier mutated to the appellant. Another reason for the marital discord was the respondent's second marriage.

After separation, the appellant filed a suit for maintenance for herself and the children. In response to the suit, the respondent pronounced *talaq* on 26 June 2001. In another chain of litigation, the respondent initiated a declaratory suit for denying his paternity of the children. He made serious allegations against the chastity of the appellant in the *talaqnama* and the suit. No one except the spouses appeared as witnesses in the case. The suit was about to conclude when the respondent made an application for conducting a DNA test of the children. The trial court rejected the application. The first Appellate Court, however, allowed the test. The petitioner challenged this decision before the High Court in a writ petition, which was dismissed. Therefore, she brought her case before the Supreme Court.

The counsel of the respondent contended that in India, under section 112 of the Evidence Act 1872, the courts allowed a DNA test when a husband questioned the legitimacy of children along with the chastity of the wife. He further submitted that since Article 128 of the Qanun-e-Shahadat Order 1984 was analogous to Section 112, the same principle should be applied in Pakistan. Justice Jawad Khawaja did not accede to this argument and pointed out that due to marked differences between the two provisions, the precedent in India could not be transplanted without further reflection:

> The Article [128] is couched in language which is protective of societal cohesion and values of the community. This appears to be the rationale for stipulating affirmatively that a child who is born within two years after the dissolution of the marriage between his parents (the mother remaining un-married) shall constitute conclusive proof of his legitimacy.[9]

Justice Khawaja pointed out:

> [N]either the classical Islamic jurists nor the framers of the Qanun-e-Shahadat Order 1984 could have been oblivious [to] the scientific fact that the normal gestation period of the human foetus is around nine months. That they then extended the presumption of legitimacy to two years, in spite of this knowledge, directly points towards the legislative intent as well as the societal imperative of avoiding controversy in matters of paternity… In this regard, it is also worth taking time to reflect on the belief in our tradition that on the Day of Judgment, the children of Adam will be called out by their mother's name. It shows that the Divine Being has, in His infinite wisdom and mercy, taken care to ensure that even on a day when all personal secrets shall be laid bare, the secrets about paternity shall not be delved into or divulged.[10]

Justice Khawaja emphasised the conclusive nature of the presumption embodied in Article 128 in the following words:

> Once the relevant facts as to [the] commencement and dissolution of marriage and date of birth of a child within the period envisioned in Article 128 are proved, and the date of birth is within the period specified in Article 128(1), the Court cannot allow evidence to be given for disproving the legitimacy of a child born within the period aforesaid.[11]

Justice Khawaja deliberated upon the issue of a husband's exercise of his option to disown a child if he believes the child is illegitimate. According to Imam Abu Hanifa, paternity should be immediately denied after birth, while in the opinion of Imam Abu Yousaf, a father can deny it within the postnatal period, i.e. within forty days. No one could be allowed to deny paternity after this period. Justice Khawaja observed:

> Law does not give a free license to individuals and particularly unscrupulous fathers, to make unlawful assertions and thus to cause harm to children as well as their mothers… The wisdom of this rule of Muslim Personal Law cannot be gainsaid, considering in particular the patriarchal and at times misogynistic societal proclivities where women frequently do not receive the benefit of laws and on the contrary face humiliation and degrading treatment.[12]

In this case, the first denial of paternity was made through the *talaqnama* and according to the Supreme Court that was not the diligent and lawful exercise of a husband's exceptional option to deny paternity. The court allowed the appeal against permission of conducting a DNA test with costs. In doing so, the court also considered the fourteen years of prolonged litigation in which the legitimacy of innocent children and the chastity of their guiltless mothers were kept in perpetual jeopardy.

Malik Muhammad Rafique v Tanveer Jahan PLD 2015 Islamabad 30

A DNA test cannot be routinely ordered. There must be a *prima facie* case for conducting such a test and the person, who is to be subjected to the test, must give his/her consent.

In this case, the father did not raise the question of paternity during his lifetime; rather, his brother brought it forth after his death. In consonance with the settled principle, the court denied the application for conducting a DNA test to determine the legitimacy of a child.

A renowned academic, Professor Dr Khalid Alvi, died in 2008 and left behind his widow and a son who appeared as respondents no. 1 and no. 2 respectively. The petitioner was the brother of the deceased. After his death, the respondents sought a succession certificate from the court which was granted. According to that certificate, the petitioner was not entitled to gain anything from the deceased's estate. Therefore, the petitioner questioned the paternity of respondent no. 2. The petitioner argued that respondent no. 2 was an adopted son and therefore he was not entitled to any share in the deceased's estate. During the course of the proceedings, the petitioner applied for a DNA test and other medical tests in order to ascertain the paternity of the son. The trial court rejected his application, and the Appellate Court upheld this decision. Thereafter, the petitioner brought the matter before the High Court.

The petitioner's counsel argued that the lower courts had not applied their mind judiciously. Therefore, a DNA test should be allowed because it is in the interest of justice and equity. The High Court denied the petition and imposed costs on the petitioner for frivolous litigation. The court relied upon the following grounds for dismissing the petition: (i) a DNA test could not be routinely ordered; (ii) the petitioner had failed to establish *prima facie* case by failing to provide convincing evidence necessitating a DNA test; and (iii) the requisite consent for conducting a DNA test was not given by the party who was to be subjected to the test. The court provided the following rationale for its decision:

> The Courts do not lightly entertain attempts of persons who may appear to be on fishing expedition. Entertaining applications for DNA test under such circumstances would open the flood gates, allowing relatives to carry out roving enquiries in the hope that they may find a share in the property of the deceased… Passing an order in routine and compelling a person to undergo a DNA test can have serious consequences, besides interference with personal liberty… Allowing an opportunity to fish for a cause to create doubts regarding the paternity of a person can neither be encouraged nor taken lightly.[13]

Khizar Hayat v Additional District Judge, Kabirwala PLD 2010 Lah 422

Since there is a possibility of human error in conducting a DNA test, it cannot be ordered when the fact of the birth of a child during the marriage is already proved.

In addition to following the judicial aversion to conducting a DNA test in cases of alleged illegitimacy, the present case goes further to point out that human error in conducting the DNA test could result in dangerous consequences for an innocent child.

The petitioner was married to respondent no. 2. A child, respondent no. 3, was born during wedlock in 1997. After their marriage was dissolved in 1998, respondent no. 2 filed a suit for the recovery of dowry articles and maintenance allowance for herself and respondent no. 3. The petitioner defended the suit on many grounds including alleged illegitimacy of respondent no. 3. The trial court decreed the suit in favour of the respondents and the first Appellate Court confirmed it in appeal. Thereafter, the petitioner brought the matter before the High Court.

The petitioner contended that refusal to conduct a DNA test to verify the paternity of respondent no. 3 caused substantial injustice and material loss to him. The court observed that the petitioner admitted to having the knowledge of the birth of respondent no. 3, and the entry of respondent no. 3's name in the petitioner's *shajrah nasab* (pedigree table) had been made by the *halqa patwari* (revenue official). In light of these observations, the court concluded that the petitioner's denial was a ploy to avoid payment of maintenance. The court held that once the fact of a child's birth during the marriage was proved, the burden of proof shifted to the one who denied it according to the combined reading of Articles 128, 117, 118, and 119 of the Qanun-e-Shahadat Order 1984. Since the petitioner was unable to discharge the burden of proof, the lower courts rightly dismissed his suits. The court observed:

> It has been observed by this Court that it has become a common practice that when the relationship between the parties become strained after marriage and even extreme hatred is developed between the spouses and the same is dissolved, the parties do not spare each other and even go to this extent that often father refuses to acknowledge the child for the reason either to evade maintenance or to deprive the child from inheritance in case of his second marriage at the insistence of his second wife or pressure of the elders of the family and this trend is not only damaging but also very dangerous for the society and in such a situation request for DNA test is not proper.[14]

Regarding the reliability of the DNA test, the court remarked that although medical science has developed tremendously in the modern era, it had not attained the desired level of accuracy, especially in Pakistan where there are not enough sufficiently skilled persons who can conduct an accurate DNA test. Hence, the possibility of error in conducting the test could not be ruled out. The court noted that a human error in conducting this test could result in a disaster not only for a child but also for the entire society. As a result of a wrong DNA test, the life of the child will become miserable without his fault, and he would be stigmatised as illegitimate in the society.

Muhammad Shahid Sahil v State PLD 2010 FSC 215

A DNA test can be conducted to establish the offence of rape.

In this case, the Federal Shariat Court allowed a DNA test to prove the offence of rape by determining the biological relationship between the child born of rape and the alleged rapist. The petitioner had allegedly raped the victim. She lodged an FIR in 2005 against him under sections 10 and 11 of the Offence of Zina (Enforcement of Hudood) Ordinance 1979. In her complaint, she claimed that she had given birth to a baby girl due to the alleged rape. After the investigation, the police presented the requisite challan to the court for the prosecution of the petitioner. During the trial, the victim made an application for determining the biological relationship between the baby girl and the alleged offender through a DNA test. The court accepted the application. The petitioner filed the present petition to impugn the order of the trial court.

The petitioner contended that the alleged victim did not disclose the factum of rape earlier and that she had only done so when her husband divorced her because she gave birth to a baby girl after five months of her marriage. He questioned the admissibility of a DNA report at the trial court under the Code of Criminal Procedure 1908. The court rejected these contentions and observed:

> In criminal cases the identity of the actual accused is an element of primary importance. A lot of pre-meditation, improvements and tactical delays on the part of [the] complainant party can be checked if [the] scientific analysis is resorted to. Apart from saving time and ensuring quick disposal of cases particularly of sexual assault, such an exercise can act as a deterrent in future. Many genuine complaints remain unresolved due to stereotype method of investigation. From the point of view of a new born it is his right to be born with known paternity. The law, be it enacted or judge made, must come to the rescue of the aggrieved.[15]

The court observed that the Qur'an and Sunnah do not forbid the use of scientific or analytical methods in discovering the truth. Rather, several verses of the Qur'an recommend the discovery and investigation of truth. The court referred to the doctrine of *ijtihad* to support its argument for the admissibility of a DNA test in criminal cases related to the Hudood Ordinance. Consequently, the court dismissed the petition and ordered the petitioner to submit to the DNA test.

This case is different from the cases discussed above. In those cases, the courts denied resorting to DNA tests since a presumption of truth is attached to the paternity of children born during wedlock. In the present case, however, a rape victim applied for the test of the alleged rapist and the child to substantiate the fact that the child was an outcome of the alleged offence. Moreover, the previously discussed cases are civil in nature and the denial of a DNA test is meant to deter those who resort to this plea with the intent to avoid their responsibility of providing maintenance to their children despite having no cogent evidence for their denial of paternity.

6.5.3 Acknowledgement. The Islamic legal principle of acknowledgement can be invoked to confer the right of paternity upon a child of an unknown lineage. It means that a child who has been proven to be legitimate or illegitimate cannot be acknowledged as his/her lineage is already established. This principle proceeds upon the assumption that the acknowledged child is the offspring of the acknowledger. Once acknowledged, the person cannot deny the paternity of the child on any ground.

Asma Naz v Muhammad Younas Qureshi 2005 SCMR 401

An adopted child could be given the right of paternity under the principle of acknowledgement.

Acknowledgement is a valid mode of establishing legitimacy and paternity. The present case is one of the rare cases in which the Supreme Court applied this principle. The court highlighted the distinction between adoption and acknowledgement. Under Islamic law, an adoption is a simple act of adopting a child without interfering with his/her lineage. On the other hand, acknowledgement is a concept that holds greater value. It confers paternity upon a child of unknown lineage and merges him/her into the family of the acknowledger as if s/he was born into that family.

The respondent and his wife were issueless when a family friend handed them a child in 1965. The friend had found the child lying abandoned near his house in Karachi and got her custody by an order of a magistrate. As he already had children, he decided to give the child to the respondent. After taking custody of the child, the respondent and his wife started to treat her as if she had been born during their wedlock. The respondent had given her parentage in all relevant documents including school and college records as well as other official records, e.g. B-Form, ID card, and her *Nikahnama*.

After the petitioner's marriage in 1985, rumours arose about her paternity and legitimacy. Upon the insistence of her in-laws, the petitioner asked the respondent-father to disclose her identity and parentage, but he was persistent in his claim that she was his daughter.

During this time, the petitioner asked the respondent to hand over the documents of a particular plot situated in Karachi which the latter had purchased in her name. The respondent was reluctant to do so for undisclosed reasons. This attitude of the respondent infuriated the petitioner who had already been stressed by the rumours about her legitimacy. In reaction, she filed a criminal petition against her father, the respondent, for fraud, deceit, and defamation. The courts dismissed her petition. However, during the judicial proceedings, she discovered the fact of her adoption. The disclosure of this fact deeply disturbed her, and she filed a civil suit against the respondent to restrain him from denying her paternity.

The lower courts did not accept her suit and ultimately, she appealed before the Supreme Court. Justice Iftikhar Muhammad Chaudhry, as he then was, found that the respondent and his wife had been treating and acknowledging the petitioner as their daughter since her adoption in 1965. This fact was quite apparent from numerous documents, some of which have been mentioned above. Justice Chaudhry observed that legitimacy in Islamic law is determined by birth, but if this fact could not be ascertained or is clouded in mystery then the same status could be extended by acknowledgement. Justice Chaudhry relied upon various precedents and held that acknowledgement has similar implications as if the acknowledger was the father of the child. Furthermore, once the status of paternity is conferred by acknowledgement it cannot be taken away.

Justice Chaudhry observed that the trial court had wrongly placed the burden of proving herself as legitimate upon the petitioner. In view of abundant documentary evidence, the respondent should have been required to prove that the petitioner was not his legitimate daughter. Since the respondent had once conferred the status of paternity on the petitioner, in accordance with settled principles of acknowledgement, he was not entitled to deprive her of the same. Justice Chaudhry refused to rely upon the document through which the respondent's family friend acquired custody of a child from a magistrate in Karachi as it could not be established that the child mentioned in that document and the petitioner were the same person. Consequently, the court accepted the appeal of the petitioner and restrained the respondent from denying her legitimacy and paternity. The court declared the petitioner to be entitled to all the rights of a legitimate child.

Muhammad Allahdad Khan v Muhammad Ismail Khan 1888 ILR 10 All 289

Acknowledgement proceeds upon the assumption that the acknowledged child is the offspring of the acknowledger and the issue of a lawful union.

This case deals with the important question regarding the legitimacy of a child who was proven illegitimate because of a disapproved marriage between his parents, or because their marriage was unlawful.

The main contention involved in this case was regarding the status of the plaintiff, Allahdad Khan and the effect of acknowledgement of his paternity by his father, Ghulam Ghaus Khan. Moti Begum was lawfully married to Ghulam Ghaus Khan. There was no evidence to indicate that she had been married to anyone other than Ghulam Ghaus Khan. Evidence showed that Moti Begum cohabited with Ghulam Ghaus Khan for a number of years and was treated by him as his lawful wife. However, the exact date of Moti Begum's marriage to Ghulam Ghaus Khan with reference to the birth of the plaintiff could not be ascertained in the absence of trustworthy evidence. Ghulam Ghaus Khan acknowledged the plaintiff as his son and treated him as such. There was no express specification as to whether the plaintiff was a stepson, a legitimate son, or an illegitimate son. Similar acknowledgment or treatment was accorded to him by the defendant, Ismail Khan, and the rest of thc family. The lower court held that the plaintiff was an illegitimate son of Ghulam Ghaus Khan because he was born before the marriage of his parents. Consequently, an appeal was filed before the Allahabad High Court.

In his detailed judgment, Justice Syed Mahmood clarified the Islamic rule of acknowledgement. One of the issues addressed by the court was whether the rule of acknowledgement of parentage is a rule of the Muhammadan substantive law of inheritance or merely a rule of evidence. In the former case, the issue was to be discussed under Muhammadan law, and in the latter, it was to be discussed under the Evidence Act 1872. In order to answer this question, Justice Mahmood consulted classical textbooks of Muhammadan law. These authorities revealed that Muslim jurists do not treat the subject of an acknowledgement as forming part of the rules of evidence though they recognise the fact that acknowledgements resemble admissions. He observed:

> This peculiarity of such acknowledgements, that is, the permanency of their effect when duly made, upon the personal status of the persons in respect of whom such acknowledgements are made, is in itself sufficient to justify the conclusion that the acknowledgement of parentage, though it has reference to evidential presumptions and other considerations, is in effect a rule of personal status in the eye of Muhammadan law.[16]

Justice Mahmood subsequently moved on to discuss legitimacy as a qualification for a child to inherit from his father. He observed that the right of inheritance under Muhammadan law is based on three grounds as described by Baillie:

> [*N*]*asub* [*sic*], which is *kurabat*, or kindred; special cause, which is marriage, that is, a valid marriage, for there are no mutual rights of inheritance by a marriage that is invalid or void, according to all, and *wula* [*sic*], which is of two kinds, *wula* [*sic*] of emancipation and *wula* [*sic*] of *moowalat* [*sic*], or mutual friendship.[17]

This case concerned only *nasab* or relationship by consanguinity of descent, which in Muhammadan law means legitimate descent only as far as an inheritance from the father's side is concerned. It should be noted that marriage between the parents of the inheritor is a condition precedent to his legitimacy.

This led Justice Mahmood to question whether the paternity of a child can be proved only by establishing a marriage between his parents at the time of his birth. He deliberated upon the question of whether Muhammadan law recognises any other method whereby such marriage and legitimate descent can be presumed, inferred, or held to be established as a matter of substantive law for the purposes of inheritance. While addressing this question, he relied upon various rulings of the Privy Council. He noted that in all the rulings, their Lordships never intended to lay down the rule that a child who is illegitimate, either in consequence of marriage between his parents being disproved, or being unlawful, could be legitimated by an acknowledgement. All the cases before their Lordships were of such nature where the fact or the exact time of the alleged marriage was uncertain; consequently, their Lordships applied the principle of acknowledgement of parentage to ascertain legitimacy for the purposes of inheritance.

It was argued before the court that Muhammadan law regarding the acknowledgement of parentage was nothing more or less than a substitute for affiliation by adoption as recognised by Roman law or Hindu law—an affiliation which has no reference either to the consanguinity of descent of the acknowledged child from the acknowledger or to the legitimacy of such descent. Justice Mahmood held that this contention is not warranted by any of the rulings of the Privy Council, and it is in fact opposed to Muhammadan law. He observed:

> The Muhammadan law of acknowledgement of parentage with its legitimating effect has no reference whatsoever to cases in which the illegitimacy of the child is proved and established… The doctrine relates only to cases where either the fact of the marriage itself or the exact time of its occurrence with reference to the legitimacy of the acknowledged child

> is not proved in the sense of the law as distinguished from disproved. In other words, the doctrine applies only to cases of uncertainty as to [the] legitimacy, and in such cases, acknowledgement has its effect, but that effect always proceeds upon the assumption of a lawful union between the parents of the acknowledged child.[18]

This means that, under Muhammadan law, there is no justification for the view that a child proven to be the offspring of fornication, adultery, or incest could be legitimated by any act of acknowledgement by the father. The rule is limited to cases involving the uncertainty of legitimate descent and operates entirely upon an assumption of legitimacy and the establishment of such legitimacy by the principle of acknowledgement.

Justice Mahmood subsequently moved on the impugned judgment which had held the plaintiff to be the illegitimate son of Ghulam Ghaus Khan as he was born before the marriage of Ghulam Ghaus Khan with Moti Begum:

> [T]he entire question of the descent, birth, and legitimacy of Allahdad [the plaintiff] is involved in obscurity owing to the exact date of his mother's marriage with Ghulam Ghaus being unascertainable, and that, therefore, this case presents all those conditions to which the Muhammadan law as to the acknowledgement of parentage is most appropriately applicable.[19]

Hence, in view of the facts and circumstances of the case, the court held the plaintiff to be the legitimate son of Ghulam Ghaus Khan, and therefore, he was entitled to inherit from him.

6.6 Conclusion

Parentage is one of the most important rights of a child because other rights such as maintenance, guardianship, and inheritance depend upon it. The parentage includes both paternity and maternity. However, paternity is far more important as it is established only for a legitimate child, unlike maternity which is established regardless of a child's legitimacy. Article 128 of the Qanun-e-Shahadat Order 1984 determines the minimum and maximum periods of gestation. It provides that any child born during the continuance of a valid marriage between his/her mother and a man and not earlier than the expiration of six lunar months from the date of the marriage, or within two years after its dissolution, the mother remaining unmarried, shall be conclusive proof that s/he is the legitimate child of that man.

Analysis of case law suggests that Pakistani courts tend to lean in favour of the presumption of paternity unless proved otherwise by strong evidence. In deciding paternity and legitimacy cases, the courts do not adhere to rigid technicalities rather they consider the broader social ramifications associated with declaring a child illegitimate. This is why a husband has not been given any right to nonchalantly deny paternity of a child born to him by his wife. A father cannot deny paternity of a child unless he expressly does so within forty days of the child's birth. The courts have also been quite wary of ordering DNA tests in cases where the paternity or legitimacy of a child is challenged. The courts are even more careful with respect to the validity of a DNA test as there is a lack of requisite expertise in Pakistan in collecting and handling adequate evidence that could be subjected to DNA testing. Any minor error can stigmatise both the mother and the child for the rest of their lives. In several reported cases, fathers have asked for DNA tests of the children in defence of a suit for the maintenance of the children. The courts have discouraged this practice by refusing permission to conduct DNA tests in these cases. The case law does not leave any room for unconscientious fathers to make bald assertions of the illegitimacy of their children. On the other hand, in criminal cases, the courts are willing to accept the evidence based on DNA tests for determining the offence of rape.

In various decisions of the superior courts, the presumption of legitimacy of children born during wedlock is clearly established. In one important case, the Supreme Court creatively applied the Islamic legal principle of acknowledgement to protect the interests of an allegedly adopted child whose descent and familial origin was not established with conclusive evidence, and she was treated as a natural-born child throughout her life.

Questions

1. What are the implications of legitimacy and how does an illegitimate child suffer owing to his/her status?
2. Critically evaluate the judicial approach that refuses to entertain requests for DNA profiling in cases of alleged illegitimacy. Can evidence based on a DNA test be denied in all types of cases or can it be used as circumstantial evidence in criminal cases?
3. What is the principle of acknowledgement in Islamic law and is it an alternative to adoption?

📖 Further Reading

Books/Articles

Cheema, S.A., 'DNA Evidence in Pakistani Courts: An Analysis', *LUMS Law Journal* (2016) 3, 1–15.

Pollack, D., M. Bleich, C.J. Reid, and M.H. Fadel, 'Classical Religious Perspectives of Adoption Law', *Notre Dame Law Review* 693 (2004) 79 (2). See Section III: Adoption under Islamic law, 732–53.

Cases

Ambreen Khatoon v Mumtaz Bibi 2020 SCMR 643 (The DNA evidence proved, in addition to other evidence, that the minor was the son of the deceased; therefore, he was entitled to inheritance.)

Bibi Amu v Mst Asiat PLD 1958 Kar 420 (Legitimacy presupposes a valid marriage between the child's parents. In case direct evidence of the marriage is not available, then continued cohabitation between the parents and the acknowledgement of the child by the father provides strong presumptive evidence for extending legitimacy.)

Maj. (Retd) Abdul Akbar v Maryam Khushboo PLD 2011 Pesh 78 (Muslim law recognises acknowledgement as a method for establishing paternity.)

Mst. Benish Liaquat v Station Police Officer 2020 MLD Karachi 740 (If no issue is raised regarding the legitimacy of the child by the parties, the courts should not raise the same.)

Mst. Laila Qayyum v Fawad Qayyum PLD 2019 SC 449 (No person can be compelled to undergo the DNA test to ascertain his/her legitimacy because it would violate his/her privacy and the DNA test would not be conclusive evidence.)

Mst. Safia Bibi v Muhammad Akbar PLD 2018 Lah 758 (The court can order the DNA test with the consent of the party. In cases of inheritance, DNA is not the only evidence to determine the disputes relating to paternity that can be proved through oral and documentary evidence.)

Muhabat v Abdullah PLD 1970 Lah 303 (Prolonged cohabitation between the parents, conduct of the father along with his written acknowledgement as to paternity, and repute and notoriety amongst the family and respectability of the locality were regarded as convincing evidence for proving legitimacy.)

Muhammad Khalid v State 2018 PCrLJN 29 Lahore (Acknowledgement renders a child legitimate and Islamic law favours legitimisation rather than stigmatisation.)

Nandlal Wasudeo Badwaik v Lata Nandlal Badwaik (2014) 2 SCC 576 [The Supreme Court of India] (The presumption attached to legitimacy under section 112 of the Evidence Act 1872 will have to give way to the scientifically valued and trusted evidence such as DNA. Presumptions could attain significance in the absence of evidence, but in those cases where reliable evidence could be procured through modern scientific techniques, presumptions would lose force or relevance.)

Noor Jamal v The State PLD 1990 SC 656 (A child born after *li'an* is attributed to the mother and not the father.)

Zaheer Ahmad v Nasiman Bibi 2007 CLC 1145 [Lah] (The husband who wishes to repudiate the child, can only do so by the procedure of *li'an*. Such a husband is required to disown the child immediately upon the birth of the child or upon having the knowledge of such birth.)

Zarmeen Abid v NADRA, Islamabad 2022 PLD 39 (Lah) (A child of unknown parentage was adopted and assigned different parentage first in her educational documents, and then on her CNIC due to two marriages of her foster mother in succession. On the cancellation of CNIC by NADRA on the application of the second adopted father without hearing the petitioner, the court termed this process as unconstitutional, and directed NADRA to reissue the petitioner a new CNIC with the first adopted father in line with her educational testimonials.)

Notes

1. PLD 1975 SC 624, 651–52.
2. Ibid., 652.
3. PLD 2008 Lah 302, 304.
4. PLD 1975 SC 624.
5. PLD 2008 Lah 302, 305.
6. 2003 SCMR 1183, 1185.
7. PLD 1989 SC 362.
8. PLD 2010 Lah 422.
9. PLD 2015 SC 327, 333.
10. Ibid., 333–34.
11. Ibid., 334.
12. Ibid., 335.
13. PLD 2015 Islamabad 30, 33.
14. PLD 2010 Lah 422, 426.
15. PLD 2010 FSC 215, 219.
16. 1888 ILR 10 All 289, [14].
17. Ibid., [16].
18. Ibid., [25].
19. Ibid., [29].

7

GUARDIANSHIP, CUSTODY, AND WELFARE OF MINORS

7.1 Introduction

The terms guardianship and custody are often used interchangeably. They denote taking care of a minor or his/her property, or both. If an individual is declared both a guardian and a custodian of a minor, s/he will bear the cost of all financial and physical needs of the minor until the latter attains the age of majority. If two different persons assume the guardianship and custody of a minor, the guardian will bear all expenses of the minor, whereas the person who has custody will take care of the minor without the responsibility to incur any expenses while doing so. Under Islamic law, *hadanah* (custody) belongs to the mother, while the father is regarded as the natural guardian (*wali*). Thus, even when a child is in the custody of the mother, s/he is considered to be under the guardianship (*wilayah*) of the father.

The issues of custody and guardianship of minors often arise in cases of the dissolution of a marriage or separation of spouses from each other during the subsistence of their marriage. The law puts the responsibility of guardianship upon the father, whereas the mother is awarded custody until minors attain a specific age. The responsibility of guardianship is linked to the minor's right to be maintained. Under Islamic law, it is the duty of the father to maintain his children; and if he is unable to do so then the paternal grandfather has to fulfil this duty provided that he is in an affluent position. The mother is not obliged to maintain her children.

Under the Hanafi school, a mother has a preferential right to the custody of her son until he attains the age of 7 and her daughter until she attains puberty. Under the Shia school, a mother has a right to the custody of her son until he attains the age of 2 and of her daughter until the age of 7. Generally, the mother and her female relatives (e.g. her mother, grandmother, and sisters) are given preference over the father and other male relatives as regards the custody of a minor.

Under classical Islamic law, a mother or any other female relative who has custody of a child loses this right upon her marriage to a man who is not related to the child within the prohibited degree of marriage. This rule, however, does not apply in the case of the father or other male relative entitled to the right of custody. Other grounds that may disqualify a female from the custody of the minor include: (i) if she is leading an immoral life, such as where she is a prostitute; or (ii) if she neglects to take proper care of the child. A male is only given the custody of a female child when he stands within the prohibited degree of marriage to her. Likewise, a female relative is given custody of a male child when she is related to him within the prohibited degree of marriage. If there is no one to take custody of a minor, the court appoints an appropriate person as a guardian.

In cases where a mother loses the right to custody, the following relatives become entitled to the custody of the minor:

1. Mother's mother, how high so ever
2. Father's mother, how high so ever
3. Full sister
4. Uterine sister
5. Consanguine sister
6. Full sister's daughter
7. Uterine sister's daughter
8. Consanguine sister's daughter
9. Maternal aunt
10. Paternal aunt

In the absence of any female relatives, or where the female relatives are not considered fit to be given the right of custody, the custody of the minor belongs to the following male relatives:

1. Father
2. Paternal grandfather, how high so ever
3. Full brother
4. Consanguine brother
5. Full brother's son
6. Consanguine brother's son
7. Full brother of the father
8. Consanguine brother of the father
9. Son of father's full brother
10. Son of father's consanguine brother

It is important to note that the overarching principle for deciding custody and guardianship is the 'welfare of the minor'[1] as enshrined in the Guardians and Wards Act 1890. Under section 17 of the Act, this principle has to be applied consistently with the personal law of the minor. Under the same section, while considering the welfare of the minor, the court takes into account the age, sex, and religion of the minor; and the character, capacity, and relation of the guardian to the minor along with the wishes, if any, of the deceased parent. The court may consider the preference of the minor if s/he is old enough to form an intelligent preference. Such a preference, however, is subject to the principle of the welfare of the minor.[2] Article 3(1) of the United Nations Convention on the Rights of the Child 1989 provides that 'the best interests of the child shall be a primary consideration' regarding 'all actions concerning children, whether undertaken by public or private social welfare institutions, courts of law, administrative authorities or legislative bodies'.[3]

7.2 Outline of Case Law

7.2.1 Factors to be Considered for Determining Custody

Iram Shahzad v Additional District Judge, Lahore PLD 2011 Lah 362

Welfare of a minor is the supreme consideration in deciding custody matters.

Dr Tahir married Iram in 2001. The following year, a child, Hamza Tahir, was born whose custody was contested in this case. In 2005, the wife sought dissolution on the basis of *khula*. Upon this, the father took his son to Saudi Arabia where he was working as a doctor. Thereafter, he took his son to the United Kingdom. The mother, who remarried and had children from her second marriage, initiated proceedings for the custody of her son. She succeeded in getting the custody of her son in 2007 through a decision of the High Court of Justice Family Division, UK.

In 2008, the father filed an application under section 25 of the Guardians and Wards Act 1890 with the Guardian Judge, Lahore for the custody of the son. The court decided in his favour and the mother was granted periodic visitation rights. The mother appealed against the decision in the first Appellate Court. The court, while maintaining the Guardian Judge's decision, ordered to increase the frequency of visitation by the mother, and directed the father not to take the son out of the jurisdiction of the Guardian Judge without his permission. Both parties felt aggrieved by the decision of the first Appellate Court and approached the Lahore High Court through writ petitions.

The decisions rendered by the courts below (the Guardian Judge and the first Appellate Court) were primarily influenced by two considerations: first, the age of the son was above seven, and second, the mother's second marriage and her children from it. After arriving back in Pakistan from the UK, the son lived with his maternal grandmother who resided a few miles away from the son's mother. The son was admitted to a school and the mother paid regular visits to look after him. On the other hand, the father did not attempt to pay a single penny towards his son's maintenance since his arrival in Pakistan. The father had remained unmarried since the dissolution of marriage with the petitioner, which was his third marriage. When the son was with him in Saudi Arabia, he had appointed a maid for him and stated in his pleadings that he would do the same once the custody was given to him.

Taking into consideration the above-mentioned facts and after a careful analysis of the precedents, the High Court reversed the decisions of the lower courts and allowed the son to remain with his maternal grandmother under his mother's direct supervision. The father was permitted to visit his son through the Guardian Court periodically but was not to take him beyond the jurisdiction of the court except on the condition of him depositing his passport with the court.

The court observed that the welfare of the minor is of paramount importance and the sole determining factor for the custody of children. The age, gender, and marital status of the parties are taken into consideration for arriving at a conclusion as to how the interest and welfare of a minor can be best protected. These aspects are not to be considered in contradistinction to the welfare of a minor. Furthermore, there is no absolute rule or mathematical formula available to determine the welfare of a minor. It is equally a settled law that for determining the right to custody, mere age is not sufficient. If it was so, the Guardian Court would not be required to exercise its parental jurisdiction. Rather, the matter might have been left to ministerial officers to merely examine the birth certificate of the minor. The court held:

> The ostensible wealth of a father can never be a ground entitling him to the custody of his minor child. It is the bounden duty of a Muslim father to maintain his children, whether they are in his custody or of his spouse... Furthermore, in the eventuality of divorce and a mother on remarrying,

the child being brought up in the care of the mother through the maternal grandmother is also not unacceptable, and may be the preferred option.[4]

7.2.2 Welfare of Minor—Definition

Feroze Begum v Lt. Col. Muhammad Hussain 1983 SCMR 606

The welfare of the minor means his/her financial, moral, spiritual, and intellectual well-being.

This case is important because it defines what actually constitutes 'the welfare of a minor', which is the supreme consideration of a court in deciding any issue pertaining to the custody of a minor. This case has established that it is not just a minor's material or financial well-being that counts in deciding custody issues, but his/her moral, spiritual, and intellectual development has equal importance.

Briefly, the facts of the case are that the respondent was married to the petitioner and two children were born. Later, the relations between the spouses became strained and the parties were divorced in 1966. The two minors remained in the custody of their mother. In 1967, Muhammad Hussain, the respondent, remarried and had three children from his second marriage. The petitioner filed a suit for maintenance and in response Muhammad Hussain initiated a suit for the custody of the two minor children. The suit was decreed in favour of the respondent on the grounds that he was well-educated with a steady source of income as opposed to the petitioner who was an illiterate lady without any source of income of her own. The petitioner brought the case before the High Court. The High Court attempted to bring about a settlement between the parents for the welfare of the minors but did not succeed. Thereafter, without considering the evidence, the court accepted the respondent's offer to put both the minors in good boarding schools as it was considered *bona fide* and in the interest of the minors. As a result, the petitioner's appeal was dismissed. The petitioner filed an application for special leave to appeal before the Supreme Court.

After hearing arguments and perusing the record, the Supreme Court noted that both the children clearly expressed their wish to remain with their mother. The Supreme Court held that the courts below did not proceed on the basis of the evidence led by both parties and based their decision on other irrelevant considerations. In the courts below, the respondent had tried to prove that he was Shia by faith, but his cross-examination suggested otherwise. Additionally, he levelled allegations of bad character against the petitioner but there were no findings of the courts below to substantiate his claim. This was important, because if the petitioner was of bad character, then it was not appropriate to give her custody of the minors. However, if the allegation levelled by the respondent was ill-founded, then it reflected negatively on his character. The Supreme Court observed that the respondent initiated the suit for the custody of the children only after the mother filed a suit for maintenance.

The courts below only emphasised the fact that the respondent was an educated person of means, as opposed to the petitioner who was an illiterate poor woman. The Supreme Court observed that there was nothing on record to show that the minors were not being duly taken care of in their mother's custody; in fact, the evidence suggested otherwise. The court held that the mere inability of a mother to maintain her children could not be a ground for depriving her of the custody of her children, because under the law it is the obligation of the father to provide maintenance for the children. The welfare of the minor is the supreme consideration in deciding custody matters, which 'means his material, intellectual, moral and spiritual well-being'.[5] The High Court had accepted the respondent's offer to put the minors in boarding school without even considering whether or not it would be advisable to do so, especially in the case of a female minor who was about to attain puberty. For the foregoing reasons, the court allowed the appeal and gave the custody of the minors to the mother.

7.2.3 Power of the Court to Appoint a Guardian—Repugnancy to the Injunctions of Islam

Mrs Ambreen Tariq Awan v Federal Govt. of Pakistan 2013 MLD 1885 (FSC)

Law authorising a court to appoint a guardian for a minor is not repugnant to the Injunctions of Islam.

The principle, in this case, provides that the Qur'an and Sunnah have not laid down detailed rules and regulations on the appointment and removal of guardians in various circumstances, therefore, any Islamic polity may decide how guardians of a person and property should be appointed and removed.

In this case, the petitioner challenged sections 7, 17, and 27 of the Guardians and Wards Act 1890 before the Federal Shariat Court on the basis of their alleged repugnancy to the Injunctions of Islam. These sections deal with the power of a court to appoint a guardian of a person or property, or both of a minor and undertake necessary proceedings for his/her welfare. The petitioner placed reliance on several verses of the Qur'an (2:133, 31:14, and 46:15) and sayings of the Prophet (PBUH) in addition to certain passages from the *Hidaya* relating to the concept of natural guardianship. During the court proceedings, it transpired that the petitioner had no interest in the proceedings of the case and the attorney deputed by her had withdrawn her *wakalatnama* (power of attorney). Therefore, the court was left with no option but to scrutinise the matter on its own. The court, after referring to the Qur'anic verses 5:42, 4:58, 16:90, and 6:152, held:

> [I]t is the duty of persons in authority (legislature/judges/executive) to appoint or terminate guardianship of person and property belonging to minors and disabled persons according to the norms of justice, principles of 'Ihsan' and, besides also forbid harmful acts, evil deeds, oppressive conduct and fulfil the Commands of Allah as laid down in the Holy Qur'an and Sunnah of the Holy Prophet (SAW). Islamic Shariah empowers the ruler or Imam through 'Shura' to enact laws according to requirements of various circumstances and employ sound and valid legal methodology in matters which come within the purview of permissible matters (i.e. Mubah), if not specifically prohibited in the 'Nass' (text) of the Holy Qur'an and Sunnah. An 'Imam' is thus vested with powers which he shall exercise for the welfare or 'Maslaha' of 'Ummat'.[6]

The court pointed out that the verses relied upon by the petitioner did not relate to the issue under consideration. So far as the reference to the *Hidaya* was concerned, a matter of repugnancy could not be decided on the basis of various juristic opinions. The court observed:

> [T]he sections impugned by her (i.e. the petitioner) which clearly authorise the Court to appoint a guardian of a person for a person or property or both for safeguarding interests of the minor, are just for his/her welfare and the Court is duty bound to consider all facts and circumstances of each case and pass an appropriate order in accordance with norms of justice as deemed appropriate for the welfare of a minor.[7]

Consequently, the petition was dismissed as being devoid of any merit, declaring the courts competent to appoint and remove guardians in light of the welfare of the minor.

7.2.4 Relevance of a Compromise Agreement between the Parties in Matters of Custody. The judges recognise the welfare of a minor as the paramount principle while dealing with compromise agreements on the custody of children. The courts hold that such agreements cannot be given any legal effect unless they promote the welfare of the minor.

Hameed Mai v Irshad Hussain PLD 2002 SC 267

The welfare of a minor supersedes any private agreement between the parties on the matter of custody.

The daughter of Hameed Mai (appellant) was married to Irshad Hussain (respondent). The daughter died during childbirth. The baby, Humera Khurshid lived with her father after the death of her mother. Her maternal grandmother, Hameed Mai got her custody through a writ of *habeas corpus*. Thereafter, the respondent filed a suit for custody of his minor daughter in the Guardian Court, which was disposed of on the basis of an agreement between the parties. According to the agreement, Humera would remain in the custody of her grandmother (appellant) until she reached seven years of age. The parties also amicably decided to settle some financial matters pertaining to Humera's deceased mother through the same agreement. The respondent did not adhere to the agreement and attempted to avoid paying the entire settled amount. Thereupon, the court issued a warrant for the respondent's arrest, which forced him to discharge his liability.

After Humera attained the age of seven, the respondent filed a suit in the Guardian Court for her custody. He asked for her custody on the basis of his agreement with the appellant and his status as her natural guardian. The appellant contested the suit on the ground that the situation had changed significantly since the conclusion of the agreement, as the respondent had remarried and had children from that marriage. Moreover, his financial status was not stable as compared to the appellant's family. Therefore, it would not be wise to comply with the agreement. The Guardian Court enforced the terms of the agreement and handed over the custody of Humera to her father. The appellant challenged the decision in the first Appellate Court, and thereafter, through a writ petition before the High Court, but both courts upheld the decision of the Guardian Court by giving overrated importance to the agreement between the parties.

Aggrieved by these decisions, the appellant brought her case before the Supreme Court, which granted the leave to appeal to decide whether the Guardian Court was bound to consider the welfare of the minor irrespective of the agreement between the parties. The appellant's counsel argued that the Guardian Court should have decided the matter on merit considering all the relevant facts and not on the basis of the agreement alone. The respondent defended his case on the basis of the agreement and his status as a natural guardian. The Supreme Court observed:

> It is a settled proposition of law that in such cases the paramount consideration is [the] welfare of the minor. No doubt initially the parties had settled the dispute as above, the fact, however, remains that later on the circumstances, stood materially changed and the question of [the] welfare of [the] minor again cropped up in a more serious manner than before. [The] [i]ssue of custody of minor[s] in all cases cannot be effectively settled by private compromise.[8]

The court further observed:

> The court's powers with regard to custody of minor are in nature of parental jurisdiction. Therefore, the court must act in a way a wise parent would do. The expression 'welfare' shall be construed in a way to include in its compass all the dominant factors essential for determining the actual welfare of the minor. Technicalities of law are not adhered [to] in such like cases.[9]

The court remanded the case to the Guardian Court for a fresh decision on merits within six months. However, the decision left some important issues unresolved: if all the material relevant for determining the matter of custody of the minor was placed before the Supreme Court, what was the logic of remanding the case to the Guardian Court for another series of litigation? When the Supreme Court was not satisfied with handing over the custody to the father by the subordinate courts, then the only remaining aspirant for custody was the maternal grandmother. Why was she not awarded custody? On the one hand, the Supreme Court has been warning the subordinate courts not to be swayed by the technicalities of law while deciding the cases of guardianship, and on the other, it observed such technicalities itself. It is pertinent to state that under Article 187 of the Constitution of the Islamic Republic of Pakistan, the Supreme Court has been bestowed with power and authority to do 'complete justice'. And there is no best way to exercise such authority than to safeguard the interests of underprivileged and disadvantaged segments of society, such as children and women. It is worthwhile to highlight that the Supreme

Court has occasionally resorted to this provision with the aim to provide complete and substantial justice to such segments unencumbered by the technicalities of law.[10] It is advisable to make it a norm in cases of guardianship.

Mehmood Akhtar v District Judge, Attock 2004 SCMR 1839

The welfare of a minor supersedes any private settlement between the parties pertaining to the custody of a minor.

Mehmood Akhtar (petitioner/appellant) was married to Yasmeen (respondent) in 1991. During the wedlock, a daughter Shazia was born. In 1995, the respondent filed a suit for dissolution of marriage on the basis of *khula*, which was decreed. As far as the custody of the minor daughter was concerned, the same was settled by an agreement in the following terms:

> The minor shall remain in the custody of [the] respondent and the petitioner shall be liable to pay [the] maintenance allowance of [the] minor at the rate of Rs. 600 per month. In case the respondent contracts second marriage, she will hand over the custody of [the] minor to the petitioner, but if the petitioner fails to pay maintenance allowance, the respondent notwithstanding any other condition will be entitled to retain the custody of [the] minor permanently.[11]

Upon the appellant's failure to discharge his liability of paying maintenance, the respondent initiated a suit for recovery of maintenance on behalf of the minor daughter, which was decreed in her favour. When the decree was being executed, the appellant filed an application before the Guardian Judge for the custody of the minor. The Guardian Judge dismissed the application of the appellant. Consequently, he brought an appeal before the first Appellate Court. The first Appellate Court reversed the decision of the Guardian Judge and held that the appellant was entitled to his minor daughter's custody. Aggrieved by the decision, the respondent challenged the same before the High Court. The Court declared it to be without lawful authority and upheld the decision of the Guardian Judge in favour of the respondent. The appellant was dissatisfied with this outcome and applied for leave to appeal before the Supreme Court.

The appellant's counsel argued his case on two grounds: (1) the status of the appellant as natural guardian; (2) the respondent's second marriage with a person not falling within the prohibited degree of marriage with the minor daughter. The counsel relied upon passages from Mulla's *Principles of Muhammadan Law* to establish that once a mother enters into a second marriage with a stranger, she loses her right of custody. The counsel further contended that the appellant's status as natural guardian could not be taken away on the pretext of the welfare of the minor. The Supreme Court rejected these arguments and held:

> The right of custody of [the] minor is not an absolute right rather it is always subject to the welfare of the minor. The Court in the light of [the] law on the subject, facts and circumstances of each case considers the question of custody on the basis of [the] welfare of minors and there can be no deviation from the settled principle of law… No doubt the general principle of Islamic law is that a Muslim father being the natural guardian of the minor, has the preferential right of custody of [the] minor but such rule is always subject to the welfare of the minor which is the prime consideration in [the] determination of the question of custody. The right of custody of [a] minor being not an absolute right, the father or the mother as the position may be, may abandon such right.[12]

After reiterating the settled principle, the court analysed the arguments and evidence on record. The record showed that the appellant was negligent in maintaining his minor daughter. The court noticed the fact that the appellant and the respondent had contracted second marriages and observed that the minor daughter thus had no choice in the present case except to live either with a stepfather or a stepmother. In such a situation, it would be better to allow her to live with the step-relation with whom she had already developed familiarity over the years under the supervision of her real mother. Forcing the minor daughter into a new environment managed by her stepmother would likely cause difficulties for her. In light of these reasons, the court maintained the decision of the High Court and refused the leave sought by the appellant.

Mst. Beena v Raja Muhammad PLD 2020 SC 508

Surrendering the custody of a minor as consideration for *khula* is unlawful and against the principles of public policy as stipulated in section 23 of the Contract Act 1872 as well as the injunctions of Islam.

This case involved a contest over the custody of a child. The appellant, Mst Beena, sought the physical custody of the minor and the Guardian Judge granted her petition. The respondent, the father, challenged the decision but his application was dismissed. Thereafter, the Peshawar

High Court exercising jurisdiction under Article 199 of the Constitution set aside the judgment and handed over the custody of the minor to the father. It was against this backdrop that the appellant brought the case to the Supreme Court.

The appellant's counsel argued that the appellant had obtained *khula* from the respondent forgoing her dower (*haq mehr*) and signed an agreement that she will not claim custody of her child. The Supreme Court observed that Muslim personal law prescribes rules for custody (*hizanat*) under which a mother cannot be compelled to surrender custody of her child, nor can such surrender constitute consideration for an agreement of *khula*. Furthermore, if the object or consideration of an agreement is against public policy, it is void under section 23 of the Contract Act 1872. The insertion of such a condition in an agreement of *khula* is also contrary to the injunctions of Islam.

While appraising the evidence, the Supreme Court held that the High Court overlooked the law, Sharia, and precedents to support its judgment. Moreover, the High Court was not sensitive in handling the case as it used improper words by referring to the mother as 'a crippled/disabled lady having no income'. Appreciating the work of the mother, the Supreme Court stated that she works in an embroidery shop to earn an honest living and does not beg despite her physical impairment. In view of these reasons, the Supreme Court set aside the judgment of the High Court and ordered to hand over the custody of the minor within seven days to the mother.

7.2.5 Who Will Have the Custody of a Minor? The courts give paramount importance to the welfare of the minor in deciding issues related to custody and guardianship. Working on the assumption that the mother is usually the most suitable person for ensuring the well-being of the minor, the courts have shown a tendency to give her a preferential right to the custody of the minor. However, she loses this preferential right upon a second marriage with a stranger but retains her ordinary right.

7.2.5.1 Father's Custody

Ammara Waseem v Syed Khawar Hussain 2011 SCMR 148

A father, who remains unmarried after divorce and has some other female relation to take care of a minor is entitled to custody in case the mother remarries and resides abroad.

Ammara Waseem (appellant) was married to Syed Khawar Hussain (respondent) in 2004 and a son, Syed Muhammad Ahmad Hussain, was born. The marriage did not last long and was dissolved on the basis of *khula* in 2007. The minor son had been living with his mother at his grandparents' residence since the dissolution of the marriage. Thereafter, the mother entered into a second marriage with a person settled in the US. Consequently, she relocated there with her husband, leaving the minor son in his maternal grandmother's custody. The respondent filed an application for the custody of the minor which was decided in his favour. Meanwhile, the respondent secured an order from the High Court restraining the appellant from taking the minor out of the country. The appellant assailed the decision of the Guardian Judge in the first Appellate Court and thereafter impugned this decision in the High Court. Both courts upheld the respondent's right to the custody of the minor.

The decisions of the three courts were influenced by the circumstances of the mother's second marriage and her leaving the minor in his maternal grandmother's custody and thereafter making calculated efforts to remove the minor from the country by securing his immigration visa. When the appellant brought the case before the Supreme Court, the court issued a restraining order prohibiting the appellant from taking the minor out of the country as was done by the High Court.

During the proceedings before the Supreme Court, the appellant went abroad leaving the minor with his maternal grandmother. The counsel for the appellant argued that the minor had developed a cordial relationship with the maternal grandmother and other family members as he had been residing with them since his birth. It would not be in consideration of the welfare of the minor to hand over his custody to the respondent who had not developed such a bond with the minor. The court was also informed that no female member resided in the house of the respondent to look after the minor.

On the other hand, the respondent's counsel relied on the status of the respondent as a natural guardian who remained unmarried after the dissolution of the first marriage and made a solemn affirmation that he would go to any extent for the minor's appropriate upbringing. It was also brought to the notice of the court that an unmarried younger sister of the respondent had been living with him and she would make every possible effort to ensure the welfare of the minor. Above all, the apprehension of removing the minor from the country by the appellant, which the court had already recognised, was a consideration that urged the Supreme Court not to interfere with the concurrent conclusions of the courts below. Hence, the court dismissed the appeal and upheld the decision of the High Court. The court observed that the minor's welfare lay in giving his custody to the respondent. The court further ordered that the grandmother would have the right to visit the minor and bring him to her residence for a day each week.

7.2.5.2 Mother's Custody

Razia Bibi v Riaz Ahmad 2004 SCMR 821

Mere poverty of a mother, leaving all other pertinent factors aside, cannot be the sole factor for denying her the custody of her child.

The case deals with an important issue: whether the poverty of a mother is a relevant consideration for deciding the welfare of a minor in cases of custody. Razia (appellant/petitioner) was married to Riaz Ahmad (respondent) in 1989, and the couple was blessed with a son, Ijaz Ahmad after one year. The relationship between the spouses became strained after the minor's birth and the mother along with the minor moved to her village leaving the matrimonial house of the father located in the city. Ultimately, the respondent dissolved the marriage through divorce in 1997.

The appellant filed an application for the custody of the minor in the Guardian Court. The respondent resisted the application on the ground that the mother had been living in the village and such an atmosphere would not be suitable for the proper upbringing of the minor. In addition to the respondent's dwelling in the city, the fact that he was unmarried led the court to grant him the minor's custody. The appellant assailed the decision by filling an appeal before the first Appellate Court which accepted the appeal and reversed the decision of the Guardian Court.

Thereafter, the respondent successfully invoked the writ jurisdiction of the High Court to gain custody of the minor. This decision was impugned in the Supreme Court. The court served notices to the respondent to appear, but he did not appear because he had gone abroad. Hence, the court was constrained to decide the controversy *ex parte* regarding the mother's entitlement to the custody of the minor in the context of her residence in the village as well as her indigence. Another important fact that came to the notice of the court was that the respondent had contracted a second marriage during the pendency of the proceedings. On the contrary, the appellant remained unmarried, devoting herself to the upbringing of her minor child. It was in these circumstances that the court observed:

> The learned Single Judge of the Lahore High Court has been mainly swayed by the so-called better facilities enjoyed by the respondent disentitling the petitioner lady from the custody of the minor. The petitioner lady has been looking after her minor son since his birth and maintaining him in a good environment. The father, who is under the law to maintain his child, has not provided any maintenance till date. The minor is living since his birth with his mother and [the] welfare of the child in the circumstances also lies in favour of the petitioner. It is true that non-maintenance on the part of the father would not automatically disentitle him from the custody of his child but this would be one of the circumstances for determining the welfare of the minor.[13]

The Supreme Court decided the matter in favour of the mother by implying that the mere poverty of a mother should not be given precedence over other pertinent factors in determining the custody of a minor. This is so because under Islamic law it is the responsibility of a father to provide maintenance to his children irrespective of their mother's financial circumstances.

Haji Muhammad Shafi v Maqbool Afza 1986 SCMR 1634

A mother who has been divorced thrice and was presently working as a maidservant should not get custody of the child.

This case highlights the circumstances, which may affect a mother's right to the custody of a child. It established that a mother who had been divorced thrice and was working as a maidservant should not have custody of the child, as it is not in the welfare of the minor, especially when the minor is being looked after well in the father's custody.

The brief facts of the case are such that the petitioner, Haji Muhammad Shafi, and respondent no. 1, Maqbool Afza were married in 1976 and were blessed with a daughter who at the time of the decision of the Supreme Court was about 8 years old. The daughter was living with her father/petitioner and her grandmother. The mother of the minor daughter, (respondent no. 1) filed an application for the custody of the child which was not entertained due to lack of jurisdiction. She subsequently filed another application on the grounds that the petitioner lived in Kuwait and in his absence, the minor was being ill-treated by her stepbrothers. The grandmother of the minor, being an old lady, could not protect her. The Guardian Judge accepted the petition and directed the restoration of the minor to her mother. The district judge dismissed the father's appeal.

The petitioner filed a constitutional petition, which was also dismissed. Ultimately, the matter was brought before the Supreme Court.

The minor girl was produced before the court and was asked whether she wanted to live with her father or mother. She preferred to remain in her father's custody, as her father and grandmother were taking good care of her. The counsel for the petitioner contended that the welfare of the minor had not been given due consideration by the two courts below and alleged that the mother of the minor did not have a good character as she had been divorced thrice; hence, the custody of the minor should not be handed over to her. The court noted that the petitioner was well-off while the mother of the minor (respondent no. 1) was working as a maid and had also been divorced thrice. The court observed that, in view of the circumstances of the present case, the minor's welfare was best served if she continued to live with her father. Hence, the appeal was accepted, and custody was given to the father.

Amar Ilahi v Rashida Akhtar PLD 1955 Lah 412

By marrying a stranger, a mother does not lose her right to custody of her child absolutely; she only loses her preferential right but retains an ordinary right.

This case sheds light on the issue of whether a mother's remarriage to a stranger disqualifies her from being the custodian of her child. The appellant, Amar Ilahi married the respondent, Rashida Akhtar in 1936 and a daughter, Kishwar Sultana was born. Soon thereafter, the relations between the parents became strained and a protracted litigation ensued between them.

The appellant divorced the respondent and the parties entered into a compromise during the litigation whereby the respondent gave up her claim to dower and her daughter's claim to maintenance. In return, the appellant renounced his right to the custody of the minor girl. Since then he did not see his daughter. The appellant contracted a second marriage and had five children from the second marriage. Thereafter, when the respondent also remarried the appellant filed an application for the custody of the minor.

It was brought out in evidence that the income of the respondent was only Rs 150 per month and that for some time the minor had been living with her maternal aunt whose husband was the brother of the appellant. The minor was in eighth grade. In view of these circumstances, the Guardian Judge held that it was not in the welfare of the minor that her custody should be given to the appellant. Hence, the present appeal was filed.

The counsel for the appellant contended that by remarrying a person who was not related to the minor within the prohibited degree of relationship, the respondent disqualified herself from being the custodian of the minor. The court noted that in the chapter on 'Hizanat' in Baillie's *Digest of Moohummudan Law*, it is stated that 'the rights of all the women before mentioned are made void by marriage with strangers'.[14] The court observed:

> Keeping in view the entire scheme of Muslim law regarding Hizanat, there can be no doubt that "the right" referred to in this sentence is the preferential right of certain female relations of the minor to its custody… The right referred to above can only mean the right of a particular female who, failing those mentioned prior to her, has a right to the custody of the minor, in preference to those whose rights have been subordinated to hers… [W]hen it is said that the right of a certain relation has been lost, it can only mean that all things being equal, he or she, as the case may be, must be relegated to a position in the order of priority below those who follow him or her. Thus there can be no room for supposing that the Muslim Law does not permit a disqualified relation to rank even with strangers.[15]

The court then relied upon the dictum in *Mst Samiunnisa v Mst Zaida Khatun*,[16] and held:

> The whole law on the subject seems to have been developed on a reply by the Prophet to a woman, who had separated from her husband, that she had a right in the custody of the child in preference to that of her husband so long as she did not marry with a stranger. The reason given in the *Hedaya* is that the stranger to whom the mother may be married will not have the same affection for the child and may ill-treat her and the context in which the whole matter is discussed is the respective merit of the various relation[s] and the central idea is as to who is more likely to look after the welfare of the minor. There seems to be nothing in that chapter to indicate that it is a sort of punishment to the mother when she, by reason of the fact that she has remarried a stranger, is to be punished by not being allowed to have the custody of the child even though there may not be any other person capable of looking after the minor.[17]

Therefore, by marrying a stranger, a mother, or any other female relation only loses her preferential right to the custody of the child. This means that if there is another relation of the minor, who under Islamic law possesses a right to the custody of the minor and to whom the welfare of the minor can be safely entrusted, such a female relation cannot claim the custody of the child as of right.

In the instant case, the appellant in order to evade his liability to maintain the child and to pay his wife's dower, totally relinquished his right to the custody of the child and never even cared to see his daughter. This reflected how much the appellant cared for the child. On the contrary, the mother had done a lot for her daughter. The child also refused to live with her father. The father/appellant claimed the custody of the girl only to get her married to someone of his own choice but given the circumstances of the case, he was not the right person to do so. In light of the foregoing reasons, the appeal was dismissed.

Roshni Desai v Jahanzeb Niazi PLD 2011 Lah 423

Islamic law allows a non-Muslim mother to exercise the same rights of custody as enjoyed by a Muslim mother.

In this case, Ms Roshni Desai filed a writ petition under Article 199 of the Constitution read with section 491 of the CrPC for the recovery of her son, Azan Sohail Niazi, aged three and a half years. The child was born in Montreal, Canada in 2007. In 2010, the petitioner left the respondent due to some differences. The respondent had visitation rights to meet the child once a week. The respondent wanted full custody, and in March 2011 brought the child unlawfully to Pakistan from Canada without the knowledge and consent of the petitioner. After learning about this, she filed a petition before the Superior Court (Family Division), Canada, which granted legal custody of the minor to the petitioner and directed the respondent to hand over the custody of the minor to her. The Canadian Mounted Police issued a warrant for the arrest of the respondent for the abduction of the minor.

Before the High Court, the petitioner's counsel argued that the respondent did not have the right to custody of the minor under Pakistani law because the petitioner and the respondent did not contract a legal marriage and were simply living together. The counsel of the respondent rebutted this claim by arguing that as the couple lived together with their free consent their relationship should be deemed as a lawful marriage. He averred that the respondent took the minor to Pakistan with the consent of the petitioner. He further contended that the petitioner, being a non-Muslim, was unfit to have the custody of the minor and the welfare of the minor required that he should stay with his Muslim father who was a Pakistani citizen.

The court observed that the parties lived together without any marriage or civil union solemnised between them and their marriage was a *de facto* union described as a common law marriage. About the validity of such marriage, Justice Asad Munir observed:

> The question of a minor's custody has to be addressed by reference to his status under the applicable Pakistan Law, more appropriately the Islamic law, which does not recognize a common law marriage or partnership as a valid marriage with the result that a child born to parents, having a common law marriage, is born outside marriage and cannot be regarded as a legitimate child. Under Islamic Law, the father of an illegitimate child has no legal tie with the child even though he is the biological father and the blood tie between the two is undisputed. Such a father has no legal relationship whatsoever with the minor so much so that the child does not inherit from his father or vice versa which is otherwise in the case of a legitimate offspring. However, an illegitimate child has a full legal tie with his mother and there is no obstacle in the way of the child inheriting from his mother or vice versa. In fact, the mother of an illegitimate child is not only entitled to the custody of the child but is also regarded as the guardian of the child to the total exclusion of the father....[18]

On the issue of the right of a non-Muslim mother to the custody of a minor, the court held:

> A non-Muslim mother suffers no disability as Islamic Law allows a non-Muslim mother to exercise the same rights of custody as are enjoyed by a Muslim mother. If any support is needed, reference can be made to Ameer Ali's *Muhammadan Law*, page 223, where it is stated that the right of a mother to the custody of her child is established even if she is a non-Muslim and is not even a Christian or a Jew. This only means that Islamic law protects the rights of custody of a non-Muslim mother regardless of whether the child is legitimate or is otherwise....[19]

The petitioner assured the court that she intended to retain the present Muslim name of the minor and that she would ensure that the minor is brought up as a Muslim and imparted the basic Islamic teachings. She further stated that she would convert to Islam if she found it necessary for the sake of bringing up the minor as a Muslim.

The court referred to *Peggy Collin v Muhammad Ishfaque Malik*[20] where the facts were the same but the issue of the legitimacy of the child was not involved. In this case, the Lahore High Court refused the father's plea that a Christian mother was not entitled to the custody of the minor. The court held that since religion had not mattered to the respondent when falling in love with a Christian girl and settling in France, he was merely taking shelter behind faith to gain custody of the child.

The court allowed the petition by granting the custody of the minor to his mother who was free to take him back to Canada.

We find the part of the judgment relating to the legitimacy of the child problematic. The circumstances of the case did not require the learned judge to make a declaration about the paternity and legitimacy of the child. It is indeed unfortunate that the child was denied all the rights related to paternity, i.e. maintenance and inheritance in a battle of his custody among his parents.

Farooq Siddiqui v Farzana Naheed PLD 2013 Lah 254

Pakistani law does not recognise paternity on the basis of surrogacy in the absence of evidence. If surrogacy is not proven, the surrogate mother would be entitled to the custody of the child.

This is an interesting case, which demonstrates the humane approach of Pakistani courts in deciding emerging legal problems. The petitioner was a surgeon based in the US. He sued for the custody of a baby girl on the ground that he was her father, and the respondent was only a surrogate mother. He claimed that the respondent surrogate mother had left the new-born child with him and disappeared. She later filed an application under section 491 of the Criminal Procedure Code 1898 (CrPC) for the recovery of the child. The court handed over the baby to her. The petitioner subsequently filed an application under section 25 of the Guardians and Wards Act 1890. The trial court dismissed the application, and the Appellate Court upheld that decision. The petitioner filed a constitutional petition before the High Court.

He contended that he was not married to the respondent. Although a *nikahnama* was produced as evidence, he asserted that there was a contract between them whereby the respondent agreed to act as a surrogate mother for a huge consideration. Therefore, the respondent did not have any right to the custody of the child. He argued that the welfare of the child required that he should be given custody to bring her up in the US. He further stated that he professed Shia faith, which vests the custody of a female child in the father after her attaining the age of 7 years. He asserted that the respondent was a tramp who rented her uterus.

After hearing these arguments, Justice Ijaz Ahmad observed that the basic legal question, in this case, was whether the petitioner was the father of the child. The petitioner denied that he was married to the respondent. He asserted that a third person transplanted the fertilised egg into the womb of the respondent. Since he did not produce this third person as a witness, Justice Ahmad held that the case of surrogacy was not proved:

> The law of [the] land does not recognise the surrogation. Even if the surrogation is recognised by the law of the land and the transplantation of a fertilised egg is proved, there is no evidence that the sperm that fertilised the egg, originated from the petitioner. Thus the petitioner has no right over the child not born in consequence of a lawful marriage.[21]

On the facts of the case, Justice Ahmad observed that the petitioner denied marriage with the respondent but craved for the custody of the child. In the *nikahnama*, he entered his abridged name so that he should not lose his wealth to the poor bride. Justice Ahmad observed that in such circumstances:

> [W]hether marriage is established or not, the child belongs to the bed. An adulterer may be convicted and punished but the custody of the child will go to the mother who housed the fetus for nine months. All that is sure is that the baby was born to the respondent. Her motherhood is undeniable. The petitioner, whether he is or is not the father of the child through marriage or the source of the sperm that fertilised the egg, has no right to the custody of the minor girl.[22]

In this way, the court upheld the decisions of the lower courts with the observation that the poverty of the mother does not disentitle her from claiming custody of the child. As she was already financially deprived, she should not be deprived of the custody of her child to multiply her woes.

After failing to get any relief from the High Court, the petitioner brought his case before the Federal Shariat Court. The judgment of the FSC is discussed below.

Farooq Siddiqui v Farzana Naheed PLD 2017 FSC 78

A baby produced through medical intervention by the sperm and egg of duly wedded couples [without involving a third party] is permissible under Islamic law.

This case also deals with the issue of surrogacy in Pakistan. It determines if the practice of surrogacy is in conformity with the injunctions of the Qur'an and Sunnah.

Farooq Siddiqui, the petitioner, was a Pakistani-born American citizen. Before the court, he stated that he was a doctor and dealt with surrogacy cases. Since his own wife was unable to give birth, he published an advertisement in the newspaper for procuring a surrogate mother. The respondent, Mst. Farzana Naheed, responded to the advertisement by agreeing to be a surrogate mother in exchange for money. The respondent was paid Rs 25,000 for medical tests which deemed her fit for a surrogacy procedure. She later gave birth to a baby girl, Fatima Siddiqui. According to the petitioner, the whole agreement was oral. Since this procedure was taboo in Pakistan and likely to evoke strong reactions in society, a story of a false drama of marriage was concocted to cover up the matter. After giving birth, the respondent refused to adhere to her contractual obligation and did not hand over the baby to the petitioner. The respondent contended that the whole claim of surrogacy was false and fabricated and that she was the legally wedded wife of the petitioner. The daughter was born from their wedlock and the petitioner was liable to pay the expenses of the child.

The petitioner's appeals in the Guardian Court, Rawalpindi, in 2011, and thereafter before the High Court and Supreme Court were also dismissed. The courts had granted the respondent's petition for custody and maintenance. As a last resort, the petitioner filed a petition before the Federal Shariat Court. He argued that since he has been accepted as a father of the baby in the maintenance petition, he should be handed over the custody of the child. Since the case involved an important legal question regarding surrogacy, the court admitted the petition for a hearing.

The court referred to a famous US case on surrogacy known as the *Baby M* case.[23] In this case, Mary Beth Whitehead had agreed to become a surrogate mother for a couple. For this purpose, the sperm was obtained from the husband and the egg from Mary Beth. After the birth of a baby girl, Mary Beth refused to hand over the custody of the child to the hiring couple and claimed that her own husband was the father of the child. She accepted that she had entered into a contract of surrogacy with the couple but during pregnancy developed an emotional attachment with the child. She contended that she was ready to return the money that she had been paid as a consideration for being a surrogate. Upon her refusal, the couple went to the court of New Jersey. In the trial, the court decided against Mary Beth, but in appeal, the judgment was reversed. Mary Beth was declared the real mother and was given custody of the child, while the hiring couple was given visitation rights.

In the context of the facts of the instant case, the court framed the legal issue: whether the surrogacy contract is a valid contract and whether the surrogacy by itself is in accordance with the Injunctions of Islam as laid down in the Qur'an and Sunnah. The court held that where the egg and sperm are obtained from the actual mother and father, are then fertilised in a test tube, and placed into the actual mother's womb, the child will belong to the actual mother and father. This process can by no means be illegal or against Islamic injunctions as the egg and sperm both are of the real parents. However, in all other cases, where a surrogate is arranged in exchange for monetary compensation to give birth, such birth would be illegal and against the injunctions of the Holy Qur'an and Sunnah.

Chief Justice Riaz Ahmad Khan authored the main judgment. He observed that surrogacy involves social and ethical dilemmas, as it is exploitative of poor women who bear the physical and emotional pain of pregnancy. Such surrogate mothers develop an emotional attachment with the baby they nurture in their wombs. He pointed out that a child needs the natural love and affection of family which may not be available through a party that pays a surrogate mother for the birth of the child. In this way, according to him, surrogacy is a threat to the institution of family which is the basic unit of the society. He contended that hiring women and giving them monetary compensation to act as surrogate mothers reduces their status to emotionless machines. The exploitation becomes worst when wealthy people from developed countries come to third-world countries to arrange for cheap surrogate mothers who are not provided sufficient medical facilities and medical insurance. Justice Khan argued that marriage is the only means through which children should be produced under Islamic law. He observed that surrogacy is likely to give rise to innumerable legal problems regarding paternity and maternity of the surrogate children: the relationship between actual children and surrogate children and inheritance rights.

In the end, the court directed that an amendment must be made in section 2 of the Contract Act 1872, which should specifically provide that any surrogacy agreement would not be legally enforceable as it would involve unlawful proposal and consideration. The court further directed that the Pakistan Penal Code 1860 should be amended to declare surrogacy an offence punishable by imprisonment and a fine. The required amendments must be made by 15 August 2017.

As far as the case of the petitioner was concerned, the court did not pass any judgment because under Article 203–D of the Constitution of Pakistan; the Federal Shariat Court cannot provide any personal relief.

The petitioner's case had already been decided by the Civil Courts of ordinary jurisdiction and the Federal Shariat Court could not interfere in their findings.

7.2.5.3 Maternal Grandparents' Custody

Firdous Iqbal v Shifaat Ali 2000 SCMR 838

It is better for a minor to be under the custody of his grandmother with the supervision of his real mother rather than having him/her live with his stepmother.

The mother, Firdous Iqbal (appellant), was married to Shifaat Ali (respondent) in 1989 and a son named Muhammad Mudassur, whose custody was being contested in this case, was born. The marriage was dissolved in 1990 and the minor was left with his mother. After the second marriage of the appellant the minor lived with his maternal grandmother and his mother was thoroughly engaged in supervising his affairs.

The appellant filed a suit for maintenance against the respondent for their son. The respondent reacted to the suit by initiating an application for the custody of the minor arguing that the minor had passed the age of 7 years and the respondent being the natural guardian was entitled to his son's custody. The application was resisted by the appellant, contending that it was initiated after the suit for maintenance was filed against the respondent and was hence motivated to avoid payment of the minor's maintenance. The Guardian Court dismissed the application for the custody of the minor. Subsequently, the first Appellate Court maintained this decision. Therefore, the respondent filed a writ petition before the High Court, which held that the appellant had forfeited her right of *hizanat* (custody) on contracting the second marriage.

The appellant sought leave to appeal before the Supreme Court. The appellant's counsel, in addition to controverting the mother's right to custody on the basis of her second marriage, raised an important question: 'Whether under Muslim Law a mother absolutely loses the right of Hizanat of her male minor children who are aged more than seven years or there are some exceptions to this general rule'.[24]

The judgment of the Supreme Court is well-crafted and is based on the analysis of some books of authority such as Baillie's *Digest of Moohummudan Law*, Ameer Ali's *Commentaries on Muhammadan Law*, the *Fatawa i Alamgiri*, and Tayabji's *Muhammadan Law*. The court also reproduced the tabulated rule 354 from Mulla's *Principles of Muhammadan Law* which deals with the disqualification of a mother from claiming the custody of her minor children on various grounds including her second marriage. The court observed that Mulla's presentation on the subject suffered from 'over simplification'.[25]

The court held that 'the welfare of the minor remains the paramount consideration in determining the custody of a minor notwithstanding the right of the father to get the custody after seven years of age of the male minor child'.[26] While reiterating that the father is a natural guardian of a minor, the court observed that his right to custody of the minor could not be termed as an absolute right even after the minor was above 7 years of age. This right of the father would always be determined considering his conduct in the peculiar circumstances of each case.

The court subsequently evaluated the circumstances of the case and the conduct of the respondent. It highlighted that the respondent had been negligent towards his minor son who was taken care of by the appellant and even after her remarriage she had managed to look after the affairs of the minor through her parents. On the other hand, the respondent was serving in the army and his second wife along with their children were settled in a village. In such circumstances, if the minor's custody was given to the respondent, he would lodge him with his second wife and children in the village. Therefore, the option of leaving the minor in direct control of the stepmother in comparison with allowing him to live with his maternal grandparents under the supervision of the mother would not be conducive to the welfare of the minor. Consequently, the court accepted the appeal and granted the custody of the minor to the appellant (mother).

Zafar Iqbal v Rehmat Jan 1994 SCMR 339

In case a mother and a father are not suitable for appointment as guardians of a minor, a willing grandmother is to be appointed as a guardian.

This case involved litigation over the custody of a minor, Shahbaz Iqbal. The minor was born in 1984 to Zafar Iqbal (appellant) and Naureen Kausar. Their marriage was dissolved in 1985. Thereafter, both the father and the mother contracted their second marriage and had more children from their respective marriages. Both were living abroad at the time of the present litigation before the Supreme Court, and the minor was residing with his maternal grandmother. The father was serving in Somalia along with his new family and the mother was settled in London.

The case went through many phases of litigation before reaching the Supreme Court. The appellant initiated the first phase of litigation for the custody of the minor. The Guardian Judge disposed of the application with the direction that the minor should be admitted to a good boarding school and the expenses of schooling should be borne by the appellant. In case he failed to do so, the maternal grandmother would be entitled to the custody of the minor until he reached seven years of age. The mother assailed the decision in the first Appellate Court and during its pendency the maternal grandmother Rehmat Jan (the respondent in the present litigation) applied to be impleaded. The court, while refusing to implead her maintained the decision of the Guardian Judge.

Thereafter, the respondent initiated another phase of litigation by filing an application for custody of the minor in the Guardian Court, which was accepted; and the maternal grandmother was declared to be the guardian of the minor. This decision was challenged in the first Appellate Court, which reversed it. The respondent filed a writ petition before the High Court, which restored the decision of the Guardian Judge and declared the maternal grandmother as a guardian.

It was against this background that the appellant brought the case to the Supreme Court, assailing the maternal grandmother's appointment as guardian. The appellant's counsel argued that the High Court had not properly appreciated the evidence on record and proceeded on a wrong presumption that upon the disqualification of a father and a mother, the maternal grandmother had the right to the custody of a minor.

The court observed that only three parties had shown their interest to be appointed as guardians—the father, the mother, and the maternal grandmother. As the father and the mother were disqualified from being guardians owing to their residence abroad with their respective families, the only eligible contestant appeared to be the maternal grandmother. In such circumstances, her appointment by the High Court did not warrant any interference as the decision was in the welfare of the minor. Consequently, the court upheld the decision of the High Court.

Ahmad Bilal v Khurram Javed Writ Petition No. 2383/2021 Islamabad

A father shall have the custody of the minor unless found unfit to act as a guardian by the Guardian Court.

This case involved litigation over the guardianship and custody of the minor between the real father and the grandmother. The minor was 2 years old when her mother passed away due to epilepsy. After three months of her demise, the dispute regarding custody of the minor arose when the grandmother refused to hand over the custody to her father. The Family Court ruled in favour of the grandmother on the ground that the petitioner had remarried and the respondent, the grandmother, was better educated. Thereafter, the Additional District Court endorsed the judgment of the Family Court.

The petitioner filed a writ petition challenging the order of the Family Court. The counsel for the petitioner contended that the petitioner neither abandoned his daughter nor was he unfit for guardianship. Therefore, the Family Court erred in handing over the custody to the grandmother.

The important legal question before the Islamabad High Court was whether a relative of a minor or third party could be appointed as a guardian when the biological parent was alive and not declared unfit for custody by the Family Court. Justice Babar Sattar emphasised the established jurisprudence that the welfare of a minor is the supreme consideration in matters of guardianship and custody. He explained that any person having the care of a minor or his property could be appointed as a guardian under the Guardians and Wards Act 1890. He observed that the ICT Child Protection Act 2018 empowers the state to uphold the life, liberty, and dignity of children guaranteed under Articles 9 and 14 of the Constitution. By virtue of this Act, any person other than the biological parent can be appointed as guardian if the child is at risk of significant harm, abuse, or exploitation in the presence of biological parents. Justice Babar Sattar held that the provisions of the ICT Child Protection Act 2018 and Guardians and Wards Act 1890 are to be read together in matters of guardianship and custody.

Justice Babar Sattar held that a third person can be appointed as guardian only when the biological parents are found to be unfit for guardianship. In cases where the mother is handed over the custody of a child, it does not imply that guardianship of the father vanishes; rather, he provides for the maintenance of the child. The contest of guardianship between natural parents is different from the contest between a natural parent and a third-party relative. Justice Babar Sattar held that the welfare of the minor lies with the natural parent, and a natural parent cannot be deprived of guardianship unless the Family Court find him/her unfit for this purpose. Justice Babar Sattar observed that the emotional and psychological well-being of the child and the parent claiming guardianship need to be evaluated by a psychiatrist or established authority. Therefore, it is not under the authority of a judge to declare a person unfit for guardianship without the evaluation of relevant established authorities.

In the instant case, there was no evidence presented by the respondents to indicate that the petitioner father was unfit for the guardianship of the minor. The Family Court erred in holding that the maternal grandmother would provide more love to the minor and that her welfare lay with the respondent. Mere poverty of the petitioner or less education would not amount to the fact that the welfare of a minor would be compromised by staying with the father. Justice Babar Sattar concluded that a natural parent could not be deprived of guardianship to the third party when the biological parent is alive and fit. In a contest of custody between natural parents, even if the mother retains the custody, the father acts as the natural guardian and cannot be replaced unless deemed unfit.

In light of these circumstances, the court allowed the petition and directed to hand over the guardianship to the father and visitation rights to the grandmother so that the sudden transition would not affect the mental health of the child.

7.2.5.4 Real Parents' Custody v Adopted Parents' Custody

Mrs Shaukat Khalid v Additional District Judge, Rawalpindi 1991 SCMR 19

It is natural for a minor to pass the most important years of adolescence with her real parents than with a foster mother, as the same is in consonance with Islamic Injunctions.

This case involved litigation over the custody of a minor between her real parents and her foster mother. The minor was a 16–year-old girl when the Supreme Court heard the case. At the time of her birth, she was handed over by her father (respondent no. 3) to his brother (paternal uncle) and the latter's wife, Mrs Shaukat Khalid (appellant), as the couple did not have any children. After the death of the paternal uncle of the minor, the appellant along with the minor moved to her sister's house. The parties in the case had a number of other issues between them and because of this, the minor was kept away from her natural parents and siblings. During court proceedings, when the minor was inquired about her siblings, she was unable to tell those particulars which a brother or sister would be expected to know in normal circumstances.

The Supreme Court assisted the parties in reaching an amicable solution and drew up an agreement for them in the form of a court order. In addition to handing over the minor to respondent no. 3, the court held that the minor would be allowed to have lunch with the appellant every Friday at her sister's residence, where the appellant was residing. The appellant was also permitted to visit the house of respondent no. 3 to meet the minor at least twice a week.

Respondent no. 3 assailed the order of the court regarding the appellant's visitation rights on the ground that it would not be in the welfare of the minor. However, due to the efforts made by the court, respondent no. 3 offered the appellant to stay at his residence instead of staying at her sister's house. However, the appellant was not willing to leave her sister's house and insisted on getting custody of the minor. The appellant claimed that being the minor's foster mother she had brought her up like her own daughter. She argued that it would be unnatural to deprive her of the minor's custody because an unmatched love and affection had developed between them.

At various hearings of the case, the Supreme Court noted that the minor's conduct and attitude were not demonstrative of good manners. The court attributed these ill mannerisms to three different factors: first, the parents' extra care due to prolonged litigation over the custody of the minor; second, the unsatisfactory upbringing of the minor by the appellant; and third, the failure of the school authorities in the performance of their duties.

At another hearing, the respondent's counsel appraised the court that the minor had started to live happily at her natural parents' house and mixed amicably with her own family. Considering the fact of prolonged litigation and its ill effect on the well-being of the minor, the court observed:

> Be that as it may[,] even if it would have been [a] little indifferent, she sharing with her own parents, their joys and worries, would be more natural than her passing these very important years of adolescence with a foster mother. And this [is] in accord with the principles enunciated by Islam and contained in [the] Qur'an and Sunnah. The adopted parents have never been treated as the same or equal to the real parents. In this context, therefore we do not accept the contention of the learned counsel (of the appellant) that it was "unnatural" to transfer the custody of the minor from her foster mother to [her] real mother and father. What Islam enjoins and teaches, in our system of law, is natural and not unnatural.[27]

In light of these reasons, the court ultimately refused the custody of the minor sought by the appellant.

7.2.5.5 Maternal Aunt's Custody

Nighat Firdous v Khadim Hussain 1998 SCMR 1593

A father's negligent conduct along with the minor's wish to live with his maternal aunt may disentitle the father from the custody of the minor.

This case involved a contest over the custody of a minor, Adrian Khadim, between his father (Khadim Hussain, as the respondent) and his maternal aunt (Nighat Firdous, as the appellant). The mother of the minor died at the time of his birth in 1983 and since then the appellant brought him up under an agreement between the parties. The father entered into another marriage and had a son from that marriage. On the other hand, the appellant was also married with a daughter.

The respondent filed an application for the custody of the minor before the Guardian Judge, which was decided in his favour. The appellant assailed the decision on the basis that the minor's choice was not recorded by the trial court. The first Appellate Court remanded the case for recording the minor's choice. Then the minor expressed his choice to live with his maternal aunt (appellant) before the Guardian Judge but again the Guardian Court decided in favour of the respondent. The appellant did not succeed in getting any relief in an appeal before the first Appellate Court and the writ jurisdiction before the High Court.

Then before the Supreme Court, the appellant argued for the custody of the minor on various grounds including the fact that the respondent's application for custody of the minor was filed in reaction to a suit for maintenance initiated by the appellant against him. The appellant contended that she had agreed to bring up the minor on the condition that the respondent would not demand custody of the minor afterwards.

The respondent did not appear before the court to plead his case. From the record, it appeared that his main argument was that once the minor had attained seven years of age the father has an absolute right to his custody under Muslim Personal Law. The court observed:

> The custody of a minor can be delivered by the Court only in the interest and welfare of the minor and not the interest of the parents. It is true that the Muhammadan father is the lawful guardian of his minor child and is ordinarily entitled to his custody provided it is for the welfare of the minor. The right of the father to claim custody of a minor is not an absolute right, in that, the father may disentitle himself to custody on account of his conduct depending upon the facts and circumstances of the case… The

> preference of the minor, in guardianship cases, is ordinarily taken into consideration but it is not always relevant because the minor is not [the] best judge of his/her welfare. It is for the Court to determine as to whom the custody of the minor should be delivered in his/her welfare.[28]

Moreover, the court analysed the peculiar facts of the case including the initiation of the guardianship litigation by the respondent after the appellant's suit for maintenance; the respondent's continuous absence from the Supreme Court demonstrated his non-serious attitude towards the minor and the minor's choice to be in the custody of his maternal aunt which he made when he attained fifteen years of age. In light of the aforementioned circumstances, the court handed over the minor's custody to the appellant and gave the respondent visitation rights which were to be determined by the Guardian Court.

7.2.5.6 Non-Appointment of Relatives as Guardians. It is generally accepted that the welfare of minors lies in handing over their custody to their relatives. In some situations, the courts award custody to relatives, such as grandparents. The Guardian Courts may appoint non-relatives or government officials as guardians considering the paramount principle of the welfare of the minor. At the same time, the courts may deny the right of custody to such relatives who are motivated solely by their financial interests.

Bashir Ahmad v Incharge (Female) Darulaman, District Mianwali 2011 SCMR 1329

A non-relative is to be given the custody of a minor who has been serving as her *de facto* guardian since her birth, especially when the real mother does not have any shelter or source of income.

A dispute over the custody of the female child, Muqqadus Bibi, arose between her real mother (respondent no. 2) and an issueless person Bashir Ahmad (petitioner) who was not related to the minor. The mother, with her free consent, handed over the minor to the petitioner in her infancy. She was unable to bring up her daughter as she was a beggar and had no stable place of residence. She was also blind. On the other hand, the petitioner was a retired army officer who was issueless.

The dispute arose when the mother (respondent no. 2) and the petitioner applied to the Guardian Court to be appointed as the minor's guardian. The court decided the matter in favour of the mother and dismissed the application submitted by the petitioner. Thereafter, the matter went to the first Appellate Court which maintained the decision of the Guardian Court but directed the Incharge Darulaman (respondent no. 1) to take the responsibility/custody of the minor until she attained the age of majority. The petitioner filed an appeal before the High Court, which was dismissed. Hence, the matter came before the Supreme Court.

The Supreme Court sent notices to respondent no. 2 for the appearance and presentation of her version, but she did not appear. Therefore, the court proceeded in her absence. The counsel for the petitioner argued that he had been bringing up the minor since his assumption of her responsibility as if she was his own daughter. The petitioner told the court that respondent no. 2 did not have any fixed abode or a source of income. The court observed that the petitioner was financially stable as he was drawing a retirement pension from the army. The minor who was aged 12/13 years at that time and a student in sixth grade, appeared before the court. As the minor looked confident enough to be asked about her preference, the court inquired of her in this regard. The minor stated that the petitioner had been taking proper care of her and she would prefer to live with him instead of going to the Darulaman.

The court observed that in these circumstances, handing over the minor's custody to the Darulaman would not be conducive to her welfare because she would not get the quality of education she was receiving while she was in the petitioner's custody. The court appointed the petitioner as the guardian of the minor considering that he had been serving as her *de facto* guardian in a proper manner from the moment he was given her custody by respondent no. 2. Considering the fact that the petitioner was not related to the minor, the court directed that he should bring the minor before the Guardian Court each month and the judge would determine as to whether or not she was being taken proper care of. The court observed the fact that the minor's real mother was alive and held that she would be entitled to meet the minor whenever she wished to do so.

Naveed Munir v Additional District & Sessions Judge, Lahore 2014 SCMR 1446

A court may not appoint any relative as a minor's guardian if his interest is motivated by the property inherited by the minor rather than by any love and affection.

Nasir Ahmad Shahid was married to Rehmat Bibi and a son, Sanaullah Siddique was born in 2003. The marriage was dissolved some time later. The mother left for her native area Chitral leaving the son with his father and contracted another marriage. No one had any information about her beyond this fact. The Supreme Court made efforts to procure her presence in the court but could not succeed. The father entered into another marriage with Kausar Parveen (respondent no. 2) who had an offspring from her previous marriage. The father had considerable property which after his death in 2007 was the entitlement of his sole son, Sanaullah Siddique, whose custody was in contest in this case.

The person appearing as the appellant/petitioner, Naveed Munir, was a nephew of the father of the minor and was interested in being appointed the guardian of the minor. He submitted an application in this regard to the Guardian Court and secured a guardianship certificate *ex parte*. When the *ex parte* decision came to the knowledge of respondent no. 2, she assailed it through various applications: one challenging the decision on the ground of fraud by the petitioner and another for setting aside the *ex parte* decision, but both these applications were dismissed. Consequently, respondent no. 2 appealed before the first Appellate Court, which remanded the matter to the Guardian Court for a fresh decision.

This was not an acceptable outcome for the petitioner, and he impugned it before the High Court. The court did not find any infirmity in the decision and dismissed the petition. Therefore, an appeal was filed before the Supreme Court. The court did not go into the procedural intricacies and pointed out at the outset that none of the courts below had paid any consideration to the main issue in this matter, that is, the welfare of the minor.

Some facts of material consequence were that the petitioner disputed the status of respondent no. 2 as the widow of the late Nasir Ahmad Shahid. It was also brought to the notice of the court that the relatives of the deceased had initiated some other litigation in respect of the deceased's properties. Money had also been withdrawn from the accounts of the deceased through fraud and misrepresentation.

In this context, the Supreme Court directed an assistant commissioner to prepare the record of the properties owned by the minor and deputed a commission to report on the minor's condition and quality of living. After interviewing the minor and collecting the information about his living conditions, the commission reported that the minor was confident and living a happy life with his stepmother. The minor's life was affected by the danger he was exposed to due to huge properties he was heir to. It was this last aspect which put tremendous effect on the quality of life of the minor. Though he was living with his stepmother, he was not allowed to play outside the house and most of his leisure time was spent playing on the roof of the house. The stepmother along with the minor had been living under constant threats to the latter's life and were forced to move from one rented house to another. This shifting had adversely affected the minor's education.

The case was brought before the court on many occasions because the court was of the view that its parental jurisdiction required it to resolve the matter in the best interest of the minor without violating any provision of the law and the rights of any other person. During the course of the proceedings, the court persuaded the parties and other relatives to amicably settle their suits and if they had grabbed any property/finances that belonged to the minor, then it should be returned. Due to the efforts of the court, some cases initiated by the petitioner and some other relatives were withdrawn and some amount was also deposited back to the minor's account.

Thereafter, the court constituted a committee to look after the affairs of the minor including his admission to Aitchison College. During these proceedings the parties, particularly the petitioner, softened his attitude towards respondent no. 2 and accepted her as the widow of the deceased, Nasir Ahmad Shahid. The parties instead of litigating their respective controversies in the various courts submitted before the Supreme Court to decide whatever it deemed appropriate in the circumstances of the case. While deciding the matter, the court observed:

> [T]he interests of the various parties in the minor may well be motivated by the property that he has inherited rather than any love and affection. If the minor had not inherited such property, he would perhaps have ended up in an orphanage or abandoned in the street. The conduct of the petitioner and other paternal relatives as well as the respondent no. 2 has not been aboveboard.[29]

Though the court made efforts to resolve conflicts regarding the minor's properties and accounts, it was unable to do so because the parties, through their negligence and financial interests, had complicated the issues to such an extent that it made their resolution impossible. After concluding that none of the relatives was suitable to be appointed as the guardian, the court held:

> A formalistic approach commonly associated with the adjudication of adversarial civil disputes may not be conducive to the exercise of parental jurisdiction by this Court. A more proactive role may have to be adopted so as to ensure the protection of the best interest of the minor.[30]

The court referred to the provisions of the Punjab Courts of Wards Act 1903 and directed the competent authority/commissioner to exercise *suo moto* powers for the superintendence of the minor's person and property until the time he reached 18 years of age. By disposing of the present matter, the court also directed the competent authority/commissioner to report to the court every three months about the upbringing, education, and property of the minor.

7.3 Conclusion

Parents have joint responsibility for the physical, spiritual, moral, and social well-being of their children. However, when parents get separated for any reason their responsibilities as to the upbringing of their children also split up. Consequently, child custody and guardianship often become contentious issues following the separation or dissolution of a marriage. While the father is regarded as a natural guardian, the right of custody of minor children rests with the mother who is entitled to the custody of her male child until he attains the age of seven and her daughter until she attains puberty under the Hanafi school. However, a mother's second marriage or her immoral lifestyle may cause her to lose her right to the custody of her children.

In Pakistan, the Guardians and Wards Act 1890 is the law under which courts operate for resolving the issues of guardianship and custody. This law, however, is not exhaustive and leaves some discretionary power for the courts. The superior courts have evolved a jurisprudence of benevolence and compassion for minors and have arrogated to themselves a parental role to ensure the well-being of children and safeguard their interests in whatever way possible. Analysis of case law demonstrates that the welfare of the minor is the supreme consideration of the courts in deciding custody issues. Due to this, factors such as financial stability, conduct, and character of a person desirous of having custody of a child are given primary importance while deciding custody matters. Moreover, the courts also consider the age, sex, religion, and preference of the minor. In this regard, the welfare of the minor is important enough to justify any apparent deviation from the stringent principles of personal law regulating this area. The cases discussed in this chapter illustrate various instances where a father, despite being a natural guardian was denied custody and other instances when a mother was given custody when the welfare of the minor demanded so. Similarly, in the interest of the minor, the courts often ignore the poverty of the mother, her second marriage, and private agreements between the parties. The courts have put the welfare of the minor above everything else, going as far as to appoint non-relatives and government officials as guardians instead of a close relative of the minor.

The FSC has declared surrogacy against the Injunctions of Islam as laid down in the Qur'an and Sunnah. It declared surrogacy detrimental to the proper upbringing of a child as it deprives a child of the natural love and affection of his/her parents.

Questions

1. Who has the right to the guardianship and custody of a child/minor? What are the main considerations of the courts while deciding these cases?
2. What is the principle of welfare of a minor and how is it applied in disputes regarding the custody of children?
3. Write a note on the right of a mother to the custody of her children. State whether this right can be extended to a stepmother, non-Muslim mother, and surrogate mother.
4. Why should a mother lose custody of her child when she enters into a marriage with a stranger? Are there any exceptions to this principle?
5. Who should have the custody of a surrogate child and why? Critically analyse the Federal Shariat Court judgment on surrogacy.

Further Reading

BOOKS/ARTICLES

Ishaque, S., and M.M. Khan, 'The Best Interests of the Child: A Prevailing Consideration within Islamic Principles and a Governing Principle in Child Custody Cases in Pakistan', *International Journal of Law, Policy and the Family* (2015) 29, 78.

Davis, M.F., 'Child Custody in Pakistan: The Role of Ijtihad', *Boston College Third World Law Journal* (1984) 5(2), 119.

CASES

Akbar Bibi v Shaukat Ali 1981 CLC 78 [Lah] (If the minor is old enough to make an intelligent preference in the matter of his/her custody, then his/her preference plays a decisive role in determining the suitability and desirability of a person desirous of custody of a minor.)

Mohammad Deen Malik v IInd Additional District Judge, Karachi 1982 CLC 441 (A mother's ill health is not a ground to refuse her the custody of a minor.)

Mst. Ayesha Abdul Maleek v Additional District Judge, Sahiwal 2020 YLR 401 (Lah) (Where a court finds that a minor is competent enough to use his/her intelligence, the principle of 'intelligence preference' can be used to decide the custody of the minor.)

Nazeer Begum v Abdul Sattar PLD 1963 Kar 465 (Where a mother contracts a second marriage and the father does not claim the infant within a reasonable time from the date of such marriage or from the date of his knowledge thereof, he should be presumed to have abandoned his right. This proposition is subject to the welfare of the minor.)

Rahimullah Choudhry v Mrs Syeda Helali 1974 SCMR 305 (Welfare of the minor is a question of fact and it has to be resolved on the basis of the material placed before the court and not on the basis of any presumption.)

Rashida Begum v Shahab Din PLD 1960 Lah 1142 (Marriage of a mother to a person not within the prohibited degree of relationship with the minor does not disentitle her from the right to custody.)

Shabana Naz v Muhammad Saleem 2014 SCMR 343 (A mother loses the right of custody when she marries a person, who does not fall within the prohibited degree of relationship with the child unless there are exceptional circumstances which justify departure from this rule on the basis of the welfare of the minor.)

Uzma Wahid v Guardian Judge 1989 MLD 3064 [Lah] (Where the stepmother is issueless, her presence in the house does not stand in the way of the welfare of the minor especially when a minor's grandparents also live in the same house as the stepmother.)

Zohra Begum v Sheikh Latif Ahmad Munawwar PLD 1965 Lah 695 (Where there is a conflict of views in authentic books of Muslim law on a mother's right of custody, a court is competent to differ from the views of jurists to form its own opinion.)

Notes

1. Also described as the principle of the best interest of the child, which is enshrined in Article 3 of the Convention on the Rights of the Child 1989. Pakistan is a party to this convention.
2. *Mst Aisha v Manzoor Hussain* PLD 1985 SC 436.
3. Pakistan ratified this Convention in 1990 and its Optional Protocol on Sale of Children, Child Prostitution and Child Pornography in 2011. To fulfil its obligations under these instruments, the legislature passed the National Commission on the Rights of the Child Act 2017.
4. PLD 2011 Lah 362, 371.
5. 1983 SCMR 606, 610.
6. 2013 MLD 1885, 1889.
7. Ibid., 1890.
8. PLD 2002 SC 267, 269.
9. Ibid., 270.
10. In *Mst. Laila Qayyum v Fawad Qayyum* PLD 2019 SC 449, the Supreme Court invoked its ancillary powers under Article 187 of the Constitution to dismiss a suit of declaration to conduct a DNA test.
11. 2004 SCMR 1839, 1843.
12. Ibid., 1842.
13. 2004 SCMR 821, 823.
14. PLD 1955 Lah 412, 415.
15. Ibid.
16. AIR 1944 All 202.
17. PLD 1955 Lah 412, 415–16.
18. PLD 2011 Lah 423, 429.
19. Ibid., 429–30.
20. PLD 2010 Lah 48.
21. PLD 2013 Lah 254, 256.
22. Ibid.

23. *In re Baby M* 109 NJ 396 (1988). In their judgments, Pakistani courts should also keep the identity of the child anonymous to protect them against stigmatisation and for the protection of their rights in future.
24. 2000 SCMR 838, 842.
25. Ibid.
26. Ibid., 843.
27. 1991 SCMR 19, 23.
28. 1998 SCMR 1593, 1596.
29. 2014 SCMR 1446, 1454.
30. Ibid., 1455.

Part III
PERSONAL PROPERTY

8

HIBA (GIFT)

8.1 Introduction

A *hiba* is a transfer of the ownership of property without any consideration. It is a gratis transaction in which one person voluntarily transfers his/her property to another. Every Muslim who is a major and of sound mind is capable of making a *hiba*. A gift can be made to any person. If an intended donee is either insane or a minor, possession must be delivered to his/her legal guardian. Since *hiba* entails the absolute transfer of ownership rights in a property, it cannot be made to an unborn person as there is no one to take possession of his/her interests.

Under Islamic law, the disposing capacity of the donor of *hiba* is not limited. During one's lifetime, a Muslim may gift all or part of his/her property to whomsoever s/he wishes without any restriction (gift *inter vivos*). However, this is in contradistinction to wills where a person cannot dispose of more than one-third of his/her property. Another restriction under Sunni law is that a gift through testamentary disposition (will) is not allowed in favour of a legal heir. A testamentary gift of more than one-third of the property or in favour of a legal heir can only take effect if all the other legal heirs give their consent. A gift made during *marz-ul-maut* (death sickness) takes effect as a will, which means it cannot consume more than one-third of the property and the gift property should be transferred immediately. Under Shia law, however, a bequest in favour of a legal heir can be made within the limit of one-third of the property without the consent of other legal heirs.

8.2 Elements of a Valid *Hiba*

For a gift to be valid, the following elements must be present:

1. Declaration of the gift by the donor (*ijab*).
2. Acceptance of the gift by the donee (*qabul*).
3. Delivery of possession (*qabza*).

The declaration of a gift must be express and unequivocal; it cannot be implied and should be endorsed by the entire relinquishment of the possession. However, the acceptance can be either express or implied. Depending upon the nature of the property, the delivery of possession may be actual or constructive (construed by the law, not by fact). In the case of the former, the property is physically handed over to the donee. This is the usual mode of delivery of possession of tangible property. On the other hand, constructive possession means possession in the construction of the law. It amounts to an act in the eyes of the law when the act is not actually or apparently performed. This is usually done in the case of intangible property, but a donor must exhibit a clear intention of relinquishing his rights over the property in favour of the donee. Constructive possession is also an acceptable mode of delivery of possession where the property is tangible but physical possession is not possible. The transfer of possession, however, is not necessary in the following exceptional cases:

1. When a donor and donee reside in the same house.
2. When the gift is from a husband to a wife, or vice versa.
3. A parent's gift to a child.
4. A guardian's gift to a ward.
5. A gift to a bailee in possession.

The third requirement of a valid gift (transfer of possession) implies that a future or contingent interest, such as an expectation of succeeding to the estate of a living person (*spes successionis*), cannot be a valid subject matter of a gift. The controversy about the validity of a gift of limited interests under Islamic law also stems from this requirement.

It is necessary for a donor to possess the gift at the time of making the gift. In addition, the subject matter of the gift must exist at the time when the gift is being made. Therefore, future, conditional, and contingent gifts are not valid. Future gifts are purported to be transferred to a donee in future. On the other hand, conditional gifts depend upon the fulfilment of some condition by a donee, whereas contingent gifts depend upon the happening of an uncertain event in future. Similarly, any condition attached to a gift that hinders its completeness and is derogatory to the proprietary interests of the donee is void, but the gift itself is valid. Furthermore, a property, which is held adversely to the interests of a donor cannot be gifted, as the possession, one of the necessary ingredients of a valid gift, cannot be delivered in such a case. However, after the declaration of the law of adverse possession as un-Islamic by the Shariat Appellate Bench of the Supreme Court of Pakistan, this perspective has lost relevance.[1] Therefore, a donor may transfer in any manner he is capable of transferring his proprietary rights in a given situation that lawfully satisfies the requirement of delivery of possession.

8.2.1 Subject matter of *Hiba*. As far as the subject matter of a *hiba* is concerned, Islamic property law recognises a distinction between the substance/corpus (*'ayn*) and the usufruct/fruit (*manfa'a*). The transfer of substance along with usufruct is called *hiba*, while a transfer of usufruct without substance is called *ariya* (commodate loan). *Ariya* is the grant of a license, without consideration, to a person to use and enjoy the usufruct of a certain thing for a limited period of time. Such a gift is revocable at the option of the grantor.

8.2.2 *Mushaa*. An undivided share in the property, called *mushaa*, can also be a valid subject matter of a gift in certain cases. A gift of an undivided share in a property, which is not capable of division, is considered valid under all schools of thought. However, there is no unanimous view among different schools of Islamic law on the gift of an undivided share in a divisible property. Under Shafi'i and Ithna Ashari laws, such a gift is valid if a donor withdraws his control over the property in favour of the donee. However, under Hanafi law, such a gift, with certain exceptions, is irregular (*fasid*), but can be made valid by subsequent partition and delivery of possession.

The doctrine of *mushaa* is limited in its application, and is subject to the following exceptions:

1. Gift of *mushaa* to a co-heir.
2. Gift of shares in *zamindari*.
3. Gift of shares in a land company.
4. A joint gift to two or more persons where their shares are clearly and distinctly specified.
5. Gift of shares in freehold property in a commercial town.[2]

8.2.3 Revocation of *Hiba*. A donor can revoke a gift at any time before the delivery of possession. The rationale for this rule is that the gift is not complete before the delivery of possession. However, after the delivery of possession, a gift can only be revoked by the intervention of a competent court or by mutual consent of the donor and the donee. There are certain situations in which a gift becomes irrevocable, such as:

1. When a donor or a donee is dead.
2. When a donor and a donee are related within the prohibited degrees of relationship. Under Shia law, a gift made to any blood relation is irrevocable.
3. When a donor and a donee are tied in a marital relationship.
4. When a donee has disposed of the subject matter of a gift through sale or a gift.
5. When the subject matter of a gift is lost or destroyed or so changed as to lose its identity.
6. When the subject matter of a gift increases in its value and the increment is inseparable.
7. When the gift is a *sadaqah*.
8. When a donor has received something in return (consideration/ *iwaz*).[3]

Hiba must be distinguished from *sadaqah*, which is a gift made with a religious motive to obtain merit in the eyes of God. Like *hiba*, delivery of possession is essential in the case of *sadaqah*; but unlike *hiba*, *sadaqah* is irrevocable because of its religious object.

8.2.4 *Hiba Bil-Iwaz.* *Hiba* is different from a sale transaction, which involves consideration. There is, however, a concept of *hiba bil-iwaz*, which is a gift for consideration. It literally means a gift for an exchange. This transaction consists of two mutual gifts between a donor and a donee, that is, one gift from a donor to a donee and the other from a donee to a donor. The gift (*hiba*) and consideration (*iwaz*) are two independent transactions and when both are completed, the entire transaction is called *hiba bil-iwaz*. This kind of *hiba bil-iwaz* is generally known as true *hiba bil-iwaz*. There is another version of *hiba bil-iwaz* known as false *hiba bil-iwaz*. It was developed by Muslim scholars of South Asia for avoiding the requirement of the transfer of possession for a valid gift and the strict rules regarding a gift of undivided property (*mushaa*). There are two requisites of a false *hiba bil-iwaz*: (1) actual payment of consideration on the part of a donee; and (2) *bona fide* intention on part of a donor to divest himself of the gifted property. In a true *hiba bil-iwaz*, consideration is not stipulated at the time of *hiba*. The consideration is an independent transaction of *hiba*. For example, A gives his house to B without a stipulation of any return and delivers the house to B. Subsequently, B gives his shop to A without saying that it is in return for the house and delivers it to A. In this example, A's gift of house is independent of B's gift of shop. In South Asian (or false) *hiba bil-iwaz*, however, A gives his house to B as a gift on the condition that B would give him a shop as a gift.

8.2.5 *Hiba Bi-Shart Al-Iwaz.* *Hiba bi-shart al-iwaz* is a gift made with the stipulation for a return. In this way, it may resemble South Asian *hiba bil-iwaz*. However, unlike the latter, delivery of possession is essential in *hiba bi-shart al-iwaz*.[4] The main advantage of South Asian *hiba bil-iwaz* is that it provides the donor with the advantage of transferring the ownership of the gifted property to a donee without the delivery of possession. The consideration from the donee may be a token, for example, a prayer rug or a rosary, which in comparison with the value of the main gift may have trivial or insignificant value converting it into a gratuitous transaction. In this way, the donor nominally parts with the ownership of the property but continues to enjoy its benefits during his lifetime. Historically, this transaction has been used to circumvent the strict rules of the transfer of undivided property (*mushaa*) and Islamic inheritance law.[5]

8.2.6 Legal Formalities. Writing is not required for the validity of any gift under Islamic law. It can be made orally provided that the three basic ingredients of a gift are satisfied. However, for evidentiary purposes, it is desirable for a gift transaction to be made in writing. Under the Transfer of Property Act 1882, a gift of immovable property is required to be witnessed and registered. Section 123 of the Act states that a gift of immovable property must be made by a registered instrument signed by or on behalf of the donor and it must also be attested by two witnesses. However, section 129 of the same Act exempts Muslim law from the application of the Act. This means that gifts made under Muslim law are not required to fulfil the requirements of writing, registration, and witnessing.[6] Likewise, a written instrument of a gift is not required to be registered under the Registration Act 1908.[7]

When a person makes a gift under Muslim law, it may be presumed that s/he fully understands what s/he is doing, but this presumption does not apply in the cases of a *pardanashin* lady. In such cases, it is the onus of the donee to satisfy the court that the gift made by such a donor was voluntary and free from coercion or undue influence. In the case of a *pardanashin* lady, such an onus of proof is usually discharged by proving that the woman had access to independent advice.

8.3 Outline of Case Law

8.3.1 Essentials of a Gift and Onus of Proof. Traditionally, the donor is legally capable of gifting his/her property to whomsoever s/he wants provided that the essential requirements of a valid gift, i.e. declaration, acceptance, and the delivery of possession are met. However, case law suggests that the courts have adopted a flexible approach towards these stringent requirements, particularly with respect to the delivery of possession. The courts have held that actual possession need not be transferred for a valid gift; delivery of constructive possession will suffice in certain circumstances. In case the validity of a gift is challenged, the donee is required to prove the same through cogent and reliable evidence. The validity of a gift is a mixed question of law and fact and has to be assessed by considering all relevant circumstances of a case.

Shafqat Parveen v Muhammad Iftikhar Amjad 2012 SCMR 1602

The onus to prove the validity of a gift is upon the donee.

This case lays down the three necessary ingredients of a valid gift: offer by the donor, acceptance by the donee, and delivery of possession. It also establishes that the onus to prove these ingredients is upon the beneficiary of the transaction, the donee.

In this case, Shafqat Parveen, the petitioner/donee was married to respondent no. 4 in 1965. The *nikahnama* mentioned that the father-in-law, the donor transferred his house to her as a gift in lieu of her dower. Another unregistered document, purported to be prepared in 1966 supported the alleged gift. The respondents in the case were the petitioner's husband and other children of the donor.

After the death of the donor, the petitioner filed a suit for declaration of her proprietary right on the suit property on the basis of the alleged gift made in her favour. She also sought a permanent injunction restraining respondents from interfering with the suit property. All three courts—the trial court, the first Appellate Court, and the High Court—rejected the petitioner's claim on the basis of the evidence adduced by the parties. Some important pieces of evidence militating against the claim of the petitioner were: the donor remained in the disputed house till his death in

1987, he had been exercising his proprietary right on the disputed house during his life, he paid the property tax himself throughout that period, all utility meters were in his name, and the petitioner did not make any effort to get the house transferred in her name through a registered document for more than two decades after her marriage in 1965 up to the donor's death in 1987.

The respondents argued that the entry in the *nikahnama* regarding the gift was made through fraud and collusion. The petitioner was unable to prove its genuineness by producing relevant witnesses, viz. the *Nikah* Registrar and its scribe. The one witness who supported the plea of the petitioner was her husband, respondent no. 4 who was himself a beneficiary of the alleged transaction. In view of the foregoing circumstances, the Supreme Court dismissed the petition while observing that 'in Muhammadan Law, offer, acceptance and delivery of possession are the three essential ingredients of a valid gift and the onus was on the petitioner to prove these components'.[8]

Riaz Ullah Khan v Asghar Ali 2004 SCMR 1701

Transfer of possession is not required in case of a gift from a father to a minor child, from a guardian to a ward, and a husband to a wife and *vice versa*.

This case lays down the principle that the delivery of possession is not required for a valid gift in case of a gift from a father to a minor child, from a guardian to a ward, and a husband to a wife and *vice versa*.

The husband (donor) transferred his property to his wife (donee) through a registered deed in 1989. The same was also mutated and subsequently attested in her name in 1991. After the death of the donee in 1991, her legal heirs inherited the disputed property. The petitioner, who was a nephew of the donor instituted a suit against the legal heirs of the donee in order to have the gift declared invalid, and thereby secure his legal share in the gifted property. During the proceedings in the trial court, the scribe of the registered deed and marginal witnesses appeared to prove the authenticity of the alleged gift deed. Consequently, the trial court and both appellate forums—first Appellate Court and the High Court—dismissed the petitioner's case.

The petitioner appealed to the Supreme Court. In his plea before the Supreme Court, the petitioner contended that the alleged gift was never completed because possession was not delivered to the donee. Hence, the entire transaction was liable to be set aside. The court rejected this contention by observing that 'such argument is not at all available to the petitioner because in case of [a] gift to a wife and to a ward, the delivery of possession is immaterial'.[9]

Abrar Ahmed v Irshad Ahmed PLD 2014 SC 331

Delivery of constructive possession is valid for a gift.

Delivery of possession is an important ingredient of a valid gift under Islamic law. Therefore, the manner of the delivery of possession is also important. The issue, in this case, was whether a gift can be completed by the delivery of constructive possession or physical possession is absolutely necessary.

Babu Khan (donor) bestowed his house upon one of his sons Irshad Ahmad (donee), the respondent. The donor executed a declaration of gift in favour of the donee in 2001, which was subsequently reinforced by a registered deed of gift in 2002. The appellants were two other sons of the donor who were residing in the gifted house along with the respondent. With reference to the gifted house, the donor made an unambiguous statement, admitting the previously mentioned gift in another suit initiated by the appellants against him in 2000.

In 2002, the respondent filed a suit for securing possession of the house and mesne profit against the appellants. The trial court dismissed the suit mainly on the ground that no physical possession was delivered to the donee by the donor; hence the gift was not valid. The respondent challenged the decision in the first Appellate Court which reversed it. Thereafter, the appellants assailed the decision of the first Appellate Court in the High Court, which maintained the impugned decision. In this background, the appellants brought the case before the Supreme Court. The Court initially granted a leave to consider the validity of the alleged gift as physical possession was not delivered, but eventually, the petition was dismissed.

During the regular hearing of the case, the appellants contended that the suit for possession was not maintainable on the basis that the alleged gift lacked delivery of physical possession. The court took into account the fact that the appellants did not raise this contention in their written statements and observed that the appellants being bound by their pleadings could not take such a defence at this stage. Considering the two declarations of gift and the donor's statement in another litigation regarding the gift, the court held that in the circumstances of the case, the status of the appellants could not be termed better than that of licensees who were in occupation of the house of the licensor with his permission.

When the donor cancelled the license of the appellants to reside in the gifted house, he was deemed to have acquired the sort of possession which was capable of being transferred further without any legal hindrance. The court held:

> Obviously, a licensee cannot question the validity of the gift on the basis that the possession of the property was with him, especially when at the time of making [an] oral gift he has no enforceable right or interest in the property. This is so because the appellants at the time of the gift, for all intents and purposes, were strangers to the gift, either being the licensee of Babu Khan (donor) or being his prospective legal heirs.[10]

The court stated that an important factor in the case was the donor's consistency in articulating on various occasions that he had completed the gift in favour of the donee. Consequently, the case of the appellants was dismissed as being devoid of any merit.

It is worth observing that in this case the court did not insist upon the delivery of physical possession, rather, it treated constructive delivery of possession as sufficient for a gift to be valid. It can be inferred that a donor may make a valid gift by transferring what he is capable of transferring at the time of making a gift provided he is the legitimate owner of the gifted property.

Nasrullah Khan v Rasul Bibi 2001 SCMR 1156

The donee must prove the validity of a gift.

It is the responsibility of a donee to establish the validity of a gift by cogent and reliable evidence. Any deficiency in establishing the validity of a gift would hamper his claim. In this case, the donee failed to discharge the onus and consequently lost his claim to the property as a donee.

Allah Ditta had two daughters, Rasul Bibi and Nazir Bibi, from Barkat Bibi. After her dissolution of marriage with Allah Ditta, Barkat Bibi contracted another marriage and had children from that marriage as well. The appellant, Nasrullah Khan, was the son of Nazir Bibi. Rasul Bibi, the respondent filed a suit in the Civil Court for a declaration of her right to her father's property and for a permanent injunction against the appellant restraining him from interfering with the property. In her pleadings, she stated that the land in dispute had been in possession of her real sister's son, and he had been paying her rent. However, he stopped paying the rent two months before the institution of the present suit. She claimed that he had stopped paying the rent as he intended to file a suit to claim the entire land on the basis of a false gift. She contended that there was nothing to prove that any such gift was made by her father in favour of Nasrullah Khan.

The appellant took a different stance altogether by arguing that the land in dispute had already been gifted in his favour through mutation and therefore, he was its rightful owner. Moreover, he asserted that Rasul Bibi was not Allah Ditta's real daughter, and she was born from another marriage of Barkat Bibi, hence she did not have any right to the property.

The Civil Court dismissed the suit of Rasul Bibi, and the first Appellate Court maintained the decision of the trial court. Thereafter, she approached the High Court and assailed the concurrent findings of the lower courts. The court after evaluating the evidence on record concluded that the appellant had failed to establish that Allah Ditta made the alleged gift in his favour. The appellant brought the case before the Supreme Court.

The Supreme Court, after going through the record and decisions of the courts below, pointed out some critical deficiencies within the appellant's case. It held that it was the responsibility of the appellant to establish the voluntary nature of the alleged gift by convincing evidence. The appellant, however, failed to do so. He was unable to prove that the donor, Allah Ditta presented himself before the revenue authorities for the purpose of admitting the gift. This was significant as the mutation of the alleged gift was not carried out and attested in a routine fashion. The appellant secured the mutation from another revenue estate than the one in which the land in dispute was actually located. In these circumstances, the court dismissed the appeal and confirmed that the land in dispute devolved on the respondent through inheritance.

Syed Mohsin Raza Bukhari v Syed Gulzar Hussain Kazmi PLD 2004 SC 520

A donor can gift his property to whomsoever s/he wants during his/her lifetime.

The matter in dispute was a house located in a posh residential area of Lahore owned by Syed Altaf Hussain Bukhari (donor/father) who died on 18 November 1986. Syeda Azra Zaineb Bukhari (respondent/donee) alleged that her father had bestowed the house upon her, disentitling the appellants from any share in the suit property and the same fact had been acknowledged through an acknowledgement of disposition of property dated 30 October 1986. The appellants were the legal heirs of the donor and because of the gift they were deprived of their prospective shares in the inheritance. They initiated a suit in the Civil Court challenging the transaction on numerous grounds including *marz-ul-maut* (death sickness) of the donor. The court, after recording the evidence, decided in favour of the respondent holding that the gift was validly made to the donee and the donor had not been suffering from *marz-ul-maut* when he made the gift. An appeal was preferred to the division bench of the High Court, which did not find any merit in the appeal, and therefore dismissed the same.

The case was brought before the Supreme Court. The appellants vehemently argued that the courts below failed to appreciate the evidence. There was nothing on record to prove the authenticity of the acknowledgement of the disposition of property. It could not be established that an oral gift was made earlier to the said acknowledgement because in the absence of an oral gift the piece of paper acknowledging it was of no avail. Moreover, as the donor was suffering from imminent fear of death any transaction made by him in that situation could not be regarded as valid. The appellants also attempted to assail the gift on the basis of its preferential nature favouring one legal heir while depriving all the other legal heirs including sons and unmarried daughters. The respondents contended that the decisions by the lower courts did not suffer from any illegality because the gift was proved with cogent and reliable evidence.

The court thoroughly perused the evidence on record. It observed that all witnesses appearing on behalf of the respondents including marginal witnesses of the acknowledgement, an official from the excise and taxation department and the tenant residing in the house, had been consistent throughout their testimonies and supported the factum of the gift in favour of the donee. The marginal witnesses confirmed their signatures on the acknowledgement. The excise official testified that the property tax had been paid by the donee from the time of the gift until her death. Similarly, the tenant stated that he was asked by the donor to pay rent to the donee. All witnesses testified that the donor was in good health at the relevant time. This can be evidenced by the fact that he used to drive his car which would have been impossible had he not been in his senses.

Considering such convincing evidence before it, the court did not see any reason to interfere in the decision rendered by the trial court and confirmed by the Appellate Court. The court refuted the contentions of the appellants by observing that the donor was not afflicted with *marz-ul-maut* when he gifted his house. Moreover, under Islamic law, the donor is the exclusive owner of his house, and he can dispose of it during his lifetime to whomsoever he likes. And, in doing so, he could also deprive his prospective heirs by preferring one over the others.

8.3.2 Corpus and Usufruct. Islamic law distinguishes between the corpus and the usufruct of the property. A donor can donate the usufruct of the property while keeping the corpus for his/her personal use. Moreover, even if the donor keeps using the usufruct after the mutation of the gifted property, the courts have held that such utilisation will not automatically invalidate the gift. In order to have such a gift declared invalid, the claimant will have to establish through convincing evidence that the same was not valid on grounds of fraud and coercion.

Muhammad Nawaz v Muhammad Khan 2005 SCMR 710

A valid gift of usufruct can be made without its corpus.

The case involves numerous relatives. All of them were the children and grandchildren of Noor Khan (donor). The donor gifted his property to one of his daughters, Mehr Bhari in 1941. She was unmarried then and remained so till her death. She further transferred the property to the son of her brother, Muhammad Khan (respondent), in 1973. Noor Khan died in 1980 and after his death, his legal heirs initiated the process of succession to his legacy. During this process, it transpired that the property gifted to the donee was further mutated to the respondent. All the aggrieved legal heirs filed a suit for the cancellation of the mutation in favour of Muhammad Khan. Their main contention was that Noor Khan had made a lifetime gift of the usufruct of the disputed property to Mehr Bhari because she was unmarried. Hence, she did not have any legitimate right to transfer the property to the respondent. Therefore, the alleged mutation ought to be cancelled and the petitioners be awarded their share in the property. On the other hand, the respondent argued that Mehr Bhari was the exclusive owner of the gifted property, and she was legally competent to transfer the same to him.

After going through the different stages of litigation, the case was finally heard by the Supreme Court. After analysing numerous decisions of the superior judiciary, the court tabulated the following main principles: (a) that besides the gift of the corpus, Islamic law also recognises the gift only of the usufruct of the property; (b) that a determination of whether the gift was of the corpus or of the usufruct of the property, depends upon the facts of each case to be inferred from the relevant evidence oral/documentary after discovering the real intention of the donor and no hard and fast rule could be laid down for the said purpose; (c) that if it was found that what had been gifted was the corpus of the property then any condition attached to such a gift would be illegal while the gift itself would be perfectly valid; and (d) that the mere fact that the gift was '*Umra*' and '*Rikba*' would not be sufficient by itself to hold that the gift is only for the usufruct and not of the corpus.[11]

Having explained the principles in this regard, the court carefully analysed the evidence on record. It observed that the report of the *patwari* dated 28 November 1941 regarding the mutation of the suit land carried the statement of Noor Khan which showed that Mehr Bhari would only be entitled to the *paidawar*/usufruct of the gifted property till her death because of the fact that she was unmarried. It was supported by the factual evidence that the donee remained unmarried throughout her life. From this, the court concluded that the donee was only gifted the usufruct of the suit property by the donor and the unambiguous intention of the latter in this respect was easily discernible from his statement. Hence, she did not have any right to transfer the corpus of the gifted property to the respondent. Consequently, the appeal of the petitioners was accepted, and they were declared entitled to their respective shares in the gifted property.

Muhammad Amir v Mst Beevi 2007 SCMR 614

The enjoyment of the usufruct of a property by the donor during his lifetime does not invalidate a gift if the possession of the property is transferred.

This case highlights the legal consequences of the enjoyment of usufruct of the property by a donor after it has been transferred as a gift. The case involves a dispute over a gift of 277 *kanals* of land made in 1966 by Lala (donor), who died in 1990, to Muhammad Amir (donee). The donor was the maternal uncle of the donee and the latter had resided in the former's house since his childhood because the former did not have any male issue. The donor had female children from two wives, Mst Jallan and Mst Aisha. The donee was married to Mst Manzooran who was the daughter of Mst Aisha. The appellants, in this case, included the donee, his wife, the brother of the donee, Mst Aisha, and another daughter from Mst Aisha. On the other hand, the respondents were the daughters of Lala from Mst Jallan.

The gift in dispute was mutated in 1966 and after the death of the donor, the respondents filed a suit to assail that mutation on the ground of forgery and fraud. The trial court dismissed the suit of the respondents on the basis that it was time-barred and devoid of any credible evidence. Thereafter, the respondents approached the first Appellate Court. The Appellate Court reversed the decision of the trial court on the ground that the donor remained in possession of the gifted property throughout his life and had been sustaining himself from that property. The appellants being aggrieved by the decision, assailed it in the High Court which did not find any reason to interfere in the impugned judgment of the Appellate Court. The fact, which weighed extensively in the decisions of the first Appellate Court and the High Court, was that the donor enjoyed the usufruct of the gifted property even after making the alleged gift.

Eventually, the appellants brought their case before the Supreme Court. The Supreme Court found numerous flaws in the decision of the High Court including not giving due regard to the evidence adduced by the relatives of the donee who happened to be the appellants in the case, the revenue official, and the tenant of the gifted property.

The Supreme Court observed that it was not unusual for the donor to enjoy the usufruct of the gifted property during his lifetime because it did not obstruct the completeness of the gift in any manner. And on this basis alone, the gift could not be declared invalid when all the essential ingredients had been proven. As to the contention of the respondents regarding the non-delivery of the gifted property, the court noted that this argument was never raised in their pleadings and hence it did not merit consideration at this stage of the proceedings. The court specifically pointed out an important piece of evidence regarding the delivery of possession that the tenant of the same property had stated that he had been paying produce to the donee.

The court further observed that once the appellants proved the transaction of the gift and its mutation it was for the respondents to challenge the same by producing convincing evidence that it was an outcome of fraud. The respondents had not brought such evidence in support of their plea. Therefore, the court dismissed the judgment of the High Court and allowed the appeal.

8.3.3 Gift of *Mushaa*. The undivided share in the property is termed as '*mushaa*'. It is classified into two categories: (1) the property which is incapable of division: the gift of this kind of property is complete when the donor transfers what he is capable of transferring, taking into account the nature of property; (2) the property which is capable of division: the gift of this category of property is not completed unless possession is delivered. Two cases in this section show that a gift of undivided property is valid and the doctrine of *mushaa* is to be restrictively applied in commercial towns.

Haji Muhammad Ali v Muhammad Akram PLD 2007 SC 319

A gift of undivided property, *mushaa*, is valid.

This case establishes the principle that a gift of an undivided property is valid. Noor Nishan was married twice and had children from both marriages. The petitioner in this case was a child from the second marriage, while the respondents were related to Zohra who was born from the first marriage. Noor Nishan (donor) owned some agricultural land in a joint *khata* (joint holding), and she gifted the same to Zohra (donee) by way of a registered deed executed in 1976 and subsequently mutated it in the same year. The donee died sometime thereafter.

In 1988, the respondents on the basis of the alleged gift to the donee, filed a suit for procuring possession of the gifted property and restraining the petitioner from transferring the property without partition. The petitioner also instituted a suit for the declaration of the alleged gift as invalid because it was never completed by the delivery of possession. The trial court after consolidating both suits dismissed the case of the respondents and passed judgment in favour of the petitioner. The respondents' appeal before the first Appellate Court was also dismissed. Thereafter, they filed two revision petitions in the High Court, which reversed the concurrent decisions of the lower courts. The petitioner brought the matter before the Supreme Court.

The counsel for the petitioner argued that the alleged gift made by Noor Nishan to the donee was invalid because of the fact that the property in dispute was part of a joint holding, which prevented the completion of the gift through the delivery of possession. He further contended that the property in question was agricultural land and hence divisible by nature. Therefore, the gift should have been validated by delivery of possession. On the other hand, the counsel of the respondents argued that delivery of possession was not required for the validity of the gift of a joint holding property (*mushaa*). It was interesting to note that both counsels relied upon the same passages of Mulla's *Principles of Muhammadan Law*:

> Gift of *mushaa* where property divisible:
>
> A gift of an undivided share (*mushaa*) in property which is *capable of division* is irregular (*fasid*), but not void (*batil*). The gift being irregular, and not void, it may be perfected and rendered valid by subsequent partition and delivery to the donee of the share given to him. If possession is once taken the gift is validated.

Exceptions.—A gift of an undivided share (*mushaa*), though it be a share in property capable of division, is valid from the moment of the gift, even if the share is not divided off and delivered to the donee, in the following cases:—

1. where the gift is made by one co-heir to another;
2. where the gift is of a share in a *zamindari* or *taluka*;
3. where the gift is of a share in freehold property in a large commercial town;
4. where the gift is of share in a land company.[12]

The court observed that the gift of an undivided share (*mushaa*) in property, which was capable of division, was only irregular and not void. Thereafter, the same could be validated by delivery of possession. However, there are some exceptions to this rule; that is, a gift from one co-heir to another, and a gift of share in *zamindari* or *taluka*. The court noted that it was an admitted fact that the property in dispute was a share in *zamindari* or *taluka*. Moreover, both the donor and the donee were related to each other as heirs. On the basis of these exceptions, the court concluded that delivery of possession was not required to make a valid gift of undivided property (*mushaa*). Consequently, the court dismissed the petition for leave to appeal.

Begum v Mst Kazbanoo PLD 1957 Kar 884

The doctrine of *mushaa* is to be restrictively applied in commercial towns.

This case deals with a gift of an undivided share (*mushaa*). Muhammad Saleh gifted his share in freehold properties situated in Hyderabad to his wife and children who appeared as respondents in the case. The respondents filed a suit for partition and possession of their gifted property in the Civil Court. The suit was decreed in their favour.

The appellant, Begum (who was the defendant in the suit) brought the present appeal to assail the validity of the alleged gift on many grounds, *inter alia,* the doctrine of *mushaa*. She contended that the alleged gift was invalid because the same was never completed by the delivery of possession by the donor to the respondents (donees).

The court, while disagreeing with the contention of the appellant, observed:

> It is well established that this doctrine is wholly unadapted to a progressive state of society and must be confined within the strictest rules. The Privy Council refused to apply the principle in [the] case of share in companies and freehold properties in a commercial town vide Ibrahim Goolam Ariff v. Saiboo and others (34 Ind. App. 167). Following this decision, the Courts have refused to apply the rule of *mushaa* to gifts in respect of properties in commercial towns and Hyderabad is undoubtedly a commercial town. … The rule of *mushaa* is in the nature of restraint to transfer one['s] property and should be limited to properties to which it had been actually applied in the past.[13]

The court also responded to an important question as to the manner in which a property should be delivered in the case of *mushaa*. It was observed that delivery of possession was not necessary. 'What is required is that a donor should wipe himself off and put donee in the same kind of possession as he himself had or which the property gifted is susceptible of.'[14] The donor in the present case had accomplished this by executing the registered deed declaring therein to have delivered the possession to the donees and mutating the said property in their names.

8.3.4 *Hiba Bil-Iwaz*

Mehr Bhari v Bhag Bhari 1991 SCMR 897

There are two main ingredients of *hiba bil-iwaz*: actual payment of consideration by the donee; and *bona fide* intention of the donor to divest himself of the possession and confer the same on the donee.

A gift involving *iwaz* (consideration) is not required to be delivered and is deemed to be complete even before the physical possession of the gifted property is given to the donee.

In this case, Amir Khan (donor), predecessor-in-interest of the appellants, requested the father of Bhag Bhari (respondent no. 1/donee) to marry her to his son, Muhammad Khan. The father of Bhag Bhari demanded that some agricultural land be transferred to her before she married Muhammad Khan. He assured him that Bhag Bhari would render good services after becoming his daughter-in-law. In 1979, the land in dispute was transferred in favour of respondent no. 1 by a registered gift deed. Thereafter, respondent no. 1 was married to Muhammad Khan. The marriage continued for about three and a half years and then the spouses got separated followed by multiple rounds of civil and criminal litigation between them. Meanwhile, respondent no. 1 transferred the gifted property to her brother-in-law who appeared as respondent no. 3 in this case.

In 1984 the donor, Amir Khan initiated a civil suit for declaration of the gift deed as invalid on the ground of undue influence and assailed the transfer made by the donee/respondent no. 1 to respondent no. 3 as illegal and ineffective. He averred that the gift was never completed due to lack of delivery of possession, hence it could be revoked. The trial court concluded that the alleged gift could not be invalidated on the ground of lack of free consent. However, the court held the gift invalid on the ground of lack of delivery of possession and confirmed the right of revocation of the donor.

On appeal in the first Appellate Court, the decision of the trial court was reversed. The court held that the gift was made in consideration of the marriage, and after the marriage, the possession of the donor would be regarded as if the same was held on behalf of the donee (respondent no. 1). Furthermore, the donor was related to the donee (respondent no. 1) within the prohibitory degree, hence he was not entitled to revoke it. The legal heirs of the donor challenged the decision of the first Appellate Court, but the High Court maintained the impugned decision.

Before the Supreme Court, the appellants argued that the donor did not merely gift the property to respondent no. 1 in order to get her married to his son, rather he was persuaded by the promise of being looked after in his old age by the donee (respondent no. 1). However, when the promised services were not rendered, the donor refused to deliver the possession of the gifted property. Therefore, the gift was not valid.

On the other hand, the counsel of the respondents argued that the gift was *hiba bil-iwaz* and the *iwaz* in this transaction was the marriage of the donee to the son of the donor. Once the marriage was concluded and continued for about three and a half years, the donee rendered consideration. Furthermore, the relationship between the donor and donee was fiduciary in nature and the possession of the gifted property by the donor in such circumstances would be considered to be on behalf of the donee.

After hearing the arguments of the parties, the court explained that there were two main ingredients of *hiba bil-iwaz*: (1) actual payment of consideration by the donee; and (2) *bona fide* intention on the part of the donor to divest himself of the possession and confer the same on the donee. The court observed that the alleged gift satisfied both these ingredients in terms of the donee's marriage to the donor's son and its continuity for a reasonable period of time. The court observed that it could not be argued that the consideration ought to have been continued for the entire life of the donor and in case the same was not extended as such, the donor was entitled to revoke the gift. Considering the fiduciary nature of the relationship between the donor and the donee, the court held that the possession of the disputed property by the donor after the marriage between his son and the donee was on behalf of the latter. Therefore, the court dismissed the appeal.

8.3.5 Preferential Gift

Nusrat Zohra v Azhra Bibi PLD 2006 SC 15

An *inter vivos* [made during a lifetime] gift can be made in favour of one legal heir while depriving others.

This case discusses the validity of a preferential gift—a gift made by a donor during his lifetime in favour of one or more legal heirs while excluding others.

Khair Muhammad (respondent no. 3) had two wives from whom he had three daughters: Azhra Bibi and Sughran Bibi (respondents no. 1 and 2) from one wife, and Nusrat Zohra (petitioner) from another. The mother of Nusrat Zohra was abducted and was thereafter divorced. Sometime later, she contracted another marriage.

Khair Muhammad gifted his entire property to respondents no. 1 and 2 and got the same mutated in their favour. Aggrieved by this, Nusrat Zohra initiated a civil suit for the cancellation of the mutation and prayed for the award of her share in the gifted property. She asserted that respondent no. 3 had gifted his property orally to all of his daughters including her. However, due to undue influence, the mutation was only affected in favour of respondents no. 1 and 2. On the other hand, in their written statements, respondents no. 1 and 2 asserted that the alleged gift was validly made in their favour and the petitioner did not have any right to challenge the same. After recording evidence and hearing the arguments of the parties, the trial court decided in favour of the petitioner awarding her legal share in the suit property.

The trial court did not consider the fact that respondent no. 3 himself appeared in the witness box to state that he had made the gift only to respondents no. 1 and 2. The first Appellate Court reversed the trial court's decision. The High Court also confirmed the decision of the first Appellate

Court. Against this backdrop, the petitioner brought the matter before the Supreme Court.

It was assiduously argued on behalf of the petitioner that the gift was invalid on the sole ground of being preferential in nature by depriving one legal heir and unjustifiably enriching the others. A tradition of the Prophet (PBUH) was presented, which narrated that once someone requested him to be witness to a transaction of gift in favour of his son. The Prophet (PBUH) inquired if he had some other children. When he replied affirmatively, the Prophet (PBUH) refused to be a witness to such a transaction of gift and stated: 'Fear God and observe equality amongst your children'.[15] Taking this tradition as a foundation stone of his argument, the counsel for the petitioner requested the court to reconsider the trend of upholding the validity of preferential gifts in order to prevent *zulm* and ensure justice to all heirs. After analysing the chain of decisions on the subject and referring to *fiqh* books, the court did not agree with the contentions of the petitioner.

The court noted that there had been some decisions and passages in some books giving the impression of the sinfulness of preferential gifts. However, each sinful act does not warrant the state to declare it illegal; and the sinfulness attached to a preferential gift is of this nature.

The court observed that a Muslim donor has the power to alienate his property by way of a gift during his lifetime, subject to the condition that he should be in a proper state of health and the gift should be made voluntarily without any coercion or inducement. The court refuted the argument of *zulm* by stating that no one could be prevented from exercising his proprietary right over his own property during his lifetime for the protection of prospective legal heirs. The court observed:

> [The p]owers of a Muslim to dispose of his property by way of gift are unfettered. A gift cannot be invalidated only because the heirs are deprived of their shares, but where material facts are concealed by donee, such gift can be declared invalid on such account. The policy of Mahomedan law appears to be to prevent a testator interfering by Will with the course of devolution of property according to law among his heirs, although he may give a specified portion, as much as one-third to a stranger. But it also appears that a holder of property may, to a certain extent, defeat the policy of law by giving in his lifetime the whole or any part of his property to one of his sons, provided he complies with certain forms.[16]

8.3.6 Gift by a Pardanashin Lady

Rasheeda Bibi v Mukhtar Ahmad 2008 SCMR 1384

A *pardanashin* lady must receive friendly advice from a person whom the court considers as being genuinely interested in her welfare before executing the gift deed.

This case involves an alleged gift made by a *pardanashin* lady. It deals with two main questions. First, what kind of safeguard should be adopted by the courts to protect the interests of a *pardanashin* lady? And second, should the courts differentiate between the cases of *pardanashin* ladies and other routine cases?

The appellants were three daughters and a widow of Ghulam Muhammad. The respondents were legal heirs of Muhammad Shafi, who was a son of Ghulam Muhammad's widow from her earlier marriage. Hence, he was the stepbrother of the three appellants. Muhammad Shafi managed the land left by Ghulam Muhammad as a tenant after the latter's death. In 1977, Muhammad Shafi took all the appellants to nearby courts giving them the impression that someone else had transferred their property and they needed to get it revoked through a document known as *abtaal-nama* (revocation deed). All the appellants put their thumbmarks on the paper presented in this regard and appeared before the registrar for the registration of that document. They were unaware that under the pretext of the *abtaal-nama* Muhammad Shafi had made them donate all their inherited property to him.

When this fraud came to their knowledge, they initiated a suit for declaration of their rights to the allegedly gifted property and annulment of the alleged gift deed. On the other hand, the respondents maintained that the property had been gifted to their predecessor-in-interest after the fulfilment of relevant legal formalities. All the courts—the trial court, the first Appellate Court, and the High Court—dismissed their suit and ensuing appeals on the ground that the appellants could not convincingly establish their claim of fraud in the alleged transaction of gift.

The counsel for the appellants argued before the Supreme Court that they had challenged the alleged gift since the inception of the present litigation as being invalid on the ground of non-fulfilment of legal formalities under Islamic law. However, to their misfortune, the trial court had not framed the issues on the basis of relevant legal and factual controversies which precluded the appellants from bringing relevant evidence on record. It was also contended that the appellants were simple and illiterate village women (*pardanashin* ladies); hence, their case ought to have been looked into from a different perspective. The respondents, however, held that the impugned decisions were rendered after observing all substantive and procedural requirements.

The court examined the evidence and found it supported the appellant's version. For instance, one of the appellants adduced that they were brought to the courts for registering the alleged gift deed under the false impression that they were revoking another transaction. Similarly, the action of the scribe of the alleged gift deed created doubts about the authenticity of the alleged gift deed as he claimed that he did not know the donors personally and he had not demanded their national identity cards from them to ascertain their identity. Thus, the court observed that no presumption of truth could be attached to the deed registered under these circumstances, especially when the appellants were neither able to understand the nature of the transaction personally nor did they have any independent advice available to them at that time.

The court also found numerous flaws in the issues framed by the trial court and expressed its surprise that none of the appellate forums had identified these lacunae.

The court also tabulated some important questions that need to be answered by the courts when they deal with cases involving *pardanashin* ladies. These are as follows:

1. Did the plaintiff have any friendly advice before executing the deed and from a person whom the court considers as being genuinely interested in her welfare?
2. Was the document explained to her and did she really have the capacity to understand its consequences?
3. Was it a mental act, that is, did the mind accompany the hand that executed it?
4. Was the entire transaction free from circumstances throwing any shadow of doubt or suspicion on the inception, execution and application of the deed?

Considering the above lacunae, the court remanded the case to the trial court with a directive to frame relevant legal and factual issues for providing a fair opportunity for the parties to bring their evidence.

8.4 Conclusion

The concept of *hiba* is linked with a charitable spirit and act of giving in Islam. A donor has unfettered powers to gift his property to whomsoever s/he wants during his/her lifetime provided s/he acts voluntarily and is not under any kind of duress, undue influence, or coercion. The only exception to this is that a gift made in contemplation of death by a person on his/her deathbed only operates to the extent of one-third of his/her estate. The law requires that the donee should not be given false hope by mere declaration of a gift in his/her favour without any *bona fide* intention on the part of the donor to actually deliver the same. Therefore, such intention along with the delivery of possession of the property to the donee is made necessary to fulfil the essentials of a valid gift.

The law of *hiba* has also been influenced by the local context. The ingenuity of Muslim scholars helped avoid some strict rules, e.g. non-delivery of possession would not invalidate a *hiba* if the element of consideration, however insignificant it may be, is tactfully involved in a transaction. Moreover, the rigours of the traditional doctrine of *mushaa* have also been softened by carving out some exceptions and thereby relieving this institution from becoming redundant because of unnecessary and unwarranted restrictions on the exercise of proprietary rights.

The review of the cases in the chapter has demonstrated that the concept of *hiba* overwhelmingly follows and is shaped by the principles of Islamic law, especially in matters of capability and eligibility of donors and donees, the extent of the donor's disposing power, essential requirements of *hiba*, and the nature of gifted property. The case law shows that the courts have developed principles to protect the interests of both the donee and the donor. In this respect, the courts require that *pardanashin* ladies receive independent and friendly advice before executing a deed of gift. Such ladies must also be capable of understanding the transaction and the said transaction should be free from any doubt of genuineness of intention. Likewise, case law illustrates that the courts ensure that the donee is able to enjoy the gift without any encumbrance. Hence, any condition attached to the gift, which is derogatory to the proprietary interests of the donee, has been declared void.

Questions

1. What are the ingredients of a valid gift under Islamic Law?
2. How significant is the delivery of possession in a transaction of a gift? Discuss the circumstances in which delivery of possession is not required to validate a gift and why?
3. Can a Muslim make a gift of usufruct without its substance/corpus? If so, how are these gifts ascertained by the courts?
4. What is *hiba bil-iwaz* and how is it different from a simple gift under Islamic law?
5. Who is required to prove an alleged transaction of a gift and how?
6. How do the courts determine the genuineness of a gift involving a *pardanashin* lady?

Further Reading

Books/Articles

Carroll, L., 'Life Interests and Inter-Generational Transfer of Property Avoiding the Law of Succession', *Islamic Law and Society* (2001) 8(2), 245–86.

Mulla, D.F., *Principles of Mahomedan Law*, 20th edn (Haryana: LexisNexis, 2013), 151–95.

Cases

Abdul Aziz v Zaib-un-Nissa PLD 2022 SC 504 The Supreme Court observed that the rules pertaining to the protection of *pardanashin* ladies must not be confused with the doctrines of fraud, duress, and undue influence. In these doctrines, the burden of proof is placed on those who challenge any transaction on these grounds. However, in cases of *pardanashin* ladies, the burden to prove with convincing evidence that the transaction is carried out with free and informed consent of such ladies is on the one who is a beneficiary of such a transaction.

Abdul Hameed v Muhammad Mohiyuddin PLD 1997 SC 730 (In case of a gift of the corpus of a property, any condition derogatory to the proprietary interests of the donee is treated as void and the gift is considered as valid.)

Abdul Majeed Khan v Ms Maheen Begum 2014 SCMR 1524 (The question of the validity or otherwise of a gift mutation is not the domain of the revenue hierarchy but falls exclusively within the plenary jurisdiction of the Civil Court. Disputed questions of fact cannot be entertained by the revenue hierarchy.)

Abid Hussain v Muhammad Yousaf C.P.No.1647/2018 [Decided on 03–02–2022] (A gift cannot be revoked when the donor and donee are related within the prohibited degree of relationship.)

Baja v Mst Bakhan 2015 SCMR 1704 (When the alleged donor of a gift is an illiterate *pardanashin* lady, who disputed the very genuineness of the gift on the allegation of fraud, the courts must look into the surrounding circumstances so as to ascertain its validity in order to ensure that women are not deprived of their property through frivolous or fraudulent means due to their illiteracy, weak social background, and other compelling circumstances and have been taken advantage of.)

Faqir Ali v Sakina Bibi PLD 2022 SC 85 (Generally, courts do not inquire into the reasons and justifications for making a gift. However, for the gift transactions that are orchestrated to deprive female members of the family of their inheritance rights, courts may inquire into reasons and justifications for making such gifts so that legitimate heirs might not be subjected to injustice.)

Khalid Hussain v Nazir Ahmad 2021 SCMR 1986 (Registration of a gift deed is of no legal use if it does not fulfil three essential conditions of validity of gifts under Islamic law.)

Muhammad Farukh Iqbal v Mrs Ayesha Iram 2021 SCMR 1341 (No oral gift can be made for the immovable property as section 123 of the Transfer of Property Act 1882 provides that gift of immovable property can only be made through a registered instrument.)

Muhammad Ibrahim v Province of Sindh through DCO, Revenue PLD 2013 Sindh 501 (It is a well-established principle that a gift should be absolutely unconditional, and in case any condition is imposed by a donor, the gift becomes void.)

Naseeb Rana v Hazrat Hilal PLD 2015 Pesh 111 (Depending upon the peculiar circumstances of a case, it is not important to use the word 'gift' in a document establishing the same, rather the intention of the donor is to be looked into.)

Nisar Akbar Khan v Jamil Nasir PLD 2014 Lah 417 (There is no bar against the transfer of land by way of a gift by a co-owner to the extent of his share in the property.)

Provincial Government through District Coordination Officer, Swabi v Fazal Rahim 2016 YLR 233 (Pesh) (Writing is not essential to the validity of a gift either of movable or immovable property. The gift must be expressed and unequivocal and the intention of the donor should be demonstrated by his entire relinquishment of the item given. A gift is null and void if the donor continues to exercise any act of ownership over the subject matter of a gift.)

Rab Nawaz v Ghulam Rasul 2014 SCMR 1181 (Evidence regarding the mental health of a donor, where he is of old age and unsound mind and is living at the mercy of a donee, can shake the very basis of a gift.)

Rehmat Ali v Dr Muhammad Hussain 1988 MLD 847 (Lah) (It is not necessary that a gift deed must be proved by the evidence of two male or one male and two female witnesses. Though Islamic law of evidence is applicable to gifts, its interpretation is not as stringent in civil cases as it is in cases of *hudood*.)

Sadar Abbas v Province of Punjab 2015 CLC 822 (Lah) (Mere declaration of a gift by a donor in favour of a donee does not fulfil the essentials of a valid gift unless a *bona fide* intention to give is established on the record. Also, no gift can be made or pleaded if the sole object of making such a gift is to deprive heirs of inheriting the property as per their Qur'anic shares.)

Sardar Arshid Hussain v Mst Zenat Un Nisa 2017 SCMR 608 (Mere registration of a gift deed does not exonerate or relieve the beneficiaries of such transaction from proving its three basic ingredients, i.e. offer, acceptance, and delivery of possession.)

Notes

1. *Maqbool Ahmed v Hakoomat-e-Pakistan* 1991 SCMR 2063.
2. D.F. Mulla, *Principles of Mahomedan Law*, 20th edn (Haryana: LexisNexis, 2013), 176–79.
3. Ibid., 187–88.
4. Ibid., 192–93.
5. L. Carroll, 'Life Interests and Inter-Generational Transfer of Property Avoiding the Law of Succession', *Islamic Law and Society* (2001) 8(2), 245–55. Under s 2(d) of the Punjab Preemption Act 1991, *hiba bil-iwaz* and *hiba bi-shart al-iwaz* are included in the definition of sale. It means that the incidences of sale are applicable on these kinds of *hiba* under the Act and they are liable to pre-emption rights.

6. *Umar Bibi v Bashir Ahmad* 1977 SCMR 154; *Abdullah v Abdul Aziz* 1987 SCMR 1403.
7. *Muhammad Ejaz v Khalida Awan* 2010 SCMR 342.
8. 2012 SCMR 1602, 1605.
9. 2004 SCMR 1701, 1703.
10. PLD 2014 SC 331, 334.
11. 2005 SCMR 710, 714.
12. PLD 2007 SC 319, 322.
13. PLD 1957 Kar 884, 886.
14. Ibid., 887.
15. PLD 2006 SC 15, 22.
16. Ibid., 23.

9

WAQF

9.1 Introduction

Waqf is an important Islamic legal institution. Literally, *waqf* means to stop or detain, whereas in Islamic law it is a settlement or a permanent endowment of property for charitable purposes or an Islamic trust. Historically, the institution of *waqf* has been used for myriads of religious, pious, and charitable purposes such as the establishment of mosques, shrines, hospitals, schools, libraries, orphanages, and travel lodges. *Waqf* is also used as a family settlement to provide for the maintenance of relatives.

There are three major parties in a *waqf*. The founder, also known as *waqif*, creates a *waqf* either through writing or pronouncing his intention to make a *waqf* of his property in favour of the beneficiary/beneficiaries called *muwqoof alayh*. The third party is the administrator, also called *mutawalli,* who manages and controls a *waqf*. A *waqf* can be created for a specific purpose such as the promotion of religious education, and the welfare of the needy, poor, captives, and travellers.

A valid *waqf* must be perpetual, irrevocable, and unconditional. Any Muslim who has attained majority and is of sound mind may create a *waqf* during his/her lifetime (*inter vivos*), or by will (testamentary). However, a *waqf* made during death sickness (deathbed *waqf*) and a testamentary *waqf* shall not exceed one-third of the founder's property without the consent of the heirs. A testamentary *waqf* is revocable during the lifetime of the founder. Such a revocation functions as the revocation of a will.

In a *waqf*, the substance of the property is reserved while its usufruct is spent for the specific purposes expressed by the *waqif*. Therefore, the subject matter of a *waqf* should be such that it generates revenue. Jurists define a *waqf* as the extinction of ownership of a founder in the dedicated assets, which are detained in the implied ownership of God and the profits are utilised for the benefit of humanity.[1] Dr Tanzil-ur-

Rahman defined *waqf* as 'a transfer of the corpus of valuable property to the ownership of Allah with a declaration of dedicating its usufruct perpetually for religious, charitable, or pious purposes as recognised by Shari'at'.[2] It should be noted that the *waqf* property cannot be sold, gifted, or inherited, neither by the founder nor beneficiaries. Thus, in effect, the substance of the *waqf* property ceases to be private property.

Jurists unanimously agree that a *waqf* for a mosque is irrevocable and perpetual as mosques are for God.[3] Therefore, the land of a mosque cannot be sold in any case, even if the building has fallen into ruins and it becomes impossible to reconstruct it.[4] However, if the authorised *mutawalli* of a mosque buys property with the money of the *waqf*, according to the majority opinion, the new property will not become part of the *waqf* property but will be considered property of the mosque that can be sold.

9.2 Types of *Waqf*

There are two main types of *waqf* under Islamic law: public and private/family *waqf*. In practice, however, public and private interests are intermixed as a *waqf* may benefit the family members of a founder along with the public. According to a general rule, the ultimate beneficiaries of a private *waqf* are the poor after the death of specified beneficiaries. During the colonial period, the validity of the family *waqf* was questioned because the British judges regarded it as a family settlement, distinct from a charitable trust. In the famous case, *Abul Fata Mahomed Ishak v Rasamaya Dhur Chowdhry*, the Privy Council held that the family *waqf* was invalid because its main objective was to enrich the family as in such a *waqf* the benefit to the poor is illusory and too remote.[5] This judgment led to political agitation by the Indian Muslims and the Mussalman Wakf Validating Act 1913 was passed to declare the family *waqf* valid. Unlike a private trust, a family *waqf* is perpetual and inflexible because its terms cannot be modified by either the administrator or the beneficiaries except with the permission of the court under exceptional circumstances. Therefore, it is rarely used in current times. Old family *awqaf* (plural of *waqf*), however, continue to operate.

9.2.1 Regulatory Framework of *Awqaf*. The regulatory regime in Pakistan witnessed a great transformation from the colonial policy of minimal state intervention to absolute state control through Ayub Khan's modernisation, Z.A. Bhutto's nationalisation, Zia ul-Haq's Islamisation, and Imran Khan's 'spiritualisation'. This transformation has been led by the peculiar political and economic contexts in Pakistan. Massive landholdings in the form of religious endowments by *pir*s (holy men) and *sajjadanashin*s (curators of the shrine) were not only a source of religious and economic influence, but they also culminated in political power by providing a vote bank to influential 'electables' from rural areas.[6] The educated urban elite lobbied for the state regulation of religious endowments during the British colonial period. The colonial administrators, however, were cautious because any intervention in the regulation of endowments could have led to mass agitation on the pretext of the intervention of the state in the religious affairs of Muslims. Therefore, the state regulation was limited to a very loose supervision of public *awqaf* through an oversight by the courts. The Wakf Act 1923 required the submission of the particulars of *awqaf* and their annual accounts with the state functionary and did not impose any official supervision on *awqaf*. After the creation of Pakistan in 1947, the Punjab Muslim Auqaf Act 1951 was passed to 'provide for the proper administration of Muslim Auqaf in the Punjab'. The Act established a Board which had limited supervisory powers over *awqaf*. The main functions of the Board were limited to the registration of *awqaf*, conducting inquiries about the administration of *awqaf*, and appointment of *mutawalli*s. The military regime of Ayub Khan promulgated the West Pakistan Waqf Properties Ordinance 1959 and the West Pakistan Waqf Properties Rules of 1960 with the aim to regulate religious endowments. The Ordinance enabled the Awqaf Administrator to take over the control of *awqaf* properties. In 1976, the government federalised all Provincial Awqaf Departments through the Awqaf Federal Control Act 1976. This policy of centralisation was short-lived as the power was given back to the provinces in 1979 under the Awqaf Federal Repeal Ordinance 1979. This Ordinance granted power to the Administrator Awqaf of provinces to completely take control over *awqaf*. The Waqf Ordinances were promulgated for the four provinces of Punjab, Sindh, Khyber Pakhtunkhwa (then NWFP), and Balochistan in 1979. The main function of the Provincial Awqaf Departments was to take over the administration and control of the waqf properties in order to ensure better management.

In 2020, the federal legislature passed the Islamabad Capital (ICT) Territories Waqf Properties Act 2020 in line with the recommendations of the Financial Action Task Force (FATF) to prevent money laundering through trusts, awqaf, and cooperative societies. Subsequently, the federal government issued directions to the provincial governments to ensure compliance with the FATF regulations. The Balochistan and Sindh governments repealed their respective Waqf Ordinance 1979 and adopted the Waqf Properties Act 2020. Whereas Khyber Pakhtunkhwa and the Punjab government did not repeal their Waqf Ordinance 1979 but amended it through the Waqf Amendment Act 2020. Under the new amendments, registration of *waqf* properties has been made compulsory and failure to do so has been rendered a crime punishable with fine and imprisonment. The legal changes have also enhanced the powers of the Chief Administrator and authorised the Commissioner to observe and monitor *waqf* properties. The new changes require the Chief Administrator to submit an annual report to the government and provide information to the authorities and reporting entities. To ensure transparency, the authorities and supervisory agencies formed under the Anti-Money Laundering Act 2010, have been empowered to monitor the activities of *awqaf*. In addition, a person creating a *waqf* or manager of *waqf* is obligated to disclose his status to reporting entity before entering into transactions.

9.3 Outline of Case Law

9.3.1 Definition and Nature of a *Waqf*. *Waqf* is a dedication of any property for religious, pious, and charitable purposes. Once established, it cannot be subsequently revoked unless it is a testamentary *waqf*, which is revocable at any time before the death of the *waqif*. Being mindful of the historical significance of this institution, the courts have held that property which has been used for a long period for charitable purposes can be regarded as a *waqf* even in the absence of cogent evidence to this effect.

Faraz Ahmad Bhutta v Additional District Judge PLD 2011 Lah 483

Waqf is a permanent dedication of any property for religious, pious, and charitable purposes. Once established, it cannot be subsequently revoked unless it is a testamentary *waqf*.

This case addresses the issue of whether a *waqf* property can be sold. The petitioner, Faraz Ahmad, filed an ejectment petition under section 13 of the Punjab Urban Rent Restriction Ordinance 1959 against the respondent, Sughran Begum. The petitioner asserted that he along with his brothers purchased the suit property through a registered sale deed dated

22 March 2002 from Haji Nawab-ud-Din and Muhammad Sharif. The petitioner served a notice under section 13–A of the Ordinance, informing the respondent regarding the change of ownership of the suit property. The petitioner claimed a monthly rent of Rs 8,000. He contended that since the respondent failed to pay the rent from 22 March 2002, she was a defaulter, and an order of ejectment must be passed against her. The respondent argued that the relationship of landlord and tenant did not exist between the petitioner and the respondent as the suit property was a family *waqf* (*waqf ala al-aulad*) which could not be sold and hence the sale to the petitioner was illegal. The respondent admitted that she was a tenant of Haji Nawab-ud-Din and had been paying monthly rent to him.

Thereafter, the Rent Controller concluded that the property in question was a *waqf* property that could not be alienated in favour of the petitioner and hence dismissed the petition. An appeal was preferred against the judgment before the Additional District Judge who concurred with the findings of the Rent Controller. During the pendency of the appeal, the petitioner also filed an application, seeking permission to place on record the revocation of a *waqf* deed dated 26 November 1946. After observing that the document had not been previously placed on record and the copy placed on record was unattested, the Additional District Judge turned down the application. Furthermore, the Additional District Judge held that the *waqf* of the suit property was a permanent dedication which could not be withdrawn by the founder at a later stage. The petitioner, aggrieved by the said decision, assailed it as in the instant constitutional petition.

The counsel for the petitioner argued that the *waqf* deed was never implemented and the founder himself subsequently revoked it through a registered deed. Therefore, the two sons of the founder, Nawab-ud Din, and Muhammad Sharif, were entitled to alienate the property in favour of the petitioner. On the contrary, the counsel for the respondent argued that once a *waqf* had been created, the founder (*waqif*) had no authority to revoke it as it was a permanent dedication made for charitable purposes.

The court referred to various principles of *waqf* law as laid down in Mulla's *Muhammadan Law*:

> According to section 173 of Muhammadan Law, a waqf is a permanent dedication by a person professing the Muslim faith of any property, recognized by the Muslim Law as religious, pious or charitable. Section 174 of the Muhammadan Law directs a waqif to make a permanent waqf without limiting the period while the object of the waqf has been described in [section] 178 mentioning that it should be religious, pious and [for]

> charitable purposes and [a] waqf could be in favor of settlor's family, children and descendants.[7]

The court noted that only a testamentary *waqf* can be revoked at any time before the death of the founder. A *waqf* property cannot be alienated except where the *mutawalli* sells or mortgages it with the permission of the court, or if such power has been given expressly in the *waqf* deed. In the instant case, Shahab Din, the father of the sellers had created the *waqf* in 1931 and executed the *waqf* deed in 1953. The *waqf* deed showed that it was a permanent dedication to the charitable and pious purpose of establishing a school for children. The deed also restrained the successive *mutawalli*s from alienating the whole or part of the property. The court held that once the *waqf* is created, then the property does not vest in the founder but the same is transferred to Allah and the *waqif* has no authority to revoke it. The courts below had rightly held that the relationship of a landlord and tenant did not exist between the parties. Therefore, the court dismissed the petition.

Lahore Development Authority v Naimat Saleem Trust PLD 2004 Lah 270

Waqf property vests in Allah Almighty.

This case reiterates the legal principle that the ownership of *waqf* property vests in Allah Almighty. According to the facts of this case, the Lahore Development Authority, the appellant, required land to establish a housing scheme. For the acquisition of land, a notice under section 4 of the Land Acquisition Act 1894 was issued in 1988. As per the notification, the land in question measuring 42 *kanal*, 16 *marla*, was to be acquired. However, before further proceedings took place the respondent, a registered trust, purchased the land in 1998. The sales were also registered in the revenue records. Thereafter, the appellant issued a notification to the respondent under section 17(4) of the Act and took over the possession of the land. However, before the possession could be taken, the respondent trust had already constructed a boundary wall around the suit land and obtained the sanction of the site plan from the Union Council for the purposes of establishing a school for disabled children.

Aggrieved by the acquisition of the land by the appellant, the respondent trust filed a writ petition seeking exemption from the acquisition. A single judge of the Lahore High Court allowed the petition. It was held that, under the Act, the land could be acquired for public purposes, but in this case, the purpose of God had intervened, and no public purpose is holier and nobler than that of God. Since the land was dedicated to charitable, religious, and pious purposes, its acquisition for a housing society was void and ineffective. The appellant filed an intra-court appeal against this decision.

The counsel for the petitioners argued that the transfer of land to the respondent trust for the purpose of establishing a school for disabled children was *mala fide* because the owners of the land wanted to save their land from state acquisition. Furthermore, he contended that after the issuance of the notification under section 4 of the Act, land could not be validly transferred. The Double Bench of the High Court rejected these arguments and agreed with the decision of the single judge that the property in question was *waqf* property vested in Allah Almighty and hence, the appellant could not acquire such a property. It was held that there is no better public purpose than establishing a school for disabled children, the most neglected section of society. The suit property purchased by the respondent trust had become a part of the *waqf* and could not be acquired by the appellant irrespective of the fact that the sale transaction took place after the issuance of the notification for acquisition. Therefore, the court dismissed the appeal.

Amina Bai v Karachi Metropolitan Corporation 1994 SCMR 804

A building used as a charitable hostel (*musafir khana*) for poor travellers for a long period of time can be regarded as a public trust (*waqf*) and can only be used for charitable purposes.

This case establishes the legal principle that the long use of the property for charitable purposes gives it a status of a public *waqf* without any express declaration to this effect. A *musafir khana* known as Moledina Musafir Khana was constructed on a plot in Karachi in 1893. The appellants were the legal heirs of Haji Moledina who contributed towards the construction of the *musafir khana*. This *musafir khana* was constructed for poor Muslim travellers, coming to Karachi from interior Sindh and other parts of the Indo-Pak subcontinent. A marble stone at the *musafir khana* read that it was built by the joint costs of Haji Moledina and the Karachi municipality. The appellants claimed that after the death of Haji Moledina, his elder son took over the management of the *musafir khana*. However, in 1922, due to some financial difficulties, he handed over the supervision and management to the respondent corporation, a municipality at that time.

In 1966, the respondent published a public notice in a newspaper to dispose of the suit property on a 99–years lease. The appellants filed a suit in a Civil Court against this action of the respondent, contending that the respondent could not use the disputed property and the construction thereon for any commercial purpose. The court decreed the suit in favour of the appellants holding that the respondent was not the exclusive owner of the suit property and hence not entitled to such disposal. The respondent could not demolish or destroy the *musafir khana* that was built for the purpose of providing shelter to poor Muslim travellers. The respondent appealed against the decision before the Additional District Judge who upheld the decision of the trial court. The respondent subsequently filed a revision application before the High Court, which was allowed and the findings of the two courts below were reversed. The High Court held that the inscription on the marble stone alone did not prove the appellant's ownership of the suit property without any other convincing evidence. Hence, the respondent corporation was entitled to use the property.

The appellants challenged the High Court decision before the Supreme Court. The counsel for the appellants argued that Haji Moledina and the respondent corporation constructed the *musafir khana* for charitable purposes, hence the respondent does not have any right to demolish or dispose of the property for any commercial use. On the contrary, the counsel for the respondent corporation argued that the suit property was the property of the respondent corporation and Haji Moledina only contributed to the construction of the building of the *musafir khana*. The building was in a state of disrepair and disuse; hence the respondent could develop it for better purposes.

The court observed that Haji Moledina and the respondent corporation had jointly constructed the *musafir khana* in order to accommodate poor Muslim travellers. This charitable purpose and public use of the *musafir khana* had continued for a long time until the son of Haji Moledina handed over its supervision to the respondent. Since 1922, the respondent corporation remained in full control and management of the *musafir khana*. After partition, people occupied large parts of open areas for residential purposes but the building of the *musafir khana* stood in a state of disarray and in bad need of repair. The court pinned the entire responsibility of damage to this historical monument upon the respondent as it was in sole control of the *musafir khana* since 1922. The court also noted that the *musafir khana* was not constructed for the purpose of temporary public charity, rather it was a well-thought-out and organised plan to which Haji Moledina contributed. The building was constructed on the plot of the respondent, but they failed to bring evidence relating to its construction. The inscription on the marble stone bearing the name of Moledina showed that a major part of the costs was borne by him. The building was constructed for the sole purpose of dedication to charitable use and was so used for decades. Hence, it was a public trust. The court observed that the building might not have the legal attributes of a *waqf* in the strict sense, still, the principles of *waqf* law could be applied because of its close resemblance to a *waqf*. The court concluded:

> It is thus clear that property dedicated for charitable purpose recognised by Islam or any other pious object or of general public utility and remains under such use for decades or for a long period, shall be treated as trust property. The nature and purpose of such property cannot be changed at the discretion of the person making the trust or in control or management thereof, nor can such building be demolished and obliterated thereby destroying the very object of the dedication or trust. In Muslim Law such dedication is permissible.[8]

In light of the foregoing reasons, the court held that the respondent could neither demolish the building nor put it to any commercial use that was different from the purpose for which it had been originally constructed. If the utility of the *musafir khana* was completely diminished, the same could be put to use for any other charitable purpose having nexus to the original purpose of dedication under the doctrine of cy-pres.[9] The court allowed the appeal.

9.3.2 Modes of the Establishment of a *Waqf*. The case law suggests that a valid *waqf* can be created orally and the *waqif* need not part with the possession of the immovable property. A valid *waqf* can also be established through long use.

Abdul Samad v Shista Khan 1998 CLC 171 [Quetta]

A valid *waqf* can be created orally and without parting with the possession of the immovable property.

This case shows the application of the principle that a valid *waqf* can be created by mere declaration. According to the facts of the case, Maulvi Abdul Daim, predecessor-in-interest of petitioner no. 3, died issueless leaving only a widow. He, being a religious scholar, created a *waqf* of his immovable property for the benefit of children, for them to receive religious education. He also spent his income for the benefit of students in this manner. After his death in 1995, respondent no. 1, with the connivance of respondent no. 2, claimed their shares in the estate of Maulvi Daim as his legal heirs. In addition, respondent no. 3 claimed that during his lifetime Maulvi Daim had donated the suit property to him. In 1996, the petitioners filed a suit for declaration against the respondents, which was decreed in their favour. The respondents, except respondent no. 4, filed an appeal against the decision in which the Appellate Court set aside the judgment of the trial court. Hence, the present revision petition was filed.

The counsel for the respondents argued that the alleged *waqf* created by Maulvi Daim was invalid as the possession of the property remained with him. The counsel for the petitioners rebutted this argument by contending that a *waqf* cannot be declared invalid solely on this ground. The court, after hearing the witnesses and perusing the record, observed:

> [U]nder the Muslim Personal Law there is no provision of creating *waqf* by [a] testator in [a] particular form. It could be verbal or in writing. If the court feels satisfied in view of the material placed before it that a *waqf* was created by the deceased for a valid object it has no authority to question as to why the same was not reduced into writing.[10]

> In this case, testimonies of the petitioners' witnesses clearly suggested that Maulvi Abdul Daim created a *waqf* of his immovable property. On the contrary, the testimonies of the respondents' witnesses suffered from many discrepancies making them unreliable. The Court also addressed the question [of] whether, without parting with the possession of the *waqf* property, a valid *waqf* could be created. The Court relied upon certain judicial authorities and concluded that for the completion of a *waqf*, mere declaration is sufficient and no delivery of possession of the *waqf* property is required. In the light of [the] foregoing reasons, the Court held that Maulvi Abdul Daim had created a valid waqf, and it could not be declared invalid just because he did not part with the possession of the *waqf* property.

Anjuman Masjid-i-Farooqia v Fazal Begum 1991 SCMR 2112

Long use of a property as a *waqf* is good evidence for treating it as *waqf* property.

This case applies the principle that the long use of a property as a *waqf* is in itself good evidence for treating it as *waqf* property. The respondents filed a suit against the appellants for the declaration that the suit property was not a *waqf* property and the disputed entries showing it as such were liable to be cancelled. The respondents contended that their father purchased the suit property from the provincial government in 1902 and constructed shops on the property. After his death, the property devolved to the respondents as his legal heirs. In 1968, when they intended to sell the suit property, they learnt that it was entered in the record of rights as a *waqf* maintained by respondent no. 3. Therefore, the respondents sought a declaration to the effect that the said entry was illegal, void, and ineffective. The appellants resisted the suit and contended that the suit property was attached to a mosque and was being used as a *waqf* for a very long time. The trial court and the first Appellate Court decided against the respondents, while the High Court ruled in favour of the respondents. Therefore, the appellants took their case before the Supreme Court.

The real controversy before the Supreme Court was whether the predecessor-in-interest of the respondents had dedicated the property in dispute as a *waqf* for the benefit of a mosque adjacent to the suit property. The court observed:

> [L]ong use of a property is by itself good evidence for declaring or treating a property as a *Waqf*, it has to be remarked that it depends upon the circumstances of each case; as to whether the long use was as a *Waqf* or not. And secondly, even if it is established that the long use was as of Waqf, it would depend upon the circumstances of each case whether the property itself was treated as *Waqf* or its income only was being used for purposes of *Waqf*.[11]

In the instant case, there were many missing links in the evidence adduced by the appellants. The court observed that the predecessor-in-interest of the respondents might have used the rent of the shops for the purpose of maintenance of the mosque or he might have given the rent to the managers for the same purpose. However, there was no evidence that the income was dedicated permanently to the maintenance of the mosque. Therefore, the appellants could not establish the plea of long use of the suit property as a *waqf* by reliable evidence. In these circumstances, the appeal was dismissed, though the court recognised that the long use of a property as a *waqf* is good evidence for declaring it as such.

Ashiq Hussain v Anjuman Islamia, Kamalia Regd. 2007 CLC 71 (Lah)

A *waqf* could be established through long use and the rule of limitation does not apply to *waqf* property.

This case shows the application of the principle that prolonged use of a property as a *waqf* is one of the accepted modes of establishing it as a *waqf* under Islamic law. The brief facts of the case are that respondent no. 1, Anjuman Islamia, was managing the affairs of the Jamia Masjid and the other respondents were the office bearers of the Anjuman. The respondents filed a suit for declaration against the petitioners. The respondents claimed that the Anjuman had been managing the affairs of the Jamia Masjid which had been established during the days of the Mughals and had been existing for several centuries. They contended that the suit property formed part of the Jamia Masjid and had been in the use of the *imam* of the masjid, Ghulam Muhammad, who was the predecessor-in-interest of the petitioners. After the death of Ghulam Muhammad, the suit property came under the control of his descendants, that is, the petitioners. Presenting this set of facts the respondents prayed that a decree for declaration should be passed to the effect that the suit property was the property of the Jamia Masjid. The trial court decreed the suit in favour of the respondents. The Appellate Court upheld the decree. Hence, the present revision petition was filed before the High Court.

The counsel for the petitioners argued that the respondents should prove their title to the suit property since they sought a declaration and possession of the same. He further argued that according to evidence on record, the petitioners were in fact the owners of the suit property. On the contrary, the counsel for the respondents argued that the suit property formed a part of the Jamia Masjid, and the documents relied upon by the petitioners were not documents of title. The court noted that it was an undisputed fact that the disputed property formed part of the composite structure of the Jamia Masjid which dated back to the Mughal period. The documents relied upon by the petitioners only showed the name of the occupant and not the owner. There is nothing on record identifying the owner. Therefore, the courts below were correct in holding that the disputed property formed part of the Jamia Masjid. The petitioners' argument that the suit was time-barred did not hold in the case of *waqf* property. The court observed:

> One of the accepted modes for [the] creation of a *Waqf* under the Islamic Law is through immemorial use. Even in the absence of an express

> dedication where land is being used from times immemorial for a religious purpose e.g. a mosque, such land shall be deemed to be a *Waqf*.[12]

Therefore, the court dismissed the revision petition.

9.3.3 Family *Waqf*. Historically, the institution of waqf has also been used to provide for one's family. The courts have held that a *waqf* can be established in favour of some members of a family to the exclusion of all others. However, even in a family *waqf*, the ultimate charitable purpose must not be illusory and unsubstantial. Similar to a *waqf* for charitable purposes, the ownership of property, that forms the subject of a family *waqf*, vests in Allah Almighty and therefore cannot be sold or attached for the personal debts of the *waqif*.

Haji Mian Muhammad v Tila Muhammad PLD 1959 Pesh 152

In a family *waqf*, the gift for a charitable purpose must not be illusory and unsubstantial.

This case discusses the validity of a *waqf* where the ultimate benefit reserved for charitable purposes was unsubstantial and illusory. Haji Mian Muhammad registered a *waqf* deed in 1949 for the benefit of his four children and their descendants. In the deed, along with other conditions, he set out that in case the *waqf* property is leased out the heirs would be entitled to the lease money, but out of the lease money Rs 10 per mensem would be spent on charitable purposes. In 1956, he sold some of the *waqf* property to his son, Haji Fazal Ilahi. This led to the other three sons and the wife of Haji Mian Muhammad bringing a suit for declaration that after having established a family settlement dedicating the property as a *waqf* he could not sell the property and hence the sale was illegal and void. The court decreed the suit in favour of the petitioners by declaring the suit property as a family *waqf* and held that the *waqif* could not sell any part of it after the creation of the *waqf*.

Haji Mian Muhammad filed an appeal against the decision before the High Court. The most important question before the High Court was whether the *waqf* deed was valid. The court referred to the Mussalman Waqf Validating Act 1913 which defined a *waqf* as 'the permanent dedication by a person professing the Muslim faith of any property for any purpose recognised by Muslim law as religious, pious or charitable'. The court observed that the purpose of the impugned *waqf* was to maintain, wholly or partially, the *waqif*'s family, children, or descendants, amongst other purposes, which is a valid purpose under the Act. However, in such a *waqf* the ultimate benefit should be explicitly or impliedly reserved for the poor or for any other purpose recognised under Muslim law as being religious, pious, or charitable of a permanent character. Under the Act, such purpose can validly be postponed until after the extinction of the family, children, or descendants of the *waqif*. The court subsequently examined the *waqf* deed in light of these principles and observed that there should be a clear overriding charitable intention expressly or impliedly stated in the *waqf* deed.

> The word "impliedly" used in the proviso [to] section 3 of the Mussalman Validating Act VI of 1913 only means that the reservation can be indirectly inferred from the recitals in the deed coupled with the surrounding circumstances. There must be some indication, either in the introductory portion of the deed, or in recitals of the facts, or the recitals of the object and purpose, from which a reasonable inference can be drawn that the waqif had a possible ultimate benefit to the poor, or any religious, pious or charitable purpose, in his mind.[13]

The deed at hand was executed for the maintenance of Haji Mian Muhammad's daughter and sons. During his lifetime, Haji Mian Muhammad as *mutawalli* had not paid anything to his children or to the poor or for any religious, pious, or charitable purposes. After his death, his children were to occupy his property according to Islamic inheritance law without paying anything for any religious or pious purpose until and unless the property was leased out. The condition that Rs 10 per mensem would be paid to charity did not specify any charity. The court observed:

> If the preponderating feature of the waqf is intended to be the benefit of the settlor's family, and the reservation for the purpose recognized by the Muslim Law as religious, pious, or charitable is only illusory, then the waqf, in spite of the use of the word "waqf" in the deed, will not be a waqf validated under the Musslaman Waqf Validating Act… In the deed of waqf, there should be a clear overriding charitable intention, either expressed in clear words, or by implication.[14]

The court held that the payment of Rs 10 per mensem, which was not absolute but conditional, was illusory and unsubstantial. The court observed:

> There is no mention in the deed that the property will be applied ultimately for the benefit of the poor or for any other purpose recognised by the Muslim Law as religious, pious or charitable either during the lifetime of his family, children and descendants, or on their complete extinction. All that the settlor intended to achieve under the deed in hand was to protect the whole of the property from alienation so that it may remain preserved perpetually for the use and benefit of his family, children and descendants. There is no recognition either in Muhammadan Law or in the Mussalman Waqf Validating Act 1913 for an arrangement of this kind as a waqf. It is a device to preserve property for the benefit of the settlor's family under the cloak of a waqf and no system of civilized law would encourage it. Muhammadan Law does not prevent members of the settlor's family, his children and descendants from being beneficiaries from a waqf, but when they are the exclusive beneficiaries or beneficiaries in substantial measure, the law enjoins that a provision must exist in the deed that in the event of the extinction of such beneficiaries the property will be wholly applied for the benefit of the poor or for purposes which according to Muslim Law are charitable, pious or religious.[15]

The court did not find any provision for the benefit of the poor in the *waqf* deed and held that it was not a valid *waqf* deed under the Mussalman Waqf Validating Act 1913. Therefore, the appeal was accepted.

Muhammad Yaqub v Ali Muhammad PLD 1957 Lah 544

The property, subjected to a family *waqf*, vests in Allah Almighty and cannot be attached to the personal debts of the *waqif.*

This case highlights the issue of the attachment and sale of a family *waqf* in the execution of a decree. The appellant, Muhammad Yaqub, and the deceased, Shahab-ud-Din, were running a business in a partnership. Muhammad Yaqub filed a suit for the rendition of accounts against Shahab-ud-Din in 1948. Shahab-ud-Din died during the pendency of the suit and his heirs were brought on record as his legal representatives. In 1953, the court passed a decree in favour of the appellant against the estate of the deceased which was in the hands of his legal representatives. In the execution of this decree, the court attached one house, eight shops, and a plot of land in Sialkot.

Two applications objecting to the attachment were filed: one by Ali Muhammad, son of the deceased, and the other by Barkat Bibi, daughter of the deceased. Their contention was that the deceased had created a family *waqf* (*waqf ala al-aulad*) of his entire property through a *waqf* deed and they were the *mutawalli* of the *waqf*. On the contrary, the decree-holder contended that the *waqf* deed was never acted upon and it was subsequently cancelled. He further contended that under the *waqf* deed, the deceased was entitled to run the partnership business and that the decree of execution was passed in respect of that business, which was liable to attachment, even though it was a *waqf* property.

The trial court held that the *waqf* deed had been acted upon; and even if it was cancelled, such a cancellation was illegal and hence ineffective. Furthermore, the court held that the decree-holder did not prove that the decree was related to the business which had been declared to be a *waqf* and in any case the *waqf* property was not liable to attachment in execution of a personal decree against Shahab-ud-Din. The decree-holder appealed against this decision.

The counsel of the appellant presented two arguments before the High Court: (1) although the corpus of the property was a *waqf*, the founder of the *waqf* had the power to dispose of the income of the property. In fact, he had given direction in the deed as to how this income was to be distributed amongst his heirs after his death and that the income of the property should be regarded as the property of the deceased in the hands of his legal representatives and was liable to attachment and sale; (2) the liability was incurred in connection with and for the benefit of the business, which was *waqf*; and for such debt, the *waqf* property was liable to attachment and sale.

On the first contention of the appellant counsel, Justice B.Z. Kaikaus noted that it must be remembered that the decree was against the estate of the deceased in the hands of his legal representatives. In order for the decree-holder to succeed he had to show that there was property which the deceased owned at the time of his death, and which passed to his heirs. The court rejected the appellant's contention that when a testator gave a direction in the *waqf* deed regarding the distribution of income from the property after his death he was still the owner of the income of the property and that the direction he gave with respect to the distribution of income was given by virtue of his right as an owner of the usufruct of the property, who was entitled to make a testamentary disposition. The court observed that the moment a *waqf* is made, the *waqif* ceases to be the owner of the corpus and the usufruct of the dedicated property vests in Almighty Allah. This cessation takes place even where the *waqif* is to maintain himself out of the income generated from the *waqf* property. He takes that income as a beneficiary, not as an owner and the income is used for the purpose of the *waqf*. The direction given by the *waqif* in the *waqf* deed on the application of income for the maintenance of his descendants is not a direction in the nature of a will by a person who owns the property; rather it is a direction by the founder of the *waqf* as to the purpose of the *waqf* and the manner of application of the income. In this case, after the perusal of the *waqf* deed, it was clear that the *waqif* retained no right in the *waqf* property as an owner after the creation of the *waqf*.

The appellant's second argument was that the decree was in respect of the business of the *waqf*, and the late Shahab-ud-Din was sued in his capacity as a *mutawalli*. Under the *waqf* deed, the coffee shop was to be a *waqf* business and Shahab-ud-Din was entitled to contract debts and to alienate the property if money was needed for the purpose of the *waqf* business. The court rejected this argument after observing that there was no proof that the suit in which the decree was passed related to the coffee shop business. In addition, the suit was filed against the deceased in his personal capacity and the decree passed against him was a personal decree. Therefore, it was only executable against his estate and the *waqf* property did not form part of his estate. It meant that if the appellant wanted to attach the *waqf* property, a suit against the *waqf* had to be filed. The judgment debtor, Shahab-ud-Din established the family *waqf* in 1930 and the appellant did not deny the existence of this *waqf*. Before dismissing the appeal Justice Kaikaus clarified that the appellant should file a separate suit to enforce his claims against the *waqf* property and this dismissal would not serve as *res judicata*.

Ghulam Shabbir v Nur Begum PLD 1977 SC 75

A *waqf* can be established in favour of some members of a family to the exclusion of others.

This case presents a classic example of some of the motivations behind establishing a family *waqf* and the legal problems associated with it. Haji Faiz Baksh executed a *waqf* deed in November 1948. The reason for establishing a family *waqf* under the deed was the profligate and spendthrift nature of his son. In January 1948, he had left to perform pilgrimage entrusting the management of his business to his son. In his absence, his son mismanaged the business and wasted money on merry-making and visiting prostitutes. This experience made the old man apprehensive about the future of his family after his death. Therefore, he established a *waqf ala al-aulad* of all his property and appointed himself as a *mutawalli*. The ultimate benefit of the *waqf* was reserved for an orphanage and religious schools. After his death, the *waqf* was to be managed by Abdul Ghafoor, the brother of his daughter-in-law and after him by one of his two grandsons, Ghulam Shabbir (the appellant) and Abdul Qadir. His only son, Hussain Baksh was deprived of all rights in the property. Soon after the death of Haji Faiz Baksh, his son sold a part of the property to Nur Begum (the respondent). The *mutawalli* of the *waqf*, however, challenged this sale. After going through various stages of the judicial process, the matter was placed before the Supreme Court.

The validity of the *waqf* was assailed on the basis that it deprived a legal heir of his rights, and it was a fictitious transaction which should be voidable at the option of the creditors who were defrauded. The court rejected these arguments. First, the court held that a valid *waqf* could be established in favour of some members of a family excluding others. Second, the court observed that the actual purpose of the founder for establishing the family *waqf* was to protect the property from his spendthrift son. It was held that once a valid *waqf* is created even subsequent action by the founder against the objectives of the *waqf* does not invalidate the *waqf*. Regarding the process of the establishment of a *waqf*, the court held that the law does not require that the property should be transferred to the *mutawalli* in the register of mutations or other documents.

As a last resort, the counsel for the respondent argued that the respondent was a *bona fide* purchaser for value and referred to section 41 of the Transfer of Property Act 1882 which protects the rights of a purchaser who enters into a sale transaction in good faith and after taking reasonable care about the title of the property. The Supreme Court rejected this argument by pointing out that the respondent could have with reasonable care and due diligence discovered that the property she purchased was subject to a registered *waqf*. The seller from whom she purchased the property did not even have possession. The court declared the *waqf* as valid and allowed the appeal of the *mutawalli*.

Anjuman Himayat-e-Islam, Lahore v Dr Syed Farooq Hassan PLD 2007 SC 352

When clear wording of a family *waqf* deed leads to an irresistible conclusion that upon the demise of the last *mutawalli*, the management would vest in a specified charitable institute, these words will be given effect.

This case deals with the nature and scope *of waqf ala al-aulad*. It also establishes that a valid *waqf* can be created in favour of some family members to the exclusion of others.

Rehmat Ali Khan was the owner of the property which is the subject matter of the present petition. He created a *waqf ala al-aulad* in respect of the property through a registered deed in 1931. The *waqf* deed provided that the executant, Rehmat Ali Khan would be the first *mutawalli*, and upon his death, his wife, Taj Begum would be the second *mutawalli*. Thereafter, upon her death, Qamar Sultan and Daisy Dilara, the children of his pre-deceased daughter, Rehmat Jehan, would be the joint *mutawalli*s. It was further stipulated that upon the death of the joint *mutawalli*s the Anjuman Himayat-e-Islam (the petitioner) would be the *mutawalli* of the *waqf* property. The respondent, Dr Farooq Hassan was the son of Daisy Dilara who died in 1992. The other joint *mutawalli* Qamar Sultan had died earlier.

After the death of Daisy Dilara, the petitioner filed a suit for permanent injunction in 1992 praying that the respondent be restrained from interfering in the management of the *waqf* property and from demanding rent from its tenants. The respondent took the plea that according to the terms of the *waqf* deed, after the death of Daisy Dilara, he would be the *mutawalli* of the *waqf* property and the management of the property would rest with the petitioner only after the extinction of the line of descendants of the founder of the *waqf*. The respondent raised a preliminary objection as to the maintainability of the suit on three technical grounds: (i) that the suit was not properly framed as the relief of gaining possession of the property was not claimed; (ii) that the suit did not bear the requisite court fee; and (iii) that the suit was not filed through a duly authorised representative of the Anjuman.

The case went through several rounds of litigation. First, the trial court rejected the suit, which was challenged in appeal. The Appellate Court remanded the case with a direction to frame issues and decide afresh. The trial court framed issues but dismissed the suit again. The Appellate Court maintained the dismissal. Thereafter, a civil revision was filed before the High Court. The High Court reversed the concurrent judgments of the lower courts and remanded the case for a fresh trial. The trial court framed issues and again dismissed the suit on the same technical grounds on which it had initially done so. The court held that the petitioner, Anjuman Himayat-e-Islam, was not entitled to be the *mutawalli* of the property on merit. The judgment was challenged in appeal, which was also dismissed by the first Appellate Court and subsequently, the civil revision was dismissed by the High Court. Thereafter, the judgment was challenged before the Supreme Court in a civil appeal, which was allowed with a direction to the High Court to decide the matter afresh on merit.

This time the High Court, after considering the *waqf* deed, decided the question regarding the nature of the *waqf* in favour of the petitioner. It held that after the demise of Daisy Dilara, the management of *waqf* property was to be vested in the petitioner. However, the High Court dismissed the petitioner's civil revision holding that the suit was not maintainable on the earlier-mentioned technical grounds.

Before the Supreme Court, the petitioner's counsel argued that having decided the case on merit in favour of the petitioner, the High Court could not dismiss it merely on technical grounds that an authorised representative of the Anjuman did not file the suit and that relief of possession was not claimed. In addition, the onus to prove the issue pertaining to the maintainability of the suit was upon the respondent who had failed to discharge it. He further contended that if the court deemed it necessary to claim relief of possession of the property in the plaint, the court should have allowed the petitioner to amend the plaint accordingly.

On the contrary, the respondent's counsel supported the impugned judgment of the High Court so far as it dismissed the suit as being non-maintainable on technical grounds. However, he opposed the impugned judgment for declaring that the petitioner was entitled to be the *mutawalli* of the *waqf*. He contended that the mere title of the *waqf* as *waqf ala al-aulad* indicated that it was not confined to the immediate descendants of the executant, Rehmat Ali, but included his descendants that followed thereafter. According to him, any other interpretation would defeat the purpose of the *waqf*. Since the *waqf* was declared as *waqf ala al-aulad* for the executant's offspring and descendants, it could not be terminated on the death of grandchildren, that is, Qamar Sultan and Daisy Dilara, the mother of the respondent.

After perusing the record and hearing the arguments, Justice Tassaduq Hussain Jillani noted that the concept of *waqf ala al-aulad* is recognised in Muslim law and validated by section 3 of the Mussalman Waqf Validating Act 1913. Clause (a) of the section makes it lawful for a Muslim to create a *waqf* 'for the maintenance and support wholly or partially of his family, children or descendants'. However, the proviso to this section states that 'the ultimate benefit is in such cases expressly or impliedly reserved for the poor or for any other purpose recognised by the Musslaman law as religious, pious or charitable purpose of a permanent character'. Justice Jillani referred to the judgment in *Mubarak Jan v Taj Begum*[16] which pertained to a similar *waqf* that was the subject matter of the petition in this case. In that case, the court had concluded that a valid *waqf* could be created in favour of some family members to the exclusion of others.

It means that such a *waqf* is not legally required to cater for the needs of the *waqif*'s descendants till the extinction of his lineage as argued by the respondent unless the same is expressly stated in the *waqf* deed. Furthermore, the court highlighted that according to the *waqf* deed the *waqf* would completely vest in the Anjuman Himayat-e-Islam after the death of Rehmat Ali's grandchildren. The Supreme Court reproduced the impugned findings of the Lahore High Court about the nature of the *waqf* and held that they were neither against the evidence on record nor the applicable law. The findings are reproduced as under:

> It may be noted that Wakf in clear and unambiguous terms states that upon the demise of Daisy Dilara and Qamar Sultan, the management and related benefits of the property would vest in Anjuman Himayat-e-Islam. Furthermore, any terms or words to the effect that the benefit or the management of the property would vest in the descendants of Qamar Sultan and Daisy Dilara are conspicuous by their absence.
>
> The clear wording of the Wakf deed leads to an irresistible conclusion that upon [the] demise of the last *mutawalli* Daisy Dilara, the management of the property would vest in Anjuman Himayat-e-Islam, and the benefits therefrom are to be used for the upkeep of Muslim orphans.[17]

As to the maintainability of the suit on the ground that an unauthorised person filed it, the court noted that the Anjuman was a registered society which could file a suit or be sued in its own name. No objection was raised to the effect that the society was not registered; the only objection raised was that an unauthorised representative of the Anjuman filed the suit. The onus to prove the said ground was upon the respondent who failed to produce any evidence that Asmat Ullah, the person who filed the suit lacked authorisation to do so. Furthermore, a power of attorney authorising Asmat Ullah to file and defend suits on behalf of the Anjuman was filed along with the suit. The courts below overlooked this important document in rendering adverse findings as regards the Anjuman. Hence, the respondent's objection in this regard was not tenable.

Furthermore, the objection that the suit was liable to be dismissed as the possession of the property was not claimed was also found to be untenable. The court relied upon an authority in this regard which established that 'suit for possession *qua* a building under tenancy need not have been filed'.[18] In addition, it was observed that 'suit for declaration that property in suit is wakf without relief for possession is not barred under S. 42 [of the Specific Relief Act 1877]'.[19]

In light of the foregoing reasons, the Supreme Court reversed the judgment of the High Court and decreed the petitioner's suit for a permanent injunction.

9.3.4 Legal Effects of the Establishment of a *Waqf*. Once established, *waqf* property becomes vested in Allah Almighty and cannot be subjected to commercial transactions for profitable purposes unless they are in the interest of the *waqf*, and duly authorised by the courts or the *waqf* deed itself.

Muhammad Ramzan v The State 2013 SCMR 737

A village common property owned by a mosque cannot be sold even with the consensus of the entire village.

This case answers the legal question of whether the former owner of a *waqf* property or his legal heirs can reclaim or retrieve it. The appellant instituted a suit for the specific performance of a contract with respect to certain property in a trial court. The suit was decreed in favour of the appellant. As the issue related to a *waqf* property attached to a mosque, various members of the public questioned the decree through their applications under section 12(2) of the Civil Procedure Code 1908 but later on they withdrew these applications. One of the orders permitting the withdrawal of such applications was questioned before the High Court but it was also withdrawn. This alerted the judges of the High Court to exercise *suo moto* jurisdiction. After hearing the parties and perusing the record, the High Court held that once it has been established that the land is owned by the mosque then even if the entire proprietary body of the village orally agrees to sell the land, such a sale is invalid. The mosque in Islamic law is a *waqf* and *waqf* property cannot be sold without the permission of the court. The court relied upon the principle laid down in *Zahid Farooq v Anjuman Jamia Masjid* wherein Justice Fazal Karim held that a plot dedicated to a mosque cannot be sold.[20]

Before the Supreme Court, the counsel for the appellant argued that the owners of the village did not dedicate the disputed property to the mosque, only its usufruct was allowed to be retained by the mosque for the maintenance of the *imam* and the employees. When the suit property became barren and of no use to the mosque the owners retrieved it with mutual consensus. The mosque or its administration could not assert any right over the property. Senior Supreme Court advocate, Syed Sharifuddin Pirzada, appearing as a counsel on behalf of one of the respondents argued that the respondent was a *bona fide* purchaser, and his rights were protected. He contended that where a portion of the village common land had once been dedicated by general consent to a particular use, it could be retrieved with the will of the majority. Furthermore, he contended that if the income of the property was dedicated to the benefit of a mosque, the property does not become the ownership of the mosque along with the income. For this, he relied upon the dictum laid down in *Anjuman Masjid-i-Farooqia v Mst Fazal Begum*.[21] In this case, Chief Justice Muhammad Afzal Zullah held that it would depend upon the circumstances of each case whether the property itself was treated as the *waqf* or only its income was used for the purposes of the *waqf*. The counsel of respondent no. 5 rebutted these arguments by contending that the suit property stood vested in the mosque since 1891–92 as was evident from the entry made in the record of rights. These entries had been repeated since the late 19th century, which bore ample testimony to the fact that the original settlers of the village had not only dedicated this property to the mosque, but they had also forsaken the rights they had in it. Therefore, the suit property being a *waqf* could not be retrieved.

After hearing the arguments and perusing the record, the Supreme Court reached the conclusion that the property in dispute was a village common property which had been dedicated to the mosque. At no point did any member of the village interfere with the rights of the mosque over the property. Therefore, it was a *waqf* for all intents and purposes. The court held that once the nature of the property as a *waqf* was established, there was no back door of intrusion into the same by a former owner or his legal heirs. The *waqf* property could not be reclaimed or retrieved. The appeal was, therefore, dismissed.

Muhammad Hashim v Chief Administrator Auqaf, Punjab, Lahore 2010 CLC 1674 [Lah]

A *waqf* property cannot be leased out for more than three years.

In this case, the suit land was bequeathed by the ancestors of the petitioner to Khanqah Makhdoom Abdul Rasheed for charitable and religious purposes. Subsequently, it was used as a school playground for the benefit of the inhabitants and the students. The grievance of the petitioner was that a piece of land donated by the donor for religious trust was leased out for thirty years by respondent no. 1 for the establishment of a petrol pump to be installed by respondent no. 5, the lessee. This portion was carved out in such a way that the remaining land lost its utility as a playground. In this way, a religious trust was put to commercial use. The present petition assailed the lease of the *waqf* property.

The counsel for the respondent argued that the proposed site for the establishment of a petrol pump was outside the boundary wall of the playground and the proceeds from the lease money were to be used for charitable purposes. He further argued that to save the suit land from the *qabza* (encroachment) groups, respondent no. 1 deemed it necessary to lease out the land for a petrol pump. It was also contended that due authorisation for the lease was obtained under the law with the approval of the Chief Minister.

After hearing the arguments and perusing the record, the court found that despite objections from the Finance Department the land in question had been leased out in a dubious manner. It observed that land donated for religious purposes can only be employed for educational purposes and there is no justification to put it to commercial use. The court further noted that under sections 15 and 16 of the Punjab Waqf Properties Ordinance 1979, the Chief Administrator has the jurisdiction to prepare a scheme for the administration of the *waqf* property. However, the *waqf* property cannot be leased out for more than three years in ordinary circumstances. Therefore, the petition was allowed, and the lease was cancelled.

Noor Shah Filling Station (Regd.) through Manager v Auqaf Department through Chief Administrator Punjab 2009 CLC (Lah) 1148

A lease of *waqf* property for more than three years could be granted in exceptional circumstances where it is in the interest of the *waqf.*

The judgment in this case applied various principles of *waqf* law. First, the status, duties, and functions of the Chief Administrator Auqaf were highlighted. Second, it established that the *waqf* property can be leased out for more than three years in exceptional circumstances if it is in the best interest of the *waqf*. Third, it laid down that the subject matter of a *waqf* may include movable property.

The petitioner, through the manager of Noor Shah Filling Station, filed a writ petition against the Auqaf Department and its officer who were impleaded as respondents no. 1 to 3. The *Nazim*, Union Council Ferozpur, and DPO Sheikhupura were also impleaded as respondents no. 4 and 5 respectively. The petitioner contended that the land measuring 11 *kanal* and two *marla* situated in village Chahr was vested in the auqaf department. Four *kanals* of the land were auctioned to the petitioner who offered the goodwill of Rs 3,020,000 and a monthly rent of Rs 4,000. Pursuant to the grant of the lease, the petitioner claimed to have obtained all the required no-objection certificates and permission to establish a petrol station at the site. The grievance of the petitioner was that the Nazim, respondent no. 4 had started to interfere in the construction of the petrol pump. Respondent no. 1 also issued a notice through a letter dated 13 December 2006 directing the petitioner to suspend the work at the petrol station. The petitioner challenged the letter and asked the court that respondents no. 1 to 4 be restrained from acting in detriment to the legal rights of the petitioner.

The legal counsel of the Auqaf Department submitted that the constitutional petition had become infructuous as the impugned letter directing the petitioner to suspend work at the petrol station had been withdrawn vide a subsequent letter dated 17 January 2007. Respondent no. 4 contended that the petrol station was being built within the boundary of a *durbar* and its construction would hurt the religious sentiments of the people. Furthermore, respondent no. 4 pointed out that the area leased out was used for the performance of rituals and rites during the *urs* of the saint buried in the *durbar*. During the pendency of the present writ petition, respondent no. 4 filed another writ petition challenging the grant of lease to the petitioner by the Auqaf Department. Both the petitioner and the Auqaf Department resisted the petition. They maintained that the lease was strictly in accordance with the law and in the interest of the *durbar*, as the income generated therefrom would be used for the upkeep of the *durbar*. They also denied that the disputed property was transferred to the *durbar* for any particular purpose.

After the perusal of various provisions of the Punjab Waqf Properties Ordinance 1979 and certain judicial precedents, the court commented:

> [T]he status of the Chief Administrator Auqaf and his subordinates is that of a Mutawalli, whose authority is circumscribed by the provision of the law i.e. the Punjab Waqf Properties Ordinance, 1979 and the rules framed hereunder. The Chief Administrator Auqaf is vested with the administration, control, management and maintenance of the Waqf Properties and is authorised to prepare a scheme for the administration and development of such Waqf properties, but such authority is neither absolute nor unfettered. The discretion in this behalf is strictly structured by law and is always justifiable. The Chief Administrator is required to give effect to the wishes of a person dedicating the Waqf to the extent that such wishes can be

> ascertained and reasonably be given effect to… Only where such wishes of the dedicators are not ascertainable or impossible to give effect thereto, the Waqf property may be used for any purpose recognised by Islam as religious, pious or charitable.[22]

The court further noted that in the instant case, the land in dispute was sold to the *durbar*. It was not a case of dedication or creation of a *waqf* for any particular purpose, but it was in fact a property acquired by a *waqf* through its funds. Hence, there is no specified purpose for which the property was dedicated which needs to be given effect. The counsel for respondent no. 4 argued that the disputed property could not be leased out for a period of more than one year or at best three years. On this point, the court observed:

> Rule 7 of the Punjab Waqf Properties (Administration) Rules, 2002, prescribes that ordinarily such lease of Waqf property should not exceed three years which provision is in consonance with the classical Islamic Law with reference to powers of a Mutawalli to lease the property. However, a proviso has been added whereby the Chief Administrator Auqaf may grant a lease for a longer period if in his opinion such action is necessitated by the best interest of the Waqf property. That proviso obviously requires conscious application of mind and determination and disclosure of reasons as to why the lease in a particular case is being granted for a longer period of time.[23]

The court clarified the nature of a *waqf* property holding that a *waqf* not only comprises the property that is used for the purposes of the *waqf* but it could also include revenue-generating property:

> [T]he law recognises the creation of Waqf where the property is not itself directly to be used for a purpose recognised by Islam as religious, pious or charitable … but the purpose is that the income generated therefrom be used for a religious, pious or charitable… The aforesaid becomes even more obviously [sic] as not only an immovable property but also movable property such as stocks, shares and cash can also form subject matter of a Waqf.[24]

The court disposed of the petition by referring it back to the Chief Administrator, Auqaf. He was directed to determine whether the suit land had been used since time immemorial for a purpose recognised as religious, pious, or charitable and whether the establishment of a petrol station would interfere with the performance of the rites and rituals at the *durbar*.

9.4 Conclusion

Waqf is an important institution under Islamic law. It is not necessary for a *waqf* to be made in writing; it may be made orally. It is not necessary that the word '*waqf*' be employed to establish a valid *waqf*. However, the intention to dedicate the property for religious, pious, or charitable purpose must be clear. Properties that have been used for a long period for charitable purposes can also be regarded as a *waqf*. Moreover, the subject matter of a *waqf* can be any property, movable or immovable.

Waqf is used for both public and private purposes. A public *waqf* is required to be perpetual, irrevocable, and unconditional for religious, pious, or charitable purpose. On the other hand, a family *waqf* is used as a settlement or private trust for the benefit of the family with a terminal object of dedicating the benefits to some religious, pious, or charitable purposes. This feature of the private *waqf* relates it to wills and inheritance law. *Waqf* resembles a gift and charity as the founder gives away his property to either some specific persons or charitable institutions. It is because of these features that a *waqf* is treated as being under personal law. Perpetuity is an essential condition of a *waqf* and the ultimate beneficiaries, even in a private *waqf*, are to be the poor or some charitable purpose. This makes a *waqf* an efficient mode to dispose of personal property in cases where it is necessary to prevent it being squandered in the hands of some profligate heir(s). However, as an institution *waqf* is not very flexible because the conditions of a *waqf* cannot be changed after it is established unless the founder reserves the right to change these conditions or after authorisation by the courts. This leads to myriads of legal problems. Therefore, family *waqf* is rarely used nowadays; only the old family *awqaf* continue to operate.

In Pakistan, the courts apply traditional principles of Islamic law in matters pertaining to *awqaf*. Religious institutions such as mosques, shrines, and graveyards are still regulated under classical Islamic law. However, during colonial and post-colonial periods, various statutes were passed to provide for effective state regulation of religious *awqaf*. At present, an elaborate regulatory framework is established in each province under the Wakf Properties Ordinance 1979. These ordinances are similar in regard to the institutional framework as well as jurisdictional capacities and functions of *waqf* authorities at provincial levels.

Questions

1. What is a *waqf* and how is it different from other modes of disposing of properties under Islamic law?
2. What are the different modes of the establishment of a valid *waqf*? Please explain the legal effects of the creation of a *waqf*.
3. Discuss the various kinds of *waqf* with particular reference to the family *waqf* and its chequered history in the Indian subcontinent.
4. Can a *waqf* property be retrieved or sold or rented out by the founder/*waqif* or his/her legal heirs?

Further Reading

Articles

Abbasi, M.Z., 'The Classical Islamic Law of Waqf: A Concise Introduction', *Arab Law Quarterly* (2012) 26, 121.

Malik, S.J., 'Waqf in Pakistan: Change in Traditional Institutions', *Die Welt des Islams* (1990) 30 (1/4), 63.

Ewing, K., 'The Politics of Sufism: Redefining the Saints of Pakistan', *The Journal of Asian Studies* (1983) 42 (2), 251.

Cases

Abid Arif Nomani v Chief Administrator, Auqaf, Punjab 2004 SCMR 1050 (A *mutawalli* or *sajjadanashins* without explicit authorisation in a *waqf* deed cannot exchange the *waqf* property with another unless he has sought specific permission from a court to do so.)

Allama Maqsood Ahmad v Government of Punjab 2005 SCMR 816 (Only the government can prepare a scheme for the sale or disposal of a *waqf* property under the Punjab Waqf Properties Ordinance 1979.)

Asghar Bin Shahid Jafry v Defence Housing Authority PLD 2017 Lah 347 (The place allocated by a housing authority for a graveyard cannot be treated as a *waqf* for the public at large; even if it is considered as a *waqf* for the specific purpose of serving the needs of those who are members of that particular housing authority.)

Chief Administrator Auqaf v Abdul Qadeer Khan 2004 MLD 532 [Lah] (The conditions laid down in the *waqf* deed prevail over the Punjab Waqf Properties Ordinance 1979.)

Chief Administrator Auqaf, Sindh v Masooma Begum PLD 2001 SC 75 (The establishment of a *waqf* must be proved with convincing evidence and the erroneous payment of rent for a short period of time to the *auqaf* authorities cannot make a certain property a *waqf*.)

Mueen-ud-Din v Administrator General of Auqaf, Pakistan, Islamabad PLD 2007 Lah 583 (A *waqf* is a permanent dedication for religious and pious purposes and a *khanqah* could be a private property.)

Muhammad Zaman Shah v Chief Administrator Auqaf 1991 SCMR 2152 (In this case, the *waqif/sajjadanashins* bequeathed all of his self-acquired property to the *waqf* and then during his lifetime kept on drawing some income from the *waqf* for meeting his own and his family's expenses. Subsequently, a question arose as to the nature of his dedication, whether it was a simple *waqf* or *waqf ala al-aulad*. The court held that without having any specific evidence to prove that such dedication was in nature of *waqf ala al-aulad*, the transaction would be treated as *waqf*.)

Sh. Inayat Ullah v M.A. Khan PLD 1964 SC 126 (The Chief Administrator Auqaf cannot prohibit absolutely the established religious practices and ceremonies in a *waqf* property.)

Sher Bahadur v Ghulam Qamar Din 2016 MLD 1749 (Pesh) (The status of *sajjadanashin*s is different from a *mutawalli* as the former has to perform religious and spiritual services in addition to managerial and administrative duties usually assigned to the latter.)

Ulfat Butt v Muhammad Arif 2000 YLR 2753 [Lah] (A graveyard is a *waqf* through long use.)

Zahid Farooq v Anjuman Jamia Masjid 1995 SCMR 1584 (*Waqf* property is vested in God and the *qazi*, His delegate, is assigned the task of executing and looking after its affairs. Hence, no part of the *waqf* property can be sold without having prior approval from *qazi* unless such authority has been explicitly entrusted in the *waqf* deed itself.)

Notes

1. See Ibn al-Humām, *Sharh Fatah al-Qadir ala al-Hedaya*, 6th vol (Beirut: Dar al-Kutub al-Ilmiyya, 2003), 187–191; Ibn Abidin, *Radd al-Muhtar*, 6th vol (Beirut: Dar al-Kutub al-Ilmiyya, 2003), 517; Muhidin Abu Zakaria Yahya ibn Sharif En Nawawi, *Minhaj Et Talibin* (Calcutta: W. Thacker & Co., 1914), 232.
2. Dr Tanzil-ur-Rahman, *Code of Muslim Personal Law*, vol. 2, 101.
3. Al-Zuhayli, *Al-Fiqh ul-Islami*, vol. 10 (Dar al-Fikr 2004), 7602. In order to establish an irrevocable *waqf* for a mosque, prayer must be offered by a group of two or more persons and in one opinion attributed to Abu Hanifa there should be *azan* (call for prayer) and an undisclosed offering of prayer for making the establishment of *waqf* public. Al-Shaykh Nizam, *Al-Fatawa al-Alamgiriyya*, vol. 2 (Calcutta: Nawal Kishawr, 1865), 1030.
4. Nawawi, *Minhaj*, 233.
5. [1894] 22 IA 76.
6. Katherine Ewing, 'The Politics of Sufism: Redefining the Saints of Pakistan', The Journal of Asian Studies (1983) 42 (2), 251–268; A. Malik and T. Malik, 'Pīrs and Politics in Punjab, 1937–2013', *Modern Asian Studies* (2017) 51 (6), 1818–1861.
7. PLD 2011 Lah 483, 487.
8. 1994 SCMR 804, 810.
9. Under the doctrine of *cy-pres* (literally, 'as near as possible'), where the intention to create a *waqf* is clearly expressed in a *waqf* deed, the *waqf* will not fail because the specified objects are impossible to achieve, but the income will be utilised for other charitable purposes or objects similar to the unattainable objects mentioned in the deed. JE Penner, *The Law of Trusts*, 6th edn (Oxford: Oxford University Press, 2008), 457–58.
10. 1998 CLC 171, 177.
11. 1991 SCMR 2112, 2113.
12. 2007 CLC 71, 75.
13. PLD 1959 Pesh 152, 156.
14. Ibid., 155.
15. Ibid., 158.
16. AIR 1938 Lah 452.
17. PLD 2007 SC 352, 359.
18. *Gian Chand v Bhagwan Singh* AIR 1932 Lahore 97. Ibid., 361.
19. Ibid.
20. 1995 SCMR 1584.
21. 1991 SCMR 2112.
22. 2009 CLC 1148, 1157.
23. Ibid., 1158.
24. Ibid.

10

WILLS

10.1 Introduction

A Muslim, under Sunni law, can bequeath his/her property through a will subject to two conditions regarding its quantum and legatees. First, the bequest cannot consume more than one-third of the estate after the payment of debts and funeral charges unless the heirs give their consent after the death of a testator. Once given, such consent cannot be revoked. Second, a bequest to an heir whose shares are specified under Islamic inheritance law is invalid. However, such a bequest becomes valid if other legal heirs give their consent after the demise of the testator. The consent need not be expressed and may be inferred from the conduct of the heirs. However, mere silence or inaction on the part of the legal heirs cannot be construed as implied consent. An individual legal heir's consent is only binding on his own share.

Under Shia law, a testator may bequeath his property to a legal heir as long as it does not exceed one-third of his/her estate. Such a bequest does not need the consent of other heirs in order to be valid. However, for a bequest exceeding one-third of an estate, the consent of legal heirs is required. This consent may be given before or after the death of the testator.

The above principles have been drawn from the following two sayings of the Prophet (PBUH):

> 'No bequest for an heir'.[1]
>
> It is narrated that the Prophet (PBUH) visited Sa'd bin Abi Waqqas and he told him, 'O Messenger of Allah, my ailment has overcome me as you can see and I have wealth, but no one inherits me except a daughter that I have. Do I, then bequeath two-thirds of my wealth?' The Messenger of Allah (PBUH) said, 'No'. Sa'd said to him, 'Half?' He said, 'No'. The Messenger of Allah (PBUH) then said, 'A third, a third is (more than) enough. If you

leave your heirs rich, it is better than leaving them indigent and dependent on people'.[2]

10.2 Validity of a Will

The testator must be sane, rational, and a major to make a valid will. A will should be made voluntarily. Any element of undue influence, coercion, or fraud will render the will invalid. It can be made in favour of any person capable of holding property, to an institution, or for a charitable and religious purpose not opposed to Islam. The general rule is that a legatee must be in existence when the bequest is made, not merely at the time of the testator's death. However, a bequest in favour of a child conceived but not born is regarded as valid. The unborn child becomes a legatee and is presumed to be in existence provided s/he is born within six months of the making of the will.

10.2.1 Subject Matter of a Will. The subject matter of a bequest can be any property, which is capable of being transferred and exists at the time of the testator's death. It should be noted that such property need not exist at the time when the will is made. However, as in the case of gifts, future and contingent bequests are void. A bequest with a condition which obstructs its completeness takes effect as if no condition was attached to it, meaning thereby that the condition is void but the will is valid. The bequests may be of the corpus of a property or its usufruct, as it is possible to give the usufruct to one person and the corpus to another.

Although a bequest is similar to a gift, unlike a gift it becomes operative only after the death of a testator. Hence, there is a requirement that the legatee should accept a bequest expressly or impliedly. According to the Hanafi school, if a legatee predeceases the testator, the bequest lapses. However, under Shia law, it goes to the legal heirs of the legatee, but lapses if there are no legal heirs.

Under Islamic law, a will can be made orally, in writing, or even through gestures, provided that the intention of the testator is sufficiently manifest. In a case where a will is in writing, it need not be signed or attested as long as the testator's intention is ascertainable.

10.2.2 Revocation of a Will. A testator may revoke a bequest at any time, either expressly or impliedly. A revocation is expressed if the testator revokes the bequest in express terms either orally or by means of a written instrument. However, a bequest can be revoked impliedly by an act which amounts to either extinction of the testator's proprietary rights or an addition to the subject of a bequest, provided that the addition is of such a nature that the bequest cannot be delivered without it. For instance, if the testator constructs a house on the bequeathed land, the bequest will lapse. Similarly, any non-testamentary transaction, gift, or sale of the bequeathed property will revoke the will automatically. However, in such cases, the intention of the testator regarding the interpretation of the will is given paramount importance. A will may be revoked by a subsequent will. Moreover, where the same thing is bequeathed to two different persons in a will, the parties will share the property in equal proportions.

10.2.3 Interpretation of a Will. A Muslim will must be interpreted in accordance with the principles and rules laid down in Islamic law. The intention of the testator is the most important factor in the construction of a will. In the case of an oral will, an earnest effort should be made to ascertain the exact words of the testator so that the will may be implemented accordingly. In the case of a documentary will, then rules pertaining to the interpretation of documents must be adhered to. The surrounding circumstances and the prevalent social conditions must also be considered.

10.2.4 Procedural Law Regarding a Will. Detailed procedures regarding the administration of the movable and immovable property of the deceased have been laid down in the Succession Act 1925. Although, this Act deals largely with the personal laws of non-Muslim communities, however, its procedural parts apply to Muslims as well. Similarly, the powers and duties of executors under the Act are also applicable to the wills of Muslims.

10.3 Outline of Case Law

10.3.1 Interpretation of a Will. The intention of the testator is ascertained from the document if the will is in writing. The courts have laid down the rule that the intention of the testator must be clearly ascertainable from the document which is interpreted as a whole. The courts may consider the surrounding circumstances and the conduct of legatees in order to construe a document of will.

Shirin Bai v Muhammad Ali PLD 1970 Kar 450

If the will is in writing, it is not required to be signed and witnessed. However, the intention of the testator must be clear and ascertainable from the document.

The judgment in this case lays down the principle regarding the form of wills under Islamic law. The petitioner, Shirin Bai, prayed for the grant of the Succession Certificate in respect of the debts and securities of her deceased sister, Fatima Jinnah, who died on 10 July 1967. The petitioner claimed the whole estate as the only surviving full sister of the deceased who died as a Shia and without leaving a will. Six respondents opposed the petition and claimed half of the estate as residuaries of the deceased. They claimed that the deceased died as a Sunni and, according to Sunni inheritance law, they were entitled to half of the estate of the deceased. They also asserted that the deceased left a will which was presented before the court. Thus, the court had to determine whether the will produced was valid.

There were three documents before the court as Exhibits 12, 13, and 14. The counsel for the objectors conceded that the first two documents could not be treated as a 'valid will' because they were mere drafts. He contended that only the third document, Exhibit 14, was relevant and it was in the handwriting of the deceased. This document contained only notes of the deceased regarding cash amounts. Justice Abdul Qadir Shaikh summarised the applicable law as follows:

> As to the form of a 'Will', it is well settled that a Muslim is not obliged to observe any special formality in making his 'Will', the Muhammadan Law not having prescribed any form in this regard. The 'Will' of a Muslim need not even be in writing, an oral 'Will' is perfectly valid; but the intention with respect to the property which the testator desires to be carried out after his death must, in whatever form they are declared, be with sufficient clarity, so as to be capable of being ascertained. If the 'Will' is in writing, it need not even be signed by the testator or attested by witnesses, because the verse in the Holy Quran regarding witnesses is considered nearly as a recommendation, and is not mandatory…[3]

Justice Shaikh observed that for evidentiary purposes wills are in writing because otherwise, the burden of proof is on the person alleging the will to prove 'with the utmost precision, the words [of a deceased man] on which he relied, with every circumstance of time and place'.[4] In the circumstances of the case, Justice Shaikh held that the alleged document of the will did not make the intentions of the deceased clear as the document only showed a few notes of the sums of moneys which she wanted to give to certain persons upon her death. Therefore, the court directed that the Succession Certificate should be issued to the petitioner.[5]

Khairan Bibi v Ghulam Hassan 2007 CLC 167 (Lah)

A document should be interpreted as a whole as opposed to focusing on isolated expressions.

This case concerns the interpretation of a document that was relied upon by both the contesting parties. The court discussed whether the respective document was a will or a gift. The parties were legal heirs of Charagh Din. The petitioners were his widow and a daughter, while the respondents were legal heirs of his brother who died during the litigation. In 1986, Charagh Din executed a document termed as *Tamleek-e-Warasat*. Through this document, he transferred his entire property in favour of the petitioners. Thereafter, he appeared before the revenue authorities for the attestation of the mutation on the basis of the above document. During this process, he employed the word '*wassiyat*' (will) in his statement and did not use the word *hiba* (gift). Charagh Din was also declared a landless person after the mutation as his entire property was transferred to the petitioners. This transaction was recorded in the *Roznamcha Waqiati* prepared by the revenue authorities.

After the death of Charagh Din in 1987, his brother assailed the mutation before the revenue authorities. However, when he could not get it set aside, he initiated a suit for declaration and possession of his share in the property of Charagh Din. He contended that the entire property was wrongly transferred to the petitioners to deprive him of his legitimate share mandated under Islamic law of inheritance. Hence, the mutation should be set aside, and he should be awarded his due share. The Civil Court decreed the suit, and the first Appellate Court dismissed the appeal of the petitioners.

The petitioners subsequently presented a revision petition before the High Court. They argued that the transaction was a gift in their favour. This fact was evident from the transfer of the property during the lifetime of Charagh Din and the mere use of the word '*wassiyat*' by Charagh Din would not convert the transaction into a will. It was further submitted that a will takes effect after the death of a testator and in this case, the property was actually transferred to the petitioners while Charagh Din was alive. The respondents, however, defended the decisions rendered by the courts below.

After hearing the parties and perusing the record, the court noted that both the courts below had drawn their conclusions of *Tamleek-e-Warasat* as a will from the use of the word '*wassiyat*' in the *Roznamcha Waqiati*. The transaction should not have been construed by banking upon a solitary expression and ignoring the document as a whole. The court held that 'it is a settled law that terms of document and intention of parties as to the character of the document must be gathered from considering the document as a whole and not from any isolated expression'.[6] The courts below had not given appropriate weightage to the fact that Charagh Din had appeared before the revenue authorities and was declared a landless person after the attestation of the mutation. Considering the document in its entirety and lapses in the appreciation of evidence, the High Court accepted the revision petition by holding the transfer of the entire property of Charagh Din as a gift in favour of the petitioners.

Haji Murad Khan v Abdul Ghafoor 1987 CLC 7 [Pesh]

The discovery of the intention of the testator was of paramount importance; also the conduct of legatees was a relevant factor in the construction of a bequest.

Abdul Ghafoor and others filed a suit for a declaration that they were the owners of 123/192 share in the estate of Abdul Manan and a preliminary partition decree passed on 3 July 1968 was based on fraud and was ineffective against their rights. The trial court partly decreed the suit. However, the appeals against the decree could not succeed. Therefore, the issue was brought before the High Court.

The court noted that the contesting parties admitted that originally Abdul Manan was the owner of the disputed property. He died in 1942 and was survived by his two sons: Abdul Ghafoor (plaintiff no.1) and Abdul Sattar (succeeded by defendants no. 2 to 8); four daughters: Mst Zafro (plaintiff no. 2), Mst Khairul Wara (plaintiff no. 3), Mst Noor ul Huda (succeeded by plaintiffs 2 to 6), and Mst Wadduha (defendant no. 1) and two widows: Mst Radifa and Mst Zarira.

Upon the death of Mst Zarira, she was succeeded by Abdul Ghafoor solely. Mst Radifa died in 1969 and was succeeded by plaintiffs 2 to 6, defendant no. 1, and defendants no. 3 to 8. When the shares were calculated, the share of the plaintiffs came out to be 123/192 and the remaining 69/192 share was of defendants no. 1 to 8. The plaintiffs contended that they were deliberately not made a party to a collusive suit decided in 1968 between the heirs of Mst Radifa and Abdul Sattar. The defendants, on the other hand, contended that Abdul Manan had divorced his wife, Mst Zarira, and alienated the entire suit property in favour of his other wife, Mst Radifa, during his lifetime. She transferred the urban property in favour of her son, Abdul Sattar, and the agricultural land in favour of her daughter, Mst Wadduha, via registered deeds. The trial court held that Abdul Manan had validly bequeathed the land and the house only as a life estate to Mst Radifa and, upon her death the property was to revert to his legal heirs. The plaintiffs were held entitled to 35/64 share. Their claim with respect to the rest of the property was dismissed.

The court noted that the main issue between the parties pertained to the construction of the disputed deed. Both lower courts found that the first part of the deed pertaining to the rural property was a will for life estate and the second part relating to the urban property was an unconditional will. One of the parties in this case contended that the deed was a will while the other party averred that it was a gift. Therefore, the court found it necessary to look at the original deed so that the intention of the testator could be determined. The court held:

> The guiding principle in construing a bequest is to ascertain the intention of the testator reflected in the language of the deed and the surrounding circumstances. The discovery of the intention of the testator is of paramount importance and the conduct of the legatee is a relevant factor in this context.[7]

The court noted that a perusal of the deed showed that Abdul Manan had intended to make a will in favour of Mst Radifa. The opening sentences of the deed showed that Abdul Manan had attained the age of 80 years and had 'no trust in cunning life'; hence he decided to make a will. It was stipulated in the will that he had bequeathed the agricultural land and the house situated in a village to Mst Radifa for life and the proprietary and possessory rights were to vest in her after his death. But upon her death, the property was to be distributed amongst his heirs. However, no such condition was found to be attached to the urban property and she was to be deemed to be its absolute owner. The deed did not mention the word gift or *tamleek*. The terms and conditions of the deed made it clear that Abdul Manan intended to make a will in the favour of his wife Mst Radifa. Furthermore, the deed had been described as a will in the divorce deed Exh. D dated 15 May 1941. Moreover, the legatee Mst Radifa described the disputed deed as will more than once. She had executed a registered sale deed dated 17 July 1965 in favour of her son, Abdul Sattar, with regard to the disputed urban property, and had described the disputed deed as a will in the aforesaid sale deed. She had done the same when she transferred some agricultural land to her daughter Mst Wadduha. The court observed that both Abdul Manan and Mst Radifa treated the disputed deed as a will and decided accordingly.

Regarding the consent of the legal heirs for a will exceeding one-third property of the legator, the court observed that such consent need not be express, it may be signified by a conduct showing fixed and unequivocal intention.

In the end, the court held that the finding of the lower courts regarding the nature of the deed being a will was well-founded. Furthermore, the first part of the will pertaining to the rural property created a life estate in favour of Mst Radifa, which upon her death reverted to Abdul Manan's legal heirs. The second part of the will regarding the urban property was held to be impliedly consented to by other legal heirs. Therefore, both appeals were dismissed.

10.3.2 Testamentary Powers. A full owner has the testamentary power to bequeath all his/her property. However, the effectiveness of the will to the extent of more than one-third of the property is subject to the consent of the legal heirs.

Nawab Din v Bagh 1994 SCMR 1975

A full owner of a land has the testamentary power to bequeath one-third of his/her property to anyone without the consent of the legal heirs.

In 1960, Fetah Bibi bequeathed one-third of her estate to Noor Din, the predecessor-in-interest of the respondents. The will was duly registered to avoid any future conflict. It is important to note that the legatee was not a legal heir of the testator: hence, the consent of legal heirs was not required for the will to be effective. In 1973–74, after the death of Fetah Bibi, the petitioners colluded with the revenue authorities to disregard the will and carried out some mutations of the estate.

The aggrieved respondents instituted a suit in the Civil Court for the mutations to be declared illegal and for their due share in the estate. The suit was decreed entitling the respondents to their due share under the will. Thereafter, both appellate forums, the first Appellate Court, and the High Court, maintained the decision. The petitioners subsequently sought leave to appeal before the Supreme Court. It was argued that Fetah Bibi was not the full owner of the land. Rather, she possessed it as a limited owner. Therefore, she was not competent to dispose of the land by way of a will. The court went through the record and observed that she was the full owner of the land in India and after migrating to Pakistan she was allotted the disputed land in lieu of the property that she had left in India. Hence, she had complete proprietary rights over the land. Moreover, the will registered by her in favour of the predecessor-in-interest of the respondents was beyond any reproach. It was within her testamentary power and the consent of the legal heirs was not required. Consequently, the Supreme Court refused the leave to appeal.

Sardar Muhammad v Faqir Muhammad 1996 CLC 916 (Lah)

A will can operate to the extent of 1/3rd of the property in favour of non-legal heirs. The consent of the legal heirs is required if a will exceeds one-third of the property.

In this case, the court elucidated upon the scope and object of a will in Islamic law. The judgment, in this case, is a second round of litigation between the parties. In the first round, the petitioners could not succeed in getting their due share under a will. Nabi Bakhsh, predecessor-in-interest of the parties, had sizeable agricultural property. He had one son and six grandsons from another predeceased son. In 1953, he executed a will of half of his estate in favour of the legal heirs of his predeceased son who were petitioners in this case. He died in 1957 and thereafter a legal conflict arose between his son and the legal heirs of his predeceased son. The dispute related to the distribution of the estate including the implication of the will executed in favour of the latter.

In the first round of litigation, which concluded at the Supreme Court, the estate of Nabi Bakhsh was divided equally among the litigants and the will was not taken into consideration for awarding the petitioners their due share under it. It was against this background that the petitioners filed a declaratory suit for having their rights under the will enforced. However, the objective was not achieved before the subordinate courts. Hence, the matter was brought before the High Court. The court accepted their contention and gave effect to the will by awarding them one-third of the estate, not one-half as mentioned in the will. The court held that the testator was not entitled to make a will of more than one-third of his estate without the consent of other legal heirs. After analysing the Qur'anic verses and other books of authority, the court observed:

> Making of Will is a divine institution and it is sanctioned by Holy Qur'an and Sunnah of the Holy Prophet (PBUH) that it is a settlement of property gratuitously made on the legatee after the death of testator; that it is not only confined to the property but it includes any usufruct of the property or any advantage arising out of the property; that making a Will is desirable and virtuous; that underlying object of this mode of transfer is better the lot of those relatives who were/are not legal heirs; that another object of making Will is to help the noble causes in the services of community and in the causes of God Almighty; that there can be no Will beyond 1/3rd [one-third] of the legal estate left by the testator and its should not be designed to injure the rule of inheritance; that the Will can be made with respect to a property which may not be in existence at the time of Will but may be acquired by testator before his death and he left after the death and is capable of being delivered to the legatee.[88]

Gul Zaman v Maula Dad 2014 CLC 635 (Pesh)

A will of one's entire estate is not void *ab initio*. Its effectiveness to the extent of more than one-third is subject to the consent of legal heirs.

In this case, Maula Dad claimed that Qadir Bakhsh bequeathed his entire land to him in 1976 through a will. Since then, he was in possession of the suit land and any mutation not conforming to his rights under the will was liable to be set aside. The Civil Court dismissed the case. Thereafter, he filed an appeal before the first Appellate Court, which modified the decision of the Civil Court to the extent of one-third of the suit land giving due regard to the will of Qadir Bakhsh.

The decision of the first Appellate Court was assailed before the High Court on the ground that law and facts did not warrant the same. On the other hand, Maula Dad, the respondent, was content to have at least one-third of the testator's land and argued that no illegality was committed by the first Appellate Court. The High Court did not find any illegality or misappreciation of evidence in the impugned decision and, therefore, maintained the same.

The High Court observed that certain facts were proved on the basis of evidence adduced by the parties. These facts were that Qadir Bakhsh executed a will in favour of Maula Dad. The entire land of the testator was bequeathed to the legatee through that will, and the will was not confirmed by the consent of the legal heirs. Against this background, only one question was left unanswered: whether a testator could bequeath more than one-third of his/her property without the consent of the legal heirs. By reproducing the relevant passage from Mulla's *Principles of*

Muhammadan Law, the court observed that the testator's testamentary power would only be effective to the extent of bequeathing one-third of his/her property if the excess was not approved by the legal heirs. Therefore, the decision of the first Appellate Court granting one-third of the suit land to Maula Dad was legally valid. In other words, the court declared that a will of one's entire estate is not void *ab initio*, though its effectiveness to the extent of more than one-third is subject to the consent of legal heirs. If the requisite consent is not given the will/bequeath will automatically be reduced to one-third of the estate.

10.3.3 Consent of Legal Heirs. A testator has the power to bequest one-third of his/her property to non-legal heirs without the consent of legal heirs. However, if s/he chooses to make a bequest in favour of a legal heir, even if that bequest is less than one-third of the property, the will cannot be operative unless all other legal heirs give tangible and voluntary consent after the testator's death. Mere silence on the part of other legal heirs for a long period will not amount to their implied consent to the will. However, no such consent is required if the bequest is in favour of the testator's orphaned grandchildren as they are not regarded as legal heirs of the deceased.

Zakirullah Khan v Faizullah Khan 1999 SCMR 971

A will in favour of legal heirs even to the extent of one-third of property is inoperative without the consent of other legal heirs and mere silence on part of other legal heirs for a long period of time does not amount to their implied consent to the will.

Saadullah Khan died leaving behind two widows and children from both of them. The petitioners were children from one widow and the respondents were the offspring of the other. After the death of Saadullah Khan, his entire estate was mutated in favour of the petitioners on the basis of three deeds, while the respondents were deprived of any share in the property.

The respondents' declaratory suit to get their share in the estate was dismissed by the trial court. In appeal, the first Appellate Court modified the decision of the trial court and declared that, according to the deeds, that were wills in reality, the petitioners were only entitled to one-third of the estate. The rest of the estate would be distributed among the petitioners and the respondents in accordance with their respective shares under the Islamic law of inheritance.

The respondents challenged this decision before the High Court, which further modified the decision of the first Appellate Court. It held that the entire estate of the deceased, Saadullah Khan, would be distributed according to the law of inheritance and the petitioners would not have any preferential treatment under the wills even to the extent of one-third because the same were not consented to by other legal heirs.

On being deprived of their share in the property under the wills, the petitioners agitated the matter before the Supreme Court. Their case was based on two grounds: first, the deeds, regarded by the courts below as wills, were not wills. Second, even if these instruments were wills, the respondents by not assailing the mutation for a reasonable period, had impliedly given the requisite consent for the effectiveness of these wills.

The court did not accede to the arguments of the petitioners and dismissed the appeal. The court held that since these words '*wasiat haza per bad az wafat amal daramad ho ga*' (this will shall take effect after the death [of the testator]) were mentioned at the end of each deed, it was not possible to treat them as any other transaction. The court further observed that the mere silence of the respondents for a long period would not amount to implied consent. There had to be some specific evidence of consent of the respondents because it related to their valuable right. Therefore, the wills in favour of some legal heirs even to the extent of one-third were not implemented without the consent of other legal heirs and a mere lapse of time was not regarded as implied consent by other legal heirs.

Muhammad Shoaib v Razia Bibi 2002 YLR 2895 (Lah)

A bequest to an heir is not valid unless other heirs consent to it after the death of the testator. Such consent has to be tangible and voluntary.

This case establishes the principle that a bequest to an heir is not valid unless other heirs provide their consent after the death of the testator. Any heir may consent to bind his/her own share only. However, such consent has to be tangible and voluntary. This case also lays down the rule that a testator cannot deprive a legal heir of inheritance through a will.

This case involved a controversy relating to the division of property left by Khurshid Muhammad Chishti who died on 14 September 1993. He contracted two marriages during his lifetime: first with Firdous Begum and the second with Razia Bibi. Petitioners no. 1 and 2 were sons of the deceased from his first wife, and petitioner no. 3 was the sister of the deceased. The other petitioners were legal heirs of Aziz

Fatima, another sister of the deceased. On the other hand, respondent no. 1 was the second widow of the deceased and respondents no. 2 to 5 were her sons and daughters. After the death of Khurshid Muhammad, a mutation of inheritance was entered into by the Revenue Department for the distribution of the estate among the legal heirs as per their entitlements according to Islamic inheritance law.

The respondents filed a civil suit and claimed the entire landed property left by the deceased on the basis of a will. The petitioners contested the suit. The trial court partially decreed the suit. It held that the respondents were entitled to one-third share in the legacy of the deceased on the basis of a will, and the rest of the property should be distributed among all legal heirs of the deceased. Both parties challenged the decree of the trial court. The respondents were aggrieved because they laid claim to the entire landed property of the deceased, while the petitioners were aggrieved because the courts accepted the will to the extent of one-third share in the property. The Appellate Court dismissed both the appeals, hence the two parties filed instant civil revision petitions before the High Court. The petitions were consolidated as the parties and the subject matter remained the same.

The respondents argued that the deceased made a will on 22 December 1991 bequeathing his entire estate to his wife Razia Bibi and four minor children. It was also averred that Firdous Begum was the wife of the deceased to whom he gave a one-half share in his bungalow involved in the suit; however later, in 1985 the deceased divorced her. It was also stated that the two sons of the deceased from his first wife were given three acres of land each during the lifetime of the deceased. According to the respondents, these two sons of the deceased and Zubada Bibi, mother of the deceased (who died during the pendency of the proceedings) had accepted the will.

The petitioners maintained that the will dated 22 December 1991 was fraudulent and was an unregistered document and resisted the suit. They further stated that as the legal heirs of the deceased, they were entitled to their respective shares in the estate.

The main issue was the validity of the will. The counsel for the petitioners argued that under Islamic law, a testator does not possess a right to make a bequest in favour of one of the legal heirs to the exclusion of others. He maintained that any will made with the sole intention of depriving the heirs of the right to inherit the property of their predecessor-in-interest was invalid. The petitioners' counsel also argued that the written statement filed by the mother of the deceased, Zubada Bibi, accepting the will could not be taken as a piece of evidence and the presumption of undue influence was to be drawn in her case. On the contrary, the counsel for the respondents argued that there is no rule according to which a testator can only bequeath one-third of his property. He stated that the will made in favour of one or more legal heirs would be a valid will in respect of the entire estate left by the deceased when other legal heirs accept the same. On the other hand, the respondents' counsel drew support from the statements of petitioners no. 1 and 2 (the sons from the first wife) and from the written statement of consent filed by Zubada Bibi, mother of the deceased. The court observed:

> [A] Muslim testator enjoys the power to bequeath his property to the extent of 1/3rd [one-third] share of his estate in favour of any other person except his legal heirs. However, he may bequeath 1/3rd [one-third] share in favour of any one or more of the legal heirs but such bequeath in favour of one or more legal heirs shall only be valid and enforceable if the same is assented to by other legal heirs after the death of the testator.[9]

The respondents' counsel argued that petitioners no. 1 and 2 did not object to the will, rather they assented to the same on the *rasm-i-soyem* and *rasm-i-chehlum* of the deceased. However, there was no documentary evidence to this effect. The only witnesses who deposed the factum of assent were either the relatives of respondent no. 1, Razia Bibi, or were under her control. There was no evidence of any overt act of petitioners no. 1 and 2 showing consent on their part. The court held:

> [T]he essence behind the principle that a bequeath to an heir is not valid unless the other heirs consent to the bequeath after the death of testator conveys that there should be a tangible voluntary consent.[10]

Such consent was missing in the present case. Even the evidence that the respondents produced to prove the same did not inspire any confidence nor was it probable in the circumstances of the case.

The court also referred to the will itself. The deceased testator stated in his will that his son Shahbaz (from his first wife) tried to kill him and his sons from his second wife and was still determined to kill them all. The said will was executed against this background. First, the testator had declared his son, Shahbaz 'deprived' (*aaq*) of his inheritance. Then, he made his second wife and the children from her the legal heirs of his entire property through the will. The court observed that the will showed that the deceased testator did not have cordial relations with the petitioners. Hence, one of the reasons for executing the will, as stated by the testator, was the threat to his life as well as the lives of his second wife and children from her. These facts, however, did not impact the law. The law requires that if a will is made in favour of legal heirs, then the consent of other legal heirs is required.

Therefore, the courts dismissed the civil revision filed by the second wife and her children.

The judgment, in this case, leaves an interesting and important question unanswered: whether a legator can deprive a legal heir who threatens to kill him for his legacy. A murderer is deprived of his share of the inheritance of the deceased under Islamic law. In *Beguman v Saroo*, the Lahore High Court extended this principle by holding that a murderer or his progeny cannot benefit from the crime of murder committed with a design to inherit property.[11] If the legator would have been properly advised, he should have transferred all his property to the intended beneficiaries during his lifetime. In the *Beguman* case, the judge relied upon the principles of justice, equity, and good conscience. One may argue that these principles could have been invoked to stop the son, who threatened to kill his father and his children from the second wife, from benefiting from the legacy of his father, especially if the objective of this threat was to inherit the property from the father. However, the law as it stands today is that a person cannot deprive any of his/her legal heirs of his/her legacy, even if they planned to kill him during his/her lifetime from his/her legacy.

Abdul Haq v Surrya Begum 2002 SCMR 1330

Orphaned grandchildren are not considered legal heirs of a grandfather, hence a will in their favour does not require the consent of other legal heirs.

This case establishes an important principle of Islamic law that a will in favour of non-heirs becomes effective to the extent of one-third of an estate, even though the same has not been consented to by the legal heirs.

In 1960, Samad Khan died and left behind one son, Atta Muhammad and several other legal heirs including a widow and Atta Muhammad's sons and the daughters of another predeceased son, Ali Muhammad. The deceased executed a will in favour of the legal heirs of his predeceased son (his orphaned grandchildren). Subsequently, the mutation of his estate was carried out in accordance with the will. Atta Muhammad disputed the factum of the will, but the revenue authorities mutated the estate in favour of the legal heirs of his predeceased son as per the will. Atta Muhammad did not raise any objection against his deprivation from the estate during his lifetime.

The parties in this case were the legal heirs of the predeceased son, Ali Muhammad. The petitioners were his sons, whereas the respondents were his daughters who were collectively the beneficiaries of the estate under the will of the deceased. In 1979, the petitioners filed a declaratory suit claiming therein that the respondents were not entitled to any share in the estate of Samad Khan because they were not the real daughters of Ali Muhammad; rather, they were born from their mother's previous wedlock. The petitioners' mother also supported their claim in the court. The suit was dismissed by the trial court.

On appeal before the first Appellate Court, the suit was decreed. The court held that upon the death of Samad Khan, Atta Muhammad should have inherited the entire estate as he was the sole legal heir then. However, after the latter's death, the estate should have gone to the petitioners exclusively as the legal heirs of Atta Muhammad. The court also observed that the will, according to which the mutation was attested, could not be effective because the same was not consented to by Atta Muhammad and, therefore, the respondents could not get any property. In reaching this conclusion, the first Appellate Court assumed that the orphaned grandchildren (daughters of predeceased son, Ali Muhammad) were the legal heirs of Samad Khan and therefore they could not benefit under the will without the consent of other legal heirs (Atta Muhammad).

The High Court restored the decision of the trial court. It held that the respondents were entitled to the share in the estate as daughters of Ali Muhammad under the will of their grandfather. The petitioners filed an appeal before the Supreme Court. The court maintained the decision of the trial court as confirmed by the High Court. It observed that there was no defect in the mutation according to the will in favour of the legal heirs of the predeceased son, Ali Muhammad, because they were not the legal heirs of the deceased, Samad Khan, in the presence of his living son, Atta Muhammad. Hence, the consent of the latter for awarding them any property under the will was not required. Therefore, the observation of the first Appellate Court in this regard was a misreading of Islamic law on this point.

It must be noted that the propositus in this case died before the promulgation of the MFLO. Section 4 of the MFLO grants orphaned grandchildren inheritance rights. It is unclear whether courts will treat orphaned grandchildren as 'legal heirs' after the promulgation of the

MFLO and hence will require the consent of other legal heirs in case a grandfather leaves a will in favour of his orphaned grandchildren within the prescribed limit of one-third of his estate. By relying upon the purposive interpretation of section 4 of the MFLO, it may be argued that since its objective is to expand rather than limit the inheritance rights of orphaned grandchildren, the courts will interpret it beneficially for them. Therefore, consent of other legal heirs will not be required under Sunni law if a grandfather leaves a will in favour of his grandchildren while they also inherit under section 4 of the MFLO. Moreover, this section pertains to the rights of inheritance exclusively and was never intended to affect the law of wills under Islamic law.

Nasreen Begum v A 2006 MLD 1988 (Kar)

A will in favour of legal heirs cannot operate without the consent of other legal heirs even to the extent of one-third of the property.

This case sheds light on some important points concerning the testamentary power of a testator and the consent of legal heirs. However, the decision rendered was not exclusively based on these principles.

Ch. Baduddin died in 1973 leaving behind a widow, five sons, and two daughters. The petitioner in the case was one of the daughters who applied for Letters of Administration of the property of the deceased after about thirty years of his death. During this period, some of the legal heirs of the deceased had also died and an updated list of all legal heirs was presented before the court.

As per the law, the court had to dispose of the matter in summary proceedings following a settled procedure. It advertised a notice in a newspaper for procuring the attendance of all legal heirs of the deceased. In response to the notice, a relative appeared before the court and presented a will, which was asserted to have been made by the deceased. The alleged will stated that the deceased had bequeathed his estate in entirety to his sons and excluded the daughters including the petitioner as they had already been given their due share in cash.

On the basis of the alleged will, it was prayed by the relative producing the will that the Letters of Administration should not be issued in summary proceedings instead the matter should be dealt with by the Civil Court in a regular suit. Interestingly, none of the legal heirs supported the factum of the existence of the alleged will. They vehemently extended their support for the issuance of the Letters of Administration to the petitioner and submitted affidavits for this purpose.

The petitioner's counsel argued that the will was an afterthought that was fabricated for ousting the daughters of the deceased from their due share, and it was not credible because it was never made public before its production in the court after decades of its alleged drafting. The counsel submitted that the alleged will could not be regarded as valid because it disposed of the entire estate of the deceased, whereas his testamentary power was only limited to one-third of his estate. He further submitted that even if it was considered genuine, it could not be given effect to for more than one-third of the estate and that was also dependent on the consent of the legal heirs. There was nothing on record to show that the heirs consented to the alleged will, instead they had demonstrated their utter ignorance about it. In this context, the mere silence of the daughters, including the petitioner, was not enough to deprive them of their valuable rights.

In the circumstances of the case, the High Court issued the Letters of Administration as applied for and refused to accept the contention of the relative for not issuing the same in summary proceedings and left the matter to be decided by the Civil Court.

10.3.4 Revocation of a Will. A will can be revoked at any time during the lifetime of a testator, either by way of express declaration or through the testator's conduct.

Tauqeer Ahmed v Bashir Ahmed 2001 YLR 3153 (Kar)

A will can be revoked during the lifetime of a testator even if it was initially intended to be irrevocable.

This case deals with the maintainability of a suit regarding a will during the lifetime of the testator. Defendant no. 1 was the father of the plaintiff and another defendant, whereas the other two defendants were the wife and brother-in-law of that defendant. Defendant no. 1 owned a spacious shop and other movable properties. He executed a will on 10 June 1996 when he was aged 72 years. Under this will, he stated that all his properties, movable and immovable, should be transferred after his death to all his legal heirs including the plaintiff as per their respective shares under the Hanafi law of inheritance. It was further stated in the will that defendant no. 1 would keep on exercising his control over his properties during his life though the will would be irrevocable.

On 16 October 2000, the plaintiff came to the shop and found that its name was changed. Furthermore, he found out that the shop had been sold by defendant no. 1 to another defendant, disregarding the will he had made dated 10 June 1996. Consequently, the plaintiff instituted a suit for declaration along with injunctive relief against the defendants to protect his rights under the will.

The plaintiff claimed that the will was an irrevocable document as per its contents. Therefore, no transaction could have been carried out superseding the valuable rights created under it. Hence, the sale transaction, purporting to transfer of the shop by defendant no. 1 to another defendant, should be declared void. It was further claimed that the will could not be disregarded without its cancellation through a court proceeding under section 39 of the Specific Relief Act 1877.

The defendants' counsel argued that the plaintiff had no cause of action to file the suit. During his lifetime, defendant no. 1 was the exclusive owner of the suit property and could dispose of it in any manner he pleased. By referring to D.F. Mulla's *Principles of Muhammadan Law*, it was contended that a bequest is considered revoked once the testator extinguishes his proprietary right in the property bequeathed. Therefore, by selling his shop to another defendant, defendant no. 1 had already revoked his earlier will. He prayed that the plaint was liable to be rejected on this ground alone.

The court observed that a will takes effect after the death of the testator and during his lifetime a testator has every right to revoke it, either expressly or impliedly. With reference to the argument of cancelling the registered will through a court proceeding, the court held that there was no such requirement in Islamic law. Therefore, defendant no. 1 was competent to dispose of his properties. Hence, the petition was dismissed.

Muhammad Ibrahim v Akhtar Ali 2001 CLC 1323 (Lah)

A will can be revoked by a testator anytime during his lifetime.

Barkat Ali was married to Chiragh Bibi but remained issueless until his death on 21 September 1957. He had properties in three different villages, namely, Sharqpur, Gowinda, and Kot Mehmood. In addition to his wife, his close relatives included three brothers and one sister. On 24 September 1952, Barkat Ali executed a will for settling all his properties on his legal heirs. The property in Sharqpur was stated to be transferred to his wife after his death, while the properties in the other two villages were for his brothers and sister. On 16 August 1954, Barkat Ali sold his property located in Gowinda and the same was duly mutated in favour of the purchaser. This fact came to the knowledge of his relatives after his death. Following Barkat Ali's death, his property situated in Sharqpur was transferred to his widow as a gift, whereas the property located in village Kot Mehmood was transferred as an inheritance mutation in favour of all his legal heirs including the widow.

Unaware of the sale transaction dated 16 August 1954, the relatives (the widow on one hand and the brothers and sister on the other) executed a document on 4 October 1958. In this document, the widow agreed to relinquish her share in the property located in Kot Mehmood to Barkat Ali's brothers and sister. However, the widow was left in exclusive possession of the property located in Sharqpur. She died on 10 January 1984. After her death, a portion of her property mutated through a will in favour of some mosques, while the remainder was inherited by her brother, Muhammad Ibrahim.

After the death of the widow, Barkat Ali's brothers and sister along with their legal heirs brought a suit. They claimed that the will dated 24 September 1952 was not valid as Barkat Ali had revoked the same through a sale transaction dated 16 August 1954 by disposing of a part of his property. Moreover, as the legal heirs did not extend their consent to the will, it was liable to be considered ineffective. Furthermore, any transaction made under this will should be declared to be of no legal effect. In fact, only one transaction, that is, transferring land to the widow was purportedly carried out under the will. Therefore, the main relief claimed by them was that all properties of Barkat Ali should have been transferred under the Islamic law of inheritance by considering the will as revoked. Their suit was decreed and the same was upheld by the first Appellate Court.

In this context, Muhammad Ibrahim filed a revision petition before the High Court as he was the one who lost substantially because of the decision of the lower courts. It was argued that first, the suit was barred by limitation; and second, the will dated 24 September 1952 was confirmed by the consent of the legal heirs vide an agreement dated 4 October 1958. Hence, the decision was not sustainable under the law.

The court held that the contention of limitation was of no avail because possession of some co-heirs was considered a joint possession of all. As far as the other contention was concerned, the court held that since Barkat Ali, by disposing of a part of his property during his lifetime revoked the will relied upon by Muhammad Ibrahim, there was no question as to its confirmation by consent of legal heirs at any subsequent date. Once the will was revoked, the properties owned by Barkat Ali devolved upon his legal heirs in accordance with the law of inheritance immediately upon his death. Hence, the court dismissed the instant revision.

10.3.5 Mandatory Will. Under Islamic law, orphaned grandchildren are not legal heirs in the presence of other male offspring of the deceased grandparent. Section 4 of the Muslim Family Laws Ordinance 1961 (MFLO) was enacted to address this lacuna. The law states that the deceased parent of the orphaned grandchildren will be considered alive for the calculation of his/her share in inheritance and thereafter, that share will be distributed among the orphaned grandchildren. In some Muslim countries the doctrine of 'mandatory will' has been devised through legislation to address the disinheritance of grandchildren. The Federal Shariat Court in the following case considered the possibility of transplanting this doctrine in Pakistan. The court declared section 4 of the MFLO 1961 repugnant to the Injunctions of Islam and proposed to replace it with the doctrine of 'mandatory will'. Section 4 of the MFLO is still a valid law because an appeal against this decision has been pending in the Shariat Appellate Bench of the Supreme Court of Pakistan since 2000.

Allah Rakha v Federation of Pakistan PLD 2000 FSC 1

Property may be disposed of compulsorily by a mandatory will enacted through a legislative instrument.

In this case, the petitioner challenged numerous provisions of the Muslim Family Laws Ordinance 1961 for being against the Injunctions of Islam. We shall focus only on section 4 of the MFLO relating to the inheritance of orphaned grandchildren.

The MFLO was enacted after considering the recommendations of the Marriage and Family Law Commission constituted in 1955 to review and revise Islamic family law in Pakistan. Regarding Islamic inheritance law, the Commission observed that the disinheritance of orphaned grandchildren in the presence of their uncles and aunts was flagrant injustice which should be remedied by promulgating an appropriate law. The Commission suggested that the rule of representation could be employed to grant the orphaned grandchildren a share in inheritance by putting them in the shoes of their deceased parents. The Commission pointed out that there was neither any Qur'anic Injunction nor authoritative provision in the Sunnah prohibiting this arrangement to protect the rights of orphaned grandchildren in inheritance. Consequently, the law was enacted in 1961. Although the law was not welcomed by the majority of Muslim scholars due to its alleged repugnancy to traditional Islamic law, nonetheless it remained in force for more than three decades, as it was protected from Islamic judicial review under the Constitution of Pakistan 1973.

The Federal Shariat Court reviewed the MFLO after expanding its jurisdiction through a novel interpretation of the various provisions of the Constitution. After analysing section 4 of the MFLO and the rationale behind it as provided in the report of the Commission, the court held that this section violated the Injunctions of Islam and, therefore, it should be amended. The court was of the view that this section, though based on the concept of compassion and kindness tended to turn the entire structure of Islamic inheritance law upside down. Thereafter, the court delved into the analysis of various alternatives for substituting section 4 of the MFLO and put its weight in favour of the 'mandatory will'.

One of the reports of the Council of Islamic Ideology with respect to section 4 of the MFLO suggested that the uncles and aunts of the orphaned grandchildren should be made responsible for taking care of them instead of giving the latter a share in the inheritance. If the uncles and aunts failed to perform their responsibility, a legislative provision sanctioning penal consequences might be enacted. The court observed that this suggestion was not appropriate as it went against the self-respect of the orphaned grandchildren.

Referring to Egypt and Kuwait, the court suggested that the doctrine of 'mandatory will' could be adopted as a suitable alternative to the representation rule owing to its consistency with Islamic Injunctions. According to this doctrine, the orphaned grandchildren would be entitled to 1/3rd of the estate or to the extent of their deceased parent's share under a mandatory will deemed to have been made in their favour at the time of the death of their grandparent. This alternative would not interfere with the Islamic structure of inheritance as sanctioned by the Qur'an and Sunnah of the Holy Prophet (PBUH). It would be supported by the Qur'anic principle enshrined in verse 2:180 for bequeathing some estate in favour of those near relatives who are unlikely to have any share through inheritance. This doctrine would not be inconsistent with the Islamic inheritance law as it would only be implemented as a will. After presenting the above analysis, the court left it open for the legislature to debate this alternative and enact a suitable provision as a substitute for section 4 of the MFLO.

It should be noted that since this decision of the Federal Shariat Court is pending adjudication before the Shariat Appellate Bench of the Supreme Court of Pakistan, section 4 of the MFLO is still a valid law. The suggestion of the court as to the 'mandatory will' seems plausible, but the court failed to address an important issue: how can a will, which is primarily a voluntary institution, be converted into a mandatory/compulsory transaction by virtue of a piece of the legislative instrument?

10.3.6 Enforcement of Wills

Malik Khan Muhammad alias Khanay v Moulvi Luqman 1993 CLC 1552 (Quetta)

Wills executed by Muslims are not to be enforced or regulated under the Succession Act of 1925.

This case establishes the principle that wills executed by Muslims are not to be enforced or regulated under the Succession Act 1925. Respondent no. 1, Maulvi Luqman filed a civil suit before Qazi Bori Sinjavi in Loralai for a declaration and permanent injunction to the extent of one-third share of the landed property owned by the late Muhammad Rasool. He averred that Muhammad Rasool executed a will in his favour bestowing the property to the extent of one-third on the condition that after his death the respondent will perform spiritual rites on his behalf. The defendant/appellant contested the suit. In his written statement, the defendant stated that he himself is in possession of a will executed by Muhammad Rasool in his favour and denied the existence of any other will. During the examination of one of the respondent no. 1's witnesses, the defendant made an application mentioning therein that if the said witness made his statement on the Qur'an, then the suit be decreed. Respondent no. 1 agreed to it and the witness recorded his statement on the Qur'an. Consequently, the trial court decreed the suit.

The defendant subsequently filed an appeal, which was dismissed. Instant proceedings have been initiated challenging both the judgments and decrees passed by the trial and the Appellate Court.

The appellant's counsel contended that in view of the provisions of sections 211 and 213 of the Succession Act 1925, the court of *qazi* functioning under the Balochistan Shariat Application Regulation 1976, did not have the jurisdiction to adjudicate upon the matter. Respondent no. 1's counsel countered this argument by stating that sections 211 and 213 of the Succession Act 1925 were not applicable in the cases where the parties were Muslims because their cases were to be decided according to Muslim Personal Law. Justice Iftikhar Muhammad Chaudhry, as he then was, observed:

> As far as Wills executed by Muhammadans [Muslims] are concerned these are not to be enforced or regularized under the various provisions of [the] Succession Act, 1925, in view of section 58 of the Act, because under the principles of Muslim Personal Law a Muhammadan [Muslim] has been authorized to make a Will in any form i.e. oral or written and if it is in writing it need not be attested nor a probate thereof is required to be obtained from the competent Court of jurisdiction.[12]

In light of the above discussion, it was held that sections 211 and 213 of the Succession Act 1925 have no relevance in matters where a Muslim has executed a will.

10.4 Conclusion

Will, an important instrument for disposing of property, holds a distinct position in Islamic law. To some extent, a will is similar to a *hiba* as a testator may pronounce it *inter vivos*. While in another respect, it is akin to inheritance as its implementation is deferred until the death of a testator. However, the restrictions placed on testators' testamentary powers make it a unique transaction. Its importance is highlighted in cases where it is used to transfer property to orphaned grandchildren, adopted children, foster children, and foster parents who have a close and affectionate relationship with the deceased but are not entitled to inherit as legal heirs. In this way, such a will plays a dynamic function in making the law protective and considerate of such relations.

It is an established legal principle that a person cannot bequeath more than one-third of his estate to a non-legal heir without the consent of other legal heirs. However, in the case of a bequest to a legal heir, even a bequest to the extent of one-third of the estate requires the consent of other legal heirs under Sunni law. Such consent must be voluntary and cannot be implied from the silence of legal heirs. This requirement protects the rights of inheritance of legal heirs from being adversely affected by way of a will. Furthermore, a testator can revoke a will at any time during his life; such revocation can be through express declaration, or it can be implied through his conduct.

The legislature and judiciary in Pakistan have struggled to protect the interests of orphaned grandchildren. In its landmark judgment in the *Allah Rakha* case, the Federal Shariat Court suggested the adoption of the doctrine of a 'mandatory will' to the extent of one-third of the property in favour of orphaned grandchildren. It declared section 4 of the MFLO as repugnant to the Injunctions of Islam. This section provides orphaned grandchildren with a right to inheritance to the extent of the share of their parents in inheritance. An appeal against this decision is still pending before the Shariat Appellate Bench of the Supreme Court of Pakistan. Therefore, section 4 of the Muslim Family Laws Ordinance 1961 continues to be a valid law until the appeal is decided.

Questions

1. Write a detailed note on testamentary powers under Islamic law.
2. How is a will proved and interpreted in court?
3. Can a testator revoke his will, if yes, how? Does a prospective beneficiary have a right to prevent modification and revocation of a will adversely affecting his future share?
4. Why does Islamic law impose restrictions on testamentary powers of a testator and how can such restrictions be circumvented?
5. What is the concept of 'mandatory will'? Should it be incorporated into the MFLO in place of its section 4 to protect the inheritance rights of orphaned grandchildren but without affecting the inheritance rights of other legal heirs?
6. Under section 4 of the Muslim Family Laws Ordinance 1961, orphaned grandchildren are entitled to the share of their predeceased parents. The Federal Shariat Court declared this section repugnant to the Injunctions of Islam. Critically analyse this issue in the light of juristic opinions, recommendations of the Marriage and Family Law Commission Report 1956, and case law.

Further Reading

Articles

Carroll, L., 'Orphaned Grandchildren in Islamic Law of Succession: Reform and Islamization in Pakistan', *Islamic Law and Society* (1998) 5(3), 409–47.

Carroll, L., 'The Pakistan Federal Shariat Court, Section 4 of the Muslim Family Laws Ordinance, and the Orphaned Grandchild', *Islamic Law and Society* (2002) 9(1), 70–82.

Munir, M., 'The Share of Orphaned Grandchildren under Islamic Law and Pakistani Legal System: A Re-evaluation of Representational Succession in Section 4 and Its (Mis) interpretation by Courts', *The Asian Yearbook of Human Rights and Humanitarian Law* (2018) 2, 95–116.

Cases

Muhammad Akbar Shah v Muhammad Yusuf Shah PLD 1964 SC 329 (A testator must be of a sound disposing mind at the time of executing a will. A sound disposing mind means the capacity to comprehend the nature and effect of the will that the person concerned is executing. A paralysis attack may affect the intellect of a person to some extent, but it does not necessarily prevent the existence of a sound disposing mind, making a person unable to understand his affairs or incapable of transacting business or of executing a will for that matter.)

Raj Bibi v Mst Shahzadi PLD 2003 Quetta 53 (A bequest to an heir is not valid unless other heirs consent to it after the death of the testator, whereas, any single heir may consent so as to bind his/her own share only. Also, a bequest with a condition which derogates from the completeness of the grant takes effect as if no condition was attached to it, for such a condition is deemed void.)

Sardar Bibi v Abdul Latif PLD 1952 Lah. 294 (A bequest can be revoked by implication. It may be revoked by the extinction of the proprietary right of the testator, for example, if he gifts away the entire subject matter of the will.)

Shahnaz Begum v Additional District Judge PLD 2021 Lah 69 (Upon the discretion of the court, a succession certificate may be granted to those legal heirs who may have a prima facie title subject to the furnishing of bond with sureties equal to the sum likely to be drawn under the said succession certificate.)

Srimati Priyabala Mazumdar v Nalini Mohan Mazaumdar PLD 1957 Dacca 513 (Those who benefit under a will and have been instrumental in preparing or obtaining the same, have the onus to prove the righteousness of the transaction. Where circumstances exciting suspicion of the court exist, it is for those who propound the will to prove affirmatively that the testator knew and approved the contents of the document. It is only when this is done that the burden of proof shifts on those opposing the will to prove fraud, undue influence, or whatever ground they rely upon.)

Notes

1. Imam Abu Dawud Sulaiman bin al-Ash'ath Sijistani, *Sunnan Abu Dawud*, vol. 2, Book 11, Hadith No. 2864 (Ahmad Hasan tr, Lahore: Sh Muhammad Ashraf Publishers and Booksellers, 1984), 808.
2. Muhammad bin Ismail al-Bukhari, *Sahih al-Bukhari*, vol. 8, Book 80, Hadith Number 725 (Dr Muhammad Muhsin Khan tr, Lahore: Kazi Publications, 1979), 477.
3. PLD 1970 Kar 450, 451.
4. The judge quoted from the Privy Council decision in *Baboo Beer Partab v Maharajah Rajender Pertab* (1867) 12 MIA 1.
5. Whether Fatima Jinnah and Mohammad Ali Jinnah were Shias or Sunnis was left to be decided in other suits. For details, see *Hussain v Mansoor Ali* PLD 1977 Kar 320 and *Amir Ali v Gul Shaker* PLD 1985 Kar 365.
6. 2007 CLC 167, 170–71.
7. 1987 CLC 7, 10.
8. 1996 CLC 916, 932.
9. 2002 YLR 2895, 2901.
10. Ibid., 2902.
11. PLD 1964 Lah 451.
12. 1993 CLC 1552, 1554.

11

DEATH ILLNESS GIFTS

11.1 Introduction

Death illness (*marz-ul-maut*) is a malady which induces an apprehension of death in the person suffering from it and which eventually results in his/her death. Death-illness or death bed gift is made in contemplation of death, and it falls in between the categories of gift (*hiba*) and will. For its validity, the essentials of a gift are required to be fulfilled whereas its consequences resemble a will. Just like a gift (*hiba*), a death illness gift is not valid unless the gifted property is delivered to the donee. At the same time, a death illness gift is subjected to two limitations of a will. First, it cannot comprise more than one-third estate of a donor after the payment of debts and funeral charges unless the legal heirs give their consent and second, it is invalid in favour of a legal heir unless other legal heirs give their consent after the death of the donor. Under Shia law, the second limitation does not apply, and a death illness gift can be made in favour of a legal heir without the consent of other legal heirs as long as it does not exceed one-third of the estate of the donor. Under Sunni law, the consent of legal heirs can only be extended after the death of the donor while under Shia law such consent can be given during the lifetime of the donor or after his/her death.[1]

According to the Maliki school, one of the four Sunni schools, death illness gifts are invalid.[2] An important authoritative book in Shia law titled *Jama-ush-Shattat* quoted by Ameer Ali states that death illness gifts will not be reduced to one-third of an estate provided the possession was transferred to the donee and the donor was in his/her senses.[3] On the other hand, another authoritative book of Shia law namely *Sharaya* describes the impact of death illness in line with the Hanafi school, i.e. without the consent of legal heirs, the gift will be reduced to one-third of the estate.[4] This last position was followed by the courts in British India.[5]

11.2 Death Illness or *Marz-ul-Maut*

Whether a particular illness can be termed as *marz-ul-maut* is a mixed question of law and fact.[6] According to Ameer Ali,

> [u]nder the Hanafi law, the term *Marz-ul-Maut* is applicable not only to diseases which actually cause death, but to diseases from which it is probable that death will ensue, so as to engender in the person affected with the disease an apprehension of death.[7]

The same author explains with reference to cases decided by British Indian High Courts that where a malady is of a long continuance or it has lasted over a year and there is no immediate apprehension of death, a sick person can dispose of his entire estate by way of gift.[8] Mahomed Ullah has summarised some cases of the British Indian era to highlight that a disease with which a sick person is accustomed and that does not imminently cause apprehension of death cannot be considered as *marz-ul-maut*, e.g. long-standing trouble of asthma, any long lingering disease, albuminuria for longer than a year, bursting of a blood vessel, and paralysis.[9] Pre-condition of one year period is mentioned in various law books as a constituent element for ascertaining a death illness, it was pointed out that it 'does not lay down any hard and fast rule regarding the character of illness; it only indicates that a continuance of the malady for that length of time may be regarded as taking it out of the category of a mortal illness.'[10]

In *Fatima Bibee v Ahmad Baksh*,[11] the court observed that according to Muhammadan law, three conditions are necessary to constitute *marz-ul-maut* or death illness: (a) illness, (b) expectation of fatal issue, and (c) certain physical incapacities that indicate the degree of the illness. The second condition cannot be presumed to exist when the first and the third conditions are ascertainable. For instance, if a person does not expect to die in a particular state of health though he could not stand up to say his prayers. With reference to one year rule, the court noted that ordinarily a malady lasting more than a year is considered to be of long continuance that does not immediately engender an apprehension of death. However, if sickness increases to give rise to an apprehension of death in the mind of the donor that increase may be treated as death illness.

The Bombay High Court laid down the following conditions for constituting the death illness:

a. Proximate danger of death so that there is a preponderance of *khauf* or apprehension that at the given time death must be more probable than life.
b. There must be some degree of subjective apprehension of death in the mind of the sick person.
c. There must be some external indicia, chief among which is the inability to attend to ordinary avocations.[12]

Pregnancy *per se* is not considered a death illness,[13] but actual pains of childbirth may be treated as *marz-ul-maut*.[14]

While defining *marz-ul-maut*, an emphasis is placed on the 'subjective apprehension of death' by the donor. The eminent Muslim jurist, Abdur Rahim, disagrees with this and argues:

> [i]t is [a] cardinal principle of Muhammadan jurisprudence that the law takes note only of perceptible facts. The original authorities do not lay down that the fear entertained by the sick man himself form[s] any criterion of death-illness. In fact, it is an event of nature, the character of which cannot depend upon what the patient might think of it. The law in placing an embargo on a sick person's juristic acts puts it on the ground of illness, and not on the apprehension of death by the sick man. The reason or motive underlying the law is that illness weakens a man's physical and mental powers, and he is likely, as experience shows, to act under such circumstances to the detriment of his spiritual interests by disappointing his heirs in their just expectations. But this is a general presumption on which the law on the point is founded and according to the principles of Muhammadan jurisprudence, it is not to be proved as a fact in each particular case.[15]

In some of the cases referred below and more particularly judicial opinions expressed by Justice B.Z. Kaikaus lay emphasis on the subjective element of death illness, i.e. apprehension of death in the mind of the donor. He argues that what has been accumulated under the doctrine of death illness beyond the sole essential primarily belongs to the domain of the law of evidence. On the other hand, we have the view of Abdur Rahim criticizing those who have underlined the subjective element in this regard and downplayed the objective aspect of death illness. He is of the opinion that without external manifestation of the subjective element, the law could not be applied.

The way in which the doctrine of death illness has evolved in British India and then in Pakistan, it takes into account both subjective and objective/external elements: though the principal element is subjective, the rules of evidence forming the objective element have been so interwoven with it that no other manner can be devised to ascertain the existence of the subjective element. Hence, both elements have their own significance and salience in the determination of death illness and any one of them should not be over-evaluated so as to downplay the importance of the other.

11.2.1 Disease Which Comes Under *Marz-ul-Maut*. The first condition for *marz-ul-maut* is that the donor or testator must be sick or ill. The determination of the *marz-ul-maut* is a question of fact and varies in every case. However, the apprehension of death is the major test and factor in determining *marz-ul-maut*. In modern days, there are many diseases and one can die from cold or cancer, which are both very different. In addition, there is no condition that a sick person should be confined to bed, but a sick person should not be able to attend day-to-day avocations. With advancement and technology in medicine it is noticed that the life period is increased, therefore, one year rule should carefully be applied when sickness has become mortal. To determine whether a sickness is mortal or not is a question of fact and should be determined by the physician on a case-to-case basis to apply the doctrine of *marz-ul-maut*.

One must be careful that simple disease like blood pressure does not fall under the umbrella of mortal diseases because it can be cured by ordinary medication. In addition, the diseases like asthma, diabetes, and paralysis cannot be categorised as mortal diseases unless the condition becomes very serious and medical recovery becomes extremely narrow. In *Raja Nazar Hussain v Nawazish Ali* 2016 YLRN 46, the Lahore High Court held that a donor who died of fever could not be said to be suffering from *marz-ul-maut*. In *Muhammad Gulshere K.V. Mariyam B* (1881) 3 All 73, it was ruled that 'long and lingering diseases which makes the person familiar to the effects over a period of more than one year, which ultimately dilutes the apprehension of death cannot be considered as a sickness for *marz-ul-maut*.' However, the diseases which lead to rapid consumption, galloping or pneumonia which render a person helpless are considered *marz-ul-maut*. For some contemporary Muslim jurists, the death sentence can be regarded as *marz-ul-maut*.[16]

11.2.2 Transaction with Consideration During Death Illness. The application of the doctrine of death illness is confined to transactions without consideration. It does not have any consequences for transactions which involve consideration. In *Ghulam Mustafa v Hurmat*,[17] it was held that the provisions of Mahomedan law applicable to gifts made by persons labouring under a fatal disease do not apply to a so-called gift made in lieu of dower debt, which is really in the nature of a sale.[18] But if a transaction is in reality a gift though concluded in a manner to give an impression of sale, then it is to be governed by the doctrine of death illness.[19]

11.2.3 Debt-Related Acknowledgement/Release During Death Illness. According to D.F. Mulla, debt can be acknowledged by any person at any stage of his life including death illness. Acknowledgements of debt made during health and those confirmed by independent evidence are preferred over those made during death illness. However, an acknowledgement of a debt made during death illness in favour of an heir is no proof at all of the debt, and no effect can be given to it.[20]

A person may lawfully acknowledge a debt in favour of a person who is not an heir even to the extent of his entire estate.[21] Under Islamic law, debts are paid before the execution of legacies and distribution of inheritance. Considering the importance of debts, some unblemished evidence should confirm the existence of debt. But if a debt is spoken of by a terminally ill person without any independent confirmation, it raises questions as to the very existence of a debt.

Death illness acknowledgement of debt similar to death illness gift assumes that the architect of the transaction might not be in a fit state of mind to exercise his proprietary rights rationally and he might be motivated to unduly enrich someone and deprive other expectant heirs. Such considerations necessitate that some sort of embargos should be imposed to safeguard the rights of expectant heirs, though it is not legally mandatory to prove the existence of any of the above considerations in case of a death illness acknowledgement.

If someone has acknowledged a debt during death illness which is not proved by any other evidence, there is a probability that such acknowledgement might be fictitious or unrealistically proffered with the sole object of benefitting the so-called creditor. Hence, such debts which were acknowledged and proved to have been due against the acknowledger before death illness must be discharged before reverting to death illness acknowledgements of debt. But if the beneficiary of death illness acknowledgement is an heir and there is no other evidence except an acknowledgement, then such acknowledgement will not be implemented unless assented to by other heirs.[22] However, under Shia law, an acknowledgement of debt in death illness in favour of an heir is valid to the extent of one-third of the estate even without the consent of other legal heirs.[23]

A release of debt during death illness is lawful and implemented to the extent of bequeathable one-third of the estate.[24] But if a release of debt exceeds one-third and the same is confirmed by other independent evidence, it can be enforced.

This area of Muslim law can be appreciated well if divided into two: (i) one dealing with the principles and (ii) the other related to procedure which mainly comprises rules of evidence. So far as the principles are concerned, there is no prohibition on the acknowledgement of debt during death illness. In the absence of any other proof, an acknowledgement in favour of an heir is similar to a testamentary transaction, i.e. will, which is subject to consent by other heirs and that too to the extent of one-third. It is within the domain of the law of evidence to protect debts proved by independent evidence in comparison to those debts which are dependent on the acknowledgement of a terminally ill person exclusively. Hence, the first category of debt is preferred over the latter.

11.3 Outline of Case Law

11.3.1 Nature of Death Illness

Shamshad Ali Shah v Syed Hassan Shah PLD 1964 SC 143

The most important pre-requisite for determining a death illness is that the transaction should be made under the pressure of the imminence of death.

The donor (mother/grandmother/mother-in-law of the parties) gifted her property to some legal heirs excluding the others. The alleged gift was made on 18 December 1939, and its registration was completed on 21 December 1939. After a couple of hours from the registration process, the donor breathed her last and died. The donor was then 65 years of age and suffering from pneumonia. According to one of the witnesses, she was extremely weak at the time of the execution of the gift deed and was lying on a cot.

Two important points with respect to death illness gift were debated in detail in the judgment: first, if a death illness gift is not accompanied by delivery of possession, it will be considered void *ab initio*, and second, what is the criterion for determining *marz-ul-maut*. Considering the individual circumstances of the donor, the court concluded that she was on death bed at the time of making the gift, and the non-delivery of possession has rendered the alleged gift illegitimate. The counsel representing the appellants drew the attention of the court to the diversity of opinion on the delivery of possession in the Shia school to which the parties belonged. However, the court noted that this controversy had been settled in favour of the perspective emphasising on delivery of possession as an essential element of a death illness gift fifty years ago by the Allahabad High Court, and it did not see any justification to get into that debate once again.

The Supreme Court of Pakistan, relying upon a decision of the Privy Council,[25] summarised the criteria for treating a gift as made during *marz-ul-maut*:

1. 'Was the donor suffering at the time of gift from a disease which was the immediate cause of his death?
2. Was the disease of such a nature or character as to induce in the person suffering the belief that death would be caused thereby, or engender in him the apprehension of death?
3. Was the illness such as to incapacitate him from the pursuit of his ordinary avocations—a circumstance which might create in the mind of [the] sufferer an apprehension of death?
4. Had the illness continued for such a length of time as to remove or lessen the apprehension of immediate fatality or to accustom the sufferer from the malady?'[26]

Justice B.Z. Kaikaus wrote his independent note raising some pertinent points to ponder as to a gift made during death illness. According to him, the sole requisite of such gifts is that they should be made 'under the pressure of the sense of imminence of death'. The rest of the jurisprudence developed around the subject of *marz-ul-maut* primarily falls within the domain of the law of evidence, i.e. how to ascertain that a particular person is suffering from death illness. Justice Kaikaus noted, according to some commentaries on the subject, that the person should eventually die from the illness which has caused him apprehension of death. However, while expressing his unwillingness to agree with this proposition he wrote:

> [i]f a person was suffering from galloping tuberculosis and was therefore under apprehension of death when he made the gift, but he was shot dead by some person or died of an accident, or of cholera or some other epidemic a short time after the gift, I do not see why the doctrine of *marz-ul-maut* should not be applicable.[27]

He further extended his emphasis on the pre-eminence of the subjective element in death illness to its logical conclusion by saying:

> [t]ruly speaking even the fact that a person survives and does not die at all should not validate a gift which he made under apprehension of death. The validity of the gift is to be determined with reference to the circumstances as they exist at the time of making the gift. Subsequent failure to die cannot have a retrospective effect, so as to validate an invalid transaction… The reason why a gift in *marz-ul-maut* operates as a will is that the intention is to make a testamentary alienation only.[28]

Hussain Jan v Asmat Begum PLD 1964 SC173

Apprehension of death in the mind of the donor is the sole determining factor of death illness and that is to be proved by circumstantial evidence in each and every case. The rules relating to non-attending daily avocations and not more than one year of prolonged illness are basic rules of evidence.

A transaction of gift was made by a donor thirteen days before his death. The gift was in favour of the donor's mother to the exclusion of his sister, wife, and daughter. The wife was living separately due to some domestic issues and the daughter was born a few days before his death about which the donor was kept ignorant. The donor was suffering from tuberculosis, and according to one of the doctors who attended him in the sanatorium he was in a 'hopeless' condition. The condition of the donor, as per another doctor, was that he was unable to move, and the sub-registrar was brought to the house for the registration of the gift deed.

The daughter (Asmat Begum) initiated the suit for acquiring a half share in her father's property against her grandmother, her father's sister, and her mother. The suit was not decided in her favour in the subordinate courts, but the High Court declared the transaction of gift to the grandmother as a death illness gift, against which this appeal was filed in the Supreme Court.

Dismissing the appeal, speaking on behalf of the court Justice B.Z. Kaikaus held that direct evidence as to the apprehension of death, which is the sole determinant for death illness transaction, cannot be procured due to the deceased's death. Therefore, the court has to rely on circumstantial evidence only. The court further held:

> no hard and fast rule can be laid down as to when such a state of mind can be inferred and every case has to be decided on its own facts… It is

> said for instance that in order that a malady may be a death-illness the patient should be unable to attend to his ordinary avocations. It should be understood that the fact which is to be established in accordance with Muslim Law is only the apprehension of death resulting from a malady and any other proposition laid down in judgments as to the circumstances which establish death-illness is really a proposition relating to evidence. It is not impossible to conceive of a malady in which the patient can till last carry on his avocations particularly when those avocations do not call for various physical effort[s].[29]

The court further clarified that the extended duration of malady is not treated as death illness because the apprehension it has generated in the beginning would gradually disappear and the patient would become accustomed to such illness. This rule does not relate to the doctrine of *marz-ul-maut*, in reality, it is relevant for proof of the apprehension of death according to the learned judge. In short, the court emphasised the subjective criterion for the ascertainment of *marz-ul-maut* and termed the main objective markers (such as non-attending to daily avocations and prolonged illness) as rules pertaining to evidence and proof, primarily.

Shahbaz v Ali Begum 1988 CLC 1507 [Lahore]

An illness that does not cause an apprehension of imminent death is not a death illness.

In this case, the deceased donor, who was aged 60 years, gifted his property to his daughters to the exclusion of his brothers and sisters (collaterals). The plaintiffs/appellants questioned the transaction on the ground that the donor was suffering from death illness, so his gift could not be implemented beyond one-third of his estate. The revenue authorities got the statement of the donor recorded through a local commissioner, and at the time of making his statement, he was in his senses and sound disposing mind. The plaintiff was present during the visit of the local commissioner, but he did not object to the transaction made by the donor on the ground that the donor suffered from death illness. It is pertinent to mention that the donor died before the completion of the official formalities of the gift. As per the register of deaths, his death occurred due to fever. Furthermore, there was no evidence that the donor before his death had been treated for some serious illness by any doctor or *hakeem* (traditional medical practitioner).

The Lahore High Court did not find the alleged transaction to be afflicted with the doctrine of death illness. The court's decision was characterised by two kinds of arguments. The first pertained to the nature of the legal obligation on plaintiffs for proving death illness, and the other nature of death illness itself.

With respect to the first, the court pointed out that the plaintiffs were under a legal obligation to produce evidence establishing that the donor was labouring under serious and imminent apprehension of death at the time of making the alleged transaction. This responsibility has to be discharged by them independently, and they could not be given the benefit of any lapse in the evidence produced by the beneficiaries of the alleged death illness transaction.

With respect to the second, the Lahore High Court observed that all diseases did not qualify to be treated as death illness. *Marz-ul-maut* means 'the disease of death' or 'the disease which causes death'...

> In order to constitute a disease as "the disease of death", [the] following conditions are necessary:
>
> i. The illness must cause the death of the diseased,
> ii. The illness must cause apprehension of death in the mind of the diseased,
> iii. There must be some external indicia of a serious illness.[30]

The court further observed:

> objective consideration of external indicia of the deceased suffered may provide an important clue to the subjective consideration of the mind of its sufferer. Mere weakness or immobility would not necessarily import death malady.[31]

Chiragh Bibi v Karim Bakhsh 1987 MLD 3055 [Lahore]

If a person was not in imminent danger of death despite being bedridden, his gift is not termed as a death illness gift.

In this case, the donor made a gift to his nephew and son-in-law on 17 January 1956 and died on 26 December 1957. The donor remained bedridden for almost three years, but his disease worsened only two months prior to his death. He was additionally afflicted with some pain in his ankle.

The trial court concluded that the gift was completed by delivery of possession, but it was only effective to the extent of one-third of the estate because the donor was apprehending imminent death at the time of making it. The first appellate court reversed the decision on this last point and found no evidence to substantiate it. It led to the second appeal before the high court.

The high court found itself in agreement with the first appellate court while observing that pain in the ankle was not of that nature to reduce the gift to the prescribed extent of one-third of the donor's estate. The court highlighted the facts of the prolonged nature of the donor's illness and that the transaction was made two years before his death. It observed that '[i]n such a situation, feeling of imminent danger of death is not usually entertained by the person concerned unless some event has aggravated the illness to give rise to such feeling.'[32] Hence, the main essential of the death illness, i.e. the apprehension of death, was not ascertainable at the time of making the gift.

11.3.2. Death Illness and Burden of Proof. The party alleging that the gift was made during death illness is under an obligation to prove that the donor was under the pressure of imminent death at the relevant time, and mere old age of the donor without positive evidence as to his apprehension of death would not lead to an inference that the transaction was actually made during death illness. Sometimes peculiar knowledge of the beneficiary of the death illness gift may oblige him/her, particularly under suspicious circumstances, to prove that the donor was not afflicted with the death illness.

Chanan Bibi v Muhammad Shafi PLD 1977 SC 28

Old age and illness, such as paralysis, are not *per se* sufficient to draw a conclusion that the donor was suffering from fear of imminent death: the fact of his apprehension of death is required to be proved with evidence.

In this case, the donor had suffered paralysis that rendered him bedridden and immobile, but it did not injuriously affect his mental capabilities. According to the evidence adduced by the sub-registrar, sub-treasurer and vendor of the stamp papers, the donor was in a fit and healthy state of mind at the time of execution of the gift deed. At the stage of the trial court, it was erroneously assumed that paralysis *per se* was enough to cause an apprehension of death as if it was a proposition of law to be followed without requiring any evidence like other questions of law. This approach was not approved by the high court against which the matter was brought before the Supreme Court.

The Supreme Court made some important observations relating to the doctrine of *marz-ul-maut*. It was pronounced that the ascertainment of an apprehension of imminent death is in reality a question of fact and that should be determined on the basis of evidence. And the one who has asserted the death illness and resulting apprehension of death has to prove the same with convincing evidence. Moreover, considering the difficulty to produce direct evidence on the apprehension of death in the mind of a donor in all circumstances, the court held that inference is to be drawn from available evidence, and the issue of whether an accurate inference has been drawn is an issue of law or at least mixed issue of law and fact. So, a court may inquire into the propriety of inference/s in a given situation.

The court held that if the donor was suffering from paralysis, his actual medical condition has to be proved by the evidence of someone who belonged to the medical profession. In this case, it was asserted that the donor was treated by a *hakeem*, but he was not produced to give evidence, nor any other medical attendant came before the court. On the other hand, there was evidence from some official personnel mentioned above that the donor was in a proper state of mind which had a presumption of regularity on its side unless rebutted by cogent evidence.

The court also noted that a donor's illness which was confined to his physical health and did not bear any adverse impact on his mental faculty, and that physical infirmity might become a constitutive part of the donor's being progressively making him learn how to live with it. Consequently, it was bound to alleviate the apprehension that might have arisen at the beginning of such illness. The court held that merely mentioning in the recital that the donor was an ailing person and intended to make a gift in favour of the donees with an object to avoid future dispute could not be read to generate an absolute inference that the donor had an apprehension of imminent death. In short, the court concluded that old age and ailment simpliciter could not necessarily engender an apprehension of death in the mind of a donor and convert a transaction as carried out during death illness.

Mst. Pathani v Ramzan 1999 MLD 3374 [Lahore]

The proximity of the death of a donor with the transaction of the gift does not absolve a complainant/plaintiff to produce positive evidence as to his apprehension of death.

The donor died five days after making an oral gift to his sole daughter who is the appellant in the present case. The revenue official who recorded the oral gift deposed that he was in a fit state of mind at the time of making the statement. However, the respondents in the present case did not produce a medical certificate or any other kind of evidence to discharge their burden to establish the main constitutive element of death illness, i.e. an apprehension of imminent death. Despite such an important lapse in the evidence of the respondents, the courts below, taking into account the sole fact of the death of the donor five days after his making of an oral gift, held it as invalid.

As per the rules of evidence, the burden to invalidate a gift on the basis of death illness is on the party challenging it. In the instant case, the evidence of the revenue official about the donor's fit state of mind duly supported by other witnesses was sufficient to set aside the decision of the subordinate courts. In this background, the high court observed that the subordinate courts had committed an error of law by declaring the gift invalid without discharging the burden of proof by the plaintiffs/respondents. It further underscored that under the doctrine of death illness, mental incapacity was more important and far more consequential than physical incapacity: if despite physical incapacity the donor was taking intelligent decisions, they could not be subjected to the restrictions imposed under the doctrine of death illness.

Saleem Akhtar v Muhammad Ashraf PLD 1997 SC 308

Under special circumstances, a conclusion may be drawn with the support of evidence produced on behalf of the donee that the donor was suffering from an imminent fear of death in case the complainant/plaintiff could not exclusively discharge his primary burden.

It is a settled rule of evidence that the burden of producing evidence as to the apprehension of death of a donor while making a gift during death illness primarily lies on the party asserting so. However, exceptionally, this burden may be shared by the other party to absolve the complainant/plaintiff from producing evidence of such nature exclusively. The present case is a good illustration of this phenomenon.

The donor/deceased was left alone in his village by his children and wife (plaintiffs/respondents), who were tired of his illness. He was then taken care of by his maternal nephews (defendants/petitioners), who rendered services to the deceased till his death. Before 16/17 days of his death, the deceased executed a gift deed of his property in favour of his nephews.

The plaintiffs instituted a declaration suit for getting the gift deed as void and illegal. It was specifically averred in the plaint that the donor was suffering from death illness at the time of the transaction. The same was admitted by the donees in the written statement that the deceased fell ill in the later part of his life. On the basis of the pleadings and evidence, all courts below treated the transaction as a death illness gift and reduced the entitlement of the donees to the extent of one-third of the suit property. Against this background, a leave to appeal was filed in the Supreme Court which was turned down affirming the earlier decisions.

Two important points were raised on behalf of the donees in the apex court. Firstly, no specific issue was framed by the trial court pertaining to the death illness of the donor, and secondly, the burden of proving that the gift was executed during the death illness was on the plaintiffs which they could not discharge. So far as the first objection was concerned, the court highlighted that both parties were sufficiently aware of the nature of the dispute and that awareness reflected not only in their pleadings but also in their evidence, particularly in cross-examination. Hence, the non-framing of specific issues has not caused any prejudice to the donees' case/defence. With respect to the burden of proof on the plaintiffs, the court pointed out that at the time of his death, the deceased was in the custody and care of his maternal nephews, and they could have special knowledge as to the nature of his illness and the circumstances of his death. And they in their evidence spoke as to the deceased's illness which was ample to support that the donor at the time of the transaction was suffering from death illness. Therefore, in the face of such evidence, the plaintiffs cannot be burdened to establish the death illness of the donor independently of the donees' evidence.

Mst. Sharifan Mai v Khuda Bakhsh 2022 YLR 147 (Lah)

Whosoever contends that the donor was suffering from *marz-ul-maut*, the onus to prove rests on him.

This case deals with the gift made by the husband to his wife. The petitioner, Mst Sharifan Mai, filed a suit for a declaration that she was the legally wedded wife of Imam Bakhsh and was entitled to her share in his estate. She also claimed that the property delivered to her as a dower through a deed belonged to her. The respondents, sons and daughters of the deceased's brothers and sisters, contested the claim on the basis that Imam Bakhsh was suffering from cancer which constituted *marz-ul-maut*. Therefore, the alleged dower deed had no legal effect. The trial court framed necessary issues and ruled in favour of the petitioner. The respondents appealed and the order of the trial court was reversed; therefore, the petitioner brought the matter before the Lahore High Court through a revision petition.

The counsel for the petitioner contended that the petitioner had proved the gift through cogent and reliable evidence, whereas the defendants had failed to prove that Imam Bakhsh was a cancer patient and was suffering from *marz-ul-maut*. In addition, the dower was debt and that was to be paid from the estate of the deceased. In addition to the contention of *marz-ul-maut*, the respondents' counsel argued that the alleged gift was not registered so it should be declared void.

In light of these facts, there were two legal questions before the High Court: (i) whether registration of the alleged transfer of land in lieu of dower was necessary under the Registration Act 1908, and (ii) whether Imam Bakhsh was suffering from *marz-ul-maut*. Justice Ahmad Nadeem observed that since the property was given as a gift in lieu of a dower, it constituted *Hiba Bil-iwaz*. Therefore, it was not necessary to register it. However, for the second question, the onus to prove that Imam Bakhsh was suffering from *marz-ul-maut* was on the alleging party, i.e., the respondents. They failed to prove that Imam Bakhsh was suffering from cancer or a fatal disease. Hence, the Lahore High Court accepted the revision petition and set aside the earlier order of the appellate court.

11.3.3 Death Illness and Undue Influence. A death illness transaction may prefer some at the cost of others, and in this context, it is likely to cause injustice to those who might have inherited under the law of inheritance had the transaction not been carried out. Furthermore, the doctrine of death illness assumes the lack of capacity of a donor due to the looming apprehension of death and prescribes that in such a situation, the gift must not take effect beyond one-third of the estate. It is pertinent to note that some common law rules which are similarly founded on the lack of capacity of a contracting party may have an effect of vitiating the transaction, e.g. undue influence. In both death illness and undue influence, a donor does not have the capacity to independently formulate his rational opinion for one reason or another and may not have independent advice for concluding a transaction: but in the former, his transaction is given effect to the extent of one-third of the estate, while in the latter the transaction is declared void. It is noteworthy that both of these pleas are generally argued together for vitiating a transaction, but the consequences that ensue are different in nature. Moreover, the burden of proof for establishing death illness is generally placed on the one who questions the transaction, whereas in case of undue influence, the beneficiary has to establish that the transaction was not afflicted with any vitiating factor. In short, death illness transaction is made during the cognitively weak moments, and similarly, those are the weak moments that give rise to the apprehension that undue influence has been exercised.

Rab Nawaz v Ghulam Rasul 2014 SCMR 1181

When a donor was living with a donee and was not in sound disposing mind to gift his property at an advanced age, the transaction may be afflicted with undue influence.

The donor in the present case was the predecessor in the interest of the parties. He allegedly gifted his property to one of his sons excluding the others. The gift mutation was attested on 18 June 1992 and the donor died on 17 November 1993. At the time of the transaction, the donor was about 92/93 years of age and was residing with the donee. He was not in a sound state of mental health and was also physically incapacitated due to various reasons including old age and fracture of vertebrae. After routing through various judicial forums, the dispute came before the Supreme Court.

The petitioners presented twofold arguments. Firstly, the donee was in a dominant position to exercise his undue influence over the donor who did not have any independent advice at the time of the alleged gift. The donor was in his advanced age and was prone to undue influence because of his mental and physical infirmities. Secondly, if the donor was supposed to have transacted a gift, then it remained incomplete because of a lack of delivery of possession. Moreover, if there was no delivery of possession, then there was no justification to treat the transaction as a death illness gift. On behalf of the respondent/donee, it was argued that without any specific disease capable of engendering an apprehension of death and preventing the donor from pursuing his usual occupation, the transaction was an ordinary gift and not a death illness gift.

The Supreme Court found no medical evidence of any disease that could induce the donor an apprehension of death. Further, fracture of vertebrae was not of that kind which either became the immediate cause of death or was capable to induce the apprehension of imminent death. The real issue was that the donor was not enjoying sound mental health when he purportedly made the gift and lack of mental health brought the case into the realm of undue influence. The court noted that when the donor was old, infirm, and incapacitated living at the mercy of the donee, the element of undue influence could not be ruled out.

The court while referring to a case of the Privy Council[33] reproduced the general principles for the determination of undue influence in the cases like the present one: '(a) whether the gift in question is one which a right-minded person might be expected to make; (b) is it or is it not an improvident act on the donor's part; (c) is it such as to have required advice, if any, obtained by the donor; and (d) whether the intention to make the gift originated by the donor.'[34] With reference to another case,[35] the apex court pointed out that when a presumption of undue influence is raised in a gift, the donee has to prove that it was a spontaneous act of a donor based on his independent will. In the absence of such evidence, the case of the donee would not succeed.

In addition to the above, the court did not find any evidence in support of delivery of possession to make the alleged gift a lawful transaction, and the donee was supposed to bring such evidence before the courts. In the circumstances of the case, the court held that no valid gift was ever transacted in favour of the donee.

Noor Muhammad Khan v Habibullah Khan PLD 1994 SC 650

A donor who is neither suffering from *marz-ul-maut* nor was under undue influence may transfer all his property to some of his legal heirs to the exclusion of others by way of gifts during his lifetime.

This case deals with the gifts allegedly made in contemplation of death. The brief facts of the case are that Muhammad Aslam Khan (the donor) who owned a large number of properties was married thrice. One wife was issueless and another's only son passed away. He had four daughters from his third wife. One of his daughters remained unmarried and looked after her father. Therefore, her father gifted her many properties. Out of jealousy, Col. Muhammad Hasan Khan, one of the sons-in-law, murdered the carer's daughter. Aggrieved and saddened by the death of her daughter, the donor decided to deprive the progeny of Muhammad Hasan Khan and gifted his properties to the children of other daughters. After the death of the donor, a suit was filed by one of the remote collaterals for his share in inheritance which was dismissed by the trial court and an appeal against it was dismissed by the High Court as well. Thereafter, the controversy was brought before the Supreme Court.

The counsel for the appellants (legal heirs of the original plaintiff) challenged the legality of the gifts. Appellants argued that the donor was sick and was suffering from diabetes, enlarged prostate, and high blood pressure and his mental condition was broken because of the unfortunate incident of the murder of his beloved daughter. In addition, the donor was excluded from all social contacts by one of his sons-in-law whose children had been beneficiaries of the alleged gifts which amounted to undue influence on the donor. Apart from the shock of the death of her daughter, the deteriorating health of the donor indicated that he was suffering from *marz-ul-maut*.

The legal question before the Supreme Court was whether gifts were the result of undue influence, duress and fraud, and whether the donor was suffering from *marz-ul-maut*. Justice Saleem Akhtar held that the appellants failed to prove duress or undue influence. Further, the donor was found to be in good health at the time of his death as he was frequently travelling to Rawalpindi from his native town (Mardan) for legal advice. The donor even submitted an application during the process of making gifts that he was making such gifts with a free mind and voluntarily to ward off any controversy after his death. There is no denying that grandchildren could have some influence; however, they could not dominate the will of their grandfather. There is no evidence showing that the gift was made under the imminent pressure or apprehension of death. Moreover, the gift made to some heirs to the exclusion of other legal heirs is a preferential gift and it is not void under Islamic law. Justice Saleem observed that the only restraint placed on a Muslim regarding alienation of his property is a death illness gift and will. In light of these reasons, the Supreme Court dismissed the petition.

11.4 Conclusion

Death illness gift is made in contemplation of death. The term *marz-ul-maut* comprises both subjective and objective elements; however, the emphasis is placed on the subjective apprehension of death in the mind of a donor. Death illness gift resembles a gift in a way that all essentials of a gift are to be fulfilled, and it resembles will in terms of its consequences. Just like a gift, a death illness gift is invalid when a property is not transferred to a donee. Death illness gifts can comprise one-third of the estate after payment of debt and funeral charges without the consent of legal heirs; however, if made more than one-third of the estate, consent is necessary. If the death illness gift is made to the legal heirs, the consent of other legal heirs is necessary even if the property is less than one-third. In Shia law, this limitation does not apply as a legal heir can get one-third of the estate without the consent of other legal heirs. The limitation imposed by Islamic law is to protect the rights of the expectant legal heirs.

It must be noted that a transaction with consideration during death illness is valid. The doctrine of death illness applies when a transaction is made without consideration. Similarly, if a person acknowledges debt during death illness which cannot be proved by any other evidence, such debts must be discharged. However, if the beneficiary of the acknowledgement of death illness debt is an heir and there is no evidence except the acknowledgement, then such acknowledgement will not be implemented unless assented to by other legal heirs. However, in Shia law, the acknowledgement of debt during death illness without any other evidence to the heir is valid to the extent of one-third of the estate.

As regards the *marz-ul-maut*, the courts have observed that three elements are necessary to constitute a disease as a death illness: the illness causes the death of the donor within a year, the illness produces subjective apprehension of death in the mind of the diseased, and there is some evidence of external indicia, such as serious illness or physical or mental infirmities. The courts have established that subjective apprehension of death in the mind of the donor is the determining factor for death illness, and the same is proved by the circumstantial evidence in each case. There are no specific diseases to be considered as *marz-ul-maut* since it depends on the severity of the disease, and it is a mixed question of law and fact. As far as evidentiary requirements are concerned, the courts have ruled that the onus to prove that the donor was under the pressure of imminent death at the relevant time is on the party alleging the fact and mere old age is not sufficient in this regard. Undue influence can be exerted during death illness because the donor lacks the capacity to enter into a transaction in both cases. It is noteworthy that the burden of proof for establishing death illness is placed on the one who questions the transaction, whereas, in case of undue influence, the beneficiary has to establish that the transaction was not afflicted with vitiating factor.

Questions

1. What is a death illness gift? How is it different from a gift and will?
2. Is a death illness gift valid under Islamic law? If yes, to what extent?
3. What is *marz-ul-maut*? What significance does it have with regard to the validity of the gift?
4. Can a person at death illness enter into a valid transaction without consideration?
5. Discuss the issue of the burden of proof in cases of death illness and undue influence?

Further Reading

Cases

Abdul Majeed v Abdul Rashid 2006 CLC 819 (Lah) (A gift made two days before the donor's death by way of the registered document will not be treated as a death illness gift unless it is proved by cogent evidence that he was actually on death bed and his mind was indisposed to carry out any such transaction of property.)

Mian Maqboolur Rehman v Mst. Munawar-un-Nisa 2001 CLC 1804 (Pesh) (To constitute a malady *marz-ul-maut*, three elements have to be satisfied: there was a preponderance of apprehension of death, some degree of subjective apprehension in the mind of a sick person, and some external indicia, chief among would be the inability to attend the ordinary avocations.)

Mst. Asiya Bibi v Muhammad Yousaf 2017 CLCN 41 (Lah) (Where a father was suffering from throat cancer and died within a year, the doctrine of *marz-ul-maut* was applicable to the alleged transaction.)

Mst. Shagufta Shireen v Mst. Mariam Bibi PLD 2005 Quetta 127 (Where a person had executed the gift two years prior to the death, that person's suffering from a specific disease would not be regarded as *marz-ul-maut*.)

Muhammad Imran v Muhammad Afzal 2016 MLD 1505 (Lah) (In an alleged transaction of gift by a fatally ill donor under circumstances engendering an impression of undue influence, the beneficiaries of such transaction have to prove all ingredients of a valid gift.)

Nisar Ahmad v Muhammad Anwar 2022 MLD 85 (Pesh) (The onus to prove that a gift mutation is made by a person suffering from *marz-ul-maut* is on the party alleging the fact.)

Syed Ghulam Hyder Shah alias Umaz Shah v Mst. Bibi Amirunnissa PLD 2011 Kar 183 (The doctrine of *marz-ul-maut* is applicable in cases of gifts not sale.)

Notes

1. Various authors have used terms such as death-bed gifts or death-sickness gifts. For the sake of consistency, we use the term death illness (*marz-al-maut*) in this chapter.
2. S.A. Ali, *Tagore Law Lectures–1884: The Law relating to Gifts, Trusts, and Testamentary Dispositions among the Mahommedans* (Calcutta: Thacker, Spink & Co, 1885), 58.
3. Ibid., 58–59.
4. Ibid., 60–61.
5. *Khurshed Husain v Faiyaz Husain* (1914) 36 All 289; R.K. Wilson, *A Digest of Anglo-Muhammadan Law*, 1st edn. (Calcutta: W. Thacker & Co, 1895); F.B. Balchin and Aisharaty between is titled, Muslim Family Law (New Delhi: 2015) teh was adjudication. pon khula, a wife has to reTyabji, *Principles of Muhammadan Law*, 2nd edn (Calcutta: Butterworth & Co. 1919).
6. Tyabji (n 4), 373–374.
7. Ali (n 1), 64.
8. Ibid.
9. Wilson (n 4), 45; A. Rahman, *Institutes of Mussalman Law* (Thacker, Spink & Co, 1907), 289.
10. *Hassarat Bibi v Golam Jaffar* 3 C.W.N., 57 (1898); Rehman (n 8), 246.
11. (1904) I.L.R. 31 Cal 319.
12. *Rashid Karmalli v Sherbanoo* (1907) I.L.R. 31 Bom 264.
13. Tanzil-ur-Rehman, *A Code of Muslim Personal Law* (Hamdard Academy, 1978).

14. *Shams-ul-Hasan v Syed Hasan* 71 I. C. 296 (All 1922).
15. A. Rahim, *The Principles of Muhammadan Jurisprudence* (Luzac & Co, 1911), 256.
16. Muhammad Akbar Khan & Zohaib Hasan Makwal, *The Legal Effects of Death-Illness on the Formation and Dissolution of Marriages in Islamic Law* (2018) 5 LUMS L.J. 72.
17. ILR 2 All 854 (1880).
18. Rehman (n 8), 246.
19. *Fazl Ahmad v Raheem Bibi* (1918) 40 All 238; D.F. Mulla, *Principles of Mahomedan Law* (LexisNexis 2013), 149.
20. D.F. Mulla, *Principles of Mahomedan Law* (PLD Publications 1995, Edited by Dr M.A. Mannan), 204.
21. Rehman (n 8), 290.
22. Ibid.
23. Tyabji (n 4), 818.
24. Ibid.
25. *Ibrahim Goolam Ariff v Saiboo* 34 IA 167.
26. PLD 1964 SC 143, [150].
27. Ibid., 159.
28. Ibid.
29. Ibid., 144.
30. 1988 CLC 1507 Lahore [4].
31. Ibid.
32. 1987 MLD 3055 Lahore, [3].
33. *Muhammad Bakhsh Khan v Hosseini Bibi* ILR 15 PC 684.
34. 2014 SCMR 1181, [8].
35. *Inche Noriah v Shaikh Allie bin Omer* 1929 AC 127.

12

INHERITANCE LAW

12.1 Introduction

Inheritance is the involuntary devolution of the property of a deceased person to his/her legal heirs. It comes into operation after the death of a person. Inheritance applies to all movable and immovable properties of the deceased. Debts, funeral expenses, and will are deducted before the distribution of property through inheritance. Contrary to popular perception, Islamic law does not recognise a person's right to disinherit (*'aaq*) his/her legal heirs, *inter vivos* (through testamentary disposition).

In pre-Islamic Arabia, females could neither inherit nor dispose of property. Rather, females were considered as property, inheritable by males. A brother or a stepson took possession of a dead man's widow(s) along with his property. Adult male agnate(s) (*'aṣaba*—from a male ancestor) inherited the entire estate, while the females and cognates (from female ancestors) were excluded. Descendants were preferred to ascendants. Ascendants were preferred to collaterals. An adopted son who was able to carry arms inherited like a real son. Mutual inheritance between two men based on their vows was considered acceptable.

Under Islamic legal reforms, females are given a share in inheritance, generally, 1/2 of the share of a male. In some circumstances, cognates are also declared to be entitled to inherit. The husband and wife are made legal heirs. Parents and ascendants are also given a specific share in inheritance in the presence of male descendants.

12.1.1 Qur'anic Verses on Inheritance. The following are translations of verses from the Qur'an that deal with the subject of inheritance.

> **Inheritance of Children and Parents.** Allah (thus) directs you as regards your children's (inheritance): to the male, a portion equal to that of two females: if only daughters, two or more, their share is two-thirds of the

inheritance; if only one, her share is a half. For parents, a sixth share of the inheritance to each, if the deceased left children; if no children and the parents are the (only) heirs, the mother has a third, if the deceased left brothers (or sisters) the mother has a sixth. (The distribution in all cases is) after the payment of legacies and debts. Ye know not whether your parents or your children are nearest to you in benefit. These are settled portions ordained by Allah; and Allah is All-knowing, All-Wise. (Surah 4, An-Nisa: Verse 11. The Holy Quran translation by A. Yusuf Ali)

Inheritance of Spouses and Siblings. In what your wives leave your share is a half if they leave no child; but if they leave a child ye get a fourth; after payment of legacies and debts. In what ye leave their share is a fourth if ye leave no child; but if ye leave a child they get an eighth; after payment of legacies and debts. If the man or woman whose inheritance is in question has left neither ascendants nor descendants but has left a brother or a sister each one of the two gets a sixth; but if more than two they share in a third; after payment of legacies and debts; so that no loss is caused (to anyone). Thus is it ordained by Allah and Allah is All-Knowing Most Forbearing. (Surah 4 An-Nisa: Verse 12. The Holy Quran translation by A. Yusuf Ali)

Inheritance of Siblings. They ask thee for a legal decision. Say: Allah directs (thus) about those who leave no descendants or ascendants as heirs. If it is a man that dies leaving a sister but no child she shall have half the inheritance: if (such a deceased was) a woman who left no child her brother takes her inheritance: if there are two sisters they shall have two-thirds of the inheritance (between them): if there are brothers and sisters (they share) the male having twice the share of the female. Thus doth Allah make clear to you (His law) lest ye err. And Allah hath knowledge of all things. (Surah 4 An-Nisa: Verse 176. The Holy Quran translation by A. Yusuf Ali)

12.1.2 The Occasion of Revelation of the Verse of Inheritance. The most significant verse regarding inheritance is Surah An-Nisa verse 11 which is known as 'the verse of inheritance'. It was revealed when a companion of the Prophet (PBUH) was martyred leaving behind his wife and two daughters. After his martyrdom, his brother took control of all his property in accordance with the prevailing Arabian custom. Thereupon, the wife along with her daughters came to the Prophet (PBUH) and complained that she would not be in a position to wed her daughters without having anything from her husband's estate. In this context, the above-referred verse was revealed. Thereafter, the Prophet (PBUH) ordered the paternal uncle to give away 2/3 of his deceased brother's estate to his daughters and 1/8 to his wife.

12.2 General Principles

In cases where the deceased and heirs belong to different religions or sects, the applicable law is the law of *propositus*, not the law of legal heirs. Therefore, if a non-Muslim embraces Islam and dies as a Muslim his property will be divided according to Islamic law.

The right to succeed accrues after the death of the *propositus*, not at the birth of a legal heir. Right to inheritance becomes vested at the death of the *propositus* and is not lost at the death of the heir before the distribution of the property. Moreover, mere expectancy to inherit—*spes successionis*—is not a valid transferable right. Heirs are tenants in common and not joint tenants with rights of survivorship.

Islamic law recognises the rule of primogeniture (preference given to the first male heir) to a limited extent. Under Shia, Shafi'i, and Maliki schools, the eldest sound-minded son inherits certain articles of the father (wearing apparel, Qur'an, ring, and sword) provided the deceased left other property.

12.2.1 Bar to Inheritance. The following circumstances deprive a legal heir from getting a share in the inheritance:

1. Homicide: murder of a *propositus* (intentional under Shia law, and intentional or unintentional under Hanafi law) by a legal heir/beneficiary of a will excludes him/her along with his/her descendants.
2. Illegitimacy: under Hanafi law, an illegitimate child inherits only from the mother and *vice versa*. Such a child cannot inherit from either parent under Shia law.
3. Difference of religion: non-Muslims cannot inherit from a Muslim. Likewise, a Muslim does not inherit from a non-Muslim. The property of an apostate is distributed to his legal heirs during his lifetime.
4. Estoppel in succession: a person who denied a relationship with the *propositus* cannot subsequently claim inheritance.

12.3 Distribution of an Estate under the Sunni and Shia Schools

There are two main schools of Islamic law: Sunni and Shia. Each school provides a logically coherent system of inheritance. Therefore, we shall discuss them separately in two different sections.

12.3.1 Sunni Inheritance Law

Under Sunni inheritance law, there are three types of legal heirs: (i) Sharers (Qur'anic heirs); (ii) Residuaries; and (iii) Distant kindred. The order of priorities in inheritance is as follows:

1. Sharers (Qur'anic heirs)
2. Residuaries (Agnatic heirs)
3. *Radd* (Return to Sharers)
4. Distant Kindred (Uterine heirs)
5. *Radd* (Return to Spouse)
6. Universal Legatee (a person who is not a legal heir and, in whose favour, the property is left under a will)
7. Bait ul Maal

12.3.1.1 Sharers (Qur'anic heirs). The share of each of the Sharers is specifically provided in the Qur'an. Therefore, they are also called Qur'anic heirs. They include four male and nine female relatives. Some of them are specifically mentioned in the Qur'an (e.g. father, mother, daughter), while others are implied as such without specific reference (e.g. grandfather, grandmother, son's daughter).

MALES	SHARE
Father	1/6
Grandfather	1/6 (in the absence of the father)
Husband	1/2 (in the absence of children) or 1/4 (in the presence of children)
Uterine brother(s)	1/6 (in the absence of the father) or 1/3 (where two or more than two)

FEMALE	SHARE
Mother	1/6 (in the presence of children of the deceased)
Paternal grandmother	1/6 (in the absence of the mother)
Maternal grandmother	1/6 (in the absence of the mother)
Wife	1/8 (in the presence of children) 1/4 (in the absence of children)
Daughter	1/2 (in the absence of a son, and alone) 2/3 (where two or more than two)
Son's Daughter	1/2 (in the absence of daughter, and alone) 2/3 (where two or more than two)
Full sister (s)	1/2 (in the absence of father and children, and alone) 2/3 (where two or more than two)
Consanguine sister(s)	1/2 (in the absence of a father, children, and full sister, and alone) 2/3 (where two or more than two)
Uterine sister(s)	1/6 (in the absence of a father, and alone) 1/3 (where two or more than two)

12.3.1.2 Residuaries (*Asbat*). Their right to inheritance was well-founded in pre-Islamic customs and was retained after certain corrective measures were introduced by the Qur'an and Sunnah. They are divided into three categories:

Residuaries in their own right	This category includes the following male relatives: (1) Male descendants, how low so ever (e.g. son and son's son). (2) Male ascendants, how high so ever (e.g. father and true grandfather). (3) Deceased's brother, how low so ever (e.g. full and consanguine brother and their son[s]). (4) Brother of male ascendants, how low so ever (e.g. full uncle and consanguine uncle and their son).

Residuaries in another's right	These are female sharers who are converted into residuaries in the presence of their male counterparts provided the latter possess the same level and same proximity of relationship with the deceased: (1) Daughter[s] along with son[s]. (2) Son's daughter along with son's son. (3) Full sister along with full brother. (4) Consanguine sister along with consanguine brother.
Residuaries together with another	(1) Daughter[s] converts sister[s] (full as well as consanguine) into a residuary. (2) Daughters remain as Sharers even after the conversion of sisters as residuaries. Once daughters have their prescribed share, the rest will be inherited by sisters. (3) After conversion, sisters start behaving like their male counterparts (e.g. full sister excludes consanguine brother and full brother's son).

12.3.1.3 Distant Kindred. They are divided into two types: (i) maternal relatives (e.g. maternal grandfather, maternal uncles and aunts, and their children); and (ii) paternal relatives other than sharers and residuaries (e.g. daughter's children, sister's children, and paternal uncle's wife).

There are three ways of distribution among distant kindred: (i) *Ahl al-Rahm* (now obsolete); (ii) *Ahl al-Tanzil* (followed by the Hanbali, Shafi'i, and Maliki schools); and (iii) *Ahl al-Qarabah* (followed by the Hanafi school and applied in Pakistan).

According to *Ahl al-Qarabah*, the legal heirs are divided into the following categories:

(i)	Descendants of a deceased (daughter's children)	The legal heirs placed in this category will exclude the legal heirs of the rest of the categories.
(ii)	Ascendants of a deceased (false grandfather, false grandmother)	Legal heirs in this category will not allow the remaining categories (iii and iv) to inherit anything.
(iii)	Relatives of a deceased's parent (sister's children, brothers' daughter, and uterine brother's son)	The legal heirs of this category will exclude the legal heirs of category (iv).

(iv)	Relatives of a deceased's grandparents (paternal uncle's wife, maternal uncles and aunts, and their children)	

Once we have the legal heirs of one category entitled to have their share, they will be given the share on the principle that a male will have double the share of a female.

12.3.1.4 Principle of Exclusion. Under the principle of exclusion, one legal heir is excluded by another from inheritance on the basis of nearness in a relationship with the deceased. Exclusion could be partial or complete.

Under this principle, the nearer relative excludes the more remote relative. Thus, a father excludes the grandfather, a son excludes the son's son, and a mother excludes the paternal/maternal grandmother. After the sharers are given their prescribed share, the property is distributed among the residuaries in such a way that descendants exclude ascendants (son excludes father) and ascendants exclude collaterals (father excludes brother, and brother excludes uncle).

Six legal heirs viz. father, mother, son, daughter, husband, and wife, cannot be completely excluded. They will inherit something from the estate although their shares are susceptible to variation.

12.3.1.4.1 Principle of *Radd* (Return). This principle is applied when the estate is to be distributed among sharers only in the absence of residuaries. Sharers may not consume the entire estate in the first round of distribution. Hence, they are once again given some share in the estate as per their original prescribed share. Spouses are not entitled to have any share in the property under the principle of *radd* in the presence of any sharer, residuary, or distant kindred. However, if there is no legal heir from any of the categories above-mentioned, they are entitled to benefit under the principle of *radd*.

12.3.1.4.2 Principle of *Awl* (Increase). When the calculated shares of sharers exceed the total number of supposed shares of the estate, the latter shares are also increased to accommodate the ratios of the calculated shares. After the application of *awl*, even though the number of the shares of each heir remains the same, the quantity of each share decreases, sometimes substantially. Under this principle, six supposed shares may convert into seven, eight, nine, and ten; twelve may convert into thirteen, fifteen, and seventeen, and twenty-four may convert into twenty-seven.

12.3.2 Shia Inheritance Law Like Sunni inheritance law, Shia law of inheritance recognises sharers and residuaries. However, there are nine sharers in Shia law as opposed to thirteen sharers under Sunni law (four females and nine males). Grandparents and sons' daughters are not regarded as sharers under Shia law. It should also be noted that residuaries do not play a significant role in the Shia scheme of inheritance. Furthermore, Shia law does not recognise distant kindred. All legal heirs are classified into three main classes in addition to being sharers and residuaries under Shia law. Following are the details of these classes:

Class 1	Parents Children (male and female), and children of male and female descendants, how low so ever
Class 2	Grandparents (true or false), how high so ever, and Brothers and sisters (full, consanguine, and uterine) and their descendants, how low so ever irrespective of their gender
Class 3	Paternal uncles and aunts Maternal uncles and aunts Their children, how low so ever irrespective of their gender

Legal heirs of Class 1 exclude legal heirs of Class 2, and legal heirs of Class 2 exclude legal heirs of Class 3. Legal heirs of the same class are entitled to their share irrespective of their gender, except that the male will have double the share of a similarly placed female. For example, there is no distinction between true and false grandparents, son's children and daughter's children, and brother's children and sister's children. Another important feature of Shia law is that a female legal heir located in Class 1 will exclude a male heir situated in Classes 2 and 3 despite the fact that the latter is regarded as a residuary. For example, a daughter deprives her grandfather, brothers, and uncles.

The principle of *awl* is not resorted to in Shia law. The principle of representation is applied for distribution among the more distant degree of relatives. For example, the daughter's children may represent the share of the inheritance of the daughter and the sister's children inherit in the right of the sister and so forth. Generally, Shia law is more gender sensitive than Sunni law.

12.3.2.1 Principle of Exclusion. The basic premise of the principle is shared by both Shia and Sunni schemes of inheritance law, but this principle is more often resorted to in Shia law than in Sunni law due to the three-tiered classification of legal heirs under Shia law. For example, a female legal heir nearer in the degree of relationship with the deceased excludes a male legal heir who is more remote in the degree of relationship (e.g. daughter excludes son's son though they both belong to the same class and full sister excludes consanguine brother).

12.3.2.2 Principle of Representation. Distant legal heirs inherit through their predeceased connecting link from the patrimony of the deceased (e.g. the son's children through the son; the daughter's children through the daughter, the brother's children through the brother, and uncle's children through the uncle). Such legal heirs do not inherit per capita as if they are entitled personally. They inherit per stripes as if they are representatives of their predeceased parent/connecting link. For example, a son's daughter and a daughter's son receive the shares of their parent. The son's daughter will have 2/3, while the daughter's son will receive 1/3. Likewise, one grandson from one son and two grandsons from another son get the share of their fathers. The first grandson will have half of the property, while the other half will be distributed among the two grandsons equally.

12.3.2.3 Principle of *Radd* (Return). The application of this principle is also more frequent in Shia law than in Sunni law. Its application, however, adversely affects the entitlement of the residuaries. Whenever there are legal heirs belonging to more than one class, only the legal heirs belonging to the superior class will inherit the estate as per their prescribed shares. In case the entire estate is not consumed, they will also receive a share under the principle of *radd* and practically nothing would be left for the residuaries of the lower class.

Examples

If a deceased leaves behind a daughter, grandfather, and uncle, the daughter inherits the entire property as she belongs to Class 1. The grandfather and uncle are excluded as they belong to Classes 2 and 3 respectively. Under Sunni law, in this situation, the daughter will inherit 1/2 as a sharer and the grandfather will inherit 1/2 as a residuary.

In a different scenario, if a daughter and father are the only legal heirs, both fall in Class 1. In such case, both will have their prescribed share first and then will have the remainder under the principle of *radd*. Thus, the daughter will get 1/2 (3/6) and the father 1/6. After giving them their due shares, only 4/6 of the estate is consumed. Therefore, we shall apply the principle of *radd* which will convert the daughter's share to 3/4 and the father's share to 1/4. Under Sunni law, in this situation, the daughter inherits 3/6 and the reminder, that is, 3/6, will be inherited by the father as a residuary.

12.3.2.4 Principle of *Awl* (Increase). Shia law does not recognise the principle of *awl*. It divides legal heirs into two categories: (a) legal heirs whose shares are susceptible to reduction (e.g. daughter, sister), and (b) legal heirs whose shares are not liable to any reduction (e.g. parents, spouses, and uterine brother/sister). In cases where the calculated shares of the sharers exceed the supposed shares, the entire burden is put upon the first category. The second category legal heirs take their prescribed shares.

Example

A husband and two sisters are the legal heirs. The husband's share is 1/2, and the two sisters' share is 2/3. The least common multiple (LCM) is 6. The husband is entitled to 3/6 and the sisters to 4/6. The collective share of legal heirs is 7, but the actual number of shares is 6. Under Shia law, the share of two sisters will be reduced to 3/6 from 4/6. This is in contrast with Sunni law where the collective share is increased from 6 to 7. Thus, the husband gets 3/7, and two full sisters get 4/7. Thus in Shia law, the decrease in the supposed shares is borne by daughters and sisters; whereas in Sunni law all the legal heirs collectively bear the reduction caused by the occurrence of *awl*.

12.4 Customary Law of Inheritance in Pakistan

During the colonial period, customary law was given priority over Muslim Personal Law under section 5 of the Punjab Laws Act 1872 and section 27 of the NWFP Justice Regulation 1901. Under customary law, agnatic relatives are preferred over cognate relatives. In this way, female relations, with the exception of widows, are excluded. Female relatives, e.g. daughters and sisters, had limited life interests only. Property held by a female beneficiary as an heir, or a donee reverted to the male heirs of the last male owner on the termination of the life interest (marriage or death) of the female beneficiary. Unlike the male legal heirs, the female legal heirs did not have a right to challenge the alienation of ancestral property under customary law. However, since the 1930s through the introduction of various legislative instruments the law of inheritance has been progressively Islamised. Currently, inheritance law in Pakistan is based on Islamic Injunctions as enshrined in the Qur'an and the Sunnah.

12.5 Legislation on Inheritance

Some relevant legislative instruments are as follows:

- The NWFP Shariat Act 1935.
- The Muslim Personal Law (Shariat) Application Act 1937 (agricultural land was excluded because it was a provincial subject) under the Government of India Act 1935.
- The West Pakistan Muslim Personal Law (Shariat) Application Act 1948 (applied to agricultural land but did not apply to testate succession).
- The West Pakistan Muslim Personal Law (Shariat) Application (Amendment) Act 1951 (applied to testate succession and terminated estates held under wills). A similar Act was passed in Sindh in 1950.
- The Muslim Family Laws Ordinance 1961 (provided representation right to an orphaned grandchild).
- The West Pakistan Muslim Personal Law (Shariat) Application Act 1962 (consolidated various Muslim Personal Law Application Acts in West Pakistan but created confusion).
- The Punjab Muslim Personal Law (Shariat) Application (Removal of Doubts) Ordinance 1972 (tried to clarify the confusion regarding the termination of life estates rights).
- The Punjab Muslim Personal Law (Shariat) Application (Removal of Difficulties) Act 1975 (clarified that the refugee females who were allotted evacuee property are limited owners under custom).
- Under the Criminal Law (Third Amendment) Act 2011 section 498A was added to the Pakistan Penal Code 1860 which prescribes the punishment of ten years or a fine of one million or both for depriving women of their right to inheritance.
- The Transgender Persons (Protection of Rights) Act 2018 (This legislation, in addition to the protection of other rights, ensures that a transgender person is not discriminated against with respect to inheritance rights. Transgender males and females are mandated

to be granted their respective share as male and female, whereas in case of ambiguous sexual orientation/characteristics, the self-perceived identity of a transgender person would be taken into consideration for the determination of inheritance rights.

- The Enforcement of Women's Property Rights Act 2020 [For the Islamabad Capital Territory] (The Ombudsperson appointed under the Protection against Harassment of Women at the Workplace Act 2010 is authorised to initiate inquiries relating to the matters in which the women have been illegally deprived of ownership and possession of the property, and to take necessary measures for the enforcement of their proprietary rights in an expeditious manner).
- The Punjab Enforcement of Women's Property Rights Act 2021 [Punjab Statute] (The Ombudsperson appointed under the Protection against Harassment of Women at the Workplace Act 2010 is authorised to initiate inquiries relating to the matters in which the women have been illegally deprived of ownership and possession of the property, and to take necessary measures for the enforcement of their proprietary rights in an expeditious manner).
- The Muslim Family Laws (Amendment) Act 2021 (MFLO 1961 is amended to recognise under Shia law the share of widow/s [1/4 or 1/8 in the absence and presence of children respectively] and widower [1/2 or 1/4 in the absence and presence of children respectively] in both moveable and immovable properties of their deceased spouses.)

12.6 Letters of Administration and Succession Certificates

The letters of administration and succession certificates had been exclusively issued by civil courts till 2020. This authority has been partially delegated to the National Database and Registration Authority (NADRA) by simplifying the procedure. Upon the death of any person, legal heirs may initiate a process for seeking the letter of administration and succession certificate. NADRA issues such documents after verification. However, in cases of any controversy requiring the recording of evidence or where one of the legal heirs is a minor, the matter is decided by the civil courts. The procedure to be followed by NADRA in all the legislations is substantially similar. The following are the titles of the relevant laws:

- The Letters of Administration and Succession Certificates Act 2020 [Islamabad Capital Territory]
- The Sindh Letters of Administration and Succession Certificates Act 2021
- The KPK Letters of Administration and Succession Certificates Act 2021
- The Punjab Letters of Administration and Succession Certificates Act 2021
- The Balochistan Letters of Administration and Succession Certificates Act 2022

12.6.1 Procedure of Devolution. Upon the death of a landowner, proceedings for inheritance mutations shall proactively be initiated by the Revenue Officer forthwith, without any application being moved by any of the parties and he shall sanction the mutation as soon as possible. Reference to CNIC and B-Form is mandatory while sanctioning inheritance mutation to ensure that no legal heir is deprived of his/her fundamental right to property.[1] Stamp duty has been waived for partition made effective through inheritance for both rural and urban properties. Only a token amount of Rs 500 per mutation is imposed replacing the 2 per cent stamp duty.

12.7 Outline of Case Law

12.7.1 Distribution of Estate. The case law in this section highlights the application of Islamic inheritance law by the superior courts. Several judgments have been identified where the courts did not apply the correct law. Furthermore, one can also see excellent examples of the prudent application of law by the superior courts such as in the *Beguman* case where a murderer and his progeny were disinherited.

Beguman v Saroo PLD 1964 Lah 451

A murderer or his progeny cannot benefit from the crime of murder committed with a design to inherit property

This case lays down the rule that under the principles of equity, justice, and good conscience, a murderer or his progeny cannot be allowed to benefit from the crime of murder committed with the intention to inherit property.

The disputed property belonged to Rehman who died on 25 August 1951. He left behind a widow Beguman and two daughters, Rasulan and Sardaran. He also had two sons, Ahmad Bakhsh and Allah Yar who were killed in 1948. The respondent, Manak, and his father, Dara were prosecuted for the murders of the two sons. Consequently, Dara was sentenced to death. Upon the death of Rehman, the inheritance mutation of his property was sanctioned in favour of his widow, and two daughters and a 5/24 share of the property was mutated in favour of Saroo and Manak, sons of Dara, as collaterals of Rehman. On this, the widow and the two daughters filed a suit for declaration to the effect that the respondents being the murderers or abettors of the murderers of the two sons of Rehman could not inherit from his property and the plaintiffs were entitled to the whole property. During the pendency of the suit Beguman died, leaving behind her daughters who were contesting in their personal capacities as heirs of Rehman and as legal representatives of their mother, Beguman.

The respondents contested the suit. They denied that either they or their father committed the murder of Rehman's sons and argued that they were entitled to the property of Rehman as he had died two years after the murders of his sons. At the time of his death, the Muhammadan law of inheritance was applicable, and they, as collaterals were entitled to succeed to the extent of 5/24 share in their own right.

The court noted that Manak and his father, Dara, were actually prosecuted as murderers of Rehman's sons in which the latter was convicted. These murders were committed to get the deceased's property. The court held:

> The rule of law is well-settled that under principles of justice, equity and good conscience a murderer or his progeny cannot be allowed to benefit by his crime of murder. The murderer may be the father alone but if the descendants claim through him even though not merely from him their title becomes tainted as the source or channel through which the inheritance has to flow to them becomes blocked and extirpated by reason of the crime committed by that source.[2]

Waris Ali v Rasoolan Bibi PLD 2014 SC 779

The sisters take the Qur'anic share of 2/3 and the deceased brother's son (nephew) the rest of the property (the remaining 1/3) as a residuary in his capacity as the nearest male agnate of the deceased.

Amina Bibi died leaving behind three legal heirs: two sisters, Rasoolan Bibi (respondent) and Ghulam Fatima (appellant no. 2) and a nephew, the son of the full brother Waris Ali (appellant no. 1). One-half of the estate was mutated to appellant no. 1 and the other half was divided equally between the respondent and appellant no. 2. Thereafter, appellant no. 1 transferred his share to another person impleaded as appellant no. 3 in the case.

The respondent initiated a civil litigation to set aside the mutation in favour of appellant no. 1 and the subsequent transfer of the share to appellant no. 3. She was of the view that appellant no. 1 was not entitled to any share in the estate since his father—full brother of the deceased Amina Bibi—died before the deceased. The Civil Court decreed the suit by ordering the cancellation of the mutation in favour of appellant no. 1.

Appellant no. 1 assailed the decision in the first Appellate Court and was successful in getting a declaration to his entitlement to the estate. Thereafter, the respondent brought the matter before the High Court, which confirmed the decision of the Civil Court, thus reversing the first Appellate Court's judgment. Against this background, the appellants brought the dispute before the Supreme Court. The court elaborated upon the issue by identifying the following principles:

> The issue regarding the distribution of inheritance between the two real sisters of the deceased and the son of a pre-deceased brother (nephew) attracts two fundamental principles of Islamic Law of inheritance accepted by the Sunni Fiqh. The first principle is that the Qur'anic Sharers are to be given their prescribed shares unless a Qur'anic Sharer is excluded by another heir according to the Rules of Exclusion prescribed in the Qur'an and Sunnah and elaborated upon by Islamic Jurisprudence (Shari'a). The second principle is that after the Qur'anic Sharers have been given their shares the rest of the estate is divided amongst the nearest male agnates of the deceased as residuaries.[3]

The court further observed, '[Considering the status of the nephew as a residuary] the deceased brother's son (nephew) neither excludes the sisters of the deceased (whereas a son would have done so) nor does he agnatize the sisters of the deceased (as a brother of the deceased would have done)'.[4] Consequently, the sisters will take their Qur'anic share of 2/3 of the estate. The deceased brother's son (nephew) will inherit the rest (the remaining 1/3) as a residuary in his capacity as the nearest male agnate of the deceased.

After appraising the Islamic law on the subject, the court concluded the respective shares of the parties to the estate in the above manner. Taking into account the fact that appellant no. 2 did not object to the mutation in favour of appellant no. 1, rather sided with the appellants, the court held that she would be deemed to have waived her right to her original entitlement to the estate in favour of appellant no. 1. Hence, the court enforced the respective share of the respondent according to her legitimate share, that is, 1/3 of the estate, but did not do the same for appellant no. 2.

Saadullah v Gulbanda 2014 SCMR 1205

A consanguine brother would not inherit any share in presence of full sisters of the deceased as the full sisters would inherit as sharers as well as under the principle of *radd*.

Badshah Mir died issueless leaving behind his mother, three full sisters including the respondent and one consanguine brother. The appellants in the title were legal heirs of the consanguine brother. In 1973, the suit land was mutated in favour of the legal heirs of Badshah Mir as follows: the mother 1/6; three full sisters 2/3; and the consanguine brother 1/6.

There was no dispute as to the shares of the mother and the full sisters, but the respondent (one of the sisters) was not satisfied with the award of 1/6 share to the consanguine brother. Therefore, she filed a civil suit to get the share granted to him set aside. The suit was decreed by the court and the mutation in favour of the consanguine brother was invalidated as the court was of the opinion that the same was not warranted by Islamic law. The court reverted 1/6 share to the full sisters in addition to their prescribed share, that is, 2/3, according to the principle of *radd* (return).

The appellants challenged the decision in the first Appellate Court and thereafter filed a revision petition before the High Court. Both courts confirmed the Civil Court's decision. The appellants afterwards brought the matter before the Supreme Court.

The appellants were of the view that the consanguine brother should have been awarded 1/6 share in the estate left by Badshah Mir. On the other hand, the respondent argued that the full sisters were entitled to 1/6 share under the principle of *radd*.

After perusing the Qur'anic verse 4:176 and a table of residuaries from Mulla's *Principles of Mahomedan Law*, the court observed that the full sisters were nearer in the degree of relationship with the deceased than the consanguine brother. In fact, the full sisters were shown at serial no. 6, whereas the consanguine brother stood at serial no. 7 in the table. Hence, the court applied the principle of return (*radd*) and the rule of exclusion, holding thereby that the three full sisters of the deceased would not only inherit 2/3 share as sharers from thc estate of their deceased brother but being nearer in the category of residuaries the remaining 1/6 share would also devolve upon them in such capacity. The consanguine brother, in the presence of the full sisters, would not inherit anything from the estate as a residuary.

This case sets a bad precedent as it misconstrues two important principles of inheritance: *radd* and exclusion. The principle of *radd* cannot apply in the presence of even a single residuary.[5] On the one hand, the court treated the full sisters as residuaries and on the other, it applied the principle of *radd*. It appears that the table of residuaries referred to in Mulla's *Principles of Mahomedan Law* can cause confusion. The court noted the sequence mentioned therein and applied the principle of exclusion for depriving the consanguine brother but overlooked the conditions stated there for treating the full sisters as residuaries. Full sisters become residuaries and exclude consanguine brother(s) when they (the full sisters) inherit along with the deceased's daughter/s or son's daughter/s.[6] In this case, despite the fact that no daughter or son's daughter of the deceased was alive, the Court converted the full sisters into residuaries and adversely affected the right of the consanguine brother who was eligible to get 1/6 of the property as a residuary.

The Supreme Court followed this case in its recent judgment in *Muhammad Sharif v Naimat Bibi* 2021 SCMR 1355 wherein an inheritance dispute involved a sister and a consanguine paternal uncle's son. The Supreme Court awarded half of the estate to the sister as a sharer and other the half as residuary, while excluding the consanguine paternal uncle's son. However, in *Shah Jahan Begum v Zafar Ahmed* PLD 2018 Lahore 426, the Lahore High Court pointed out that the Supreme Court was not provided with full reference to Mulla's *Principles of Mahomedan Law* on which it purportedly relied in *Saadullah v Gulbanda*, and consequently, reached an incorrect conclusion. In *Shah Jahan Begum v Zafar Ahmed*, an inheritance dispute involved a widow, a sister, and nephews (sons of the predeceased brother). The High Court held that the widow and sister would have their prescribed shares as sharers and the residue would be given to the nephews.

Abdul Khaliq v Fazalur Rehman PLD 2004 SC 768

A sharer inherits twice in the absence of any residuary: once as a sharer and subsequently under the principle of *radd* (return).

In this case, the Supreme Court clarified the controversy regarding the inheritance of distant kindred after a long-drawn legal battle. The owner of the estate, Najo died leaving behind his children, Abdul Ghafoor and Roshanai. Thereafter, Abdul Ghafoor died issueless, and his share was transferred to Roshanai who gifted the entire property to Abdul Khaliq and others appearing as petitioners in the case.

Aggrieved by the transaction, the respondents in the present case, relatives of Abdul Ghafoor filed a civil suit. They claimed that being collaterals of Abdul Ghafoor they were entitled to inheritance in his estate. The trial court dismissed their claim. The first Appellate Court and the High Court awarded them 3/4 share in the estate and that share was reduced to 1/2 by the Supreme Court. The petitioners were not satisfied by the decision of the Supreme Court. Hence, they filed a review petition.

In the review petition, the Supreme Court referred to the important fact missed in earlier judicial proceedings that respondents were distant kindred. Therefore, they were not entitled to any share in the presence of a sharer (i.e. Roshanai). The petitioners' counsel argued that Roshanai was entitled to 1/2 of the estate as a sharer and the remainder ought to have been transferred to her under the principle of *radd* (return). Thus, the transaction of gifts in favour of the petitioners was not illegal.

After pursuing the pedigree chart, the Supreme Court noted that the respondents were related to the deceased, Abdul Ghafoor, through one distant kindred. Hence, their status of being the latter's descendants was that of the distant kindred. The Court also reproduced the relevant sections from Mulla's *Principles of Mahomedan Law* to conclude that distant kindred could not inherit in the presence of a sharer or a residuary. The one exception to this rule is the presence of a spouse.

Considering the fact that the sister of the deceased as a sharer was alive and the respondents belonged to the category of distant kindred, the court decided that they were not entitled even to 1/2 of the estate awarded to them in the impugned decision. The entire estate of the deceased would be inherited by his sister: 1/2 as a sharer and the other half under the principle of *radd*. Therefore, the gift of the entire estate by Roshanai to the petitioners was declared to be valid.

Sher Muhammad v Mahmood Bakhsh 2000 SCMR 672

Under the Sunni and Shia schools, collaterals get nothing in the presence of a daughter, children of a deceased daughter, and a sister.

Allah Diwaya died in 1977. He was survived by a daughter, children from another daughter, and a sister. The estate left by the deceased was mutated to all the legal heirs (2/3 to the daughter and the children of another daughter, while 1/3 to the full sister). Afterwards, they transferred the entire estate through various transactions.

The petitioners were collaterals of the deceased, Allah Diwaya. They filed a suit to challenge the inheritance mutation and claimed that they were also entitled to their due share in the estate of the deceased. The case was defended by the daughter, the children of another daughter and the sister of the deceased along with their subsequent transferees. They argued that the collaterals were not entitled to anything from the estate of the deceased since the latter belonged to the Shia school of thought. According to the Shia law of inheritance, they were liable to be excluded in the presence of the deceased's children. The trial court concluded, from the evidence adduced that the deceased professed Shia *fiqh* and hence, his estate had to be distributed according to that law. The court dismissed the suit while observing that the petitioners, being collaterals, were not entitled to inherit from the estate of the deceased.

The petitioners assailed the decision in the first Appellate Court and thereafter, in the High Court. Both courts dismissed their appeals. Therefore, they brought the matter before the Supreme Court.

The petitioners argued that the deceased was a follower of the Sunni school of thought and that his estate ought to have been distributed in accordance with Sunni law. They had hopes of getting a share in the estate if it was distributed under Sunni law since they were the deceased's nearest male agnates.

The Supreme Court, while referring to the categories of legal heirs of Shia law mentioned in Mulla's *Principles of Mahomedan Law* concluded that the petitioners would not inherit from the estate of the deceased. The mutation in favour of one daughter and another daughter's children to the extent of 2/3 and the remainder 1/3 for the surviving sister was a legally accurate distribution of the estate. The court elaborated that if the deceased was presumed to be a Sunni even then the petitioners were not entitled to inherit from him. This was so because after awarding the prescribed share to the daughter and the children from another daughter, the remaining 1/3 had to be given to the sister. According to Sunni law, a sister is converted into a residuary in the presence of daughter(s) provided the surviving collaterals are remoter in their degree of relationship with the deceased. Considering this scenario, the court dismissed the petition by observing that the petitioners were not entitled to inherit from the deceased regardless of the application of Shia or Sunni law.

The Supreme Court was right in its conclusion that the petitioners were not entitled to anything from the estate in either situation. However, there was an important point with respect to the Shia law of inheritance that the court misconstrued. According to Shia law, a brother and a sister do not inherit in the presence of a deceased's children irrespective of their gender.[7] In this case, the surviving sister who had inherited 1/3 of the estate was not entitled to that share had the case been decided correctly. The remainder ought to have been reverted to the daughter and the children from another daughter under the principle of *radd* (return). This is so because the children (son, daughter, and their children) of a deceased fall in Class 1, while a sister is placed in Class 2, and in the presence of a legal heir from Class 1, the legal heirs in Class 2 and 3 are excluded and deprived of any share. Both the Court and the parties missed this point and hence, the sister was successful in retaining the remainder (1/3) of the estate.

Muhammad Khalid v Noor Bibi 2005 SCMR 1717

Among the distant kindred, the nearer the degree of relationship with a deceased would exclude the more remote relations.

Muhammad Sharif died issueless. The petitioners in the case were daughters and sons of the paternal uncle and an aunt of the deceased. They initiated a civil suit to inherit his estate. The respondents were maternal uncles of the deceased. The petitioners maintained that the respondents could not inherit anything from the estate of the deceased. All three courts—Civil Court, Appellate Court, and the High Court—dismissed the case of the petitioners. Hence, they brought it before the Supreme Court.

The court, relying upon the relevant passages from Mulla's *Principles of Mahomedan Law*, concluded that there was no sharer and residuary alive to have a preferential right of inheritance over the estate left by the deceased. All the claimants were from the category of distant kindred mentioned in section 68 of Mulla's *Principles of Mahomedan Law*. Therefore, the nearer the degree of relationship with the deceased would exclude the remoter relations. In the circumstances of the instant case, the respondents were found to be nearer in the degree of their relationship with the deceased and, on this basis alone, the petitioners were excluded from the estate. Consequently, the court dismissed their petition.

An important point not considered by the court and probably not highlighted by the petitioners was that the sons of the paternal uncle were residuaries, not distant kindred. Therefore, they ought to have inherited the entire estate excluding all legal heirs contesting the case from both sides because the rest of the aspirants of the estate were all distant kindred.

Amir v Bashiran Bibi 2004 SCMR 832

A daughter inherits 1/2 of the property and the other half goes to the brothers of the deceased as residuaries.

The respondents in this case claimed to be the daughter and the widow of the deceased, Mohabat, who died in 1954. Their claim was disputed by the collaterals of the deceased who appeared as petitioners in the title of the case. The estate of the deceased was initially mutated in favour of the collaterals depriving the respondents. The respondents assailed the mutation before the revenue authorities but could not get their share.

Consequently, the respondents filed a suit for declaration of their title to the estate of the deceased in 1989. They claimed that they were entitled to 5/8 of the estate (the daughter 4/8 and the widow 1/8). The suit was dismissed and thereafter the respondents went to the first Appellate Court. The court found respondent no. 1 entitled to 1/2 of the estate because she was proven to be the daughter of the deceased. On the other hand, respondent no. 2, the alleged widow, was not entitled to anything because she was divorced by the deceased before his death, hence she could not be termed as the widow of the deceased. The High Court affirmed the decision of the first Appellate Court.

Against this background, the matter was brought before the Supreme Court and leave to appeal was sought. It was argued by the petitioners that since respondent no. 2 was never married to the deceased respondent no. 1 could not be regarded as the daughter of the deceased. The court observed that there was ample evidence to support the conclusion arrived at by the first Appellate Court and affirmed by the High Court. The court relied upon the First Information Report (FIR) lodged by the cousin of respondent no. 2 against the deceased for maltreating her and expelling her out of his house. The last-mentioned piece of evidence established the factum of marriage between the deceased and respondent no. 2, though it did not conclusively prove that the same was subsisting at the time of the death of the deceased. Therefore, the court concluded that it was proved that respondent no. 1 was the daughter of the deceased, hence she was entitled to her prescribed share. But, due to inconclusive evidence of subsistence of the marriage at the time of death of the deceased, respondent no. 2 could not be treated as a widow of the deceased. Consequently, the court refused the leave to appeal the application and maintained the judgments of the first Appellate Court and the High Court.

Qazi Fazal Ahmad v Riaz-ur-Rahim 2004 SCMR 432

Two daughters as sharers inherit 2/3 and a brother as a residuary gets 1/3 of the property.

Mehr migrated from India and in lieu of the property he left behind, he was allotted land in Pakistan. Mehr died in 1955 and his estate was mutated in favour of his two daughters. Budha, who was Mehr's brother and alive at the time of the latter's death, did not object to the inheritance mutation. The land devolved to the legal heirs of Mehr's daughters who in 1976 sold the entire land to Muhammad Ramzan. In 1978, the legal heirs of Budha, the appellants in the present case, presented an application to the revenue authorities for challenging the mutation and seeking their share. They were advised to approach the Civil Court and they filed a suit in 1980.

The appellants argued that the mutation was carried out by fraud, misrepresentation, and concealment of facts. Hence, it was liable to be cancelled. The Civil Court framed issues pertaining to relevant controversies including the alleged illegality of the mutation and the *bona fide* nature of the sale of the land to Muhammad Ramzan. On the basis of the evidence adduced, the court held that the mutation was not a result of fraud and concealment of facts. It was further decided that the sale of the land to Muhammad Ramzan did not suffer from any illegality.

The appellants assailed the decision before the first Appellate Court and, thereafter, before the High Court, but both courts dismissed their claim. Against three adverse concurrent decisions, the appellants approached the Supreme Court.

The court did not find any substance in the main argument advanced by the appellants that the pedigree table wrongly attributed the daughters to Mehr, though they were not his real daughters. However, the court noticed an important fact which was neglected by all the courts below, that the brother of Mehr was alive at the time of his death. Budha should have been given his share as a residuary after disbursing the prescribed share to the daughters. The prescribed share of the daughters was, in the circumstances, 2/3 of the land and the remaining 1/3 ought to have been awarded to him. Therefore, the court partly accepted the appeal to the extent of 1/3 of the land and declared that the same should be distributed among the legal heirs of Budha. Consequently, the sale to Muhammad Ramzan was held to be legal to the extent of 2/3 of the land only.

Umar Nawaz v Mst Alam Khatoon 2011 CLC 736

Legal heirs under Sunni law generally inherit per capita, whereas under Shia law in some situations they are entitled to inheritance as per stripes.

In this case, an important question arose as to whether residuaries of the same category, but descending from different ascendants, would get an equal share (per capita) or they would step into the shoes of their ascendants (per stripes) for the purpose of inheritance. The parties belonged to Sunni/Hanafi sect, so their rights had to be decided according to their personal law. The deceased, in this case, left behind a widow and three sons of his two brothers (two from the same brother and a third from another). In such a situation, the widow would have 1/4 share and the rest would be distributed among the residuaries (i.e. three sons of the deceased's brothers).

The court of first instance distributed the residue equally among all residuaries. When the case was brought before the first Appellate Court, it decided that the residuaries were not entitled to equal shares as they represented their ascendants. According to the first Appellate Court, the sole son of one brother would have double the share of each son of another brother. This is because he was the only son of his father, and his share would be equivalent to what his father would have inherited had he been alive.

Aggrieved from this decision, the two sons of the same brother of the deceased brought the case before the Lahore High Court. The court, after perusing the record of the case, affirmed the principle of Sunni law as the *propositus* was a Sunni. The court held that if all residuaries belong to the same category but are linked to the deceased from different ascendants, they will inherit equally in the estate. It means that their rights to inheritance are given effect on the basis of per capita distribution and not per stripes. Had the propositus been Shia, distribution of the estate in this situation would have been carried out as per stripes and not per capita.

M. Sohail Kiyani v Raja M. Anwar PLD 2017 Islamabad 162

If a missing person has not been heard of for seven years, he would be considered dead and his estate will be distributed among his legal heirs.

The Islamabad High Court dealt with a complicated proposition about the distribution of inheritance of a missing person. Since 1973, Mr A had been unheard of and all of his legal heirs including his mother, brothers, and sisters except one brother Mr B, died at the time of the institution of a civil suit in 2013 for distribution of the missing person's estate. Mr B argued that the missing person should have been considered dead from the time of the pronouncement of the decision by a competent court to that effect. This contention if acceded to would have made him the sole beneficiary of the estate left by the missing person. On the other hand, it was pleaded by the rest of the interested parties that since the missing person was not heard to be alive since his disappearance in 1973, he should be treated as dead from 1980 and those legal heirs who were alive at that time should be given their respective shares in his estate.

After hearing the arguments and delving into the law enacted as well as laid down by the superior courts, the court observed that once a person is proved to be missing and unheard of for seven years, he would be presumed to be dead after the lapse of seven years from that fateful incident. And if someone argues a different date and time for the death of such a missing person, he would be required to prove that by producing cogent and convincing evidence. As Mr B pleaded that though Mr A went missing in 1973 and he should not be treated as dead until a decision was rendered by a competent court, then Mr B was under an obligation to produce evidence to show that he was alive from 1980 onwards and died at the time when he instituted the case. Resultantly, the court directed that the estate of the missing person should be distributed among those heirs who were alive in 1980 including his mother, sisters, and brothers by considering him dead after the lapse of seven years of his disappearance.

12.7.2 Determination of Religion and Sect. The following case law suggests that the courts have formulated a multi-tiered presumption to facilitate the determination of the religion and sect of a litigant regarding issues of inheritance. The courts presume all persons as Muslims unless proven otherwise and a Muslim will be presumed to be a follower of the Hanafi school unless proven otherwise, e.g. follower of any other Sunni school, i.e. Maliki, Shafi'i, or Hanbali or Shia. Similarly, if a person is a Shia Muslim, the court will presume him/her to be a follower of the Athna Ashari'a school as the majority of Shia Muslims in Pakistan are the followers of this school. In determining the religion and the sect of the litigant, the courts take into account the surrounding circumstances such as his/her way of life, parental faith and the faith of his/her kith and kin.

Latifan Bibi v Rehmat Ali 2012 SCMR 1251

All persons are presumed to be the followers of the Hanafi school and burden of proof is on the one who claims otherwise.

Upon the death of the predecessor-in-interest, his estate was mutated in favour of the appellant/defendant, Latifan Bibi who was an Ahmadi. She claimed the entire estate of the deceased on the basis that the deceased was also an Ahmadi. The respondents/plaintiffs, who were the nephews of the deceased claimed that the deceased was a Muslim. The appellant/defendant was the niece of the deceased. She benefitted under the mutation and asserted that the deceased converted and became an Ahmadi before his death. The respondents/plaintiffs filed a declaratory suit to establish their claim and to get the mutation of the deceased's estate set aside. The suit was dismissed by the trial court. Thereafter, both Appellate Courts decided the matter in their favour.

Against this background, the appellant/defendant brought the dispute before the Supreme Court on the ground that gross misreading and non-reading of the evidence had been committed by the Appellate Courts. The appellant/defendant argued that the impugned mutation was duly carried out after a proper inquiry conducted by the *tehsildar*. It was contended that mere mentioning of the deceased as a Muslim in the National Identity Card (NIC) would not suffice to declare him a Muslim.

The Supreme Court drew attention to numerous pieces of evidence on record supporting the case of the respondents/plaintiffs regarding the faith of the deceased. In addition to his NIC, the deceased's name was registered as a voter in the Muslims' voters list. He was born into a Muslim family and used to offer Friday prayer behind a Muslim *imam*. Upon his death, his funeral prayer was led by a Muslim *imam* and he was buried in a Muslim graveyard. There was no documentary evidence in the form of the deceased's affidavit confirming his conversion. Moreover, he was not established to be a member of any Ahmadi organisation. Hence, the court dismissed the appeal holding that the impugned decision did not suffer from any misreading or non-reading of evidence.

The court observed that in cases like this, the courts have to weigh evidence with care keeping in mind the fact that a great majority of people in Pakistan are Hanafi Muslims; and the party alleging otherwise is under a heavy onus to dispel the initial presumption. Since this onus had not been discharged, the court dismissed the appeal.

Ghulam Shabbir v Bakhat Khatoon 2009 SCMR 644

Considering the great majority of the Hanafi-Sunni population in Pakistan, a deceased would be presumed to be a Hanafi-Sunni.

Fateh Muhammad died leaving behind two widows, Bakhat Khatoon and Sultana Bibi and other relatives including collaterals. After the death of Fateh Muhammad, his immovable property was transferred on the basis of considering him to have been a Shia and the mutation was attested to this effect. Since a childless widow is not entitled to any share in the immovable property of her deceased husband according to the Shia law of inheritance, the mutation deprived the widows of the immovable property.[8] One of the widows, Bakhat Khatoon, challenged the mutation before the revenue authorities. She claimed that the deceased was a Sunni Muslim, and she was entitled to a share in his immovable property. Her plea was accepted by the revenue authorities and an order was passed granting her share in the immovable property.

The collaterals (appellants in the present case) filed a civil suit to have the order passed by the revenue authorities set aside and the litigation went up to the Supreme Court. The collaterals presented evidence in the court that the deceased was a Shia, and his funeral ceremonies were performed according to the rites and rituals observed by the Shia community. The other widow of the deceased, Sultana Bibi also supported the contentions of the appellants. On the other hand, there were many other pieces of evidence adduced before the court proving that the deceased was a Sunni. For instance, there was an official record of him having paid *ushr*; many of his close relatives including his brother, sister, and widows were Sunni and his funeral prayer was led by a Sunni prayer leader.

The Supreme Court relied upon the presumption that all Muslims living in Pakistan are presumed to be Sunnis unless proved otherwise. In this case, the collaterals could not rebut this presumption through reliable evidence. Hence, the deceased was rightly declared by the revenue authorities to be a Sunni and his widow was entitled to her share in his immovable property.

In this case, had the deceased been proven to be a Shia, his widow would have been excluded from inheriting his immovable property. This was the main reason for the contention of the collaterals that he followed the Shia faith. They got a mutation attested to this effect and contended the same unambiguously in the judicial proceedings despite the fact that most of them were Sunni Muslims themselves.

The Supreme Court laid down some important presumptions as to the determination of faith of any deceased person in cases of inheritance. First, considering the great majority of the Sunni population among Muslims in Pakistan, a deceased would be treated as a Sunni, unless proven otherwise. Second, as there are many sub-sects among Sunnis, but the majority among them follow the Hanafi school, a deceased would be considered to be a Hanafi unless the contrary is proved. Third, since the overwhelming majority of the Shia population in Pakistan follows the Ithna Ashari school, a Shia deceased would be presumed to be a follower of the Ithna Ashari school unless proven otherwise.

Muhammad Bashir v Latifa Bibi 2010 SCMR 1915

A deceased's faith can be determined by considering the surrounding circumstances, his way of life, parental faith, and the faith of his kith and kin.

Imam Bakhsh died issueless leaving behind his widow, a real sister, and collaterals. The deceased's immovable properties were transferred to his sister on the basis of considering him to have died a Shia. The collaterals were deprived of their share in the deceased's estate. Therefore, they challenged the mutation in the Civil Court. The Civil Court dismissed their suit, but the first Appellate Court reversed the decision of the Civil Court.

Thereafter, the matter was brought before the High Court which was reported as *Latifa Bibi v Muhammad Bashir*.[9] The court reversed the decision of the first Appellate Court and declared the deceased to be a Shia. In reaching this conclusion, the court relied predominantly on the statement of the widow of the deceased that he was a Shia and used to participate in the religious ceremonies of the Shia community. The deceased was a *patwari* and was posted in a village which was largely inhabited by the Shia community. There was no direct evidence to establish his conversion from Sunni to Shia.

The case was brought before the Supreme Court, which reversed the decision of the High Court and restored the judgment of the first Appellate Court by declaring the deceased to be a Sunni. In doing so, the court analysed the entire evidence on record in detail. Some important pieces of evidence were underscored by the court in its judgment. The statement of the Sunni *imam masjid* of the village, where the deceased used to say his prayers under his *imamat*, was worth consideration because ordinarily, a person who was Shia by faith does not offer prayer under the *imamat* of a Sunni *imam*. Moreover, the *namaz-e-janaza* (funeral prayer) of the deceased, which was attended by a majority of his relatives was led by a Sunni *imam*. The evidence presented from the sister's side did not point out that the *namaz-e-janaza* of the deceased was performed by a Shia *imam* in accordance with Shia rituals. The court observed that this was an additional factor for determining the question as to the faith of the deceased because if he had been a Shia his relatives would not have allowed his *namaz-e-janaza* to be performed by a Sunni *imam*.

The Supreme Court held that there was no principle of universal application for determining the faith of any person. Such determination ordinarily 'depends on surrounding circumstances, way of life, parental faith, and faith of kiths and kins'.[10]

Qamar Sultan v Bibi Sufaidan 2012 SCMR 695

The evidence of a mother, motivated to support her daughter against the brother of the deceased, does not have any legal value.

Fateh Khan died as an unmarried person. He left behind his mother Anwar Sultan, his sister Qamar Sultan, and a collateral, Mumraiz Khan. After his death, a mutation was sanctioned regarding his estate considering the deceased to be a Shia. His estate was distributed entirely in favour of his mother and sister, while the collateral was excluded. The collateral initiated a suit contending that the deceased was a Sunni Muslim, and he was entitled to 1/6 share in the deceased's estate. Both parties adduced evidence and presented witnesses in court to prove their divergent contentions. The collateral presented evidence in the court that the deceased's funeral prayer was led by a Sunni *imam* which showed that he was a Sunni. On the other hand, the mother of the deceased appeared in the witness box and stated that her son was a Shia.

According to the High Court,[11] there was not much difference as to the reliability of the evidence adduced by the parties except that the evidence of the mother was motivated to financially benefit her daughter (the deceased's sister) and to exclude her rival (the deceased's collateral) from inheritance. Considering the financial interest of the mother to enrich her daughter, the court refused to rely on this piece of evidence and declared the deceased to be a Sunni. This entitled the collateral to his share in the estate.

The decision of the High Court was challenged before the Supreme Court. The Supreme Court, after going through the evidence on record concluded that the substantial piece of evidence presented by the sister/ appellant in the case was the evidence of the deceased's mother which appeared to be motivated by financially benefiting her daughter (the deceased's sister). Hence, the Supreme Court dismissed the petition of the deceased's sister and accepted the plea of the deceased's collateral granting him the residue of the estate which was calculated to be 1/6 share.

Farah Chaudhry v Shahid Mahmood Malik 2005 YLR 29

Section 4 of the MFLO does not apply to Ahmadis because the MFLO applies only to Muslim citizens of Pakistan.

The judgment, in this case, addresses the issue of whether section 4 of the MFLO is applicable to non-Muslims. Mahmood Ahmed Malik died and left behind several legal heirs including a daughter of his predeceased son namely, Mehwish Khalid. Both the courts below concurrently decided that all legal heirs would be entitled to the deceased's estate as per applicable law.

In the civil revision before the High Court, the counsel for the petitioners contended that Mehwish Khalid, who was a granddaughter of the deceased, belonged to the Ahmadi faith. He referred to the provisions of the MFLO and argued that the MFLO was applicable only to Muslim citizens of Pakistan. Therefore, Mehwish Khalid who was admittedly an Ahmadi, was not entitled to inherit from her grandfather. The counsel for the respondent rebutted this argument by stating that a granddaughter was entitled to inherit from her grandfather under *Fiqha Ahmadia* and she could not be disinherited because section 4 of the MFLO did not apply to her because she was an Ahmadi.

Justice Mian Hamid Farooq of the Lahore High Court framed the question as to whether the provisions of the MFLO are applicable to Ahmadis. He observed that the parties, in this case, admitted to being Ahmadis by faith and section 1 of the MFLO provided that it applies to all Muslim citizens of Pakistan wherever they may be. Therefore, after the Constitutional Amendment which declared Ahmadis non-Muslims, the MFLO does not apply to Ahmadis.

Justice Farooq further observed that even if it is assumed that Ahmadis follow Hanafi law, Mehwish Khalid would not be entitled to a share in the estate of her grandfather because according to the Hanafi law nearer in degree excludes the more remote relation. According to this principle, the daughter of a predeceased son is not entitled to inherit from her grandfather in the presence of other sons and daughters of the deceased. He examined the book known as *Fiqha Ahmadia* which purported to support the argument that even in the absence of the application of the MFLO an orphaned granddaughter inherits from her grandfather. He noted that according to this book, this rule is applicable only when no other son and daughter of the *propositus* is alive. In this case, the sons and daughters of the deceased were alive. According to another rule in the book, a *qazi* could give to the extent of 1/3 to the orphaned grandchildren from the estate of the grandfather provided this did not affect the share of other legal heirs. Since the application of this rule in the instant case adversely affected the share of other legal heirs it was inapplicable. Therefore, the court partially allowed the revision petition.

12.7.3 Muslim Family Laws Ordinance 1961. The following case law discusses the jurisprudence related to section 4 of the Muslim Family Law Ordinance (MFLO) 1961. Contrary to Sunni and Shia laws, section 4 provides the orphaned grandchildren a share in the inheritance of the deceased as per the share of their parent(s). In *Bhaggay Bibi v Razia Bibi*,[12] the Supreme Court held that section 4, while protecting the interests of orphaned grandchildren does not affect the rights of other legal heirs. However, the Federal Shariat Court declared this section repugnant to the Injunctions of Islam in *Allah Rakha v Federation of Pakistan*.[13] An appeal against this decision is still pending in the Shariat Appellate Bench of the Supreme Court. Since the *Allah Rakha* case, the Supreme Court has applied the respective section in a number of cases. However, while doing so it has been held that the section must be construed strictly in light of the Islamic law of inheritance.

Sarwar Jan v Mukhtar Ahmad PLD 2012 SC 217

Section 4 of the MFLO does not operate retrospectively.

This case deals with the issue of retrospective/retroactive application of the MFLO. In this case, the Supreme Court rejected the plea that the MFLO could have a retrospective application.

Briefly, the facts of the case are that Ilam Din died in 1956. One of his sons had died a year before his death. The descendants of the predeceased son applied on 19 November 1984 for their share in the estate of their grandfather on the basis of the right created under section 4 of the MFLO. The trial court decreed their suit, but the Appellate Court reversed the decision of the trial court. On the revision petition, the High Court upheld the decision of the trial court. Therefore, the matter was brought before the Supreme Court. The court held that the MFLO would only be applied prospectively. The matters relating to inheritance, which had been settled before the promulgation of the MFLO would not be reopened to benefit orphaned grandchildren. Justice Mian Saqib Nisar, as he then was, held:

> In order to examine if as per its own force section 4 ibid [MFLO] has a retrospective effect, it is settled rule that any statute or a provision thereof forming part of substantive law, which creates or extinguish or affect the rights of the persons/citizen shall ordinarily have a prospective effect, except where by the clear command of the law, it is made applicable retrospectively. From the language of section 4 ibid [MFLO] we do not find such to be the intention of the legislature, therefore, in our considered view, the application of the section for all intents and purposes is prospective in nature and by no rule of interpretation can it be given a retrospective effect, so as to undo or reopen the past and closed settlements of inheritance, which had been concluded prior to the coming into force of the Ordinance, otherwise, there shall be no sanctity and conclusiveness attached to all or any of the successions, which have been settled under the Mohammedan Law, much before the enforcement of the Ordinance, 1961, even those successions finalized 50 or 100 years prior thereto shall have no protection. This has never been the object of section 4 ibid [MFLO] and the intendment of the legislature.[14]

In the circumstances of the case, the court observed that since Ilam Din died in 1956, therefore the legal heirs of his pre-deceased son would not be entitled to inherit his estate under Islamic law. As such, the court allowed the appeal and set aside the judgment of the High Court.

Bhaggay Bibi v Razia Bibi 2005 SCMR 1595

Section 4 of the MFLO does not affect the rights of other heirs while protecting the interests of orphaned grandchildren.

This is an important case on the conflict between the general provisions of Islamic law of inheritance and section 4 of the MFLO. According to the facts of the case, Mughla died and left behind his son, Khizar Hayat, and legal heirs (a widow and two daughters) of another son, Maula Dad who had predeceased him. Khizar Hayat inherited half of his estate, while the other half was distributed to the legal heirs of Maula Dad. Maula Dad's, widow was entitled to 1/8 and his daughters to 2/3 from his half share as sharers. The residue of Maula Dad's half share was inherited by Maula Dad's brother Khizar Hayat.

The widow and the daughters of Maula Dad were not happy with the above distribution and argued that nothing should have been given to the brother of the deceased, namely, Khizar Hayat, from the estate devolved upon Maula Dad under section 4 of the MFLO. The residue given to the brother of the deceased ought to have been inherited by them under the doctrine of *radd* (return).

The Supreme Court observed that the application of section 4 of the MFLO was meant to protect the rights of descendants of the predeceased children of a *propositus*; the same could not be extended to override the shares of other eligible heirs under the general provisions of Islamic law. Thus, the application of the MFLO will be tolerated only to the extent that it does not interfere with the shares of other heirs under Islamic law. Consequently, it was held that the brother of the deceased was rightly awarded the residue after giving the widow and the daughters their due from the half share of Maula Dad.

Mukhtar Ahmad v Rasheeda Bibi 2003 SCMR 1664

Section 4 of the MFLO is to be construed subject to Islamic inheritance law.

In this case, the issue in dispute was regarding the extent of the share of inheritance of a daughter of a pre-deceased son. After the death of the deceased, the daughter of the predeceased son claimed her share in the property of her grandfather under section 4 of the MFLO. All the courts below concurrently granted the entire share of the predeceased son to the daughter.

The Supreme Court noted that the daughter of the predeceased son was entitled to the share of her father in her grandfather's estate under section 4 of the MFLO. The court, however, did not stop here and went on to observe that since the daughter was the only child of the predeceased son, she would be entitled to 1/2 and the other 1/2 from the share of her father (i.e. pre-deceased son) would be given to the collaterals.

The Supreme Court followed the same line of reasoning adopted in *Bhaggay Bibi v Razia Bibi*[15] and reduced the share of the daughter to the extent of 1/2 from the estate of the pre-deceased son (her father). The rest of his estate was given to the collaterals.

The manner of interpretation of the Supreme Court in the last two cases is in line with the overall approach of the Pakistani courts which favour strict application of Islamic law. This approach, however, appears to go against the literal construction of section 4 of the MFLO and adversely affects the shares of those who have been legislatively intended to be the beneficiaries of the provision.

Hassan Aziz v Meraj ud Din C.P.3011/2021

The great-grandchildren of a propositus are not entitled to inheritance rights under section 4 of the MFLO because it is limited to the children of predeceased son/daughter.

This case was a leave to appeal before the Supreme Court against the order of the Islamabad High Court[16] which had held that the great-grandchildren of a propositus do not fall within the category of 'the children of such [predeceased] son or daughter' under section 4 of the MFLO. The Supreme Court upheld the judgment of the Islamabad High Court.

According to the facts of the case, the propositus died in 2015, while her two sons predeceased her. One of them, namely Nawab ud Din, died in 1992, and his son Aziz ur Rehman also died in 2005. The petitioners, in this case, are the children of the deceased Aziz ur Rehman. So, they are the great-grandchildren of the propositus. According to the plain reading of section 4 of the MFLO, only the grandchildren of a propositus are entitled to represent their predeceased father/mother.

The petitioners argued that the phrase 'per stirpes' used in section 4 of the MFLO was suggestive to make the children of any predeceased son/daughter 'a compact unit'. And if anyone from such a compact unit died before the opening of the succession, his/her children would have replaced him/her. In this manner, the great-grandchildren were entitled to have a share from the proportionate share of the predeceased grandson Aziz ur Rehman.

The case was heard by a three-member bench of the Supreme Court and Justice Munib Akhtar wrote the judgment. Justice Akhtar presented the following arguments. Firstly, the phrase 'the children of such [predeceased] son or daughter, if any, '*living at the time the succession opens*' must be understood in its normal implication that only those grandchildren who had been alive at the time of the death of the propositus were entitled to have share under the provision. If this meaning was not adhered to, it would make these words redundant which was not warranted by the rules of statutory interpretation. Secondly, section 4 of the MFLO is itself a well-worded exception to the Islamic law of inheritance that does not allow its liberal extension. Thirdly, section 4 of the MFLO employs the phrase 'children' of the predeceased son/daughter and not 'legal heirs' which prevents extending its benevolent implications to other legal heirs of the predeceased son/daughter including spouse. Fourthly, section 4 of the MFLO does not employ the phrase 'how low so ever' as is generally used in Islamic law of inheritance to extend the rights of inheritance from one generation to subsequent generations. Hence, there was no justifiable ground to give any share to the great-grandchildren under section 4 of the MFLO.

12.7.4 Superior Courts and Women's Right to Inheritance. The following case law suggests that the courts tend to adopt a pro-women approach regarding their right to inheritance. For example, traditionally according to Shia law, an issueless widow of a Shia deceased was not entitled to any share in the immovable property of her deceased husband. However, in *Khalida Shamim Akhtar v Ghulam Jaffar*[17] the Lahore High Court observed that Islamic law places no such bar on the issueless widow of a Shia deceased. It was held that an issueless widow of a Shia deceased was as much entitled to a share in the immovable property of her deceased husband as any other legal heir. Similarly, mindful of the patriarchal nature of Pakistani society, the courts have held that the brothers of female co-sharers in possession of land are required by the law to protect the property rights of their sisters.

Ghulam Ali v Ghulam Sarwar Naqvi PLD 1990 SC 1

Brothers of female co-sharers in possession of land are required by law to protect the property rights of their sisters.

This is a landmark case on the subject of the right of inheritance of women in Pakistan. The principles established in this case are that as soon as the owner dies, his property devolves upon his heirs and no state intervention is required to pass the title of the property to the heirs. It further establishes that the law requires brothers of female co-sharers to protect the property rights of their sisters if the brothers come into possession of the land in any capacity.

In this case, the petitioners were the three sons of Ghulam Ahmad Shah, and the respondent was their sister. Ghulam Ahmad Shah died in 1903. Mutations, as regards his property, were entered, and sanctioned in all estates except one, in respect of which the mutation was sanctioned in 1963. The rest of the property was duly mutated in favour of both the petitioners and the respondent. The respondent's share in the land under mutation no. 1231 was stated as 7 *kanal* and 12 *marla*. However, her name was omitted from the pedigree table made on this mutation. Consequently, she was deprived of her share in her father's property covered under this mutation.

The petitioners tried to justify this discriminatory treatment on the basis of their expenditure on the respondent's two marriages as there was an intervening divorce. In addition, they had to spend some money on the murder case in which they had got involved in on account of her divorce. They further claimed some amount for maintaining their sister for five years. They maintained that, owing to these considerations, the respondent relinquished her claim in the inheritance of her father as far as it related to one estate only. The main argument of the petitioners' counsel was that the mutation sanctioned in 1903 against the respondent and her failure to challenge it for a long period of time would constitute such a conduct which would render the petitioners' possession as adverse to her. The trial court dismissed the suit of the respondent seeking her share in the land covered under the disputed mutation. She filed an appeal against the decision which was accepted by the Appellate Court. The petitioners filed a civil revision before the High Court which was dismissed. Therefore, the present petition for leave to appeal was filed before the Supreme Court.

Justice Muhammad Afzal Zullah cited several judicial authorities on this issue, and held:

> As soon as owner dies, succession to his property opens. There is no State intervention or clergy's intervention needed for the passing of title immediately to the heirs. Thus it is obvious that a Muslim's estates legally and juridically vests immediately on his death in his or her heirs and their rights respectively come into separate existence forthwith. The theory of representation of the estate by an intermediary is unknown to Islamic Law of inheritance as compared to other systems … Thus the brother, the father, husband, son or *vice versa*, does not or cannot intervene as intermediary. Here we are dealing with the brother trying though illegally, as if a guardian-in-inheritance-so-called, of a *sui juris* sister, on allegedly "moral" basis, to oust her. It is clearly prohibited by Islam. The females cannot be treated so in our system.[18]

The court delved deeper into the status of women in various foreign systems and compared them to the Islamic system showing how Prophet Muhammad (PBUH) changed the status of women and gave them their full independence and rights. The court also noted that the respondent in this case was not only deprived of her share in the property under the garb of the alleged relinquishment, but her name was also not mentioned in the pedigree table, meaning that even her existence as a daughter, though not otherwise denied, was not acknowledged in the documentation pertaining to inheritance. The court observed that Islam does not recognise any such treatment of women. The court held that the recognition and enforcement of law of inheritance by the state agencies, including courts, *vis-à-vis* female heirs is a matter of public policy. In this regard, the court placed reliance upon Hadiths which enjoins upon men to protect women's rights in every field, and inheritance is no exception.

The court also noted that section 23 of the Contract Act 1872 provides that 'the consideration or object of an agreement is lawful, unless it is forbidden by law or … the court regards it as immoral, or opposed to public policy'. In view of these considerations the court held:

> Here in the light of foregoing discussion on the Islamic point of view, the so-called "relinquishment" by a female of her inheritance as has taken place in this case, is undoubtedly opposed to "public policy" as understood in the Islamic sense with reference to Islamic jurisprudence. In addition, it may be mentioned that Islam visualized many modes of circulation of wealth of certain types under certain types of strict conditions. And when commenting on one of the many methods of achieving the object, almost all commentators on Islamic System agree with variance of degree only, that the strict enforcement of laws of inheritance is an important accepted method in Islam for achieving circulation of wealth. That being so, it is an additional object of public policy. In other words, the disputed relinquishment of right of inheritance, relied upon from the petitioner's side, even if proved against [the] respondent, has to be found against public policy. Accordingly, the respondent's action in agreeing to the relinquishment (though denied by her) being against public policy the very act of agreement and contract and contract constituting the relinquishment, was void.[19]

The court rejected the pleas of estoppel, waiver, and adverse possession on the basis of Islamic principles. It was noted that the petitioners being the brothers of the respondent were required by the Islamic law to protect the property rights of their sister when they came into possession of the land in any capacity. Therefore, the one who was enjoined with the protection of the other's property cannot lay claim adverse to the interests and rights of the latter. In conclusion, the court held that the plea of adverse possession was not available against a sister. Likewise, the rule of public policy and the principle of devolution of property immediately upon the death of her father negated the pleas of estoppel and waiver. Therefore, the petition was dismissed.

Khalida Shamim Akhtar v Ghulam Jaffar PLD 2016 Lah 865

A childless widow of a deceased Shia is entitled to her share of the land.

According to the traditionally understood and applied version of Shia law of inheritance in South Asia, an issueless widow is not entitled to any share in the immovable estate of her deceased husband. This rule deprives the females from their prescribed share in inheritance. Neither the legislature nor judges challenged this rule, as it was perceived to be sanctioned by religious precepts. However, the Lahore High Court in this judgment held that this rule is not supported by religious texts and hence, need not be implemented by the courts. The court observed that this rule should have been amended by the legislature as pointed out by the Supreme Court in *Syed Muhammad Munir v Abu Nasar, Member (Judicial) Board of Revenue Punjab, Lahore*;[20] but this step had not been taken. The court assumed the jurisdiction to rectify the ensuing discrimination and injustice.

In this case, two brothers of the deceased husband deprived an issueless widow from her share in the inheritance of her Shia husband. The Civil Court declared the widow to be entitled to the share in her deceased husband's estate, but the first Appellate Court reversed the decree following the traditionally applicable law. Consequently, the widow brought her case before the Lahore High Court and successfully got her share. Before reproducing the excerpts from the Lahore High Court decision, it would be beneficial to replicate here the imperative part of the decision of the Supreme Court in the above-mentioned case. The Supreme Court held:

> In view of this difference in the interpretation of the Qur'anic text itself, we feel that it would not be proper on our part at this stage to attempt to put our own construction in opposition to the express ruling of commentators of such great antiquity and high authority. To depart from a rule of succession which the Shia community has universally been following ever since the days of Imam Jafar Sadek, as evidenced by the unanimous opinions of the Shia Jurists on this point, would be wrong. It is not open to us to change a settled rule of succession, having the force of Ijma' behind it at this late stage. If a change is desired to be made this work should be undertaken by the Legislature itself after consulting the Shia Community.[21]

Justice Ibad-ur-Rehman Lodhi of the Lahore High Court observed that the applicable law of exclusion of a childless widow in the Shia school is against the explicit meaning of verse no. 12 of Surah 4 of the Qu'ran. The verse does not differentiate on the basis of nature of property the widow would be entitled to. While reaching this conclusion, the court also found support from an *amicus curiae* belonging to the Shia community, who relied on various books of authority to substantiate his argument. With respect to D.F. Mulla's the *Principles of Mahomedan Law* and its articulation of the impugned rule, the court observed that this book should not be considered an enacted law, particularly when any part of it is found to be contrary to the Injunctions of Islam. Justice Lodhi held:

> The question of competence of a childless widow from Fiqa-e-Jafariya has not yet been adjudicated upon by the Judiciary and unless the Legislature, by performing its duty, legislate any codified law in this respect, it is declared that even a childless widow from Fiqa-e-Jafariya would be entitled to claim 1/4th share from the leftover estate of her husband.[22]

Before concluding this decision Justice Lodhi further observed:

> It is expected that, the Government of Pakistan in Ministry of Law, would take legislative measures to promulgate a codified law in this regard in order to protect the rights of childless widows from Ahl-e-Tashih, in getting their due shares from the inheritance of their deceased husbands.[23]

In response to this judgment, the legislature passed the Muslim Family Laws (Amendment) Act 2021 which added subsections to section 4 of the MFLO to recognise the inheritance right of a childless widow of a Shia husband in immovable property. The new law however did not give a childless widow the right to inheritance in the corpus of the property but limited it to 'one-fourth share of the fixed price or value of the property.'[24] The law provides that she shall become entitled to her due share 'in the corpus of immovable property if the legal heirs of the deceased do not give the widow her due share.[25] The new law also provides for arbitration in case of dispute by a 'juris-consult, religious scholar or doctor of Shia school of thought well versed with Shariah having international repute'.[26]

Atta Mohammad v Mst. Munir Sultan 2021 SCMR 73

The deprivation of inheritance rights of the females by their male relatives through sham devices is not only against Sharia, it also contravenes the constitutionally guaranteed rights and numerous principles of policy.

According to the facts of this case, the mother of Mst. Munir Sultan was divorced by Fateh Muhammad who contracted another marriage and had two sons and four daughters from that marriage. Fateh Muhammad gifted his property to his second wife and two sons through three gift mutations. As a result of these gifts, the rest of the legal heirs that included the daughter from the first marriage, Mst. Munir Sultan, along with four daughters from the subsequent marriage, were deprived of their inheritance rights. Mst. Munir Sultan filed a suit for securing her inheritance rights. The Lahore High Court decided in her favour. Against the judgment of the Lahore High Court, the present leave to appeal was filed before the Supreme Court.

The Supreme Court rejected the leave to appeal on the grounds of non-discharge of burden of proof for establishing genuine gifts. The Court observed that the propositus was of over 90 years of age when he died, and the gifts were allegedly made a few months before his death. The Court observed that unusual circumstances of alleged mutations of gifts must have put the revenue authorities on alarm and they should have brought such attempts into the notice of the daughters, but unfortunately that course was not taken. Considering the lapse of twenty-two years from the claim to the final determination of the rights of the daughters, the Supreme Court directed to impose the costs of this process on the petitioners.

Going beyond the facts, the most important feature of the judgment is that it articulated vigorously that any attempt to deprive women from their inheritance rights is in contravention of Sharia, fundamental rights enshrined in the Constitution, and the principles of policy. The author of the judgment Justice Faez Isa reproduced the verses of the Qur'an (9:4, 10:4, and 152:6) with an object to highlight that the proprietary rights of orphans must be protected, and no one should be allowed to deal with such rights to their detriment. He specifically referred to Articles 24(1) and 25(3) of the Constitution that deal with the protection of property including inherited property and the protection of women and children, respectively.

Justice Isa emphasised the unique nexus between the principles of policy and the protection of women's rights of inheritance and observed:

> The Constitution sets out the goals which the people of Pakistan have set out for themselves in the "Principles of Policy", which include the protection of "mother and the child" (Article 35) and require the "promotion of social justice and eradication of social evils" (Article 37). Depriving a mother and her child from their inheritance does not protect them but preys on them. Such conduct is a prevalent social evil and inherently unjust. It is expected that the organ and authority of the State will act in accordance with the Principles of Policy as provided by Article 29(1) of the Constitution. Therefore, claims by orphans and widows alleging that they have been deprived of their inheritance must be expeditiously decided by the concerned organ and authority of the State, including the courts.

It is worth mentioning that Justice Isa, in recent years, in line with the celebrated case dealing with inheritance rights of women, namely *Ghulam Ali v Ghulam Sarwar Naqvi*,[27] has time and again underlined the inextricable relationship between Sharia, fundamental rights, and principles of policy in the protection of inheritance rights of women and orphans.[28]

Justice Isa further refined the relationship between the principles of policy and the protection of inheritance rights of women and orphan in *Ghulam Qasim v Razia Begum*.[29] He argued that under Article 31(1), the citizens should be provided an enabling atmosphere to live their lives in accordance with Islam, and under Article 31(2)(b), 'Islamic moral standards' should be promoted. These provisions are violated when women are deprived of inheritance rights since their rights are mandated by Islamic law. The denial of inheritance rights to women leads to their economic dependence, decline in their standard of living, and concentration of wealth in the hands of males. These three untoward and evil consequences must be avoided under Article 38(a) of the Constitution. Furthermore, the economic dependence of women debars them from taking part in all spheres of life which is another mandatory aspiration of the principles of policy under Article 34 of the Constitution.

12.7.5 Burden of Proof and Acquiescence. Case law demonstrates that the courts tend to place the onus of proof on the claimant whenever it is asserted that a female legal heir has relinquished her share in inheritance. Hence, it has been held that the relinquishment must be by way of positive action(s); mere knowledge of mutation and silence of a female heir would not constitute a valid relinquishment. After all, such an acquiescence may deprive a female heir of her share in the inheritance property.

Gohar Khanum v Jamila Jan 2014 SCMR 801

Onus of proof is on the claimant that a female heir has relinquished her share in inheritance: mere knowledge of mutation and silence of a female heir would not constitute a relinquishment.

In this case, some important issues relating to inheritance were settled. First, when males exclusively inherit an estate, they have to prove that the females have either relinquished or transferred their share in the property to them. Second, the question of limitation is of no consequence in such circumstances.

The deceased left behind a son and a daughter. The estate was mutated in favour of his son to the exclusion of the daughter. The property had been in exclusive possession of the son since the death of the deceased. The son developed the estate by constructing a house on it. This was within the knowledge of the daughter. After about fifty years from the mutation, the daughter claimed her share in the property by filing a suit. The son resisted the suit mainly on two grounds: period of limitation, and the voluntary relinquishment of the share by the daughter. The case was eventually brought before the Supreme Court.

The court observed that the onus to prove that the daughter had relinquished her share or transferred it by any transaction to benefit the son was upon the son. Mere knowledge of the mutation and not opting to assail it for about five decades would not constitute a relinquishment in the eyes of law. In order to relinquish or transfer her share in the estate there had to be a positive and affirmative act, which could be proved by producing documentary evidence of relinquishment, sale, transfer, or gift. In the absence of any such affirmative act on part of the daughter, it could not be said that the property vested entirely in the son. Hence, the court held that the son failed to discharge such onus.

The court further observed that despite the fact that the estate of the deceased was mutated wholly in favour of the son, and he had been in exclusive possession of the same since the death of their father, the daughter was actually a co-owner of the property. Moreover, the occupation of the property by the son as the other co-owner could only be construed as possession on behalf of all co-owners including the daughter. Therefore, the suit filed by the daughter was not time-barred in circumstances. According to the Islamic law of inheritance, the son became the owner of 2/3 of the estate, while the daughter became owner of the remaining 1/3 share. In addition, 1/3 share of the daughter was a product of the operation of law, not dependent on any illegal or faulty mutation. The court held that the mutation was erroneously made in favour of the son in absence of the cogent evidence substantiating the relinquishment or transfer of the daughter's share.

Grana v Sahib Kamala Bibi PLD 2014 SC 167

Acquiescence may deprive a female heir from her share in inheritance.

The law of limitation does not have any relevance in cases of inheritance as pointed out in the above-mentioned case. There is, however, an important exception to this dictum and that is acquiescence. In appropriate cases, acquiescence of a claimant might deprive him/her of his/her share. The present case is a good illustration of this principle.

The plaintiff filed a suit in 1991, which was eventually dismissed by the Supreme Court. In this case, the plaintiff assailed the registered sale deed dated 8 June 1916 and the sale mutation dated 23 December 1917. The plaintiff had also challenged the inheritance and gift mutations dated 5 December 1930, 1 September 1949, and 11 November 1959 respectively, along with further mutations attested from time-to-time until 1987. The plaintiff was more than 80 years old at the time of filing the suit, and according to evidence, she was 6–7 years old when she inherited the property as a limited owner. The plaintiff married in 1930 and as a result she had to give up her share in the property in favour of her stepsister. Subsequently, the plaintiff remained out of possession of the suit property.

It was in the knowledge of the plaintiff how the property was handled thereafter and of her rights therein. The plaintiff was well aware of the transfer of the suit property made by her stepsister and the subsequent gift transfer, but never questioned the sale deed of 1916 until filing of the suit in 1991. The suit property was further sold and re-sold, constructed, and re-constructed upon, but the plaintiff did not take any action for the annulment or prevention of the transfers of the suit property. When the plaintiff filed the suit in 1991 there were as many as 251 transferees of the suit property. In these circumstances, the court observed that the conduct of the plaintiff clearly demonstrated acquiescence in all the impugned transfers of the property which amounted to waiver of her right. Because of the plaintiff's inaction, the transferees of the suit property were led to believe that the defendant had a valid title to the same. Consequently, the Supreme Court dismissed the appeal of the plaintiff.

In deciding the matter, the court held that the law of limitation was not to be ignored entirely whenever any property was claimed on the basis of inheritance. In this regard, the conduct of a claimant-heir might become relevant and material when the defendant argued against the bar of time limitation. On the other hand, the defendant might show that the claimant-heir by his/her acts, overt or implicit, demonstrated acquiescence towards the defendant's title to the suit property thereby allowing him to deal with it as an exclusive owner, in which process he regularly and openly disposed of parts of the property or developed it at his own expense over a long period of time. In such circumstances, when the defendant transferred the suit property for valuable consideration, the transferee was justified in believing that the defendant/transferor had a valid title to the property and a legally vested right to dispose of the same.

12.8 Conclusion

Historically, the domain of inheritance in Pakistan has been regulated by a combination of customary law, Islamic law, and statutory law. Since the 1930s, there is a growing trend of replacing customary law with Islamic law through the introduction of various legislative instruments such as the Muslim Personal Law (Shariat) Application Acts of 1937, 1948, 1962, 1972, and 1975.

As Islamic inheritance law is based on the personal faith of individuals, there are two main types of Islamic laws of inheritance in Pakistan: Sunni and Shia. A majority of Sunnis in Pakistan follow the Hanafi school, while Shias follow the Ithna Ashari (Twelver) school. As the scheme of inheritance under each school differs and the determination of the personal faith of a deceased materially affects the share of legal heirs, the courts have evolved a three-tiered formula of presumptions for determining the sect of a person: first, all Muslims living in Pakistan are presumed to be Sunnis unless proven otherwise; second, all Sunnis are presumed to be Hanafis unless proved otherwise; and third, all Shias are presumed to be Ithna Asharis (Twelvers) unless proved otherwise.

Section 4 of the MFLO protects the rights of orphaned grandchildren by providing them with a share in the estate of their grandfather. Since such a right is not provided under classical Islamic law of both the Sunni and Shia schools, this section has generated much controversy. In the *Allah Rakha* case, the Federal Shariat Court declared this section as repugnant to the Injunctions of Islam and recommended its replacement with a 'mandatory will' to the extent of the one-third property of the grandfather.[30] An appeal against this decision is still pending before the

Shariat Appellate Bench of the Supreme Court. Therefore, section 4 of the MFLO is still a valid law. However, Pakistani courts construe this section in a strict manner so that the scheme of Islamic inheritance law is not disturbed.

The courts in Pakistan have developed various principles to protect the property rights of women in inheritance. It has been emphasised by the Supreme Court that the deprivation of women from their inheritance rights is not only against Sharia/Islamic law, but it is also in conflict with numerous fundamental rights and principles of policy enshrined in the 1973 Constitution. The law of limitation is not applied to protect the proprietary rights of women when they initiate suits for recovery of their property held by their male relatives. In case the male relatives aver that females relinquished their share in the estate they are required to prove it by adducing convincing evidence. In the absence of such evidence, women are put in possession of their inherited property even decades after the death of a *propositus*. Despite this benevolent approach of the superior judiciary, we observe numerous instances of disinheritance of women. There is a widespread custom of disinheriting women in society. Many instances of disinheritance go unnoticed by the legal system as a large number of women do not bring their cases before the courts due to fear of being deprived of the support of their ancestral family for the rest of their lives, especially during hard times.[31]

Questions

1. Please elaborate on the major categories of legal heirs under the Sunni law of inheritance.
2. How does the Shia law of inheritance specify the legal heirs in various classes for the ascertainment of their respective shares?
3. Briefly describe the major differences between the Hanafi Law of Inheritance and the Ithna Ashari Shia Law of Inheritance.
4. What are the principles laid down by the superior courts of Pakistan for determining the faith and sect of a deceased person for the distribution of inheritance?
5. What is the impact of the difference of sect of a *propositus* on the share of the inheritance? Please elaborate through examples.
6. What are the implications of section 4 of the MFLO for the Islamic law of inheritance in Pakistan?
7. Please elaborate on the contribution of Pakistani courts to the protection of the right of inheritance of women.

Further Reading

Books/Articles

Carroll, L., 'Application of the Islamic Law of Succession: Was the Propositus a Sunnī or a Shī'a?', *Islamic Law and Society* (1995) 2, 24–42.

Carroll, L., 'The Hanafi Law of Intestate Succession: A Simplified Approach', *Modern Asian Studies* (1983) 17, 629.

Carroll, L., 'The Ithna Ashari Law of Intestate Succession: An Introduction to Shia Law Applicable in South Asia', *Modern Asian Studies* (1985) 19, 85.

Carroll, L., 'The Pakistan Federal Shariat Court, Section 4 of the Muslim Family Laws Ordinance, and the Orphaned Grandchild', *Islamic Law and Society* (2002) 9 (1), 70–82.

Cheema, S.A., 'Distribution of Inheritance under Islamic Law: An Appraisal of Online Inheritance Calculators', *Journal of Islamic Thought and Civilization* (Spring 2021) 11 (1), 1–20.

Cheema, S.A., 'Inheritance of Full Sister/s with Consanguine Brother/s in Pakistan: A Critical Analysis of Saad Ullah v Gulbanda', *Pakistan Journal of Islamic Research* (2021) 22 (1), 13–28.

Cheema, S.A., 'Shia and Sunni Laws of Inheritance: A Comparative Analysis', *Pakistan Journal of Islamic Research* (2012) 10, 69–82.

Cheema, S.A., 'Socially Abhorrent but Legally Acceptable: A Study of Alleged Conversions of Sunnis and Shias in Cases of Inheritance in Pakistan', *South Asian Studies: A Research Journal of South Asian Studies* (2014) 29 (1), 259–268.

Cheema, S.A., *Islamic Law of Inheritance: Practices in Pakistan* (Islamabad: Shariah Academy, 2017).

Fyzee, A.A.A., *Outlines of Muhammadan Law*, 5th edn (New Delhi: Oxford University Press, 2008) Chapters 12 to 14, 304–369.

Mulla, D.F., *Principles of Mahomedan Law*, 20th edn (Haryana: LexisNexis, 2013), Chapters 6 to 8, 50–131.

Cases

Abdul Khaliq v Fazalur Rehman PLD 2004 SC 768 (Distant kindred can only inherit in the absence of sharers or residuaries. If a sharer or residuary exists, distant kindred are completely ousted.)

Ambreen Khatoon v Mumtaz Bibi 2020 SCMR 643 (The Supreme Court, in an inheritance related dispute, in addition to other evidence, such as CNIC, birth register, also took into consideration the results of DNA tests for the purpose of conclusively establishing the relationship of the deceased with his widow and son.)

Ch. Muhammad Boota v Bano Begum 2003 CLC 485 [Lah] (In this case, the contest was between a brother and a sister, and the brother claimed the entire property to the exclusion of his sister on the basis of an alleged gift made by his mother. The court observed that mothers are ordinarily much more concerned about the welfare of their daughters and are not expected to deprive them of their share in inheritance without having exceptionally strong reasons. Since such extraordinarily strong reasons did not exist to satisfy the judicial conscience as to the disinheritance of the daughter, the petition was dismissed.)

Dubai Islamic Bank v Saima Yasin 2020 CLD 518 [Lah] (The category of joint account in which authorisation to manage account is vested in either of joint account holders or survivor is against the Powers of Attorney Act, Islamic law of inheritance, and article

2A of the Constitution of Pakistan. The court noted that once a propositus dies, his entire estate vests in the collective ownership of all legal heirs, and the said type of account if allowed to remain operative unilaterally is in violation of such collective ownership.)

Dur Muhammad v Abdul Sattar 1996 CLC 1596 (Lah) (Where parties were neither co-heirs nor co-sharers and it was proved that the defendants had been in possession of the land in question right from the death of the deceased landowner some forty years ago and his inheritance mutation was also attested in their favour to the exclusion of the plaintiff, the plaintiff's suit filed after four decades was held to be barred by limitation.)

Gakhar Hussain v Surayya Begum PLD 2013 Lah 464 (Under Islamic law, there is no institution of abandonment (‘*aaq*’) for a disgruntled child depriving them from inheritance.)

Kullu v Faizi 2015 YLR 2014 [Lah] (In the presence of sharers, an estate of a deceased cannot devolve upon distinct kindred rather the same would return to the sharers under the principle of return (*radd*). In this case, the deceased was survived by his mother (sharer) who would get 1/3 share out of his legacy while the remaining 2/3 share in the absence of any other residuary would revert to her to the exclusion of all distant kindred.)

Mehrunnisa v Syed Muhammad Zoha 2015 CLC 738 [Kar] (A widow of an issueless deceased who does not have any other relative alive would inherit 1/4 of the estate as sharer and the remaining 3/4 would revert to her under the doctrine of return [*radd*].)

Mst Noor Bibi v Ghulam Qamar 2016 SCMR 1195 (Even if a widow has given birth to a child during her wedlock with the *propositus*, but such child died prior to the death of the *propositus*, the widow would not be entitled to inherit the immovable property of the *propositus* as she was a ‘childless widow’ under Shia personal law.)

Muqadar v Roshah 2008 CLC 43 [Pesh] (In this case, a deceased was survived by a widow, a daughter, and a collateral. The widow and the daughter being sharers, would be entitled to 1/8 and 1/2 shares respectively, while the collateral being a residuary would be entitled to the remaining estate which would be 9/24 shares.)

Slabo Bibi v Gul Rehman PLD 1996 Pesh 1 (There is no period of limitation against the co-sharers in suits for inheritance when the property in dispute was held in possession by some other co-sharers, as the latter would be deemed to possess the property on behalf of the deprived co-sharers.)

Wafaqi Hakoomat-e-Pakistan v Awam-e-Pakistan PLD 1991 SC 731 (The Benevolent Fund and Group Insurance Act 1969 is not repugnant to the Inunctions of Islam since the funds like Benevolent Fund and Group Insurance do not constitute inheritable estate ‘*Taraka*’.)

Notes

1. Rule 9 of the Punjab Land Revenue Rules 1968.
2. PLD 1964 Lah 451, 452.
3. PLD 2014 SC 779, 781.
4. Ibid.
5. D.F. Mulla, *Principles of Mahomedan Law*, 72.
6. Ibid., 76–77.
7. Ibid., 110 and S.A. Cheema, ‘Shia and Sunni Laws of Inheritance: A Comparative Analysis’, *Pakistan Journal of Islamic Research* (2012) 10, 69–82.
8. In *Khalida Shamim Akhtar v Ghulam Jaffar* PLD 2016 Lah 865, the Lahore High Court held that an issueless widow of a Shia deceased is entitled to her share in the land.

9. 2006 CLC 1076.
10. 2010 SCMR 1915, 1919.
11. *Qamar Sultan v Mst Bibi Sufaidan* 2010 YLR 2515.
12. 2005 SCMR 1595.
13. PLD 2000 FSC 1.
14. PLD 2012 SC 217, 221.
15. 2005 SCMR 1595.
16. Hassan Aziz and others v Meraj-ud-Din and others 2021 CLC 1821.
17. PLD 2016 Lah 865.
18. PLD 1990 SC 1, 12.
19. Ibid., 21.
20. PLD 1972 SC 346.
21. PLD 2016 Lah 865, 868–69.
22. Ibid., 871.
23. Ibid., 872.
24. The Muslim Family Laws (Amendment) Act 2021, section 2.
25. Ibid.
26. Ibid.
27. PLD 1990 SC 1.
28. *Farhan Aslam v Nuzba Shaheen* 2021 SCMR 179; *Ghulam Qasim v Razia Begum* PLD 2021 SC 812.
29. PLD 2021 SC 812.
30. PLD 2000 FSC 1.
31. For an ethnographic study on this point see M.A. Chaudhry, 'The Logic in the Traditional Share of the Daughter in Father's Patrimony: A Case Study of the Punjab', *Journal of Law and Social Research* (2009–10), 27–40.

Part IV
PERSONAL LAWS AND FAMILY COURT PROCEDURES

Chapter 13
PERSONAL LAWS OF NON-MUSLIMS

Chapter 14
CONFLICT OF PRIVATE/PERSONAL LAWS

Chapter 15
PROCEDURES IN FAMILY COURTS

13

PERSONAL LAWS OF NON-MUSLIMS

13.1 Introduction

Pakistan is home to various non-Muslim communities including Christians, Hindus, Jaina, Parsis, Sikhs, Buddhists, and others. The personal matters of these religious communities are largely regulated by their uncodified laws and customs. During the colonial period, a few statutes were enacted which regulate the personal and family matters of Christians, Hindus, Sikhs, and Parsis. The Christian Marriage Act 1872 and the Divorce Act 1869 provide a comprehensive regime for the regulation of the personal affairs of Christians. Certain parts of the Succession Act 1925 also apply to Christians.[1] Similarly, several statutes regulate various aspects of Hindu personal law.[2] Unlike in India, Hindu law is not codified in Pakistan and consequently it has mainly remained stagnant. It was only recently that the Hindu Marriage Act 2017 and the Sindh Hindus Marriage Act 2016 were passed. These Acts primarily deal with the registration of Hindu marriages, though the former Act does prescribe some rules for divorce within the Hindu community and the protection of the financial rights of wives and children upon divorce. Regarding the Sikh community, the Anand Marriage Act 1909 declares that the Sikh marriage ceremony called Anand shall be deemed valid in law. However, the Act does not provide further rules regarding registration of such marriages, divorce, legitimacy of children, and other issues related to inheritance. In contrast, the Parsi Marriage and Divorce Act 1936 provides detailed rules regarding marriage, divorce, rights of children, personal property, and Parsi Matrimonial Courts.

In addition to particular statutes, the Special Marriages Act 1872 regulates the marriage and divorce of persons who do not profess the Christian, Jewish, Hindu, Muslim, Parsi, Buddhist, Sikh, or Jaina religion. This Act recognises that there might be individuals who profess religions other than the ones mentioned in the Act or who profess no religion at all. In addition, the Act envisages multi-religious marriages where each party professes a different religion. The option of this type of marriage, however, is only available to persons who profess Hindu, Buddhist, Sikh, or Jaina religion. Muslims, Christians, Jews, and Parsis cannot enter into a marriage with a person professing a religion other than their own under this Act.

In the following chapter, we provide a comprehensive overview of the non-Muslim personal laws in Pakistan by summarising important statutes along with relevant case law.

13.2 Personal Law of Hindus

In Pakistan the personal matters of Hindus, in addition to their uncodified customary practices, are regulated by the Hindu Marriage Act 2017, and the Sindh Hindus Marriage Act 2016.

13.2.1 The Hindu Marriage Act 2017. The promulgation of the Hindu Marriage Act 2017 in March 2017 is a landmark development with regard to the personal laws of Hindus. This law, however, is applicable only in Punjab, Khyber Pakhtunkhwa, and Balochistan as the province of Sindh had formulated its own law—the Sindh Hindus Marriage Act 2016. The Act makes it mandatory for the parties intending to enter into a marriage to be 18 years of age or above. It also lays down that for a marriage to be solemnised, the parties must render their free consent; they must not be related to each other within a prohibited degree of relationship as per laws, religion, and customs having the force of law relating to Hindus and neither of the parties should have an existing spouse at the time of marriage. The Act declares any such marriage void if the parties are within the prohibited degree of marriage or if they have a living spouse. A Hindu husband can enter into a polygamous marriage if his wife cannot conceive a child and is medically declared to be so.[3]

According to the Act, a marriage may be declared voidable, and may be subsequently annulled by obtaining a decree of nullity, if any of the following grounds are met: (1) it has not been consummated owing to the impotence of the respondent; (2) the parties are below 18 years of age at the time of marriage; (4) the marriage was not freely consented to; (5) the consent of the petitioner was obtained by force, coercion, or fraud; or (6) the respondent at the time of marriage was pregnant by some person other than the petitioner. The option of the annulment of the marriage is not available under the Act if the petition is presented more than one year after the force or coercion ceases to operate or when the fraud has been discovered, or the petitioner, with his/her consent, continued to live with the other party as a spouse after the force had ceased to operate or the fraud had been discovered.

The Act also provides for judicial separation and divorce between the parties on the following grounds: (1) if the petitioner was treated with cruelty; (2) the respondent ceased to be Hindu by conversion to another religion; (3) the petitioner was deserted for a period of two years without reasonable cause and without the consent or against the will of the other party, and it includes the wilful neglect of the petitioner by the other party; (4) the respondent was of unsound mind; (5) the respondent was suffering from a virulent, incurable, or venereal disease; (6) the respondent renounced the world by entering a religious order; (7) there has been no resumption of cohabitation between the parties for a period of more than one year after the decree for judicial separation or order for restitution of conjugal rights; (8) the husband is sentenced to imprisonment for a period of four years or more; or (9) if the marriage, whether consummated or not, was solemnised before the wife attained the age of 18 years, she can repudiate her marriage before attaining that age. The spouses may file for a decree of the termination of marriage with mutual consent on the ground that they have been living separately for a period of one year or more because they are unable to live together. The petitions under the Act are to be filed before the Family Courts.

Under section 13 of the Act, the adverse impact of termination of marriage on a wife and children has also been considered. A wife has the right to oppose the grant of the decree of the termination of marriage on the ground that it may result in grave financial hardship to her unless arrangements have been made to the satisfaction of the court to eliminate such hardship. The court shall not pass a decree of termination of marriage unless it is satisfied that adequate provisions have been made for the maintenance of the children born during the wedlock.

Where a marriage is dissolved by a decree of divorce and the time for filing an appeal has expired or appeal has been preferred but dismissed, the Act allows for the parties to remarry after the expiry of six months from the date of final decision in this regard. Under section 17 of the Act, a Hindu widow is entitled to remarry after six months of the death of her husband.

For facilitating the proof of marriages, the Act lays down rules for the registration of marriages with the marriage registrar. The register containing the particulars of a marriage is to remain open for public inspection. However, an omission in the marriage register does not affect the validity of a marriage.

In comparison with the Hindu Marriage Act 2017, the Sindh Hindus Marriage Act 2016 is limited to registration of Hindu marriages. It does not lay down any rules regarding valid marriages, restitution of conjugal rights, divorce, remarriage of Hindu widows, legitimacy of children, and the protection of financial rights of wives and children after divorce.

13.2.2 The Sindh Hindus Marriage Act 2016. The Sindh Hindus Marriage Act 2016 is the first such legislation in the history of Pakistan whereby the Hindu community was given the right to legally register their marriages and prove their marital unions. The Act makes it compulsory for the parties intending to enter into a marriage to be 18 years of age or above. It also requires that for a marriage to be solemnised between parties: (1) the parties must give their free consent; (2) they must not be related to each other within the prohibited degree of relationship; (3) neither of the parties should have an existing spouse at the time of marriage; and (4) there should be at least two witnesses present both at the time of the solemnisation and registration of a marriage. The Act also provides that a marriage is to be solemnised according to the customary rites and ceremonies of either party to the marriage.

As for the registration of a marriage, the Act states that it must be registered with the Union Council/Ward or any other Municipal Authority, where the marriage was solemnised, within 45 days of such solemnisation. The Act also lays down the manner of registration: there shall be four copies of the marriage certificate, which after being filled out, shall be given to the Concerned Officer. The Officer, after satisfying himself that all conditions of marriage (as laid out in section 4 of the respective Act) have been fulfilled, shall endorse the marriage certificate. Furthermore, he shall keep one copy of the marriage certificate for his record and return the remaining copies to the parties. The Concerned Officer is required to maintain a marriage register for the purposes of the Act, and all the entries in the register shall bear the official stamp of the Concerned Officer and be signed by the person solemnising the marriage, both parties to the marriage, two credible witnesses, and the Concerned Officer.

The Act shall also have retrospective effect for the registration of marriages solemnised prior to its commencement and such marriages should be registered with the Concerned Officer in accordance with the procedure laid down by the Act. The provisions of the Act are to be interpreted to advance the purposes of this Act, i.e. the registration of

Hindu marriages; and the provisions of the Act take precedence over the provisions of any other law.

13.3 Personal Law of Christians

As opposed to other religious communities, the personal matters of Christians have been regulated by the state for a long time under the statutes passed during the colonial period. The Christian Marriages Act 1872, and the Divorce Act 1869 are applicable to Christian marriages and divorce in Pakistan.

13.3.1 The Christian Marriage Act 1872. The Christian Marriage Act 1872 regulates the matters related to the marriages within the Christian community in Pakistan. It applies in all those situations where either one or both the parties are Christians. According to the Act, marriages between Christians can be solemnised by any person who has received Episcopal ordination, by any clergyman of the Church of Scotland, by any minister of religion, marriage registrar, or any other person licensed under the Act. Unless a special license is obtained, the marriage must be solemnised between 6:00 a.m. and 7:00 p.m. As for the venue where the solemnisation can take place, the marriage must be solemnised at a church unless a special license is obtained to solemnise it at any other place. A notice in writing must be given to the minister, who is to solemnise the marriage, by one of the persons intending marriage. Such notice must state the full name, profession, status, home address, and duration of residence at the aforesaid address of each of the persons intending marriage and also the place where marriage is intended to be solemnised. The aforesaid notice must be affixed by the minister in a conspicuous part of the church at which the marriage is to be solemnised only if he is entitled to officiate as minister in such church. If he is not so entitled, the notice must be returned to the person who delivered it or may be sent to the minister who is entitled to officiate the marriage.

In case where one of the parties intending to marry is a minor, consent of such person's parent or guardian is required unless the parent or guardian does not reside in Pakistan. In this case, a copy of the notice sent to the minister must be forwarded to the marriage registrar of the district. The marriage registrar must affix such notice at a conspicuous place in his office.

The Act provides that on request of either party intending marriage, a certificate of the notice and declaration made by the parties in this regard can be obtained from the minister or the marriage registrar where the issuance of the certificate is neither forbidden nor does any lawful impediment exist as to its issuance. Any person whose consent is required for the marriage can prohibit the issuance of the certificate by giving a notice in this regard to the minister of religion. On the receipt of such notice, the minister must not solemnise the marriage until he examines the matter of such prohibition and satisfies himself that the person prohibiting the marriage is authorised to do so. Where a marriage is to be solemnised by the marriage registrar and the consent is unjustly withheld or the person whose consent is required is insane, the parties may apply by petition to the District Judge. The same remedy is available in a case where the marriage registrar refuses to issue the aforesaid certificate of notice. Moreover, in marriages solemnised by ministers of religion, any person whose consent is required for a marriage between parties may protest against the marriage registrar's issuance of certificate. However, if such protest is found to be frivolous, the person protesting will be held liable to pay damages to the party whose marriage was protested against. Marriages solemnised by the marriage registrar are subject to virtually similar rules as those governing ministers of religion.

Furthermore, a marriage must be solemnised within two months of the issuance of the certificate of notice; otherwise, the marriage will be void unless the certificate is reissued. It should be noted that marriages between parties must be solemnised in the presence of two credible witnesses. Marriages also need to be registered in accordance with the rules laid out in Part IV of the Act. The Act also provides penalties in case the provisions of the Act are contravened.

13.3.2 The Divorce Act 1869. The Divorce Act 1869 regulates the divorce and associated matters of Christians in Pakistan. The Act lays down several grounds on the basis of which marriage between spouses may be dissolved, annulled, or the spouses may be judicially separated. It provides that a husband may file a petition for the dissolution of his marriage on the ground that his wife has been guilty of adultery. Similarly, a wife also has a right to seek dissolution of marriage on the grounds that (1) her husband has converted to some other religion since solemnisation of marriage and has gone through a form of marriage with another woman; (2) has been guilty of incestuous adultery; (3) of bigamy with adultery; (4) of marriage with another woman with adultery; (5) of rape, sodomy, or bestiality; (6) of adultery coupled with such cruelty as without adultery would have entitled her to a divorce a *mensa et toro* (divorce from bed-and-board); (7) of adultery coupled with desertion, without reasonable excuse, for two years or more.

A husband or a wife may also seek nullity of their marriage through court: (1) if the husband was impotent both at the time of marriage and the institution of suit; (2) if parties were related to each other within the prohibited degree of relationship; (3) if either party was insane at the time of marriage; or (4) if the former spouse of either party was alive at the time of marriage and marriage with the same was still intact. The court may also pass a decree of nullity of marriage if it is proved that the consent of either party was obtained by force or fraud. The Act also allows parties to obtain a decree of judicial separation on the grounds of adultery, cruelty, or desertion without reasonable cause for two years or more. Such decree will have the effect of a divorce a *mensa et toro* (divorce from bed-and-board).

Furthermore, the Act provides for the reversal of the decree of separation if such a decree is obtained in the absence of a husband or a wife. A husband or a wife may also file a petition for the restitution of conjugal rights if either spouse is not cohabitating with the other without any reasonable cause. The parties may also remarry after the expiry of six months from the date of a decree for dissolution of marriage, or where an appeal has been filed against the decree, after the dismissal of such appeal.

Part VI of the Act relates to protection orders. A wife who has been deserted by her husband may seek orders from the court to protect any property which she may have acquired or may acquire after such desertion, against her husband, his creditors, or any person claiming to act under him. The Act also allows a husband to claim damages from a person who has committed adultery with his wife. Furthermore, the provision of the Act authorises courts to make orders regarding alimony pending the suit, permanent alimony or monthly or weekly sums for maintenance to be given to the wife by the husband. In a case where the court passes a decree for the dissolution of marriage or judicial separation on the basis of wife's adultery and the court finds out that the wife is entitled to some property, the court, as it deems fit, may order for the settlement of such property for the benefit of the husband, their children, or both.

Part XI of the Act deals with the power of the courts to issue orders regarding the custody of children in suits of judicial separation, dissolution, or nullity of marriages. The court may from time to time, before passing its decree or after passing such decree, issue such interim orders as it deems fit in regard to the maintenance, education, and custody of minor children.

13.4 Outline of Case Law

13.4.1 Marriage of *sui juris* Christians

Mst Saima v The State PLD 2003 Lah 747

The marriage of *sui juris* Christians solemnised by an authorised clergy is valid.

This case discusses the validity of a marriage solemnised by a person whose authorisation to do so was in question. Brief facts of the case, as per the prosecution, are that the complainant's daughter, petitioner no. 1, suddenly disappeared along with some jewellery and household articles. On the complaint of petitioner no. 1's mother, the Additional Session Judge Lahore, summoned the parties. Petitioner no. 1 claimed that she was the lawfully wedded wife of Qaiser Yusuf, petitioner no. 2. She maintained that she, being a *sui juris* female, did not commit any offence in marrying petitioner no. 2. On the contrary, the complainant maintained that the marriage was fake, as Father Rev. Daniel Yunus, petitioner no. 3, was not authorised under the Christian Marriage Act 1872 to solemnise the marriage. She further contended that the opinion given by the Bible Society in this regard confirmed that the marriage performed by petitioner no. 3 was not valid in the eyes of law. Hence, in light of these considerations, petitioner no. 2 and 3 have committed *zina.*

The counsel for the petitioner no. 1, on the other hand, argued that after the death of the petitioner no. 1's father, a dispute arose between the petitioner and the complainant. The complainant was not happy with the marriage of petitioner no. 1 and registered a frivolous case against her. The counsel further argued that Father Rev. Daniel Yunus had a valid appointment letter issued by the Methodist Church of Pakistan and was fully competent to solemnise the marriage. The counsel also pointed out that petitioner no. 1 had filed a declaratory suit which was pending adjudication, and it was for the Civil Court to decide the validity of the marriage, not for an investigating officer in the domain of criminal law.

After hearing counsels for both the parties, the court relied upon section 5 of the Christian Marriage Act 1872 which enlists persons authorised to solemnise a Christian marriage. The court noted that the clause (1) of section 5 states that marriage can be solemnised 'by any person who has received Episcopal Ordination, provided that marriage be solemnised according to the rules, rites, ceremonies and customs of the Church of which he is a Minister'. The letter issued by the Methodist Church of Pakistan to petitioner no. 3 explicitly authorised him to solemnise marriages. The court noted that the aforesaid letter confirmed the appointment of petitioner no. 3 as Deacon of the Methodist Church of Pakistan. It held that the letter of the Bible Society produced by the prosecution was merely an opinion by a body engaged in the publication of the Bible, having no authority to issue verdicts on such issues. The court further observed that a marriage is a union between two *sui juris* individuals and the non-performance of rituals does not invalidate it, especially in this case where petitioner no. 3 was clearly authorised to solemnise the marriage.

As the case against petitioner no. 1 and 2 was registered under sections 7, 9, and 10 of the Offence of Zina (Enforcement of Hudood) 1979, along with certain provisions of the Pakistan Penal Code 1860, the court also considered whether petitioner no. 1 and 2 had committed an offence under section 10 of the Ordinance. It observed that in terms of section 6 of the Ordinance, there are several circumstances in which a person is said to commit *zina*, one of such circumstances includes sexual intercourse 'with the consent of the victim, when the offender knows that the offender is not validly married to the victim and the consent is given because the victim believes that the offender is another person to whom the victim is or believes herself or himself to be validly married'.

The court observed that in the present case both petitioners no. 1 and 2, believed that they were validly married, and hence, the condition precedent for the alleged offence *prima facie* did not exist. It held that the case registered against petitioners no. 1 and 2 reflected both malice in fact and in law.

13.4.2 Bigamy

Nazir Yasin v Yasin Farhat PLD 2000 Lah 594

Christian marriages are monogamous and Christian law does not allow second marriage without divorcing the first wife or unless the first wife is dead.

The judgment in this case applies the legal principle that Christian law does not allow polygamy. Mst Nazir Yasin, the appellant, filed a complaint under section 200 of the Criminal Procedure Code 1898 alleging therein that she lawfully married the respondent, Yasin Farhat, in Libya according to Christian rites and with free consent. Later, the respondent contracted a second marriage. He subsequently filed a suit for the dissolution of the first marriage under section 10 of the Divorce Act 1869. The appellant filed an application for the rejection of the plaint which resulted in the plaint being rejected by the civil judge. Thereafter, the appellant filed an application for the registration of a criminal case against the respondent under sections 494 and 495 of the Pakistan Penal Code 1860 before the Superintendent of Police who marked it to the Station House Officer, but no action was taken, hence this complaint.

After recording preliminary evidence, the trial magistrate summoned the respondent and charge-sheeted him, but he pleaded not guilty. Both the respondent and the appellant produced witnesses in support of their claims. The respondent also appeared as his own witness and stated that the complainant herself had left the respondent without any legal justification and also avoided giving birth for thirteen years of their marriage, therefore, he contracted a second marriage. After considering the evidence, the trial magistrate acquitted the respondent which led to the present appeal.

The counsel for the appellant submitted that the order of the trial court was illegal and against the record. He relied upon section 4 of the Christian Marriage Act 1872 to argue that the second marriage of the respondent was void and illegal. The aforesaid section lays down that any marriage which is not solemnised in accordance with the provisions of the Act shall be void. The counsel also relied upon other provisions of the Christian Marriage Act 1872 and the Divorce Act 1869. Reliance was also placed upon section 60(2) of the Christian Marriages Act 1872, which lays down certain conditions that are required to be met in order for the marriage between native Christians to be certified. According to one of the conditions, 'neither of the persons intending to be married shall have a wife or husband still living'. Similarly, section 19(4) of the Divorce Act 1869 lays down the grounds on the basis of which a marriage can be nullified: it states that a decree may be passed if 'the former husband or wife of either party was living at the time of marriage and marriage with such former husband or wife was then in force'.

The court noted that, from the above-quoted provisions of the law, it was clear that Christian law does not allow second marriage without divorcing the first wife or unless the first wife is dead. The court also found support for this conclusion from the written views submitted by the Bishop of Lahore, who citing various sources established that Christian marriages are monogamous. In light of the foregoing reasons, the court accepted the appeal.

13.4.3 Dissolution of Marriage on the Ground of Irretrievable Breakdown of Marriage

Ameen Masih v Federation of Pakistan PLD 2017 Lah 610

A Christian couple can invoke section 7 of the Divorce Act 1869 in order to seek divorce on grounds available under UK Matrimonial Causes Act 1973, including the ground that the marriage is irretrievably broken down.

This case examines the constitutionality of the repeal of section 7 of the Divorce Act 1869 through Federal Laws (Revision & Declaration) Ordinance 1981 (XXVII of 1981) on the touchstone of minority rights guaranteed under the Constitution.

The petitioner was a Christian who wished to divorce his wife. However, he could not do so under the Divorce Act 1869 (Act) as it stood at that time, because in order to get divorced he had to prove adultery on part of his wife as per section 10 of the Act, an option he did not wish to invoke. He stated that under the repealed section 7 of the Act, grounds of divorce provided under the UK Matrimonial Causes Act 1973 (UK Act), including the ground that the marriage had broken down irretrievably were available to him. However, section 7 of the Act had been repealed through Federal Laws (Revision & Declaration) Ordinance 1981 (XXVII of 1981) (Ordinance). He prayed that item 7(2) of the Second Schedule to the Ordinance, whereby section 7 of the Act was repealed, be declared unconstitutional, and section 7 be restored to its original position.

He further contended that Christians in Pakistan are a minority, and it is a duty of the state to safeguard the legitimate interests of the Christians, over and above the fundamental rights, which are guaranteed to them as citizens of Pakistan. He prayed that, by reviving section 7 of the Act, the grounds of divorce available to a Christian under the UK Act be made available to the petitioner. He argued that section 7 of the Act was omitted during the undemocratic era of General Zia ul-Haq without any consultations with the Christian community. The repeal was meant to force Christians to abandon their faith as in order to go around section 10 of the Act, many Christians have, over the years faked conversions in order to divorce their spouses.

Assistant Attorney General for Pakistan, Ms Hina Hafeezullah Ishaq contended that Pakistan has ratified the Convention on the Elimination of all Forms of Discrimination Against Women (CEDAW) and has thus committed to end discrimination against women. She stated that Article 25 of the Constitution empowers the State to make special provisions for women and Article 8 provides that any law or custom or usage inconsistent with fundamental rights will have no force of law. She further submitted that Divorce Act 1869 is a pre-constitutional legislation and is almost 147 years old. Despite several attempts to introduce amendments in the Act, the State has remained unsuccessful to this effect. She maintained that even though the Federal Law (Revision & Declaration) Ordinance 1981 stands validated under Article 270–A of the Constitution, this validation fails to pass the test of fundamental rights. Moreover, all laws need to be brought in conformity to the fundamental rights guaranteed under the Constitution. She argued that when the Divorce Act 1869 was prevalent, the English law of the time was the Matrimonial Act 1857, which had limited grounds of divorce. Then came the Matrimonial Causes Act 1923 and finally the Matrimonial Causes Act 1973 which allowed for divorce if the marriage had irretrievably broken down. She submitted that the Divorce Act 1869 must be in line with the developments in the divorce law as in rest of the Christian world so that Christians in Pakistan have the same relief.

Additional Advocate General Punjab, Anwaar Hussain submitted that the government has made efforts to amend the Act in order to include other grounds for divorce besides adultery. However, consensus could not be reached because the representatives of Catholic Church, Presbyterian Church, and Church of Pakistan contended that amendment in section 10 of the Act would be in contravention of their holy scriptures. He further submitted that in the Christian majority countries around the world, the law of divorce has undergone an immense change; Christians all over the world can now divorce their spouses on grounds other than adultery. He cited examples of many countries where no-fault divorce has been introduced thus providing grounds for divorce other than adultery.

In order to reach out to the Christian community and to ensure maximum participation, public notices were published in different local newspapers and notices were also issued to some prominent members of the Christian community. In their responses to the public notices, most of the representatives of the Christian community supported the contention of the petitioner and submitted that no-fault divorce has been introduced all over the world and must also be available to the Christians in Pakistan. It was further submitted that the current law of divorce for the Christians is in violation of the conventions signed by the Government of Pakistan, namely the Universal Declaration of Human Rights and International Covenant on Civil and Political Rights.

Addressing the contention of various stakeholders that divorce, other than on the ground of adultery, was not permitted in the holy scriptures and the judicial examination of the impugned Ordinance by this court amounted to judging personal/Biblical law of Christians; the court noted that Biblical law was not being examined in this case; rather it was state law, i.e. the Federal Laws (Revision & Declaration) Ordinance 1981 which was under review, whereby section 7 of the Act was deleted. Therefore, 'the distinctiveness of state law and personal law has to be borne in mind in order to understand the scope of this judgment'.[4] This court was only to judicially review the existing State law on the touchstone of constitutional values and fundamental rights guaranteed to the minorities-cum-citizens of this country under the Constitution.

Discussing the development of Christian divorce law in various countries, Chief Justice Syed Mansoor Ali Shah of the Lahore High Court noted:

> Divorces under Christian law are generally of two distinct types: Absolute divorce, or divorce "*a vinculo matrimonii*" is a judicial dissolution of the marriage ordered as a result of marital misconduct or other statutory cause arising after the marriage ceremony, whereas limited divorce, sometimes referred to as divorce "*a mensa et thoro*," "divorce from bed and board," or legal separation is a change in status by which the parties are separated and are precluded from cohabitation, but the actual marriage is not affected. Limited divorce is sometimes termed a judicial separation, which suspends the marriage relation and modifies its duties and obligations, leaving the bond in full force.[5]

Trying to trace the global change in the Christian divorce law in some of the Christian majority countries, Justice Shah noted that the countries with a majority Christian population have introduced the no-fault divorce based on the concept of irretrievable breakdown of marriage, where either one or both parties are unable or refuse to cohabit and there are no prospects for reconciliation. To this end, the court examined the UK Matrimonial Causes Act 1973 and noted that the UK law shows that no-fault divorce or irretrievable breakdown of marriage is an established ground of divorce in Christian majority countries of the world.

After appraising various international human rights instruments to which Pakistan is a party, Justice Shah turned his attention towards the Pakistani Constitution and noted:

> The preamble of the Constitution, as well as, the Objectives Resolution, which forms substantive part of the Constitution under Article 2A of the Constitution, provide that adequate provisions shall be made for the minorities to freely profess and practice their religion and develop their culture. And adequate provision shall be made to safeguard the legitimate interests of the minorities. Article 20 of the Constitution, as a fundamental right, provides that every citizen shall have the right to profess, practice and propagate his religion subject to law, public order and morality. Principle of Policy under Article 36 provides that State shall safeguard the legitimate rights and interest of minorities. Under Article 29 of the Constitution, it is the responsibility of the State, and of each person performing functions on behalf of an organ or authority of the State, to act in accordance with those Principles. Members of the minority also enjoy fundamental rights guaranteed to every citizen under the Constitution. Therefore, inter alia, right to life, liberty, dignity and non-discrimination are also available to the minorities of this country being citizen of Pakistan. Minority rights are, therefore, a basket of fundamental rights, constitutional values, State obligations under the Principles of Policy, international conventions like ICCPR (duly ratified by Pakistan) and the rich jurisprudence developed over the years.[6]

Justice Shah contended that the impugned amendment in the Act, whereby section 7 was deleted, was to be reviewed and examined on the touchstone of these minority rights available to the petitioner:

> The wisdom and experience behind the liberalization and emancipation of the Christian Divorce law around the world has been the protection of the right to a happy family life and right to dignity of a human being, who cannot be left chained to a dead marriage forever or forced to convert to another religion just to be released of the bondage of an unhappy marriage.[7]

Justice Shah noted that human dignity demands that the state must establish a legal system that recognises the right of every person to create a familial relationship as s/he desires, which includes the right of the individual to choose his/her partner and to establish a family with him/her. It was held that the impugned amendment limits the choice of a person to divorce thus perpetuating a dead marriage which impairs the quality of life and curtails the liberty of a person by forcing him to live an unhappy family life against his free choice. 'The limited grounds of divorce under the State divorce law when compared with the rights enjoyed by the Christians in the world, amounts to discriminating [against] the Christian minority in Pakistan'.[8] This gap in the state law can best be filled by extending the same rights enjoyed by Christians in the rest of the world to the Christians in Pakistan. This can be easily achieved by restoring section 7 of the Act. The impugned amendment, therefore, does not pass the test of minority rights and is violative of the fundamental rights to life, liberty, dignity, and non-discrimination.

In light of the above discussion, Justice Shah held that the impugned amendment was an affront to minority rights of the petitioner, the constitutional values, fundamental rights, principles of policy, and the international obligations of Pakistan. Hence, the impugned amendment did not enjoy the constitutional immunity under Article 270–A. Consequently, section 7 of the Divorce Act 1869 was restored, in the manner it stood in the year 1981, making the relief based on the principles and rules of divorce under UK Matrimonial Causes Act 1973 available to the Christians of Pakistan. It was held that the restored section 7 is to be read harmoniously with section 10 of the Act. This means that the ground of divorce on the basis of adultery is available to anyone who wishes to invoke it but those who wish to seek divorce on the ground of irretrievable breakdown of marriage can rely on section 7 of the Act and avail the additional grounds of divorce available under the UK Matrimonial Causes Act 1973.

13.4.4 Standard of Proof for Dissolution of Marriage

Mst Parveen Amanual v Additional District Judge-III, Rahimyar Khan PLD 2009 Lah 213

A Christian woman's claim for the dissolution of marriage should be based on concrete facts supported by reliable and cogent evidence.

This case highlights the application of the principle that the wife's claim for dissolution of marriage should be based on concrete facts supported by cogent evidence. This case was decided before the landmark case of the Lahore High Court discussed above and accurately depicts the legal scenario in the absence of no-fault dissolution of Christian marriage in Pakistan. The petitioner, Mst Parveen Amanual, filed a suit for the dissolution of marriage against her husband, Razzaq Shakir, respondent no. 3. The Family Court decreed the suit for the dissolution of marriage. Aggrieved by the judgment, respondent no. 3 appealed before the District Judge. The District Judge remanded the case to the Family Court on the ground that the marriage was not dissolved in accordance with the provisions of the Divorce Act 1869. The wife filed an appeal before the High Court against the decision of the District Judge.

After perusing the record and hearing the arguments, the court noted that the order of the Family Court was based on the petitioner's statement that she was not ready to live with respondent no. 3 at any cost. The order reflected that in making the same, the judge of the Family Court was influenced by the provisions of the Muslim Family Personal Laws 1961. The court observed:

> There is no provision in the nature of Khula in the Divorce Act, 1869 and as such the mere statement of the petitioner that she was not willing to live as a wife with respondent no. 3, is not sufficient for the purpose of dissolution of Christian marriage … The bond of marriage between Christian husband and wife is of a permanent nature and as such the wife has to prove her case on the concrete facts after leading reliable and cogent evidence to the facts on which the claim of dissolution of marriage is based. Only then the Court can grant a decree for a judicial separation within the meaning of section 22 of the Divorce Act, 1869 or to dissolve the marriage under section 10 of the same Act.[9]

In light of the foregoing reasons and circumstances of the case, the court held that the District Judge rightly remanded the case to the Family Court, and the instant petition was accordingly dismissed.

Mushtaq v Fareeda 1979 CLC 457 (Karachi)

A Christian marriage should not be dissolved on the ground of adultery in the absence of cogent corroborative evidence.

In this case, the husband filed a petition under section 10 of the Divorce Act 1869 for the dissolution of a marriage on the ground of adultery. The petitioner stated that his marriage with the respondent was solemnised in 1962 as per Christian rites. He had six children from the wedlock and only four of them were alive at the time of the filing of the present petition. His eldest daughter was 8 years of age, and the youngest son was 3 years old. The petitioner further stated that three years before filing the instant petition, the petitioner's family permanently shifted to Chak no. 11,

Sanghar. He claimed that immediately after they took up residence in the area people unknown to him started visiting the respondent. They used to stay with her in their house and committed adultery with the respondent. The petitioner reprimanded her, but the respondent did not stop. He also alleged that as a result of the adultery the respondent became pregnant. Six months before filing the instant petition in the petitioner's absence, the respondent left the petitioner's house and went to her father's home taking with her clothes, ornaments, and some cash. The petitioner claimed that he took two or three men of his village along with him to bring the respondent back, but she refused to return and confessed that she became pregnant due to adultery.

The respondent did not appear in the court; thus the District Judge passed the decree *nisi* for dissolution of marriage *ex parte* on acceptance of the petitioner's affidavit as *ex parte* proof. The petitioner repeated all the aforesaid allegations in the affidavit but did not mention anything about the confession of adultery made by the respondent in the presence of villagers. Therefore, it was to be examined whether the petitioner proved adultery via an affidavit filed by him as an *ex parte* proof.

The court evaluated the allegations made by the petitioner in detail. It noted that, according to the petitioner's allegation, some strangers committed adultery with his wife in his home to the extent that she became pregnant. This sounded improbable. The court observed that if these allegations were true, the petitioner must have known the names of these adulterers and stated them in the petition and joined them as co-respondents. The court further noted that it was quite unlikely that the petitioner had let his wife commit adultery in his own house unless he was an accessory to the same. Moreover, the court noted that the petitioner's claim in the affidavit that he rebuked the respondent, but she did not listen to him, seems to have been made only to avoid the attraction of section 13 of the Act, which provides that the court shall dismiss a petition for dissolution of marriage if the petitioner connived in or has been an accessory to the adultery committed by his wife.

The court held that the allegation that the respondent became pregnant due to adultery did not hold true. It observed that the marriage between the parties was solemnised in 1962 and on the date of filing of the petition on 7 August 1973 the petitioner had four children alive, the eldest of whom was 8 years old and the youngest was 3 years old. It was reasoned that the petitioner maintained that three years before filing the present petition he had moved to Chak no. 11, Sanghar; therefore, it is clear that no child was born during their three-year stay at Sanghar. If the respondent had been impregnated due to adultery, she must have given birth to a child either before the filing of the petition or before the filing of the affidavit which was done about nine months after relocating. But there was no mention of any such child being born to the respondent during this period. The court noted that the real reason behind the filing of the instant petition seemed to be the failure of the petitioner to convince the respondent to resume co-habitation with him. The court also stated that even if the allegations of adultery were true, the petitioner had condoned the same by persuading the respondent to return to live with him after knowing about her alleged adultery, which made the petition liable to be dismissed under section 13 of the Act.

The court also looked into another aspect of the case. It observed that the petitioner was at liberty to verify his case by affidavit as per section 51 of the Act. However, ordinarily such affidavits should not be accepted without corroborative evidence of adultery either by a witness or by surrounding circumstances. Therefore, the district judge should not have passed the decree *nisi* on the basis of the affidavit alone.

Additionally, the court noted that the petitioner was required to join the adulterer as a co-respondent as required by section 11 of the Act unless he was excused from doing so on the grounds mentioned in the section. These grounds are: (1) that the respondent is leading a life of a prostitute and the petitioner knows of no person with whom the adultery has been committed; (2) that the name of the alleged adulterer is unknown to him although he has made efforts to discover the same; or (3) that the alleged adulterer is dead. The petitioner made an application to excuse himself from joining the adulterer as a co-respondent on the grounds that the respondent was leading an immoral life and he did not know the adulterer or his name despite his efforts to find out the same. The court noted that the district judge should not have granted this application as the allegation that the respondent was living an immoral life is not the same as her leading a life of a prostitute, as required by the section. The court held that it is improbable that the petitioner did not know of the alleged adulterers when, according to him, they used to stay in his own house. The court did not confirm the decree *nisi* and dismissed the petition.[10]

Francisco Xavier Pinto v Julie Pinto PLD 1979 (Karachi) 716

An inference of the commission of adultery may be drawn from the evidence of association coupled with the opportunity to commit adultery and the evidence of illicit affection.

This case deals with the standard of evidence required to prove adultery which is one of the grounds for the dissolution of marriage and judicial separation under the Divorce Act 1869. The petitioner, Francisco Xavier Pinto, filed a petition under section 10 of the Act on the grounds of adultery committed by his wife, Julia Pinto, with the co-respondent, Philip D. Silva. The petitioner also claimed Rs 2000 as damages. Both the respondent and the co-respondent denied the allegations of adultery. The District Judge, Karachi pronounced a decree for dissolution of marriage subject to confirmation by the Karachi High Court under section 17 of the Act.[11]

The petitioner stated that during the period between September 1968 and the middle of December 1968 the respondent committed adultery with the co-respondent in Karachi and thereafter, the co-respondent left for Chittagong and was followed by the respondent who stayed with him for ten days as learned by the petitioner via a telegram sent by a person called Rozario. On being asked by the petitioner, the respondent admitted going to Chittagong. Upon the return of the co-respondent to Karachi, the respondent again started meeting him and was found with him at several places including some secret spots. The petitioner claimed that the respondent had taken up a job in a local medical clinic and purposefully opted for night duties with the intention of committing adultery with the co-respondent. The respondent used to write love-letters to the co-respondent and she neglected her household affairs as well as the children.

The respondent, in her written statement denied the allegations of adultery. However, she admitted that the co-respondent, who was the friend of the petitioner, was in Chittagong for about ten months in the year 1968–69 and she went there to seek his help in order to mend the petitioner's ways. She denied staying with the co-respondent while she was in Chittagong; she maintained that she had stayed with Rozario and his wife. She further counter-charged the petitioner of having illicit relationships with other women. She stated that she started working as a nurse in a local clinic owing to the bad attitude of the petitioner towards her. As far as the love-letters were concerned, she said that she wrote them under the threat of life and coercion by the petitioner. The stance taken by the co-respondent, in his written statement was virtually the same as that of the respondent.

The court noted that in a petition for the dissolution of marriage on the grounds of adultery, the onus of proving that the respondent committed adultery was upon the petitioner. The court relied upon several cases in order to determine the standard of proof required for proving the charge of adultery as direct evidence in such cases was rarely available. It was noted that inference has to be drawn in such cases and the court commented upon how such inference was to be drawn:

> [Such inference] cannot be drawn from evidence of association coupled with opportunity [to commit adultery], but from such evidence together with evidence of illicit affection or illicit familiarity. 'Illicit' is a strong word. However, as to what is illicit affection and what is illicit familiarity must depend on the circumstances of each case, and these circumstances necessarily include the manners and habits of the parties concerned and of the community to which they belong and in which they live.[12]

The court, however, noted that there may be cases where association coupled with opportunity may lead a reasonable person to infer commission of adultery. It observed that such cases are generally called 'hotel cases', where a person having a home in that city locks himself/herself in a hotel room with a stranger of the opposite sex.

In light of the case law, the court examined the evidence and circumstances of the instant case. The petitioner produced a few witnesses who confirmed seeing the respondent with the co-respondent holding hands and kissing. In rebuttal, only the respondent and the co-respondent appeared as their own witnesses. The court observed that the four letters written by the respondent to the co-respondent as available on record reflected a rather intimate relationship between the two. It observed that the respondent's contention that she was coerced by the petitioner into writing these letters did not hold true as these letters were written on different occasions and in different ink and the content thereof seemed to be spontaneous, depicting their emotional involvement with each other.

The court further noted that the respondent's contention that she had gone to Chittagong but did not meet the co-respondent, rather was in correspondence with him, was contradicted by her conflicting stances taken in her cross-examination and written statement. In her cross-examination, she admitted that she had gone to Chittagong to meet the co-respondent and had sought his help by requesting him to go to India to see her mother. While in her written statement, she maintained that she went there to seek the help of the co-respondent, who was a common friend, to use his influence in persuading the petitioner to mend his ways. The court held that the said plea did not hold true as the petitioner and the respondent had common friends and relations in Karachi also, therefore, there was no need to go all the way to Chittagong to seek the help of the co-respondent. The court noted that the co-respondent admitted accompanying the respondent to several places and escorting her to the hospital where she worked. This was supported by the testimony of the hospital ward boy who claimed to have seen the two of them together and kissing each other, and he was told by the co-respondent that he was the respondent's husband. This statement remained unchallenged in the cross-examination. This background led the court to the conclusion that the respondent had illicit relationship with the co-respondent. Therefore, the court concluded that the respondent committed adultery with the co-respondent and dissolved the marriage by making the decree *nisi* absolute.

Inayat Bibi v Harbans Lal PLD 1966 Pesh 13

The standard of proof in matrimonial offenses is the same as that required in criminal offense, i.e. the offense must be proved beyond reasonable doubt.

The case deals with several issues but only those dealing with the standard of proof in matrimonial offenses shall be the subject of discussion. The brief facts of the case are that the appellant instituted a suit for the dissolution of marriage against her husband, respondent, on three grounds: (1) the husband compelled the appellant to commit adultery with his brother-in-law; (2) the respondent co-habited with several women in Mardan and committed adultery with them; and (3) he deserted the appellant. The respondent denied all these allegations. The District Judge dismissed the appellant's petition holding that the appellant failed to make a reliable case for getting a decree for the dissolution of marriage.

The court looked into the allegations levelled by the appellant against the respondent and concluded that the appellant had failed to prove the aforementioned three grounds on which she sought the decree for the dissolution of marriage. It further observed:

> The standard of proof for matrimonial offenses is as stringent as in criminal cases that is the case must be proved "beyond reasonable doubt" and not the one required in a civil suit, i.e. "preponderance of probability". The language of section 14 (which deals with the power

> of court to pronounce decree for dissolving marriage), in particular the words "satisfied on the evidence" and further the word "proved" make it abundantly plain that the proof in matrimonial offenses must be at par with the one required in criminal offenses, i.e. beyond reasonable doubt, for if it were not so the words "satisfied" and the "proved" would not have been used in section 14.[13]

The court observed that the first ground, that the respondent forced the appellant to commit adultery, did not seem to be true as only the appellant testified to this effect. It was hard to believe that a husband can stoop so low to offer his wife for adultery to the husband of his own sister and more so when his sister was alive and living under the same roof with the respondent and the appellant. The court also noted that the appellant lost her credibility when she gave conflicting statements on material points in the case. For example, at one point she said that she had been subjected to sexual intercourse by the respondent's brother-in-law two to three times, and on the other she stated that only an unsuccessful attempt of adultery was made on her. The court noted that the second ground that the respondent had illicit relations with other women had also remained unproven. The appellant's evidence on this point was vague and she admitted during cross-examination that she could not name any woman with whom the respondent allegedly had illicit relations with. Furthermore, she admitted that she has never seen the respondent with any other woman as she never visited the quarters where the respondent used to live. The testimonies of other witnesses produced by the appellant were equally vague to prove adultery on the part of the respondent. In light of these considerations, the appeal was dismissed.

This decision was made when section 7 of the 1869 Divorce Act was still part of the legal system and in that background such a stringent interpretation is vindicated to some extent. But after the deletion of section 7 in 1981, the court could have switched to the lenient construction of the provision as the word 'proved' in the Evidence Act 1872 (Qanun-e-Shahadat Order 1984) encompasses both the meanings, i.e. 'beyond reasonable doubt' and 'preponderance of evidence'.

13.4.5 Collusion between Parties

Pamela Ambrose Martin v Ambrose Frank Anthony Martin PLD 1976 (Karachi) 565

Collusion between the parties may be inferred if the agreement is supported by corrupt intention and has the effect of perverting the course of justice.

The parties involved in the present case were married in 1969 according to Christian rites. In 1974, the wife moved an application under section 23 of the Divorce Act 1869 for judicial separation from the respondent. According to the facts disclosed in the petition, after marriage the appellant started living in the respondent's flat. However, the respondent's mother mistreated her. In order to save her marriage the appellant purchased another flat where she could live with the respondent, but the respondent showed complete indifference towards her. The respondent left the appellant at her parents' house without making any provision for her maintenance. Efforts made for reconciliation also failed and thus, the appellant resorted to the court for judicial separation. The respondent denied all the allegations levelled against him. He instead alleged that the appellant was a rude and aggressive lady who ruined the peace of his home. He further claimed that the appellant had herself left the respondent's house to live with her parents.

Before the evidence was recorded, an application for compromise between the parties was submitted in the court. The application stated that in the interest of justice and public policy and to avoid further bitterness between the parties, the respondent has agreed that the judicial separation be granted to the appellant as prayed for by her. The district judge, however, dismissed both the application for compromise and the petition for judicial separation on the ground of collusion between the parties. The appellant being aggrieved by the dismissal filed the instant appeal.

The counsel for the appellant argued that the district judge was not justified in dismissing the petition on the sole ground that the parties submitted a compromise application. He stated that the learned judge misconstrued the purpose of the application and incorrectly inferred collusion from the same, as it was a sincere attempt on part of the parties to end litigation. The counsel also maintained that since it was a petition for judicial separation and not divorce, collusion had been incorrectly imputed into this matter. This was because collusion was a pre-requisite for the dismissal of the petition for divorce but not judicial separation.

The counsel for the respondent also questioned the inference of collusion drawn by the district judge in the absence of any evidence.

After hearing the arguments, the court observed that although it is true that there is no specific provision in the act making collusion between parties a ground for the compulsory dismissal of the petition for judicial separation, it is incorrect to say that this consideration is totally irrelevant in the matters of judicial separation. The court noted that section 47 of the Act provided that every petition, under the Act, be it for dissolution of marriage, nullity of marriage, or judicial separation must state that there was no collusion between the petitioner and the other party to the marriage.

The next point considered by the court was whether there was evidence on record to infer collusion between the parties to the instant appeal. Relying upon several cases in this regard, the court formulated a gist of the test to draw inference of collusion. The test was that 'the court must find evidence from the agreement (compromise/bargain) whether there was a corrupt intention and if it had the effect of perverting the course of justice'.[14]

After applying the test to the circumstances of the instant case, the court did not find any collusion between the parties. The court noted that according to the compromise between the parties, the appellant would not claim any alimony or cost of the suits from the respondent and in return respondent would agree to their judicial separation. This did not disclose any dishonest intention or an object to pervert the course of justice on part of the parties. It was further stated that in the case of divorce, if one party accepts remuneration to agree to a decree of divorce, then it may lead the court to infer collusion between them as it would free them from the bond of marriage. But this is not true in the case of a judicial separation where a marriage remains intact. This conclusion was further bolstered by the fact that parties had in fact been living in separation for five years. The parties' counsel stated that the initiative to strike a compromise between the parties was taken by them and the parties only listened to their honest advice, hence there was no reason to disbelieve them. The appeal was accordingly accepted, and a decree for judicial separation was granted in terms of the compromise.

13.4.6 Alimony *Pendente Lite*

Mrs Marie Antoinette Palmer v Oswald Robert Palmer PLD 1957 (Lahore) 235

Misconduct on the part of the wife is not a sufficient ground to disentitle her from claiming alimony pending the suit.

This case establishes that misconduct of a wife is not a sufficient ground to disentitle her from claiming alimony pending the suit.

Mrs M.A. Palmer, the petitioner, filed a suit for dissolution of marriage and for judicial separation in the alternative. She also claimed alimony *pendente lite* and costs of the suit from the husband, the respondent. The court directed the husband to pay alimony pending the suit, costs already incurred by the petitioner in respect of the petition, costs of the petitioner's counsel and witnesses and the security costs for the petitioner.

The court noted that section 36 of the Divorce Act 1869 lays down that in any suit, whether presented by a husband or a wife, the wife may ask for alimony pending the suit and the court may make any order as it may deem fit in this regard. This is subject to one condition that alimony thus granted shall not 'exceed one-fifth of the husband's average net income for the next three years preceding the date of the order and shall continue in the case of a decree for dissolution of marriage or nullity of marriage until the decree is made absolute or is confirmed, as the case may be'.[15]

The grounds on which the respondent resisted the petitioner's claim for alimony *pendente lite* included committing adultery, deserting the respondent, and having income of her own. The respondent's counsel argued that if the court was convinced that the petitioner committed adultery and deserted her husband then she should not be granted alimony *pendente lite* until the final disposal of the petition. The court, however, did not agree with this contention. It stated:

> The section [section 37 of the Divorce Act 1869] empowers the Court to grant alimony *pendete lite* even if the petition is by the husband, and as the petition for dissolution of marriage by the husband may allege adultery it is obvious that the misconduct of the wife was not intended by the legislature to be a sufficient ground to disentitle her from claiming alimony *pendente lite*.[16]

Moreover, the court did not agree with the respondent's contention that the petitioner had income of her own. It noted that although the petitioner had worked as a teacher for some time, her statement in the court reflected that she has been out of work and did not have the means to sustain herself. This statement was not rebutted by the respondent by appearing as a witness. However, the respondent filed an affidavit in which he stated that the petitioner was in a position to work and had some funds of her own. The court observed that when the petitioner made a statement in the court and subjected herself to cross-examination, the better course of action for the respondent was to appear in the witness box and controvert the same. The court held that even if the aforesaid omission was ignored, the statement of the petitioner represented the truth about her financial status. The court ordered that the petitioner was entitled to alimony pending the suit.

13.5 Personal Law for Special Religious Communities

The Special Marriage Act 1872 provides a form of marriage for persons who belong to religions other than Christianity, Judaism, Islam, Zoroastrianism, Buddhism, Sikhism, or Jainism, or marriages between people each of whom professes one of following religions: Hinduism, Buddhism, Sikhism, or Jainism. To validate a marriage under the Act, (1) neither party must, at the time of marriage, have a husband or wife living; (2) the man must be above 18 years of age and the woman must be above 14 years; (3) each party, if below 21, must have the consent of his/her father or guardian; and (4) parties must not be related to each other in any degree of consanguinity or affinity, which would, depending on the law that applies to the parties, render a marriage between them illegal.

Section 4 of the Act provides that when a marriage is intended to be solemnised, one of the parties must give notice in writing to the registrar before whom it is to be solemnised. Section 6 of the Act states that a marriage can be solemnised fourteen days after the notice has been given to registrar, unless any person objects that the above-mentioned conditions have been contravened. Such objection shall be recorded in writing by the registrar and shall be signed by the person making the objection. According to section 7 of the Act, the registrar cannot solemnise the marriage until fourteen days have passed from the receipt of such objection. Additionally, an objector can file a suit in any Civil Court having local jurisdiction for a decree declaring that such marriage is in contravention of the above-listed conditions. Under section 9, the court can fine the objector if it appears that the objection was not reasonable and *bona fide*.

The Act provides a procedure for the solemnisation of a marriage and the place where it may be solemnised. Under section 10 of the Act, the parties and their witnesses shall in the presence of registrar sign a declaration to the effect that they do not profess the Christian, Jewish, Hindu, Muslim, Parsi, Buddhist, Sikh, or Jaina religion, or as the case may be, that they profess the Hindu, Buddhist, Sikh, or Jaina religion when they enter into a marriage with a person professing religion other than their own. And if the parties are not yet the age of 21 years, such declaration shall be signed by their father or guardian. The Act provides that once the marriage has been solemnised, the registrar shall enter a certificate certifying the marriage in the Marriage Certificate Book.

Section 17 provides that the Divorce Act 1869 applies to the marriages under this Act. Likewise, according to section 24, the property of the persons and their progeny is governed under the Succession Act 1925. Section 22 of the Special Marriage Act 1872 provides that the marriage under this Act, of any member of an undivided family who professes the Hindu, Buddhist, Sikh, or Jaina religion shall be deemed to affect his severance from such family. Section 25 of the Act provides that no person professing Hindu, Buddhist, Sikh, or Jaina religion who marries under this Act shall have any right of adoption.

Section 15 of the Act declares that any person who, being at the time married, procures a marriage of himself to be solemnised under this Act, shall be deemed to have committed an offence under sections 494 and 495 of the Pakistan Penal Code 1860, and such marriage shall be void.

The Special Marriage Act 1872 had limited application in Pakistan. However, this Act has acquired new significance after the constitutional declaration of Ahmadis/Quadianis as non-Muslims and the criminalisation of their calling themselves Muslims under the Anti-Islamic Activities of the Quadiani Group, Lahori Group, and Ahmadis (Prohibition and Punishment) Ordinance 1984. In the absence of any legislation to register their marriages with the state machinery, some members of the Ahmadi/Quadiani community made recourse to this Act to register their marriages in order to get official recognition of such marriages.[17] In order to get their marriages registered under this Act, the parties are required to declare that they do no profess Christian, Jewish, Hindu, Muslim, Parsi, Buddhist, Sikh, or Jaina religion.

13.6 Conclusion

The statutory law regulating the personal affairs of non-Muslim communities in Pakistan presents a picture of anachronistic rules during the 19th and early 20th century. In Pakistan, neither the legislature has reformed these laws to keep them in pace with changing circumstance, nor have the courts laid down new legal principles to provide a fresh interpretation of old statutes. There are only a few reported cases under these statutes. This area has also received minimum academic attention. The focus of reported cases and academic research has been on the conflict of personal laws. Consequently, the non-Muslim communities have mostly relied upon communal justice to resolve their family related problems. This state of affairs is far from ideal. In a modern nation state, citizenship rights require equal access to justice which can only be ensured through fair laws. Article 25 of the Constitution of the Islamic Republic of Pakistan 1973 provides that all citizens are equal before law and are entitled to equal protection of law. Moreover, other constitutional provisions, specifically Article 14, ensures dignity of man. Article 20 provides freedom to profess religions, the Objectives Resolution, and the Principles of Policy ensure that non-Muslim minorities have the right to profess their religions with dignity and honour. Pursuant to these constitutional mandates and in order to protect the rights and interests of women and children belonging to non-Muslim communities, their personal laws should be updated and reformed to bring them in line with the requirements of modern society and give the followers of minority religions a fair opportunity to profess and practice their religions.

Questions

1. Write a note on the personal laws of non-Muslims in Pakistan.
2. Critically evaluate the Hindu Marriage Act 2017 and the Sindh Hindus Marriage Act 2016.
3. Analyse the case law on Christian divorce. Do you think that the judiciary has taken enough measures to reform Christian divorce law and there is no need for its further reform?

Further Reading

Cases

Asif Raza v Mst. Sofia alias Pinky PLD 2021 Peshawar 41 (Mere assertion by a Christian wife that she does not want to live with the husband is not sufficient to dissolve marriage because bond of marriage between Christian husband and wife is of permanent nature and there be should a ground for dissolution.)

Jagsi v Shr. Marwan PLD 2005 Kar 334 (Under the Family Courts Act 1964, the Family Courts have the jurisdiction to adjudicate upon the personal matters of the non-Muslim citizens of Pakistan in accordance with their customary practices.)

Marina Pushong v Derick Noel Pushong PLD 1975 Lah 793 (Christians do not have personal law governing custody of minors. Therefore, the matter must be decided by equity and good conscience, generally interpreted to mean the rule of English law if found applicable to society and circumstances in the country.)

Masood Sadiq v Mst Shazia PLD 2008 Lah 398 (In the absence of any specific provision for the grant of maintenance to minor(s) in the Christian Divorce Act 1872, they can be granted maintenance under the provisions of Family Courts Act 1964.)

Miss Lilian Sen v Mrs Phyllis Merlin Xavier PLD 2003 Kar 270 (Adoption does not create any kindred relationship between the child and adoptive parent under Islamic law and Christian law. Under the Succession Act 1925, adopted child is not entitled to inherit the estate of deceased adoptive parent.

Mrs Yvonne Anna Carman v Mr Leon Carman PLD 1960 Lah 381 (The court can pass a decree of dissolution of marriage only if the parties to the marriage are domiciled in Pakistan at the time the petition is presented.)

Mst. Shagzana Walayat v Mst. Shabnam Tabassum 2021 CLC 1761 (Islamabad) (The law of divorce relating to Christian marriage did not grant or authorised any individual or Jirga to pronounce divorce between husband and wife and grant permission for second marriage without following mandates of Christian Marriage Act 1872.)

Riaz Javaid v Sheraz Ahmed 2010 CLC 1925 [Lah] (Under the Family Courts Act 1964, the Family Courts have jurisdiction over all religious personal laws, including Ahmadi, arising out of non-codified personal laws.)

Notes

1. The Marriages Validation Act 1892 supplements the Christian Marriage Act 1872 to validate marriages of the Native Christians. The Married Women's Property Act 1874 also applies to Christians.
2. These included: the Hindu Widow's Marriage Act 1856; the Arya Marriage Validation Act 1892; the Hindu Disposition of Property Act 1916; the Hindu Inheritance (Removal of Disabilities) Act 1928; the Hindu Law of Inheritance (Amendment) Act 1928; the Hindu Marriage (Disabilities Removal) Act 1946; the Hindu Married Women's Right to Separate Residence and Maintenance Act 1946; and the West Pakistan Hindu Women's Right to Agricultural Law Ordinance 1959.
3. Proviso to s 4 of the Hindu Marriage Act 2017.
4. 2017 LHC 2488, [23].
5. Ibid., [26].
6. Ibid., [40].
7. Ibid., [41].
8. Ibid., [42].

9. PLD 2009 Lah 213, 214–15.
10. Under section 17 of the Divorce Act 1869, a decree of the dissolution of marriage required confirmation by the High Court. Therefore, the petitioner brought this suit before the High Court. This section was repealed in 1975. [Confirmation of decree for dissolution by District Judge.] Omitted by the Divorce (Amdt.) Act 1975 (IV of 1976), s 11.
11. Ibid.
12. PLD 1979 Kar 716, 720.
13. PLD 1966 Pesh 13, 14.
14. PLD 1976 Kar 565, 570.
15. PLD 1957 Lah 235, 237.
16. Ibid.
17. See *Re: M* [2011] EQHC 2132 (FAM). This case was decided by the High Court of Justice in the UK. The father of the bride had acquired a certificate of marriage under the Special Marriage Act 1872 to facilitate the immigration of her daughter to the UK.

14

CONFLICT OF PRIVATE/PERSONAL LAWS

14.1 Introduction

A conflict of laws arises when the court is faced with a case where the parties belong to more than one legal system. In such instances, the court is required to adjudicate upon the questions of jurisdiction and applicable law with regard to the particular circumstances of each case. Most of these cases relate to international commercial transactions where the court has to choose amongst competing state laws. However, more complex issues of conflict of laws arise in cases pertaining to the personal laws of the parties. Termed as conflict of interpersonal laws, such cases usually involve issues relating to marriage, maintenance, custody of children, divorce, gifts, wills, and inheritance among the parties proclaiming adherence to more than one system of personal law. These conflicts usually arise in more religiously diverse populations such as those of India, Pakistan, and Bangladesh where various religious denominations have interacted for centuries.

14.2 Conflict of Law Rules

Some rules of conflict of laws such as *lex domicilii* (law of the domicile); *lex loci celebrationis* (law of the land where the marriage was solemnised); and *lex situs* (law of the place where the property is situated) have been developed under Private International Law. However, various jurisdictions differ as to the application of these rules endorsing the view that 'every country has its own private international law'.[1] Particularly in the context of interpersonal conflict of laws, the states are hesitant to give credence to such personal laws which might compromise their territorial sovereignty. For example, in England, the state applies a particularly restrictive approach towards the recognition of personal laws of Muslims and Hindus, describing them as 'cultural practices' of ethnic minority communities.[2]

Similarly, the attitude of South Asian polities such as India and Pakistan toward the conflict of interpersonal laws is not quite distinct from that of England. In Pakistan, for instance, the case law shows a predominant tendency of the courts to apply Muslim personal law—endorsed as state law under the Muslim Family Laws Ordinance 1961—in almost all conflict of interpersonal laws cases pertaining to marriage, maintenance, divorce, gifts, wills, and inheritance. In doing so, the courts usually rely upon the transnational nature of Islamic law arguing that a Muslim citizen of Pakistan, wherever s/he may be, is regulated under section 1(2) of MFLO 1961.

It should be noted, however, that this tendency of favouring Muslim law over other personal laws does not necessarily lead to inequitable results. For instance, in *Caroline Rehman v Chairman, Union Council*,[33] the court validated the exercise of the delegated right to divorce of a Christian wife who might not be able to have her marriage dissolved under Christian personal law. Likewise, in the custody of children cases, the courts give paramount importance to the welfare of the child rather than strictly applying Muslim law. In *Peggy Collin v Muhammad Isfaque Malik*, the Lahore High Court rejected the defendant's father's plea that he was the natural guardian of his son under Islamic law and wanted to raise him as a Muslim. The court was of the view that it was not in the welfare of the children to remain with the father who was a fugitive from law.[4]

14.3 Outline of Case Law

14.3.1 Effects of Religious Conversion on Marriage. The following case law suggests that Pakistani courts tend to apply Muslim personal law whenever a conflict of interpersonal laws arises. In this regard, the courts have held that a Christian man can validly enter into a new marriage after conversion without the dissolution of the former marital bond, as polygamy is allowed in Islam. Similarly, as regards the issue of *talaq* the courts have validated the *talaq* pronounced by a Muslim convert after conversion. It has been held that a Muslim convert renounces all ties to his previous religious identity upon conversion and, therefore, is to be treated in light of his new personal law which grants him an unfettered right to unilateral divorce.

14.3.1.1 Pronouncement of *Talaq*

Arshad Peter v Mst Shumaila PLD 2012 Lah 430

A divorce pronounced by a Christian husband after his conversion to Islam will be effective upon the expiry of the *iddat* period, and the Christian wife would be entitled to maintenance allowance till that date.

The parties involved in the case professed the Christian faith. They were married in 2003. The wife filed a suit for maintenance allowance against her husband. She also demanded maintenance for her minor daughter, Khulda Simran, and the medical expenses incurred upon the birth of the child. A decree for the payment of maintenance allowance was passed on 7 March 2007 in favour of the wife only to the extent of Rs 5,000 per month. This decree was to take effect from 11 July 2003 till her re-joining the husband or till the completion of *iddat* period in case she was divorced. The court also declared her entitled to Rs 15,000 as the expenses incurred on the birth of the child.

The wife subsequently filed an execution petition and claimed Rs 690,000 as maintenance allowance and medical expenses. The counsel for the husband argued that the wife could not claim the maintenance allowance because the husband had converted to Islam in 2007 and had divorced her on 20 February 2007. Hence, she could be entitled to maintenance allowance only till she re-joined her husband or upon completion of *iddat* in case she was divorced. On the contrary, the counsel for the wife argued that the marriage between the parties was solemnised in accordance with Christian law, therefore, the divorce could only be pronounced in accordance with that law. The counsel contended that the maintenance allowance would have to be paid to the wife till she re-joined her husband or was divorced under Christian law.

Justice Ijaz Ahmad of the Lahore High Court rejected the argument of the counsel for the wife and held:

> In a case where the spouses at the time of marriage were Christian and the wife renounces her religion and converts to Islam, she in that eventuality being a Muslim would be one married to a non-Muslim, both professing their scriptural religions. She will be on the intervention of the court, entitled to a decree for dissolution of marriage. The Court in such an eventuality would call upon the husband to embrace faith of the wife and if he refuses to do so, a Judge may pronounce the dissolution of marriage. In the case of husband renouncing the Christianity and embracing Islam,

> the convert Muslim husband would have a scriptural (Katibia) woman as his wife. Such a union is permitted by Islam and may continue till the wife obtains a decree for dissolution of marriage or the husband pronounced "Talaq" in accordance with law of the religion professed by him.[5]

Justice Ahmad observed that the divorce pronounced by the husband in accordance with his new religion was subject to the limitations and safeguards provided in the Qur'an. The divorce pronounced on 20 February 2007 would be effective after the expiry of the *iddat* period and the wife would be entitled to maintenance allowance till that date. The petition was partly accepted.

Farooq Leivers v Adelaide Bridget Mary PLD 1958 (W.P) Lah 431

A Christian who has married a Christian wife cannot divorce her under *Shariat* after embracing Islam and *talaq* pronounced by him is invalid.

This case discusses the question as to whether a husband, after converting to Islam, can validly divorce his Christian wife by the Islamic way of *talaq*.

The plaintiff, Mr Farooq Leivers, and the defendant, Adelaide Bridget, were domiciled in India when they married each other according to Christian rites. After the establishment of Pakistan, they were domiciled in Pakistan. Later, differences arose between the spouses and the defendant applied for judicial separation in the court of District Judge, Multan, in August 1951, and was granted judicial separation. The plaintiff was also directed to pay Rs 130 per month as alimony to the defendant.

About one and a half years later, the plaintiff renounced Christianity and embraced Islam. Thereafter, the plaintiff asked the defendant to embrace Islam, but she refused. Realising that there was no chance of reconciliation, the plaintiff divorced the defendant by pronouncing *talaq* in an Islamic way. The defendant was informed about it in April 1953 through a letter. The plaintiff subsequently filed the present suit in 1954 seeking a declaration that the defendant had been divorced and that the order passed by the district judge directing him to pay a monthly alimony of Rs 130 to the defendant was not binding upon the plaintiff. He also sought a permanent injunction in order to restrain the defendant from claiming and receiving any alimony under the aforesaid order of the district judge. The defendant resisted the suit on multiple grounds. Later, however, the plaintiff confined his suit only to a declaration that he had validly divorced the defendant and the defendant confined her plea only to the competency of the plaintiff to divorce her by pronouncing *talaq* in an Islamic way.

The main question before the trial court was whether the plaintiff was competent to divorce his Christian wife by pronouncing *talaq* in accordance with Muslim law. The trial court decided this question against the plaintiff and dismissed the suit. The plaintiff subsequently filed an appeal before the district judge, which also failed. The plaintiff finally approached the present court in second appeal.

The main contention of the counsel for the plaintiff was that after converting to Islam, the plaintiff had acquired a new social status and was governed by Muslim law in the matter of divorce, not by Christian law under which the parties were married. He further argued that on conversion to Islam, the convert renounces all his religious and personal laws and immediately adopts the Muslim religious and personal laws. He relied upon *The Advocate-General of Bombay v Jumbabai*[6] in support of his view. The court noted:

> It cannot be disputed that as soon as a person embraces Islam, he at once becomes subject to the Muslim personal and religious law and is completely cut off from his past. He accepts a new mode of life and enters a new domain where his deeds, words and actions are governed by the laws of his new religion. So far as his individual personality is concerned, there cannot be any doubt about it that his future in all aspects of his life becomes amenable to Muslim law, from the moment of his conversion to Islam.[7]

The court considered the effect of such conversion upon other persons who have some vested rights in the property of the convert. In doing so, the court considered the effect of conversion upon the right of inheritance of legal heirs of the convert in his/her property and held:

> [T]he effect of conversion to Islam brings about a complete change as regards the right of inheritance. His non-Moslem relations, howsoever near relations they may be are completely debarred from succeeding to the estate of the convert. Although the act of conversion is unilateral, but the legal consequences which flow from it directly affect the rights of others, which but for the conversion, they are entitled to enforce under their own personal law.[8]

The court subsequently considered the effect of such conversion upon pre-conversion marriages, and noted:

> [W]hen one of the spouses embraces Islam, then on account of the difference of religion, the ends of marriage are defeated, and therefore, except in the case of a kitabia wife, the infidel party is called upon to embrace the faith and if he or she refuses to do so, the Judge must pronounce the dissolution of the marriage.[9]

The main question involved in this case was 'whether the plaintiff, on his conversion to Islam, was competent to divorce his Christian wife by pronouncing the formula of talak [*sic*] as provided by Muslim Law?'[10] Before dealing with this question, the court considered the position of Muslim law on this point. Several Qur'anic verses such as 10:40 and commentary thereupon were relied upon in deducing that 'the marriage tie is to be dissolved in the case of unbelievers as soon as one of the spouses is converted to Islam'.[11] This view found support from instances available from the life of Hazrat Umar: Karebta and Malekta were the wives of Hazrat Umar, before his conversion to Islam and as they did not embrace Islam both of them were divorced by him. However, the marriage of a Muslim man with a woman whose religion is based on a revealed book (*kitabia*) is found permissible under 5:6 of the Qur'an. But this is only permissible to Muslim men, not to Muslim women.

The question then arose as to the effect of conversion on the earlier marriage of the convert with a *kitabia* woman. It was noted that such a marriage continued after conversion and there was no prohibition in *fiqh* on such marriages. The court noted:

> In 'Hedaya', at page 65 it is stated that the conversion of the husband of a kitabia does not occasion separation, because the marriage of a Mussalman with a kitabia being legal *ab initio*, its continuance is so a fortiori. Article 127 of Institutes of Mussalman Law (by Nawab Abdur Rahman) lays down that 'where the husband of a Christian or Jewish wife turns Muslim the marriage cannot be dissolved.' In the light of the above, it will thus be seen that in the instant case the respondent continued to be the wife of the plaintiff in spite of his conversion to Islam.[12]

The question directly involved in the case was whether the plaintiff could have legally divorced the defendant in accordance with Muslim law. There was no direct authority on the point. First, the court reached the conclusion that a Muslim man is empowered to divorce his *kitabia* wife, who had been married to him before his conversion:

> The injunctions of the Holy Qur'an do not make any distinction in the matter of divorce so far as the faith of the wife is concerned. Therefore, the only reasonable inference which can be deduced from the injunctions of the Holy Qur'an is that it is immaterial whether the wife is a Muslim or is a believer of any other revealed Book, the Muslim husband subject to the limitations and safeguards provided in the Holy Qur'an is empowered to divorce his wife in the prescribed form.[13]

The court, after establishing that a Muslim husband was empowered to divorce his *kitabia* wife sought to determine whether the plaintiff could divorce his wife by way of *talaq*. This question presented a difficulty because of the different faith of the parties. The problem was further exacerbated because as per the wife's faith the marriage could only be dissolved upon death of a spouse or by a divorce obtained in accordance with the provisions of the Divorce Act 1869. There was no direct law on the point. It was noted that section 2 of the Muslim Personal Law (Shariat) Application Act 1937 and section 2 of the West Punjab Muslim Personal Law (Shariat) Application Act 1948, did not apply in the instant case as both the parties were not Muslim. The only other provision of law which dealt with such a question was section 6 of the Punjab Laws Act 1872, which provided that 'in cases not otherwise specially provided for, the Judges shall decide according to justice, equity and good conscience'. Therefore, this provision was found to govern the instant case.

The counsel for the defendant raised the contention that the marriage between the parties was solemnised according to Christian rites, so upon the husband's conversion to Islam it cannot be terminated through *talaq*. The court noted:

> It cannot be denied that the Divorce Act of 1869 is in full force in Pakistan and section 7 of that Act enjoins the Court to give relief on principles as nearly as may be conformable to the principles on which the Court for Divorce and Matrimonial Causes in England for the time being acts and gives relief. In Re: Hammarsmith, Superintendent Registrar of Marriages; Mir Anwaruddin Ex parte ((1917) 1 K B 634), their Lordships of the King's Bench Division refused to recognize talak given by a Muslim husband to his Christian wife. In this view of the matter, no Court in prepartition India would have recognized such a talak. And as no change has been brought about so far in the existing laws of Pakistan the position appears to have remained the same even after Partition. The question of domicile does not present any difficulty in this case. At the time of their marriage, the parties were domiciled in India, but since the Partition, they are domiciled in

> Pakistan. And the law as it stands in both the countries does not make any difference as regards the questions involved in this appeal. It, therefore, follows that in view of section 7 of the Divorce Act, and the existing laws, which are at present enforceable, no Court will recognize such a talak even in the Islamic Republic of Pakistan.[14]

The position that emerged was such that on one hand, a Muslim husband, after conversion, can divorce his *kitabia* wife according to the Islamic way of *talaq*; on the other hand, the courts in Pakistan cannot recognise such *talaq* in view of the provisions of the Divorce Act 1869. In such a situation, there was no justification to prefer the faith of one party over that of the other. It was now to be considered whether the plaintiff was entitled to any relief by application of the principles of justice, equity, and good conscience as provided by section 6 of the Punjab Laws Act 1872. The court observed that in accordance with the law applicable to the parties at the relevant time, the respondent was granted an order for judicial separation and the plaintiff was directed to pay alimony to her at the rate of Rs. 130 per month. Hence, the right to realise this amount from the plaintiff is vested in the defendant. If the decree were to be granted to the plaintiff in the present case it was likely to affect her vested right. As the marriage of a Muslim with a *kitabia* woman is allowed under Muslim law, the difference in religion is no ground for recognising *talaq*. After giving thorough consideration to the issue involved, the court held that it would be against the dictates of equity, justice, and good conscience to grant a decree in favour of the plaintiff in terms of the relief sought by him. The appeal was accordingly dismissed.

14.3.1.2 Second Marriage after Conversion

Mrs C.M. Samuel v C. Samuel and the State PLD 1967 SC 334

A man who contracts a second marriage after his conversion to Islam while his first marriage with the Christian wife subsists cannot be held liable for the offence of bigamy as plurality of wives is permitted in Islam.

This case dealt with the issue of whether a husband who, after converting to Islam, contracted a second marriage with a Muslim woman while his first marriage with the Christian wife subsisted, could be held guilty of the offence of bigamy under section 494 of the Pakistan Penal Code 1860.

The parties got married in 1945 under Christian rites. At the time of marriage, the parties were Indian nationals. They acquired Pakistani domicile after partition and lived in Peshawar till 3 July 1960. Later, in July of that year the appellant, Mrs C.M. Samuel, left her husband and started living with her sister. In December 1960, the respondent embraced Islam and made a public affirmation of his new faith. He subsequently married a Muslim lady. The appellant made a complaint against the respondent and his second wife by charging them with bigamy. The trial magistrate held that the respondent had not genuinely converted to Islam and convicted him under section 494 of the Pakistan Penal Code 1860. The respondent filed an appeal before the sessions judge who found that the respondent's conversion to Islam was done merely with an object of marrying for the second time and hence upheld his conviction. The respondent subsequently challenged the orders of the trial court and the Appellate Court before the High Court of West Pakistan, Peshawar Bench. The court set aside the conviction and held that the respondent's conversion was *bona fide*. Therefore, the respondent had committed no offence by contracting a second marriage while his first marriage with the appellant subsisted because Islam allowed a plurality of wives.

Before the Supreme Court, the counsel for the appellant argued that the respondent's alleged conversion to Islam was open to question as the two courts below held that there was no genuine conversion. Therefore, these findings should have been upheld. Justice S.A. Rahman noted that the rule regarding concurrent findings did not apply to criminal cases and the High Court was competent to examine the entire evidence and come to its own findings on the point. Therefore, the court proceeded on the assumption that the respondent's conversion to Islam was *bona fide* and the only question to be determined was that despite the fact of the respondent's conversion could he be held guilty of the offence under section 494 of the Pakistan Penal Code 1860.

The main argument advanced by the counsel for the appellant was that the obligations arising out of the Christian marriage contracted by the respondent prevented him from contracting a second marriage. He relied upon *Emperor v Mst Ruri*[15] where a Christian woman was convicted of the offence of bigamy for entering into a second marriage after her conversion to Islam. However, Justice Rahman distinguished the particular case from the present one on the ground that the former dealt with a woman taking a second husband after renouncing Christianity and converting to Islam. He noted that under Islamic law women are not allowed to take a plurality of husbands, though there was no such restriction in the case of Muslim males. Justice Rahman observed that the *John Jiban Chandra Dutta v Abinash Chandra Sen*[16] was the case on point in which it was held:

> In that case a Division Bench of the Calcutta High Court ruled that under the Muhammadan law, where a Christian embraces Islam, he acquires all the rights which a Muhammadan possesses and can contract a valid marriage even if the first one with his Christian wife subsists.[17]

Justice Rahman also took note of the authority, *Advocate-General of Bombay v Jumbabai*.[18] He reproduced the relevant part of the judgment:

> On conversion to Muhammadanism, converts, no matter what their previous religion may have been, must be taken at that moment to have renounced all their former religious and personal law in so far as the latter flowed from and was inextricably bound up with their religion, and to have substituted for it the religion of Muhammad with so much of the personal law as necessarily flows from that religion.[19]

Justice Rahman distinguished the judgment laid down in *Farooq Leivers v Adelaide Bridget Mary*[20] as the judge in that case did not 'appear to be in accord with the latest judicial trends'.[21] For the latest judicial trend, he relied upon his own judgment in *Syed Ali Nawaz Gardezi v Lt. Col. Muhammad Yusuf*[22] and held:

> [T]he capacity to enter into the marriage bond, must be determined according to the law of domicile of the party concerned. It would follow, therefore, that the validity of the marriage contracted by the respondent had to be judged in accordance with the law which governed him in the matter of marriage in this country, namely, the Islamic law. Marriage being a matter of status, he was governed by his personal law in this respect. There is no provision under the Divorce Act or under the Christian Marriages Act which could stand in the way of acceptance of this second marriage as valid, even if the first one performed under Christian rites subsisted.[23]

A reference was also made to *Emperor v Atony*[24] and *Gladys Sainapatti v Sainapatti*,[25] which laid down that 'a Hindu convert to Christianity first marrying a Christian woman according to the rites of the Roman Catholic religion and subsequently during the lifetime of his Christian wife, reverting to Hinduism and marrying a Hindu woman in accordance with Hindu rites would not be guilty of bigamy'.[26]

Justice Rahman noted that the respondent could have been held guilty of the offence of bigamy only if his second marriage could be said to be void by reason of it taking place during the lifetime of his first wife, as provided under section 494 of the Pakistan Penal Code 1860, which read as:

> Whoever, having a husband or wife living, marries in any case in which such marriage is void by reason of its taking place during the life of such husband or wife, shall be punished with imprisonment of either description for a term which may extend to seven years and shall also be liable to fine.

The respondent's second marriage, in the present case, could not be held to be void by reason of the subsistence of his first marriage as the validity of his second marriage had to be judged under the law applicable to Muslims, not under the law applicable to Christians. In light of the foregoing reasons, the respondent's acquittal did not require any interference and hence, the appeal was dismissed accordingly.

Tariq Masih v The State 2004 PCrLJ 1017 (FSC)

An adult convert to Islam can enter into a valid *nikah* without a court order of the dissolution of her first marriage.

Shahbaz Masih was married to the appellant, Nagina Masih. In the absence of Shahbaz, Rakhu Masih and Saleem Masih took the appellant out of her house on the pretext of shopping. When Shahbaz returned, his wife was missing. His neighbours informed him that the two appellants (Nagina Masih and Tariq Masih) were seen with three other co-accused in a rickshaw. He went to the house of the accused and demanded the return of his wife. However, his demand was refused. As a consequence, he registered a criminal case against them. According to the medical examination record, both appellants were found to have had sexual intercourse.

The appellants contended that they had embraced Islam. The appellant, Nagina Masih did not want to spend her life with a non-Muslim, therefore, the appellants contracted marriage according to the teachings of Islam. However, the trial court convicted the appellants Tariq Masih (now Ghulam Mustafa) and Nagina Masih for offences under sections 16 and 10(2) of the Offense of Zina (Enforcement of Hudood) Ordinance 1979. The trial court based its decision on the ground that marriage between Christian spouses cannot be dissolved except through a court of law. Since a court had not annulled the marriage of the appellant, it subsisted and made the subsequent marriage invalid. The appellants appealed against this decision.

The Federal Shariat Court, in its appellate jurisdiction, found the reasoning and judgment of the trial court misplaced. It observed that there was sufficient evidence to prove that the appellants had embraced Islam. Hence, after embracing Islam the marriage between the appellant, Nagina Masih, and her Christian husband stood perpetually dissolved. The appellant Nagina did not commit any offence in contracting the second marriage with Tariq Masih. The court observed that the nature of marriage in Islam is similar to a civil contract entered into between a man and a woman and there is no requirement of a formal deed for its validity. The court held that the appellants were properly married, and their convictions were set aside.

14.3.2 Applicable Law for Marriages between Muslims and Christians

14.3.2.1 The Legal Status of an English Marriage in Pakistan

Mrs Marina Jatoi v Nuruddin K. Jatoi PLD 1967 SC 580

The *talaq* given by the husband to his Christian wife in case of a marriage solemnised in London under the (English) Marriage Act 1949, is valid.

This case dealt with a two-fold question: (i) what was the nature of the marriage contracted by the parties before the Registrar of Marriages in London, and (ii) whether the dissolution of such marriages was governed exclusively by the Divorce Act 1869? The five judges of the Supreme Court were divided and delivered a split judgment of 4:1. First, the majority judgment shall be discussed and then, the minority judgment.

The appellant, Marina Jatoi, a Spanish national and Christian by faith, married the respondent, Nur-ud-Din K. Jatoi, under the Marriage Act 1949 before a Registrar of Marriages in England in 1959. A son was born to them during wedlock. The respondent returned to Pakistan in 1960 without his wife and the child. Here, he married a Swedish lady after she converted to Islam. This was a marriage under Muslim law. Thereafter, the respondent sent a letter of divorce to the appellant on 11 May 1961. The appellant applied for the legal custody of her son and maintenance for herself and her son to the Domestic Proceedings Court, Chelsea, London. The letter of divorce sent by the respondent was exhibited in those proceedings but was not accepted. In 1963, the appellant was granted custody of her son and was awarded maintenance for herself and her son. This order was transmitted to Pakistan where it was registered in the court of District Magistrate Karachi under the Maintenance Orders Enforcement Act 1921. It was confirmed by the District Magistrate in 1964 and afterwards, a notice was sent to the respondent in this regard, who neither opposed the confirmation nor remitted anything to the appellant. After waiting a year, she came to Pakistan to seek enforcement of her maintenance order. While she was in Pakistan, the respondent sent her another notice of *talaq*, a copy of which was also sent to the Chairman, Union Council, as required under section 7 of the Muslim Family Laws Ordinance 1961. He subsequently applied to the District Magistrate for the cancellation of the maintenance order on the grounds that he had divorced the appellant. After the expiry of 90 days from the date of the notice, he filed another application before the District Magistrate repeating his aforementioned prayer. The District Magistrate dismissed his application.

The respondent challenged the order of the District Magistrate before the High Court of West Pakistan, Karachi Bench, which cancelled the maintenance order by holding that the divorce had become effective through *talaq*. Consequently, Mrs Jatoi filed an appeal before the Supreme Court.

The counsel for the appellant contended that the marriage of parties in London was a Christian marriage and could not be dissolved by the unilateral act of the husband by means of a *talaqnama*. It was urged that the marriage could have been dissolved only by a competent court. Justice S.A. Rahman noted that 'under the rules of Private International Law, the *lex loci celebrationis* as such has nothing to do with the question of divorce which is a matter solely for the law that happens to be the *lex domicili* of the parties'.[27] This law may be different from the one governing marriage in the first place. He referred to *Private International Law* by G.C. Cheshire, 6th edition. The author described that the original doctrine of the Church that a marriage was only dissoluble by death has been long abandoned and the only characteristics of a marriage that are now demanded are that a marriage should be monogamous and a union for life in the sense of not being limited in duration. The author subsequently examined 'the orthodox view that a marriage celebrated before an English public officer must always be understood to be monogamous even though the party to it may be a person who in his own country, could have contracted a polygamous marriage',[28] and quoted the observations of Lord Selborne in *Harvey v Farnie*:[29]

> When a marriage has been duly solemnised according to the law of place of solemnistaion, the parties become husband and wife. What is the character which the wife assumes? She becomes the wife of foreign husband in the case where the husband is a foreigner to the country in which the marriage is contracted. She no longer retains any other domicile than his, which she acquires. The marriage is contracted with a view to that matrimonial domicile which results from placing herself by contract in relation of wife to the husband whom she married, knowing him to be a foreigner, domiciled and contemplating permanent and settled residence abroad. Therefore, it must be within the meaning of such a contract … that she is to become subject to her husband's law, subject to it in respect of the consequences of the matrimonial relation and all other consequences depending upon the law of the husband's domicile.[30]

In support of this view, the author also cited the opinion of Lord Brougham in *Warrender v Warrender*:[31]

> An Englishman, marrying in Turkey, contracts a marriage of the English kind, that is, excluding a plurality of wives, because he is an Englishman and only residing in Turkey and under Mohammedan law, accidentally and temporarily, and because he marries with a view of being a married man and having a wife in England and for English purposes; consequently the incidents and effects, must be the very nature and essence, be ascertained by the English and not the Turkish law.[32]

He also quoted the observation made by Lord Justice of Appeal Sir Alfred Denning, as he then was, when he stated that:

> So also, if she (an English woman domiciled in England) while in England, marries a man of polygamous race, intending to go to live with him in his homeland, knowing what marriage means in that country, there would be no condition that it should be monogamous and the marriage would not be made on that basis; and she could not complain if he there took another wife.[33]

Therefore, it was not necessary that a marriage performed before a Registrar in England must necessarily be monogamous.

In the instant case, this point had to be looked at in light of the Pakistani law which happened to be the law of the domicile of the husband. The question was whether the marriage solemnised in England before a

Registrar could at all be assimilated to the position of a Muslim marriage so as to attract the provisions of the Muslim law regarding its dissolution.

Justice Rahman referred to the judgment in *Farooq Leivers v Adelaide Bridget Mary*[34] which established that a Muslim can not only marry a *kitabia* woman but can also divorce her by *talaq* under pure Muslim law. However, the courts in Pakistan could not recognise such a *talaq* in view of the provisions of the Divorce Act 1869 and the Christian Marriage Act 1872. There being a conflict in the personal laws of the parties, it was held that the dictates of justice, equity, and good conscience stood in the way of a decree of dissolution.

The appellant's counsel argued that even if Pakistani law was considered, the Divorce Act 1869 and the Christian Marriage Act 1872 taken together constituted a complete scheme of law governing all incidents of marriage where one party to the marriage was a Christian. But Justice Rahman noted that this contention rested on the supposed implications of these Acts, not on any express provision contained therein. No provision in these Acts explicitly prevented a Muslim husband of a Christian woman from resorting to his personal law for dissolving the marriage. The Acts provided a procedure for the dissolution of a marriage through the court, but nothing in them suggested that this particular procedure was exclusive.

Justice Rahman noted that as far as a Muslim husband was concerned, as per section 3 of the Punjab Laws Act 1872, in the absence of any usage or custom contrary to the law applicable to a Muslim in respect of questions relating to his marriage would be Muslim personal law. Also, the MFLO is applicable to Muslim citizens of Pakistan wherever they may be. Hence, if a Muslim man was married to a Christian woman in a form recognised by Muslim law, or to a non-citizen Muslim woman, there was no reason that provision of section 7 of the MFLO did not apply to him if he wished to divorce his wife. Justice Rahman also noted that as pointed out in *Ali Nawaz Gardezi v Lt-Col. Muhammad Yusuf*[35] even the latest judicial trend in England favours the principle that if the law of domicile permitted a dissolution of marriage solemnised in England by pronouncement of *talaq* the divorce may be recognised as valid under the rules of Private International Law.

Justice Rahman also observed that the previous case law, which was contrary to the abovementioned views, had been reviewed in *Russ v Russ*.[36] This case established the recognition of a non-judicial foreign divorce pronounced by the husband in accordance with the law of his domicile country by the English courts. Justice Rahman noted that

Professor Cheshire in the *Private International Law*, has also dealt with the question of whether an extra-judicial foreign divorce would be recognised in England:

> [A] divorce obtained in, or according to the law of, a foreign domicile, even though obtained without contentious proceedings and even though it dissolves a marriage solemnized in England, between British subjects, must be recognised by the Courts of England, since it satisfies the general principle that alteration of status are governed by the *lex domicili* … it is that law which decided, inter alia, whether the status shall cease, and it is difficult to agree that its termination, by some process adequate according to the personal law, should be disregarded, merely because it has been effected in a manner alien to English, [sic] conceptions and practice … if the cause for divorce is immaterial to its recognition in England, as the authorities indubitably establish, why should its method, judicial or extra judicial, be material.[37]

Justice Rahman also relied upon Dicey's *Conflict of Laws*, 7th edition, in which it was stated:

> In spite of early dicta to the contrary, it is now clear that English Courts will recognise non-judicial divorces, obtained unilaterally by one party to the marriage, in accordance with a religious law (e.g. a Jewish ghet), provided that the parties are domiciled in a country, the territorial laws of which permit such a method.[38]

He further stated that a pertinent factor to be noted was that divorce by way of pronouncing *talaq* was regulated in Pakistan by the procedure prescribed for it in the MFLO, so it no longer remained a purely private unilateral act of the husband. It was noted:

> The statement in Halsbury's Laws of England, Vol. 7, Third Edition, p. 112, para. 200, read with Note (q) to the effect that a marriage contracted in England, is not dissolved by mere operation of the law of the religion of the husband and without decree from the Court of Law, is also based on the older decisions and does not take account of recent judicial trends in England as evidenced in Russ v Russ.[39]

He also relied upon a decision reported as *Attorney General of Ceylon v Reid*.[40] In this case, it was established:

> [A] Christian monogamous marriage contracted in Ceylon, did not prohibit for all time, during the subsistence of that marriage, a change of faith and a personal law, on the part of the husband, resident and domiciled there. He had an inherent right to change his religion and personal law and so to contract a valid polygamous marriage, if recognised by the laws of Ceylon, notwithstanding an earlier subsisting marriage. If such inherent right was to be abrogated it must be done by statute and there was none in the case of Ceylon.[41]

In the instant case too, the right of the Muslim husband to divorce his wife in respect of the marriage being recognised by Muslim law did not appear to have been taken away by any current statute in Pakistan. Therefore, the *talaq* given by the respondent had become effective. Hence, the wife was not entitled to maintenance though she was entitled to *mahr-ul-misl* as no dower had been fixed initially.

Justice Muhammad Yaqoob Ali, however, did not agree with the majority judges (A.R. Cornelius CJ, S.A. Rahman, Fazle-Akbar, and Hamoodur Rahman JJ). He noted that the High Court in reaching the conclusion that the marriage between the parties in the instant case stood dissolved from 1 October 1965 found support from the case titled the *Gardezi* case.[42] However, he found that the question of whether a marriage solemnised under the Christian Marriage Act 1872, or its British counterpart, was liable to be dissolved by a pronouncement of *talaq* or only by the intervention of court under the Divorce Act 1869, which was as much the law of the domicile of the husband as his personal law, was neither raised nor determined in the *Ali Nawaz Gardezi* case. Therefore, the question was open to examination. The learned judge relied upon judgments in *The King v Superintendent Registrar of Marriages Hammersmith*, *Ex parte Mir Anwaruddin* which held that 'a marriage performed in England in the office of the Superintendent Registrar was not dissolved by declaration of the husband operating or purporting to operate solely according to his personal law'.[43] On these premises, a certified marriage performed by a Superintendent Marriage Registrar under the British Marriage Act 1949 could not be assimilated into a Muslim marriage which could be dissolved by the pronouncement of *talaq*. Furthermore, the decision in the *Gardezi* case proceeded on the premise that a marriage between a Muslim male and a non-Muslim, non-citizen female can be dissolved by a pronouncement of *talaq*. This would hold true only where the marriage was performed in accordance with

Muslim law and not where the marriage was performed under the British Marriage Act 1949 or the Christian Marriage Act 1872. He further stated:

> The view that a marriage between a Muslim male and a non-Muslim and non-Pakistani female may be dissolved by [a] pronouncement of talaq can be rested on the doctrine that a marriage being [a] matter of personal status the personal law of the husband shall apply to its dissolution. It does not, however, follow that section 7 of the Muslim Family Laws Ordinance becomes applicable to such a marriage. Section 2 is in definite terms that the Ordinance applies to Muslim citizens of Pakistan wherever they may be. The personal status which the appellant acquired as a married woman under the British Marriage Act, 1949, would not, therefore, be affected by the provisions of the Ordinance unless an express provision was made to that effect in the Ordinance.[44]

Justice Ali subsequently looked at the relevant provisions of the Divorce Act 1869, the British Marriage Act 1949 and the Christian Marriage Act 1872 and observed:

> [A] marriage between a Muslim male and Christian female though permitted by Islam can be performed in Pakistan under Act XV of 1872 and to that extent the application of personal law stands excluded by statute. Reference may be made to section 5 of the Punjab Laws Act and other similar enactments … it is for this reason that a Christian female is usually converted to Islam before being married to a Muslim male. Consequently a marriage between a Muslim male and a Christian female can be dissolved only under the Divorce Act and not by pronouncement of talaq under the personal law of the husband….[45]

The learned judge endorsed the principle laid down in the *Farooq Leivers* case wherein it was held that the Courts in Pakistan cannot recognise such a *talaq* by a Muslim husband to his Christian wife, in view of the provisions of the Divorce Act 1869.[46] He held that the marriage between the parties solemnised in London subsisted and was not dissolved by the pronouncement of *talaq* and service of notice under section 7 of the MFLO. Therefore, the order of the District Magistrate confirming maintenance should be restored.

14.3.2.2 Delegated Right to Divorce a Christian Wife

Caroline Rehman v Chairman Union Council 1985 CLC 2855 [Lah]

A Christian wife can validly divorce herself by exercising the right to delegated divorce explicitly given to her by a Muslim husband.

This case addressed two issues: (i) whether a Christian wife can validly exercise her right to delegated divorce explicitly given to her by a Muslim husband; and (ii) whether the Chairman, Union Council, is bound to take cognizance of the notice of *talaq* sent by the wife in such a case?

The petitioner, Caroline Rehman, married a Muslim named Atiq-ur-Rehman. The marriage was solemnised by the Senior Marriage Registrar Lahore and a certificate was issued under section 79 of the Christian Marriages Act 1872. The husband Atiq-ur-Rehman, in the exercise of the powers granted to him under Muslim Personal Law, delegated the right to divorce to the petitioner. Later the petitioner divorced her husband by exercising this right. She also sent a notice of the pronouncement of *talaq* to the Chairman, Union Council, respondent no. 1, who subsequently issued notices to the parties for the nomination of their representatives to the Arbitration Council. The petitioner appeared before the Council through her nominated representative, while Atiq-ur-Rehman did not respond to the notice. The Chairman sought advice from his legal advisor in the matter and refused to take cognizance of the notice of the pronouncement of *talaq* of the petitioner. The petitioner, through the present constitutional petition, challenged this order and prayed it to be declared illegal and without lawful authority. She also prayed that the *talaq* be declared effective between Atiq-ur-Rehman and herself.

The counsel for the petitioner argued that the order passed by respondent no. 1 was illegal as the Muslim Family Laws Ordinance 1961 was applicable to Atiq-ur-Rehman, who delegated the right to divorce to the petitioner in accordance with Muslim Personal Law. Moreover, the petitioner exercised the delegated right to *talaq* on behalf of her husband, not in her own right.

The court noted that Atiq-ur-Rehman, being a Muslim, was governed by his own personal law in the matter of divorce. He had specifically delegated the right to divorce to the petitioner in the exercise of which the petitioner divorced herself. The petitioner did not exercise this right in her own right, but on behalf of her Muslim husband who was governed by the Muslim Family Laws Ordinance 1961. Therefore, the refusal of respondent no. 1 to take cognizance of the notice of *talaq* was illegal and without lawful authority. The matter was, consequently, sent back to respondent no. 1 to be proceeded in accordance with the law.

As regards the matter of declaring the *talaq* effective, the court noted that such an order being declaratory in nature cannot be passed in its constitutional jurisdiction. Also, since Atiq-ur-Rehman has not been impleaded as a respondent, no adverse declaration could be made in his absence.

14.3.3 The Legal Status of Foreign Judgments in Pakistan. In custody of children cases, Pakistani courts give paramount importance to the principle of the welfare of the child. This principle is also endorsed under Private International Law.

Dr Viktor Hacker v Dr Shahida Mansoor PLD 2013 Isb 34

A foreign judgment cannot be enforced in Pakistan if it was not passed on merits and if an appeal was pending against it in the apex court of the respective jurisdiction.

The petitioner, a citizen and resident of Austria, married respondent no. 1, a citizen of Pakistan, in 1999. Two daughters were born to the couple in wedlock. The petitioner alleged that he was the sole lawful custodian and guardian of the minors. Such sole custody was granted to him by the District Court of Graz, Austria vide its decision dated 3 May 2012, which was affirmed by the Provincial Court Graz vide its decision dated 29 June 2012. The minors were unlawfully removed by respondent no. 1 from Austria and were brought to Pakistan on 12 February 2012 in violation of the orders of the Austrian courts. Through the instant criminal petition, the petitioner prayed that the detention of the minors by respondent no. 1 be declared unlawful and improper; respondent no. 1 be directed to produce the detenues before the court; and directions be issued for the release of the minors from respondent no. 1's illegal confinement.

The petitioner's counsel argued that respondent no. 1 sought divorce from the petitioner and instituted court proceedings in Austria in 2009. However, the divorce had not taken effect as yet and the marriage between the parties subsisted. As per Austrian law, the court stepped in to resolve the matter of custody of the children and the custody was allowed to be joint as per an order dated 8 September 2010. Vide order 26 July 2011, the court allowed the custody to be joint, but the residence of the minors was declared to be with the mother. Respondent no. 1 assailed the order dated 26 July 2011 by filing an appeal before the Provincial Court, which was accepted, and the sole custody was granted to respondent no. 1 subject to the condition that the minors would not be removed from the jurisdiction of the Court of Graz, Austria. But on 12 February 2012, respondent no. 1 removed the minors from the Court of Graz's jurisdiction. Respondent no. 1's counsel kept representing her in the court even in her absence, but the custody of the minors was given to the petitioner vide order dated 3 May 2012. Respondent no. 1 filed an appeal against the order which was dismissed on 26 June 2012. Respondent no. 1 subsequently filed an appeal before the Supreme Court in Austria, which was pending at the time of the institution of the instant suit and no injunction order was issued in this regard. The District Court Graz also initiated criminal proceedings against respondent no. 1. The petitioner's counsel argued that respondent no. 1 removed the minors from their jurisdiction unlawfully and in violation of the orders of the Austrian courts. Furthermore, the minors were Austrian citizens and could not be brought to Pakistan without the consent of the petitioner. Respondent no. 1 was illegally detaining them in violation of the law and against the will of the minors.

On the other hand, the counsel for respondent no. 1 argued that the petitioner had converted his faith from Christianity to Ahmadiyya. It was also contended that an appeal in respect of the custody of the minors was still pending in the apex court in Austria. It was further argued that the petition was not maintainable: first, because the foreign judgment has not become conclusive; and second, because the decision upon which the present petition had been filed was obtained in the absence of respondent no. 1. The counsel submitted that respondent no. 1 had been given the custody after a long period of four years during which she was required to undergo several physical and psychological tests which checked her fitness for the custody of the minors. Furthermore, the welfare of minors was reliant upon the mother and the judgment given by the lower court in Austria was not conclusive as the appeal arising therefrom was still pending. As for the judgment passed by the Provincial Court in Austria, it was against the principles of natural justice because it was passed in the absence of respondent no. 1, and hence was not passed on merits. He also contended that there was no restriction placed by the court regarding removing minors from the jurisdiction of the Austrian court. If the judgment of the Austrian court was taken to be conclusive even then the present court had no jurisdiction to entertain the matter, as the proper forum to address this issue was the court of Guardian Judge. Moreover, it was contended that since the matter involved a factual controversy which could not be decided without recording evidence and as the instant court was not an executing court, therefore the instant petition was not maintainable.

After hearing the arguments and perusing the record, the court noted that as far as the petitioner's prayer to the extent of directing respondent no. 1 to produce the minors before this court was concerned, the respondent had been so ordered and she has produced the minors before this court. The second prayer of the petitioner was about the declaration of custody held by respondent no. 1 as illegal and the issuance of directions for the release of minors from the illegal confinement. The court observed that the petitioner had maintained that he had been awarded the sole custody of the minors vide the order dated 3 May 2012 by the District Court of Graz, Austria; therefore, the detention of the minors by respondent no. 1 was illegal. The court looked at section 13 of the Code of Civil Procedure 1908, which relates to foreign judgments:

> Section 13: When foreign judgment are not conclusive. A foreign judgment shall be conclusive as to any matter thereby directly adjudicated upon between the same parties or between parties under whom they or any of them claim litigating under the same title except:

a. where it has not been pronounced by a Court of competent jurisdiction;
b. where it has not been given on the merits of the case;
c. where it appears on the face of the proceedings to be founded on an incorrect view of international law or a refusal to recognise the law of Pakistan in cases in which such law is applicable;
d. where the proceedings in which the judgment was obtained are opposed to natural justice;
e. where it has been obtained by fraud;
f. where it sustains a claim founded on a breach of any law in force in Pakistan.

The court noted that it was clear from section 13 that the judgment passed by the Court of Graz, Austria was not conclusive because it was not delivered on the merits of the case and the appeal from the decision was still pending in the apex court in Austria. Furthermore, the present court did not have jurisdiction to deal with the matter of custody of the minors who were in the custody of their real mother', so it cannot be said that they were in illegal confinement. Also, the present court could not assume the jurisdiction of an executing court to enforce the judgment passed by the District Court of Graz, Austria.

Moreover, the petitioner filed the instant petition under section 491 of the Criminal Procedure Code 1898. The proceedings under section 491 are summary in character and the jurisdiction of the High Court can be invoked under section 491 if a person is alleged to be in illegal confinement, but in the instant case, the minors were in their real mother's custody which cannot be held illegal under any circumstances. This matter involved an appointment of a guardian and such jurisdiction solely lay with the Guardian Judge. Furthermore, in the instant case, the petitioner did not allege that respondent no. 1 removed the minors from his custody. And as a consequence, the petitioner could only resort to making an application under section 25 of the Guardians and Wards Act 1890. In light of the foregoing reasons, the petition was dismissed.

Peggy Collin v Muhammad Isfaque Malik PLD 2010 Lah 48

In light of a decree regarding custody passed in a foreign jurisdiction, the custody of a child can be handed over to a non-Muslim mother of foreign domicile if she is found capable of ensuring the child's welfare and the conduct of the father is in blatant disregard of the child's welfare.

The petitioner, Peggy Collins, a French national, married respondent no. 1, Muhammad Isfaque Malik, a Pakistani national, in 1995. The couple started living in France and respondent no. 1 obtained dual nationality. The couple was blessed with a son in 2000 who was named Omer. Sometime later, the parties got separated and respondent no. 1, surreptitiously brought Omer to Pakistan without the knowledge and consent of the petitioner. Ultimately, the parties reached an agreement and Omer was brought back to France by respondent no. 1. The agreement was produced before a French court which turned it into a judgment in 2003. As per the agreement, Omer was to ordinarily reside with the petitioner and respondent no. 1 was to have visitation rights, but he could not remove Omer from the territorial jurisdiction of the court without the consent of the petitioner. Later, respondent no. 1 sought a variation in the agreement which was not allowed by the court in 2005. An appeal was filed against the refusal which was also dismissed by the court in 2006. It was at that time that respondent no. 1 decided to disregard the law and brought Omer to Pakistan without the knowledge and consent of the petitioner.

When this whole incident came to the knowledge of the petitioner, she came to Pakistan and filed a *habeas corpus* petition. The court did not succeed in recovering Omer, on which the petitioner withdrew her application and filed a writ petition for issuance of a direction to the local police to register a criminal case against respondent no. 1 in respect of kidnapping and removing Omer from her lawful guardianship. As a result of the issuance of this direction by the court, an FIR was registered against respondent no. 1 under section 363, Pakistan Penal Code 1860. Upon the failure of the police to find and produce respondent no. 1 before the court, the petitioner filed the present petition on 17 March 2008. On 19 March 2008, it was reported to the court that Omer had been recovered on which the court directed the police to hand over his custody to the petitioner, but respondent no. 1 again managed to slip away from the police with Omer. Finally, on 13 October 2009, respondent no. 1 was produced before the court.

The counsel for the petitioner argued that respondent no. 1 removed his minor child surreptitiously and in blatant violation of the orders of the French court from its jurisdiction, thus his custody of the child was illegal and improper. The counsel maintained that respondent no. 1 removed the child illegally from France in utter disregard for his welfare. The child had not received any education and had been hidden in different cities in appalling and frightful conditions as respondent no. 1 was being chased by the police.

On the contrary, the counsel for respondent no. 1 argued that by virtue of Articles 4 and 5 of the Constitution of the Islamic Republic of Pakistan 1973, despite being a French national, the petitioner was under an obligation to obey the laws and Constitution of Pakistan 1973; and under the laws of Pakistan, a father is always the legal and natural guardian of a child and a Christian mother cannot claim custody of the child after the expiry of the period of *hizanat.* It was emphasised that respondent no. 1 was a Muslim while the petitioner was a Christian and the Islamic ethos of this society did not warrant a Muslim Pakistani boy to be handed over to a Christian mother as it would risk the loss of the boy's Muslim and Pakistani identity. It was further argued that as per section 13 of the Civil Procedure Code 1908, foreign judgments are ineffective if they come in conflict with the laws of Pakistan. Furthermore, where there is a danger of the minor being taken out of the country, Pakistani courts are quite reluctant to transfer custody in such matters. Also, a petition under section 491 of the Criminal Procedure Code 1898 was not maintainable against a father of a minor as custody of the minor with a father could never be illegal or improper. It was submitted that the petition under section 491 was only maintainable in the matter of custody of a minor where there was real urgency. The counsel also maintained that a delay in filing a *habeas corpus* petition is usually fatal to such a petition. Lastly, the counsel submitted that the wishes of the minor had to be given due consideration, and in the instant case, the minor did not want to remain with the petitioner.

Justice Asif Saeed Khan Khosa, as he then was, observed that respondent no. 1 emphasised the conflicting faith and culture of the parties. But when it came to falling in love and marrying a Christian woman, faith had not mattered much to him. Different cultures had not disconcerted him as he had settled in France and had acquired French nationality after marriage. The religious inclinations of his spouse and the Western culture of France did not seem to make a difference to him as he had produced a child and had brought him up in France. In short, religion, culture, and nationality only had significance for respondent no. 1 when it suited him. But when the marriage between the parties came to a dead end and a legal battle ensued between them over the child's custody, respondent no. 1 quite conveniently took shelter behind religion, culture, and nationality. Justice Khosa found this conduct of respondent no. 1 offensive to justice, equity, and good conscience.

Justice Khosa further observed that respondent no. 1's actions contradicted his words and the lip service that he paid to his faith and the laws of his country. The court did not ignore the fact that both in 2001 and 2007 when respondent no. 1 removed the minor from France, a criminal case was registered against him for kidnapping. This has been done by respondent no. 1 in blatant violation of the court orders and relevant laws, which showed that he did not have much regard for the law and judicial process both in Pakistan and abroad. Respondent no. 1 was found to be a previous convict, a fugitive against whom an International Warrant for Arrest had been issued and he was also under arrest in Pakistan. Therefore, he was not in the position to invoke Articles 4 and 5 of the Constitution. Furthermore, he had been on the run with the minor and had been hiding in different cities throughout the country with little or no regard for the minor's state of mind, upbringing, and education. Respondent no. 1's conduct demonstrated that his eagerness to keep custody of the child outweighed his concern for the child's welfare. In light of respondent no. 1's actions, it could not be said that by virtue of him being Muslim and his mere incidence of birth in Pakistan that he could be relied upon for the proper welfare of the minor. The welfare of the minor would rather lie in living with a Christian mother of French origin whose actions were found to be spotless; whose love and care for her child has dragged her into a foreign land facing trials and whose character was well-suited for inculcating good values in the minor. With these findings, the petition was disposed of.

Christine Brass v Dr Javed Iqbal PLD 1981 Pesh 110

In Private International Law, the principle of the welfare of the child determines the jurisdiction of a court.

The petitioner, Christine Brass, a Canadian national and a Christian was married to the respondent, Dr Javed Iqbal, who was a Muslim and held dual nationality of Pakistan and Canada. Their marriage took place in Ontario, Canada, in 1968. Four children, two sons (Rahim and Dean) and two daughters (Kristen and Sonya), were born to them during the wedlock. According to the petitioner, the respondent along with his wife and their four children moved to Washington, USA, where the petitioner instituted proceedings against him for divorce and custody of their children. The petitioner was granted a decree for dissolution of marriage and was given the custody of two children, a daughter (Sonya) and a son (Dean), while the custody of the other two children was given to the respondent. As per the petitioner, when the respondent obtained access to all four children pursuant to the terms of the decree, he abducted the children and brought them to Kohat, Pakistan. She further alleged that the respondent did not let her communicate with or meet her children. Therefore, she returned to Ontario, Canada, and started living with her mother. Sometimes later, she came to Peshawar and filed the present petition under Article 199(1)(b)(i) of the Constitution of Pakistan 1973, read with section 491 of the Criminal Procedure Code 1898 (CrPC), praying that the custody of all four children be entrusted to her as they had been detained by the respondent in an unlawful manner.

In his written statement, the respondent stated that it would be unsafe for the children to be given in the custody of the petitioner as she was a negligent woman who hardly took an interest in their upbringing. He further stated that the petitioner filed divorce proceedings in Washington, USA, as a no-cause divorce was possible there, not in Canada where the respondent and the petitioner had been living. He further submitted children's school certificates in order to show that the children were receiving proper education in his custody.

The petitioner, in her rejoinder, stated that the respondent had submitted himself to the superior court of the state of Washington for King County.

She further maintained that the respondent violated the decree passed by the court as to the care, control, and custody of the children.

The counsel for the petitioner submitted that, under Article 199(1)(b) of the Constitution, on the application of any person the High Court may make an order directing that a person in custody within the territorial jurisdiction of the court be brought before it. He further stated that this provision applied to all forms of custody, private or public. He also submitted that, under section 491 of the CrPC, the High Court may, whenever it deems fit, direct that a person illegally or improperly detained in public or private custody within such limits be set at liberty. He further stated that withholding minors from the custody of their legal guardian constitutes illegal detention attracting the application of section 491, CrPC, and relief under this section could not be refused merely because another remedy may be open to a person. The petitioner's counsel also submitted that the judgment by the court of Washington qualified as a foreign judgment under section 2(6) of the CPC and was not governed by the definition of 'judgment' given in section 2(9) of the CPC. He stated that, subject to compliance with certain requirements, the decision of a foreign court imposes a legal duty upon a party, against whom a decision was given, to obey the same.

On the contrary, the respondent's counsel argued that the petitioner was a Canadian national, who after obtaining the decree for dissolution of marriage from a court in Washington, USA, had gone back to Canada. She was seeking the custody of children before this court solely on the basis of the aforesaid foreign court's decision. He argued that, first, the foreign court's decision was a copy of a decree, not a judgment; and even if it is treated as a judgment, it had no binding effect in Pakistan. This is because such judgment was to be made a cause of action in a suit in a Pakistani court and if the court affirmed it, only then it would be enforceable in Pakistan. Second, he argued that a foreign judgment acquired a status of a decree in Pakistan and was liable to be attacked on the basis of exceptions provided under section 13 of the CPC. He submitted that the petitioner, without initiating a civil action in a competent court in Pakistan for converting a foreign judgment into a decree, had come directly to the High Court and made that decision a foundation of her prayer, which was illegal. He argued that even if it was assumed that the petitioner could bring a civil suit within the limitation period specified under Article 117 of the Limitation Act 1908, the petitioner would still fail. The judgment was only a copy of a foreign decree and a suit on the strength of section 13 of the CPC could not succeed in a Civil Court in Pakistan unless the judgment was attached with the decree so that the propriety of the same could be scrutinised in the light of exceptions provided under section 13 of the CPC. Furthermore, even if it was assumed that the decision given by a court in Washington conclusively decided the issue of dissolution of marriage between the parties, its finality could not be extended to the issue of children's custody because the direction in respect of the same was an order, which by its very nature could not be final.

The court noted that both the parties temporarily went to the USA and came back to Canada, from where the respondent came to Pakistan along with his children. It observed that, under the Private International Law it is the welfare of the children which controls the jurisdiction of a court whenever a case is brought before it. In the instant case, the minors were Pakistanis, and their welfare was of paramount consideration. The father being a Muslim had a legal right, both under domestic law and international law, to see that his children were brought up in accordance with the Muslim faith and no order/decree should stand in his way. The court noted that it was an admitted fact that the petitioner was outside the jurisdiction of both the Washington Court and the High Court of Pakistan. The petitioner claimed the relief on the basis of the decree/judgment of the Washington Court which had not been given additional force by a decree obtained in Pakistan by the petitioner. Even otherwise, the court had to take the welfare of the minors in consideration and 'it will be against the intention of law if the minor children residing in Pakistan under a Muslim father are entrusted to the petitioner who is a Christian and who is living outside Pakistan to be taken to Canada'.[47] This amply showed that it was in the interest of the minors to be in the custody of their father. In addition, the petitioner's prayer that children's present custody under the respondent be declared illegal was not maintainable. The petition was dismissed accordingly.

14.3.4 Application of the MFLO to Pakistani Citizens Living Abroad

Yusuf Abbas v Mst Ismat Mustafa PLD 1968 Kar 480

The MFLO applies to Pakistani citizens living abroad and the Pakistani courts have jurisdiction to administer the estate of a Pakistani deceased situated in Pakistan and abroad. Beneficiaries of such estate could include foreigners as well.

The judgment, in this case, laid down important legal principles regarding the application of Pakistani family law to the estate of Pakistanis living abroad. The dispute in this case related to the administration of the estate of a wealthy merchant, Mustafa Bin Abdul Latif, whose business empire spread across Pakistan and various Gulf States of Bahrain, Dubai, and Sharjah. He died in Karachi on 5 May 1964. The plaintiffs were his orphaned grandchildren who claimed a share in the estate through their pre-deceased mother, Mariam Mustafa under section 4 of the Muslim Family Laws Ordinance 1961 (MFLO). The defendants denied the claims of the plaintiffs on the grounds that the MFLO did not apply to the estate of the deceased and the Sindh High Court did not have the jurisdiction to administer his estate situated outside Pakistan.

Justice Noorul Arifin analysed the issue of the jurisdiction of the court regarding estates outside Pakistan and the applicable law by taking into account the principles under English law. He observed:

> The distinction in the English system of conflict of laws between immovables and movables for the purpose of succession and jurisdiction of Courts, has its roots in the feudal law, under which the feudal lords did not allow the descent of their land to be affected if vassals should acquire a foreign domicile. Accordingly, the principle of scission was developed, by which the deceased's movable property was governed by *lex domicilii*, while his immovable were governed by the *lex situs*. The rule of scission is peculiar to the countries whose legal system is based on the AngloSaxon system of jurisprudence. Countries like Italy, Germany, Netherlands, Spain, Portugal, Sweden have, however, followed Roman Law rule of Universal Succession, and accordingly apply a unitary law to the whole of the deceased's property, immovable and movables. Under this system, the heirs succeed per *Universtitatem* and, not by a series of particular acts to each item. In other words[,] for movables and immovable alike, one system of law is applied, which in the case of some countries, that is, Germany, Italy, Spain, Portugal, Netherlands, Sweden, Poland, Egypt, Japan, China and Greece, is his personal law, and in countries like Switzerland, Norway, Denmark and Argentine, it is the law of the deceased's domicile; Wolf's Private International Law, Second Edn. 567–568—The advantage of the Unitary Law is that the law applied in the succession to the deceased's estate is simple, and complications are avoided which would be inevitable when several items of property included in one estate have to be distributed under different rules.[48]

Justice Arifin noted that English Courts have realised the inconvenience in the application of the principle of scission (*lex situs* for immovable; and *lex domicilii* for movables) and have developed several exceptions to it. By referring to Amir Ali's *Muhammadan Law*, Vol. 2, 1965 Edition,

p. 134, the learned judge held that Islamic law does not recognise the principle of scission:

> Thus, if a Moslem dies domiciled in England, the Courts in this Country [Pakistan], will apply, not *lex domicillii* but his personal law that is, Islamic Law as administered in this country to succession to his movables in Pakistan. Even the will with regard to these movables, though valid in English law, will be recognised by the Courts of this country only so far as it is consistent with Islamic Law.[49]

Justice Arifin further observed that the principle of scission is disregarded in the MFLO because its section 1(2) provides that it 'extends to the whole of Pakistan, applies to all Muslim citizens of Pakistan, wherever they may be'. Therefore, if a Muslim citizen of Pakistan dies domiciled in a foreign country, the law of his domicile cannot be applied to his estate in Pakistan. Under the same principle:

> If a Muslim citizen dies domiciled in Pakistan and leaves property, both immovables and movables, in foreign jurisdiction, the succession to his estate will be according to the rule or Islamic law as modified be section 4 of the Ordinance. The Courts in Pakistan, in matters of succession to the estate of [a] Muslim citizen, can apply only his personal law, irrespective of the rules of *lex domicilii* or *sites*. The only limitation on the jurisdiction of the Courts to regulate succession according to the personal law of the *propositus*, is the effectiveness of their judgments.[50]

Justice Arifin rejected the argument of the counsel for the defendant that under section 1(2) of the MFLO, both the *propositus* and the beneficiary under section 4 of the MFLO should be citizens of Pakistan and held:

> I would interpret section 1(2) and section 4 of the Ordinance to mean that if a citizen of Pakistan, wherever he may be, dies after the promulgation of the Ordinance, then his succession opens not only for persons who are heirs according to the ordinary rules of Islamic Law relating to inheritance and a succession, but also for the benefit of the children of his predeceased son or daughter. The Muslim Family Laws Ordinance would not, therefore, exclude foreigners from the benefit of succession under section 4. Such exclusion should have been by express language or by necessary implication. The language of section 1(2) and section 4 of the Ordinance does not suggest that it was intended to exclude foreigners from succession under the Ordinance. Moreover, the Islamic Law, as administered in this

> country, does not exclude foreigners from succession to a deceased Muslim citizen of Pakistan, and the Muslim Family Laws Ordinance, in matters of succession, does not make any departure from this rule.[51]

Therefore, the court held that the plaintiffs were entitled to the decree for the administration of the estate of Mustafa Bin Abdul Latif within Pakistan and abroad.

14.4 Conclusion

Given the multi-religious nature of Pakistani society, judges of Pakistani courts are faced with the issues of conflict of personal laws where parties profess more than one religion. Similarly, the large number of overseas Pakistanis gives rise to legal issues related to transnational families regulated under multiple legal systems. Generally, in such cases Pakistani courts give precedence to Islamic law and state law over foreign laws. In this respect, they seek guidance from the principles laid down by English courts. Despite the preponderance of judgments favouring the application of Islamic law in cases of interpersonal conflict of laws, Pakistani judges do not hesitate to deviate from such application if the circumstances of the case require so. In this respect the judges are guided by the principles of equity, fairness, and justice. The equivalents of these principles could be found in Islamic law under the doctrines of *istihsan* (juristic preference) and *maslaha* (public welfare).

Questions

1. Do Pakistani courts recognise a marriage that has taken place abroad between a Pakistani citizen and a foreigner? Please analyse the case law on the validity of dissolution of such marriages in Pakistan.
2. Can a Muslim, as a convert from Christianity, dissolve his marriage with a Christian woman through *talaq*? Please elaborate the development of Pakistani case law on this point.
3. What are the principles that the Pakistani courts apply while deciding the custody of children cases regarding transnational families?

Further Reading

Book

Pearl, D. and W. Menski, *Muslim Family Law*, 3rd edn (New Delhi: Sweet & Maxwell, 1998), 84–87, 106–117.

Cases

Hina Jilani v Sohail Butt PLD 1995 Lah 151 (A mother does not lose her right of custody of a child if, after the dissolution of marriage, she takes away the child to her native country.)

Louise Anne Fairley v Sajjad Ahmed Rana PLD 2007 Lahore 300 (The Pakistani courts shall exercise their jurisdiction only with regard to minors who are ordinarily residing here. As the child was not an ordinary resident of Pakistan and her custody matter was pending adjudication before the Court in Scotland, Pakistani courts did not interfere in the jurisdiction of the competent court.)

Ms Sadaf Munir Khan v Chairman Reconciliation Committee PLD 2019 Lah 285 (The divorce certificate issued by the Chairman Reconciliation Committee in Pakistan is of no legal effect because *talaq* was given when parties were residing abroad.)

Mst. Asma Bibi v Chairman Reconciliation Committee PLD 2020 Lah 679 (When *talaq* is pronounced abroad, the functions of the Chairman union council are performed by the officers of Pakistan mission abroad.)

Muhammad Ramzan v Nasreen Firdous PLD 2016 SC 174 (Courts in Pakistan are bound to apply the principles of Private International Law wherever necessary. Pakistani courts do not have jurisdiction over properties situated outside Pakistan. Since the parties were domiciled in England, English courts have jurisdiction over the properties situated in England.)

Roshni Desai v Jahanzeb Niazi PLD 2011 Lah 423 (Islamic law allows a non-Muslim mother to exercise the same rights of custody as enjoyed by a Muslim mother.)

Zubair Hussain Siddiqui v Shakeela Khanum 2006 CLC 1099 (A Muslim female marrying a Christian shall not become non-Muslim merely by the fact of such marriage though it would be a sinful act, and she shall not be deprived of her right of inheritance from her Muslim parents.)

Notes

1. D. Pearl and W. Menski, *Muslim Family Law*, 3rd edn (New Delhi: Sweet & Maxwell 1998), 106.
2. Ibid., 85.
3. 1985 CLC 2855.
4. PLD 2010 Lah 48.
5. PLD 2012 Lah 430, 433.
6. ILR 41 Bom 181.
7. PLD 1958 (WP) Lah 431, 436.
8. Ibid., 437.
9. Ibid., 437–38.
10. Ibid., 439.
11. Ibid., 441.
12. Ibid., 442.
13. Ibid.
14. Ibid., 447.
15. AIR 1919 Lah 389.
16. AIR 1939 Cal 417.
17. Ibid., 419.
18. ILR 41 Bom 181.
19. Ibid., [5].
20. PLD 1958 Lah 431.
21. PLD 1967 SC 334, 339.

22. PLD 1963 SC 51.
23. Ibid., [14].
24. ILR 38 Mad. 371.
25. AIR 1932 Lah. 116.
26. PLD 1967 SC 334, 339–40.
27. PLD 1967 SC 588, 599.
28. Ibid., 600.
29. (1882) 8 AC 43.
30. Ibid., 50.
31. (1835) 2 Cl. & Fin 488; [1835] 6 All ER 1239.
32. Ibid.
33. Ibid., [11].
34. PLD 1958 Lah 431.
35. PLD 1963 SC 51.
36. (1962) 3 AER 193.
37. PLD 1967 SC 580, 604–05.
38. Ibid., 605.
39. Ibid., 606.
40. 1965 LR 720.
41. PLD 1967 SC 580, 606.
42. PLD 1963 SC 51.
43. (1917) 1 KBD 634.
44. Ibid.
45. Ibid.
46. PLD 1958 Lah 431.
47. PLD 1981 Pesh 110, 117.
48. PLD 1968 Kar 480, 501.
49. Ibid., 502.
50. Ibid., 503.
51. Ibid., 510.

15

PROCEDURES IN FAMILY COURTS

15.1 Introduction

Family Courts established under the Family Courts Act 1964 (Act) are Civil Courts. To avoid procedural technicalities and delays in the adjudication of family disputes, the Code of Civil Procedure 1908 (CPC) does not apply to the proceedings before Family Courts except for sections 10 and 11 which deal with the principles of *res sub judice* and *res judicata,* respectively. Likewise, the Qanun-e-Shahadat Order 1984 also does not apply to the proceedings before these courts.[1] These courts have special procedures because of their inquisitorial jurisdiction. The Family Courts regulate their own proceedings and have wide powers to use any procedure unless it is prohibited by law. The Family Courts conduct the trial of an offence under the Act, the Muslim Family Laws Ordinance 1961, and the Child Marriage Restraint Act 1929 in accordance with the provisions of Chapter XXII of the Code of Criminal Procedure 1898. An offence, other than contempt of the Family Courts, is cognizable on the complaint of the Union Council, Arbitration Council, or the aggrieved party.[2] The Family Courts also exercise jurisdiction under the Guardians and Wards Act 1890, and when functioning in this capacity, they are termed as Guardian Courts.[3]

15.2 Jurisdiction of Family Courts

The Family Courts have jurisdiction to entertain, hear, and adjudicate upon civil matters such as (1) dissolution of marriage; (2) dower; (3) maintenance; (4) restitution of conjugal rights; (5) custody of children and the visitation rights of a non-custodial parent; (6) guardianship; (7) jactitation of marriage; (8) dowry; (9) the personal property and belongings of a wife and a child living with his mother; and (10) any other matter arising out of the *Nikahnama.*

The Family Courts have the jurisdiction to try the offences under sections 337A(i), 337F (i), 341, 342, 343, 344, 345, 346, 352, and 509 of the Pakistan Penal Code, 1860. These provisions relate to offences against the human body, unlawful confinement, criminal assault, and harassment of women. This special procedure is meant to provide speedy justice to the victims.[4]

15.2.1 Territorial Jurisdiction of Family Courts. Under Rule 6 of the Family Courts Rules 1965, a Family Court has jurisdiction to try suits where the cause of action, in whole or in part, arises within its local limits or where the parties reside or last resided together. In suits relating to the dissolution of marriage or recovery of dower, the court within the local limits in which the wife ordinarily resides will have the jurisdiction. Generally, the residence of a wife is a determining factor for deciding the jurisdiction of the Family Court. Under section 9 of the Guardians and Wards Act 1890, the minor's ordinary residence determines the jurisdiction of the Guardian Court.

In cases where there are multiple suits between the same parties, courts consolidate such suits to avoid further delays.

15.2.2 Appeals. An appeal against the decision of the Family Court lies before the District Court. However, an order of the Family Court cannot be subjected to revision under section 115 of the CPC. A decision given or a decree passed by the Family Court is appealable in the High Court when a case is decided by a District Judge or his equivalent, but in all other cases, an appeal will be presented before the District Judge. However, in the following cases, no appeal lies against the decision of the Family Court:

1. For dissolution of marriage, except where the husband treats his wife with cruelty, that is to say, he habitually assaults her or makes her life miserable by cruelty of conduct even if such conduct does not amount to physical ill-treatment.
2. For dower or dowry not exceeding Rs 100,000.
3. For maintenance of Rs 5,000 or less per month.

Moreover, no appeal lies against an interim order passed by the Family Court. The Appellate Court is required to dispose of the appeal within four months.[5] Due to the non-availability of the right of second appeal and revision before the High Court, a large number of writs are filed against the decisions of the Appellate Courts. High Courts exercise this jurisdiction restrictively and tend not to interfere with the decision of the Family Courts and the Appellate Courts unless their judgments are based on misreading or non-reading of the evidence or misconception of law.

15.2.3 Institution of Suits in Family Courts. A suit before the Family Court is instituted by presentation of a plaint or in any other manner as may be prescribed by law. The plaint is required to contain all the material facts pertaining to the dispute and a schedule giving a list of witnesses, along with their names and addresses, who are to be produced in support of the plaint. However, with the permission of the court, the parties may call any witness at a later stage, if the court considers his/her evidence/testimony expedient in the interests of justice. In addition, a plaint for dissolution of marriage may contain all claims relating to dowry, maintenance, dower, personal property and belongings of a wife, custody of children, and visitation rights to avoid multiplicity of proceedings.[6]

Section 7 of the Act provides that where a plaintiff relies upon a document in his possession as evidence in order to support his claim, he must produce it in a court when the plaint is presented and deliver the document or a copy thereof to be filed with the plaint. However, in a case where he relies upon any document not in his possession, he must enter such document in a list appended to the plaint and must provide reasons for the relevancy of such document to the claim. Lastly, the plaint must be accompanied by as many duplicate copies of the schedule, and the lists of documents being relied upon as there are defendants in the suit for the purpose of service upon them.

15.2.4 Intimation to the Defendant. After a plaint is presented to the Family Court, it fixes a date which should not be more than fifteen days for the appearance of the defendant. Within two days of the presentation of the plaint, the summons is issued to the defendant with a copy of the plaint, schedule, and a list of documents that are relied upon by the plaintiff. While issuing the summons, the Family Court requires the defendant to submit a written statement on the day mentioned in the summons.[7]

15.2.5 Written Statement. On the date fixed by the Family Court, the defendant appears before the court and files a written statement, a list of witnesses, and gist of evidence. In case he fails to do so on the fixed date, the Family Court may allow the defendant to submit the same and other required documents on the next date which does not exceed fifteen days from the earlier date, provided that the defendant gives sufficient reasons that prevented him from filing the written statement.[8]

Section 9 of the Act provides that a defendant husband may, where no earlier suit for restitution of conjugal rights is pending, claim a decree for restitution of conjugal rights to a suit for dissolution of marriage or maintenance in his written statement, which will be deemed as a plaint and no separate suit will lie for it. Similarly, a defendant wife may in a written statement to a suit for restitution of conjugal rights make a claim for dissolution of marriage including *khula*, which will be deemed as plaint and no separate suit will lie for it.

As far as the production of documents is concerned, where a defendant relies upon a document in his possession, he must produce a copy thereof forthwith in the court along with his written statement. However, where he relies upon a document not in his possession/power, he is required to enter such document in a list to be appended to the written statement and give reasons as to its relevancy to the defence in the written statement. Copies of the written statement, list of witnesses, précis of evidence, and the documents being relied upon by the defendant in support of his defence must be given to the plaintiff, his agent, or advocate present in the court.

In a case where it is proved that the summons/notice was duly served on the defendant and the defendant fails to appear before the court on the fixed date, the court may proceed against him *ex parte*. However, if the court had adjourned the hearing of the suit *ex parte* and the defendant at or before such hearing appears and shows good cause for his earlier non-appearance he may, upon the terms directed by the court, be heard as if he had appeared on the date fixed for his appearance. However, if it is not proved that the summons/notice was duly served on the defendant, the court will issue a fresh summons. If the defendant does not submit his written statement at all, either on or before the fixed date, his defence will be struck off and the court shall decide the case as per the law. After passing an *ex parte* decree, the court shall send the notice to the defendant regarding the same along with a certified copy of the decree within three days of the passing of the decree.

A defendant can apply to the Court to set aside the *ex parte* decree within thirty days of the service of the previously mentioned notice of the passing of the decree. In that case, he will have to satisfy the court that he was not duly served, or he was prevented by sufficient cause from appearing when the suit was heard. After service of notice on the plaintiff and on such terms and costs as it deems fit, the court may make an order for setting aside the decree against the defendant and will appoint a day for proceeding with the suit.

15.2.6 Pre-trial Proceedings. After the written statement is filed, the court fixes a date for the pre-trial hearing of the case, in which it examines the plaint, the written statement, the précis of evidence, documents filed by the parties and, if needed, hear the parties and their counsels. At this stage, the court ascertains the points of dispute between the parties and attempts to effect a compromise. If a compromise is not possible between the parties the court may, if necessary, frame precise points of dispute and record evidence of the parties.

However, in a case of dissolution of marriage, if compromise fails, the court immediately passes a decree for dissolution of marriage and in case the marriage is dissolved through *khula*, the court may direct the wife to give up fifty per cent of her deferred dower or up to twenty-five per cent of her admitted prompt dower to the husband. The court will direct the husband to pay the whole or part of the outstanding deferred dower to the wife.[9]

15.2.7 Power of Family Courts to Summon Witnesses. The Family Courts may issue summons to any person to appear and give evidence or to produce or cause the production of any document. Moreover, if a person to whom the court has issued summons to appear and give evidence or to cause the production of any document before it, wilfully disobeys such summons the court may take cognizance of such disobedience and after giving the person an opportunity to explain, sentence him to a fine of Rs 5,000.[10]

15.2.8 Recording of Evidence. On the date fixed for the recording of evidence, the court examines the parties' witnesses in such order as it deems fit. The court records or causes to be recorded the substance of the statement of witnesses. The same can also be recorded through audio or video recording. The court does not issue a summons for the production of any witness unless, within three days of framing of issues any party intimates the court that it desires any particular witness to be summoned through the court, or the court itself is satisfied that it is not practicable for such party to produce such witness. The witnesses give evidence in their own words, but parties or their counsels may further examine, cross-examine, or re-examine them. However, the court may forbid any question that it considers indecent, scandalous, frivolous, or which appears to be intended to insult or annoy or is needlessly offensive in form. The court itself may also ask any question from any witness for the purpose of elucidation of a point material to the case. The court may also permit the evidence to be given in the form of an affidavit and if it deems fit, the court may call such witness for the purpose of examination.[11]

15.2.9 Conclusion of a Trial and Cases to be Disposed of within a Specified Period. After the closing of evidence of both parties, the court again attempts to effect a compromise between parties within a period not exceeding fifteen days. If such a compromise is not possible, the court announces its judgment and passes a decree.[12] The court is required to dispose of a case, including a suit for dissolution of marriage, within six months from the date of institution of the suit. However, if a case is not disposed of within this period, either party has a right to approach the High Court for necessary direction as it may deem fit.[13]

15.2.10 Enforcement of Decrees. The Family Court passes a decree in such form and manner as may be prescribed, and enters its particulars in the prescribed register. If any money is paid or any property is delivered towards the satisfaction of the decree in the presence of the court, it enters the fact of the payment or the delivery of the property in its register.

Where a decree relates to the payment of money and the amount is not paid within the time specified by the court, not exceeding thirty days, the same is, if directed by the court, recovered as arrears of land revenue, and is paid to the decree-holder on recovery. The decree is executed by the court passing it or by such other Civil Court as the district judge may direct by special or general order. If it deems fit, the Family Court may direct the money to be paid in instalments.[14]

15.2.11 Contempt of Court. A person is guilty of contempt of the Family Court if he, without lawful excuse: (i) insults the Court; (ii) causes an interruption in the work of the Court; (iii) misbehaves with any person in the Court premises, uses abusive language, threats or physical force or intimidates in any manner; (iv) refuses to answer any question put by the Court that he is bound to answer; or (v) refuses to take oath or to state the truth or to sign any statement made by him in the Court. The court may try such a person for contempt and sentence him to a fine not exceeding Rs 2,000.[15]

15.2.12 Suit for Maintenance. In a suit for maintenance, on the date of the first appearance of the defendant, the court fixes an interim monthly maintenance for a wife or a child. If the defendant fails to pay such maintenance by the fourteenth day of each month, the defence of the defendant stands struck off and the court decrees the suit for maintenance based on averments in the plaint and other supporting documents available on the record. Moreover, in a decree for maintenance, the court may fix a maintenance amount higher than the amount prayed for in the plaint and may prescribe an annual increase in maintenance. However, if the court does not prescribe the annual increase in maintenance, the maintenance allowance fixed by the court automatically stands increased at an annual rate of ten per cent. For fixing the maintenance allowance, the court may summon relevant documentary evidence from any organisation or body to determine the resources of the defendant.[16]

15.2.13 The Appearance of a Pardanashin Lady through Agents. If a person is required under the Act to appear before the Family Court, other than as a witness and the said person is a *pardanashin* lady, the court may permit her to be represented by a duly authorised agent.[17]

15.2.14 Court Fee. The court fee to be paid on any plaint or memorandum of appeal is Rs 15 for any kind of suit or appeal under the Act.[18]

15.2.15 Intimation to Arbitration Council. In a case where the Family Court decrees the dissolution of a Muslim marriage, the court immediately, but not later than three days from the passing of the decree, sends by registered post or by other means, a certified copy of the decree to the concerned Chairman, Arbitration Council. Upon receipt of the decree, the Chairman proceeds as if he had received intimation of divorce under the Muslim Family Laws Ordinance 1961.[19]

15.3 Outline of Case Law

15.3.1 Restitution of Conjugal Rights. Each spouse has a right to sue the other when either of them refuses to live with the other without a lawful excuse. The Federal Shariat Court held that this right is not repugnant to the Injunctions of Islam.

Nadeem Siddiqui v Islamic Republic of Pakistan PLD 2016 FSC 1

The jurisdiction of Family Court to issue a decree for restitution of conjugal rights is not repugnant to the Injunctions of Islam.

In this case, the Federal Shariat Court tested the validity of a decree of restitution of conjugal rights and did not find it repugnant to the Injunctions of Islam. The petitioner challenged section 5 of the Family Courts Act 1964 on the ground that it is repugnant to the Injunctions of Islam. The impugned section states as follows:

> Subject to the provisions of the Muslim Family Laws Ordinance, 1961, and the Conciliation Court Ordinance, 1961, the Family Courts shall have exclusive jurisdiction to entertain, hear and adjudicate upon matters specified in the Schedule.

The Schedule included matters pertaining to the restitution of conjugal rights. The petitioner relied upon several verses of the Qur'an, specifically verse 35 of Surah An-Nisa. He argued that the Family Court could not force a wife to live with her husband against her will. At best, the court can make an effort for reconciliation between the spouses whose relationship is constrained. He contended that a wife who is living away from her husband without a reasonable justification loses her right to maintenance. Under Islamic law, a court cannot force her to perform her marital obligations without her consent.

The court considered the contentions raised by the petitioner in light of verse 35 of Surah An-Nisa, which reads as follows:

> If you fear a breach between them twain [husband and wife], appoint (two) arbiters, one from his family, and the other from hers; if they wish for peace, Allah will cause their reconciliation: For Allah hath full knowledge, and is acquainted with all things. (The Holy Qur'an translation Abdullah Yusuf Ali)

The court noted that a bare perusal of the verse made it clear that reconciliation is preferred if both spouses desire to make peace and resolve their differences. It was further observed that the Act has already provided reconciliation mechanisms both at the pre- and post-trial stages, in conformity with the Injunctions of Islam. However, in case the reconciliation efforts fail or are not possible for some reason, the Act also provides a way to settle the matter one way or the other. The court held:

> It will be appreciated that the Courts are constituted to resolve the conflicts and settle the disputes which crop up between various individuals including the spouses, from time to time. The Courts are bound by the Constitution as well as by the Injunctions of Islam to observe and administer justice between the litigants/individuals in all circumstances. In case of the spouses, the jurisdiction to resolve their differences has been granted to the Family Courts.[202]

The court observed that the petitioner failed to satisfy the court as to how the impugned section authorising the Family Courts to issue decrees for restitution of conjugal rights is repugnant to the Injunctions of Islam. He could not cite any verse or hadith prohibiting a Family Court to pass such an order when a wife is not ready for the dissolution of marriage on the basis of *khula*.

In view of the foregoing reasons, the court found the instant Shariat Petition misconceived and dismissed it accordingly.

Nadeem Siddiqui v Islamic Republic of Pakistan PLD 2016 FSC 4

The mechanism provided for the execution of a decree for restitution of conjugal rights against a wife, which involved attaching her property and making periodical payments to the husband, is not repugnant to the Injunctions of Islam.

The petitioner challenged Order XXI, Rules 32 and 33 of the CPC on the ground of their repugnancy to the Injunctions of Islam. The impugned Rule 32 of the Order, besides other things, provides that in a case for a decree of restitution of conjugal rights where the party against whom a decree has been passed fails to satisfy the decree despite having an opportunity to do so, such decree will be enforced by attaching the property of the defaulting party. Rule 33 provides that in case the judgment-debtor fails to satisfy the decree for restitution of conjugal rights within the time period specified, the judgment-debtor will make periodical payments, as may be just, to the decree holder.

The counsel for the petitioner argued that in a case of the decree for restitution of conjugal rights the provision of attachment of a wife's property if she fails to satisfy the decree, puts her through immense misery and torture. Similarly, as per Rule 33, directing the wife to make certain payments to the husband on her non-compliance of obeying the restitution of conjugal rights decree, amounts to coercing her to yield to her husband's desire for cohabitation. The counsel for the petitioner placed reliance upon verse 231 of Surah Al-Baqarah and two Hadiths in this regard. The court held:

> … [the] decree of a Court has much sanctity in Islam and great significance and sanctity [h]as been attached to a decree passed by a competent court. The parties go to a court to settle disputes including matrimonial matter. If … a decree passed and judgment delivered is not complied with or not taken to its logical end, the whole exercise becomes meaningless. Therefore, there should be some mechanism to execute the judgment so delivered or decree so passed. The relevant impugned Order and Rules are just for the same purpose.[21]

The court noted that if a wife willingly enters into *nikah*, in the presence of witnesses, and expresses her willingness in writing, she is bound by the terms of *nikah*. However, if she does not want to live with her husband, she can move the court to dissolve her marriage on the basis of *khula*. In addition, verse 231 of Surah Al-Baqarah, upon which the petitioner relied, dealt with the situation where divorce has already been pronounced. The verse reads as follows:

> When you divorce women, and they (are about to) fulfil the term of their (*'iddah*), either retain them on equitable terms or set them free on equitable terms; but do not retain them to injure them, (or) to take undue advantage; if anyone does that, he wrongs his own soul. Do not treat Allah's Signs as a jest; but solemnly rehearse Allah's favours on you, and the fact that He sent down to you the Book and Wisdom, for your instruction. And fear Allah, and know that Allah is well acquainted with all things. (The Holy Qur'an translation Abdullah Yusuf Ali)

Similarly, the two Hadiths upon which the petitioner's counsel relied also dealt with the matters of *khula* and divorce. Thus, the petitioner failed to point out any specific provision in a verse, *hadith*, or even *fiqh* to support his contentions.

Furthermore, the court noted that under Article 203–B(c) of the Constitution, the Federal Shariat Court was only authorised to examine any law or provision of a law on the touchstone of the Islamic Injunctions as contained in the Qur'an and Sunnah of the Prophet (PBUH). However,

Muslim Personal Law fell outside the jurisdiction of the court. Since the impugned Order and Rules were procedural in nature they were excluded from the jurisdiction of this court. Therefore, the petition was dismissed *in limine*.

15.3.2 Institution of Suits and Additional Evidence

Roman Asghar v Samina Yasmin 2010 YLR 619 (Lahore)

Admission of evidence at later stages of a case is permissible if the court considers it expedient in the interest of justice.

This case sheds light on the scope and nature of power exercised by Family Courts under section 7(2) of the Family Courts Act 1964. Under the Act, the parties may with the permission of the court call any witness or produce any document at any stage, if the court considers such evidence expedient in the interest of justice. In this case, the court issued an interim order while the suit for dissolution of marriage, recovery of dower amount, dowry articles, and maintenance allowance were pending adjudication. The present writ petition challenged the interim order. The petitioner's counsel maintained that the suit was fixed for recording respondent no. 1's evidence on 22 October 2008. On this date, the petitioner's counsel approached respondent no. 2 (judge, Family Court) and upon his request, the judge fixed a time for recording the evidence of respondent no. 1. Respondent no. 1, on the basis of her affidavit was cross-examined by the petitioner's counsel. After the cross-examination, the petitioner's counsel inquired about the documentary evidence and respondent no. 2 told him that it was completed. The petitioner's counsel objected that respondent no. 2 had not adopted proper procedure and exhibited fake documents in the absence of the counsel. He argued that the provisions of section 7(3)(4) of the Act had not been adhered to and prayed for recalling the interim order passed by respondent no. 2 as the documents exhibited were allegedly fake and should be de-exhibited. He also contended that the documents exhibited were not mentioned in the list of documents/ reliance attached to the plaint.

After hearing arguments and perusing the record, the court noted that the proviso to section 7 of the Act states, 'provided further that the parties may with the permission of the Court may call any witness at any later stage if the Court considers such evidence expedient in the interest of justice.' The court held:

> It is settled that Family Courts are vested with the powers to allow any witness to produce any documents on record and to pass orders they deem expedient and just for the decision of a case. The Family Courts make it clear that family disputes are to be decided expeditiously without being burdened with the strict technicalities of law and it is for this reason that the Qanun-e-Shahadat 1984 has been barred under section 17 of the West Pakistan Family Courts Act 1964. The only requirement under the law is that proper procedure should be adopted by the Family Courts to decide it within a reasonable time and after hearing both the parties. Family Courts being special Courts can regulate their own procedure which is more flexible so that family matters can be settled by way of administration of Justice in its true sense unhindered by technicalities.[22]

The record of the case showed that the petitioner's counsel was present and cross-examined respondent no. 1, but he stated that it was some other counsel. Even if that was the case, the petitioner's counsel in the writ petition admitted that he cross-examined respondent no. 1. He should have objected to the documentary evidence at that time. The petitioner's counsel did not object at the time of cross-examination to cover up his own negligence and consequently, was obstructing the course of justice. The court noted that the record showed that respondent no. 1 in her list of documents had mentioned the documents to be exhibited. Had it not been so, even then respondent no. 1 had the right under section 7(2) of the Act to put the same on file with the permission of the court. The mode of evidence was at the discretion of the Family Court and it was 'bound to allow what is in the interest of justice and exercise its own powers to prevent the course of justice from being deflected from the path that leads to fair and just decision.'[23] The petition was dismissed accordingly.

Khurram Zulfiqar v Mst Benish Mubarak 2009 MLD 766 (Lahore)

Presenting a document in a court and exhibiting it thereafter does not amount to acknowledging its veracity.

This case established some important principles regarding the presentation and acceptance of documentary evidence in a court of law. It established that presenting a document in a court and exhibiting it thereafter does not always mean acceptance of its contents without checking its veracity.

The petitioner and respondent no. 1 contracted marriage in 2006, but it could not last due to forgery in the *Nikahnama* in columns no. 10, 17, 19, and 20 by the father of respondent no. 1. The petitioner, therefore, lodged a criminal case. Respondent no. 1 also filed a suit for recovery of the dower, dowry articles, and gold ornaments and filed receipts of the dowry articles. The petitioner objected that the receipts were forged and filed an application challenging the same; maintaining that they should not be allowed to be exhibited. The petitioner relied upon case law in support of his argument, but the same was held to be inapplicable in the present case as the entire case law relied upon by the petitioner revolved around the Qanun-e-Shahadat Order 1984 and the Code of Civil Procedure 1908 which are not applicable in family cases. The petitioner then argued that there must be some procedure for appreciating the evidence. The court found this objection invalid because every judicial officer understands the procedure that should be adopted in deciding a matter at hand. The court noted:

> The important factor which needs consideration is that presentation of document by one person and exhibiting it would not always mean acceptance of its contents also especially in a family case. As already mentioned law of evidence and Civil Procedure Code not being applicable the concept of exhibiting a document in a civil case would not apply in a family matter either. Even otherwise, the permission to allow to exhibit a document even in [a] civil case does not amount to its acceptance as an alternate [*sic*] evidence. It is only a receipt and the acknowledgement and the permission to make it a part of [the] record. One can always challenge its validity, correctness or genuineness during the cross-examination or thereafter at the time of [the] final argument. In fact if somebody wants to bring on record certain piece[s] of evidence he should not be deprived from doing so. Every authority as far as possible should not refuse to entertain the evidence produced by the parties before them in support of their claim. However, it obviously does not mean acceptance of the same without checking its veracity as well as correctness and justification. The authorities, therefore, need to be benevolent in receiving, however, prudent in accepting its evidential value.[24]

The court held that the writ petition does not lie against an interlocutory order. Hence, it was dismissed.

15.3.3 Setting Aside *Ex Parte* Decree

Aziz-ur-Rehman v Alia Munir 2010 YLR 269 (Lahore)

If a person does not appear before a court despite having knowledge about the pendency of the suit, his subsequent application for setting aside *ex parte* decision cannot be accepted.

In this case, the petitioner was married to respondent no. 1. Both parties were Pakistanis, but they were residing in the USA. They were also granted citizenship of the USA in 1991. After some time, the relations between the spouses became strained. Respondent no. 1 returned to Pakistan and instituted a suit for dissolution of marriage. She stated that the petitioner could not be served a notice and an *ex parte* decree was passed against him on 11 June 2007. Thereafter, the petitioner filed an application before the trial court seeking the *ex parte* decree to be set aside, but it was dismissed; hence, the present writ petition.

The petitioner's counsel argued that the summons was sent to the USA at the address given in the plaint, but he did not receive it. He argued that the signatures of the petitioner on the summons were forged. He also objected to the institution of the dissolution of marriage petition on the basis of the dual nationality of respondent no. 1 and her competency to institute a suit in Pakistan.

After perusing the record, the court observed that in his application under section 9(6) of the Family Courts Act 1964, the petitioner disclosed that he was prevented by sufficient reasons to appear before the court owing to his preoccupation in the USA and his financial constraints. The direct admission made in the pleadings by the petitioner established that he had knowledge about the pendency of the suit and the date of the hearing. From abroad, he requested the trial judge for adjournment. Hence, it could not be argued that the petitioner did not have any knowledge of the date of the hearing or the pendency of the suit. Owing to the conscious inactivity of the petitioner, he allowed the *ex parte* decree to be passed against him. Therefore, there was no sufficient reason for setting aside the *ex parte* decree passed by the trial court.

15.3.4 Pre-trial Proceedings. A Family Court is required to take all steps to effect reconciliation between the spouses. However, if such efforts fail or the Court is satisfied that such efforts are bound to fail even at the stage of conclusion of the judicial proceedings, then the marriage can be dissolved at the pre-trial stage without following the normal procedure prescribed for the conduct of proceedings.

Shakeel Ahmad v Judge, Family Court 2010 CLC 1 (Lahore)

A Family Court can dissolve a marriage on the basis of *khula* even without following the normal procedure of framing issues and recording evidence if it satisfies itself that there is no possibility of reconciliation between the spouses.

This case sheds light on the power conferred upon a Family Court under proviso to section 10(4) of the Family Courts Act 1964, whereby it is authorised to pass a decree for dissolution of marriage forthwith, in case reconciliation between the spouses fails. It established that the Family Court is not obligated to follow the sequential order of proceedings given in section 10 of the Act in the event of failure of reconciliation between the parties.

Arooj Lateef, respondent no. 2, was married to the petitioner. Shortly after the marriage between the parties, their relations became strained, and respondent no. 2 filed two suits, one for dissolution of marriage and the other for recovery of maintenance, dowry articles and their child's birth expenses. On 30 June 2009, respondent no. 2 made a statement before the Family Court to the effect that she did not wish to reconcile with the petitioner and that her suit for dissolution of marriage should be decreed on the basis of *khula*. In view of respondent no. 2's statement and after having satisfied itself that reconciliation between the parties had failed, the Family Court passed an order for the dissolution of marriage on the basis of *khula* in terms of section 10(4) of the Act.

The petitioner's counsel challenged this order before the High Court on the ground of it being illegal. He argued that the order was passed without affording the petitioner an opportunity to be heard. He contended that the provisions of section 10 of the Act are mandatory in nature and after following the procedure laid down in sub-sections (1), (2), and (3) of section 10, the court is required to frame issues and fix a date for recording of evidence. Since the previously mentioned requirements had not been fulfilled in the instant case, the order of the court was illegal and liable to be set aside.

After hearing the arguments, the court did not agree with the interpretation of section 10 as put forward by the petitioner's counsel. The court held that the proviso to section 10(4) had an overriding effect, whereby the Family Court had been granted the power to pass a decree for dissolution of marriage forthwith in the event the reconciliation between spouses failed. The Family Court was not obligated to follow the sequential order of proceedings given in section 10 of the Act in the event of failure of reconciliation between the parties where a decree for dissolution of marriage was sought. The court observed:

> The proviso to subsection (4) of section 10 of the We[s]t Pakistan Family Courts Act, 1964 had conferred powers and jurisdiction on Family Courts to dissolve a marriage on the basis of "Khula" if despite efforts made by it for reconciliation no scope was left for spouses to live together. Proviso to section 10(4) is couched in such language, containing a non-obstante clause giving wide power to the Family Court to dissolve the marriage when facts of the case would permit such course. The provision was enacted to avoid unnecessary delays which occurred in the past when suits for dissolution of marriage were tried like ordinary civil suits and it took years for such suits to reach a conclusion causing hardship and misery for the woman who was dragged through endless litigation involving a union that had practically come to an end.[25]

In the instant case, the perusal of the order dated 30 June 2009 and the statement of respondent no. 2 clearly suggested that pre-trial reconciliation had failed. Hence, the court rightly exercised its jurisdiction under section 10(4) of the Act in granting *khula*. The petition was dismissed.

Abdul Hameed v Rubina Bibi 2010 CLC 1681 (Lah)

Decree for dissolution of marriage can be passed by a Family Court in case reconciliation between the spouses fails.

This case focuses upon the nature and scope of section 10(4) of the Family Courts Act 1964, whereby a Family Court is authorised to pass a decree for dissolution of marriage forthwith in case reconciliation between the spouses fails.

Respondent no. 1 filed a suit for dissolution of marriage on the basis of *khula*, recovery of dowry articles, and maintenance against the petitioner. The trial court, after the failure of the reconciliation proceedings, decreed the suit for dissolution of marriage on the basis of *khula* on return of dower by respondent no. 1 to the petitioner and framed issues regarding other controversies between the parties. The petitioner raised several legal and factual objections against the order. He argued that the trial court had not made concrete efforts to bring about reconciliation between the parties and thus had failed to act in accordance with the law. He further argued that the proviso to section 10(4) of the Act was against Islamic Injunctions as the marriage could not be dissolved merely upon the wife's contention that she could not live with her husband within the limits prescribed by Allah; evidence had to be recorded in this regard to effect dissolution. He further argued that this provision had given wives undue advantage over their husbands who were being deprived of their fundamental right of fair trial under due process of law. Moreover, the insertion of the proviso to section 10(4) of the Act had rendered the scheme of the Act regarding the recording of evidence and post-trial reconciliation meaningless.

As far as the petitioner's argument regarding the failure of the court to take concrete steps to effect a compromise between the spouses was concerned, the court noted that the record showed that the parties were given time to effect a compromise. However, respondent no. 1 categorically stated that she had developed extreme aversion towards her husband and could not live with him within the limits prescribed by Allah. Moreover, the court took notice of her insulting attitude towards the petitioner and granted *khula*. The court held that the petitioner's contention that the insertion of a proviso to section 10 of the Act rendered other provisions meaningless was without force as these provisions are applicable to the trial of those suits only in which the proceedings are required to be recorded after the stage of reconciliation proceedings. The petitioner's right to fair trial was not infringed in any way as the proceedings were conducted in accordance with law. The final argument of the petitioner's counsel was that the passing of the decree on the basis of *khula* was against the Islamic Injunctions and this amendment (proviso to section 10(4) of the Act) in the Act was invalid under the Enforcement of Shari'ah Act 1991. The court noted that the Qur'anic verse 229 of Sura Al-Baqarah provided the basis for *khula*. The court observed:

> To keep the husband and wife in a hateful and unwanted union leads to many social evils. If the spouses cannot live amicably and in complete harmony and the wife categorically asserts that she wants divorce, then the court may safely presume that they cannot live within the limits of God.[26]

Hence, the petitioner's contention was found to be without force, and the petition was dismissed accordingly.

15.3.5 Recording of Evidence

Mian Shaukat Ali v Naseem Bibi 2009 CLC 848 (Lah)

If a party does not produce its witnesses on the last opportunity given for bringing witnesses in the court, the court may deny such party to produce them afterwards.

This case deals with the power of the court to close the evidence of a party which despite being given the last opportunity to produce evidence failed to do so without sufficient cause.

Respondent no. 1 filed a suit against the petitioner for recovery of maintenance for herself and three minors. The petitioner contested the suit, denied the relationship between the parties, and filed a suit for the jactitation of marriage. The Family Court consolidated both these suits. After framing the issues, the court recorded the evidence led by respondent no. 1, but the petitioner failed to cross-examine respondent no. 1's witnesses. The petitioner filed an application for acceptance of his list of witnesses, which was contested by respondent no. 1 and the Family Court dismissed it. The petitioner filed a writ petition against the order which was dismissed *in limine*. The suit for maintenance proceeded further and the petitioner was given a final opportunity to lead his evidence. On the next date of hearing on 22 December 2008, he did not produce any evidence and failed to give any justification in this regard, hence, his right to evidence was closed, which was challenged through the instant petition.

The petitioner's counsel argued that the petitioner's absence on 22 December 2008 was not wilful, rather he failed to produce his witnesses owing to some unavoidable circumstances. Therefore, the trial court should have granted him another opportunity to produce his evidence. The court, after hearing the arguments, held:

> There is no provision in [the] Family Court Act, 1964 to the effect that evidence of the party shall not be closed in any case. The very purpose of the enactment is to ensure expeditious disposal and Court can close the evidence of a party who fails to adduce evidence without sufficient cause. Section 11 provides that on the date fixed for evidence, the Family Court shall examine the witnesses produced by the parties in such order as it deems fit. In this case, despite a caution of [the] last opportunity to produce the evidence, the petitioner as [the] defendant had failed not only to appear in Court, but also produce the witnesses. It was thus a case of double default committed with a view to gain more time.[27]

The court noted that the matter had been pending in the court for the last ten years. Hence, the trial court was justified in closing the evidence.

15.3.6 Conclusion of a Trial

Muhammad Bakhsh Masood v Aysha Mai 2009 CLC 905 (Lah)

Non-conducting of a post-trial reconciliation by a Family Court may amount to an irregularity which does not vitiate the decision rendered on merits.

This case deals with the consequences of the failure of the court to make an effort for reconciliation between the parties after their evidence is closed as required under section 12 of the Family Courts Act 1964.

Respondent no. 1 filed a suit for recovery of dower, gold ornaments, and maintenance allowance against the petitioner. As the trial began, the evidence produced by respondent no. 1 was recorded, but the petitioner failed to produce any evidence and his right to do so was thus closed. Respondent no. 1's suit was partially decreed by the trial court. Both parties filed appeals against the decision of the trial court. In the appeal, respondent no. 1's suit was decreed by modifying the trial court decree, while the petitioner's appeal was dismissed. Hence, the present petition challenging the legality of the judgments/decrees of the two courts is mentioned below.

One of the petitioner's arguments was that after the petitioner's evidence was closed, the trial court did not make any effort to effect a compromise between the parties and hence, violated the mandatory provisions of section 12 of the Act. The court observed:

> It is correct that reconciliation proceedings, both pre-trial and post-trial, are requirements of the Family Courts Act, 1964 but the circumstances of the case clearly indicate that there was no chance of any reconciliation between the parties on the issues on which they were contesting the suits. The learned trial court did not record evidence about the failure of the reconciliation but such omission is only of technical nature when the Court after close [sic] of evidence of the defendant-petitioner did not make an effort for reconciliation, it was merely an irregularity not affecting the decision of the Court on merits, especially, as already stated, when it was apparent from the record of the case that such an effort had no chance of success.[28]

In light of these reasons, the petition was dismissed.

15.3.7 Enforcement of Decrees

Tauqeer Ahmad Qureshi v Additional District Judge, Lahore PLD 2009 SC 760

While executing a decree, the executing court may introduce appropriate amendments to the decree to make it executable.

This case deals with the nature and scope of an executing court's power to execute a decree. The case reached the present stage after multiple rounds of litigation.

Respondent no. 2 and 3 filed a suit for maintenance against the appellant who was their father. The suit was decreed, and maintenance was fixed at a certain rate with 20 per cent annual increase. The appellant's counsel argued that he did not object to the rate of maintenance fixed by the court, rather he urged the non-executability of the second part of the decree whereby the court ordered a 20 per cent annual increase in the amount of maintenance. He contended that such an increase was neither just nor reasonable, as the total maintenance allowance payable by the appellant with the annual increase of 20 per cent, would come to 6.88 crores at the end. Hence, this part of the decree was not executable. The Family Court had ordered such an increase in the maintenance allowance on the basis of mere speculation keeping in mind the rising rate of inflation in future; the trend may reverse in which case the minors can always approach the court for enhancement in the maintenance allowance. He stated that the appellant was a schizophrenic and had been temporarily employed from which he merely earned Rs 20,000 per month.

The court, after hearing the arguments and going through the record, noted that the Family Court had no basis to order such an exorbitant annual increase in the amount of maintenance. Such unjust enrichment of minors could not be permitted at the cost of the father. There is nothing on record to show that the appellant was rich enough to pay 6.88 crores towards the maintenance of the respondents. The court held:

> There is no cavil in the proposition that executing Court cannot go behind [*sic*] the decree but at the same time the executing Court can look into the questions [of] whether the decree or part thereof is executable or inexecutable and if for any reason the decree has become inexecutable, the executing Court is empowered to declare so and if a part of the decree is inexecutable and that part is severable from other part(s) of the decree then the executing Court is empowered to refuse the execution of the

> inexecutable part of the decree and may proceed with the execution of the rest of the decree.[29]

In view of the circumstances of the case, the Court reduced the annual increase in the maintenance allowance from 20 to 5 per cent.

15.3.8 Appeals. An appeal against the decision of a Family Court lies before the District Judge. However, remedy by way of a writ petition cannot be availed as a substitute for appeal.

Tayyaba Yunus v Muhammad Ehsan 2010 SCMR 1403

An appeal can be filed against the Family Court decision rejecting the suit for the recovery of dower.

In this case, the petitioner wife filed a suit for the dissolution of marriage, recovery of dower amounting to Rs 150,000, dowry articles amounting to Rs 250,000, and maintenance allowance. In her plaint, she asserted that she was treated with cruelty by both her husband and her in-laws. Her husband did not provide her clothing and she had to ask her parents for it instead. In June 2007, her husband beat her and drove her out of his house. In response, respondent no. 1 instituted a separate suit for restitution of conjugal rights and recovery of valuables including cash and gold ornaments. The Family Court decreed the suit of the petitioner by dissolving her marriage on the basis of *khula*, granting her dowry articles and maintenance allowance during the period of *iddat*. However, the petitioner's suit for the recovery of the dower was dismissed. The petitioner challenged the decision to the extent of recovery of the dower before the District Court which granted the dower amount of Rs 150,000. Against this decision, respondent no. 1 filed a writ petition before the High Court, which reversed the decision of the District Court regarding the recovery of the dower. The High Court justified its decision as:

> A perusal of record would show that the judgment and decree for dissolution of marriage on the basis of khula was not appealable. The learned Appellate Court conveniently ignored this important aspect, though the ground of competency of appeal was agitated by petitioner in his arguments as mentioned in the impugned judgment but the same was dealt with in a slipshod manner. The learned Appellate Court failed to appreciate that in the instant case the relief of dower amount could not be considered in isolation but the same had nexus with the dissolution of marriage based on khula

> and, therefore, the findings of trial Court for not granting dower could not be reversed without disturbing the ground of khula which essentially would tantamount to an appeal against dissolution.[30]

The petitioner challenged the High Court decision before the Supreme Court. The petitioner's counsel argued that the suit of the petitioner was instituted, among other things, for the recovery of a dower amounting to Rs 150,000 and since the trial court did not accept it, the petitioner could file an appeal against it as the bar to appeal under section 14(2)(b) of the Act did not apply. Therefore, the Appellate Court rightly granted her the dower amount and the High Court under a misconception of the law reversed the findings of the Appellate Court.

The question before the Supreme Court was whether the petitioner could file an appeal against the decision of the trial court. Section 14(2)(b) provides that no appeal against the decree of a Family Court shall lie if the dower or dowry amount did not exceed Rs 30,000. In this case, the petitioner had claimed a dower amounting to Rs 150,000. After hearing the arguments of both parties, the Supreme Court observed:

> Admittedly the appeal is a continuity of the original proceedings of a suit, therefore, in our estimation, there could not be any restraint on the petitioner to prefer an appeal claiming the amount of dower, when the trial Court on misreading, non-reading or lack of proper appraisal of the facts and circumstances of the case makes a wrong decision, therefore, it would be wrong to perceive that subsection (2) of section 14 puts a restraint to a woman or her legal heirs demanding the dower which is a condition *sine qua non* for a valid Muslim marriage.[31]

The court noted that the reasoning of the High Court, in denying the petitioner her right to recover dower, was not based on the correct interpretation of the law. The Supreme Court found force in the arguments of the petitioner's counsel that since the dower, as claimed by the petitioner, was not allowed by the trial court the petitioner could competently prefer an appeal and the bar appearing in subsection (2) of section 14 would not apply. The Supreme Court converted the petition into appeal, set aside the judgment of the High Court, and remanded the case to the High Court for a fresh decision.

Muhammad Munir v Kaneez Fatima 2010 YLR 2691 (Lah)

Remedy by way of a writ petition cannot be allowed to be availed as a substitute for an appeal.

This case addresses the question of whether a remedy by way of a writ petition could be availed as a substitute for appeal. Respondent no. 1 filed a suit for recovery of maintenance, dower amount, and four *tolas* of gold before the Family Court. The court decreed the suit to the extent of maintenance and dower on 16 December 2008. The petitioner remained silent until 14 April 2010, when the period for filing an appeal had lapsed. Then instead of filing an appeal, the petitioner filed an instant writ petition. The petitioner's counsel argued that the impugned judgment was challenged in the writ petition since he could not file an appeal within the prescribed period of limitation. The court rejected this argument, and held:

> An appeal is a statutory right, which could be exercised only if it has been specifically provided in a statute. Section 14 of the Family Court Act provides that against the judgment and decree passed by the Judge Family Court, appeal will lie to the learned District Judge. If the remedy of appeal is available to a party under statute. Remedy by way of writ petition cannot be allowed to be availed as substitute of appeal. Particularly when the alternative remedy in shape of appeal was available to the petitioner.[32]

The court observed that the attitude of the petitioner negated the principles of equity, which helps the vigilant, not the indolent. Hence, the petition was dismissed accordingly.

15.4 Conclusion

The Family Courts are established to ensure speedy resolution of family disputes. Therefore, these courts are not bound to follow strict procedures as laid down in the CPC and Qanoon-e-Shahadat Order 1984. The judges of these courts have inquisitorial powers, and they can adopt any procedure which is not prohibited by law. These courts try to resolve family disputes amicably without being bound by the technicalities of procedural law. Therefore, the Family Court judges make an effort to help parties reconcile their differences through compromise. Such an effort for a compromise or reconciliation is made before the beginning of the regular trial and after its conclusion. However, parties are not forced to reconcile, and, in a case decided by the Lahore High Court, it was held that failure of the court to conduct post-trial reconciliation does not amount to an illegality which would adversely affect the decision.[33] This and many other decisions of the superior courts show that the superior courts have liberally construed the Family Courts Act 1964 to ensure justice. The courts also discourage prolonged litigation by penalising the defaulting parties, generally husbands, who try to evade the fulfilment of their obligations towards their wives and children. Despite these efforts of the superior court judges, a large number of family-related cases remain pending before the courts for lengthy periods. According to the Lahore High Court Annual Report 2015, ninety-three thousand family cases were pending before the Family Courts in Punjab. This number has increased manifold during the past few years. Therefore, we suggest that some of the functions of the Family Courts should be delegated to local union councils which should try to reconcile the differences of the parties at the community level through alternative dispute resolution mechanisms. The disputes should be brought to the Family Courts only after such efforts do not succeed.

Questions

1. Please write a detailed note on the jurisdiction, powers, and procedures of the Family Courts.
2. Whether extended rights to appeal should be provided against the decisions of the Family Courts to avoid writ petitions before the High Court?
3. Do you think that the simplified procedure of the Family Courts has resulted in judicial efficiency in the disposal of family cases?
4. Discuss how the procedure enacted in the Muslim Family Act 1964 is at variance from the regular and normal procedure provided for civil suits.

Further Reading

The Family Courts Act 1964.
The Family Courts Rules 1965.

Cases

Amanat Masih v Najma Bibi 2010 YLR 2711 (Lah) (Objection to the jurisdiction of the Family Courts must be raised at the earliest possible stage.)

Amjad Iqbal v Mst Nida Sohail 2015 SCMR 128 (An immovable property attached for the execution of a maintenance decree cannot be transacted by way of gift/*hiba* to deprive the decree-holder of realisation of his/her rights.)

Ejaz Ahmad Butt v Samreena 2022 CLC 233 (Lah) (There is no classification of jurisdiction on a pecuniary basis for adjudication of family matters by the Family Courts.)

Farzana Rasool v Dr Muhammad Bashir 2011 SCMR 1361 (The Family Court may refer any family dispute including maintenance to mediation, arbitration to a third party for effecting a compromise, or amicable settlement between the parties on assurance of the parties to abide by such compromise/settlement. Once such compromise has taken place, no party would be allowed to backtrack from it.)

Fazal Rehman v Mst. Fahmida PLD 2022 Peshawar (The Family court has the power to change the mode of dissolution of marriage on any other available ground in order to facilitate the wife for the recovery of the dower.)

Mst. Bensih Liaquat v Station Police Officer 2020 MLD Karachi 740 (The Family court is not authorised to bring the issue of legitimacy in the case unless pleaded by the parties themselves.)

Muhammad Arshad Anjum v Mst. Khurshid Begum 2021 SCMR 1145 (The exclusion of the proceeding of Civil Procedure Code 1908 from the Family courts is to circumvent delays in the disposal of suits and does not derogate the status of courts.)

Muhammad Rehman v Fatima Bibi 2010 MLD 746 (Peshawar) (Constitutional jurisdiction would not substitute the remedy of appeal and would not be exercised except when the order/judgment was patently illegal without jurisdiction and lawful authority.)

Muneeza Waqar v Civil and Family Judge, Karachi East 2017 CLC 1718 (Appearance in the Family Court through agent is permissible and if plaintiff did not appear before the Family Court, then no adverse inference could be drawn against her. Even if the plaintiff did not appear in spite of direction by the Family Court for the participation in reconciliation proceedings her suit could not be dismissed for non-prosecution. If the Family Court was of the view that the wife's wish with regard to reconciliation proceedings should be found out by asking her personally then it could have proceeded to ascertain such fact through a video link.)

Notes

1. Section 17 of the Family Courts Act 1964.
2. Section 20, ibid.
3. Section 25, ibid.
4. Section 5, ibid.
5. Section 14, ibid.
6. Section 7, ibid.
7. Section 8, ibid.
8. Section 8, ibid.
9. Section 10, ibid.
10. Section 15, ibid.
11. Section 11, ibid.
12. Section 12, ibid.
13. Section 12A, ibid.
14. Section 13, ibid.
15. Section 16, ibid.
16. Section 17A, ibid.
17. Section 18, ibid.
18. Section 19, ibid.
19. Section 21B, ibid.
20. PLD 2016 FSC 1, 3.

21. PLD 2016 FSC 4, 7.
22. 2010 YLR 619, 620.
23. Ibid., 622.
24. 2009 MLD 766, 768.
25. 2010 CLC 1, 3.
26. 2010 CLC 1681, 1685.
27. 2009 CLC 848, 850.
28. 2009 CLC 905, 908.
29. PLD 2009 SC 760, 767.
30. 2010 SCMR 1403, 1405.
31. Ibid., 1407.
32. 2010 YLR 2691, 2692.
33. 2009 CLC 905.

16

CONCLUSION

Our analysis of the judgments on family law in Pakistan shows that the Pakistani courts have responded to the changing circumstances not only by reforming the existing principles but also by developing new ones with the passage of time. During the colonial period, *fiqh* was transformed into Muslim Personal Law through the processes of translation, legislation, and adjudication. The translations of the *Hidaya* and *al-Fatawa al-Alamgiriyya* were supplemented with administrative, procedural, and reformative legislation. However, it was the process of adjudication which played the most important role in this transformation. Judges replaced *mufti*s as the oracles of law, while judicial precedents rather than *fatawa* became the binding instruments of law. As is evident from the preceding chapters, this colonial legacy continues to have a significant impact on the development of family laws in Pakistan. In this chapter, we evaluate the case law that has been discussed in the book and identify the patterns of legal developments which influence and are influenced by the socio-political landscape of post-colonial Pakistan.

We observe that, after independence, the Pakistani courts faced a dual challenge: first, to achieve legitimacy within the newly established Muslim polity which had the baggage of the colonial past on her shoulders; and second, to act as an organ of the state and ensure effective functioning of state institutions. The courts responded to this challenge in a novel way by drawing a balance between the modern and the traditional/classical. In the context of Islamic family law, the modern is the state legislation and the traditional/classical is un-codified *sharia/fiqh* as understood by *ulama*. The by-product of this process of balancing the modern and the traditional has been highlighted in our analysis of case law. In this process, the courts adopted for themselves the role of traditional Muslim jurists and assumed the authority to re-interpret the sources of Islamic law (*fiqh*), making it adaptable to the requirements of the modern nation-state. The gradual change in women's rights to no-fault divorce (*khula*) illustrates this phenomenon. Since the judgment of the Lahore High Court in the

Balqis Fatima case,[1] other High Courts, the Supreme Court, and the Federal Shariat Court have consistently laid down such legal principles that ensure gender equality in Islamic divorce law as much as possible.[2]

The most significant aspect of the role of the Pakistani courts in the application and development of family law is manifested in what we describe as the Women Protection Principle. According to this principle, whenever courts come across conflicting, ambiguous, or unsettled legal rules, they tend to decide in a way that best protects or promotes the interests of women. There are several manifestations of the application of this principle. It explains the ambivalent judicial attitude towards the validity of 'triple *talaq*': the courts accept this form of divorce if it protects the divorced wife's right to dower, dowry, and maintenance,[3] but reject the same when its application is likely to compromise a wife's right to inheritance[4] and maintenance.[5] Such a flexible approach of the courts towards women's rights also explains the contradictory judgments regarding the requirement of sending a notice by the husband to the Chairman Union Council under section 7 of the MFLO. In the *Gardezi* case,[6] the SC declared the requirement of sending the notice mandatory in order to prevent hasty dissolutions of marriages by husbands. However, in another case regarding the maintenance right of a wife, the SC reprimanded the husband for claiming that he had orally divorced his wife without giving notice to the Chairman Union Council.[7] Likewise, to protect women against accusations of unlawful sex under the Offense of Zina (Enforcement of Hudood) Ordinance 1979, the SC reformulated its stance on sending the notice of divorce.[8] Similarly, the Pakistani courts accept the evidence based on a DNA test in criminal cases of rape[9] but they refuse to accept it to question the paternity and legitimacy of a child.[10]

The judgment of the Lahore High Court in the *Khalida Shamim Akhtar* case,[11] granting a childless widow the right of inheritance in the immovable property of her Shia husband is another instance of the application of the women protection principle. Like the *Balqis Fatima* case,[12] this judgment rectifies the legal principle under which a childless widow was deprived of her share in the immovable property of her deceased husband.[13] Despite being in conflict with clear Qur'anic injunctions on inheritance, this principle prevailed for more than a century in South Asia. Other examples of the application of this principle include: (i) the Supreme Court judgment in the *Abdul Majid* case,[14] wherein the court extended the presumption of continuity of marriage to prostitutes who were previously excluded from the benefits of this presumption; (ii) the Lahore High Court judgment in the *Muhammad Sajjad* case,[15] wherein the court held that deferred dower without specification of period or stipulation shall be payable at any time upon demand; (iii) the Peshawar High Court judgment in the *Abdul Rashid* case,[16] wherein the court held that the life spent by a wife with her husband could be considered as consideration for *khula*; (iv) the Lahore High Court judgment in the *Amar Ilahi* case,[17] wherein it was held that the marriage of a mother to a person who does not fall within the prohibited degree of relationship with the minor does not absolutely disentitle her from the custody of her child; (v) the Lahore High Court judgment in the *Farooq Siddiqui* case,[18] wherein a surrogate mother was given preference for the custody of her child; and (vi) the Supreme Court judgment in the *Ghulam Ali* case,[19] wherein it was held that the male relatives holding the inherited property of their female relations will be deemed to hold such property for and on behalf of the latter. Therefore, the pleas of estoppel, waiver, and adverse possession of brothers against the inheritance rights of their sisters should be rejected. The application of the women's protection principle, however, is not limited to Islamic family law. In a recent judgment, the Lahore High Court granted the right to divorce on the ground of the irretrievable breakdown of marriage to the Christian community of Pakistan.[20]

The above are only a few illustrations of the application of the women's protection principle by the Pakistani courts; further examples of the application of this principle can be found in almost every chapter of this book. It should be noted that this principle is not a specifically recognised judicial principle. We have drawn this general principle from reported judgments related to family law. We argue that this principle not only helps us conceptualise the conflicting judicial authorities on various contentious legal issues e.g., triple *talaq*, but it is also useful to draw new rules in hard cases where legal rules are found to be conflicting, ambiguous, or unsettled. Notwithstanding its generality, this principle provides a useful guide to navigating through conflicting and ever-increasing case law. This principle conforms with the overall function of the legal system to protect the weak and vulnerable in society and bears close resemblance with the celebrated principle of the welfare of the child.

Pakistani courts consistently follow the principle of the welfare of the child and have extended it further. In the *Muhammad Nazir* case,[21] the Supreme Court held that the law has an inclination towards the presumption of paternity rather than illegitimacy.[22] Similarly, in the *Ghazala Tehsin Zohra* case,[23] the Supreme Court held that a father cannot question the paternity of a child by asking for a DNA test of the child. The novel application of the Islamic legal principle of acknowledgement to protect the interests of an adopted child in the *Asma Naz* case by the Supreme Court is yet another example of the benevolent attitude of the superior courts towards children's rights.[24] Similarly, the Lahore High Court ingeniously applied the principle of constructive guardianship in order to make the adopting father liable for the maintenance of adopted children after divorce.[25]

While highlighting the achievements of judges in ensuring the protection of the weak and vulnerable within the institution of marriage (generally women, children, and the elderly), we also want to point out the areas of family law where positive developments are still needed. Case law shows that on many occasions, the courts chose not to adopt a women-friendly approach despite having the choice to do so. This attitude is best exemplified in two judgments of the FSC regarding the restitution of conjugal rights.[26] In almost every petition of a wife for maintenance, divorce, or custody of children, the husband responds by filing a petition for restitution of conjugal rights.[27] Interestingly, the genesis of a husband's right to restitution of conjugal society with his wife is found in Canon law which regards marriage as a covenant that cannot be easily dissolved. In fact, legal historians have pointed out that it was under the influence of Western colonialism that this principle was introduced in the Muslim world.[28]

The FSC had the occasion to rid Islamic family law in Pakistan of this menace in the two petitions which challenged the legality of restitution of conjugal rights. However, the FSC upheld this right and declared that the jurisdiction of the Family Court to issue a decree for restitution of conjugal rights is not repugnant to the Injunctions of Islam.[29] Likewise, the FSC declared that the mechanism provided for the execution of a decree for restitution of conjugal rights against a wife, which involved attaching her property and making periodical payments to the husband, is also not repugnant to the Injunctions of Islam.[30] It should be noted that this declaration of the FSC is not in conformity with its dictum laid down in the *Saleem Ahmad* case, wherein it affirmed the contractual nature of marriage in Islam and acknowledged gender equality in Islamic divorce law. It is indeed unfortunate that our legal system still recognises such misogynist judicial remedy which finds no support from Islamic jurisprudence. Since the FSC does not have the jurisdiction under the Constitution to declare a law relating to the procedure of a court as invalid on the ground of its repugnancy to the Injunctions of Islam,[31] we hope that either the legislature will take the initiative and repeal the provisions regarding restitution of conjugal rights or the High Courts or Supreme

Court will declare them inconsistent with the constitutional guarantees of fundamental rights.

Similarly, the FSC adopted a rather restrictive approach regarding the issue of surrogacy.[32] Chief Justice Riaz Ahmad Khan went so far as prescribing criminal penalties for the couple and the doctor who arranged the surrogacy as well as for the surrogate mother. We observe that while suggesting criminal sanctions for surrogacy, Justice Khan did not take into account the delicate balance between various competing rights, since an absolute ban on surrogacy is unlikely to be enforced without infringing the right to privacy and family life.[33] The FSC could have analysed the legality of surrogacy under Islamic law by invoking the principles of adoption, acknowledgement, and fosterage. Alternatively, given the absence of legislation on surrogacy and the difference of juristic opinions regarding its legal status, the FSC could have exercised judicial restraint;[34] the kind of restraint it exercised in order to refrain from declaring as un-Islamic section 8 of the MFLO, which provided the right to delegated divorce to a wife.[35]

In the context of legal reforms, we observe that the efforts of the Pakistani judiciary have been supplemented by the legislature which has responded to the changing needs of the society by enacting statutes to update family laws. In this regard, the Muslim Family Laws Ordinance 1961 (MFLO) remains the most influential enactment. The MFLO is partially based on the recommendations of the Family and Marriage Law Commission which was constituted in 1956. It is a progressive legislation that provides a comprehensive legal mechanism for the protection of the rights of women and children. However, because of its non-conformity with classical *fiqh*, traditionalist and conservative sections of the Pakistani society remain sceptical about its validity. In the *Allah Rakha* case,[33] the FSC approved many provisions of the MFLO including the ones which require the registration of marriage and divorce and regulate a husband's right to polygamy. However, the provisions of the MFLO laying down a fixed period for *iddat* and providing the right of representation to orphaned grandchildren in the inheritance of their grandfather were declared as un-Islamic. The appeal against this decision has been pending adjudication before the Shariat Appellate Bench of the Supreme Court since 2000. Meanwhile, the superior courts tend to construe the respective provisions restrictively. In *Bhaggay Bibi v Razia Bibi*,[36] the Supreme Court held that section 4 of the MFLO, while protecting the interests of orphaned grandchildren, does not affect the rights of other legal heirs and thus reduced the share of orphaned granddaughters. In another case, the Supreme Court noted that, under this section, the daughter of a pre-deceased son was entitled to the share of her father in her grandfather's estate; however, since the daughter was the only child of the pre-deceased son, she was declared entitled to 1/2 of the property, while the other 1/2 from the share of her father (i.e. the pre-deceased son) was given to the collaterals.[37] We observe that this interpretation of section 4 of the MFLO does not provide the maximum benefit to orphaned grandchildren. Further, this verdict is not in conformity with the intention of the legislature which purported to put the orphaned grandchildren in the shoes of their deceased parents by providing them 'a share equivalent to the share which such son or daughter [deceased parent], as the case may be, would have received if alive'.[38]

Notwithstanding this restrictive attitude of the Supreme Court as regards section 4 of the MFLO, the jurisprudence of benevolence is also reflected in the interpretation of the Dowry and Bridal Gifts (Restrictions) Act 1976 which put a limit to the monetary value of dowry and bridal gifts. In this regard, the courts have rejected husbands' reliance on this Act to devour the dowry items of the wives,[39] and have repeatedly reprimanded them by holding that once dowry articles are accepted at the time of marriage, no objection could be raised subsequently on the ground of the violation of the Act.[40]

The preceding analysis suggests that, in the project of Islamic family law reform, judges and parliamentarians have been equal partners. However, given the religious nature of family law in Pakistan, politicians often fail to develop a consensus on pressing legal issues in order to protect the rights and interests of vulnerable parties (i.e. women and children) within the institution of the family. Considering competing political interests in the society, it seems that the future developments in family laws will be led by the judiciary, rather than the legislature. To keep abreast of these developments, our readers will do well if they keep themselves updated with the latest judicial trends in case law. We observe that in recent years, the judges of the superior courts, particularly of the Supreme Court, have started to refer to constitutionally guaranteed fundamental rights and the principles of policy in family cases with an objective to protect the rights of women, children, specially-abled, socially marginalised persons, and the elderly. This reliance is significant in two respects. Firstly, Pakistani courts have been accustomed to applying the rules of Muslim personal law as developed during the British colonial period since independence. Human rights, however, were not enshrined in the legal system during the colonial period. Hence, references to human rights would have an effect on the decolonisation of Muslim personal law. Secondly, such references are likely to support the well-founded jurisprudence, firmly grounded in the supreme law of the land i.e. the Constitution, to protect and promote the rights of the weak and vulnerable especially that of women, children, specially abled, socially marginalised persons, and the elderly. This trend is expected to come down to the level of the high courts and the subordinate courts which would have a beneficial effect on aggrieved parties in family cases.

Notes

1. *Balqis Fatima v Najam-ul-Ikram* PLD 1959 Lah 566.
2. *Khurshid Bibi v Baboo Muhammad Amin* PLD 1967 SC 97; and *Saleem Ahmad v Government of Pakistan* PLD 2014 FSC 43.
3. *Sardar Iqbal v Tahira Parveen* 2010 YLR 582.
4. *Sardar v Malik Khan* 2003 YLR 2623.
5. *Farah Naz v Judge Family Court* PLD 2006 SC 457.
6. *Syed Ali Nawaz Gardezi v Lt. Col. Muhammad Yusuf* PLD 1963 SC 51, 75.
7. *Manzoor Ahmad v Nargis Mirza* PLD 2004 SC 132.
8. *Mst Bashiran v Muhammad Hussain* PLD 1988 SC 186.
9. *Muhammad Shahid Sahil v State* PLD 2010 FSC 215.
10. *Ghazala Tehsin Zohra v Mehr Ghulam Dastagir Khan* PLD 2015 SC 327.
11. *Khalida Shamim Akhtar v Ghulam Jaffar* PLD 2016 Lah 865.
12. PLD 1959 Lah 566.
13. The Muslim Family Laws (Amendment) Act 2021 added subsection 2 in section 4 of the MFLO to recognise this right.
14. *Abdul Majid Khan v Anwar Begum* PLD 1989 SC 362.
15. *Muhammad Sajjad v Additional District and Session Judge* PLD 2015 Lah 405.
16. *Abdul Rashid v Shahida Parveen* 2013 YLR 2616.
17. *Amar Ilahi v Rashida Akhtar* PLD 1955 Lah 412.
18. *Farooq Siddiqui v Farzana Naheed* PLD 2013 Lah 254.
19. *Ghulam Ali v Ghulam Sarwar Naqvi* PLD 1990 SC 1.
20. *Ameen Masih v Federation of Pakistan* PLD 2017 Lah 610.
21. *Muhammad Nazir v Ali Muhammad* 2003 SCMR 1183.
22. The FSC has also acknowledged this principle in an earlier judgment. *Abdul Rashid v Safia Bibi* PLD 1986 FSC 10.
23. *Ghazala Tehsin Zohra v Mehr Ghulam Dastagir Khan* PLD 2015 SC 327.
24. *Asma Naz v Muhammad Younas Qureshi* 2005 SCMR 401.
25. *Mariam Bibi through Abida Parveen v Naseer Ahmad* PLD 2015 Lah 336.
26. For details see Shahbaz Ahmad Cheema, 'Islamisation of Restitution of Conjugal Rights by the Federal Shariat Court of Pakistan', *Islamic Studies* (2019) 58(4), 535–50.
27. Muhammad Zubair Abbasi, 'Dead at Home, Alive Abroad: Restitution of Conjugal Rights in South Asia', *Islamic Studies* (2022) 61(1), 9–24.
28. K.M. Cuno, *Modernizing Marriage: Family, Ideology, and Law in Nineteenth-and Early Twentieth-Century Egypt* (New York: Syracuse University Press, 2015), 196–98. It is unfortunate that while in the UK this right was abolished in 1970, it continues to exist both in India and Pakistan. See The Law Commission, 'Proposal for the Abolition of the Matrimonial Remedy of Restitution of Conjugal Rights' (London: Her Majesty's Stationary Office, 1969). *Smt. Saroj Rani v Sudarshan Kumar*

Chadha AIR 1984 SC 1562 (the Indian Supreme Court refused to declare restitution of conjugal rights unconstitutional because it 'serves a social purpose as an aid to the prevention of break-up of marriage'.

29. *Nadeem Siddiqui v Islamic Republic of Pakistan* PLD 2016 FSC 1.
30. *Nadeem Siddiqui v Islamic Republic of Pakistan* PLD 2016 FSC 4.
31. Art 203B(c), The Constitution of Islamic Republic of Pakistan 1973.
32. *Farooq Siddiqui v Mst Farzana Naheed* PLD 2017 FSC 78.
33. J. Areen, 'Baby M Reconsidered', *Georgetown Law Journal* (1987) 76, 1741, 1752 (arguing that the enforcement of the legal prohibition of surrogacy will involve intrusion in privacy and family life). In *Ghulam Mustafa v Judge Family Court* 2021 CLC 204 the Lahore High Court held that the right of privacy is protected under Islamic law, human rights law, and constitutional law. The Family Court can only order the medical examination of the person for the determination of their sex if it is absolutely necessary.
34. Shia jurists, despite some differences, do not regard surrogacy as un-Islamic. See C. Harrison, 'Who is your Mother? Who is your Father? Assisted Reproductive Technologies in the Light of Sunni and Shi'a Law', *Journal of Shi'a Islamic Studies* (2014) 17(1), 23; M.C. Inhorn, 'Making Muslim Babies: IVF and Gamete Donation in Sunni v Shi'a Islam', *Culture, Medicine and Psychiatry* (2006) 30(4), 427; Z.B. Ardakani et al., 'Embryo Donation in Iranian Legal System: A Critical Review', *Journal of Reproduction & Infertility* (2015) 16(3), 130.
35. *Khawar Iqbal v Federation of Pakistan* 2013 MLD 1711 (FSC). The FSC observed that the Shia Jafaria school did not allow such a delegation. Therefore, section 8 of the MFLO fell within the definition of Muslim Personal Law, which is based on the interpretation of the Qur'an and Sunnah by each sect. Under Art 203B(c), the FSC does not have jurisdiction over Muslim Personal Law.
36. 2005 SCMR 1595.
37. *Mukhtar Ahmad v Rasheeda Bibi* 2003 SCMR 1664.
38. S 4, the Muslim Family Laws Ordinance 1961.
39. *Muhammad Tazeel v Mst Khair-un-Nisa* 1995 SCMR 885.
40. *Dr Muhammad Ali Chohan v Fakhur-un-Nisa* 2009 CLC 255 (Pesh).

Glossary

Aaq	Depriving an heir of inheritance; this is not recognized in Islam.
Acknowledgement of Paternity	It establishes parentage through a man's acknowledgement of paternity of a child whose paternity is not established or shrouded in mystery, subject to certain conditions.
Agnates	Also known as *asbat*—descendants from male ancestors.
Areet* or *Ariya	To enjoy the usufruct of a thing for a temporary period of time with the permission of the owner.
Asbat	Also known as agnates—descendants from male ancestors.
As-sum'at	Public announcement of dower that is in excess of privately agreed dower.
Ayn	Corpus of property
Bait-ul-Maal	State treasury
Batil	Void
Bequest	Property given through a will.
Cognates	Descendants from female ancestors.
Conditional Gift	A gift that depends upon the fulfilment of some condition by a donee.
Consanguine	Related by blood—from the same male ancestor.
Constructive Possession	Possession is construed by law, not by fact.
Contingent Gift	A gift depends upon the happening of an uncertain event in future.
Deferred Dower	Dower becomes payable after a specified period or upon dissolution of marriage by divorce or death of either party or demand of the wife.
Distant Kindred	People who are entitled to inheritance in the absence of sharers and residuaries.
Doctrine of Constructive Guardianship	Doctrine carved out by the courts to create fiduciary obligation/relation between the adopting parents and the adopted child, thereby making the adopting father liable for the maintenance of the adopted child.
Doctrine of Cy-pres	Where the intention to create a *waqf* is clearly expressed in a *waqf* deed, the *waqf* will not fail if the specified objects are impossible to achieve, but the income will be utilized for other charitable purposes or objects similar to the unattainable objects mentioned in the deed.
Dowry	Also known as *jahez*; refers to the gifts given to the bride by her parents at the time of marriage.
Fard	Obligation
Fasid	Irregular
Faskh	Dissolution of marriage through a court decree.
Filius Nullius	Child of nobody—refers to a child born out of wedlock; for instance,

	when a married woman commits adultery or when an unmarried woman has sexual intercourse with a man.
Firash	A child belongs to the marriage bed. The paternity of a child born in wedlock is presumed to be in the husband of the mother without any acknowledgement and affirmation of parentage by the husband.
Hadith	Sayings of the Prophet Muhammad (PBUH).
Halala	Intervening marriage contracted and consummated by a divorced wife before she can contract a second marriage with her ex-husband.
Haram	Prohibition
Hiba bi-shart al-iwaz	A gift made with the stipulation for a return.
Hiba bil-Iwaz	Gift for consideration.
Hiba	Gift—transfer of property without any consideration.
Hizanat	Refers to a mother's preferential right to custody of her children.
Hurmat e Masaharat	Prohibition of affinity based on marriage between each spouse and certain relatives of each other.
Ibadat	Worship or religious rituals.
Iddat	Prescribed waiting period for a woman to observe upon the dissolution of her marriage. It is the practice whereby a woman, whose marriage is dissolved by divorce or death, remains in seclusion and does not marry for a specific period of time.
Ijab	Literally means an offer. But in the context of a gift, it is the declaration of the gift by the donor.
Ijtihad	The process of deriving rules from the Qur'an and *Sunnah*.
Ila	Vow of continence—the husband vows to abstain from sexual intercourse with the wife.
Inda al-Talab (Mahr)	Payable on demand. Refers to a dower that is payable on the demand of a wife.
Inter vivos	A transaction made during one's lifetime.
Iqrar	It means to admit or acknowledge. In the context of family law, it refers to the acknowledgement of paternity of a child.
Istihsan	Juristic preference
Isitishab	Presumption of continuity
Kafa'a	It literally means equality
Khalwa Sahiha	Valid retirement. Getting the husband and wife together at a place where there is no legal, moral, or physical impediment to their having sexual intercourse.
Khiyar al-Bulugh	Option of puberty. It is a right of a Muslim minor, who is married during minority by a guardian, to repudiate the marriage upon attaining majority/puberty.
Khula	No-fault divorce initiated by the wife, whereby she may be required to give up the dower in return for dissolution of marriage.
Kitabi* or *Kitabiya	Jews and Christians, adherents of both these religions in a sacred scripture.
Lex domicilii	Latin for the law of the domicile.
Lex loci celebrationis	Latin for law of the land where the marriage was solemnised.
Lex Situs	Latin for the law of the place where the property is situated.
Li'an	Imprecations—the dissolution of marriage by the judge when the husband accuses his wife of *zina* (adultery) and the wife does not accept the accusations as true. Literally means mutual cursing.
Lifetime interest in a property	Refers to the right of a beneficiary to enjoy the usufruct of the

	property during his or her life.
Mahr	A gift by a husband that a wife is entitled to receive at the time of marriage.
Mahr Ghair Mu'ajjal* or *Mu'akhar	Deferred dower payable on demand of a wife.
Mahr Mithal	Literally, 'dower of the like'; also known as 'proper dower'. A wife is entitled to receive a proper dower where the amount of the dower is not specified.
Mahr Mu'wajjal	Deferred dower; dower that is payable after a specified time or upon dissolution of marriage by death or divorce.
Mahr Mu'ajjal	Prompt dower; dower that is payable at the time of marriage.
Mahr Musammat	Specified dower; dower amount fixed at the time of marriage contract.
Mahram	A family member who falls within the prohibited degree of marriage.
Mandub	Recommended act or omission.
Manfa'a	Usufruct of a property.
Marz-ul-Maut	Sickness leading to death.
Maslaha	Welfare
Mata'a	Parting gift or consolatory gift. It is paid by a husband to his wife as a compassionate gift to lessen her difficulties caused by a divorce due to no fault of her own.
Maternity	The legal relationship between a mother and her child.
Mithaq ghaliz	A firm covenant. Used in the Qur'an to describe a marriage contract as one that has a religious aspect to it, unlike an ordinary civil contract.
Muamalat	Civil transactions or worldly affairs.
Mubarat	Dissolution of marriage by mutual consent of spouses.
Mushaa	An undivided share in the property.
Muta	A temporary marriage recognized under Shia Ithna Ashariya law.
Mutawalli	An administrator who manages and controls a *waqf.*
Muwqoof Alayh	A beneficiary of a *waqf.*
Nafaqa	Maintenance; includes food, clothing, lodging, and other necessary expenses for the mental and physical well-being of a person.
Nasab	Relationship by consanguinity.
Nashiza	Disobedient. Commonly employed to refer to disobedient wives.
Panchayat	Council of influential elders of a locality or community that adjudicates disputes between parties who voluntarily submit to it.
Pardanashin	Women who live in the seclusion of the veil.
Parentage	The legal relationship of the parents with their children.
Parol Evidence Rule	Bars the parties to a written contract or agreement from introducing extraneous evidence that modifies the terms of the written agreement.
Paternity	The legal relationship between a father and his child.
Period of Gestation	The development period of the foetus from the date of conception till birth.
Preferential Gift	A gift made by a donor during his lifetime in favour of one or more legal heirs while excluding others.
Principle of *As-sum'at*	Refers to the arrangement where a higher amount of dower is declared in public while in actuality a lower amount is paid in private.
Principle of *Awl*	Reduction. This principle is applicable when the calculated shares

	of Sharers exceed the supposed shares.
Principle of Exclusion	Under this principle, a legal heir is excluded by another from inheritance on the basis of nearness in a relationship with the deceased.
Principle of *Radd*	Return. This principle is applicable when the estate is distributed among only the Qur'anic sharers, in the absence of residuaries.
Principle of Representation	Under this principle, distant legal heirs inherit through their predeceased connecting link from a deceased (e.g. son's children through son, daughter's children through daughter, brother's children through brother, uncle's children through uncle).
Private *Waqf*	Also known as a family *waqf*—a *waqf* created for the benefit of family members with a terminal object of dedicating the benefits to religious, pious, and charitable purposes.
Public *Waqf*	A *waqf* for religious, charitable, and pious purposes as opposed to a private *waqf*.
Qabul	Literally means acceptance, but in the background of the gift it is made by the donee in response to *ijab* by the donor.
Qabza	Literally, it means possession, but in the context of the transfer of property, it means delivery of possession.
Qiyas	Analogy
Qur'anic Heirs	Also known as sharers. They are entitled to a prescribed share specifically provided in the Qur'an.
Residuaries	They are not entitled to a prescribed share. They are given a share in inheritance after the claims of the sharers are satisfied.
Res Judicata	Something that has been already judicated. A case that has been decided.
Restitution of Conjugal Rights	Right of a spouse to sue the other when he or she refuses to live with him or her without a lawful excuse.
Rukhsati	Departure of a bride from parental home to the matrimonial home.
Rule of Primogeniture	Under this rule, the eldest male offspring inherits the entire or main estate to the exclusion of younger heirs.
Sadaqa	A gift made with a religious motive. It is completed by delivery of possession and is irrevocable.
Sahih	Valid.
Sharers	Also known as Qur'anic Heirs. They are entitled to a prescribed share specifically provided in the Qur'an, Sunnah, and ijma.
Sunnah	Sayings, deeds, or tacit approvals of the Prophet Muhammad (PBUH).
Surrogacy	The medical process whereby a woman bears and delivers a child for another couple.
Talaq	Unilateral divorce by a husband.
Talaq as-Sunna	Recommended mode of *talaq* that includes *talaq-e-ahsan* and *talaq-e-hasan*.
Talaq i Ba'in	Also known as *talaq-e-bidat*. Three pronouncements of divorce on a single occasion at any time (during menstruation or non-menstruation period). It is also commonly referred to as a triple *talaq* or instant divorce.
Talaq Tafwiz	Right of *talaq* that is delegated to the wife or a third party by the husband.
Talaq-e-Ahsan	A single pronouncement of divorce made during a period between menstruations followed by abstinence from sexual intercourse

	during the period of *iddat*.
Talaq-e-Bidat	Three pronouncements of *talaq* by a husband on a single occasion at any time (during menstruation or non-menstruation period of the wife). It is also commonly referred to as a triple *talaq*.
Talaq-e-Hasan	Three successive pronouncements of divorce during three successive periods between menstruations with no sexual intercourse during the period between menstruations.
Talaqnama	Divorce deed.
Testator	Refers to a person who dies leaving behind a will.
Usul al-fiqh	Science of Islamic Jurisprudence
Urf	Custom.
Wakalatnama	Power of Attorney.
Wali	Guardian—a father is regarded as a natural guardian.
Waqf ala al-aulad	Family *waqf*
Waqf	A permanent endowment made by a Muslim of property (moveable or immovable) for a purpose recognized by Muslim Law as religious, pious, or charitable.
Wasiyat	Will.
Welfare of minors	The paramount principle considered by the court when deciding custody cases. It is defined as the financial, moral, spiritual, and intellectual well-being of the minor.
Wilayah	Guardianship.
Zihar	Injurious assimilation—when the husband solemnly states that, to him, his wife is like 'the back of his mother'.
Zina	Illicit sexual intercourse
Zina bil jabr	Rape.

Bibliography

Abidin, I., *Radd al-Muhtar*, Vol. 6 (Damascus: Dar al-Kutub al-Ilmiyya, 2003).

Ahmad, K. (ed.), *Marriage Commission Report X-Rayed: A Study of the Family Law of Islam and a Critical Appraisal of the Modernist Attempts to 'reform' it* (Karachi: Chiragh-e-Rah Publications, 1959).

Ahmad, M.B., *The Administration of Justice in Medieval India* (Allahabad: The Aligarh Historical Research Institute, 1949).

Al-Bukhari, Muhammad bin Ismail, *Sahih al-Bukhari*, vol. 8, tr. Dr Muhammad Muhsin Khan (Lahore: Kazi Publications, 1976).

Al-Humām, I., *Sharh Fatah al-Qadir ala al-Hidaya*, vol. 6 (Beirut: Dar al-Kutub al-Ilmiyya, 2003).

Ali, A., *Mahomedan Law* (Lahore: Imran Law Book House, 2012).

Ali, Kecia, 'Marriage in Classical Islamic Jurisprudence: A Survey of Doctrines', in Asifa Quraishi and Frank Vogel (eds.), *The Islamic Marriage Contract* (Harvard University Press, 2008), 11–45.

Ali, S., *Gender and Human Rights in Islam and International Law: Equal before Allah, Unequal before Man* (The Hague: Kluwer Law International, 2000).

Ali, S.A., *Mahommedan Law* (First published in 1892; Lahore: Law Publishing Company, 1976).

Ali, S.S., *Modern Challenges to Islamic Law* (Cambridge: Cambridge University Press, 2016).

Al-Zuhayli, W., *Al-Fiqh ul-Islami*, 10 vols. (Damascus: Dar al-Fikr, 2004).

An-Na'im, A.A., *Islam and the Secular State* (Cambridge: Harvard University Press, 2008).

An-Na'im, A.A., 'Shari'a and Positive Legislation: Is an Islamic State Possible or Viable?', in Abu Ghazaleh (ed.), *Intellectual Property Laws of the Arab Countries* (The Hague: Kluwer Law International, 2000).

Arshad, R., *Islamic Family Law*, South Asian Edition (London: Sweet & Maxwell, 2016).

Baderin, M.A., *International Human Rights and Islamic Law* (Oxford University Press, 2003).

Balchin, C. (ed.), *A Handbook on Family Law in Pakistan* (Lahore: Shirkat Gah, 1994).

Bhatia, M.L., *Administrative History of Medieval India (A Study of Muslim Jurisprudence under Aurangzeb)* (New Delhi: Radha Publication, 1992).

Bhatti, M.I., *Barr-i Saghir Pak-o Hind mein 'Ilm-i Fiqh* (Lahore: Institute of Islamic Culture, 1973).

Cuno, Kenneth M., *Modernizing Marriage: Family, Ideology, and Law in Nineteenth-and Early Twentieth-Century Egypt* (New York: Syracuse University Press, 2015).

Fitzgerald, S.V., *Muhammadan Law: An Abridgement* (Oxford: Oxford University Press 1931).

Fyzee, A.A.A., *Outlines of Muhammadan Law*, 5th ed. (first published Oxford: Oxford University Press 1949, 5th ed. New Delhi: 2008).

Fyzee, A.A.A., *The Reform of Muslim Personal Law in India* (Bombay: Nachiketa Publications 1971).

Gladwin, F., *An Epitome of Mohammedan Law*, Translated from the original Persian (Calcutta: William Mackay, 1786).

Grady, S.G., Charles Hamilton's *The Hedaya, Or Guide: A Commentary on the Mussulman Laws*, 2nd ed. (London: W.H. Allen, 1870).

Guenther, A.M., 'Hanafi Fiqh in Mughal India: The *Fatāwá-i 'Ālamgīrī*', in R.M. Eaton (ed.), *India's Islamic Traditions* (Oxford: Oxford University Press, 2003).

Hallaq, W.B., *The Impossible State: Islam, Politics, and Modernity's Moral Predicament* (New York: Columbia University Press, 2013).

Hamilton, C., *The Hedaya, or Guide; A Commentary on the Mussulman Laws*, vol. 4 (London: T. Bensley. 1791).

Hodkinson, K., *Muslim Family Law: A Sourcebook* (London: Croom Helm Ltd., 1984).

Hoexter, M., 'Qāḍī, Muftī and Ruler: Their Roles in the Development of Islamic Law', in R. Shaham (ed.), *Law, Custom, and Statute in the Muslim World* (Brill, 2007).

Iqbal, S.M., *The Reconstruction of Religious Thought in Islam* (Oxford: Oxford University Press, 1934).

Mansoori, M.T., *Family Law in Islam* (Islamabad: Shari'ah Academy, 2012).

Masud, M.K., *Shatibi's Philosophy of Islamic Law* (Islamabad: Islamic Research Institute, Islamabad, 1995).

Mayer, A.E., *Islam and Human Rights: Tradition and Politics* (Oxford: Westview Press, 1991).

Mulla, D.F., *Principles of Mahomedan Law* (First published Calcutta: W. Thacker & Co. 1905, 20th ed. Haryana: LexisNexis, 2013).

Mumtaz, K., '*Political Participation: Women in National Legislatures in Pakistan*', in F. Shaheed, S. A. Warraich, C. Balchin and A. Gazdar (eds.), *Shaping Women's Lives: Laws, Practices & Strategies in Pakistan* (Shirkat Gah 1998).

Nawawi, M.A., *Minhaj Et Talibin* (Calcutta: W. Thacker & Co., 1914).

Nizam, A.S., *Al-Fatawa al-Alamgiriyya*, vol. 2 (Calcutta: Nawal Kishawr, 1865).

Opwis, F.M.M., *Maṣlaḥa and the Purpose of the Law: Islamic Discourse on Legal Change from the 4th/10th to 8th/14th Century* (Leiden: Brill, 2010).

Pal, R., *The History of the Law of Primogeniture with Special Reference to India, Ancient and Modern* (Calcutta: University of Calcutta, 1929).

Pearl, D., and W. Menski, *Muslim Family Law* (London: Sweet & Maxwell, 1998).

Pearl, D., *A Textbook on Muslim Personal Law*, 1st ed. (London: Croom Helm, 1979).

Prior, K., 'Macnaghten, Sir William Hay, baronet (1793–1841)', *Oxford Dictionary of National Biography* (OUP, 2004).

Rahim, A., *The Principles of Muhammadan Jurisprudence* (London: Luzac & Co., 1911).

Rahman, A., *Institutes of Mussalman Law* (Calcutta: Thacker, Spink & Co., 1907).

Rahman, T., *Muslim Family Laws Ordinance: Islamic & Social Survey* (Karachi: Royal Book Company, 1997).

Serajuddin, A.M., *Muslim Family Law, Secular Courts and Muslim Women of South Asia* (Oxford: Oxford University Press, 2011).

Sijistani, Imam Abu Dawud Sulaiman bin al-Ash'ath, *Sunnan Abu Dawud*, vol. 2, tr. Ahmad Hasan (Lahore: Sh Muhammad Ashraf Publishers and Booksellers, 1984).

Schacht, J., 'On the Title of the *Fatāwā al-'Ālamgīriyya*', in C. Bosworth (ed.), *Iran and Islam* (Edinburgh: Edinburgh University Press, 1971).

Sezgin, Y., *Human Rights under State-Enforced Religious Family Laws in Israel, Egypt and India* (Cambridge: Cambridge University Press, 2013).

Shah, N.A., *Women, the Koran and International Human Rights Law: The Experience of Pakistan* (Leiden: Martinus Nijhoff Publishers, 2006).

Siddique, O., *Pakistan's Experience with Formal Law: An Alien Justice* (Cambridge: Cambridge University Press, 2013).

Sircar, S.C., *Tagore Law Lectures—1873: The Muhammadan Law* (Calcutta: Thacker, Spink and Co., 1873).

Tahir, Q.M., *Aali Qawanin* (Lahore: Jang Publishers, 1999).

Tanzil-ur-Rahman, *A Code of Muslim Personal Law* (Karachi: Hamdard Academy, 1978).

Tyabji, F.B., *Principles of Muhammadan Law*, 2nd ed. (Calcutta: Butterworth & Co., 1919).

Usmani, M.T., *Islām Mein Khul' Ki Ḥaqīqat* (Karachi: Maiman Islamic Publishers, 1996).

Welchman, L., *Women and Muslim Family Laws in Arab States* (Amsterdam: Amsterdam University Press, 2007).

Wilson, R.K., *A Digest of Anglo-Muhammadan Law*, 1st ed. (Calcutta: W. Thacker & Co., 1895; 5th ed. 1921).

Zaman, M.Q., *The Ulama in Contemporary Islam: Custodians of Change* (Princeton: Princeton University Press, 2002).

Journal Articles

Abbasi, M.Z., 'Judicial *Ijtihād* as a Tool for Legal Reform: Extending Women's Right to Divorce under Islamic Law in Pakistan', *Islamic Law and Society* (2017) 24, 384.

Abbasi, Abbasi., 'Dead at Home, Alive Abroad: Restitution of Conjugal Rights in South Asia', *Islamic Studies* (2022) 61(1), 9–24.

Abbasi, M.Z., 'The Classical Islamic Law of Waqf: A Concise Introduction', *Arab Law* Quarterly (2012) 26, 121.

Abbott, F., 'Pakistan's New Marriage Law: A Reflection of Qur'anic Interpretation', *Asian Survey* (1962) 1(11), 26.

Afsah, E., 'Contested Universalities of International Law: Islam's Struggle with Modernity', *Journal of the History of International Law* (2008) 10, 259.

Ali, S.S., 'Rights of the Child under Islamic Law and Laws of Pakistan: A Thematic Overview', *Journal of Islamic State Practice in International Law* (2006) 2(1), 1.

Ansari, S., 'Polygamy, Purdah and Political Representation: Engendering Citizenship in 1950s Pakistan', *Modern Asian Studies* 43 (2009), 1421.

Areen, Judith, 'Baby M Reconsidered', *Georgetown Law Journal* (1987) 76, 1741.

Azahari, R., and Ali, H.M., 'Mahr as a Form of Economic Security: A Preliminary Study', *Arab Law Quarterly* (2015) 29 (3), 296.

Behjati-Ardakani, Zohra, et al., 'Embryo Donation in Iranian Legal System: A Critical Review', *Journal of Reproduction & Infertility* (2015) 16(3), 130.

Carroll, L., 'Application of the Islamic Law of Succession: Was the *Propositus* a Sunnī or a Shī'a?', *Islamic Law and Society* (1995) 2, 24.

Carroll, L., 'Life Interests and Inter-Generational Transfer of Property Avoiding the Law of Succession', *Islamic Law and Society* (2001) 8, 245.

Carroll, L., 'Qur'an 2: 229: "A Charter Granted to the Wife"? Judicial *Khul'* in Pakistan', *Islamic Law and Society* (1996) 3, 91.

Carroll, L., 'The Hanafi Law of Intestate Succession: A Simplified Approach', *Modern Asian Studies* (1983) 17, 629.

Carroll, L., 'The Ithna Ashari Law of Intestate Succession: An Introduction to Shia Law Applicable in South Asia', *Modern Asian Studies* (1985) 19, 85.

Carroll, L., 'The Pakistan Federal Shariat Court, Section 4 of the Muslim Family Laws Ordinance, and the Orphaned Grandchild', *Islamic Law and Society* (2002) 9, 70.

Cheema, S.A., 'Shia and Sunni Laws of Inheritance: A Comparative Analysis', *Pakistan Journal of Islamic Research* (2012) 10, 69.

Cheema, S.A., 'Socially Abhorrent but Legally Acceptable: A Study of Alleged Conversions of Sunnis and Shias in Cases of Inheritance in Pakistan', *South Asian Studies: A Research Journal of South Asian Studies* (2014) 29, 259.

Cheema, S.A., 'Islamisation of Restitution of Conjugal Rights by the Federal Shariat Court of Pakistan', *Islamic Studies* (2019) 58(4), 535–50.

Cohn, B.S., 'Anthropological Notes on Disputes and Law in India', *American Anthropologist* (1965) 67, 82.

Davis, M., 'Child Custody in Pakistan: The Role of Ijtihad', *Boston College Third World Law Journal* (1984) 5(2), 119.

Ewing, K., 'The Politics of Sufism: Redefining the Saints of Pakistan', *The Journal of Asian Studies* (1983) 42, 251.

Fadel, M., 'A Tragedy of Politics or an Apolitical Tragedy?', *Journal of the American Oriental Society* (2011) 131(1), 109.

Fadel, M., 'The Social Logic of *Taqlīd* and the Rise of the *Mukhataṣar*,' *Islamic Law and Society* 3 (1996), 193.

Giunchi, E., 'The Reinvention of Sharia under the British Raj: In Search of Authenticity and Certainty', *The Journal of Asian Studies* (2010) 69, 1119.

Hallaq, W.B., 'Juristic Authority vs. State Power: The Legal Crises of Modern Islam', *Journal of Law and Religion* (2003) 19, 243.

Hallaq, W.B., 'Was the Gate of *Ijtihad* Closed?', *International Journal of Middle East Studies* (1984) 16, 3.

Harrison, Cathy, 'Who is your Mother? Who is your Father? Assisted Reproductive Technologies in the Light of Sunni and Shi'a Law', *Journal of Shi'a Islamic Studies* (2014) 17(1), 23.

Inhorn, Marcia C., 'Making Muslim Babies: IVF and Gamete Donation in Sunni v Shi'a Islam', *Culture, Medicine and Psychiatry* (2006) 30(4), 427.

Ishaque, S., and M. Khan, 'The Best Interests of the Child: A Prevailing Consideration within Islamic Principles and a Governing Principle in Child Custody Cases in Pakistan', *International Journal of Law, Policy and the Family* (2015), 15.

Korson, J. Henry, and Sabzwari, M.A. 'Age and Social State at Marriage, Karachi, Pakistan 1961–64 and 1980: A Comparative Study', *Journal of Comparative Family Studies* (1984), 257, 272.

Kugle, S., 'Framed, Blamed and Renamed: The Recasting of Islamic Jurisprudence in Colonial South Asia', *Modern Asian Studies* (2001) 35, 257.

Layish, A., 'The Transformation of the Sharī'a from Jurists' Law to Statutory Law in the Contemporary Muslim World', (*Die Welt des Islams* 2004) 44, 85.

Lewis, T.E., 'The History of Judicial Precedent,' *Law Quarterly Review* 46 (1930–32), 207–24, 341–60; *Law Quarterly Review* 47, 411–27; *Law Quarterly Review* 48, 230–47.

Libson, G., 'On the Development of Custom as a Source of Law in Islamic law', *Islamic Law and Society* (1997) 4, 131.

Liebesny, H., 'English Common Law and Islamic Law in the Middle East and South Asia: Religious Influences and Secularization', *Cleveland State Law Review* (1985) 34, 19.

Malik, S.J., 'Waqf in Pakistan: Change in Traditional Institutions', *Die Welt des Islams* (1990) 30, 63.

Meron, Y., 'The Moslem Marriage Between Status and Contract', *Studia Islamica* (2001) 92, 197.

Munir, M., 'Stipulations in a Muslim Marriage Contract with Special Reference to Talaq Al-Tafwid Provisions in Pakistan', *Yearbook of Islamic and Middle Eastern Law* (2005–2006) 12, 235.

Nizami, K.A., 'Socio-Religious Movements in Indian Islam, 1763–898', *Islamic Culture* (1970) 44, 131.

Peters, R., 'From Jurists Law to Statute Law or What Happens When the Shari'a is Codified', *Mediterranean Politics* (2002) 7, 82.

Shalakany, A., 'Islamic Legal Histories', *Berkeley Journal of Middle Eastern & Islamic Law* (2008) 1, 2.

Usmani, T.M., 'The Islamization of Laws in Pakistan: The Case of Hudud Ordinances', *The Muslim World* (2006) 96, 287.

Wilson, R.K., 'Should the Personal Laws of the Natives of India be Codified?', *Asiatic Quarterly Review* (1898) 6, 225.

Yefet, K.C., 'The Constitution and Female-Initiated Divorce in Pakistan: Western Liberalism In Islamic Garb', *Harvard Journal of Law & Gender* (2011) 34, 553.

Reports

Council of Islamic Ideology, Report on Muslim Family Laws (Islamabad: Council of Islamic Ideology, Government of Pakistan, 1983 & 1993).

EU Access to Justice Project, Public Knowledge, Attitudes and Perceptions of Justice: Report of a Household Survey in Southern Punjab Districts (Punjab Access to Justice Project, 2015).

Law and Justice Commission of Pakistan, Report 103 on Post-Divorce Mata'a for Wife, available at <http://ljcp.gov.pk/lfr/103/> (accessed 25 July 2016).

Rashid, M.A., 'Report of the Commission on Marriage and Family Law,' in Khurshid Ahmad (ed.), *Studies in the Family Law of Islam* (Chirag-e-Rah Publications, 1959).

The Law Commission, 'Proposal for the Abolition of the Matrimonial Remedy of Restitution of Conjugal Rights' (London, Her Majesty's Stationary Office, 1969).

Unpublished PhD Theses

Esposito, J.L., 'Muslim Family Law in Egypt and Pakistan: A Critical Analysis of Legal Reform, its Sources and Methodological Problems' (PhD Thesis, Temple University, 1974).

Guenther, A.M., 'Syed Mahmood and the Transformation of Muslim Law in British India' (PhD Thesis, McGill University, 2004).

Hussin, I.R., 'The Politics of Islamic Law: Local Elites, Colonial Authority and the Making of the Muslim State' (PhD Thesis, Washington University, 2008).

Khan, F., 'Traditionalist Approaches to Sharī'ah Reform: Mawlana Ashraf 'Ali Thānawi's Fatawa on Women's Right to Divorce' (PhD Thesis, The University of Michigan, 2008).

Kozlowski, G.C., 'Muslim Endowments and Society in British India' (PhD Thesis, University of Minnesota, 1980).

Lau, M. W., 'The Role of Islam in the Legal System of Pakistan' (PhD Thesis, School of Oriental and African Studies, University of London, 2002).

Nelson, M.J., 'Land, Law, and the Logic of Local Politics in the Punjab, 1849–1999' (PhD Thesis, Columbia University, 2002).

Reyes, A.F.T., 'English and French Approaches to Personal Laws in South India, 1700–1850' (PhD Thesis, Cambridge University, 1986).

Sharafi, M.J., 'Bella's Case: Parsi Identity and the Law in Colonial Rangoon, Bombay and London, 1887–1925' (PhD Thesis, Princeton University, 2006).

Singh, A., 'The Divergence of the Economic Fortunes of Hindus and Muslims in British India: A Comparative Institutional Analysis' (PhD Thesis, University of Southern California, 2008).

Thiessen, J.G., 'Orientalism and the East India Company, 1773–1858' (PhD Thesis, The John Hopkins University, 1992).

Legislation

Balochistan Letters of Administration and Succession Certificates Act 2022
British Marriage Act 1949
Child Marriages Restraint Act 1929
Christian Marriage Act 1872
Code of Civil Procedure 1908
Contract Act 1872
Dissolution of Muslim Marriage Act 1939
Divorce Act 1869
Dowry and Bridal Gifts (Restrictions) Act 1976
Enforcement of Women's Property Rights Act 2020 [For the Islamabad Capital Territory]
Evidence Act 1872
Family Courts Act 1964
Federal Laws (Revision and Declaration) Ordinance 1981 (XXVII of 1981)
Government of India Act 1935
Guardians and Wards Act 1890
Indian Succession Act 1925
Indian Succession Act 1925
KPK Letters of Administration and Succession Certificates Act 2021
Land Acquisition Act 1894
Letters of Administration and Succession Certificates Act 2020 [Islamabad Capital Territory]
Limitation Act 1908
Muslim Family Laws (Amendment) Act 2021
Muslim Family Laws (Second Amendment) Act 2021
Muslim Family Laws Ordinance 1961
Muslim Personal Law (Shariat) Application Act 1937
Mussalman Wakf Act 1923

NWFP Justice Regulation 1901
NWFP Shariat Act 1935
Punjab Courts of Wards Act 1903
Punjab Enforcement of Women's Property Rights Act 2021
Punjab Family Courts (Amendment) Act 2015
Punjab Laws Act 1872
Punjab Letters of Administration and Succession Certificates Act 2021
Punjab Muslim Personal Law (Shariat) Application (Removal of Difficulties) Act 1975
Punjab Muslim Personal Law (Shariat) Application (Removal of Doubts) Ordinance 1972
Punjab Preemption Act 1991
Qanun-e-Shahadat Order 1984
Registration Act 1908
Sindh Child Marriages Restraint Act 2013
Sindh Letters of Administration and Succession Certificates Act 2021
Special Marriage Act 1872
Special Marriage Act 1954
Specific Relief Act 1877
Transfer of Property Act 1882
Transgender Persons (Protection of Rights) Act 2018
Wakf Properties Ordinance 1979
West Pakistan Muslim Personal Law (Shariat) Application (Amendment) Act 1951
West Pakistan Muslim Personal Law (Shariat) Application Act 1948
West Pakistan Muslim Personal Law (Shariat) Application Act 1962

Table of Cases

A

Abdul Aziz v Zaib-un-Nissa PLD 2022 SC 504
Abdul Hameed v Muhammad Mohiyuddin PLD 1997 SC 730
Abdul Haq v Surrya Begum 2002 SCMR 1330
Abdul Jabbar v Additional District Judge 2009 CLC 364 (Lah)
Abdul Kadir v Salima (1886) ILR 8 All 149
Abdul Khaliq v Fazalur Rehman PLD 2004 SC 768
Abdul Majeed Khan v Ms Maheen Begum 2014 SCMR 1524
Abdul Majid Khan v Anwar Begum PLD 1989 SC 362
Abdul Rashid v Safia Bibi PLD 1986 FSC 10
Abdul Rashid v Shahida Parveen 2013 YLR 2616 (Pesh)
Abdul Samad v Shista Khan 1998 CLC 171 [Quetta]
Abdullah v Abdul Aziz 1987 SCMR 1403
Abid Arif Nomani v Chief Administrator, Auqaf, Punjab 2004 SCMR 1050
Abrar Ahmed v Irshad Ahmed PLD 2014 SC 331
Abrar Hussain v Mehwish Rana PLD 2012 Lah 420
Abul Fata Mahomed Ishak v Rasamaya Dhur Chowdhry [1894] 22 IA 76
Aftab Ahmad v Judge Family Court 2009 MLD 962 (Lah)
Ahmad Bilal v Khurram Javed Writ Petition No. 2383/2021 Islamabad
Ajab Gul v Rahim Gul 1991 SCMR 2500
Akbar Bibi v Shaukat Ali 1981 CLC 78 [Lah]
Alaf Din v Parveen Akhtar PLD 1970 SC 75
Ali Abbas Khan v Palwasha Khan 2010 YLR 1632 [Islamabad]
Ali Adnan Dar v Judge Family Court PLD 2016 Lah 73
Ali Haider v Syed Muhammad Asghar Shah 2015 YLR 511
Allah Banda v Khurshid Bibi 1990 CLC 1683 (Lah)
Allah Dad v Mukhtar 1992 SCMR 1273 (Shariat Appellate Bench)
Allah Rakha v Federation of Pakistan PLD 2000 FSC 1
Allama Maqsood Ahmad v Government of Punjab through Chief Administrator Auqaf 2005 SCMR 816
Amanat Masih v Najma Bibi 2010 YLR 2711 (Lah)
Amar Ilahi v Rashida Akhtar PLD 1955 Lah 412
Ambreen Khatoon v Mumtaz Bibi 2020 SCMR 643
Ambreen Shah v Chairman, Union (Arbitration) Council 2002 MLD 778
Amina Bibi v Karachi Metropolitan Corporation 1994 SCMR 804
Amir Ali v Gul Shaker PLD 1985 Kar 365
Amir v Bashiran Bibi 2004 SCMR 832
Amjad Iqbal v Mst Nida Sohail 2015 SCMR 128
Amjad Khan Yousafzai v Arshad Khan 2009 CLC 1057
Ammara Waseem v Syed Khawar Hussain 2011 SCMR 148

Anisur Rehman v Mst Shehla Fatima 1988 CLC 1888 (Kar).
Anjuman Himayat-e-Islam, Lahore v Dr Syed Farooq Hassan PLD 2007 SC 352
Anjuman Masjid-i-Farooqia v Fazal Begum 1991 SCMR 2112
Arshad Peter v Mst Shumaila PLD 2012 Lah 430
Asghar Bin Shahid Jafry v Defence Housing Authority PLD 2017 Lah 347
Ashiq Ali v Mst Zamir Fatima PLD 2004 SC 10
Ashiq Hussain v Anjuman Islamia, Kamalia Regd. 2007 CLC 71 (Lah)
Asif Raza v Mst. Sofia alias Pinky PLD 2021 Peshawar 41
Asma Naz v Muhammad Younas Qureshi 2005 SCMR 401
Atta Mohammad v Mst. Munir Sultan 2021 SCMR 73
Attorney General of Ceylon v Reid 1965 LR 720
Ayesha Shaheen v Khalid Mahmood 2013 SCMR 1049
Aziz Bano v Muhammad Ibrahim Husain 89 Ind Cas 690
Aziz-ur-Rehman v Mst. Bibi Jameela 2020 CLC 380 (Quetta)
Azra Bibi v Lateef 2020 YLR 282 (Lah)
Azra Bibi v S.H.O, Police Station, Thingi, District Vehari 2005 YLR 1859 (Lah)

B
Baboo Beer Partab v Maharajah Rajender Pertab (1867) 12 MIA 1
Bai Fatima v Ali Muhammad Aiyeb ILR 37 Bom 280
Baja v Mst Bakhan 2015 SCMR 1704
Bakht-e-Rawida v Ghulam Habib PLD 1992 Kar 46
Balqis Fatima v Najam-ul-Ikram PLD 1959 Lah 566.
Basharat Ahmed v Mst Shamim PLD 2016 Lah 271
Bashir Ahmed v Muhammad Boota 1991 CLC 1153
Bashir Ahmad v Incharge (Female) Darulaman, District Mianwali 2011 SCMR 1329
Begum v Mst Kazbanoo PLD 1957 Kar 884
Beguman v Saroo PLD 1964 Lah 451
Bhaggay Bibi v Razia Bibi 2005 SCMR 1595.
Bibi Amu v Mst Asiat PLD 1958 Kar 420
Bibi Fatima v Nur Muhammad (1921) 60 IC 88 (Lah)

C
Caroline Rehman v Chairman Union Council 1985 CLC 2855 [Lah]
Ch. Muhammad Bashir v Ansarun Nisa 2012 MLD 1394 (Lah)
Ch. Muhammad Boota v Bano Begum 2003 CLC 485 [Lah]
Chief Administrator Auqaf v Abdul Qadeer Khan 2004 MLD 532 [Lah]
Chief Administrator Auqaf, Sindh v Masooma Begum PLD 2001 SC 75
Chuhar v Mst Ghulam Fatima PLD 1984 Lah 234
Christine Brass v Dr Javed Iqbal PLD 1981 Pesh 110

D
Danish v Fozia Danish PLD 2013 Sindh 209
Dr A.L.M Abdullah v Rokeya Khatoon PLD 1969 Dacca 47
Dr Asma Ali v Masood Sajjad PLD 2011 SC 221
Dr Fakhr Ud Din v Kausar Takreem PLD 2009 Pesh 92
Dr Mahmood-ur-Rehman Faisal v Govt of Pakistan PLD 1994 SC 607.
Dr Muhammad Ali Chohan v Fakhur-un-Nisa 2009 CLC 255 (Pesh)
Dr Sabira Sultana v Maqsood Sulari 2000 CLC 1384.
Dr Viktor Hacker v Dr Shahida Mansoor PLD 2013 Isb 34

Dubai Islamic Bank v Saima Yasin 2020 CLD 518 [Lah]
Dur Muhammad v Abdul Sattar 1996 CLC 1596 (Lah)

E

Emperor v Atony ILR 38 Mad. 371
Emperor v Mst Ruri AIR 1919 Lah 389

F

Faqir Ali v Sakina Bibi PLD 2022 SC 85
Farah Chaudhry v Shahid Mahmood Malik 2005 YLR 29
Farah Naz v Judge Family Court PLD 2006 SC 457
Faraz Ahmad Bhutta v Additional District Judge PLD 2011 Lah 483
Farida Malik v Khalida Malik 1998 SCMR 816
Farhan Aslam v Nuzba Shaheen 2021 SCMR 179
Farkhanda Mumtaz v Muhammad Sharif PLD 2006 Pesh 96
Farooq Leivers v Adelaide Bridget Mary PLD 1958 (W.P) Lah 431
Farooq Omar Bhoja v Federation of Pakistan PLD 2022 FSC 1
Farooq Siddiqui v Farzana Naheed PLD 2013 Lah 254
Farzana Rasool v Dr Muhammad Bashir 2011 SCMR 1361
Farzana Siddique v The State through Advocate General Azad Jammu and Kashmir 2014 CrLJ 897
Farzand Ali v Raja Muhammad Ibrahim PLD 1996 FSC 29
Fawad Ishaq v Mehreen Mansoor PLD 2020 SC 269
Fazli-e-Subhan v Mst Sabereen PLD 2003 Pesh 169
Feroze Begum v Lt-Col. Muhammad Hussain 1983 SCMR 606
Fida Hussain v Naseem Akhtar PLD 1977 Lah 328
Firdous Iqbal v Shifaat Ali 2000 SCMR 838

G

Gakhar Hussain v Surrayya Begum PLD 2013 Lah 464
Ghania Hassan v Shahid Hussain Shahid 2016 SCMR 2170
Ghazala Sadia v Muhammad Sajjad 2012 YLR 2841 (Lah)
Ghazala Tehsin Zohra v Mehr Ghulam Dastagir Khan PLD 2015 SC 327
Ghulam Ali v Ghulam Sarwar Naqvi PLD 1990 SC 1
Gakhar Hussain v Surayya Begum PLD 2013 Lah 464
Ghulam Mustafa v Judge Family Court 2021 CLC 204
Ghulam Qasim v Razia Begum PLD 2021 SC 812
Ghulam Sabir v Chairman Union Council, Ward No. 27, Samanabad Lahore, PLD 1981 Lah 232
Ghulam Shabbir v Mst. Abbas Bibi 2022 CLC 963 (Lah)
Ghulam Shabbir v Bakhat Khatoon 2009 SCMR 644
Ghulam Shabbir v Nur Begum PLD 1977 SC 75
Gohar Khanum v Jamila Jan 2014 SCMR 801
Grana v Sahib Kamala Bibi PLD 2014 SC 167
Gul Akbar v Jameela Afridi PLD 2016 Pesh 109
Gul Khatoon v Haji Muhammad Aslam 2015 PCrLJ 193
Gul Sher v Dost Muhammad 2013 YLR 1856 (Lah)
Gul Zaman v Maula Dad 2014 CLC 635 (Pesh)
Chuhar v Ghulam Fatima PLD 1984 Lah 234

H

Hafiz Abdul Waheed v Asma Jehangir PLD 2004 SC 219

Haji Mian Muhammad v Tila Muhammad PLD 1959 Pesh 152
Haji Muhammad Ali v Muhammad Akram PLD 2007 SC 319
Haji Muhammad Shafi v Maqbool Afza 1986 SCMR 1634
Haji Murad Khan v Abdul Ghafoor 1987 CLC 7 [Pesh]
Hajra Khatoon v SHO, Police Station Fateh Jang, Attock PLD 2005 Lah 316
Hameed Mai v Irshad Hussain PLD 2002 SC 267
Hamida Begum v Murad Begum PLD 1975 SC 624
Harvey v Farnie (1882) 8 AC 43
Hassan Ahmad Kanwar v Adnan Hassan 2020 CLC 1701 (Lah)
Hina Jilani v Sohail Butt PLD 1995 Lah 151
Humaira Mehmood v The State PLD 1999 Lah 494
Humayun Hassan v Arsalan Humayun PLD 2013 SC 557
Hussain v Mansoor Ali PLD 1977 Kar 320

I

In re Baby M 109 NJ 396 (1988).
Iqra Javed alias Saba v Station House Officer PLD 2013 Lah 538
Imran Anwar Khan v Government of Punjab [Shariat Petition No.4–I of 2016]
Iram Shahzad v Additional District Judge Lahore PLD 2011 Lah 362
Issa Khan v Mst Razma 1991 SCMR 2454

J

Jagsi v Shr. Marwan PLD 2005 Kar 334
Jan Muhammad v Salamat Bibi 2002 SCMR 1408
John Jiban Chandra Dutta v Abinash Chandra Sen AIR 1939 Cal 417

K

Kaneez Fatima v Wali Muhammad PLD 1993 SC 901
Kashif Akram v Mst Naila 2011 MLD 571 (Kar)
Khairan Bibi v Ghulam Hassan 2007 CLC 167 (Lah)
Khalid Bashir v Shamas-un-Nisa 2015 MLD 11 (Lah)
Khalid Hussain v Nazir Ahmad 2021 SCMR 1986
Khalida Shamim Akhtar v Ghulam Jaffar PLD 2016 Lah 865
Khawar Iqbal v Federation of Pakistan 2013 MLD 1711 (FSC)
Khizar Hayat v Additional District Judge, Kabirwala PLD 2010 Lah 422
Khurshid Bibi v Baboo Muhammad Amin PLD 1967 SC 97
Kullu v Faizi 2015 YLR 2014 [Lah]

L

Lahore Development Authority v Naimat Saleem Trust PLD 2004 Lah 270
Lata Devi v Kunta Bai 1986 MLD 1483 (Kar)
Latifa Bibi v Muhammad Bashir 2006 CLC 1076
Latifan Bibi v Rehmat Ali 2012 SCMR 1251
Loung v Allah Ditto 2002 CLC 1307 (Kar)
Lt. Col. Nasir Malik v ADJ, Lahore 2016 SCMR 1821

M

M. Ishaque v Rukhsana Begum PLD 1988 Kar 625
M. Saqlain v Zaib un-Nisa 1988 MLD 427
Maj. (Retd) Abdul Akbar v Maryam Khushboo PLD 2011 Pesh 78

Malik Amir Akbar v Mian Murid Hussain, ADJ, Lahore 2008 SCMR 505
Malik Khan Muhammad alias Khanay v Moulvi Luqman 1993 CLC 1552 (Quetta)
Malik Muhammad Rafique v Tanveer Jahan PLD 2015 Islamabad 30
Malik Tanveer Khan v Amber Liaqat 2009 CLC 1210 (Pesh)
Manzoor Ahmad v Nargis Mirza PLD 2004 SC 132
Manzoor Hussain v Safiya Bibi PLD 2015 Lah 683
Manzoor Hussain v Zahoor Ahmed 1992 SCMR 1191
Manzoor v Azizul AIR 1928 Oudh 303.
Mariam Bibi through Abida Parveen v Naseer Ahmad PLD 2015 Lah 336
Maryam Mai v Judge Family Court, D.G. Khan 2004 SCMR 1382
Mauj Ali v Safdar Hussain Shah 1970 SCMR 437.
Mehmood Akhtar v District Judge, Attock 2004 SCMR 1839
Mehr Bhari v Bhag Bhari 1991 SCMR 897
Mehrunnisa v Syed Muhammad Zoha 2015 CLC 738 [Kar]
Mian Muhammad Sabir v Uzma Parveen PLD 2012 Lah 154
Mirza Allah Ditta alias Mirza Javed Akhtar v Amina Bibi 2004 YLR 239 (Lah)
Mohammad Deen Malik v IInd Additional District Judge, Karachi 1982 CLC 441
Moonshee Buzloor Ruheem v Shumsoonnissa Begum, (Calcutta) [1867] UKPC 22
Mrs Ambreen Tariq Awan v Federal Govt. of Pakistan 2013 MLD 1885 (FSC)
Mrs C.M. Samuel v C. Samuel and the State PLD 1967 SC 334
Mrs Marina Jatoi v Nur-ud-Din K. Jatoi PLD 1967 SC 580
Mrs Shaukat Khalid v Additional District Judge, Rawalpindi 1991 SCMR 19
Mrs Yvonne Anna Carman v Mr Leon Carman PLD 1960 Lah 381
Ms Sadaf Munir Khan v Chairman Reconciliation Committee PLD 2019 Lah 285
Mst Aisha v Manzoor Hussain PLD 1985 SC 436
Mst. Asma Bibi v Chairman Reconciliation Committee PLD 2020
Mst. Ayesha Abdul Maleek v Additional District Judge, Sahiwal 2020 YLR 401 (Lah)
Mst. Benish Liaquat v Station Police Officer 2020 MLD Karachi 740
Mst. Bakhshi v Bashir Ahmad PLD 1970 SC 323
Mst. Beena v Raja Muhammad PLD 2020 SC 508
Mst. Bhagari v Khia 2006 YLR 394
Mst. Laila Qayyum v Fawad Qayyum PLD 2019 SC 449
Mst. Safia Bibi v Muhammad Akbar PLD 2018 Lah 758
Mst. Sakeena Bibi v Secretary Law Pakistan PLD 2022 FSC 64
Mst Samiunnisa v Mst Zaida Khatun AIR 1944 All 202
Mst. Shagzana Walayat v Mst. Shabnam Tabassum 2021 CLC 1761
Mst. Tuharat Firdous v Imtiaz Khan 2019 CLC 1562 (Pesh)
Mubbasher Ahmad v Talat Khurshied 1996 CLC 1963
Mubarak Jan v Taj Begum AIR 1938 Lah 452
Mueen-ud-Din v Administrator General of Auqaf, Pakistan, Islamabad PLD 2007 Lah 583
Muhabat v Abdullah PLD 1970 Lah 303
Muhammad Akbar Shah v Muhammad Yusuf Shah PLD 1964 SC 329
Muhammad Akbar v Shazia Bibi PLD 2014 SC 693
Muhammad Akram v Farman Bibi PLD 1989 Lah 200
Muhammad Ali v Judge Family Court Depalpur 2010 YLR 520 (Lah)
Muhammad Allahdad Khan v Muhammad Ismail Khan 1888 ILR 10 All 289
Muhammad Amir v Mst Beevi 2007 SCMR 614
Muhammad Arif v Saima Noreen 2015 SCMR 804
Muhammad Arshad v Additional District Judge 2015 CLC 463 (Lah)
Muhammad Arshad v Sughran Bibi PLD 2008 Lah 302

Muhammad Aslam v Ghulam Muhammad Tasleem PLD 1971 Lah 139
Muhammad Aslam v The State 2012 PCrLJ 11 (FSC)
Muhammad Bashir v Latifa Bibi 2010 SCMR 1915
Muhammad Ejaz v Khalida Awan 2010 SCMR 342
Muhammad Farukh Iqbal v Mrs Ayesha Iram 2021 SCMR 1341
Muhammad Hashim v Chief Administrator Auqaf, Punjab, Lahore 2010 CLC 1674 [Lah]
Muhammad Ibrahim v Akhtar Ali 2001 CLC 1323 (Lah)
Muhammad Ibrahim v Province of Sindh through DCO Revenue PLD 2013 Sindh 501
Muhammad Imran Ahmad v Hina Faheem 2014 MLD 1400 (Kar).
Muhammad Imtiaz v The State PLD 1981 FSC 308
Muhammad Khalid v State 2018 PCrLJN 29
Muhammad Khalid v Noor Bibi 2005 SCMR 1717
Muhammad Masood Abbasi v Mamona Abbasi 2004 YLR 482 (Lah)
Muhammad Najeeb v Talat Shahnaz 1989 SCMR 119
Muhammad Nawaz v Khurshid Begum PLD 1972 SC 302
Muhammad Nawaz v Muhammad Khan 2005 SCMR 710
Muhammad Nawazish Ali v Family Judge 2021 CLC 1841 (Lah)
Muhammad Nazir v Ali Muhammad 2003 SCMR 1183
Muhammad Ramzan v The State 2013 SCMR 737
Muhammad Riaz v Robina Bibi 2000 MLD 1886
Muhammad Sadiq Ali Khan v Fakr Jahan Begum NLR 1990 SD 541
Muhammad Sajjad v Additional District and Session Judge PLD 2015 Lah 405
Muhammad Sanaullah v Shamin Naz Kausar 1995 SCMR 1208
Muhammad Shahid Sahil v State PLD 2010 FSC 215
Muhammad Shoaib v Razia Bibi 2002 YLR 2895 (Lah)
Muhammad Tazeel v Mst Khair-un-Nisa 1995 SCMR 885
Muhammad Yaqoob v The State 1985 PCrLJ 1064
Muhammad Yaqub v Ali Muhammad PLD 1957 Lah 544
Muhammad Zafar v Kamal Fatima PLD 1981 Lah 732
Muhammad Zaman Shah v Chief Administrator Auqaf 1991 SCMR 2152
Muhammad Zaman v Mst Irshad Begum PLD 1967 Lah 1104
Mukhtar Ahmad v Rasheeda Bibi 2003 SCMR 1664
Muqadar v Roshah 2008 CLC 43 [Pesh]
Mumtaz Bibi v Qasim and others Writ Petition No. 4227 of 2021

N

Nabeela Shaheen v Zia Wazir Bhatti PLD 2015 Lah 88
Nandlal Wasudeo Badwaik v Lata Nandlal Badwaik (2014) 2 SCC 576 [The Supreme Court of India]
Naseeb Rana v Hazrat Hilal PLD 2015 Pesh 111
Nasir Ahmad Khan v Ismat Jehan Begum PLD 1969 SC 194
Nasir v Rubina 2012 MLD 1576 (Pesh)
Nasreen Begum v A 2006 MLD 1988 (Kar)
Nasrullah Khan v Rasul Bibi 2001 SCMR 1156
Naveed Munir v Additional District & Sessions Judge Lahore 2014 SCMR 1446
Nawab Din v Bagh 1994 SCMR 1975
Nazeer Begum v Abdul Sattar PLD 1963 Kar 465
Nazim Khan v Additional District Judge, Lyallpur PLD 1976 Lah 930
Naziran Begum v Khurshid Begum 1999 SCMR 1171
Nighat Firdous v Khadim Hussain 1998 SCMR 1593
Nisar Akbar Khan v Jamil Nasir PLD 2014 Lah. 417

Noor Jamal v The State PLD 1990 SC 656
Noor Shah Filling Station (Regd.) through Manager v Auqaf Department through Chief Administrator Punjab 2009 CLC (Lah) 1148
Nusrat Zohra v Azhra Bibi PLD 2006 SC 15

P

Peggy Collin v Muhammad Ishfaque Malik PLD 2010 Lah 48
Provincial Government through District Coordination Officer, Swabi v Fazal Rahim 2016 YLR 233 (Pesh)

Q

Qamar Sultan v Mst Bibi Sufaidan 2010 YLR 2515
Qamar Sultan v Bibi Sufaidan 2012 SCMR 695
Qazi Fazal Ahmad v Riaz-ur-Rahim 2004 SCMR 432

R

Rab Nawaz Ahmed v Hasina Iqbal 2011 SCMR 972
Rab Nawaz v Ghulam Rasul 2014 SCMR 1181
Rabia Khizer v Station House Officer PLD 2009 Lah 223
Rahimullah Choudhry v Mrs Syeda Helali 1974 SCMR 305
Raj Bibi v Mst Shahzadi PLD 2003 Quetta 53
Rasheeda Bibi v Mukhtar Ahmad 2008 SCMR 1384
Rashida Begum v Shahab Din PLD 1960 Lah 1142
Rasool Bibi v Waryam 1992 SCMR 1520
Razia Bibi v Riaz Ahmad 2004 SCMR 821
Riaz Javaid v Sheraz Ahmed 2010 CLC 1925 [Lah]
Riaz Ullah Khan v Asghar Ali 2004 SCMR 1701
Roshni Desai v Jahanzeb Niazi PLD 2011 Lah 423
Rukhsana Younas v Aziz-ur-Rehman 2014 CLC 1751 (Pesh)
Russ v Russ (1962) 3 AER 193.

S

Saadia Usman v Muhammad Usman Iqbal Jadoon 2009 SCMR 1458
Saadullah v Gulbanda 2014 SCMR 1205
Sadar Abbas v Province of Punjab 2015 CLC 822 (Lah)
Saifuddin v Mubarak Sawal 2009 YLR 1226 (Kar)
Saif-ur-Rehman v ADJ Toba Tek Singh 2018 SCMR 1885
Saima Gul v Haider Zaman PLD 2015 Pesh 14
Sainapatti v Sainapatti, AIR 1932 Lah. 116.
Sajjad Hussain v Judge Family Court, Mailsi 2015 CLC 1347
Saleem Ahmad v Government of Pakistan PLD 2014 FSC 43
Samreen Bibi v Judge Family Court PLD 2015 Lah 504
Sana Shehzad v Secretary Union Council PLD 2014 Lah 632
Sani Gul v Civil Judge-III, Swat 2000 CLC 1228 (Pesh)
Sardar Arshid Hussain v Mst Zenat Un Nisa 2017 SCMR 608
Sardar Bibi v Abdul Latif PLD 1952 Lah. 294
Sardar Iqbal v Tahira Parveen 2010 YLR 582 (Lah)
Sardar Muhammad v Faqir Muhammad 1996 CLC 916 (Lah)
Sardar Muhammad v Mst Nasima Bibi PLD 1966 Lahore 703
Sardar v Malik Khan 2003 YLR 2623 (Lah)

Sarwar Jan v Mukhtar Ahmad PLD 2012 SC 217
Sh. Inayat Ullah v M. A. Khan PLD 1964 SC 126
Shabana Naz v Muhammad Saleem 2014 SCMR 343
Shafqat Parveen v Muhammad Iftikhar Amjad 2012 SCMR 1602
Shah Bano Begum v Iftikhar Muhammad Khan PLD 1956 Kar 363
Shahida Parveen v Samiullah PLJ 2006 Lah 1215
Shahnaz Begum v Additional District Judge PLD 2021 Lah 69
Shahzada Begum v Sh. Abdul Hamid PLD 1950 Lah 504
Shamas Ali v Additional District Judge, Sambrial PLD 2012 Lah 183
Shamim Akhtar v Pirzada Khalil ur Rehman 2015 YLR 2176 (Islamabad)
Shamshad Begum v Abdul Haque PLD 1977 Kar 855
Sharafat Ali Ashraf v Additional District Judge Bahawalpur 2008 SCMR 1707
Shaukat Hussain v Civil Judge Multan 2006 YLR 349
Shayan through Mst Shamim v Nisar Ahmad 2010 MLD 695 (Lah)
Shazia v Muhammad Nasir 2014 YLR 1563 (Pesh)
Sher Bahadur v Ghulam Qamar Din 2016 MLD 1749 (Pesh)
Sher Muhammad v Mahmood Bakhsh 2000 SCMR 672
Shirin Bai v Muhammad Ali and others PLD 1970 Kar 450
Shoukat Ali v The State 2004 YLR 619 (FSC)
Slabo Bibi v Gul Rehman PLD 1996 Pesh 1
Smt. Saroj Rani v Sudharshan Kumar AIR 1984 SC 1562
Srimati Priyabala Mazumdar v Nalini Mohan Mazaumdar PLD 1957 Dacca 513
Sughran Mai v The State PLD 1980 Lah 386
Sultan Ahmad v Judge Family Court PLD 2012 Lah 148
Syed Abu Talib Shah v Bibi Rukhsar Zahra 2012 CLC 1272 (Pesh)
Syed Ali Nawaz Gardezi v Lt. Col. Muhammad Yousaf PLD 1963 SC 51
Syed Haroon Sultan Bokhari v Syeda Mubarak Fatima 2014 CLC 1270 (Lah)
Syed Mohsin Raza Bukhari v Syed Gulzar Hussain Kazmi PLD 2004 SC 520
Syed Muhammad v Mst Zeenat PLD 2001 SC 128
Syeda Adrish v Syed Anwar-ul-Haq PLD 2011 Lah 569

T

Tahir Ayub Khan v Mrs Alia Anwer 2017 MLD 412 [Sindh]
Tahir Hanif v Saira Kosar 2016 YLR 440
Tariq Masih v The State 2004 PCrLJ 1017 (FSC)
Tariq Mehmood v Farah Shaheen 2010 YLR 349 (Lah)
Tauqeer Ahmad Qureshi v Additional District Judge Lahore PLD 2009 SC 760
Tauqeer Ahmed v Bashir Ahmed 2001 YLR 3153 (Kar)
The AdvocateGeneral of Bombay v Jumbabai ILR 41 Bom 181.

U

Umar Bibi v Bashir Ahmad 1977 SCMR 154
Uzma Wahid v Guardian Judge 1989 MLD 3064 [Lah]

W

Wafaqi Hakoomat-e-Pakistan v Awam-e-Pakistan PLD 1991 SC 731
Waris Ali v Rasoolan Bibi PLD 2014 SC 77
Warrender v Warrender [1835] 6 All ER 1239.

Y

Yusuf Abbas v Mst Ismat Mustafa PLD 1968 Kar 480

Z

Zafar Iqbal v Rehmat Jan 1994 SCMR 339
Zaheer Ahmad v Nasiman Bibi 2007 CLC 1145 [Lah]
Zahid Farooq v Anjuman Jamia Masjid 1995 SCMR 1584
Zakirullah Khan v Faizullah Khan 1999 SCMR 971
Zarmeen Abid v NADRA, Islamabad 2022 PLD 39 (Lah)
Zohra Begum v Sheikh Latif Ahmad Munawwar PLD 1965 Lah 695
Zubair Hussain Siddiqui v Shakeela Khanum 2006 CLC 1099
Zulfiqar Ali v Shazia Bibi 2009 SCMR 1037

INDEX

K

L

M